U.S. HISTORY DOCUMENTS PACKAGE
TO ACCOMPANY
LIBERTY, EQUALITY, POWER
A HISTORY OF THE AMERICAN PEOPLE
THIRD EDITION

VOLUME I: TO 1877

John M. Murrin
Paul E. Johnson
James M. McPherson
Gary Gerstle
Emily S. Rosenberg
Norman L. Rosenberg

Prepared by
Mark W. Beasley
Hardin-Simmons University

WADSWORTH

THOMSON LEARNING

Australia Canada Mexico Singapore Spain United Kingdom United States

For more information about our products, contact us at:
Thomson Learning Academic Resource Center
1-800-423-0563

For permission to use material from this text, contact us by:
Phone: 1-800-730-2214
Fax: 1-800-730-2215
Web: www.thomsonrights.com

Asia
Thomson Learning
60 Albert Complex, #15-01
Albert Complex
Singapore 189969

Australia
Nelson Thomson Learning
102 Dodds Street
South Melbourne, Victoria 3205
Australia

Canada
Nelson Thomson Learning
1120 Birchmount Road
Toronto, Ontario M1K 5G4
Canada

Europe/Middle East/South Africa
Thomson Learning
Berkshire House
168-173 High Holborn
London WC1 V7AA
United Kingdom

Latin America
Thomson Learning
Seneca, 53
Colonia Polanco
11560 Mexico D.F.
Mexico

Spain
Paraninfo Thomson Learning
Calle/Magallanes, 25
28015 Madrid, Spain

PREFACE

Voices from the past articulate history most eloquently. Primary sources, such as those presented here, are crucial to comprehending the development of the United States because they provide firsthand descriptions of, or reflections upon, occurrences that profoundly shaped the nation. For that reason, scholars rely heavily on such material for their knowledge of the past. Unfortunately, college students usually do not have access to eyewitness accounts, and they often conclude that history is nothing more than a rather dull compilation of obscure events and even-more-obscure dates. This documents package has been prepared so that students may hear some of the distant voices for themselves and come to realize that individuals, not "facts," are the critical element in history. By studying the selections presented in these two volumes, students will understand more fully the social, cultural, and political topics developed in *Liberty, Equality, and Power: A History of the American People*, Third Edition. They will find as well that they have gained a deeper awareness of, and appreciation for, the history of the American people.

The relationships among liberty, equality, and power provide one of the major themes in U.S. history, and the documents included in this book highlight that relationship. American perceptions of liberty, equality, and power have changed markedly over time, however, and the selections will help students understand the evolution of those ideals.

Consequently, the earliest items emphasize the conflicts that occurred when European powers laid claim to the "New World." As the British gained dominance over much of North America, the English belief that power often threatened liberty became pervasive in the American colonies. The documents from the Revolutionary War era articulate that fear. Following independence, a developing market economy significantly affected attitudes toward liberty and power, while at the same time the emergence of democracy seemed to place more and more importance on the individual. During the nineteenth century, then, many Americans enjoyed the benefits of liberty and freedom. Numerous others, on the other hand, did not. The material reveals that for those people, the struggle to achieve equality has continued into the present. In addition to a growing egalitarianism during the 1900s, the expansive role of the United States in international affairs had significant implications. A number of the more recent documents therefore stress the importance of military and diplomatic efforts as the nation sought to ensure its fundamental ideals of liberty and equality while rising to a position of unprecedented world power.

Studying history can be a challenging, intimidating task, and this ancillary is designed to help students as much as possible as they explore the national heritage. Each chapter begins with an introduction that places the selections in a broad historical context and that reiterates the themes developed in the corresponding textbook chapter. Moreover, the documents have individual introductions that survey the material and describe its importance to the history of the United States. A series of questions at the conclusion of each chapter encourages students to discuss the material they have just read. Although many of the questions focus on issues of liberty, equality, and power, they all serve as springboards to a broader understanding of American history. Indeed, one of the greatest advantages of using primary sources is that they allow the reader to become the historian and discover intellectual concepts or historical themes that they find of particular interest. Students may work individually with the questions, but they will gain much more from their efforts if they work with a study partner, a small group, or the entire class. Such an approach will bring the broadest range of understanding and experience to the discussion, which will in turn help to make the material more vibrant, the history more alive, the learning more dynamic.

THE THIRD EDITION

Building on the strengths of a solid second edition collection, this revision focuses primarily on expanding the selection of sources—both in number and perspective—and on balancing the various views that comprise the American past. The additions include more pieces by or relating to women, minority groups, immigrants, and labor interests, as well as more traditional government documents and political speeches. In several instances, new selections actually incorporate two documents, highlighting opposing views on a single issue.

—Mark W. Beasley

Contents

CHAPTER 1

WHEN OLD WORLDS COLLIDE:
CONTACT, CONQUEST, CATASTROPHE

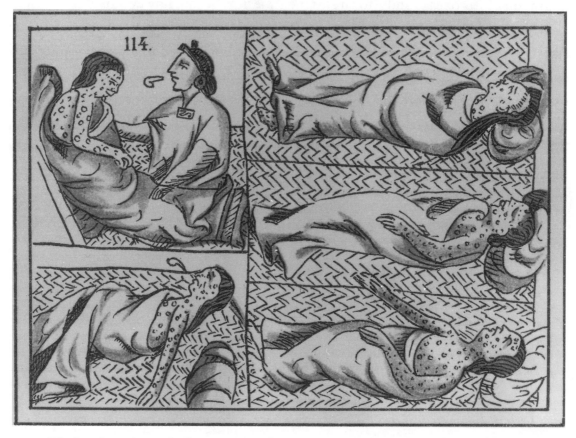

Native Americans had no acquired immunity to many of the viruses and bacteria European explorers carried, and, as a result, the native population died by the millions. Smallpox germs were the real victors in the struggle between the Aztecs and the Spanish invaders.

Liberty, equality, and power provide three currents that have profoundly shaped the history of the American people; the relationship among those forces serves as a critical theme in the national heritage. As the large-scale migration of Europeans and Africans to the Americas began, however, issues of power clearly prevailed. In particular, the Spanish claimed all of the western hemisphere, an assertion ultimately legitimized by papal authority. Spain used that blessing to create an unprecedented global empire that linked Africa, America, and Europe. On the other hand, perhaps more than 14,000 years ago, Asiatic tribes crossed Beringia, populating the vast land stretching from the Arctic to the Antarctic and creating complex societies that antedated much of Western culture. Many of these native inhabitants fiercely resisted European incursion, forcing the Spaniards to rely on legal devices and military strength to establish their power in the Americas. Consequently, contact between Europeans and Indians developed into conflicts that often had catastrophic consequences.

1. PAPAL BULL INTER CAETERAS, MAY 4, 1493*

Concern that Columbus's discoveries might have infringed on Portuguese claims led Pope Alexander VI to define the region that Spain could explore and develop. This Bull, which established a demarcation line west of the Canary Islands, served as the foundation for Spanish movement into the western hemisphere and set the stage for the long-term development of a Hispanic Latin America. The document reveals several important elements that characterized early efforts to gain control over America, including the struggle between European states to claim newly found territories, the influence of the church as a secular power, and the role of Christian zeal in the European occupation of the Americas.

To the illustrious sovereigns, our very dear son in Christ, Ferdinand, king, and our very dear daughter in Christ, Isabella, queen of Castile, Leon, Aragon, Sicily, and Granada, health and apostolic benediction. Among other works well pleasing to the Divine Majesty and cherished of our heart, this assuredly ranks highest, that in our times especially the Catholic faith and the Christian religion be exalted and be everywhere increased and spread, that the health of souls be cared for and that barbarous nations be overthrown and brought to the faith itself. . . . [R]ecognizing that as true Catholic kings and princes, such as we have always known you to be, and as your illustrious deeds already known to the whole world declare, you not only eagerly desire, but with every effort, zeal, and diligence, without regard to hardships, expenses, dangers, with the shedding even of your blood, are laboring to that end; recognizing also that you have long since dedicated to this purpose your whole soul and all your endeavors—as witnessed in these times with so much glory to the Divine Name in your recovery of the kingdom of Granada from the yoke of the Saracens—we therefore are rightly led, and hold it as our duty, to grant you . . . those things whereby . . . you may be enabled for

*From *European Treaties Bearing of the History of the United States and its Dependencies to 1648*, ed. Frances F. Davenport (Washington, D.C.: Carnegie Institution, 1917), I: 71–78.

the honor of God himself and the spread of the Christian rule to carry forward your holy and praise-worthy purpose so pleasing to immortal God. We have indeed learned that you, who for a long time had intended to seek out and discover certain islands and mainlands remote and unknown and not hitherto discovered by others, to the end that you might bring to the worship of our Redeemer and the profession of the Catholic faith their residents and inhabitants, having been up to the present time greatly engaged in the siege and recovery of the kingdom itself of Granada were unable to accomplish this holy and praiseworthy purpose; but the said kingdom having at length been regained, as was pleasing to the Lord, you, with the wish to fulfill your desire, chose our beloved son, Christopher Columbus, . . . to make diligent quest for these remote and unknown mainlands and islands through the sea, where hitherto no one had sailed; and they at length, with divine aid and with the utmost diligence sailing in the ocean sea, discovered certain very remote islands and even mainlands that had not been discovered by others; wherein dwell very many people living in peace, and, as reported, going unclothed and not eating flesh. Moreover, as your aforesaid envoys are of opinion, these very peoples living in the said islands and countries, believe in one God, the Creator in heaven, and seem sufficiently disposed to embrace the Catholic faith and be trained in good morals. And it is hoped that, were they instructed, the name of the Savior, our Lord Jesus Christ, would easily be introduced into the said countries and islands. Also, on one of the chief of these aforesaid islands the said Christopher has already caused to be put together and built a fortress fairly equipped, wherein he has stationed as garrison certain Christians, companions of his, who are to make search for other remote and unknown islands and mainlands. In the islands and countries already discovered are found gold, spices, and very many other precious things of divers kinds and qualities. Wherefore, as becomes Catholic kings and princes, after earnest consideration of all mat-ters, especially of the rise and spread of the Catholic faith, . . . you have purposed with the favor of divine clemency to bring under your sway the said mainlands and islands with their residents and inhabitants and to bring them to the Catholic faith. Hence, heartily commending in the Lord this your holy and praiseworthy purpose, and desirous that . . . the name of our Savior be carried into those regions, we exhort you very earnestly in the Lord and by your reception of holy baptism, whereby you are bound to our apostolic commands, . . . to lead the peoples dwelling in those islands and countries to embrace the Christian religion. . . . And, in order that you may enter upon so great an undertaking with greater readiness and heartiness endowed with the benefit of apostolic favor, we, . . . by the authority of Almighty God conferred upon us in blessed Peter and of the vicarship of Jesus Christ, which we hold on earth, do by tenor of these presents, should any of the said islands have been found by your envoys and captains, give, grant, and assign to you and your heirs and suc-cessors, kings of Castile and Leon, forever, together with all their dominions, cities, camps, places, and villages, and all rights, jurisdictions, and appurtenances, all islands and mainlands found and to be found, discovered and to be discovered towards the west and south, by drawing and establishing a line from the Arctic pole . . . to the Antarctic pole, . . . no matter whether the said mainlands and islands are found and to be found in the direction of India or towards any other quarter, the said line to be distant one hundred leagues toward the west and south from any of the islands commonly known as the Azores and Cape Verde. With this proviso, however, that none of the islands and mainlands, . . . beyond te said line towards the west and south, be in the actual possession of any Christian king or prince up to the birthday of the Lord Jesus Christ just past from that which the present year one thousand four hundred and thirty-three begins. And we make, appoint, and depute you and your said heirs and successors lords of them all with full and free power, authority, and juris-diction of every kind; with this proviso however, that by this our gift, grant, and assignment no right acquired by any Christian prince, who may be in actual possession of said islands and mainlands prior to the said birthday of our Lord Jesus Christ, is hereby to be understood to be withdrawn or taken away. Moreover we command you in virtue of holy obedience that, employing all due dili-gence . . . you should appoint to the aforesaid mainlands and islands worthy, God-fearing, learned, skilled, and experienced men, in order to instruct the aforesaid inhabitants in the Catholic faith and train them in good morals. Furthermore, under penalty of excommunication . . . , we strictly forbid all persons . . . to dare, without your special permit or that of your aforesaid heirs and successors, to go for the purpose of trade or any other reason to the islands or mainlands . . . towards the west and south [of the said line]. We trust in Him from whom empires and governments and all good things proceed, that, should you, with the Lord's guidance, pursue this holy and praiseworthy undertaking, in a short while your hardships and endeavors will attain the most felicitous result, to the happiness and glory of all Christendom. . . . Let no one, therefore, infringe, or with rash boldness contravene, this our recommendation, exhortation, requisition, gift, grant, assignment, constitution, deputation, decree, mandate, prohibition, and will. . . .

2. THE LAWS OF BURGOS, 1512*

*P*romulgated by Queen Juana, daughter of Isabella, these statutes institutionalized the encomienda labor system in the New World, sought to ensure the religious salvation of the natives, and defined the social and economic status of the Indians. Perhaps more importantly, the use of carefully articulated laws offered the Spanish a means to establish, and to justify their power over the natives. By passing these statutes to ensure the salvation of the Indians, the Spanish ensured the destruction of native culture. As with all legal codes, the Laws of Burgos reveal much about the attitudes and presumptions of those in power, while also providing some insight into the lives of those the laws are meant to control.

WHEREAS, the King, my Lord and Father, and the Queen, my Mistress and Mother, . . . always desired that the chiefs and Indians of the Island of Española [Hispaniola] be brought to a knowledge of our Holy Catholic Faith, and, . . .

WHEREAS, it has become evident through long experience that nothing has sufficed to bring the said chiefs and Indians to a knowledge of our Faith (necessary for their salvation), since by nature they are inclined to idleness and vice, and have no manner of virtue or doctrine (by which our Lord is discovered), and that the principal obstacle in the way of correcting their vices and having them profit by and impressing them with the doctrine is that their dwellings are remote from the settlements of the Spaniards who . . . reside in the said Island, because, although at the time the Indians go to serve them they are indoctrinated in and taught the things of our Faith, after serving they return to their dwellings where, because of the distance and their own evil inclinations, they immediately forget what they have been taught and go back to their customary idleness and vice, and when they come to serve again they are as new in the doctrine as they were at the beginning, because, although the Spaniard who accompanies them to their village . . . reminds them of it and reprehends them, they, having no fear of him, do not profit by it and tell him to leave them in idleness, since that is their reason for returning to their said village, and that their only purpose and desire is to do with themselves what they will, without regard for any virtue, and, . . .

WHEREAS, it is our duty to seek a remedy for it in every way possible, it was considered by the King . . . and by several members of my council and by persons of good life, letters, and conscience, and they . . . gave it as their opinion that the most beneficial thing that could be done at present would be to remove the said chiefs and Indians to the vicinity of the villages and communities of the Spaniards—this for many considerations—and thus, by continual association with them,

*From *The Laws of Burgos of 1512–1513: Royal Ordinances for the Good Government and Treatment of the Indians*, trans. Lesley Baird Simpson (San Francisco: John Howell Books, 1960), 11–14, 16–18, 21, 23–24, 26–28, 32, 42–45. Used by permission.

as well as by attendance at church on feast days to hear Mass and the divine offices, and by observing the conduct of the Spaniards, as well as the preparation and care that the Spaniards will display in demonstrating and teaching them, while they are together, the things of our Holy Catholic Faith, it is clear that they will the sooner learn them and, having learned them, will not forget them as they do now. . . .

THEREFORE, . . . it was agreed that for the improvement and remedy of all the aforesaid, the said chiefs and Indians should forthwith be brought to dwell near the villages and communities of the Spaniards who inhabit that Island, so that they may be treated and taught and looked after as is right and as we have always desired; and so I command that henceforth that which is contained below be obeyed and observed as follows: . . .

II

We order and command that all chiefs and Indians dwelling on the Island of Española, now or in the future, shall be brought from their present dwelling places to the villages and communities of the Spaniards who reside . . . on the said Island; and in order that they be brought of their own volition and suffer no harm from the removal, we hereby command Don Diego Columbus, our Admiral, Viceroy, and Governor of the said Island . . . to have them brought in the manner that seems best, with the least possible harm to the said chiefs and Indians. . . .

III

. . . [T]he citizens to whom the said Indians are given in encomienda shall . . . be obliged to erect a structure to be used as a church; . . . and in this said church he shall place an image of Our Lady and a bell with which to call the Indians to prayer; and the person who has them in encomienda shall be obliged to have them called by the bell at nightfall and go with them to the said church, and have them cross themselves and bless themselves, and together recite the Ave Maria, the Pater Noster, the Credo, and the Salve Regina, in such wise that all of them shall hear the said person, and the said person hear them, so that he may know who is performing well and who ill, and correct the one who is wrong. . . .

IV

Also, in order to discover how each one is progressing in things of the Faith, we command that every two weeks the said person who has them in charge shall examine them to see what each one knows particularly and to teach them what they do not know; and he shall also teach them the Ten Commandments and the Seven Deadly Sins and the Articles of the Faith, that is, to those he thinks have the capacity and ability to learn them; but all this shall be done with great love and gentleness. . . .

IX

. . . [W]hoever has fifty Indians or more in encomienda shall be obliged to have a boy (the one he considers most able) taught to read and write, and the things of our Faith, so that he may later teach the said Indians, because the Indians will more readily accept what he says than what the Spaniards and settlers tell them. . . .

X

. . . [E]ach and every time an Indian falls sick in a place where there is a priest, the priest shall be obliged to go to him and recite the Credo and other profitable things of our Holy Catholic Faith, and, if the Indian shall know how to confess, he shall confess him, without charging him any fee for it; . . . and also that they shall go with a Cross to the Indians who die and shall bury them without charging any fee for it or for the confession. . . .

XII

. . . [A]ll the Spanish inhabitants and settlers who have Indians in encomienda shall be obliged to have all infants baptized within a week of their birth, or before, if it is necessary; and if there is no priest to do so, the person in charge of the said estate shall be obliged to baptize them, according to the custom in such emergencies. . . .

XIII

. . . [A]fter the Indians have been brought to the estates, all the founding [of gold] . . . shall be done in the manner prescribed below: that is, the said persons who have Indians in encomienda shall extract gold with them for five months in the year, and at the end of these five months, the said Indians shall rest forty days; . . . and in all the said forty days no one shall employ any Indians in extracting gold. . . . And we command that . . . the persons who have the said Indians in encomienda shall be obliged, during these forty days of rest, to indoctrinate them in . . . our Faith more than on other days, because they will have the opportunity and means to do so. . . .

XVI

. . . [A]mong the other things of our Faith that shall be taught to the Indians, they shall be made to understand that they may not have more than one wife at a time, nor may they abandon her. . . .

XVIII

. . . [N]o pregnant woman, after the fourth month, shall be sent to the mines, . . . but shall be kept on the estates and utilized in housekeeping tasks, such as making bread, cooking, and weeding; and after she bears her child she shall nurse it until it is three years old, and in all this time she shall not be sent to the mines . . . or used in anything else that will harm the child. . . .

XIX

. . . [T]hat all those . . . who have Indians in encomienda . . . shall be obliged to give each of them a hammock in which to sleep continually; and they shall not allow them to sleep on the ground, as hitherto they have been doing. . . .

XXIV

. . . [N]o person or persons shall dare to beat any Indian with sticks, or whip him, or call him dog, or address him by any other name than his proper name alone; and if an Indian should deserve to be punished for something he has done, the said person having him in charge shall bring him to the visitor for punishment. . . .

3. AZTEC ACCOUNTS OF THE SPANISH ARRIVAL IN MEXICO*

*T*he conquest of Mexico proved to be one of the most dramatic contacts between Spaniards and Native Americans. Defeating the Aztecs cleared the way for the Spanish to claim Mexico and, ultimately, large portions of North America. Moreover, the Aztecs' incredible wealth dazzled the imaginations of Europeans, making the search for gold a major force in the exploration and exploitation of the entire western hemisphere. Consequently, the capture of the Aztec capital of Tenochtitlán marked a crucial step in Spain's rise to world power. The three documents that follow offer various versions of that monumental occurrence. The first account, taken from several Aztec sources, provides an Indian view of the events that took place in 1520 and 1521.

Motecuhzoma now arrayed himself in his finery, preparing to go out to meet them. The other great princes also adorned their persons, as did the nobles and their chieftains and knights. They all went out together to meet the strangers.

They brought trays heaped with the finest flowers—the flower that resembles a shield; the flower shaped like a heart; in the center, the flower with the sweetest aroma; and the fragrant yellow flower, the most precious of all. They also brought garlands of flowers, and ornaments for the breast, and necklaces of gold, necklaces hung with rich stones, necklaces fashioned in the petatillo style.

Thus Motecuhzoma went out to meet them. . . . He presented many gifts to the Captain and his commanders, those who had come to make war. Then he hung the gold necklaces around their

*From *The Broken Spears: The Aztec Account of the Conquest of Mexico*, ed. Miguel Leon-Portilla (Boston: Beacon Press, 1962, 1990), 63–69, 105–109. Originally published in Spanish under the title *Visión de las Vencidas* (Mexico City: Universidad Nacional Autónoma de México, 1959). Reprinted by permission of Beacon Press.

necks and gave them presents of every sort as gifts of welcome.

When Motecuhzoma had given necklaces to each one, Cortés asked him: "Are you Motecuhzoma? Are you the king? Is it true that you are the king Motecuhzoma?"

And the king said: "Yes, I am Motecuhzoma." Then he stood up to welcome Cortés; he came forward, bowed his head low and addressed him in these words: "Our lord, you are weary. The journey has tired you, but now you have arrived on the earth. You have come to your city, Mexico. You have come here to sit on your throne, to sit under its canopy.

"The kings who have gone before, your representatives, guarded it and preserved it for your coming. The kings . . . ruled for you in the City of Mexico. The people were protected by their swords and sheltered by their shields.

"Do the kings know the destiny of those they left behind, their prosperity? If only they are watching! If only they see what I see!

"No, it is not a dream. I am not walking in my sleep. I am not seeing you in my dreams. . . . I have seen you at last! I have met you face to face! I was in agony for five days, for ten days, with my eyes fixed on the Region of the Mystery. And now you have come out of the clouds and mists to sit on your throne again.

"This was foretold by the kings who governed your city, and now it has taken place. You have come back to us; you have come down from the sky. Rest now, and take possession of your royal houses. Welcome to your land, my lords!"

When Motecuhzoma had finished, La Malinche translated his address into Spanish so that the Captain could understand it. Cortés replied in a strange and savage tongue, speaking first to La Malinche: "Tell Motecuhzoma that we are his friends. There is nothing to fear. We have wanted to see him for a long time, and now we have seen his face and heard his words. Tell him that we love him well and that our hearts are contented."

When the Spaniards entered the Royal House, they placed Motecuhzoma under guard and kept him under their vigilance. They also placed a guard over Itzcuauhtzin, but the other lords were permitted to depart. . . .

In the morning the Spaniards told Motecuhzoma what they needed in the way of supplies: tortillas, fried chickens, hens' eggs, pure water, firewood, and charcoal. Also: large clean cooking pots, water jars, pitchers, dishes, and other pottery. Motecuhzoma ordered that it be sent to them. The chiefs who received this order were angry with the king and no longer revered or respected him. But they furnished the Spaniards with all the provisions they needed—food, beverages, and water, and fodder for the horses.

When the Spaniards were installed in the palace, they asked Motecuhzoma about the city's resources and reserves and about the warriors' ensigns and shields. They questioned him closely and then demanded gold.

Motecuhzoma guided them to it. They surrounded him and crowded close with their weapons. He walked in the center while they formed a circle around him.

When they arrived at the treasure house called Teucalen, the riches of gold and feathers were brought out to them: ornaments made of quetzal feathers, richly worked shields, disks of gold, the necklaces of the idols, gold nose plugs, gold greaves, and bracelets and crowns.

The Spaniards immediately stripped the feathers from the gold shields and ensigns. They gathered all the gold into a great mound and set fire to everything else, regardless of its value. Then they melted the gold down into ingots. As for the precious green stones, they took only the best of them; the rest were snatched up by the Tlaxcaltecas. The Spaniards searched throughout the whole treasure house, questioning and quarreling, and seized every object they thought was beautiful.

Next they went to Motecuhzoma's storehouse in the place called Totocalo, where his personal treasures were kept. The Spaniards grinned like little beasts and patted each other with delight.

When they entered the hall of treasures, it was as if they had arrived in Paradise. They searched everywhere and coveted everything; they were slaves to their own greed. All of Motecuhzoma's possessions were brought out: fine bracelets, necklaces with large stones, ankle rings with little gold bells, the royal crowns and all the royal finery—everything that belonged to the king and was reserved to him only. They seized these treasures as if they were their own, as if this plunder were merely a stroke of good luck. . . .

[The Spaniards] advanced cautiously, with their standard-bearer in the lead. . . . The Tlaxcaltecas and the other allies followed close behind. The Tlaxcaltecas held their heads high and pounded their breasts with their hands, hoping to frighten us with their arrogance and courage. They sang songs as they marched, but the Aztecs were also singing. It was as if both sides were challenging each other with their songs. They sang whatever they happened to remember and the music strengthened their hearts. . . .

Then all the Aztecs sprang up and charged into battle. The Spaniards were so astonished that they blundered here and there like drunkards; they ran through the streets with the warriors in pursuit. This was when the taking of captives began. A great many allies from Tlaxcala, Acolhuacan, Chalco, and Xochimilcho were overpowered by the Aztecs, and there was a great harvesting of prisoners, a great reaping of victims to be sacrificed. . . .

The Aztecs took their prisoners to Yacacolco, hurrying them along the road under the strictest guard. Some of the captives were weeping, some were keening, and others were beating their palms against their mouths.

When they arrived in Yacacolco, they were lined up in long rows. One by one they were forced to climb to the temple platform, where they were sacrificed by the priests. The Spaniards went first, then their allies, and all were put to death.

As soon as the sacrifices were finished, the Aztecs arranged the Spaniards' heads in rows on pikes. They also lined up their horses' heads. They placed the horses' heads at the bottom and the heads of the Spanish above, and arranged them all so that the faces were toward the sun. However, they did not display any of the allies' heads. All told, fifty-three Spaniards and four horses were sacrificed there in Yacacolco. . . .

The Spanish blockade caused great anguish in the city. The people were tormented by hunger, and many starved to death. There was no fresh water to drink, only stagnant water and the brine of the lake, and many people died of dysentery.

The only food was lizards, swallows, corn cobs and the salt grasses of the lake. The people also ate water lilies and the seeds of the colorin, and chewed on deer hides and pieces of leather. They roasted and seared and scorched whatever they could find and then ate it. They ate the bitterest weeds and even dirt.

Nothing can compare with the horrors of that siege and the agonies of the starving. We were so weakened by hunger that, little by little, the enemy forced us to retreat. Little by little they forced us to the wall.

4. REPORT OF HERNANDO CORTÉS, OCTOBER 30, 1520*

*H*ernando Cortés, commander of the Spanish conquistadors who defeated the Aztecs, provided Emperor Charles V with the following description of some of the initial events in Tenochtitlán. Cortés offered one explanation for his phenomenal success by describing the Aztec legend that prophesied a conqueror who would arrive from the East. In addition, he offered the first account of the remarkable riches that helped encourage and finance the European drive for power in the Americas.

---

*From *The Despatches of Hernando Cortés, the Conqueror of Mexico, Addressed to the Emperor Charles V. Written During the Conquest, and Containing a Narrative of its Events*, trans. George Folsom (New York: Wiley and Putnam, 1843), 85–89, 107–109.

When we had passed the bridge, the Señor Muteczuma came out to receive us, attended by about two hundred nobles, . . . in two processions in close proximity to the houses on each side of the street, which is very wide and beautiful, and so straight that you can see from one end of it to the other, although it is two thirds of a league in length, having on both sides large and elegant houses and temples. Muteczuma came through the center of the street, attended by two lords. . . . He was supported on the arms of both, and as we approached, I alighted and advanced close to salute him; but the two attendant lords stopped me to prevent my touching him, and he and they both performed the ceremony of kissing the ground; after which he directed his brother who accompanied him to remain with me; the latter accordingly took me by the arm, while Muteczuma, with his other attendant, walked a short distance in front of me, and after he had spoken to me, all the other nobles also came up to address me, and then went away in two processions with great regularity, one after the other, and in this manner returned to the city . . . [where we] reached a very large and splendid palace, in which we were to be quartered, which had been fully prepared for our reception. He there took me by the hand and led me into a spacious saloon, in front of which was a court, through which we entered. Having caused me to sit down on a piece of rich carpeting, . . . he told me to wait his return there, and then went away. After a short space of time, when my people were all bestowed in their quarters, he returned with many and various jewels of gold and silver, feather-work, and five or six thousands pieces of cotton cloth, very rich and of varied texture and finish. After having presented these to me, . . . he discoursed as follows:—

"It is now a long time since, by means of written records, we learned from our ancestors that neither myself nor any of those who inhabit this region were descended from its original inhabitants, but from strangers who emigrated hither from a very distant land; and we have also learned that a prince, whose vassals they all were, conducted our people into these parts, and then returned to his native land. He afterward came again to this country, after the lapse of much time, and found that his people had intermarried with the native inhabitants, by whom they had many children, and had built towns in which they resided; and when he desired them to return with him, they were unwilling to go, nor were they disposed to acknowledge him as their sovereign; so he departed from the country, and we have always heard that his descendants would come to conquer this land, and reduce us to subjection as his vassals; and according to the direction from which you say you have come, namely, the quarter where the sun rises, and from what you say of the great lord or king who sent you hither, we believe and are assured that he is our natural sovereign, especially as you say that it is a long time since you first had knowledge of us. Therefore be assured that we will obey you, and acknowledge you for our sovereign in place of the great lord whom you mention, and that there shall be no default or deception on our part. And you have the power in all this land, I mean wherever my power extends, to command what is your pleasure, and it shall be done in obedience thereto, and all that we have is at your disposal. And since you are in your own proper land and your own house, rest and refresh yourselves after the toils of your journey, and the conflicts in which you have been engaged, which have been brought upon you, as I well know, by all the people from Puntunchan to this place; and I am aware that the Cempoallans and Tlascalans have told you much evil of me, but believe no more than you see with your own eyes, especially from those who are my enemies, some of whom were once my subjects, and having rebelled upon your arrival, make these statements to ingratiate themselves in your favor. . . ." I answered him in respect to all that he said, expressing my acknowledgments, and adding whatever the occasion seemed to demand, especially endeavoring to confirm him in the belief that your Majesty was the sovereign that he had looked for; and after this he took his leave, and having gone, we were liberally supplied with fowls, bread, fruits, and other things required for the use of our quarters.

I one day spoke to Muteczuma and said that your Highness needed gold for certain works that he had ordered to be completed, and I wished him to send some of his people, and I would send some of mine, to the lands and abodes of those lords who had submitted themselves on that occasion, to ask them to supply your Majesty with some part of what they possessed; since besides the necessity your Majesty had for the gold, it would serve as a beginning of their fealty, and your Highness would form a better opinion of their disposition to render him service by such demonstrations; and I also requested that he himself would give me the gold he had, as well as other things, in order that I might transmit them to your Majesty. He immediately requested that I would designate the Spaniards whom I wished to send on this business, and he distributed them two by two, and five by five, among many provinces and cities; . . . and with them he sent some of his own people and directed them to go to the governors of provinces and cities, and say that I commanded each one of them to give a certain proportion of gold, which he prescribed. Accordingly all those caciques to whom he sent contributed freely what he demanded of them, as well as jewels as plates and leaves of gold and silver, and whatever else they possessed; and melting down all that admitted it, we found that the fifth part belonging to your Majesty amounted to 32,400 pesos of gold and upwards, without reckoning the jewels of gold and silver, the feather-work, and precious stones, together with many other valuable articles that I set apart for your Majesty, worth more than 100,000 ducats.

5. THE CONQUEST OF MEXICO*

Bernal Díaz del Castillo, who served in the army that captured Tenochtitlán, wrote a history of that campaign in 1568. The following passages describe first the Aztec attack that drove the Spaniards from Tenochtitlán, and then the fighting that marked the final stages of the conquest, including the carnage that accompanied the Spanish victory over the Aztecs.

[During the fighting for the city] many companies of Mexicans came to the causeway and . . . we could not fend them off, on the contrary they kept on following us thinking that this very night they would carry us off to be sacrificed.

When we had retreated near to our quarters and had already crossed a great opening where there was much water, the arrows, javelins, and stones could no longer reach us. [Then] there was sounded the dismal drum of Huichilobos and many other shells and horns and things like trumpets and the sound of them all was terrifying, and we all looked towards the lofty Cue where they were being sounded, and saw that our comrades whom they had captured . . . were being carried by force up the steps, and they were taking them to be sacrificed. When they got them up to a small square . . . where their accursed idols are kept, we saw them place plumes on the heads of many of them and with things like fans they forced them to dance before Huichilobos, and after they had danced they immediately placed them on their backs on some rather narrow stones which had been prepared as [a place of] sacrifice, and with the stone knives they sawed open their chests and drew out their palpitating hearts and offered them to the idols that were there, and they kicked the bodies down the steps, and Indian butchers who were waiting below cut off the arms and feet and flayed the faces, and prepared it afterwards like glove leather with the beards on, and kept those for the festivals when they celebrated drunken orgies, and the flesh they ate in chilmole. In the same way they sacrificed all the others and ate the legs and arms and offered the hearts and blood to their idols, as I have said, and the bodies, that is their entrails and feet, they threw to the tigers and lions which they kept in the house of carnivores. . . .

. . . [L]et us speak of the dead bodies and heads that were in the houses where Guatemoc had taken refuge. I say on my oath, Amen, that all the houses and the palisades in the lake were full of

*From Bernal Díaz del Castillo, *The True History of the Conquest of New Spain*, ed. and pub. Génaro García in Mexico, trans. Alfred P. Maudslay (London: The Hakluyt Society, 1912), 148–151, 185–187.

heads and corpses and I do not know how to describe it for in the streets and the courts of Tlatelolco there was no difference, and we could not walk except among corpses and heads of dead Indians. I have read about the destruction of Jerusalem, but I know not for certain if there was greater mortality than this, for of the great number of the warriors from all the provinces and towns subject to Mexico who had crowded in [to the city] most of them died, . . . thus the land and the lake and the palisades were full of dead bodies, and stank so much that no one could endure it, and for this reason, as soon as Guatemoc was captured, each one of the Captains went to his own camp, . . . and even Cortés was ill from the stench which assailed his nostrils, and from headache, during the days we were in Tlatelolco. . . .

[A]s there was so great a stench in the city, Guatemoc asked permission of Cortés for all the Mexican forces left in the city to go out to the neighboring pueblos, and they were promptly told to do so. I assert that during three days and nights they never ceased streaming out and all three causeways were crowded with men, women and children, so thin, yellow, dirty and stinking, that it was pitiful to see them. When the city was free of them, Cortés went to examine it and we found the houses full of corpses and there were some poor Mexicans, who could not move out, still among them, and what they excreted from their bodies was a filth such as thin swine pass which have been fed nothing but grass, and all the city was as though it had been ploughed up and the roots of the herbs dug out and they had eaten them and even cooked the bark of some of the trees, and there was no fresh water to be found, only salt water. I also wish to state that they did not eat the flesh of their own Mexicans, only that of our people and our Tlaxcalan allies whom they had captured, and there had been no births for a long time, as they had suffered so much from hunger and thirst and continual fighting.

6. THE TRAVELS OF CABEZA DE VACA, 1528–1536*

Álvar Núñez, Cabeza de Vaca, accompanied the tragic Pánfilo de Narváez expedition of 1528. The explorers traveled through Florida, but they failed to reestablish contact with their supporting flotilla and found themselves abandoned. After eight years of traveling westward, a group of survivors reached northern Mexico. Cabeza de Vaca published his observations of the journey in 1542, providing the earliest description of the southernmost region of what would become the United States. His account sparked additional explorations into the area, which provided Spain with a claim to much of North America. In their efforts to solidify that claim, the Spanish often faced powerful opposition from the Indian tribes that Cabeza de Vaca had visited.

The country between our landing place and the village and country of Apalachen [probably near the Apalachicola River in the Florida panhandle] is mostly level; the soil is sand and earth. All throughout it there are very large trees and open forests containing nut trees, laurels, and others of the kind called resinous, cedar, juniper, water oak, pines, oak and low palmetto, like those of Castilla. Everywhere there are many lagunes, large and small, some very difficult to cross, partly because they are so deep, partly because they are covered with fallen trees. Their bottom is sandy, and in the province of Apalachen the lagunes are much larger than those we found previously. There is much maize in this province and the houses are scattered all over the country. . . . The animals we saw there were three kinds of deer, rabbits and hares, bears and lions and other wild beasts, among them one that carries its young in a pouch on its belly as long as the young are small, until they are able to look for their sustenance, and even then, when they are out after food and people

*From Álvar Núñez, Cabeza de Vaca, *The Journey of Álvar Núñez, Cabeza de Vaca, and His Companions from Florida to the Pacific, 1528–1536*, ed. A. F. Bandalier, trans. Fanny Bandalier (New York: A. S. Barnes & Company, 1905), 26–28, 31–32, 117–118, 121–123.

come, the mother does not move until her little ones are in the pouch again. The country . . . has good pasture for cattle; there are birds of many kinds in large numbers; geese, ducks, wild ducks, muscovy ducks, Ibis, small white herons (egrets), herons and partridges. We saw many falcons, marsh-hawks, sparrow-hawks, pigeon-hawks and many other birds. . . .

There were men . . . who swore they had seen two oak trees, each as thick as the calf of a leg, shot through and through by arrows, which is not surprising if we consider the force and dexterity with which they shoot. I myself saw an arrow that penetrated the base of a poplar tree for half a foot in length. All the many Indians from Florida we saw were archers, and, being very tall and naked, at a distance they appear giants.

Those people are wonderfully built, very gaunt and of great strength and agility. Their bows are as thick as an arm, from eleven to twelve spans long, shooting an arrow at 200 paces with unerring aim. . . .

From the island of Ill-Fate [a coastal barrier island, perhaps Galveston] on, all the Indians whom we met as far as to here have the custom of not cohabiting with their wives when they are pregnant, and until the child is two years old.

Children are nursed to the age of twelve years, when they are old enough to gather their own food. We asked them why they brought their children up in that way and they replied, it was owing to the great scarcity of food all over that country, since it was common (as we saw) to be without it two or three days, and even four, and for that reason they nursed the little ones so long to preserve them from perishing through hunger. And even if they should survive, they would be very delicate and weak. When one falls sick he is left to die in the field unless he be somebody's child. Other invalids, if unable to travel, are abandoned; but a son or brother is taken along.

There is also a custom for husbands to leave their wives if they do not agree, and remarry whom they please; this applies to the young men, but after they have had children they stay with their women and do not leave them.

When, in any village, they quarrel among themselves, they strike and beat each other until worn out, and only then do they separate. Sometimes their women step in and separate them, but men never interfere in these brawls. Nor do they ever use bow and arrow, and after they have fought and settled the question, they take their lodges and women and go out in the fields to live apart from the others until their anger is over, and when they are no longer angry and their resentment has passed away they return to the village and are as friendly again as if nothing happened. There is no need of mediation. When the quarrel is between unmarried people they go to some of their neighbors, who, even if they be enemies, will receive them well, with great festivities and gifts of what they have, so that, when pacified, they return to their village wealthy. . . .

Those Indians are the readiest people with their weapons of all I have seen in the world, for when they suspect the approach of an enemy they lay awake all night with their bows within reach and a dozen of arrows, and before one goes to sleep he tries his bow, and should the string not be to his liking he arranges it until it suits him. Often they crawl out of their dwellings so as not to be seen and look and spy in every direction after danger, and if they detect anything, in less than no time are they all out in the field with their bows and arrows. Thus they remain until daybreak, running hither and thither whenever they see danger or suspect their enemies might approach. When day comes they unstring their bows until they go hunting.

The strings of their bows are made of deer sinews. They fight in a crouching position, and while shooting at each other talk and dart from one side to the other to dodge the arrows of the foe. In this way they receive little damage from our crossbows and muskets. On the contrary, the Indians laugh at those weapons, because they are not dangerous to them on the plains over which they roam. They are only good in narrows and in swamps.

Horses are what the Indians dread most, and by the means of which they will be overcome.

Whoever has to fight Indians must take great care not to let them think he is disheartened or that he covets what they own; in war they must be treated very harshly, for should they notice either fear or greed, they are the people who know how to abide their time for revenge and to take courage from the hearts of their enemy. After spending all their arrows, they part, going each their own way, and without attempting pursuit, although one side might have more men than the other; such is their custom.

Many times they are shot through and through with arrows, but do not die from the wounds as long as the bowels or heart are not touched; on the contrary, they recover quickly. Their eyesight, hearing and senses in general are better, I believe, than those of any other men upon earth. They can stand, and have to stand, much hunger, thirst and cold, being more accustomed and used to it than others. This I wished to state here, since, besides that all men are curious to know the habits and devices of others, such as might come in contact with those people should be informed of their customs and deeds, which will be of no small profit to them.

7. ON THE DESTRUCTION OF THE INDIES, 1542*

In 1542 Bartolomé de Las Casas (1474-1566), a Spanish Dominican priest, wrote A Short Report of the Destruction of the Indies. *In this scorching indictment, he exposes the crass motives and brutal practices of the early Spanish conquistadors. As a former settler on Hispaniola (present-day Dominican Republic and Haiti), Las Casas had witnessed such massive ill-treatment of the natives that he became a priest and devoted the remainder of his life to protecting native peoples from depredations imposed by his fellow Spaniards. His horrific descriptions were widely circulated, and contributed to an image of Spanish conquest, known as the Black Legend, that endured for more than three hundred years. In the short term, his influential writings caused both the Spanish and Portuguese governments to institute new regulations for conduct between colonists and indigenous peoples. The following selection details early Spanish settlement practices and the destruction of the people of Hispaniola.*

The Indies were discovered in the year fourteen hundred and ninety-two. The year following, Spanish Christians went to inhabit them, so that it is since forty-nine years that numbers of Spaniards have gone there: and the first land, that they invaded to inhabit, was the large and most delightful Isle of Hispaniola, which has a circumference of six hundred leagues.

2. There are numberless other islands, and very large ones, all around on every side, that were all—and we have seen it—as inhabited and full of their native Indian peoples as any country in the world.

4. God has created all these numberless people to be quite the simplest, without malice or duplicity, most obedient, most faithful to their natural Lords, and to the Christians, whom they serve; the most humble, most patient, most peaceful, and calm, without strife nor tumults; not wrangling, nor querulous, as free from uproar, hate and desire of revenge, as any in the world.

5. They are likewise the most delicate people, weak and of feeble constitution, and less than any other can they bear fatigue, and they very easily die of whatsoever infirmity; so much so, that not even the sons of our Princes and of nobles, brought up in royal and gentle life, are more delicate than they; although there are among them such as are of the peasant class. They are also a very poor people, who of worldly goods possess little, nor wish to possess: and they are therefore neither proud, nor ambitious, nor avaricious.

6. Their food is so poor, that it would seem that of the Holy Fathers in the desert was not scantier nor less pleasing.

---

*From Francis Augustus MacNutt, *Bartholomew de Las Casas: His Life, Apostolate, and Writings* (Cleveland: The Arthur H. Clark Company, 1909), 315–321.

7. They are likewise of a clean, unspoiled, and vivacious intellect, very capable, and receptive to every good doctrine; most prompt to accept our Holy Catholic Faith, to be endowed with virtuous customs; and they have as little difficulty with such things as any people created by God in the world.

8. Once they have begun to learn of matters pertaining to faith, they are so importunate to know them, and in frequenting the sacraments and divine service of the Church, that to tell the truth, the clergy have need to be endowed of God with the gift of pre-eminent patience to bear with them: and finally, I have heard many lay Spaniards frequently say many years ago, (unable to deny the goodness of those they saw) certainly these people were the most blessed of the earth, had they only knowledge of God.

9. Among these gentle sheep, gifted by their Maker with the above qualities, the Spaniards entered as soon as they knew them, like wolves, tigers, and lions which had been starving for many days, and since forty years they have done nothing else; nor do they otherwise at the present day, than outrage, slay, afflict, torment, and destroy them with strange and new, and divers kinds of cruelty, never before seen, nor heard of, nor read of, of which some few will be told below: to such extremes has this gone that, whereas there were more than three million souls, whom we saw in Hispaniola, there are to-day, not two hundred of the native population left.

10. The island of Cuba . . . is now almost entirely deserted. The islands of San Juan [Porto Rico], and Jamaica, very large and happy and pleasing islands, are both desolate. The Lucaya Isles lie near Hispaniola and Cuba to the north and number more than sixty, including those that are called the Giants, and other large and small Islands; the poorest of these, which is more fertile, and pleasing than the King's garden in Seville, is the healthiest country in the world, and contained more than five hundred thousand souls, but to-day there remains not even a single creature. All were killed in transporting them, to Hispaniola, because it was seen that the native population there was disappearing.

13. We are assured that our Spaniards, with their cruelty and execrable works, have depopulated and made desolate the great continent, and that more than ten Kingdoms, larger than all Spain, counting Aragon and Portugal, and twice as much territory as from Seville to Jerusalem (which is more than two thousand leagues) although formerly full of people, are now deserted.

14. We give as a real and true reckoning, that in the said forty years, more than twelve million persons, men, and women, and children, have perished unjustly and through tyranny, by the infernal deeds and tyranny of the Christians; and I truly believe, nor think I am deceived, that it is more than fifteen.

15. Two ordinary and principal methods have the self-styled Christians, who have gone there, employed in extirpating these miserable nations and removing them from the face of the earth. The one, by unjust, cruel and tyrannous wars. The other, by slaying all those, who might aspire to, or sigh for, or think of liberty, or to escape from the torments that they suffer, such as all the native Lords, and adult men; for generally, they leave none alive in the wars, except the young men and the women, whom they oppress with the hardest, most horrible, and roughest servitude, to which either man or beast, can ever be put. To these two ways of infernal tyranny, all the many and divers other ways, which are numberless, of exterminating these people, are reduced, resolved, or sub-ordered according to kind.

16. The reason why the Christians have killed and destroyed such infinite numbers of souls, is solely because they have made gold their ultimate aim, seeking to load themselves with riches in the shortest time and to mount by high steps, disproportioned to their condition: namely by their insatiable avarice and ambition, the greatest, that could be on the earth. These lands, being so happy and so rich, and the people so humble, so patient, and so easily subjugated, they have had no more respect, nor consideration nor have they taken more account of them (I speak with truth of what I have seen during all the aforementioned time) than,—I will not say of animals, for would to

God they had considered and treated them as animals,—but as even less than the dung in the streets.

17. In this way have they cared for their lives—and for their souls: and therefore, all the millions above mentioned have died without faith, and without sacraments. And it is a publicly known truth, admitted, and confessed by all, even by the tyrants and homicides themselves, that the Indians throughout the Indies never did any harm to the Christians: they even esteemed them as coming from heaven, until they and their neighbours had suffered the same many evils, thefts, deaths, violence and visitations at their hands.

Of Hispaniola

In the island of Hispaniola—which was the first, as we have said, to be invaded by the Christians—the immense massacres and destruction of these people began. It was the first to be destroyed and made into a desert. The Christians began by taking the women and children, to use and to abuse them, and to eat of the substance of their toil and labour, instead of contenting themselves with what the Indians gave them spontaneously, according to the means of each. Such stores are always small; because they keep no more than they ordinarily need, which they acquire with little labour; but what is enough for three households, of ten persons each, for a month, a Christian eats and destroys in one day. From their using force, violence and other kinds of vexations, the Indians began to perceive that these men could not have come from heaven.

2. Some hid their provisions, others, their wives and children: others fled to the mountains to escape from people of such harsh and terrible intercourse. The Christians gave them blows in the face, beatings and cudgellings, even laying hands on the lords of the land. They reached such recklessness and effrontery, that a Christian captain violated the lawful wife of the chief king and lord of all the island.

3. After this deed, the Indians consulted to devise means of driving the Christians from their country. They took up their weapons, which are poor enough and little fitted for attack, being of little force and not even good for defence; For this reason, all their wars are little more than games with sticks, such as children play in our countries.

4. The Christians, with their horses and swords and lances, began to slaughter and practise strange cruelty among them. They penetrated into the country and spared neither children nor the aged, nor pregnant women, nor those in child labour, all of whom they ran through the body and lacerated, as though they were assaulting so many lambs herded in their sheepfold.

5. They made bets as to who would slit a man in two, or cut off his head at one blow: or they opened up his bowels. They tore the babes from their mothers' breast by the feet, and dashed their heads against the rocks. Others they seized by the shoulders and threw into the rivers, laughing and joking, and when they fell into the water they exclaimed: "boil body of so and so!" They spitted the bodies of other babes, together with their mothers and all who were before them, on their swords.

6. They made a gallows just high enough for the feet to nearly touch the ground, and by thirteens, in honour and reverence of our Redeemer and the twelve Apostles, they put wood underneath and, with fire, they burned the Indians alive.

7. They wrapped the bodies of others entirely in dry straw, binding them in it and setting fire to it; and so they burned them. They cut off the hands of all they wished to take alive, made them carry them fastened on to them, and said: "Go and carry letters": that is; take the news to those who have fled to the mountains.

8. They generally killed the lords and nobles in the following way. They made wooden gridirons of stakes, bound them upon them, and made a slow fire beneath: thus the victims gave up the spirit by degrees, emitting cries of despair in their torture.

9. I once saw that they had four or five of the chief lords stretched on the gridirons to burn them, and I think also there were two or three pairs of gridirons, where they were burning others;

and because they cried aloud and annoyed the captain or prevented him sleeping, he commanded that they should strangle them: the officer who was burning them was worse than a hangman and did not wish to suffocate them, but with his own hands be gagged them, so that they should not make themselves heard, and he stirred up the fire, until they roasted slowly, according to his pleasure. I know his name, and knew also his relations in Seville. I saw all the above things and numberless others.

10. And because all the people who could flee, hid among the mountains and climbed the crags to escape from men so deprived of humanity, so wicked, such wild beasts, exterminators and capital enemies of all the human race, the Spaniards taught and trained the fiercest boar-hounds to tear an Indian to pieces as soon as they saw him, so that they more willingly attacked and ate one, than if he had been a boar. These hounds made great havoc and slaughter.

11. And because sometimes, though rarely, the Indians killed a few Christians for just cause, they made a law among themselves, that for one Christian whom the Indians killed, the Christians should kill a hundred Indians.

Discussion

1. How do the documents reveal, and what do they imply about, the various sources and manifestations of Spanish power in the western hemisphere?

2. What do the documents suggest about cultural differences between Spaniards and Native Americans, and how do those differences relate to the development of Spanish power?

3. How do the assertions of Spanish power implicit in the Laws of Burgos and the conquest of Mexico conform to the Papal Bull of 1493?

4. Unlike the Aztecs, some Indians resisted the Spanish for centuries. What does the account by Cabeza de Vaca reveal about the Indians' power to defend their culture?

5. What do the Laws of Burgos, the Aztec description of the conquest, Las Casas' narrative and Cabeza de Vaca's account show about Indian attitudes toward power? What do the documents disclose about Native American attitudes regarding equality?

6. Columbus assumed that Indians would be easy to convert to Christianity. The Laws of Burgos recognize that conversion will be a difficult process. What explains this change of attitude?

7. What does the Las Casas narrative reveal about Spanish attitudes towards Native Americans in terms of liberty, power, and equality?

CHAPTER 2

THE CHALLENGE TO SPAIN AND
THE SETTLEMENT OF NORTH AMERICA

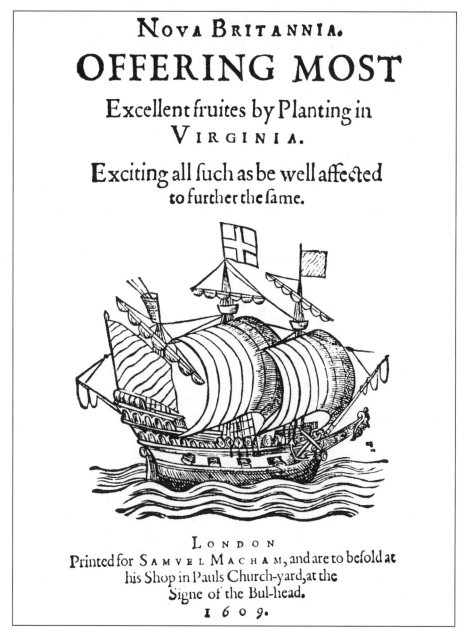

The London Company sold stock, held lotteries, and published brochures such as this to promote its Virginia colony. While these promotional efforts hinted at instant wealth, they masked the desperate need for additional settlers and laborers.

More than ten million people moved to the Americas in the three hundred years after the voyages of Columbus. In addition to those from Spain, the emigrants came from a variety of cultures, including French, Dutch, African, and English. As a result, other European states threatened Spanish hegemony in the western hemisphere, initiating power struggles in the region that lasted well into the eighteenth century. Each of these groups, furthermore, carried with them different political and economic ideals, providing a broad spectrum of settlements that significantly shaped the development of American society. For many individuals, commerce provided the primary impetus to the development of the so-called New World. Others, particularly the English, were more concerned with establishing permanent settlements. Englishmen shared a deep faith in specific civil rights that had evolved over centuries but were generally dated from the Magna Carta of 1215. As English settlers came to dominate the Atlantic coast of North America, they established a tradition of liberty that had a vital influence on the development of the United States.

8. THE CONVERSION OF THE SAVAGES IN NEW FRANCE, 1610*

The following letter, written by the Huguenot poet, lawyer, and historian Marc Lescarbot to Maria de Medici, the Catholic queen of France, touches on French attitudes toward European colonization of the Americas while providing a brief description of Acadia (modern Nova Scotia). From the early 1600s to the 1760s, North America became the prize in a monumental conflict between European powers; Lescarbot's critical comments regarding other nations portend that bitter international confrontation. This document also describes briefly the egalitarianism of tribal democracy that characterized many Indian societies.

It remains . . . to deplore the wretched condition of these people who occupy a country so large that the old world bears no comparison with it. . . . Dense ignorance prevails in all these countries, where there is no evidence that they have ever felt the breath of the Gospel, except in the last century when the Spaniard carried thither some light of the Christian religion, together with his cruelty and avarice. But this was so little that it should not receive much consideration, since by the very confession of those who have written their histories, they have killed almost all the natives of the country, who, only seventy years ago . . . numbered more than twenty millions. For more than twenty-five years, the English have retained a foothold in the country, called in honor of the deceased Queen of England, Virginia. . . . But that country carries on its affairs with so much secrecy, that very few persons know anything definite about it. . . . As to our French people, I have complained enough . . . of our lack of zeal either in reclaiming these poor erring ones, or in making known, exalted, and glorified, the name of God in the lands beyond the seas, where it never has been proclaimed. . . . But why is it that the Church, which has so much wealth; why is it that the

*From *The Jesuit Relations and Allied Documents: Travels and Explorations of the Jesuit Missionaries in New France,* 1610–1791, 73 vols., ed. Reuben Gold Thwaites (Cleveland: Burrows Brothers Company, 1896–1901), I:61–77.

Nobility, who expend so much needlessly, do not establish some fund for the execution of so holy a work? Two courageous Gentlemen, Sieurs de Monts and de Poutrincourt, have . . . shown such great zeal in this work, that they have weakened their resources by their outlays, and have done more than their strength justified them in doing. . . .

This Port Royal, the home of sieur de Poutrincourt is the most beautiful earthly habitation that God has ever made. It . . . can securely harbor twenty thousand ships. . . . Furthermore, there can be caught . . . great quantities of herring, smelt, sardines, barbels, codfish, seals and other fish; and as to shell-fish, there is an abundance of lobsters, crabs, palourdes, cockles, mussels, snails, and porpoises. But whoever is disposed to go beyond the tides of the sea will find in the rivers quantities of sturgeon and salmon, and will have plenty of sport in landing them. . . .

The people who are at Port Royal . . . are called Souriquois and . . . are governed by Captains called Sagamores. . . . At Port Royal, the name of the . . . Sagamore . . . is Membertou. He is at least a hundred years old, and may in the course of nature live more than fifty years longer. He has a number of families whom he rules, not with so much authority as does our King . . . , but with sufficient power to harangue, advise, and lead them to war, to render justice to one who has a grievance, and like matters. He does not impose any taxes upon the people, but if there are any profits from the chase he has a share of them, without being obliged to take part in it. It is true that they sometimes make him presents of Beaver skins and other things, when he is occupied in curing the sick. . . . Now this Membertou to-day, by the grace of God, is a Christian, together with all his family, having been baptized, and twenty others with him, on last Saint John's day, the 24th of June. . . .

9. THE INDIANS OF ACADIA DEFEND THEIR CULTURE*

*T*he Micmac Indians of Acadia did not agree with Lescarbot that they lived in a "wretched condition" or that "dense ignorance" prevailed among them. As Chrestien LeClercq recounted in the 1670s, they eloquently upheld their own cultural values as a superior way of life. Although their ideas of liberty contrasted with European standards, they certainly relished the freedom to preserve their own culture.

I am greatly astonished that the French have so little cleverness, as they seem to exhibit in the matter of which thou hast just told me on their behalf, in the effort to persuade us to convert our poles, our barks, and our wigwams into those houses of stone and of wood which are tall and lofty, according to their account, as these trees. Very well! But why now, . . . do men of five to six feet in height need houses which are sixty to eighty? For, in fact, as thou knowest very well thyself, Patriarch—do we not find in our own all the conveniences and the advantages that you have with yours, such as reposing, drinking, sleeping, eating, and amusing ourselves with our friends when we wish? This is not all, . . . my brother, hast thou as much ingenuity and cleverness as the Indians, who carry their houses and their wigwams with them so that they may lodge wheresoever they please, independently of any seignior whatsoever? Thou art not as bold nor as stout as we, because when thou goest on a voyage thou canst not carry upon thy shoulders thy buildings and thy edifices. Therefore it is necessary that thou preparest as many lodgings as thou makest changes of residence, or else thou lodgest in a hired house which does not belong to thee. As for us, we find ourselves secure from all these inconveniences, and we can always say, more truly than thou, that we are at home everywhere we go, and without asking permission of anybody. Thou reproachest us, very inappropriately, that our country is a little hell in contrast with France, which thou comparest to a terrestrial paradise, inasmuch as it yields thee, so

---

*From Chrestien LeClercq, *New Relation of Gaspesia, with the Customs and Religion of the Gaspesian Indians*, trans. and ed. William F. Ganong (Toronto: The Champlain Society, 1910), 103–06.

thou sayest, every kind of provision in abundance. Thou sayest of us also that we are the most miserable and most unhappy of all men, living without religion, without manners, without honour, without social order, and, in a word, without any rules, like the beasts in our woods and our forests, lacking bread, wine, and a thousand other comforts which thou hast in superfluity in Europe. Well, my brother, if thou dost not yet know the real feelings which our Indians have towards thy country and towards all thy nation, it is proper that I inform thee at once. I beg thee now to believe that, all miserable as we seem in thine eyes, we consider ourselves nevertheless much happier than thou in this, that we are very content with the little that we have; and believe also once for all, I pray, that thou deceivest thyself greatly if thou thinkest to persuade us that thy country is better than ours. For if France, as thou sayest, is a little terrestrial paradise, art thou sensible to leave it? And why abandon wives, children, relatives, and friends? Why risk thy life and thy property every year, and why venture thyself with such risk, in any season whatsoever, to the storms and tempests of the sea in order to come to a strange and barbarous country which thou considerest the poorest and least fortunate of the world? Besides, since we are wholly convinced of the contrary, we scarcely take the trouble to go to France, because we fear, with good reason, lest we find little satisfaction there, seeing, in our own experience, that those who are natives thereof leave it every year in order to enrich themselves on our shores. We believe, further, that you are also incomparably poorer than we, and that you are only simple journeymen, valets, servants, and slaves, all masters and grand captains though you may appear, seeing that you glory in our old rags and in our miserable suits of beaver which can no longer be of use to us, and that you find among us, in the fishery for cod which you make in these parts, the wherewithal to comfort your misery and the poverty which oppresses you. As to us, we find all our riches and all our conveniences among ourselves, without trouble and without exposing our lives to the dangers in which you find yourselves constantly through your long voyages. And, whilst feeling compassion for you in the sweetness of our repose, we wonder at the anxieties and cares which you give yourselves night and day in order to load your ship. We see also that all your people live, as a rule, only upon cod which you catch among us. It is everlastingly nothing but cod—cod in the morning, cod at midday, cod at evening, and always cod, until things come to such a pass that if you wish some good morsels, it is at our expense; and you are obliged to have recourse to the Indians, whom you despise so much, and to beg them to go a-hunting that you may be regaled. Now tell me this one little thing, if thou hast any sense: Which of these two is the wisest and happiest—he who labours without ceasing and only obtains, and that with great trouble, enough to live on, or he who rests in comfort and finds all that he needs in the pleasure of hunting and fishing? It is true, . . . that we have not always had the use of bread and of wine which your France produces; but, in fact, before the arrival of the French in these parts, did not the Gaspesians live much longer than now? And if we have not any longer among us any of those old men of a hundred and thirty to forty years, it is only because we are gradually adopting your manner of living, for experience is making it very plain that those of us live longest who, despising your bread, your wine, and your brandy, are content with their natural food of beaver, of moose, of waterfowl, and fish, in accord with the custom of our ancestors and of all the Gaspesian nation. Learn now, my brother, once for all, because I must open to thee my heart: there is no Indian who does not consider himself infinitely more happy and more powerful than the French.

10. CHARTER OF THE DUTCH WEST INDIA COMPANY, 1621*

*D*uring the colonial period, Americans developed a powerful faith in free enterprise and popular government. The importance of trade in the development of the Americas is evident in the following charter, granted by

*From *The Federal and State Constitutions, Colonial Charters, and Other Organic Laws of the States Territories, and Colonies Now or Heretofore Forming the United States of America*, 7 vols., ed. Francis N. Thorpe (Washington, D.C.: U.S. Government Printing Office, 1909), I:59–67.

the States General of the United Netherlands in June 1621 in an effort to gain access to the lucrative products of the western hemisphere. The selection makes clear the Dutch emphasis on commerce rather than on conquest and settlement. In its description of corporate organization and procedure, the charter also reflects the egalitarianism that marked the republican government of the Netherlands. Although American republicanism grew more directly out of English constitutionalism, the Dutch faith in liberty, property, and toleration became a significant element of American culture.

Be it known, that we knowing the prosperity of these countries, and the welfare of their inhabitants depends principally on navigation and trade, . . . and desiring that the aforesaid inhabitants should not only be preserved in their former navigation, traffic, and trade, but also that their trade may be encreased as much as possible . . . : And we find by experience, that without the common help, assistance, and interposition of a General Company, the people . . . cannot be profitably protected and maintained in their great risk from pirates, extortion and otherwise, which will happen in so very long a voyage. We have, therefore, . . . found it good, that the navigation, trade, and commerce, in parts of the West-Indies, and Africa, and other places hereafter described, should not henceforth be carried on any otherwise than by the common united strength of the merchants and inhabitants of these countries; and that for that end there shall be erected one General Company, which we . . . will maintain and strengthen with our Help, Favour and assistance . . . and moreover furnish them with a proper Charter, and with the following Privileges and Exemptions, to wit, That for the Term of four and twenty Years, none of the Natives or Inhabitants of these countries shall be permitted to sail to or from the said lands, or to traffic on the coast and countries of *Africa* from the *Tropic of Cancer* to the *Cape of Good Hope*, nor in any countries of *America*, or the *West-Indies*, beginning at the fourth end of *Terra Nova*, by the straights of *Magellan*, *La Maire*, or any other straights and passages situated thereabouts to the straights of *Anian*, as well on the north sea as the south sea, nor on any islands situated on the one side or the other, or between both; nor in the western or southern countries reaching, lying, and between both meridians, from the *Cape of Good Hope*, in the East, to the east end of *New Guinea*, in the West, inclusive, but in the name of the United Company of these United Netherlands. . . .

II. That, moreover, the aforesaid Company may, . . . make contracts, engagements and alliances with the limits herein before prescribed, make contracts, engagements and alliances with the princes and natives of the countries comprehended therein, and also build any forts and fortifications there, to appoint and discharge Governors, people for war, and officers of justice, and other public officers, for the preservation of the places, keeping good order, police and justice, and in like manner for the promoting of trade; . . . Moreover, they advance the peopling of those fruitful and unsettled parts, and do all that the service of those countries, and the profit and increase of trade shall require. . . .

V. And should it be necessary for the establishment, security, and defence of this trade, to take any troops with them, we will . . . furnish the said Company with such troops, provided they be paid and supported by the Company. . . .

VIII. That we will not take any ships, ordnance, or ammunition belonging to the company, for the use of this country, without the consent of the said company.

IX. We have moreover incorporated this company, and favoured them with privileges, . . . that they may pass freely with all their ships and goods without paying any toll to the United Provinces. . . .

XI. And that this company may be strengthened by a good government, to the greatest profit and satisfaction of all concerned, we have ordained, that the said government shall be vested in five chambers of managers; one at Amsterdam, . . . one chamber in Zealand, . . . one chamber at the Maeze, . . . one chamber in North Holland, . . . and the fifth chamber in Friesland. . . .

XIV. That the first managers shall serve for the term of six years, and then one-third part of the number of managers shall be changed by lot; and two years after a like third part, and the two next following years, the last third part; and so on successively the oldest in the service shall be dismissed; and in the place of those who go off, . . . three others shall be nominated by the managers,

. . . together with the principal adventurers . . . , from which the aforesaid Provinces, the deputies, or the magistrates, shall make a new election of a manager. . . .

XVI. That every six years they shall make a general account of all outfits and returns, together with all the gains and losses of the company; . . . which accounts shall be made public . . . , to the end that every one who is interested may, upon hearing of it, attend; and if by the expiration of the seventh year, the accounts are not made out in manner aforesaid, the managers shall forfeit their commissions, which shall be appropriated to the use of the poor. . . . And notwithstanding there shall be a dividend made of the profits of the business, so long as we find that *ten per cent* shall have been gained.

XVIII. That so often as it shall be necessary to have a general meeting of the aforesaid chambers, . . . [at least nineteen persons] shall be deputed by us for the purpose of helping to direct the aforesaid meeting of the company.

XIX. By which general meeting . . . all the business of this Company . . . shall be managed and finally settled, provided, that in the case of resolving upon a war, our approbation shall be asked.

XXXI. The manager shall not deliver or sell to the Company, in whole or in part, any of their own ships, merchandise or goods; nor buy or cause to be bought, of the said Company, directly or indirectly, any goods or merchandise, nor have any portion or part therein, on forfeiture of one year's commissions for the use of the poor, and the loss of Office.

XXXII. The managers shall give notice by advertisement, as often as they have a fresh importation of goods and merchandise, to the end that every one may have a seasonable knowledge of it, before they proceed to a final sale. . . .

XXXVI. That the . . . managers shall not be arrested, attached or encumbered, in order to obtain from them an account of the administration of the Company, nor for the payment of the wages of those who are in the service of the Company, but those who shall pretend to take the same upon them, shall . . . refer the matter to their ordinary judges. . . .

XXXIX. We have moreover promised . . . that we will defend this Company against every person in free navigation and traffic, and assist them with a million of guilders. . . .

XL. And if by a violent and continued interruption of the aforesaid navigation and traffic, the business within the limits of their Company shall be brought to an open war, we will . . . give them for their assistance sixteen ships of war, . . . with four good well sailing yachts, . . . which shall be properly mounted and provided in all respects, . . . upon condition that they shall be manned, victualled, and supported at the expense of the Company, and that the Company shall be obliged to add thereto sixteen like ships of war and four yachts . . . ; Provided that all the ships of war and merchant-men . . . shall be under an admiral appointed by us according to the previous advise of the aforesaid General Company, and shall obey our commands, together with the resolutions of the Company. . . .

XLIV. The managers of this Company shall solemnly promise and swear, that they will act well and faithfully in their administration, and make good and just accounts of their trade: That they in all things will consult the greatest profit of the Company: . . . That they will not give the principal members any greater advantage in the payments or distribution of money than the least. . . .

11. JOHN HAWKINS'S FIRST VOYAGE, 1562–1563*
RECORDED BY RICHARD HAKLUYT

Sir John Hawkins stirred English interest in the Americas with his successful voyage in the 1560s. The following account of that venture played an important role in suggesting the wealth to be made in the Atlantic

*From *Voyages of the Elizabeth Seamen: Select Narratives from the "Principal Navigations" of Hakluyt*, ed. Edward John Payne (London: Oxford University Press, 1907), 6–8.

trade, especially in what became a centuries-long commerce in slaves. The importation of African slaves had crucial implications for the United States. Slavery shaped attitudes toward liberty for more than two hundred years, and the search for racial equality has lasted well through the twentieth century. In addition, the slavery question helped generate an intense conflict over the nature of political power in the United States that culminated in civil war during the 1860s.

Master John Hawkins having made divers voyages to the isles of the *Canaries,* and there by his good and upright dealing being grown in love and favour with the people, informed himself amongst them, by diligent inquisition, of the state of the West *India,* whereof he had received some knowledge of the instructions of his father, but increased the same by the advertisements and reports of that people. And being amongst other particulars that *Negroes* were very good merchandise in *Hispaniola,* and that store of *Negroes* might easily be had upon the coast of *Guinea,* resolved himself to make trial thereof, and communicated that device with his worshipful friends in *London.* . . . All which persons liked so well of his intention, that they became liberal contributors and adventurers in the action. For which purpose there were three good ships immediately provided: . . . in which small fleet *Master Hawkins* took with him not above 100 men, for fear of sickness and other inconveniences, whereunto men in long voyages are commonly subject.

With this company he put off and departed from the coast of *England* in the month of October, 1562, and in his course touched first at *Tenriffe,* where he received friendly entertainment. From thence he passed to *Sierra Leona,* upon the coast of *Guinea,* which place by the people is called *Tagarin,* where he stayed some good time, and got into his possession, partly by the sword and partly by other means, to the number of 300 *Negroes* at the least, besides other merchandises which that country yieldeth. With this prey he sailed over the ocean sea unto the island of *Hispaniola,* and arrived at the port of *Isabella:* and there he had reasonable utterance of his English commodities, as also of some part of his *Negroes,* trusting the Spaniards no further, than that by his own strength he was able to master them. From the port *Isabella* he went to *Puerta de Plata,* where he made like sales, standing always upon his guard: from thence also he sailed to *Monte Christi,* another port on the north side of *Hispaniola,* and the last place of his touching, where he had peaceable traffic, and made vent of the whole number of his *Negroes:* for which he received in those three places, by way of exchange, such a quantity of merchandise that he did not only lade his own three ships with hides, ginger, sugars, and some quantity of pearls, but he freighted also two other hulks with hides and other like commodities, which he sent into *Spain.* And thus, leaving the island, he returned . . . , passing out by the islands of the *Caicos,* without further entering into the Bay of *Mexico,* in this his first voyage to the *West India.* And so, with prosperous success and much gain to himself and the aforesaid adventurers, he came home, and arrived in the month of September, 1563.

12. AN INDENTURED SERVANT REPORTS THE MISERIES OF EARLY VIRGINIA*

*I*n a letter to his parents written between March 20 and April 3, 1623, Richard Frethorne, an indentured servant in early Virginia, describes the deplorable conditions in the colony after Opechancanough's massacre of the previous year. As perils increased and the death toll mounted, settlers worried far more about daily survival than about their personal liberties.

---

*From *The Records of the Virginia Company,* 4 vols., ed. Susan M. Kingsbury (Washington, D.C.: U.S. Government Printing Office, 1935), IV:58–62 (modernized).

Loving and kind father and mother:

My most humble duty remembered to you, hoping in God of your good health, as I myself am at the making hereof. This is to let you understand that I your child am in a most heavy case by reason of the nature of the country, [which] is such that it causeth much sickness, [such] as the scurvy and the bloody flux and diverse other diseases, which maketh the body very poor and weak. And when we are sick there is nothing to comfort us; for since I came out of the ship I never ate anything but peas, and loblollie (that is, water gruel). As for deer or venison I never saw any since I came into this land. There is indeed some fowl, but we are not allowed to go and get it, but must work hard both early and late for a mess of water gruel and a mouthful of bread and beef. A mouthful of bread for a penny loaf must serve for four men which is most pitiful. [You would be grieved] if you did know as much as I [do], when people cry out day and night—Oh! that they were in England without their limbs—and would not care to lose any limb to be in England again, yea, though they beg from door to door. For we live in fear of the enemy every hour, yet we have had a combat with them on the Sunday before Shrovetide, and we took two alive and made slaves of them. But it was by policy, for we are in great danger; for our plantation is very weak by reason of the death and sickness of our company. For we came but twenty for the merchants, and they are half dead just; and we look every hour when two more should go. Yet there came some four other men yet to live with us, of which there is but one alive; and our Lieutenant is dead, and [also] his father and his brother. And there was some five or six of the last year's twenty, of which there is but three left, so that we are fain to get other men to plant with us; and yet we are but 32 to fight against 3000 if they should come. And the nighest help that we have is ten miles of us, and when the rogues overcame this place [the] last [time] they slew 80 persons. How then shall we do, for we lie even in their teeth? They may easily take us, but [for the fact] that God is merciful and can save with few as well as with many, as he showed to Gilead. And like Gilead's soldiers, if they lapped water, we drink water which is but weak.

And I have nothing to comfort me, nor there is nothing to be gotten here but sickness and death, except [in the event] that one had money to lay out in some things for profit. But I have nothing at all—no, not a shirt to my back but two rags (2), nor no clothes but one poor suit, nor but one pair of shoes, but one pair of stockings, but one cap, [and] but two bands. My cloak is stolen by one of my own fellows, and to his dying hour [he] would not tell me what he did with it, but some of my fellows saw him have butter and beef out of a ship, which my cloak, I doubt [not], paid for. So that I have not a penny, nor a penny worth, to help me to either spice or sugar or strong waters, without the which one cannot live here. For as strong beer in England doth fatten and strengthen them, so water here doth wash and weaken these here [and] only keeps [their] life and soul together. But I am not half [of] a quarter so strong as I was in England, and all is for want of victuals; for I do protest unto you that I have eaten more in [one] day at home than I have allowed me here for a week. You have given more than my day's allowance to a beggar at the door; and if Mr. Jackson had not relieved me, I should be in a poor case. But he like a father and she like a loving mother doth still help me.

For when we go up to Jamestown (that is 10 miles of us) there lie all the ships that come to land, and there they must deliver their goods. And when we went up to town [we would go], as it may be, on Monday at noon, and come there by night, [and] then load the next day by noon, and go home in the afternoon, and unload, and then away again in the night, and [we would] be up about midnight. Then if it rained or blowed never so hard, we must lie in the boat on the water and have nothing but a little bread. For when we go into the boat we [would] have a loaf allowed to two men, and it is all [we would get] if we stayed there two days, which is hard; and [we] must lie all that while in the boat. But that Goodman Jackson pitied me and made me a cabin to lie in always when I [would] come up, and he would give me some poor jacks [to take] home with me, which comforted me more than peas or water gruel. Oh, they be very godly folks, and love me very well, and

will do anything for me. And he much marvelled that you would send me a servant to the Company; he saith I had been better knocked on the head. And indeed so I find it now, to my great grief and misery; and [I] saith that if you love me you will redeem me suddenly, for which I do entreat and beg. And if you cannot get the merchants to redeem me for some little money, then for God's sake get a gathering or entreat some good folks to lay out some little sum of money in meal and cheese and butter and beef. Any eating meat will yield great profit. Oil and vinegar is very good; but, father, there is great loss in leaking. But for God's sake send beef and cheese and butter, or the more of one sort and none of another. But, if you send cheese, it must be very old cheese; and at the cheesemonger's you may buy very good cheese for twopence farthing or halfpenny, that will be liked very well. But if you send cheese, you must have a care how you pack it in barrels; and you must put cooper's chips between every cheese, or else the heat of the hold will rot them. And look whatsoever you send me—be it never so much—look, what[ever] I make of it, I will deal truly with you. I will send it over and beg the profit to redeem me; and if I die before it come, I have entreated Goodman Jackson to send you the worth of it, who hath promised he will. If you send, you must direct your letters to Goodman Jackson, at Jamestown, a gunsmith. (You must set down his freight, because there be more of his name there.) Good father, do not forget me, but have mercy and pity my miserable case. I know if you did but see me, you would weep to see me; for I have but one suit. (But [though] it is a strange one, it is very well guarded.) Wherefore, for God's sake, pity me. I pray you to remember my love to all my friends and kindred. I hope all my brothers and sisters are in good health, and as for my part I have set down my resolution that certainly will be; that is, that the answer of this letter will be life or death to me. Therefore, good father, send as soon as you can; and if you send me any thing let this be the mark.
ROT

Richard Frethorne,
Martin's Hundred

The names of them that be dead of the company [that] came over with us to serve under our Lieutenants: [Frethorne lists seventeen individuals, including 15 men, 2 women, and 1 child.]

All these died out of my master's house, since I came; and we came in but at Christmas, and this is the 20th day of March. And the sailors say that there is two-thirds of the 150 dead already. And thus I end, praying to God to send me good success that I may be redeemed out of Egypt. So *vale in Christo*.

Loving father, I pray you to use this man very exceeding kindly, for he hath done much for me, both on my journey and since. I entreat you not to forget me, but by any means redeem me; for this day we hear that there is 26 of [the] Englishmen slain by the Indians. And they have taken a pinnace of Mr. Pountis, and have gotten pieces, armor, [and] swords, all things fit for war; so that they may now steal upon us and we cannot know them from [the] English till it is too late—[till the time] that they be upon us—and then there is no mercy. Therefore if you love or respect me as your child, release me from this bondage and save my life. Now you may save me, or let me be slain with infidels. Ask this man—he knoweth that all is true and just that I say here. If you do redeem me, the Company must send for me to my Mr. Harrod; for so is this Master's name. April, the second day,

Your loving son,
Richard Frethorne

. . . there is no way but starving; for the Governor told us and Sir George that except the *Seaflower* [should] come in or that we can fall foul of these rogues [Indians] and get some corn from them, above half the land will surely be starved. For they had no crop last year by reason of these rogues, so that we have no corn but as ships do relieve us, nor we shall hardly have any crop this year; and we are as like to perish first as any plantation. For we have but two hogsheads of meal left to serve us this two months, if the *Seaflower* do stay so long before she come in; and that meal is but three weeks bread for us, at a loaf for four [men] about the bigness of a penny loaf in England— that is but a halfpennyloaf a day for a man. Is it not strange to me, think you? But what will it be when we shall go a month or two and never see a bit of bread, as my master doth say we must do? And he said he is not able to keep us all. Then we shall be turned up to the land and eat barks of trees or molds of the ground; therefore with weeping tears I beg of you to help me. Oh, that you did see my daily and hourly sighs, groans, and tears, and [the] thumps that I afford mine own breast, and [the way I] rue and curse the time of my birth, with holy Job. I thought no head had been able to hold so much water as hath and doth daily flow from mine eyes.

But this is certain: I never felt the want of father and mother till now; but now, dear friends, full well I know and rue it, although it were too late before I knew it.

I pray you talk with this honest man. He will tell you more than now in my haste I can set down.

Your loving son,
Richard Frethorne

Virginia, 3rd April, 1623

13. THE LAWS OF VIRGINIA, 1619*

*T*he following code constitutes the first statutes enacted by a general assembly in North America; they therefore mark an important step in the evolution of popular government. Like all laws, they mirror the society that created them, and they help the modern reader gain some understanding of life in early Virginia. At the same time, by disclosing what authorities considered to be criminal activities, the statutes shed light on perceptions of power and liberty at the beginning of English settlement in the New World.

By this present General Assembly be it enacted that no injury or oppression be wrought by the *English* against the Indians whereby the present peace might be disturbed, & ancient quarrels might be revived. . . .

Against Idleness, gaming, drunkenness, & excess in apparel, the Assembly hath enacted as followeth: . . .

Be it enacted, that if any man be found, to live as an Idler or renegade though a freed man, it shall be lawful for that Incorporation or Plantation to which he belongeth to appoint him a master to serve for wages till he show apparent signs of amendment.

Against gaming at Dice & Cards be it ordained . . . that the winner or winners shall lose all his or their winnings & both winners and losers shall forfeit ten shillings a man, one ten shillings whereof to go to the discoverer, & the rest to charitable & pious uses in the Incorporation where the faults are committed.

Against drunkenness be it also decreed, that if any private person be found culpable thereof, for the first time he is to be reproved privately by the Minister, the second time, publicly, the Third time to lie in bolts 12 hours in the House of the Provost Marshall & to pay his fees, and if he still continue in that vice, to undergo such severe punishment as the Governor & Council of Estate shall think fit to be inflicted upon him. But if any Officer offend in this crime, the first time he shall receive a reproof from the Governor, the second time he shall openly be reproved in the Church by the minister, & the third time he shall first be committed & then degraded. . . .

---

*From *Journals of the House of Burgesses of Virginia, 1619–1658/59*, ed. H. R. McIlwaine (Richmond, Virginia: State Library, 1915), 9–11, 13–14.

Against excess of apparel, that every man be assessed in the Church for all the public contributions, if he be unmarried according to his own apparel, if he be married, according to his own & his wife's, or either by their apparel.

As touching the Instruction of drawing some of the better disposed of the Indians to converse with our people & to live & labor among them, the Assembly . . . think it fit to enjoin . . . those of the Colony neither utterly to reject them, nor yet to draw them to come in. But in case they will of themselves come voluntarily . . . to do service, in killing of Deer, Fishing, beating Corn, & other works that then five or six may be admitted to every such place, and no more, & that with the consent of the Governor, provided that good guard in the night be kept upon them, for generally . . . they are a most treacherous people, & quickly gone when they have done a villainy. . . .

Be it enacted . . . that for . . . the conversion of the Indians to Christian Religion, each town, city, Borough, & particular plantation do obtain unto themselves by just means a certain number of the natives' children to be educated by them in the true Religion & civic course of life, of which children the most towardly boys . . . to be brought up by them . . . so as to be fitted for the College intended for them, that from thence they may be sent to that of conversion.

As touching the business of planting corn, the present Assembly doth ordain, that year by year, all & every householder and householders, have in store for every servant he or they shall keep, & also for his or their own persons, . . . one spare barrel of corn to be delivered out yearly either upon sale or exchange, as need shall require. . . .

About the Plantation of Mulberry trees be it enacted that every man . . . do for seven years together every year plant and maintain in growth six Mulberry trees at the least. . . .

Be it farther enacted, as concerning silk flax that those men that are . . . settled . . . do this next year plant & Dress 100 plants. . . .

For hemp also both *English* & Indian, & for *English* Flax and Anise seeds, we do require . . . all householders of this Colony, that have any those seeds, to make trial thereof the next season.

Moreover be it enacted . . . that every householder do yearly plant & maintain ten vines, until they have attained to the art & experience of dressing a vineyard, either by their own industry, or by the instructions of some [other person]. . . .

Be it further ordained . . . that all contracts made in *England* between the owners of land & their Tenants and the servants which they shall sent hither, may be caused to be duly performed. . . .

Be it established also . . . that no crafty or advantageous means . . . put in practice for the enticing away the Tenants & Servants of any particular plantation from the place where they are Seated. . . .

That no man do sell or give any Indians any piece, shot, or powder, or any other arms offensive or defensive, upon pain of being held a Traitor to the Colony, & of being hanged, as soon as the fact is proved, without all redemption.

That no man do sell or give any of the greater hounds to the Indians, or any *English* dog of quality, as a Mastiff, Greyhound, Blood hound, land or water Spaniel, or any other dog or bitches whatever, of the *English* race, upon pain of forfeiting 5 pounds *sterling* to the public uses of the Incorporation where he dwelleth.

That no man may go above twenty miles from his dwelling place, nor upon any voyage whatsoever shall be absent from thence for the space of seven days together, without first having made the Governor, or commander of the same place acquainted therewith. . . .

That no man shall purposely go to any Indian towns, habitations or places of resort, without leave from the Governor or commander of that place where he liveth upon pain of paying 40 shillings to public uses. . . .

That no man living in this Colony, but shall between this and the first of *January* next en-suing come or send to the Secretary of State, to enter . . . all his servants' names, & for what term, or upon what conditions they are to serve. . . . Also whatsoever, Masters or people do come over to this plantation, that within one month of their arrival . . . , they shall likewise resort to the Secretary of State & shall Certify him upon what terms or conditions they be come hither. . . .

All Ministers in this Colony shall once a year . . . bring to the Secretary of Estate a true account of all Christenings, burials, & marriages. . . . Likewise where there be no ministers, that the commanders of the place do supply the same duty.

No man without leave from the Governor shall kill any Neat cattle whatsoever, young or old, especially kine, Heifers, or Cowcalves, & shall be careful to preserve their Steers & Oxen, & to bring them to the plow & such profitable uses, & without having obtained leave as aforesaid shall not kill them upon penalty of forfeiting the value of the Beast so killed.

Whosoever shall take any of his neighbors' boats, oars, or canoes without leave from the owner shall be held and esteemed as a felon and so proceeded against; also he that shall take away by violence or stealth any canoes or other things from the Indians shall make valuable restitution to the said Indians, and shall forfeit, if he be freeholder, five pounds; if a servant 40 shillings, or endure a whipping. . . .

All ministers shall duly read divine service, and exercise their ministerial function according to the Ecclesiastical Laws and orders of the church of *England*, and every *Sunday* in the afternoon shall Catechize such as are not yet ripe to come to the Communion. . . .

The Ministers and Churchwardens shall seek to prevent all ungodly disorders; the committers whereof if, upon good admonitions and mild reproof they will not forbear the said scandalous offenses, as suspicions of whoredom, dishonest company keeping with women and such like, they are to be presented and punished accordingly.

If any person after two warnings, do not amend his or her life in point of evident suspicion of Incontinency or of the commission of any other enormous sins, that then he or she be presented by the Churchwardens and suspended for a time from the church by the minister. In which Interim if the same person do not amend and humbly submit him or herself to the church, he is then fully to be excommunicate and soon after a writ or warrant to be sent from the Governor for the apprehending of his person & seizing all his goods. . . .

For reformation of swearing, every freeman and Master of a family after thrice admonition shall give 5 shillings or the value upon present demands, to the use of the church where he dwelleth; and every servant after the like admonition, except his Master discharge the fine, shall be subject to whipping. Provided, that . . . the said servant shall acknowledge his fault publicly in the Church. . . .

No man shall trade into the Bay either in Shallop, pinnace, or ship without the Governor's License, and without putting in security, that neither himself, nor his Company shall force or wrong the Indians. . . .

All persons whatsoever upon Sabbath days shall frequent divine service & sermons both forenoon and afternoon; & all such as bear arms, shall bring their pieces, Swords, powder, & shot. And Every one that shall transgress this Law, shall forfeit three shillings a time to the use of the Church. . . .

No maid or woman servant . . . shall contract herself in marriage without either the consent of her parents or her Master or Mistress, or of the magistrate & Minister of the place both together. . . .

Be it enacted by the present assembly, that whatsoever servant hath heretofore, or shall hereafter contract himself in *England* . . . to serve any Master here in *Virginia*, and shall afterward, against his said former contract, depart from his Master without leave, or being once embarked, shall abandon the ship he is appointed to come in, & so being left behind, shall put himself into the service of any other man that will bring him hither; that then at the same servant's arrival here, he shall first serve out his time, with that Master that brought him hither and afterward also shall serve out his time with his former Master according to his covenant.

14. THE MAYFLOWER COMPACT, 1620*

Unsure of the legal authority for their colony, and concerned by the number of "strangers" in their midst, Pilgrim immigrants from the Netherlands and England promulgated this agreement before establishing their settlement at Plymouth, Massachusetts. Although the document is remarkably brief, the ideas expressed in the compact have exerted tremendous influence on the American people. By creating a "body politick," the emigrants put into place government by the majority with the consent of the minority. The Mayflower Compact, therefore, stands as an early American effort to provide some balance between the power of government and the liberties of individuals.

In the name of God, Amen. We whose names are under-written, the loyal subjects of our dread sovereign Lord, King James, by the grace of God, of Great Britain, France, and Ireland King, defender of the faith, etc., having undertaken, for the glory of God, and advancement of the Christian faith, and honor of our king and country, a voyage to plant the first colony in the Northern parts of Virginia, do by these presents solemnly and mutually in the presence of God, and of one another, covenant and combine ourselves together into a civil body politick, for our bettering ordering and preservation and furtherance of the ends aforesaid; and by virtue hereof to enact, constitute, and frame such just and equal laws, ordinances, acts, constitutions, and offices, from time to time, as shall be thought most meet and convenient for the general good of the Colony, unto which we promise all due submission and obedience. In witness whereof we have hereunder subscribed our names at Cape Cod the 11th of November, in the year of the reign of our sovereign lord, King James, of England, France, and Ireland, the eighteenth, and of Scotland the fifty-fourth. Anno Domino 1620.

15. A MODEL OF CHRISTIAN CHARITY, 1630**

This sermon, famous because of John Winthrop's plea that the Puritans establish a model community in New England, also shows the importance of the covenant in Calvinist thinking. The ideal of the covenant helped to shape the development of constitutional republicanism in the United States by insisting that those in power recognize the liberties of the people over whom they govern. In addition, the conviction that the Puritans were chosen by God for a unique destiny later manifested itself in the growth of a powerful United States that conquered much of North America before assuming a role as a leading international power.

Thus stands the case between God and us. We are entered into a Covenant with Him for this work. We have taken out a commission. The Lord hath given us leave to draw our own articles. We have professed to enterprise these and those ends, upon these and those accounts. We have hereupon besought of Him favor and blessing. Now if the Lord shall please to hear us, and bring us in peace to the place we desire, then hath he ratified this Covenant and sealed our Commission, and will expect a strict performance of the articles contained in it; but if we shall neglect the observation of these articles which are the ends we have propounded, and, dissembling with our God, shall fail to embrace this present world and prosecute our carnal intentions, seeking great things for ourselves and our posterity, the Lord will surely break out in wrath against us; be revenged of such a (sinful) people, and make us know the price of the breach of such a Covenant.

---

*From *William Bradford, Bradford's History of Plymouth Plantation, 1606–1646,* ed. William T. Davis (New York: Charles Scribner's Sons, 1908), 107.
**From Robert C. Winthrop, *Life and Letters of John Winthrop, Governor of the Massachusetts-Bay Company at the Time of Their Emigration to New England,* 2d ed. (Boston: Little Brown, and Company, 1869), II:18–20.

Now the only way to avoid this shipwreck, and to provide for our posterity, is to follow the council of Micah, *to do justly, to love mercy, to walk humbly with our God.* For this end, we must be knit together, in this work, as one man. We must entertain each other in brotherly affection. We must be willing to abridge ourselves of our superfluities, for the supply of other's necessities. We must uphold a familiar commerce together in all meekness, gentleness, patience, and liberality. We must delight in each other; make other's condition our own; rejoice together, mourn together, labor and suffer together, always having before our eyes our commission and community in the work, as members of the same body. So shall we *keep the unity of the spirit in the bond of peace.* The Lord will be our God, and delight to dwell among us, as his own people, and will command a blessing upon us in all our ways. So that we shall see much more of his wisdom, power, goodness, and truth, than formerly we have been acquainted with. We shall find that the God of Israel is among us, when ten of us shall be able to resist a thousand of our enemies; when he shall make us a praise and a glory, that men shall say of succeeding plantations, "The Lord make it like that of *New England.*" For we must consider that we shall be as a City upon a hill. The eyes of all people are upon us. So that if we shall deal falsely with our God in this work we have undertaken, and so cause him to withdraw his present help from us, we shall be made a story and a by-word throughout the world. We shall open the mouths of enemies to speak evil of the ways of God, and all professors for God's sake. We shall shame the faces of many of God's worthy servants, and cause their prayers to be turned into curses upon us till we be consumed out of the good land whither we are a-going. . . .

Therefore let us choose life that we, and our seed may live, by obeying His voice and cleaving to Him, for He is our life and our prosperity.

16. THE TRIAL OF ANNE HUTCHINSON, 1637*

*I*n 1634 Anne Hutchinson (1591-1643), a merchant's wife, migrated with her family to Boston. Soon she began inviting local residents into her home to discuss the Bible and the sermons of local ministers. She openly criticized ministers who apparently preached salvation by works (good behavior) over grace (faith). Her condemnation aroused the attention of political leaders who resented her criticism of local clergy as well as her growing influence in the community. In November, 1637, Hutchinson appeared before the court at Newtown to face interrogation about her beliefs and practices. During the trial her claims of receiving direct revelations from God (the "Antinomian" heresy) particularly agitated the magistrates. As a result of her trial Massachusetts authorities banished Hutchinson from the colony; she and her followers fled to Narragansett Bay and formed communities which later became part of Rhode Island. The following selection demonstrates Hutchinson's courage as she stoutly defended her actions against her determined accusers.*

Mr. Winthrop, governor. Mrs. Hutchinson, you are called here as one of those that have troubled the peace of the commonwealth and the churches here; you are known to be a woman that hath had a great share in the promoting and divulging of those opinions that are causes of this trouble, and to be nearly joined not only in affinity and affection with some of those the court had taken notice of and passed censure upon. But you have spoken divers things as we have been informed very prejudicial to the honour of the churches and ministers thereof, and you have maintained a meeting and an assembly in'your house that hath been condemned by the general assembly as a thing not tolerable nor comely in the sight of God nor fitting for your sex; and notwithstanding that was cried down, you have continued the same. Therefore we have thought good to send for you to understand how

*From Thomas Hutchinson, *The History of the Province of Massachusetts-Bay, From the Charter of King William and Queen Mary, in 1691, Until the Year 1750* (Boston: Thomas & John Fleet, 1767), 482–89, 507–09.

things are, that if you be in an erroneous way we may reduce you that so you may become a profitable member here among us, otherwise if you be obstinate in your course that then the court may take such course that you may trouble us no further . . .

Mrs. Hutchinson. I am called here to answer before you but I hear no things laid to my charge.

Gov. I have told you some already and more I can tell you. (*Mrs. H.*) Name one Sir.

Gov. Have I not named some already?

Mrs. H. What have I said or done?

Gov. Why for your doings, this you did harbour and countenance those that are parties in this faction that you have heard of. (*Mrs. H.*) That's matter of conscience, Sir.

Gov. Your conscience you must keep, or it must be kept for you. . . .

*   *   *

Gov. Why do you keep such a meeting at your house as you do every week upon a set day?

Mrs. H. It is lawful for me so to do, as it is all your practices; and can you find a warrant for yourself and condemn me for the same thing? The ground of my taking it up was, when I first came to this land, because I did not go to such meetings as those were, it was presently reported that I did not allow of such meetings but held them unlawful, and therefore in that regard they said I was proud and did despise all ordinances. Upon that, a friend came unto me and told me of it and I to prevent such aspersions took it up, but it was in practice before I came; therefore I was not the first.

Gov. For this, that you appeal to our practice you need no confutation. If your meeting had answered to the former it had not been offensive, but I will say that there was no meeting of women alone. But your meeting is of another sort, for there are sometimes men among you.

Mrs. H. There was never any man with us.

Gov. Well, admit there was no man at your meeting and that you was sorry for it, there is no warrant for your doings; and by what warrant do you continue such a course?

Mrs. H. I conceive there is a clear rule in Titus, that the elder women should instruct the younger; and then I must have a time wherein I must do it.

Gov. All this I grant you, I grant you a time for it; but what is this to the purpose that you, Mrs. Hutchinson, must call a company together from their callings to come to be taught of you?

Mrs. H. Will it please you to answer me this and to give me a rule, for then I will willingly submit to any truth? If any come to my house to be instructed in the ways of God, what rule have I to put them away?

Gov. But suppose that a hundred men come unto you to be instructed, will you forbear to instruct them?

Mrs. H. As far as I conceive I cross a rule in it.

Gov. Very well and do you not so here?

Mrs. H. No Sir, for my ground is they are men.

Gov. Men and women all is one for that, but suppose that a man should come and say, "Mrs. Hutchinson, I hear that you are a woman that God hath given his grace unto and you have knowledge in the word of God. I pray instruct me a little." Ought you not to instruct this man?

Mrs. H. I think I may.—Do you think it not lawful for me to teach women, and why do you call me to teach the court?

Gov. We do not call you to teach the court but to lay open yourself.

Mrs. H. I desire you that you would then set me down a rule by which I may put them away that come unto me and so have peace in so doing.

Gov. You must shew your rule to receive them.

Mrs. H. I have done it.

Gov. I deny it because I have brought more arguments than you have.

Mrs. H. I say, to me it is a rule.

Mr. Endicott. You say there are some rules unto you. I think there is a contradiction in yur own words. What rule for your practice do you bring, only a custom in Boston.

Mrs. H. No Sir that was no rule to me but if you look upon the rule in Titus it is a rule to me. If you convince me that it is no rule I shall yield.

Gov. You know that there is no rule that crosses another, but this rule crosses that in the Corinthians. But you must take it in this sense that elder women must instruct the younger about their business and to love their husbands and not make them to clash.

Mrs. H. I do not conceive but that it is meant for some publick times.

Gov. Well, have you no more to say but this?

Mrs. H. I have said sufficient for my practice.

Gov. Your course is not to be suffered for, besides that we find such a course as this to be greatly prejudicial to the state, besides the occasion that it is to seduce many honest persons that are called to those meetings and your opinions being known to be different from the word of God may seduce many simple souls that resort unto you, besides that the occasion which hath come of late hath come from none but such as have frequented your meetings, so that now they are flown off from magistrates and ministers and this since they have come to you, and besides that it will not well stand with commonwealth that families should be neglected for so many neighbours and dames and so much time spent, we see no rule of God for this, we see not that any should have authority to set up any other exercise besides what authority hath already set up and so what hurt comes of this you will be guilty of and we for suffering you.

Mrs. H. Sir I do not believe that to be so.

Gov. Well, we see how it is we must therefore put it away from you or restrain you from maintaining this course.

Mrs. H. If you have a rule for it from God's word you may.

Gov. We are your judges, and not you ours and we must compel you to it.

Mrs. H. If it please you by authority to put it down I will freely let you for I am subject to your authority. . . .

*   *   *

Mr. Dudley, dep. gov. Here hath been much spoken concerning Mrs. Hutchinson's meetings and among other answers she saith that men come not there. I would ask you this one question then, whether never any man was at your meeting?

Gov. There are two meetings kept at their house.

Dep. Gov. How; is there two meetings?

Mrs. H. Ey Sir, I shall not equivocate, there is a meeting of men and women, and there is a meeting only for women.

Dep. Gov. Are they both constant?

Mrs. H. No, but upon occasions they are deferred.

Mr. Endicot. Who teaches in the men's meetings, none but men? Do not women sometimes?

Mrs. H. Never as I heard, not one. . . .

Dep. Gov. . . . Now it appears by this woman's meeting that Mrs. Hutchinson hath so forestalled the minds of many by their resort to her meeting that now she hath a potent party in the country. Now if all these things have endangered us as from that foundation, and if she in particular hath disparaged all our ministers in the land that they have preached a covenant of works, . . . why this is not to be suffered. And therefore being driven to the foundation, and it being found that Mrs. Hutchinson is she that hath depraved all the ministers and hath been the cause of what is fallen out, why we must take away the foundation and the building will fall.

Mrs. H. I pray, Sir, prove it that I said they preached nothing but a covenant of works.

Dep. Gov. Nothing but a covenant of works? Why, a Jesuit may preach truth sometimes.

Mrs. H. Did I ever say they preached a covenant of works, then?

Dep. Gov. If they do not preach a covenant of grace clearly, then they preach a covenant of works.

Mrs. H. No Sir, one may preach a covenant of grace more clearly than another, so I said.

Dep. Gov. We are not upon that now, but upon position.

Mrs. H. Prove this then, Sir, that you say I said.

Dep. Gov. When they do preach a covenant of works, do they preach truth?

Mrs. H. Yes Sir, but when they preach a covenant of works for salvation, that is not truth,

Dep. Gov. I do but ask you this: when the ministers do preach a covenant of works, do they preach a way of salvation?

Mrs. H. I did not come hither to answer to questions of that sort.

Dep. Gov. Because you will deny the thing.

Mrs. H. Ey, but that is to be proved first.

Dep. Gov. I will make it plain that you did say that the ministers did preach a covenant of works.

Mrs. H. I deny that.

Dep. Gov. And that you said they were not able ministers of the new testament, but Mr. Cotton only.

Mrs. H. If ever I spake that, I proved it by God's word.

Court. Very well, very well. . . .

*   *   *

Mrs. H. If you please to give me leave, I shall give you the ground of what I know to be true. Being much troubled to see the falseness of the constitution of the church of England, I had like to have turned separatist; whereupon I kept a day of solemn humiliation and pondering of the thing; this scripture was brought unto me—he that denies Jesus Christ to be come in the flesh is antichrist—This I considered of, and in considering found that the papists did not deny him to be come in the flesh, nor we did not deny him—who then was antichrist? Was the Turk antichrist only? The Lord knows that I could not open scripture; he must by his prophetical office open it unto me. So after that, being unsatisfied in the thing, the Lord was pleased to bring this scripture out of the Hebrews. He that denies the testament denies the testator, and in this did open unto me and give me to see that those which did not teach the new covenant had the spirit of antichrist, and upon this he did discover the ministry unto me and ever since. I bless the Lord, he hath let me see which was the clear ministry and which the wrong. Since that time I confess I have been more choice, and he hath let me to distinguish between the voice of my beloved and the voice of Moses, the voice of John Baptist and the voice of antichrist, for all those voices are spoken of in scripture. Now if you do condemn me for speaking what in my conscience I know to be truth, I must commit myself unto the Lord.

Mr. Nowell. How do you know that that was the spirit?

Mrs. H. How did Abraham know that it was God that bid him offer his son, being a breach of the sixth commandment?

Dep. Gov. By an immediate voice.

Mrs. H. So to me by an immediate revelation.

Dep. Gov. How! an immediate revelation.

Mrs. H. By the voice of his own spirit to my soul. I will give you another scripture, Jer. 46. 27, 28—out of which the Lord shewed me what he would do for me and the rest of his servants.—But after he was pleased to reveal himself to me, I did presently like Abraham run to Hagar. And after that, he did let me see the atheism of my own heart, for which I begged of the Lord that it might not remain in my heart; and being thus, he did shew me this (a twelvemonth after) which I told you of before. Ever since that time I have been confident of what he hath revealed unto me. . . . You see this scripture fulfilled this day, and therefore I desire you that as you tender the Lord and the church and commonwealth to consider and look what you do. You have power over my body, but the Lord Jesus hath power over my body and soul; and assure yourselves thus much, you do as much as in you lies to put the Lord Jesus Christ from you; and if you go on in this course you begin, you will bring a curse upon you and your posterity, and the mouth of the Lord hath spoken it.

Dep. Gov. What is the scripture she brings?

Mr. Stoughton. Behold I turn away from you.

Mrs. H. But now having seen him which is invisible, I fear not what man can do unto me.

Gov. Daniel was delivered by miracle. Do you think to be deliver'd so too?

Mrs. H. I do here speak it before the court. I look that the Lord should deliver me by his providence.

Mr. Harlakenden. I may read scripture and the most glorious hypocrite may read them and yet go down to hell.

Mrs. H. It may be so. . . .

17. WILLIAM PENN'S PREFACE TO HIS FIRST FRAME OF GOVERNMENT, 1682*

Although William Penn apparently discounted the importance of any particular governmental model, he still invested considerable effort in formulating a constitutional system for his colony; numerous drafts of his First Frame of Government have survived. Consistent with his Quaker beliefs, he linked liberty, the virtue of the people, and the rule of law, declaring that "any government is free to the people under it (whatever be the frame) where the laws rule, and the people are a party to those laws."

The
PREFACE.

When the great and wise God had made the world, of all His creatures it pleased Him to choose man [as] His deputy to rule it. And to fit him for so great a charge and trust, He did not only qualify him with skill and power, but with integrity to use them justly. This native goodness was equally his honor and his happiness; and while he stood here, all went well. There was no need of coercive or compulsive means; the precept of divine love and truth in his own bosom was the guide and keeper of his innocence. But lust prevailing against duty made a lamentable breach upon it; and the law, that before had no power over him, took place upon him and his disobedient posterity, that such as would not live conformable to the holy law within, should fall under the reproof and correction of the just law without in a judicial administration.

This the Apostle teaches in divers of his epistles: the law (says he) was added because of transgression. In another place, knowing that the law was not made for the righteous man, but for the disobedient and ungodly, for sinners, for unholy and profane, for murderers, for whoremongers, for them that defile themselves with mankind, and for manstealers, for liars, for perjured persons,

---

*From *The Federal and State Constitutions, Colonial Charters, and Other Organic Laws of the States, Territories, and Colonies Now or Heretofore Forming the United States of America,* 7 vols., ed. Francis N. Thorpe (Washington, D.C.: U.S. Government Printing Office, 1909), V: 3052–54.

etc. But this is not all; he opens and carries the matter of government a little further. Let every soul be subject to the higher powers; for there is no power but of God. The powers that be, are ordained of God: whosoever therefore resists the power, resists the ordinance of God. For rulers are not a terror to good works, but to evil: will thou then not be afraid of the power, do that which is good, and thou shall have praise of the same. He is the minister of God to thee for good. Wherefore, ye must needs be subject, not only for wrath, but for conscience sake. This settles the divine right of government beyond exception, and that for two ends: first, to terrify evildoers; secondly, to cherish those that do well; which gives government a life beyond corruption, and makes it as durable in the world, as good men shall be. So that government seems to me a part of religion itself, a thing sacred in its institution and end: for if it does not directly remove the cause, it crushes the effects of evil, and is as such (though a lower, yet) an emanation of the same divine power that is both author and object of pure religion; the difference lying here, that the one is more free and mental, the other, more corporal and compulsive in its operations. But that is only to evildoers; government in itself being otherwise as capable of kindness, goodness, and charity as a more private society. They weakly err that think there is no other use for government than correction, which is the coarsest part of it. Daily experience tells us that the care and regulation of many other affairs, more soft and daily necessary, make up much the greatest part of overnment; and which must have followed the peopling of the world had Adam never fallen, and will continue among men on earth under the highest attainments they may arrive at, by the coming of the blessed second Adam, the Lord from Heaven. Thus much of government in general, as to its rise and end.

For particular frames and models, it will become me to say little; and comparatively I will say nothing. My reasons are, first, that the age is too nice and difficult for it, there being nothing the wits of men are more busy and divided upon. It is true they seem to agree in the end [of government], to wit, happiness; but in the means they differ, as to divine, so to this humane felicity; and the cause is much the same, not always want of light and knowledge, but want of using them rightly. Men side with their passions against their reason; and their sinister interests have so strong a bias upon their minds, that they lean to them against the good of the things they know.

Secondly, I do not find a model in the world, that time, place, and some singular emergencies have not necessarily altered; nor is it easy to frame a civil government that shall serve all places alike.

Thirdly, I know what is said by the several admirers of monarchy, aristocracy, and democracy, which are the rule of one, a few, and many, and are the three common ideas of government, when men discourse of that subject. But I choose to solve the controversy with this small distinction, and it belongs to all three: any government is free to the people under it (whatever be the frame) where the laws rule, and the people are a party to those laws, and more than this is tyranny, oligarchy, or confusion.

But lastly, when all is said, there is hardly one frame of government in the world so ill designed by its first founders, that in good hands would not do well enough; and [hi]story tells us, the best in ill ones can do nothing that is great or good; witness the Jewish and Roman states. Governments, like clocks, go from the motion men give them; and as governments are made and moved by men, so by them are ruined too: wherefore governments rather depend upon men, than men upon governments. Let men be good, and the government can't be bad; if it be ill, they will cure it. But if men be bad, let the government be never so good; they will endeavor to warp and spoil it to their turn.

I know some say, let us have good laws, and no matter for the men that execute them. But let them consider, that though good laws do well, good men do better; for good laws may want good men, and be abolished or evaded by ill men; but good men will never want good laws nor suffer ill ones. It is true, good laws have some awe upon ill ministers, but that is where they have not power to escape or abolish them, and the people are generally wise and good. But a loose and depraved people (which is the question) love laws and an administration like themselves. That therefore which makes a good constitution must keep it, viz.: men of wisdom and virtue; qualities, that because they descend not with worldly inheritances, must be carefully propagated by a virtuous education of youth; for which after-ages will owe more to the care and prudence of founders and the successive magistracy than to their parents for their private patrimonies.

These considerations of the weight of government, and the nice and various opinions about it, made it uneasy to me to think of publishing the ensuing Frame and conditional Laws, foreseeing both the censures they will meet with from men of differing humors and engagements, and the occasion they may give of discourse beyond my design.

But next to the power of necessity (which is a solicitor that will take no denial), this induced me to a compliance, that we have (with reverence to God and good conscience to men) to the best of our skill contrived and composed the Frame and Laws of this government to the great end of all government viz.: to support power in reverence with the people, and to secure the people from the abuse of power; that they may be free by their just obedience, and the magistrates honorable for their just administration. For liberty without obedience is confusion, and obedience without liberty is slavery. To carry this evenness is partly owing to the constitution, and partly to the magistracy; where either of these fail, government will be subject to convulsions; but where both are wanting, it must be totally subverted. Then where both meet, the government is like to endure, which I humbly pray and hope, God will please to make the lot of this of Pennsylvania. Amen.

William Penn.

Discussion

1. Based on the documents, what expressions of egalitarianism existed at the time that large-scale emigration of Europeans and Africans to the Americas began? What examples of inequality do the documents reveal?

2. Several of the selections show that efforts to capitalize on the wealth of the western hemisphere played a key role in the development of the Americas. What assertions of power and expressions of liberty exist in those documents? What does that suggest about concepts of power and liberty in early colonial America?

3. How do the documents hint that future power struggles will ensue in the Americas?

4. What do the documents suggest about different understandings of power and liberty that might have existed between the people who settled Virginia, Massachusetts, or Pennsylvania? Between the French and the Indians in New France?

5. Based on the documents and your readings, which colony would be the most attractive to you as a potential settler? Why? In what way would the documentary expressions about liberty, equality, and power influence your decision?

6. Based on the Anne Hutchinson document, how are the themes of liberty, power, and equality addressed at her trial? Why is Hutchinson perceived as a threat by the Massachusetts authorities?

CHAPTER 3

ENGLAND DISCOVERS ITS COLONIES: EMPIRE, LIBERTY, AND EXPANSION

TO BE SOLD, on board the Ship *Bance-Island*, on tuesday the 6th of *May* next, at *Ashley-Ferry*; a choice cargo of about 250 fine healthy

NEGROES,

just arrived from the Windward & Rice Coaſt. — The utmoſt care has already been taken, and ſhall be continued, to keep them free from the leaſt danger of being infected with the SMALL-POX, no boat having been on board, and all other communication with people from *Charles-Town* prevented.

Auſtin, Laurens, & Appleby.

N. B. Full one Half of the above Negroes have had the SMALL-POX in their own Country.

Public notices of slave auctions were common by the eighteenth century. Like advertisements today, they focused on what buyers of the day wanted to know: that the slaves are healthy and thus a good investment and that they originated on the "Rice Coast" of Africa and are knowledgeable in growing rice.

By the middle of the seventeenth century, England had established a firm hold on much of the Atlantic seaboard, and the American colonies became an integral part of an increasingly powerful English state. Colonial policies, therefore, became much more sophisticated during the seventeenth century as royal authorities sought to protect imperial interests by establishing a mercantilistic economy, by creating new colonies, and by organizing the Dominion of New England. Colonial Americans throughout the period continued to claim their rights as Englishmen, and England enjoyed great success in strengthening the empire while recognizing the liberties of its subjects. Nevertheless, turmoil characterized the era, particularly the disputes between Parliament and the king that led to the Civil War and to the Glorious Revolution. Intense conflicts also occurred in the colonies, generally between settlers and royal governors. By the end of the century, another source of turmoil in North America emerged as direct confrontations between the contrasting empires of Britain, France, and Spain began to erupt, foreshadowing a struggle for the continent.

18. THE NAVIGATION ACT OF 1651*

International rivalries led England to place a growing emphasis on mercantilistic commercial policies beginning in the 1650s. The following document, designed to eliminate the competition that Dutch merchants presented, was the first in a series of Navigation Acts regulating trade in the English empire. Although mercantilism often proved advantageous to Americans, many of the colonials at first feared the Navigation Acts as dangerous expressions of royal power. Restricting trade, they believed, limited their ability to gain property, which posed a dire threat to the most fundamental of their liberties. Moreover, the mercantilistic assumption that colonies existed to benefit the mother country implied that the English viewed colonists as inferiors, not as equals.

For the Increase of the Shipping and the Encouragement of the Navigation of this Nation, which under the good Providence and Protection of God, is so great a means of the Welfare and Safety of this Commonwealth; be it Enacted by this present Parliament and the Authority thereof, That from [December 1] . . . forwards, no Goods or Commodities whatsoever of the Growth, Production, or Manufacture of Asia, Africa or America; or of any part thereof; or of any Islands belonging to them . . . shall be Imported or brought into this Commonwealth of England, or into Ireland, or any other lands, . . . in any other Ship or Ships, Vessel or Vessels whatsoever, but onely in such as do truly and without fraud belong onely to the People of this Commonwealth, or the Plantations thereof, as the Proprietors or right Owners thereof; and whereof the Master and Mariners are also for the most part of them of the People of this Commonwealth, under the penalty of the forfeiture and loss of all those Goods that shall be imported contrary to this Act. . . .

---

*From C. H. Firth and R. S. Rait, *Acts and Ordinances of the Interregnum: 1642–1660*, 3 vols. (London: Wyman and Sons, 1911), II:559–61.

And it is further Enacted by the Authority aforesaid, that no Goods or Commodities of the Growth, Production, or Manufactures of Europe, or of any part thereof, shall . . . be imported or brought into this Commonwealth of England, or into Ireland, or any other Lands, . . . to this Commonwealth belonging, or in their possession, in any Ship or Ships, Vessel or Vessels whatsoever, but in such as do truly and without fraud belong only to the people of this Commonwealth, as the True Owners and Proprietors thereof, and in no other, except onely such Forin Ships and Vessels as do truly and properly belong to the people of that countrey or Place, of which the said Goods are the Growth, Production, or Manufacture; or to such Ports where the said Goods can onely be, or most usually are first shipped for Transportation; And that under the same penalty of forfeiture and loss expressed in the former branch of this act. . . .

And it is further Enacted . . . , That no sort of Cod-fish, Ling, Herring, Pilchard, or any other kinde of salted Fish, usually fished for and caught by the people of this Nation; nor any Oyl made, or that shall be made of any kinde of Fish whatsoever; nor any Whale-fins, or Whale-bones, shall from henceforth be Imported . . . but onely such as shall be caught in Vessels that do or shall truly and properly belong to the people of this Nation. . . : And the said Fish to be cured and the Oyl aforesaid made by the people of this Commonwealth. . . .

And it is further Enacted . . . That no sort of . . . salted Fish whatsoever, which shall be caught and cured for the people of this Commonwealth, shall be . . . exported from any place or places belonging to this Commonwealth, in any other Ship or Ships, Vessel or Vessels save onely in such as do truly and properly appertain to the people of this Commonwealth, as Right Owners. . . .

19. A CAPTIVITY NARRATIVE FROM METACOM'S WAR, 1676*

*M*etacom's War (1675-1676) nearly destroyed the British settlements of New England. Wampanoag sachem Metacom, called King Philip by the English, led an alliance against the rapidly expanding settlements that were encroaching on Native American lands. Atrocities on both sides characterized the conflict. Mary Rowlandson's narrative of her capture and 11-week ordeal as a prisoner of New England Indians, published in 1682, became a best-selling book about the war. The following selection portrays her initial capture and illustrates the brutality of the conflict.

A NARRATIVE OF THE CAPTIVITY AND RESTAURATION
OF MRS. MARY ROWLANDSON

On the tenth of February 1675 [1676], Came the Indians with great numbers upon Lancaster: Their first coming was about Sun-rising; hearing the noise of some Guns, we looked out; several Houses were burning, and the Smoke ascending to Heaven. There were five persons taken in one house, the Father, and the Mother and a sucking Child, they knockt on the head; the other two they took and carried away alive. There were two others, who being out of their Garison upon some occasion were set upon; one was knockt on the head, the other, escaped: Another their was who running along was shot and wounded, and fell down; he begged of them his life, promising them Money (as they told me) but they would not hearken to him but knockt him in head, and stript him naked, and split open his Bowels. Another seeing many of the Indians about his Barn, ventured and went out, but was quickly shot down. There were three others belonging to the same Garison who were killed; the Indians getting up upon the roof of the Barn, had advantage to shoot down upon them over their Fortification. Thus these murtherous wretches went on, burning, and destroying before them.

---

*From *Narratives of the Indian Wars, 1675–1699*, ed. Charles H. Lincoln (New York: Charles Scribner's Sons, 1913), 118–22.

At length they came and beset our own house, and quickly it was the dolefullest day that ever mine eyes saw. The House stood upon the edg of a hill; some of the Indians got behind the hill, others into the Barn, and others behind any thing that could shelter them; from all which places they shot against the House, so that the Bullets seemed to fly like hail; and quickly they wounded one man among us, then another, and then a third, About two hours (according to my observation, in that amazing time) they had been about the house before they prevailed to fire it (which they did with Flax and Hemp, which they brought out of the Barn, and there being no defence about the House, only two Flankers at two opposite corners and one of them not finished) they fired it once and one ventured out and quenched it, but they quickly fired it again, and that took. Now is the dreadfull hour come, that I have often heard of (in time of War, as it was the case of others) but now mine eyes see it. Some in our house were fighting for their lives, others wallowing in their blood, the House on fire over our heads, and the bloody Heathen ready to knock us on the head, if we stirred out. Now, might we hear Mothers and Children crying out for themselves, and one another, Lord, What shall we do? Then I took my Children (and one of my sisters, hers) to go forth and leave the house: but as soon as we came to the dore and appeared, the Indians shot so thick that the bulletts rattled against the House, as if one had taken an handfull of stones and threw them, so that we were fain to give back. We had six stout Dogs belonging to our Garrison, but none of them would stir, though another time, if any Indian had come to the door, they were ready to fly upon him and tear him down. The Lord hereby would make us the more to acknowledge his hand, and to see that our help is always in him. But out we must go) the fire increasing, and coming along behind us, roaring, and the Indians gaping before us with their Guns, Spears and Hatchets to devour us. No sooner were we out of the House, but my Brother in Law (being before wounded, in defending the house, in or near the throat) fell down dead, wherat the Indians scornfully shouted, and hallowed, and were presently upon him, stripping off his cloaths, the bulletts flying thick, one went through my side, and the same (as would seem) through the bowels and hand of my dear Child in my arms. One of my elder Sisters Children, named William, had then his Leg broken, which the Indians perceiving, they knockt him on head. Thus were we butchered by those merciless Heathen, standing amazed, with the blood running down to our heels. My eldest Sister being yet in the House, and seeing those wofull sights, the Infidels haling Mothers one way, and Children another, and some wallowing in their blood: and her elder Son telling her that her Son William was dead, and my self was wounded, she said, And, Lord, let me dy with them; which was no sooner said, but she was struck with a Bullet, and fell down dead over the threshold. I hope she is reaping the fruit of her good labours, being faithfull to the service of God in her place. In her younger years she lay under much trouble upon spiritual accounts, till it pleased God to make that precious Scripture take hold of her heart, 2 Cor. 12. 9. *And he said unto me, my Grace is sufficient for thee.* More then twenty years after I have heard her tell how sweet and comfortable that place was to her. But to return: The Indians laid hold of us, pulling me one way, and the Children another, and said, Come go along with us; I told them they would kill me: they answered, If I were willing to go along with them, they would not hurt me.

Oh the dolefull sight that now was to behold at this House! *Come, behold the works of the Lord, what dissolations he has made in the Earth.* Of thirty seven persons who were in this one House, none escaped either present death, or a bitter captivity, save only one, who might say as he, Job 1. 15, *And I only amescaped alone to tell the News.* There were twelve killed, some shot, some stab'd with their Spears, some knock'd down with their Hatchets. When we are in prosperity, Oh the little that we think of such dreadfull sights, and to see our dear Friends, and Relations ly bleeding out their heart-blood upon the ground. There was one who was chopt into the head with a Hatchet, and stript naked, and yet was crawling up and down. It is a solemn sight to see so many Christians lying in their blood, some here, and some there, like a company of Sheep torn by Wolves, All of them stript naked by a company of hell-hounds, roaring, singing, ranting and insulting, as if they would have torn our very hearts out; yet the Lord by his Almighty power preserved a number of us from death, for there were twenty-four of us taken alive and carried Captive.

I had often before this said, that if the Indians should come, I should chuse rather to be killed by them then taken alive but when it came to the tryal my mind changed; their glittering weapons so daunted my spirit, that I chose rather to go along with those (as I may say) ravenous Beasts, then that moment to end my dayes; and that I may the better declare what happened to me during that grievous Captivity, I shall particularly speak of the severall Removes we had up and down the Wilderness.

The first Remove.

Now away we must go with those Barbarous Creatures, with our bodies wounded and bleeding, and our hearts no less than our bodies. About a mile we went that night, up upon a hill within sight of the Town, where they intended to lodge. There was hard by a vacant house (deserted by the English before, for fear of the Indians). I asked them whither I might not lodge in the house that night to which they answered, what will you love English men still? this was the dolefullest night that ever my eyes saw. Oh the roaring, and singing and danceing, and yelling of those black creatures in the night, which made the place a lively resemblance of hell. And as miserable was the wast that was there made, of Horses, Cattle, Sheep, Swine, Calves, Lambs, Roasting Pigs, and Fowl (which they had plundered in the Town) some roasting, some lying and burning, and some boyling to feed our merciless Enemies; who were joyful enough though we were disconsolate. To add to the dolefulness of the former day, and the dismalness of the present night: my thoughts ran upon my losses and sad bereaved condition. All was gone, my Husband gone (at least separated from me, he being in the Bay; and to add to my grief, the Indians told me they would kill him as he came homeward) my Children gone, my Relations and Friends gone, our House and home and all our comforts within door, and without, all was gone, (except my life) and I knew not but the next moment that might go too. There remained nothing to me but one poor wounded Babe, and it seemed at present worse than death that it was in such a pitiful condition, bespeaking Compassion, and I had no refreshing for it, nor suitable things to revive it. Little do many think what is the savageness and bruitishness of this barbarous Enemy, I even those that seem to profess more than others among them, when the English have fallen into their hands.

20. BACON'S REBELLION, 1676*

*N*athaniel Bacon's Rebellion in Virginia was the first popular uprising as well as the largest such upheaval in colonial America before 1775. The two principal antagonists issued manifestos justifying their positions in the summer of 1676. The first document is by Bacon, the second by Governor Sir William Berkeley.

Nathaniel Bacon

If virtue be a sin, if piety be guilt, all the principles of morality, goodness and justice be perverted, we must confess that those who are now called rebels may be in danger of those high imputations. Those loud and several bulls would affright innocents and render the defence of our brethren and the inquiry into our sad and heavy oppressions, treason. But if there be, as sure there is, a just God to appeal to; if religion and justice be a sanctuary here; if to plead the cause of the oppressed; if sincerely to aim at his Majesty's honour and the public good without any reservation or by interest; if to stand in the gap after so much blood of our dear brethren bought and sold; if after the loss of a great part of his Majesty's colony deserted and dispeopled, freely with our lives and estates to endeavour to save

*From *The Virginia Magazine of History and Biography*, I (1894), 55–61; Massachusetts Historical Society, Collections, 4th series, IX (1871), 178–81.

the remainders be treason; God Almighty judge and let guilty die. But since we cannot in our hearts find one single spot of rebellion or treason, or that we have in any manner aimed at the subverting the settled government or attempting of the person of any either magistrate or private man, notwithstanding the several reproaches and threats of some who for sinister ends were disaffected to us and censured our innocent and honest designs, and since all people in all places where we have yet been can attest our civil, quiet, peaceable behaviour far different from that of rebellion and tumultuous persons, let truth be told and all the world know the real foundations of pretended guilt. We appeal to the country itself what and of what nature their oppressions have been, or by what cabal and mystery the designs of many of those whom we call great men have been transacted and carried on; but let us trace these men in authority and favour to whose hands the dispensation of the country's wealth has been committed. Let us observe the sudden rise of their estates composed with the quality in which they first entered this country, or the reputation they have held here amongst wise and discerning men. And let us see whether their extractions and education have not been vile, and by what pretence of learning and virtue they could so soon [come] into employments of so great trust and consequence. Let us consider their sudden advancement and let us also consider whether any public work for our safety and defence or for the advancement and propagation of trade, liberal arts, or sciences is here extant in any way adequate to our vast charge. Now let us compare these things together and see what sponges have sucked up the public treasure, and whether it has not been privately contrived away by unworthy favourites and juggling parasites whose tottering fortunes have been repaired and supported at the public charge. Now if it be so, judge what greater guilt can be than to offer to pry into these and to unriddle the mysterious wiles of a powerful cabal; let all people judge what can be of more dangerous import than to suspect the so long safe proceedings of some of our grandees, and whether people may with safety open their eyes in so nice a concern.

Another main article of our guilt is our open and manifest aversion of all, not only the foreign but the protected and darling Indians. This, we are informed, is rebellion of a deep dye for that both the governor and council are by Colonel Cole's assertion bound to defend the queen and the Appamatocks with their blood. Now, whereas we do declare and can prove that they have been for these many years enemies to the king and country, robbers and thieves and invaders of his Majesty's right and our interest and estates, but yet have by persons in authority been defended and protected even against his Majesty's loyal subjects, and that in so high a nature that even the complaints and oaths of his Majesty's most loyal subjects in a lawful manner proffered by them against those barbarous outlaws, have been by the right honourable governor rejected and the delinquents from his presence dismissed, not only with pardon and indemnity, but with all encouragement and favour; their firearms so destructful to us and by our laws prohibited, commanded to be restored them, and open declaration before witness made that they must have ammunition, although directly contrary to our law. Now what greater guilt can be than to oppose and endeavour the destruction of these honest, quiet neighbours of ours?

Another main article of our guilt is our design not only to ruin and extirpate all Indians in general, but all manner of trade and commerce with them. Judge who can be innocent that strike at this tender eye of interest: since the right honourable the governor hath been pleased by his commission to warrant this trade, who dare oppose it, or opposing it can be innocent? Although plantations be deserted, the blood of our dear brethren spilled; on all sides our complaints; continually murder upon murder renewed upon us; who may or dare think of the general subversion of all manner of trade and commerce with our enemies who can or dare impeach any of . . . traders at the heads of the rivers, if contrary to the wholesome provision made by laws for the country's safety; they dare continue their illegal practises and dare asperse the right honourable governor's wisdom and justice so highly to pretend to have his warrant to break that law which himself made; who dare say that these men at the heads of the rivers buy and sell our blood, and do still, notwithstanding the late act made to the contrary, admit Indians painted and continue to commerce; although these things can be proved, yet who dare be so guilty as to do it?

Another article of our guilt is to assert all those neighbour Indians as well as others, to be outlawed, wholly unqualified for the benefit and protection of the law, for that the law does reciprocally protect and punish, and that all people offending must either in person or estate make equivalent satisfaction or restitution, according to the manner and merit of the offences, debts, or trespasses. Now since the Indians cannot, according to the tenure and form of any law to us known, be prosecuted, seized, or complained against, their persons being difficultly distinguished or known; their many nations' languages, and their subterfuges such as makes them incapable to make us restitution or satisfaction, would it not be very guilty to say they have been unjustly defended and protected these many years?

If it should be said that the very foundation of all these disasters, the grant of the beaver trade to the right honourable governor was illegal, and not grantable by any power here present as being a monopoly, were not this to deserve the name of rebel and traitor?

Judge, therefore, all wise and unprejudiced men who may or can faithfully or truly with an honest heart, attempt the country's good, their vindication, and liberty without the aspersion of traitor and rebel, since as so doing they must of necessity gall such tender and dear concerns. But to manifest sincerity and loyalty to the world, and how much we abhor those bitter names; may all the world know that we do unanimously desire to represent our sad and heavy grievances to his most sacred Majesty as our refuge and sanctuary, where we do well know, that all our causes will be impartially heard and equal justice administered to all men.

Governor William Berkeley

The declaration and remonstrance of Sir William Berkeley, his most sacred Majesty's governor and captain-general of Virginia, shows: That about the year 1660 Colonel Mathews, the then governor died, and then in consideration of the service I had done the country in defending them from and destroying great numbers of the Indians without the loss of three men in all the time that war lasted, and in contemplation of the equal and uncorrupt justice I had distributed to all men, not only the Assembly, but the unanimous votes of all the country concurred to make me governor in a time when, if the rebels in England had prevailed, I had certainly died for accepting it. 'Twas, gentlemen, an unfortunate love showed to me, for to show myself grateful for this I was willing to accept of this government again, when by my gracious king's favour I might have had other places much more profitable and less toilsome than this hath been. Since that time that I returned into the country, I call the great God, judge of all things in heaven and earth, to witness that I do not know of anything relative to this country wherein I have acted unjustly, corruptly, or negligently, in distributing equal justice to all men, and taking all possible care to preserve their proprieties and defend them from their barbarous enemies.

But for all this, perhaps I have erred in things I know not of. If I have, I am so conscious of human frailty and my own defects that I will not only acknowledge them, but repent of and amend them, and not, like the rebel Bacon, persist in an error only because I have committed it; and tells me in divers of his letters that it is not for his honour to confess a fault, but I am of opinion that it is only for devils to be incorrigible, and men of principles like the worst of devils; and these he hath, if truth be reported to me of divers of his expressions of atheism, tending to take away all religion and laws.

And now I will state the question betwixt me as a governor and Mr. Bacon, and say that if any enemies should invade England, any counsellor, justice of peace, or other inferior officer might raise what forces they could to protect his Majesty's subjects. But I say again, if, after the king's knowledge of this invasion, any the greatest peer of England should raise forces against the king's prohibition, this would be now—and ever was in all ages and nations—accounted treason. Nay, I will go further, that though this peer was truly zealous for the preservation of his king and subjects, and had better and greater abilities than all the rest of his fellow-subjects to do his king and country service, yet if the king (though by false information) should suspect the contrary, it were treason in this noble peer to proceed after the king's prohibition: and for the truth of this I appeal to all the laws of England, and the laws and constitutions of all other nations in the world. And yet further, it is declared by this Parliament that the taking up arms for the king and Parliament is treason; for the event showed that whatever the pretence was to seduce ignorant and well-affected people, yet the end was ruinous both to king and people, as this will be if not prevented. I do therefore again declare that Bacon, proceeding against all laws of all nations modern and ancient, is rebel to his sacred Majesty and this country; nor will I insist upon the swearing of men to live and die together, which is treason by the very words of the law.

Now, my friends, I have lived thirty-four years amongst you, as uncorrupt and diligent as ever governor was; Bacon is a man of two years among you; his person and qualities unknown to most of you, and to all men else, by any virtuous action that ever I heard of. And that very action which he boasts of was sickly and foolishly, and, as I am informed, treacherously carried to the dishonour of the English nation. Yet in it he lost more men than I did in three years' war; and by the grace of God will put myself to the same dangers and troubles again when I have brought Bacon to acknowledge the laws are above him, and I doubt not but by God's assistance to have better success than Bacon hath had. The reason of my hopes are, that I will take counsel of wiser men than myself; but Mr. Bacon hath none about him but the lowest of the people.

Yet I must further enlarge, that I cannot without your help do anything in this but die in defence of my king, his laws, and subjects, which I will cheerfully do, though alone I do it; and considering my poor fortunes, I cannot leave my poor wife and friends a better legacy than by dying for my king and you: for his sacred Majesty will easily distinguish between Mr. Bacon's actions and mine, and kings have long arms either to reward or punish.

Now, after all this, if Mr. Bacon can show one precedent or example where such actings in any nation whatever was approved of, I will mediate with the king and you for a pardon and excuse for him; but I can show him a hundred examples where brave and great men have been put to death for gaining victories against the command of their superiors.

Lastly, my most assured friends, I would have preserved those Indians that I knew were hourly at our mercy, to have been our spies and intelligence, to find out our bloody enemies; but as soon as I had the least intelligence that they also were treacherous enemies, I gave out commissions to destroy them all, as the commissions themselves will speak it.

To conclude, I have done what was possible both to friend and enemy; have granted Mr. Bacon three pardons, which he hath scornfully rejected, supposing himself stronger to subvert than I and you to maintain the laws, by which only, and God's assisting grace and mercy, all men must hope for peace and safety. I will add no more, though much more is still remaining to justify me and condemn Mr. Bacon, but to desire that this declaration may be read in every county court in the country, and that a court be presently called to do it before the Assembly meet, that your approbation or dissatisfaction of this declaration may be known to all the country and the king's Council, to whose most revered judgments it it submitted.

Given the 29th day of May, a happy day in the 28th year of his most sacred Majesty's reign, Charles the second, who God grant long and prosperously to reign, and let all his good subjects say amen.

21. THE GLORIOUS REVOLUTION IN AMERICA, 1689*

In 1688, Parliament's fear of a Catholic dynasty under the House of Stuart led to the Glorious Revolution and the joint sovereignty of William and Mary. Americans took advantage of events in England to remove

*"Declaration of the Gentlemen, Merchants and Inhabitants of Boston, and the Country Adjacent," April 18, 1689, in *Narratives of the Insurrections, 1675–1690*, ed. Charles M. Andrews (New York: Charles Scribner's Sons, 1915), 175–82.

*Edmond Andros, governor of the Dominion of New England. James II had established the Dominion to consoli-
date his power in the northern colonies, which many colonials viewed as a dangerous threat to their political rights
and their personal liberty. Nathaniel Byfield, a New England merchant, sent an account of the overthrow of Governor Andros to friends in London in June 1689. In his letter, he included the declaration of grievances that had
sparked the uprising.*

. . . II. To get us within the reach of the Desolation [King James II] desired for us, it was no
improper thing that we should first have our Charter vacated . . . before it was possible for us to appear
at Westminster in the legal Defence of it; and without fair leave to answer for ourselves the Crimes fal-
sly laid to our Charge, we were put under a President and a Council, without any liberty for an Assembly, which the other American plantations have. . . .

III. The Commission was as Illegal for the Form of it, as the Way of obtaining it was Malicious
and Unreasonable; yet we made no Resistance thereunto as we could easily have done; but chose to
give all mankind a Demonstration of our being a People sufficiently dutiful and loyal to our King:
and . . . we took Pains to make our selves believe . . . That his Magesty's Desire was no other than
the happy Encrease and Advance of these Provinces by their more immediate dependence on the
Crown of England. And we were convinced of it by the Courses immediately taken to damp and
spoyl our Trade; whereof Decayes and Complaints presently filled all the Country; while in the
mean time neither the Honour nor the Treasury of the King was at all advanced by this new Model
of our Affairs, but a considerable Charge added unto the Crown.

IV. In little more than a half a Year we saw this Commission superseded by another yet more
absolute and Arbitrary, with which Sir Edmond Andross arrived as our Governour: who besides his
Power, with the Advice and Consent of his Council, to make Laws and raise Taxes as he pleased,
had also the Authority by himself to Muster and Imploy all Persons residing in the Territory as
occasion shall serve; and to transfer such Forces to any English Plantation in America, as occasion
shall require. And several Companies of Souldiers were now brought from Europe, to support
what was to be imposed on us . . . .

V. The Government was no sooner in these hands, but Care was taken to load Preferments
principally upon such Men as were Strangers to and Haters of the People. . . . But of all Oppressors
we were chiefly squeez'd by a Crew of Abject Persons fetched from New York, to be the tools of
the Adversary . . . ; by these were extraordinary and intollerable Fees extorted from every one upon
all Occasions, without any Rules but those of their own Avarice and Beggary; . . .nor could a small
Volume contain the other Illegalities done by these Horse-leeches in the two or three Years that
they have been sucking us. . . .

VI. It was now plainly affirmed, both . . . in open Council [and] . . . in private Converse, that
the People of New-England were all slaves, and the only difference between them and Slaves
is their not being bought and sold; and it was a Maxim delivered in open Court unto us by one of
the Council, that we must not think the Priviledges of English men would follow us to the End
of the World: Accordingly we have been treated with multiplied Contradictions to Magna Carta,
the Rights of which we laid claim unto. . . . Packt and pickt Juries have been very common things
among us. . . . Without a Verdict, yea, without a Jury sometimes People have been fined most
unrighteously; and some . . . have been kept in long and close Imprisonment without any the least
Information appearing against them, or an Habeas Corpus allowed unto them. . . .

VII. . . . [T]here was one very comprehensive Abuse given to us; Multitudes of pious and sober
Men . . . scrupled the Mode of Swearing on the Book, desiring that they might Swear with an
uplifted hand, agreeable to the ancient Custom of the Colony; and though we think we can prove
that the Common Law amongst us . . . not only indulges, but even commands and enjoins the Rite
of lifting the Hand in Swearing; yet they that had this Doubt, were still put by from serving upon
any Juries; and many of them were most unaccountably Fined and Imprisoned. . . .

Because these Things could not make us miserable fast enough, there was a notable Discovery made of we know not what flaw in all our Titles to our Lands; and tho, besides our purchase of them from the Natives, and besides our actual peaceable unquestioned possession of them for near three-scores Years, and besides the promise of K. Charles II . . . , That no man here shall receive any Prejudice in his Free-hold or Estate, . . . Yet we were every day told, That no Man was owner of a Foot of Land in all the Colony. . . .

IX. All the Council were not ingaged in all these ill Actions, but those of them which were true Lovers of their Country were seldom admitted to, and seldomer consulted at the Debates which produced these unrightous Things: Care was taken to keep them under Disadvantage; and the Governour, with five or six more, did what they would. We bore all these, and many more such Things, without making any attempt for any relief; only Mr. [Increase] Mather, purely out of respect unto the Good of his Afflicted Country, undertook a Voyage unto England; which when these Men suspected him to be preparing for, they used all manner of Craft and Rage, not only to interrupt his Voyage, but to ruin his Person too. . .

X. And yet that our Calamity might not be terminated here, we are again Briar'd in the Perplexities of another Indian War; how, or why, is a mystery too deep for us to unfold. And tho' 'tis judged that our Indian Enemies are not above 100 in Number, yet an Army of One thousand English hath been raised for the Conquering of them; which Army of our poor Friends and Brethren now under Popish Commanders (for in the Army as well as in the Council, the Papists are in Commission) has been under such a Conduct, . . . and the whole War hath been so managed, that we cannot but suspect in it a Branch of the Plot to bring us low. . . .

XI. We did nothing against these Proceedings, but only cry to our God. . . . We have been quiet hitherto, and so still we should have been, had not the Great God at this time laid us under double engagement to do something for our Security. . . . For first, we are informed that the rest of English America is alarmed with just and great Fears, that they may be attaqu'd by the French, who have lately (it is said) already treated many of the English with worse than Turkish Cruelties. . . . Moreover, we have understood, (though the Governour has taken all imaginable care to keep us all ignorant thereof) that the Almighty God hath been pleased to prosper the noble Undertaking of the Prince of Orange, to preserve the three Kingdoms from the horrible brinks of Popery and Slavery, and to bring to a condign Punishment those worst of Men, by whom English liberties had been destroy'd. . . .

XII. We do therefore seize upon the Persons of those few ill Men which have been (next to our Sins) the grand Authors of our Miseries; resolving to secure them, for what Justice, Orders from his Highness with the English parliament shall direct, lest, ere we are aware, we find . . . ourselves to be by them given away to a Forreign Power, before such Orders can reach unto us; for which Orders we now humbly wait.

22. EDMOND ANDROS'S REPORT, 1690*

Governor Edmond Andros submitted the following account of events in New England to the Lords of Trade. In the report, he emphasized his loyalty to royal policy while describing the treasonous nature of the rebels. His superiors accepted his interpretation of the uprising, and they exonerated him. More ominous to Americans, the Glorious Revolution did little to limit the king's power over the settlers. Indeed, only a few years later William III created the Board of Trade in order to centralize and strengthen his authority. As the seventeenth century ended, substantive differences concerning power and liberty existed between the crown and the colonies.

---

*"Declaration of the Gentlemen, Merchants and Inhabitants of Boston, and the Country Adjacent," April 18, 1689, in *Narratives of the Insurrections, 1675–1690*, ed. Charles M. Andrews (New York: Charles Scribner's Sons, 1915), 229–36.

That in the yeare 1686 Sir Edmond Andros was by comision under the Greate Seale of England appoynted to succeed the President Dudley and Council in the government of the Massachusetts Colony, the Provinces of Hampshire and Maine and the Narragansett Country, to w'ch was annexed the Colonys of Rhode Island New Plymouth and the County of Cornwall.

In the yeare 1687 the Collony of Connecticott was also annexed and in the yeare 1688 he received a new Commission for all New England including the Province of New Yorke and East and West Jersey. . . .

Sir Edmond Andros upon receipt of his Commission went to New Yorke and Albany of which the Indians having notice, altho' they were then mett in Councill about goeing to Canada came thither, and were setled, and confirmed under his government. . . .

The severall Provinces and Coloneys in New England being soe united, the revenue continued and setled in those parts, for the support of the government, amounted to about twelve thousand pounds per annum and all places were well and quietly setled and in good posture. . . .

He was always ready to give grants of vacant lands and confirme defective titles as authorized (the late Corporation not having passed or conveyed any persuant to the directions in their Charter) but not above twenty have passed the seal in the time of his government.

Courts of Judicature were setled in the severall parts, soe as might be convenient for the ease and benefitt of the subject, and Judges appoynted to hold the Terms and goe the Circuite throughout the Dominion, to administer justice in the best manner and forme, and according to the lawes Customes and statutes of the realm of England, and some peculiar locall prudentiall laws of the Country, not repugnant therto; and fees regulated for all officers.

That particuler care was taken for the due observance of the severall Acts made for the encouragement of navigation and regulateing the plantation trade, whereby the lawfull trade and His Majestys revenue of Customs was considerably increased.

The Indians throughout the govern't continued in good order and subjection untill, towards the latter end of the yeare 1688, by some unadvised proceedings of the Inhabitants in the Eastern parts of New England, the late rupture with the Indians there comenced, severall being taken and some killed, when Sir Edmond Andros was at New Yorke more than three hundred miles distant from that place; and upon his speedy returne to Boston (having viewed and setled all parts to the Westward) great part of the garrison soldiers with stores and other necessary were imediately sent Eastward to reinforce those parts, and vessells to secure the coast and fishery, and further forces raysed and appoynted to be under the command of Majr Gen'll Winthrop, who falling sick and declineing the service, by advice of the Councill he went with them in person and by settlement of several garrisons, frequent partyes, marches and pursuits after the enemy, sometimes above one hundred miles into the desart further than any Christian settlement, in w'ch the officers and souldiers of the standing forces always imployed, takeing and destroying their forts and settlem'ts, corne, provision, ammunicion and canooes, dispersed and reduced them to the uttermost wants and necessitys, and soe secured the Countrey, . . . not the least loss, damage of spoyle hapned to the inhabitants or fishery, and the Indians were ready to submitt at mercy. About the latter end of March 1688 Sir Edmond Andros returned for Boston, leaveing the garrisons and souldiers in the Easterne parts in good condition , sufficiently furnished with provisions and all stores and implyments of warr and vessells for defence of the coast and fishery.

On the 18th of April 1689 severall of His Maj'ties Councill in New England haveing combined and conspired togeather with those who were magistrates and officers in the late Charter Government annually chosen by the people, and severall other persons, to subvert and overthrow the government, and in stead thereof to introduce their former Commonwealth; and haveing by their false reports and aspersions gott to their assistance the greatest part of the people, whereof appeared in arms at Boston under the command of those who were Officers in the sayd former popular government, to the number of about two thousand horse and foote; which strange and sudden appearance being wholly a surprize to Sir Edmond Andros, as knowing noe cause or occasion for the same, but understanding that severall of the Councill were at the Councill Chamber where . . . they were to meet, . . . he and those with him went hither. And tho' (as he passed) the streets were full of armed men, yett none offered him or those that were with him the least rudeness or incivillity, but on the contrary usuall respect; but when he came to the Councill Chamber he found severall of the sayd former popular Majestrates and other chiefe persons then present, with those of the Councill, who had noe suitable regard to him, or the peace and quiet of the Countrey, but instead of giving any assistance to support the Government, made him a prisoner and also imprisoned some members of the Councill and other officers, who in pursuance of their respective dutyes and stations attended on him, and kept him for the space of ten months under severe and close confinement untill by His Ma'ties comand they were sent for England to answer what might be objected them, Where, after summons given to the pretended Agents of New England and their twice appearance at the Councill Board, nothing could be objected by them or others, they were discharged. In the time of his confinement being denyed the liberty of discourse or conversation with any person, his own servants to attend him, r any communication or correspondence with any by letters, he hath noe particular knowledge of their further proceedings, but hath heard and understands:—

That soone after the confinem't of his person, the Confederates [took the] fort and Castle from the Officers that had the comand of them, whom they also imprisoned and dispersed the few souldiers belonging to the two standing Companeys then there, as they did the rest, when they recalled the forces imployed against . . . the Indians Eastward . . . in w'ch service halfe a company of the standing forces at New York being also imployed, the officers were surprised and brought prisoners to Boston, and the souldiers dispersed, as the remaining part of them at New Yorke were afterwards upon the revolucion there. The other company was, and remained, at Fort Albany. . . . And the Confederates at Boston possessed themselves of all His Ma'ties stores, armes ammunicion and other implements of warr, and disabled His Ma'ties man of war the Rose frigatt by securing the Comander and bringing her sayles on shoare; and at the same time haveing imprisoned the secretary and some other officers, they broke open the Sec'rys Office and seized and conveyed away all records papers and wrightings.

Those Members of His Ma'ties Councill that were in confederacy with the before mencioned popular Majestrates and other chiefe actors in this revolucion, tooke upon them the government, by the name of a Councill, who not content with the inconveniency they had brought on themselves in the Massachusetts Colony, but to the ruine of the poore neighbours, on the twentieth of April gave orders for the drawing off the forces from Pemyquid and other garrisons and places in the Easterne parts, far without the lymitts of their Collony and where the seate of warr with the Indians was, and to seize severall of the officers, and for calling home the vessells appoynted to gard the sea coast and fishery; w'ch was done accordingly, and the forces disbanded, when most of the souldiers belonging to the standing Companys were dispersed; of which, . . . the Indians [taking] notice, (and being supplyed with Ammunicion and provision out of a vessell sent from Boston by some of the chiefe conspirators before the insurrection to trade with them) they were encouraged and enabled to renew and pursue the warr; and by the assistance of some French who have been seen amongst them and engageing of severall other Indians before unconcerned, increased their numbers, that in a very short tyme severall hundreds of Their Ma'ties subjects were killed and carryed away captive; The Fort at Pemyquid taken; the whole Cuntry of Cornwall, the greatest part of the Province of Maine, and part of the Province of New Hampshire destroyed and deserted; and the principall trade of that country, w'ch consisted in a considerable fishery, the getting of masts, yards, etc. for the supply of His Ma'tyes navy Royall, and boards and other lumber for the supply of the other West India plantacions, is almost wholy ruined.

By the encouragem't and perswasion of those of . . . Massachusetts[,] the severall other provinces and collonys in New England as far as New Yorke have disunited themselves, and set up their former separate Charter, or popular governments without Charter, and by that meanes the whole revenue of the Crowne continued and setled in the severall parts for the support of the Government is lost and destroyed.

The usuall time for election of new Majestrates at Boston comeing on in the beginning of May 1689, great controversie arose about the setling of Civill Government; some being for a new election, and others that the Majestrates chosen and sworne in 1686 before the alteracion should reassume; the latter of w'ch was concluded on by them and the pretended representatives of the severall townes of the Massachusetts, and assumed by the sd Majestrates accordingly, and thereupon the old Charter Government, tho' vacated in Westminster Hall, was reassumed without any regard to the Crowne of England, and they revived and confirmed their former laws contrary and repugnant to the laws and statutes of England, setled their Courts of Judicature, and appoynted new officers, and have presumed to try and judge all cases civill and criminall, and to pass sentence of death on severall of Their Ma'ties subjects, some of whom they have caused to be executed.

Altho in the revenue continued on the Crowne for suport of the government dureing his time, the country pay'd but the old establisht rate of a penny in the pound per Annum as given and practised for about fifty yeares past, the present Administrators have of their own authority, for not above six months, raysed and exacted from the people of the Massachusetts Collony seven rates and a half.

Since the insurrection and alteracion in New England they doe tollerate an unlimited irregular trade, contrary to the severall acts of the Plantations, Trade and Navigacion, now so little regarded as in the time of their former Charter Government; they esteeming noe laws to be binding on them but what are made by themselves, nor admitt English laws to be pleaded there, or appeales to His Ma'tie. And many shipps and vessells have since arrived from Scotland, Holland, Newfoundland, and other places prohibitted, they having imprisoned His Ma'ties Collector, Surveyor and searcher, and displaced other Customhouse officers.

That they sent to Albany to treat with the Indians in those parts, particularly with the Five Nations, Masquaes etc. and invited them to Boston; which is of ill and dangerous consequence, by makeing the sayd Indians particularly acquainted with the disunion and separate governments, and shewing them the countrey and disorders thereof, as far as Boston, giveing thereby the greatest advantage to the French of gaining or subdueing the sayd Indians and attempting Fort Albany (the most advanced frontier into the country and great mart of the beaver and peltry trade) and of infesting other parts.

The forces raysed and set out by them the last summer, notwithstanding the great encouragem't they promised of eight pounds per head for every Indian should be killed, besides their pay, proved neither effectuall to suppresse the enemy or secure the country from further damage and murthers; and upon the winters approaching the forces were recalled and the country left exposed to the enemy, who have already over runn and destroyed soe great a part thereof. And now by the assistance of the French of Canada may probably proceed further into the heart of the country, being soe devided and out of order unless it shall please His Ma'tie by his owne authority to redress the same, and put a stop to the French and Indians, and thereby prevent the ruine or loss of that whole dominion of New England and consequently of Their Maj'ties other American Plantacions, endangered not only by the want of provisions, but by the many ships, vessells, seamen and and other necessarys in New England, capable to supply and transport any force, may annoy or attempt those plantations; but may be by His Ma'ties authority and comands effectually setled and preserved, and of service against the French or any other Their Ma'ties enemys in those parts, with no greater land force then is necessary to be continued there, and a sufficient revenue raysed to defray the charge thereof, by dutyes and rates, as heretofore hath been practiced amongst them and is usual in other Their Ma'ties plantacions.

23. CREATION OF THE BOARD OF TRADE, 1696*

The following declaration reorganized the Board for Foreign Plantations, created in 1660, by centralizing control of the colonies in the hands of the king rather than in Parliament. The document stresses the role that board members played in promoting and regulating trade, but it also charged them with reviewing the acts of colonial assemblies. William III, it appeared to Americans, was as intent as his Stuart predecessors had been on asserting his power at the expense of Americans' economic and political liberties.

His Majesties Commission for promoting the Trade of this Kingdom and for inspecting and improving His Plantations in America and elsewhere.

WILLIAM the Third by the Grace of God King of England, Scotland, France and Ireland, Defender of the Faith &a. To our Keeper of oure Great Seale of England or Chancellor of England . . . , Our President of Our Privy Council . . . , Our first Commissioner of Our Treasury And our Treasurer of England . . . , Our first Commissioner of our Admiralty and Our Admirall of England . . . , And our principall Secretarys of State . . . , And the Chancellor of Our Exchequer . . . , To Our Right Trusty and Right Well beloved Cousin and Councillor John Earl of Bridgewater, and Ford Earl of Tankerville, To our Trusty and Well beloved Sir Philip Meadows, Knt, William Blaithwaite, John Pollexfen, John Locke, Abraham Hill, and John Methwen, Esquires, Greeting. . . .

KNOW YEE therefor that We reposing espetiall Trust and Confidence in your Discretions, Abilityes and Integrities . . . authorize and appoint . . . you, to be Our Commissioners during our Royal Pleasure, for promoting the Trade of our Kingdome, and for Inspecting and Improving our Plantations in America and elsewhere. . . .

And We do hereby further Impower and require you Our said Commissioners to take into your care all Records, Grants and Papers remaining in the Plantation Office or thereunto belonging.

And likewise to inform your selves of the present condition of Our respective Plantations, as well as with regards to the administration of the Government and Justice in those places, as in relations to the Commerce thereof; And also to inquire into the Limits of Soyle and Product of Our severall Plantations and how the same may be improved, and of the best means for easing and securing Our Colonies there, and how the same may be rendered most usefull and beneficiall to our said Kingdom of England.

And We do hereby further impower and require you Our said Commissioners, more particularly and in a principal manner to inform your selves what Navall Stores may be furnished from Our Plantations, and in what Quantities, and by what methods Our Royall purpose of having our Kingdom supplied with Navall Stores from thence may be made practicable and promoted; And also to inquire into and inform your selves of the best and most proper methods of settling and improving in Our Plantations, such other Staples and other Ma[n]ufactures as Our subjects of England are now obliged to fetch and supply themselves withall from other Princes and States; And also what Staples and Manufactures may be best encouraged there, and what Trades are taken up and excercised there, which are or may prove prejudiciall to England, by furnishing themselves or other Our Colonies with what has been usually supplied from England; And to finde out proper means of diverting them from such Trades, and whatsoever else may turne to the hurt of Our Kingdom of England.

And to examin and look into the usuall Instructions given to the Governors of Our Plantations, and to see if any thing may be added, omitted or changed therein to advantage; To take and Account yearly by way of Journall of the Administration of Our Governors there, and to draw-out what is proper to be observed and represented unto Us; and as often as occasion shall require to

---

*From *American History Told by Contemporaries*, 5 vols., ed. Albert Bushnell Hart (New York: The Macmillan Company, 1914), II:129–31.

consider of proper persons to be Governors or Deputy Governors, or to be of Our Councill or of Our Councill at Law, or Secretarys, in Our respective Plantations, in order to present their Names to Us in Councill.

And We do hereby further Authorize and impower you Our said Commissioners, to examin into and weigh such Acts of the Assemblies of the Plantations respectively as shall from time to time be sent or transmitted hither for Our Approbation; And to set down and represent as aforesaid the Usefulness or Mischief thereof to Our Crown, and to Our said Kingdom of England, or to the Plantations themselves, in case the same should be established for Laws there; And also to consider what matters may be recommended as fitt to be passed in the Assemblies there, To heare complaints of Oppression and maladministrations, in Our Plantations, in order to represent as aforesaid what you in your Discretions shall thinke proper; And also to require an Account of all Monies given for Publick uses by the Assemblies in Our Plantations, and how the same are and have been expended or laid out.

Discussion

1. English authorities believed that their policies preserved liberty and at the same time protected the interests of the empire. Based on the documents, why might Americans have viewed those policies as dangerous assertions of power?

2. The American colonies experienced several insurrections during the seventeenth century. According to the descriptions of Bacon's Rebellion and the overthrow of Governor Edmond Andros, what were the critical issues of power and liberty that shaped those rebellions?

3. What does Mary Rowlandson's captivity narrative reveal about the cultural differences between English settlers and Native Americans? What role did Rowlandson's religious belief play in her understanding of her captivity?

CHAPTER 4

Provincial America and the Struggle for a Continent

Encouragement given for People to remove and settle in the Province of New-York in America.

THe Honourable *George Clarke*, Esq. Lieut. Governour and Commander in chief of the Province of *New-York*, Hath upon the Petition of Mr. *Lauchline Campbell* from *Isla, North-Britain*, promised to grant him Thirty thousand Acres of Land at the *Wood-Creek*, free of all Charges excepting the Survey and the King's Quit-Rent, which is about one Shilling and Nine Pence Farthing *Sterling* for each hundred Acres. *And also,* To grant to thirty Families already landed here Lands in proportion to each Family, from five hundred Acres unto one Hundred and Fifty only paying the Survey and the King's Quit-Rent. And all *Protestants* that incline to come and settle in this Colony may have Lands granted them from the Crown for three Pounds *Sterling* per hundred Acres and paying the yearly Quit-Rent.

Dated in New-York this 4th Day of December, 1738.

GEORGE CLARKE.

Printed by *William Bradford*, Printer to the King's most Excellent Majesty for the Province of *New-York*, 1738.

After 1715 the British North American colonies expanded tremendously. Individual colonies often competed with each other for settlers. This British advertisement from 1738 encourages Scots-Irish to immigrate to New York.

During the eighteenth century the British colonist population rose markedly, creating a peculiar dilemma between the need for physical expansion and the desire for further Anglicization. In the English settlements, rapid growth led to several problems, including a greater chance of confrontation with other European settlers or Native Americans as well as the need for an expanding currency. Such a population explosion also accelerated the development of regional differentiation between the Lower South, the Upper South, the Mid-Atlantic colonies, the backcountry, and New England. On the other hand, even as society grew more sophisticated and complex, Americans continued to share a common faith in their English heritage and its emphasis on individual liberties. Americans embraced the ideals of the Enlightenment as well, which greatly influenced their understanding of those liberties. In 1754, with the hegemony of North America at stake, Britain and France renewed their long-standing imperial conflict. Many Americans viewed New France as the epitome of tyranny and welcomed the prospect of conquest. To them, the battle for the continent was also a battle to preserve liberty.

24. IN DEFENSE OF PAPER MONEY, 1729*

The British colonies, hampered by mercantilistic policy, were perpetually short of hard money or specie—gold and silver. As a result, Virginia and Maryland utilized tobacco as currency, measuring their debts by weight in tobacco, but the northern colonies were without such a staple crop to provide this function. Instead, they invented paper money, beginning in Massachusetts in 1660 and extending to Pennsylvania in 1723. In 1729 Benjamin Franklin published an eloquent defense of Pennsylvania's paper money, directed particularly at those individuals (mostly creditors) who opposed paper money out of fear that it would depreciate. His arguments demonstrated that the debate over paper currency provoked controversy and reflected partisan rifts in colonial society.

Thus much by way of apology for this present *Inquiry into the Nature and Necessity of a Paper Currency.* And if any thing I shall say may be a means of fixing a subject, that is now the chief concern of my countrymen, in a clearer light, I shall have the satisfaction of thinking my time and pains well employed.

To proceed, then,

There is a certain proportionate quantity of money requisite to carry on the trade of a country freely and currently; more than which would be of no advantage in trade, and less, if much less, exceedingly detrimental to it.

This leads us to the following general considerations.

First. *A great want of money, in any trading country, occasions interest to be at a very high rate.* And here it may be observed, that it is impossible by any laws to restrain men from giving and receiving exorbitant interest, where money is suitably scarce. For he that wants money will find out ways to

*From Benjamin Franklin, *A Modest Inquiry into the Nature and Necessity of a Paper Currency* (Philadelphia, 1729) in *The Works of Benjamin Franklin*, 10 vols., ed. Jared Sparks (Chicago: Townsend MacCoun, 1882), II:253–65.

give ten per cent, when he cannot have it for less, although the law forbids to take more than six per cent. Now the interest of money being high is prejudicial to a country several ways. It makes land bear a low price, because few men will lay out their money in land, when they can make a much greater profit by lending it out upon interest. And much less will men be inclined to venture their money at sea, when they can, without risk or hazard, have a great and certain profit by keeping it at home; thus trade is discouraged. And if in two neighbouring countries the traders of one, by reason of a greater plenty of money, can borrow it to trade with at a lower rate than the traders of the other, they will infallibly have the advantage, and get the greatest part of that trade into their own hands; for he that trades with money he hath borrowed at eight or ten per cent, cannot hold market with him that borrows his money at six or four. On the contrary, *a plentiful currency will occasion interest to be low;* and this will be an inducement to many to lay out their money in lands, rather than put it out to use, by which means land will begin to rise in value and bear a better price. And at the same time it will tend to enliven trade exceedingly, because people will find more profit in employing their money that way than in usury; and many that understand business very well, but have not a stock sufficient of their own, will be encouraged to borrow money to trade with, when they can have it at a moderate interest.

Secondly, *Want of money in a country reduces the price of that part of its produce which is used in trade;* because, trade being discouraged by it as above, there is a much less demand for that produce. And this is another reason why land in such a case will be low, especially where the staple commodity of the country is the immediate produce of the land; because, that produce being low, fewer people find an advantage in husbandry, or the improvement of land. On the contrary, *a plentiful currency will occasion the trading produce to bear a good price;* because, trade being encouraged and advanced by it, there will be a much greater demand for that produce; which will be a great encouragement of husbandry and tillage, and consequently make land more valuable, for that many people would apply themselves to husbandry, who probably might otherwise have sought some more profitable employment.

As we have already experienced how much the increase of our currency, by what paper money has been made, has encouraged our trade, particularly to instance only in one article, *ship-building,* it may not be amiss to observe under this head, what a great advantage it must be to us as a trading country, that has workmen and all the materials proper for that business within itself, to have ship-building as much as possible advanced; for every ship, that is built here for the English merchants, gains the province her clear value in gold and silver, which must otherwise have been sent home for returns in her stead; and likewise every ship, built in and belonging to the province, not only saves the province her first cost, but all the freight, wages, and provisions she ever makes or requires as long as she lasts; provided care is taken to make this her *pay-port,* and that she always takes provisions with her for the whole voyage, which may easily be done. And how considerable an article this is yearly in our favor, every one, the least acquainted with mercantile affairs, must needs be sensible; for, if we could not build ourselves, we must either purchase so many vessels as we want from other countries, or else hire them to carry our produce to market, which would be more expensive than purchasing, and on many other accounts exceedingly to our loss. Now as trade in general will decline where there is not a plentiful currency, so ship-building must certainly of consequence decline where trade is declining.

Thirdly. *Want of money in a country discourages laboring and handicraftsmen (who are the chief strength and support of a people) from coming to settle in it, and induces many that were settled to leave the country, and seek entertainment and employment in other places, where they can be better paid.* For what can be more disheartening to an industrious laboring man than this, that, after he hath earned his bread with the sweat of his brows, he must spend as much time, and have near as much fatigue in getting it, as he had to earn it? *And nothing makes more bad paymasters than a general scarcity of money.* And here again is a third reason for land's bearing a low price in such a country, because land always increases in value in proportion with the increase of the people settling on it, there being so many more buyers; and its value will infallibly be diminished, if the number of its inhabitants diminish. On the contrary, *a plentiful currency will encourage great numbers of laboring and handicraftsmen to come and settle in the country*, by the same reason that a want of it will discourage and drive them out. Now the more inhabitants, the greater demand for land (as is said above), upon which it must necessarily rise in value, and bear a better price. The same may be said of the value of house-rent, which will be advanced for the same reasons; and, by the increase of trade and riches, people will be enabled to pay greater rents. Now, the value of house-rent rising, and interest becoming low, many, that in a scarcity of money practised usury, will probably be more inclined to building; which will likewise sensibly enliven business in any place; it being an advantage not only to brickmakers, bricklayers, masons, carpenters, joiners, glaziers, and several other trades immediately employed by building, but likewise to farmers, brewers, bakers, tailors, shoemakers, shopkeepers, and, in short, to every one that they lay their money out with.

Fourthly. *Want of money in such a country as ours, occasions a greater consumption of English and European goods, in proportion to the number of the people, than there would otherwise be.* Because merchants and traders, by whom abundance of artifi[c]ers and laboring men are employed, finding their other affairs require what money they can get into their hands, oblige those who work for them to take one half or perhaps two-thirds goods in pay. By this means a greater quantity of goods are disposed of, and to a greater value; because working-men and their families are thereby induced to be more profuse and extravagant in fine apparel and the like, than they would be if they were obliged to pay ready money for such things after they had earned and received it, or if such goods were not imposed upon them, of which they can make no other sue. For such people cannot send the goods they are paid with to foreign market, without losing considerably by having them sold for less than they stand them in here; neither can they easily dispose of them at home, because their neighbours are generally supplied in the same manner. But how unreasonable would it be, if some of those very men who *have been a means* of thus forcing people into unnecessary expense, should be the first and the most earnest in accusing them of *pride and prodigality*. Now, though this extraordinary consumption of foreign commodities may be a profit to particular men, yet the country in general grows poorer by it apace. On the contrary, as *a plentiful currency will occasion a less consumption of European goods, in proportion to the number of the people*, so it will be a means of making the balance of our trade more equal than it now is, if it does not give it in our favor; because our own produce will be encouraged at the same time. And it is to be observed, that, though less foreign commodities are consumed in proportion to the number of people, yet this will be no disadvantage to the merchant, because the number of people increasing, will occasion an increasing demand of more foreign goods in the whole.

Thus we have seen some of the many heavy disadvantages a country (especially such a country as ours) must labor under, when it has not a sufficient stock of running cash to manage its trade currently. And we have likewise seen some of the advantages which accrue from having money sufficient, or a plentiful currency. . . .

It remains now that we inquire, *whether a large addition to our paper currency will not make it sink in value very much.* And here it will be requisite that we first form just notions of the nature and value of money in general.

As Providence has so ordered it, that not only different countries, but even different parts of the same country, have their peculiar most suitable productions; and likewise that different men have geniuses adapted to a variety of different arts and manufactures; therefore **commerce,** or the exchange of one commodity or manufacture for another, is highly convenient and beneficial to mankind. As for instance, A may be skilful in the art of making cloth, and B understand the raising of corn. A wants corn, and B cloth; upon which they make an exchange with each other for as much as each has occasion for, to the mutual advantage and satisfaction of both.

But as it would be very tedious, if there were no other way of general dealing, but by an immediate exchange of commodities; because a man that had corn to dispose of, and wanted cloth for it, might perhaps, in his search for a chapman to deal with, meet with twenty people that had cloth to dispose of, but wanted no corn; and with twenty others that wanted his corn, but had no cloth to suit him with; to remedy such inconveniences, and facilitate exchange, men have invented money, properly called a *medium of exchange*, because through or by its means labor is exchanged for labor, or one commodity for another. And whatever particular thing men have agreed to make this medium of, whether gold, silver, copper, or tobacco, it is, to those who possess it (if they want any thing), that very thing which they want, because it will immediately procure it for them. It is cloth to him that wants cloth, and corn to those that want corn; and so of all other necessaries, it is whatsoever it will procure. Thus he who had corn to dispose of, and wanted to purchase cloth with it, might sell his corn, for its value in this general medium, to one who wanted corn but had no cloth; and with this medium he might purchase cloth of him that wanted no corn, but perhaps some other thing, as iron it may be, which this medium will immediately procure, and so he may be said to have exchanged his cloth for iron; and thus the general change is soon performed, to the satisfaction of all parties, with abundance of facility.

For many ages, those parts of the world which are engaged in commerce, have fixed upon gold and silver as the chief and most proper materials for this medium; they being in themselves valuable metals for their fineness, beauty, and scarcity. By these, particularly by silver, it has been usual to value all things else. But as silver itself is of no certain permanent value, being worth more or less according to its scarcity or plenty, therefore it seems requisite to fix upon something else, more proper to be made a *measure of values*, and this I take to be *labor*.

By labor may the value of silver be measured as well as other things. As, suppose one man employed to raise corn, while another is digging and refining silver; at the year's end, or at any other period of time, the complete produce of corn, and that of silver, are the natural price of each other; and if one be twenty bushels, and the other twenty ounces, than an ounce of that silver is worth the labor of raising a bushel of that corn. Now if by the discovery of some nearer, more easy or plentiful mines, a man may get forty ounces of silver as easily as formerly he did twenty, and the same labor is still required to raise twenty bushels of corn, then two ounces of silver will be worth no more than the same labor of raising one bushel of corn, and that bushel of corn will be as cheap at two ounces, as it was before at one, *cæteris paribus*.

Thus the riches of a country are to be valued by the quantity of labor its inhabitants are able to purchase, and not by the quantity of silver and gold they possess; which will purchase more or less labor, and therefore is more or less valuable, as is said before, according to its scarcity or plenty. . . .

25. PAPER MONEY OUTLAWED, 1740*

*T*his proclamation by the Lords Commissioners for Trade and Plantations (the Board of Trade) made it difficult for a colony to issue paper money. The need for currency, however, remained a problem throughout the colonial era. Debtors and poor Americans, furthermore, continued to resent the policy that they viewed as an assertion of power and a danger to liberty.

WHEREAS, for preventing the many & great Inconveniences that had arisen in some of his Majesty's Colonies & Plantations in America, by passing Laws for Striking Bills of Credit, & issuing out the same, in lieu of money, the respective Governors & Commanders in chief of his

---

*From *American History Told by Contemporaries*, 5 vols., ed. Albert Bushnell Hart (New York: The Macmillan Company, 1914–), II:254.

Majesty's Colonies & Plantations for the time being, have been particularly instructed not to give their Assent to or pass any such laws for the future, without a Clause inserted in such Act, declaring that the same shall not take Effect, until the said Act shall have been approved and confirm'd by his Majesty his Heirs or Successors: and whereas notwithstanding such his Majesty's Commanders to the said Governors in that behalf, Paper Bills of Credit have been created & issued in his Majesty's said Colonies & Plantations by Virtue of Acts of Assembly there, making it obligatory on all persons to take such Bills of Credits, in payment for Debts, Dues & Demands . . . and a great Discouragement has been brot on the Com'erce of this Kingdom by occasioning a Confusion in Dealings and a lessening of Credit in those parts; And whereas an humble Address was presented, the last Session by the House of Commons, to his Majesty, That he would be graciously pleased to require & command the respective Governors of his Colonies & Plantation in America, punctually & effectually to observe his Majtys Royal Instructions not to give Assent to or to pass any Act, whereby Bills of Credit may be issued in lieu of money, without a Clause to be inserted in such Act, declaring that the same shall be approved by his Majesty:

It is therefore his Majesty's Will & Pleasure, & you are hereby also further required & commanded under pain of his Majesty's highest displeasure and of being removed, from your Governmt punctually & effectually to observe his Majesty's Royal Instruction not to give Assent to or pass any Act, whereby Bills of Credit may be issued in lieu of money without a Clause be inserted in such Act, declaring that the same shall not take Effect, until the said Act shall be approved by his Majesty, his Heirs or Successors.

26. CONSIDERATIONS ON THE NATURE OF LAWS, 1721*

This essay from Cato's Letters *provides an example of the political writing that attracted great attention in the colonies early in the eighteenth century. The document reveals many of the Enlightenment ideals regarding liberty, equality, and power that shaped American thinking during the period. According to Cato, natural law established two fundamental rights: equity, or justice, and the right to defend that equity. The premise had profound implications for colonial attitudes toward those in power, because the essay concludes that a community may resist unjust laws. In 1776, Thomas Jefferson institutionalized such concepts in the Declaration of Independence.*

The Mischiefs that are daily done, and the Evils that are daily suffered in the World, are sad proofs how much human Malice exceeds human wisdom. Law only provides against the Evils which it knows or foresees; but when Laws fail, we must have Recourse to Reason and Nature, which are the only Guides in the making of Laws. *Stirpem Juris a Natura repertam,* says Cicero; there never would have been any Law against any Crime, if Crimes might have been safely committed, against which there was no Law; For every Law supposes some Evil, and can only punish or restrain the Evils which already exist.

But as positive Laws, let them be ever so full and perspicuous, can never entirely prevent the Arts of crafty Men to evade them, or the Power of great ones to violate them; hence new Laws are daily making, and new Occasions for more are daily arising: So that the utmost that Wisdom, Virtue, and Law can do, is to lessen or qualify, but never totally abolish Vice and Enormity. Law is therefore a Sign of the Corruption of Man; and many Laws are Signs of the Corruption of a State.

Positive Laws deriving their Force from the Law of Nature, by which we are directed to make occasional Rules, which we call Laws, according to the Exigences of Times, Places, and Persons, grow obsolete, or cease to be, as soon as they cease to be necessary: And it is as much against the

*From Cato's Letters; or, Essays on Liberty, Civil and Religious, and Other Important Subjects, 3rd corrected ed., 4 vols. (New York: Russell and Russell, 1733), II:64–70.

law of Nature to execute Laws, when the first Cause of them ceases, as it is to make Laws, for which there is no Cause, or a bad Cause. This would be to subject Reason to Force, and to apply a Penalty where there is no Crime. Law is right Reason, commanding Things that are good, and forbidding Things that are bad; it is a Distinction and Declaration of Things just and unjust, and of the Penalties or Advantages annexed to them.

The Violation therefore of Law does not constitute a Crime where the Law is bad; but the Violation of what ought to be Law, is a Crime even when there is no Law. The Essence of Right and Wrong, does not depend on Words and Clauses inserted in a Code or a Statute-Book, much less upon the Conclusions and Explications of Lawyers; but upon Reason and the Nature of Things, antecedent to all Laws. In all Countries, Reason is or ought to be consulted, before Laws are enacted; and they are always worse than none, where it is not consulted. Reason is in some Degree given to all Men, and *Cicero* says, that whoever has Reason, has right Reason; that Virtue is but perfect Reason, and that all nations having Reason for their Guide, all Nations are capable of arriving at Virtue.

From this Reasoning of his, it would follow, that every People are capable of making Laws; and that Laws, where they are bad, are gained by Corruption, Faction, Fear, or Surprize; and are rather their Misfortune, than the Effects of their Folly. The Acts of *Caesar* were confirmed by the Senate and the People; but the Senate was awed, and the Tribunes and People were bribed: Arms and Money procured him a Law to declare him lawless. But, as the most pompous Power can never unsettle the everlasting Land-marks between Good and Evil, no more than those between Pleasure and Pain; *Caesar* remained still a Rebel to his Country, and his Acts remained wicked and tyrannical.

Let this stand for an Instance, that Laws are not always the Measure of Right and Wrong. And as positive Laws often speak when the Law of Nature is silent, the Law of Nature sometimes speaks, when positive Laws say nothing. . . .

It is impossible to devise Laws sufficient to regulate and manage every Occurrence and Circumstance of Life, because they are often produced and diversified by Causes that do not appear; and in every Condition of Life, Men must have, and will have, great Allowances made to their own natural Liberty and Discretion: But every Man who consents to this Proposition, that *every Man should do all the Good, and prevent all the Evil that he can.* This is the voice of the Law of Nature; and all Men would be happy by it, if all Men would practise it. This Law leads us to see, that the Establishment of Falshood and Tyranny (by which I mean the Privilege of One or a Few to mislead and oppress All) cannot be justly called Law, which is the impartial Rule of Good and Evil, and can never be the Sanction of Evil alone.

It has been often said, that Virtue is its own Reward; and it is very true, not only from the Pleasure that attends the Consciousness of doing well, and the Fame that follows it, but in a more extensive Sense, from the Felicity which would accrue to every Man, if all Men would pursue Virtue: But as this Truth may appear too general to allure and engage particular Men, who will have always their own single selves most at Heart, abstracted from all the rest; therefore in the making of Laws, the Pleasures and Fears of particular Men, being the great Engines by which they are to be governed, must be consulted; Vice must be rendered detestable and dangerous; Virtue amiable and advantageous. Their Shame and Emulation must be raised, their private Profit and Glory, Peril and Infamy, laid before them. . . .

Rewards and Punishments therefore constitute the whole Strength of Laws; and the Promulgation of Laws, without which they are none, is an Appeal to the Sense and Interest of Men, which of the two they will chuse.

The two great Laws of human Society, from whence all the rest derive their Course and Obligation, are those of Equity and Self-preservation: By the First, all Men are bound alike not to hurt one another; by the Second, all Men have a Right alike to defend themselves: . . . All the Laws of Society are entirely reciprocal, and no Man ought to be exempt from their Force; and whoever violates this primary Law of Nature, ought by the Law of Nature to be destroyed. He who observes no Law, forfeits all Title to the Protection of Law. It is a Wickedness not to destroy a Destroyer; and all the ill Consequences of Self-defence are chargeable upon him who occasioned them.

Many Mischiefs are prevented, by destroying One who shews a certain Disposition to commit many. To allow a Licence to any Man to do Evil with Impunity, is to make Vice triumph over Virtue, and Innocence Prey to the Guilty. If Men be obliged to bear great and publick Evils, when they can upon better Terms oppose and remove them; they are obliged by the same Logick, to bear the total Destruction of Mankind. If any Man may destroy whom he pleases without Resistance, he may extinguish the human Race without Resistance. For, if you settle the Bounds of Resistance, you allow it; and if you do not fix its Bounds, you leave Property at the Mercy of Rapine, and Life in the Hands of Cruelty.

It is said, that the Doctrine of Resistance would destroy the Peace of the World: But it may be more truly said, that the contrary Doctrine would destroy the World itself, as it has already some of the best Countries in it. I must indeed own, that if one Man may destroy all, there would be a great and lasting Peace when Nobody was left to break it.

The Law of Nature does not only allow us, but obliges us, to defend ourselves. It is our Duty, not only to ourselves, but to the Society. . . .

So that the Conduct of Men, who when they are ill treated, use Words rather than Arms, and practise Submission rather than Resistance, is owing to a prudential Cause, because there is Hazard in Quarrels and War, and their Case may be made worse by an Endeavour to mend it; and not to any Consession of Right in those that do them wrong. When Men begin to be wicked, we cannot tell where that Wickedness will end; we have Reason to fear the worst, and provide against it.

Such is the Provision made by Laws: They are Checks upon the unruly and partial Appetites of Men, and intended for Terror and Protection. But as there are already Laws sufficient every where, to preserve Peace between private Particulars, the great Difficulty has hitherto been to find proper checks for those who were to check and administer the Laws. To settle therefore a thorough Impartiality in the Laws, both as to their End and Execution, is a Task worthy of human Wisdom, as it would be the Cause and Standard of Civil Felicity. In the Theory, nothing is more easy than this Task: Yet who is able to perform it, if they who can will not?

No Man in Society ought to have any Privilege above the rest, without giving the Society some Equivalent for such his Privilege. Thus Legislators, who compile good Laws, and good Magistrates who execute them, do, by their honest Attendance upon the Publick, deserve the Privileges and Pay which the Publick allows them; and Place and power are the Wages paid by the People to their own Deputies and Agents. Hence it has been well said, that a chief Magistrate is . . . "above the private members of the Community, but the Community itself is above him."

Wherever, therefore, the Laws are honestly intended and equally executed, so as to comprehend in their Penalties and Operation the Great as well and as much as the Small, and hold in awe the Magistrates as much as the Subject, that Government is good, that People are happy.

27. ON SELF-DENIAL, 1734*

*A*s the preceding selection shows, political philosophers embraced virtue as crucial to society. In the following essay, which first appeared in The Pennsylvania Gazette, *Benjamin Franklin offers his reflections on*

---

*From Benjamin Franklin, "On Self-Denial," *The Pennsylvania Gazette*, February 18, 1734, in *Memoirs of Benjamin Franklin. Written by Himself, and Continued by His Grandson and Others*, 2 vols. (Philadelphia: McCarty & Davis, 1837), II:470–71.

virtue. To his contemporaries, Franklin epitomized the enlightened individual of the eighteenth century. A successful and wealthy publisher, he devoted much of his life to philosophical rumination and scientific research. Franklin, as shown in the following document, occasionally revealed an iconoclasm that in many ways reflected the independent mindedness of some colonists and a new confidence in the possibilities of human benevolence.

It is commonly asserted, that *without self-denial there is no virtue*, and that the greater the self-denial is, the greater is the virtue.

If it were said, that he who cannot deny himself any thing he inclines to, though he knows it will be to his hurt, has not the virtue of resolution or fortitude, it would be intelligible enough; but as it stands, the proposition seems obscure or erroneous.

Let us consider some of the virtues singly.

If a man has no inclination to wrong people in his dealings; if he feels no temptation to it, and therefore never does it, can it be said, that he is not a just man? If he is a just man, has he not the virtue of justice?

If to a certain man, idle diversions have nothing in them that is tempting, and therefore he never relaxes his application to business for their sake, is he not an industrious man; or has he not the virtue of industry?

I might in like manner instance in all the rest of the virtues; but to make the thing short, as it is certain, that the more we strive against the temptation to any vice, and practise the contrary virtue, the weaker will that temptation be, and the stronger will be that habit; till at length the temptation hath no force, or entirely vanishes: does it follow from thence, that in our endeavours to overcome vice, we grow continually less and less virtuous, till at length we have no virtue at all!

If self-denial be the essence of virtue, then it follows, that the man who is naturally temperate, just, &c., is not virtuous, but that in order to be virtuous, he must, in spite of his natural inclinations, wrong his neighbors, and eat and drink, &c., to excess.

But, perhaps it may be said, that by the word *virtue*, in the above assertion, is meant *merit*, and so it should stand; thus without self-denial there is no merit; and the greater the self-denial the greater the merit.

The self-denial here meant must be, when our inclinations are toward vice, or else it would still be nonsense.

By merit is understood desert; and when we say a man merits, we mean that he deserves praise and reward.

We do not pretend to merit any thing of God, for he is above our services, and the benefits he confers on us are the efforts of his goodness and bounty.

All merit then is with regard to one another, and from one another.

Taking then the proposition as it stands—

If a man does me a service, from a natural benevolent inclination, does he deserve less of me than another, who does me the like kindness against his inclination?

If I have two journeymen, one naturally industrious, the other idle, but both perform a day's work equally good, ought I to give the latter the most wages?

Indeed lazy workmen are commonly observed to be more extravagant in their demands than the industrious; for if they have not more for their work, they cannot live as well as the industrious. But though it be true to a proverb, that *lazy folks take the most pains*, does it follow that they deserve the *most money?* If you were to employ servants in affairs of trust, would you pay more wages to one you know were naturally honest, than for one naturally roguish, but who had lately acted honestly: for currents whose natural channels are dammed up, til a new course is by time worn sufficiently deep, and become natural, are apt to break their banks. If one servant is more valuable than another, has he not more merit than the other, and yet this is not on account of superior self-denial. Is a patriot praiseworthy, if public support is natural to him?

Is a pacing horse less valuable for being a natural pacer?

Nor in my opinion has any man less merit for having in general naturally virtuous inclinations.

The truth is, that temperance, justice, charity, &c., are virtues whether practised with or against our inclinations; and the man who practises them, merits our love and esteem: and self-denial is neither good nor bad, but as it is applied. He that denies a vicious inclination, is virtuous in proportion to his resolution; but the most perfect virtue is above all temptation; such as the virtue of the saints in heaven: and he who does any foolish, indecent, or wicked thing, merely because it is contrary to his inclination, like some mad enthusiasts I have read of, who ran almost in public naked, under the notion of taking up the cross, is not practising the reasonable science of virtue, but is a lunatic.

28. ELECTRICAL KITE, 1752*

Benjamin Franklin, who became an outspoken proponent of colonial unity and, eventually, independence, often represented American interests before the intellectual and political leaders of Europe. In that capacity he certainly provided an invaluable service as a powerful defender of American liberty. One reason for his accomplishments as a diplomat was the immense fame he had gained through his experiments with electricity. He described his most famous experiment in the following letter to an English colleague.

As frequent mention is made in public papers from Europe of the success of the Philadelphia experiment for drawing the electric fire from the clouds by means of pointed rods of iron erected on high buildings &c. it may be agreeable to the curious to be informed that the same experiment has succeeded in Philadelphia, though made in a different and more easy manner, which is as follows:

Make a small cross of two light strips of cedar, the arms so long as to reach to the four corners of a large thin silk handkerchief when extended; tie the corners of the handkerchief to the extremities of the cross, so you have the body of a kite; which being properly accommodated with a tail, loop, and string, will rise in the air, like those made of paper; but this being of silk is fitter to bear the wet and wind of a thunder gust without tearing. To the top of the upright stick of the cross is to be fixed a very sharp pointed wire, rising a foot or more above the wood. To the end of the twine, next the hand, is to be tied a silk ribbon, and where the silk and twine join, a key may be fastened. This kite is to be raised when a thunder gust appears to be coming on, and the person who holds the string must stand within a door or window, or under some cover, so that the silk ribbon may not be wet; and care must be taken that the twine does not touch the frame of the door or window. As soon as any of the thunder clouds come over the kite, the pointed wire will draw the electric fire from them, and the kite, with all the twine, will be electrified, and the loose filaments of the twine will stand out every way, and be attracted by an approaching finger. And when the rain has wetted the kite and twine, so that it can conduct the electric fire freely, you will find it stream out plentifully from the key on the approach of your knuckle. At this key the phial may be charged; and from electric fire thus obtained, spirits may be kindled, and all other electric experiments be performed, which are usually done by the help of a rubbed glass globe or tube, and thereby the sameness of the electric matter with that of lightening completely demonstrated.

---

*Franklin to Peter Collinson, October 16, 1752, in *Memoirs of Benjamin Franklin. Written by Himself, and Continued by His Grandson and Others*, 2 vols. (Philadelphia: McCarty & Davis, 1837), II:284.

29. REASONS FOR ESTABLISHING THE COLONY OF GEORGIA, 1733*

In the 1730s a number of influential Englishmen founded Georgia. Proprietors believed that the new settlements would protect South Carolina from the Spanish and thereby ensure British power in the region. They hoped, too, that Georgia would serve as a haven for England's "deserving" poor by providing economic opportunity—and consequently some degree of liberty—for disadvantaged Britons. Written by Benjamin Martin of London, the following essay underscores the philanthropic and practical concerns that led to the creation of the colony. The piece also expresses the benevolence that characterized many Enlightenment reformers.

If half of these [estimated four thousand persons imprisoned each year for debt, about one third of whom never recover], or only five hundred of them, were to be sent to Georgia every year to be incorporated with those foreign Protestants who are expelled their own country for religion, what great improvements might not be expected in our trade, when those, as well as foreigners, would be so many new subjects gained by England? For, while they are in prison, they are absolutely lost,—the public loses their labor, and their knowledge. If they take the benefit of the Act of Parliament that allows them liberty on their delivery of their all to their creditors, they come destitute into the world again. As they have no money and little credit, they find it almost impossible to get into business, especially when our trades are overstocked. They, therefore, by contracting new debts, must return again into prison, or, how honest soever their dispositions may be, by idleness and necessity will be forced into bad courses, such as begging, cheating, or robbing. These, then, likewise, are useless to the state; not only so, but dangerous. But these (it will be said) may be serviceable by their labor in the country. To force them to it, I am afraid, is impracticable; to suppose they will voluntarily do it, I am sure is unlikely. The Colony of Georgia will be proper asylum for these. This will make the act of parliament of more effect. Here they will have the best motive for industry; a possession of their own, and no possibility of subsisting without it.

I have heard it said that our prisons are the properest places for those that are thrown into them, by keeping them from being hurtful to others. Surely this way of thinking is something too severe. Are these people, with their liberty to lose our compassion? Are they to be shut up from our eyes, and excluded also from our hearts? Many of very honest dispositions fall into decay, nay, perhaps, because they are so, because they cannot allow themselves that latitude which others take to be successful. The ways that lead to a man's ruin are various. Some are undone by overtrading, others by want of trade; many by being responsible for others. Do all these deserve such hardship? If a man sees a friend, a brother, a father going to a prison, where felons are to be his society, want and sickness his sure attendants, and death, in all likelihood his only, but *quick* relief; if he stretches out his hand to save him from immediate slavery and ruin, he runs the risk of his own liberty, and at last loses it; is there any one who will say, this man is not an object of compassion? Not so, but of esteem, and worth preserving for his virtue? But supposing that idleness and intemperance are the usual cause of his ruin. Are these crimes adequate to such a punishment as confinement for life? But even yet granting that these unhappy people deserve no indulgence, it is certainly imprudent in any state to lose the benefit of the labor of so many thousands.

But the public loss, by throwing men into prison, is not confined to them only. They have many of them wives and children. These are, also, involved in their ruin. Being destitute of a support, they must perish, or else become a burden on their parishes by an inability to work, or a nuisance by their thefts. These, too, are useless to society.

---

*From Thaddeus M. Harris, *Biographical Memorials of James Oglethorpe, Founder of the Colony of Georgia in North America* (Boston: Freeman and Bolles, 1841), 343–45.

In short, all those who can work yet are supported in idleness by any mistaken charity, or are sustained by their parishes, which are at this time, through all England overburdened by indolent and lazy poor;—all those who add nothing by their labor to the welfare of the state, are useless, burdensome, or dangerous to it. What is to be done with these necessitous? Nobody, I suppose, thinks that they should continue useless. It will be then an act of charity to these, and of merit to the public, for any one to propose, forward, and perfect a better expedient for making them useful. If he cannot, he is surely just to acquiesce, till a better be found, in the present design of settling them in Georgia.

30. Gilbert Tennent Attacks Opponents of the Great Awakening, 1740*

*M*ost conservative clergymen opposed the religious emotionalism of the Great Awakening and emphasized orthodoxy over a personal religious experience. Revivalist "New Light" ministers, such as Gilbert Tennent (1703–1764), challenged such views. In this excerpt from a 1740 sermon, The Danger of an Unconverted Ministry, *Tennent defends the practice of seeking converts from "Old Light" congregations by identifying their highly educated ministers as "Pharisee-teachers" who lacked the emotional commitment to lead their people to salvation.*

But possibly some may again object against Persons going to hear others, besides their own Ministers; . . . Again it may be objected, That the aforesaid Practice tends to grieve our Parish-Minister, and to break Congregations in Pieces.

I answer, If our Parish-Minister be grieved at our greater Good, or prefers his Credit before it; then he has good Cause to grieve over his own Rottenness and Hypocrisie. And as for Breaking of Congregations into Pieces, upon the Account of People's Going from Place to Place, to hear the Word, with a view to get greater Good; that spiritual Blindness and Death, that so generally prevails, will put this out of Danger. It is but a very few, that have got any spiritual Relish; the most will venture their Souls with any Formalist, and be well satisfied with the sapless Discourses of such dead Drones. . . .

I would conclude my present Meditations upon this Subject, by Exhorting All those who enjoy a faithful Ministry, to a speedy and sincere Improvement of so rare and valuable a Privilege; lest by their foolish Ingratitude the Righteous GOD be provok'd, to remove the Means they enjoy, or his Blessing from them, and so at last to expose them in another State to Enduring and greater Miseries. For surely, these Sins which are committed against greater Light and Mercy, are more presumptuous, ungrateful, and inexcusable; there is in them a greater Contempt of GOD's Authority, and Slight of his Mercy; those Evils do awfully violate the Conscience, and declare a Love to Sin as Sin; such Transgressors do rush upon the Bosses of GOD's Bucker, they court Destruction without a Covering, and embrace their own Ruin with open Arms. And therefore according to the Nature of justice, which proportions Sinners Pains, according to the Number and Heinousness of their Crimes, and the Declaration of Divine truth, you must expect an enflamed Damnation: Surely, it shall be more tolerable for Sodom and Gommorah, in the Day of the LORD, than for you, except ye repent.

And let gracious Souls be exhorted, to express the most tender Pity over such as have none but Pharisee-Teachers; and that in the Manner before described: To which the Example of our LORD

---

*From Gilbert Tennent, *The Danger of an Unconverted Ministry Considered in a Sermon on Mark VI,34* (Philadelphia: Benjamin Franklin, 1740).

in the Text before us, be an inducing and effectual Incitement; as well as the gracious and immense Rewards, which follow upon so generous and noble a Charity, in this and the next State.

And let those who live under the Ministry of dead Men, whether they have got the Form of Religion or not, repair to the Living, where they may be edified. Let who will, oppose it. What famous Mr. *Jenner* observes upon this Head, is most just, 'That if there be any godly Souls, or any that desires the Salvation of his Soul, and lives under a blind Guide, be cannot go out (of his Parish) without giving very great Offence; it will be tho't a Giddiness, and a Slighting of his own Minister at home. When People came out of every Parish round about, to *John* [The Baptist], no Question but this bred Heart-brning against *John*, ay, and Ill-will against those People, that would not be satisfied with that Teaching they had in their own Synagogues.' Thus far he. But tho' your Neighbors growl against you, and reproach you for doing your Duty, in seeking your Souls Good; bear their unjust Censures with Christian Meekness, and persevere; as knowing that Suffering is the Lot of Christ's Followers, and that spiritual Benefits do infinitely overbalance all temporal Difficulties.

And 0! that vacant Congregations would take due Care in the Choice of their Ministers! Here indeed they should hasten slowly. The Church of Ephesus [In Paul's Epistle) is commended, for Trying them which said they were Apostles, and were not; and for finding them Liars. Hypocrits are against all Knowing of others, and judging, in order to hide their own Filthiness; like Thieves they flee a Search, because of their stolen Goods. But the more they endeavour to hide, the more they expose their Shame. Does not the spiritual Man judge all Things? Tho' he cannot know the States of subtil Hypocrits infallibly; yet may he not give a near Guess, who are the sons of *Sceva*, by their Manner of Praying, Preaching, and Living? Many Pharisee-Teachers have got a long fine string of Prayer by Heart, so that they are never at a Loss about it; their Prayers and Preachings are generally of a Length, and both as dead as a Stone, and without all Savour. I beseech you, my dear Brethren, to consider, That there is no Probability of your getting Good, by the Ministry of Pharisees. For they are no Shepherds (no faithful ones) in Christ's Account. They are as good as none, nay, worse than none, upon some Accounts. For take them first and last, and they generally do more Hurt than Good. They serve to keep better out of the Places where they live; nay, when the Life of Piety comes near their Quarters, they rise up in Arms against it, consult, contrive and combine in their Conclaves against it, as a common Enemy, that discovers and condemns their Craft and Hypocrisie. And with what Art, Rhetorick, and Appearances of Piety, will they varnish their Opposition of Christ's Kingdom? As the Magicians imitated the Works of Moses, so do false Apostles, and deceitful Workers, the Apostles of Christ.

I shall conclude this Discourse with the Words of the Apostle *Paul 2, Cor. 11: 14-15. And no Marvel; for Satan himself is transformed into an Angel of Light: Therefore it is no great Thing if his Ministers also be transformed as the Ministers of Righteousness; whose End shall be according to their Works.*

31. SINNERS IN THE HANDS OF AN ANGRY GOD*

Early in the eighteenth century, an emotional reaction against the rationality of the Enlightenment led to a powerful revivalism known as the Great Awakening that swept Britain and its American colonies. The revival had a monumental influence on the development of American religion, education, and society, while the evangelical rejection of established authority eventually strengthened the movement for independence. New England minister Jonathan Edwards played a dominant role in the Awakening, and his passionate message is clearly evident in the following sermon.

---

*From *Selected Sermons of Jonathan Edwards*, ed. H. Norman Gardiner (New York: The Macmillan Company, 1904), 78–97.

. . . So that thus it is, that natural men are held in the hand of God over the pit of Hell; they have deserved the fiery pit, and are already sentenced to it; and God is dreadfully provoked, his anger is as great towards them as to those that are actually suffering the executions of the fierceness of his wrath in hell, and they have done nothing in the least to appease or abate that anger, neither is God in the least bound by any promise to hold 'em up one moment; the devil is waiting for them, hell is gaping for them, the flames gather and flash about them, and would fain lay hold on them and swallow them up; the fire pent up in their own hearts is struggling to break out; and they have no interest in any Mediator, there are no means within reach that can be any security to them. In short they have no refuge, nothing to take hold of; all that preserves them every moment is the mere arbitrary will, and uncovenanted, unobliged forbearance of an incensed God. . . .

This that you have heard is the case of every one of you that are out of Christ. The world of misery, that lake of burning brimstone, is extended abroad under you. **There** is the dreadful pit of the glowing flames of the wrath of God; there is hell's wide gaping mouth open; and you have nothing to stand upon, nor anything to take hold of. There is nothing between you and hell but the air; 'tis only the power and mere pleasure of God that holds you up.

Your wickedness makes you as it were heavy as lead, and to tend downwards with great weight and pressure towards hell; and if God should let you go, you should immediately sink and swiftly descend and plunge into the bottomless gulf, and your healthy constitution, and your own care and prudence, and best contrivance, and all your righteousness, would have no more influence to uphold you and keep you out of hell than a spider's web would have to stop a falling rock. Were it not that so is the sovereign pleasure of God, the earth would not bear you one moment; for you are a burden to it; the creation groans with you; the creature is made subject to the bondage of your corruption, not willingly; the sun don't willingly shine upon you to give you light to serve sin and Satan; the earth don't willingly yield her increase to satisfy your lusts; nor is it willingly a stage for your wickedness to be acted upon; the air don't willingly serve you for breath to maintain the flame of life in your vitals, while you spend your life in the service of God's enemies. God's creatures are good, and were made for men to serve God with, and don't willingly subserve to any other purpose, and groan when they are abused to purposes directly contrary to their nature and end. And the world would spew you out, were it not for the sovereign hand of him who hath subjected it in hope. There are the black clouds of God's wrath now hanging directly over your heads, full of the dreadful storms, and big with thunder; and were it not for the restraining hand of God, it would immediately burst forth upon you. The sovereign pleasure of God, for the present, stays his rough wind; otherwise it would come with fury, and your destruction would come like a whirlwind, and you would be like the chaff of the summer threshing floor. . . .

The God that holds you over the pit of hell, much as one holds a spider or some loathsome insect over the fire, abhors you, and is dreadfully provoked; his wrath towards you burns like fire; he looks upon you as worthy of nothing else, but to be cast into fire; he is of purer eyes than to bear to have you in his sight; you are ten thousand times so abominable in his eyes, as the most hateful and venomous serpent is in ours. You have offended him infinitely more than ever a stubborn rebel did his prince: and yet it is nothing but his hand that holds you from falling into the fire every moment. 'Tis ascribed to nothing else, that you did go to hell the last night; that you was suffered to awake again in this world after you closed your eyes to sleep; and there is no other reason to be given why you have not dropped into hell since you arose in the morning, but that God's hand has held you up. There is no other reason to be given why you haven't gone to hell since you have sat here in the house of God, provoking his pure eyes by your sinful wicked manner of attending his solemn worship. Yea, there is nothing else that is to be given as a reason why you don't this very moment drop down into hell.

O sinner! consider the fearful danger you are in. 'Tis a great furnace of wrath, a wide and bottomless pit, full of the fire of wrath, that you are held over in the hand of that God whose wrath is provoked and incensed as much against you as against many of the damned in hell. You hang by a slender thread, with the flames of divine wrath flashing about it, and ready every moment to singe it and burn it asunder; and you have no interest in any Mediator, and nothing to lay hold of to save yourself, nothing to keep off the flames of wrath, nothing of your own, nothing that you ever have done, nothing that you can do, to induce God to spare you one moment. . . .

How dreadful is the state of those that are daily and hourly in danger of this great wrath and infinite misery! But this is the dismal case of every soul in this congregation that has not been born again, however moral and strict, sober and religious, they may otherwise be. Oh, that you would consider it, whether you be young or old! There is reason to think that there are many in this congregation now hearing this discourse, that will actually be subjects of this very misery to all eternity. We know not who they are, or in what seats they sit, or what thoughts they now have. It may be they are now at ease, and hear all these things without much disturbance, and are now flattering themselves that they are not the persons, promising themselves that they shall escape. If we knew that there was one person, and but one, in the whole congregation, that was to be the subject of this misery, what an awful thing it would be to think of! If we knew who it was, what an awful sight it would be to see such a person! How might all the rest of the congregation lift up a lamentable and bitter cry over him! But alas! instead of one, how many is it likely will remember this discourse in hell! And it would be a wonder, if some that are now present should not be in hell in a very short time, before this year is out. And it would be no wonder if some persons that now sit here in some seats of this meeting-house in health, and quiet and secure, should be there before to-morrow morning. Those of you that finally continue in a natural condition, that shall keep out of hell the longest, will be there in a little time! 'Tis doubtless the case that of some that heretofore you have seen and known, that never deserved hell more than you and that heretofore appeared as likely to have been now alive as you. Their case is past all hope; they are crying in extreme misery and perfect despair. But here you are in the land of the living and in the house of God, and have an opportunity to obtain salvation. What would not those poor, damned, hopeless souls give for one day's such opportunity as you now enjoy!

And now you have an extraordinary opportunity, a day wherein Christ has flung the door of mercy wide open, and stands in the door calling and crying with a loud voice to poor sinners; a day wherein many are flocking to him and pressing into the Kingdom of God. Many are daily coming from the east, west, north and south; many that were very likely in the same miserable condition that you are in are in now a happy state, with their hearts filled with love to him that has loved them and washed them from their sins in his own blood, and rejoicing in the hope of the glory of God. How awful it is to be left behind at such a day! . . .

Are there not many here that have lived long in the world that are not to this day born again, and so are aliens from the commonwealth of Israel and done nothing ever since they have lived but treasure up wrath against the day of wrath? Oh, sirs, your case in an especial manner is extremely dangerous; your guilt and hardness of heart is extremely great. . . . You had need to consider yourselves and wake thoroughly out of sleep; you cannot bear the fierceness and the wrath of the infinite God.

And you that are young men and young women, will you neglect this precious season that you now enjoy, when so many others of your age are renouncing all youthful vanities and flocking to Christ? You especially have now an extraordinary opportunity; but if you neglect it, it will soon be with you as it is with those persons that spent away all the precious days of youth in sin and are now come to such a dreadful pass in blindness and hardness.

And you children that are unconverted, don't you know that you are going down to hell to bear the dreadful wrath of that God that is now angry with you every day and every night? Will you be content to be children of the devil, when so many other children in the land are converted and are become the holy and happy children of the King of kings?

And let every one that is yet out of Christ and hanging over the pit of hell, whether they be old men and women or middle-aged or young people or little children, now hearken to the loud calls of God's word and providence. . . . God seems now to be hastily gathering in the elect in all parts of the land; and probably the bigger part of adult persons that ever shall be saved will be brought in now in a little time, and . . . the election will obtain and the rest will be blinded. If this should be the case with you, you will eternally curse this day, and will curse the day that ever you was born to see such a season of the pouring out of God's Spirit, and will wish that you had died and gone to hell before you had seen it. Now . . . the axe is in an extraordinary manner laid at the root of the trees, that every tree that bringeth not forth good fruit may be hewn down and cast into the fire.

Therefore let every one that is out of Christ now awake and fly from the wrath to come. The wrath of Almighty God is now undoubtedly hanging over great part of this congregation. Let every one fly out of Sodom. *"Haste and escape for your lives, look not behind you, escape to the mountain, lest ye be consumed."*

32. MASSACHUSETTS ASSOCIATES LIBERTY WITH EXPANSION

With hegemony over North America at stake, Britain and France resumed their long-standing imperial conflict in 1754. In the annual election sermon, Jonathan Mayhew, a prominent Congregational minister, challenged the Massachusetts General Court to prepare for war, using most of the arguments voiced by New Englanders to justify the conquest of New France. For him and many English colonists, the ideas of liberty, expansion, and conquest had become indivisible.

. . . The form of our government is justly the envy of most other nations, expecially of those [with] no parliaments at all, or such as may be banished at the word and pleasure of a tyrant. . . . We have also for several late reigns been blessed with princes too just and good to encroach upon the rights of their subjects, and too wise to think that Britons can endure a chain. . . .

Our [Massachusetts] ancestors, tho' not perfect and infallible in all respects, were a religious, brave, and virtuous set of men, whose love of liberty, civil and religious, brought them from their native land into the American deserts. . . . Tho' we are not an independent state, yet, heaven be thanked! we are a free people. . . .

. . . And what a turn may be given to the affairs of Europe should heaven permit Gallic [French] policy and perfidy to prevail here over English valor! . . . We are peaceably extending our settlements upon our own territories; they are extending theirs beyond their own by force of arms. . . . The continent is not wide enough for us both, and they are resolved to have the whole. . . .

And what horrid scene is this which restless, roving fancy . . . presents to me, and so chills my blood! Do I behold these territories of freedom become the prey of arbitrary power? . . . Do I see Christianity banished for popery! the Bible, for the mass-book! the oracles of truth, for fabulous legends! . . . Instead of a train of Christ's faithful, laborious ministers, do I behold an herd of lazy monks, and Jesuits, and exorcists, and inquisitors, and cowled and uncowled imposters! Do I see a Protestant there, stealing a look at his Bible, and being taken in the fact, punished like a felon! . . .

---

*From Jonathan Mayhew, *A Sermon Preach'd in the Audience of his Excellency William Shirley, Esq; Captain General, Governour and Commander in Chief, the Honourable his Majesty's Council, and the Honourable House of Representatives, of the Province of the Massachusetts-Bay in New England. May 29th 1754. Being the Anniversary for the Election of his Majesty's Council for the Province* (Boston: Samuel Kneeland, 1754), reprinted in *The Wall and the Garden: Selected Massachusetts Election Sermons, 1670–1775*, ed. A. W. Plumstead (Minneapolis: University of Minnesota Press, 1968), 299, 301, 310–11, 316.

[In this hour of peril, the House of Representatives must put aside factional quarrels and unite for the common good. It must vote ample taxes for] a cause wherein the glory of God, the honor of your King, and the good of your country, are so deeply concerned—I might perhaps add, a cause whereon the liberties of Europe depend. For of so great consequence is the empire of North America (and that, you are sensible, is the thing now aimed at by our neighbors), that it must turn the scale of power greatly in favor of the only monarch [Louis XV] from whom those liberties are in danger, and against that prince [George II] who is the grand support and bulwark of them. . . .

33. THE ALBANY PLAN, 1754*

*B*enjamin Franklin proposed a unified colonial government as a means to meet the French and Indian threat. The Albany Congress modified the proposal and presented it to the various general assemblies, which roundly rejected the Albany Plan. According to Franklin, the colonies feared that the president-general could assert undue power, and in 1754 colonists certainly did not trust each other enough to turn authority over to a central council. Royal authorities also ultimately ruled against the plan because they doubted that the colonists could cooperate and because they feared the precedent of such a union. Nevertheless, Franklin remained dedicated to unity, and, despite the failure of his first effort to bring the thirteen colonies together, his commitment would bear fruit in the years after 1763.

That the said general government be administered by a President-General, to be appointed and supported by the crown; and a Grand Council, to be chosen by the representatives of the people of the several colonies met in their respective Assemblies—who shall meet for the first time at the city of Philadelphia, being called by the President-General as soon as conveniently may be after his appointment.

That there shall be a new election of the members of the Grand Council every three years; and, on the death or resignation of any member, his place should be supplied by a new choice at the next sitting of the Assembly of the colony he represented.

That after the first three years, when the proportion of money arising out of each colony to the general treasury can be known, the number of members to be chosen shall from time to time, in all ensuing elections, be regulated by that proportion, yet so as that the number to be chosen by any one province be not more than seven, nor less than two.

That the Grand Council shall meet once in every year, and oftener if occasion require, at such time and place as they shall adjourn to at the last preceding meeting, or as they shall be called to meet at by the President-General on any emergency; he having first obtained in writing the consent of seven of the members to such call, and sent due and timely notice to the whole.

That the Grand Council have power to choose their speaker; and shall neither be dissolved, prorogued, nor continued sitting longer than six weeks at one time, without their own consent or the special command of the crown.

That the members of the Grand Council shall be allowed for their service ten shillings sterling per diem, during their session and journey to and from the place of meeting; twenty miles to be reckoned a day's journey.

That the assent of the President-General be requisite to all acts of the Grand Council, and that it be his office and duty to cause them to be carried into execution.

*"Plan of Union," in *The Works of Benjamin Franklin*, 10 vols., ed. Jared Sparks (Chicago: Townsend MacCoun, 1882), III:36–55.

That the President-General, with the advice of the Grand Council, hold or direct all Indian treaties, in which the general interest of the colonies may be concerned; and make peace or declare war with Indian nations.

That they make such laws as they judge necessary for regulating all Indian trade.

That they make all purchases, from the Indians for the crown, of lands not now within the bounds of particular colonies, or that shall be within their bounds when some of them are reduced to more convenient dimensions.

That they make new settlements on such purchases, by granting lands in the King's name, reserving a quit-rent to the crown for the use of the general treasury.

That they make laws for regulating and governing such new settlements, till the crown shall think fit to form them into particular governments.

That they raise and pay soldiers and build forts for the defence of any of the colonies, and equip vessels of force to guard the coasts and protect the trade on the ocean, lakes, or great rivers; but they shall not impress men in any colony, without the consent of the legislature.

That for these purposes, they have power to make laws, and lay and levy such general duties, imposts, or taxes, as to them shall appear most equal and just (considering the ability and other circumstances of the inhabitants in the several colonies), and such as may be collected with the least inconvenience to the people; rather discouraging luxury, than loading industry with unnecessary burthens.

That they may appoint a General Treasurer and Particular Treasurer in each government, when necessary; and from time to time may order the sums in the treasury of each government into the general treasury; or draw on them for special payments, as they find most convenient.

Yet no money to issue, but by joint orders of the President-General and Grand Council; except where sums have been appropriated to particular purposes, and the President-General is previously empowered by an act to draw such sums.

That the general accounts shall be yearly settled and reported to the several Assemblies.

That a quorum of the Grand Council, empowered to act with the President-General, do consist of twenty-five members; among whom there shall be one or more from a majority of the colonies.

That the laws made by them for the purposes aforesaid shall not be repugnant, but, as near as may be, agreeable to the laws of England, and shall be transmitted to the King in Council for approbation, as soon as may be after their passing; and if not disapproved within three years after presentation, to remain in force.

That, in case of the death of the President-General, the Speaker of the Grand Council for the time being shall succeed, and be vested with the same powers and authorities, to continue till the King's pleasure be known.

That all military commission officers, whether for land or sea service, to act under this general constitution, shall be nominated by the President-General; but the approbation of the Grand Council is to be obtained, before they receive their commissions. And all civil officers are to be nominated by the Grand Council, and to receive the President-General's approbation before they officiate.

But, in case of vacancy by death or removal of any officer civil or military under this constitution, the Governor of the province in which such vacancy happens may appoint, till the pleasure of the President-General and Grand Council can be known.

That the particular military as well as civil establishments in each colony remain in their present state, the general constitution notwithstanding; and that on sudden emergencies any colony may defend itself, and lay the accounts thence arising before the President-General and Grand Council, who may allow and order payment of the same, as far as they judge such accounts just and reasonable.

Discussion

1. Economic policies often involve matters of power as well as concerns for liberty or equality. How do the documents regarding paper money reveal such issues? What does the selection on Georgia suggest about the relationship between economic concerns and power and liberty?

2. What does Cato's discourse on the nature of laws imply about the legitimate power of government? What role does virtue play in society? How might the essay have influenced American attitudes toward liberty?

3. In his sermon, Jonathan Edwards described the awesome power of God, yet the Great Awakening encouraged individualism and religious toleration. Is there anything in the document that suggests how the individual might have gained importance during the revival? Does Edwards appear to advocate toleration in his message?

4. How do the documents reveal the themes of expansionism and the Anglicization of American society during the eighteenth century? Do any of the documents show the emergence of distinctive American ideals; if so, how?

5. Although the Albany Plan failed to gain ratification, it served as a model for future efforts to create intercolonial cooperation. What elements of the plan address issues of power that existed in colonial America? How and to what degree is the plan a statement of American liberties?

6. What do the Tennent and Edwards sermons reveal about the attitudes and values involved in the Great Awakening?

CHAPTER 5

Reform, Resistance, Revolution

This famous engraving appeared the day after these "well-dressed gentlemen" were shot by British soldiers. Such propaganda fueled the anger over the Boston Massacre and promoted the popular belief that British soldiers were sent to deprive citizens of their liberties—and their lives.

Victory over the French in 1763 established Great Britain as the dominant power in eastern North America. Faced with defiant Indians, a huge empire, and burdensome debt, however, royal authorities determined to enact a series of comprehensive imperial reforms. To many Americans, those reforms seemed to pose as serious a threat to their liberties as had ever been presented by the French and Spanish. Ironically, then, at the height of British power in North America, the colonies would begin to resist Parliament's authority. During the next twelve years three successive crises led to a rebellion that neither the British nor the colonists had anticipated. Confrontation had hardened the resolve of both sides and fighting broke out in 1775. A year later the colonies declared their independence.

34. THE PROCLAMATION OF 1763*

King George III announced the following proclamation in an effort to organize and manage the new empire while also honoring English promises to protect Indian territory from white encroachment. The royal order established new colonial governments, and it tried to control settlement by limiting migration west of the Appalachian watershed. Many Americans deplored, and some ignored, the proclamation, because they believed that the recent war had been fought to open the west to English colonization. Prohibiting access to that land, they believed, denied them their traditional right to acquire property. Having defeated the French, they were now dismayed to realize that their own government threatened their liberty to expand.

By the King. A Proclamation. George R.

Whereas we have taken into our royal consideration the extensive and valuable acquisitions in America, secured to our crown by the late definitive treaty of peace concluded at Paris the 10th day of February last; and being desirous that all our loving subjects, as well of our kingdom as of our colonies in America, may avail themselves, with all convenient speed, of the great benefits and advantages which must accrue therefrom to their commerce, manufactures, and navigation; we have thought fit, with the advice of our privy council, to issue this our royal proclamation, hereby to publish and declare to all our loving subjects, that we have, with the advice of our said privy council, granted out letters patent under our great seal of Great Britain, to erect, within the countries and islands ceded and confirmed to us by said treaty, four distinct and separate governments, stiled and called by the names of Quebec, East Florida, West Florida, and Grenada, and limited and bounded as follows, viz.

First, the government of Quebec . . .
Secondly, The government of East Florida . . .
Thirdly, The government of West Florida . . .
Fourthly, The government of Grenada, comprehending the island of that name, together with the Grenadines, and the islands of Dominico, St. Vincent, and Tobago.

And to the end that the open and free fishery of our subjects may be extended to, and carried on upon the coast of Labrador and the adjacent islands, we have thought fit, with the advice of our

---

The Annual Register; or a View of the History, Politicks, and Literature for the Year 1763, 5th ed. (London: J. Dodsley, 1782), 208–13.

said privy council, to put all that coast, from the river St. John's to Hudson's Streights, together with the islands lying upon the said coast, under the care and inspection of our governor of New-foundland.

We have also, with the advice of our privy council, thought fit to annex the islands of St. John and Cape Breton, or Isle Royale, with the lesser islands adjacent thereto, to our government of Nova Scotia.

We have also, with the advice of our privy council aforesaid, annexed to our province of Georgia, all the lands lying between the rivers Attamaha and St. Mary's.

And whereas it will contribute greatly to the speedy settling our said new governments, that our loving subjects should be informed of our paternal care for the security of the liberty and properties of those who are, and shall become, inhabitants thereof; we have thought fit to publish and declare, by this our proclamation, that we have, in the letters patent under our great seal of Great Britain, by which the said governments are constituted, given express power and direction to our governors of our said colonies respectively, that so soon as the state and circumstances of the said colonies will admit thereof, they shall, with the advice and consent of the members of our council, summon and call general assemblies within the said governments respectively, in such manner and form as is used and directed in those colonies and provinces in America, which are under our immediate government; and we have also given power to the said governors, with the consent of our said councils, and the representatives of the people, so to be summoned as aforesaid, to make, constitute, and ordain laws, statutes, and ordinances for the public peace, welfare, and good government of our said colonies, and of the people and inhabitants thereof, as near as may be, agreeable to the laws of England, and under such regulations and restrictions as are used in other colonies; and in the mean time, and until such assemblies can be called as aforesaid, all the persons inhabiting in, or resorting to, our said colonies, may confide in our royal protection for the enjoyment of the benefit of the laws of our realm of England; for which purpose we have given power under our great seal to the governors of our said colonies respectively, to erect and constitute, with the advice of our said councils respectively, courts of judicature and public justice within our said colonies, for the hearing and determining all causes, as well criminal as civil according to law and equity, and, as near as may be, agreeable to the laws of England, with liberty to all persons who may think themselves aggrieved by the sentence of such courts, in all civil cases, to appeal, under the usual limitations and restrictions, to us, in our privy council.

We have also thought fit, with the advice of our privy council aforesaid, to give unto the governors and councils of our said three new colonies upon the continent, full power and authority to settle and agree with the inhabitants of our said new colonies, or to any other person who shall resort thereto, for such lands, tenements, and hereditaments, as are now, or hereafter shall be, in our power to dispose of, and them to grant to any such person or persons, upon such terms, and under such moderate quit rents, services, and acknowledgments as have been appointed and settled in other colonies, and under such other conditions as shall appear to us to be necessary and expedient for the advantage of the grantees, and the improvement and settlement of our said colonies.

And whereas we are desirous, upon all occasions, to testify our royal sense and approbation of the conduct and bravery of the officers and soldiers of our armies, and to reward the same, we do hereby command and impower our governors of our said three new colonies, and other our governors of our several provinces on the continent of North America, to grant, without fee or reward, to such reduced officers as have served in North America, during the late war, and are actually residing there, and shall personally apply for the same, the following quantities of land, subject, at the expiration of ten years, to the same quit-rents as other lands are subject to in the province within which they are granted, as also subject to the same conditions of cultivation and improvement, viz.

To every person having the rank of a field officer, 5000 acres.

To every captain, 3000 acres.

To every subaltern or staff officer, 2000 acres.

To every non-commission officer, 200 acres.

To every private man 50 acres. . . .

And whereas it is just and reasonable, and essential to our interest, and the security of our colonies, that the several nations or tribes of Indians, with whom we are connected, and who live under our protection, should not be molested or disturbed in the possession of such parts of our dominions and territories as, not having been ceded to, or purchased by us, are reserved to them or any of them, as their hunting grounds; we do therefore, with the advice of our privy council, declare it to be our royal will and pleasure, that no governor, or commander in chief, in any of our colonies of Quebec, East Florida, or West Florida, do presume, upon any pretence whatever, to grant warrants of survey, or pass any patents for lands beyond the bounds of their respective governments, as described in their commissions; as also that no governor or commander in chief of our other colonies or plantations in America, do presume for the present, and until our further pleasure be known, to grant warrant of survey, or pass patents for any lands beyond the heads or sources of any of the rivers which fall into the Atlantic Ocean from the west or north-west; or upon any lands whatever, which not having been ceded to, or purchased by us, as aforesaid, are reserved to the said Indians, or any of them.

And we do further declare it to be our royal will and pleasure, for the present, as aforesaid, to reserve under our sovereignty, protection, and dominion, for the use of the said Indians, all the land and territories not included within the limits of our said three new governments, or within the limits of the territory granted to the Hudson's Bay company; as also all the land and territories lying to the westward of the sources of the rivers which fall into the sea from the west and north-west as aforesaid; and we do hereby strictly forbid, on pain of our displeasure, all our loving subjects from making any purchases or settlements whatever, or taking possession of any of the lands above referred, without our special leave and licence for that purpose first attained.

And we do further strictly forbid and require all persons whatever, who have either wilfully or inadvertently seated themselves upon any lands within the countries above described, or upon any other lands within the countries, which not having been ceded to, or purchased by us, are still reserved to the said Indians as aforesaid, forth with to remove themselves from such settlements. . . .

And we do further expressly enjoin and require all officers whatever, as well military as those employed in the management and direction of Indian affairs, within the territories reserved, as aforesaid, for the use of the said Indians, to seize and apprehend all persons whatever, who standing charged with treasons, misprisions of treasons, murders, or other felonies or misdemeanours, shall fly from justice and take refuge in the said territory, and to send them under a proper guard to the colony where the crime was committed of which they shall stand accused, in order to take their trial for the same.

Given at the court of St. James's, the 7th day of October 1763, in the third year of our reign. GOD save the KING.

35. PONTIAC JUSTIFIES WAR AGAINST THE ENGLISH, 1763*

*T*he end of the French and Indian War in 1763 deeply affected the Native Americans in the Great Lakes region. They had benefited from a long-standing trading relationship with the French and had allied with them in the war. Prompted by the British refusal to continue the French custom of annual gifts and foreseeing their territory swarming with English settlers in the future, Ohio Valley Indians united under Ottawa Chief

*From "The Pontiac Manuscript" (1763) in *Historical Collections*, comp. Michigan Pioneer and Historical Society (Lansing: 1900–1913), VIII: 273–74.

Pontiac and attacked all the western British forts in Summer 1763. The Indian alliance eventually captured nine of eleven forts, terrorized the frontier from New York to Virginia, and killed hundreds of pioneer families. In the following excerpt, Pontiac justifies going to war against the English.

The day fixed having arrived, all the Ottawas, with Pondiak at their head, and the band of the Hurons, with Také [Yaka] at their head, all proceeded to the village of the Foxes [Potawatomies], where the council was intended to be held, taking care to send the women out of the village so as not to be interrupted in their deliberations. After all these precautions had been made, each Indian took his place in a circle, in accordance with his rank, and Pondiak at the head, as the great chief of all. He took the floor, and, as chief of the league, said:

"It is important for us, my brothers, that we exterminate from our land this nation which only seeks to kill us. You see, as well as I do, that we cannot longer get our supplies as we had them from our brothers, the French. The English sell us the merchandise twice dearer than the French sold them to us, and their wares [are worth] nothing. Hardly have we bought a blanket, or something else to cover us, than we must think of having another of the kind. When we want to start for our winter quarters they will give us no credit, as our brothers, the French, did. When I go to the English chief to tell him that some of our comrades are dead, instead of weeping for the dead, as our brothers, the French, used to do, he makes fun of me and of you. When I ask him for something for our sick, he refuses, and tells me that he has no need of us. You can well see by that that he seeks our ruin. Well, my brothers, we must all swear to destroy them! Nor will we wait any longer, nothing impedes us. There are very few of them, and we can easily overcome them. All the nations who are our brothers are ready to strike a blow at them; why should we not? Are we not men like them? Have I not shown you the warbelts which I have received from our great father, the Frenchman? He tells us to strike; why should we not listen to his words? Whom fear we? It is time. Are we afraid that our brothers, the French, who are here amongst us, would hinder us? They know not our designs, and could not if they wanted to. You know as well as I do, that when the English came to our country to drive out our father, Bellestre, they took away all the guns of the Frenchmen, and that they have no weapons to defend themselves. Thus it is. Let us strike all together! If there are any French who take up for them, we shall strike them as we do the English. Remember what the Master of Life has said to our brother, the Wolf. That concerns us all as well as them. I have sent warbelts and word to our brothers, the Sauteux, of the Saginaw, and to our brothers, the Ottawas, of Michelimakinak, and to those of the river's mouth to join them with us, and they will not tarry to come. While waiting for them, let us commence the attack. There is no more time to lose, and when the English shall be defeated, we shall see what to do, and we shall cut off the passage so that they cannot come back to our country."

This address, which Pondiak delivered with a voice full of energy, made upon the whole assembly the full effect which he had desired, and all swore, as in one voice, the complete extermination of the English nation. . . .

36. A BRITISH OFFICIAL JUSTIFIES IMPERIAL REFORM, 1765*

In 1765, as colonial objections to the Sugar and Stamp Acts reaching London mounted, Soame Jenyns, a member of the Board of Trade and a minor poet, outlined the major arguments in defense of George Grenville's program of imperial reform. He firmly asserted the right of Britain to impose taxes on the colonies.

*From Soame Jenyns, *The Objections to the Taxation of our American Colonies, by the Legislature of Great Britain, Briefly Considered* (London: for J. Wilkie, 1765) in *The Works of Soame Jenyns*, 4 vols., ed. Charles Nalson Cole (London: T. Cadell, 1790), II:189–96.

The right of the Legislature of Great Britain to impose taxes on her American colonies, and the expediency of exerting that right in the present conjuncture, are propositions so indisputably clear that I should never have thought it necessary to have undertaken their defence, had not many arguments been lately flung out both in papers and conversation, which with insolence equal to their absurdity deny them both. As these are usually mixt up with several patriotic and favorite words such as liberty, property, Englishmen, etc., which are apt to make strong impressions on that more numerous part of mankind who have ears but no understanding, it will not, I think, be improper to give them some answers. To this, therefore, I shall singly confine myself, and do it in as few words as possible, being sensible that the fewest will give least trouble to myself, and probably most information to my reader.

The great capital argument which I find on this subject, and which, like an elephant at the head of a Nabob's army, being once overthrown must put the whole into confusion, is this; that no Englishman is, or can be taxed, but by his own consent: by which must be meant one of these three propositions; either that no Englishman can be taxed without his own consent as an individual; or that no Englishman can be taxed without the consent of the persons he chuses to represent him; or that no Englishman can be taxed without the consent of the majority of all those who are elected by himself and others of his fellow subjects to represent them. Now let us impartially consider whether any one of these propositions are in fact true: if not, then this wonderful structure which has been erected upon them falls at once to the ground, and like another Babel, perishes by a confusion of words, which the builders themselves are unable to understand.

First then, that no Englishman is or can be taxed but by his own consent as an individual: this is so far from being true, that it is the very reverse of truth; for no man that I know of is taxed by his own consent, and an Englishman, I believe, is as little likely to be so taxed as any man in the world.

Secondly, that no Englishman is or can be taxed but by the consent of those persons whom he has chose to represent him. For the truth of this I shall appeal only to the candid representatives of those unfortunate counties which produce cyder, and shall willingly acquiesce under their determination.

Lastly, that no Englishman is or can be taxed without the consent of the majority of those who are elected by himself and others of his fellow subjects to represent them. This is certainly as false as the other two; for every Englishman is taxed, and not one in twenty represented: copyholders, leaseholders, and all men possessed of personal property only, chuse no representatives; Manchester, Birmingham, and many more of our richest and most flourishing trading towns send no members to Parliament, consequently cannot consent by their representatives, because they chuse none to represent them; yet are they not Englishmen? or are they not taxed?

I am well aware that I shall hear Lock, Sidney, Selden, and many other great names quoted to prove that every Englishman, whether he has a right to vote for a representative or not, is still represented in the British Parliament, in which opinion they all agree. On what principle of common-sense this opinion is founded I comprehend not, but on the authority of such respectable names I shall acknowledge its truth; but then I will ask one question, and on that I will rest the whole merits of the cause. Why does not this imaginary representation extend to America as well as over the whole Island of Great Britain? If it can travel three hundred miles, why not three thousand? if it can jump over rivers and mountains, why cannot it sail over the ocean? If the towns of Manchester and Birmingham, sending no representatives to Parliament, are notwithstanding there represented, why are not the cities of Albany and Boston equally represented in that Assembly? Are they not alike British subjects? are they not Englishmen? or are they only Englishmen when they sollicit for protection, but not Englishmen when taxes are required to enable this country to protect them?

But it is urged that the colonies are by their charters placed under distinct Governments each of which has a legislative power within itself, by which alone it ought to be taxed; that if this privilege is once given up, that liberty which every Englishman has a right to, is torn from them, they are all slaves, and all is lost.

The liberty of an Englishman is a phrase of so various a signification, having within these few years been used as a synonymous term for blasphemy, bawdy, treason, libels, strong beer, and cyder, that I shall not here presume to define its meaning; but I shall venture to assert what it cannot mean; that is, an exemption from taxes imposed by the authority of the Parliament of Great Britain; nor is there any charter that ever pretended to grant such a privilege to any colony in America; and had they granted it, it could have had no force; their charters being derived from the Crown, and no charter from the Crown can possibly supersede the right of the whole legislature. Their charters are undoubtedly no more than those of all corporations, which impower them to make bye-laws, and raise duties for the purposes of their own police, for ever subject to the superior authority of Parliament; and in some of their charters the manner of exercising these powers is specifyed in these express words, 'according to the course of other corporations in Great Britain'. And therefore they can have no more pretence to plead an exemption from this parliamentary authority, than any other corporation in England.

It has been moreover alledged, that though Parliament may have power to impose taxes on the colonies, they have no right to use it, because it would be an unjust tax; and no supreme or legislative power can have a right to enact any law in its nature unjust. To this, I shall only make this short reply, that if Parliament can impose no taxes but what are equitable, and if the persons taxes are to be the judges of that equity, they will in effect have no power to lay any tax at all. No tax can be imposed exactly equal on all, and if it is not equal it cannot be just, and if it is not just, no power whatever can impose it; by which short syllogism all taxation is at end; but why it should not be used by Englishmen on this side the Atlantic as well as by those on the other, I do not comprehend. . . .

37. DANIEL DULANY ATTACKS VIRTUAL REPRESENTATION, 1765*

Daniel Dulany—a prominent Maryland lawyer, officeholder, and, by 1775, a moderate loyalist—sought to repudiate the British assertion that virtual representation justified the imposition of the Stamp Act. His efforts proved largely successful. After the publication of Dulany's much-admired pamphlet, few individuals in the British colonies tried to defend British policy in such terms.

. . . A reflection naturally arises from the instances cited. When on a particular occasion *some* individuals *only* were to be taxed, and not the *whole* community, *their* consent *only* was called for, and in the last instance it appears that they who upon an occasion of a general tax would have been bound by the consent of their *virtual representatives* (for in that case they would have had no *actual representation*) were in an affair calling for a *particular* aid from them *separate* from the rest of the community required to send their *particular deputies*. But how different would be the principle of a statute imposing duties without *their* consent who are to pay them, upon the authority of *their* gift who should undertake to give what doth not belong to them. . . .

The situation of the nonelectors in England—their capacity to become electors, their inseparable connection with those who are electors and their representatives, their security against oppression resulting from this connection, and the necessity of imagining a double or virtual representation to avoid iniquity and absurdity—have been explained. The inhabitants of the colonies are *as such* incapable of being electors, the privilege of election being exercisable only in person, and therefore if *every* inhabitant of America had the requisite freehold, not *one* could vote but upon the

*From Daniel Dulany, *Considerations on the Propriety of Imposing Taxes in the British Colonies, for the Purpose of Raising a Revenue, by Act of Parliament* (Annapolis, 1765), 9–11.

supposition of his ceasing to be an inhabitant of America and becoming a resident of Great Britain, a supposition which would be impertinent because it shifts the question. Should the colonies not be taxed by *Parliamentary impositions*, their respective legislatures have a regular, adequate, and constitutional authority to tax them, and therefore would not necessarily be an iniquitous and absurd exemption from their not being represented by the *House of Commons*.

There is not that intimate and inseparable relation between the *electors* of Great Britain and the *inhabitants of the colonies* which must inevitably involve both in the same taxation; on the contrary, not a single *actual* elector in England might be immediately affected by a taxation in America imposed by a statute which would have a general operation and effect upon the properties of the inhabitants of the colonies. The latter might be oppressed in a thousand shapes without any sympathy or exciting any alarm in the former. Moreover, even acts oppressive and injurious to the colonies in an extreme degree might become popular in England from the promise or expectation that the very measures which depressed the colonies would give ease to the inhabitants of Great Britain. It is indeed true that the interests of England and the colonies are allied, and an injury to the colonies produced into all its consequences will eventually affect the mother country; yet these consequences being generally remote are not at once foreseen. They do not immediately alarm the fears and engage the passions of the English electors, the connection between a freeholder of Great Britain and a British American being deductible only through a train of reasoning which few will take the trouble or can have the opportunity, if they have the capacity, to investigate. Wherefore the relation between the *British Americans* and the *English electors* is a knot too infirm to be relied on as a competent security, especially against the force of a present counteracting expectation of relief.

If it would have been a just conclusion that the *colonies*, being exactly in the *same* situation with the *nonelectors* of England, are *therefore* represented in the same manner, it ought to be allowed that the reasoning is solid which, after having evinced a total *dissimilarity* of situation, infers that their representation is *different*. . . .

38. THE STAMP ACT CRISIS, 1765*

The Stamp Act of 1765 brought an unprecedented unity to the American colonies. Convinced that the tax, along with the Sugar Act, was an unconstitutional assertion of power, the Pennsylvania assembly passed the following resolutions. The document reaffirmed Americans' liberties as Englishmen, including a right to actual representation in matters of taxation. The congress also called for a boycott of British goods, while mobs violently protested the tax by rioting in several cities. In the face of such resistance, Parliament repealed the act. Patriots, jubilant over their apparent success, refused to recognize the implications of the Declaratory Act, which Parliament had approved when they withdrew the stamp tax. Thus, the Americans learned a singular lesson: when government threatened their rights, concerted and violent action could preserve liberty.

The house taking into consideration, that an act of parliament lately passed in England, for imposing certain stamp duties, and other duties, on his Majesty's subjects in America, whereby they conceive some of their most essential and valuable rights as British subjects to be deeply affected, think it is a duty they owe to themselves and their posterity, to come to the following resolution, viz.

Resolved. . . . That the assemblies of this province have from time to time, whenever requisitions have been made by his Majesty for carrying on military operations for the defence of America, most cheerfully and liberally contributed their full proportion of men and money for those services.

Resolved. . . . That whenever his Majesty's services shall, for the future, require the aids of the

*The Parliamentary History of England, From the Earliest Period to the Year 1803, 36 vols. (London: T. C. Hansard, 1806–1830), XV:131–33.

inhabitants of this province, and they shall be called upon for that purpose in a constitutional way, it will be their indespensible duty most cheerfully and liberally to grant to his Majesty their proportion of men and money, for the defence, security and other public services of the British American colonies.

Resolved. . . . That the inhabitants of this province are entitled to all liberties, rights, and privileges, of his Majesty's subjects in Great Britain or elsewhere; and that the constitution of government in this province is founded on the natural rights of mankind, and the noble principles of English liberty, and therefore is, or ought to be, perfectly free.

Resolved. . . . That it is the interest, birthright, and indubitable privilege of every British subject, to be taxed only by his consent, or that of his legal representatives, in conjunction with his Majesty, or his substitutes.

Resolved. . . . That the only legal representatives of the inhabitants of this province are the persons they annually elect, to serve as members of assembly.

Resolved therefore. . . . That the laying taxes upon the inhabitants of this province in any other manner, being manifestly subversive of public liberty, must, of necessary consequence, be utterly destructive of public happiness.

Resolved. . . . That the resting an authority in the courts of admiralty to decide in suits relating to the stamp duties, and other matters foreign to their proper jurisdiction, is highly dangerous to the liberties of his Majesty's American subjects, contrary to Magna Charta, the great charter and fountain of English liberty, and destructive of one of their most darling and acknowledged rights, that of trial by juries.

Resolved. . . . That it is the opinion of this house, that the restraints, imposed by several late acts of parliament, on the trade of this province, at a time when the people labour under an enormous debt, must, of necessity, be attended with the most fatal consequences; not only to this province, but to the trade of our mother country.

Resolved. . . . That this house think it their duty thus firmly to assert, with modesty and decency, their inherent rights, that their posterity may learn and know that it was not with their consent and acquiescence, that any taxes should be levied on them by any person, but their own representatives; and are desirous, that these their resolves should remain on their minutes, as a testimony of the zeal and ardent desire of the present house of assembly, to preserve their inestimable rights, which, as Englishmen, they have possessed ever since this province was settled, and to transmit them to their latest posterity.

39. A PENNSYLVANIA FARMER, 1768*

John Dickinson, a Philadelphia lawyer who wrote a series of letters in response to the Townshend duties, struck a moderate stance in the following document. Citing the dangers of rebellion, he cautioned against those Americans advocating separation from England. The "Pennsylvania farmer" concluded, however, that, if necessary, the colonists must be prepared to take vigorous measures to protect their liberties from the misuse of royal power.

I hope, my dear countrymen, that you will in every colony be upon your guard against those who may at any time endeavour to stir you up, under pretensions of patriotism, to any measures disrespectful to our sovereign and our mother country. Hot, rash, disorderly proceedings, injure the reputation of a people as to wisdom, valour and virtue, without procuring them the least benefit. I pray God, that he may be pleased to inspire you and your posterity to the latest ages with that

*From *American History Told by Contemporaries*, 5 vols., ed. Albert Bushnell Hart (New York: The Macmillan Company, 1914), II:423–26.

spirit, of which I have an idea, but find a difficulty to express; to express in the best manner I can, I mean a spirit that shall so guide you, that it will be impossible to determine, whether an *American's* character is most distinguishable for his loyalty to his sovereign, his duty to his mother country, his love of freedom, or his affection for his native soil.

Every government, at some time or another, falls into wrong measures; these may proceed from mistake or passion.—But every such measure does not dissolve the obligation between the governors and the governed; the mistake may be corrected; the passion may pass over.

It is the duty of the governed, to endeavour to rectify the mistake, and appease the passion. They have not at first any other right, than to represent their grievances, and to pray for redress, unless an emergenc[y] is so pressing, as not to allow time for receiving an answer to their applications which rarely happens. If their applications are disregarded, then that kind of opposition becomes justifiable, which can be made without breaking the laws, or disturbing the public peace. This consists in the prevention of the oppressors reaping advantage from their oppressions, and not in their punishment. For experience may teach them what reason did not; and harsh methods, cannot be proper, till milder ones have failed.

If at length it become undoubted, that an inveterate revolution is formed to annihilate the liberties of the governed, the English history affords frequent examples of resistance by force. What particular circumstance will in any future case justify such resistance, can never be ascertained until they happen. Perhaps it may be allowable to say, generally, that it can never be justifiable, until the people are FULLY CONVINCED, that any further submission will be destructive to their happiness.

When the appeal is made to the sword, highly probable it is, that the punishment will exceed the offence; and the calamities attending on war out weigh those preceding it. These considerations of justice and prudence, will always have great influence with good and wise men.

To these reflections on this subject, it remains to be added, and ought for ever to be remembered; that resistance in the case of colonies against their mother country, is extremely different from the resistance of a people against their prince. A nation may change their King or race of Kings, and retain[ing] their antient form of government, be gainers by changing. Thus Great-Britain, under the illustrious house of Brunswick, a house that seems to flourish for the happiness of mankind, has found a felicity, unknown in the reigns of the Stuarts. But if once we are separated from our mother country, what new form of government shall we accept, or when shall we find another Britain to supply our loss? Torn from the body to which we are united by religion, liberty, laws, affections, relations, language, and commerce, we must bleed at every vein.

In truth, the prosperity of these provinces is founded in their dependence on Great-Britain; and when she returns to "her old good humour, and old good nature," as Lord Clarendon expresses it, I hope they will always esteem their duty and interest, as it most certainly will be, to promote her welfare by all the means in their power.

We cannot act with too much caution in our disputes. Anger produces anger; and differences that might be accommodated by kind and respectful behaviour, may by imprudence be changed to an incurable rage.

In quarrels between countries, as well as those between individuals, when they have risen to a certain heighth, the first cause of dissention is no longer remembered, the minds of the parties being wholly engaged in recollecting and resenting the mutual expressions of their dislike. When feuds have reached that fatal point, all considerations of reason and equity vanish; and a blind fury governs, or rather confounds all things. A people no longer regards their interest, but the gratification of their wrath. The sway of the Cleon's, and Clodius's, the designing and detestable flatter[er]s of the prevailing passion, becomes confirmed.

Wise and good men in vain oppose the storm, and may think themselves fortunate, if, endeavouring to preserve their ungrateful fellow citizens, they do not ruin themselves. Their prudence will be called baseness; their moderation, guilt; and if their virtue does not lead them to destruction, as that of many other great and excellent persons has done, they may survive, to receive from their expiring country, the mournful glory of her acknowledgment, that their councils, if regarded, would have saved her.

The constitutional modes of obtaining relief, are those which I would wish to see pursued on the present occasion, that is, by petitioning of our assemblies, or, where they are not permitted to meet, of the people to the powers that can afford us relief.

We have an excellent prince, in whose good dispositions towards us we may confide. We have a generous, sensible, and humane nation, to whom we may apply. They may be deceived: they may, by artful men, be provoked to anger against us; but I cannot yet believe they will be cruel or unjust; or that their anger will be implacable. Let us behave like dutiful children, who have received unmerited blows from a beloved parent. Let us complain to our parents; but let our complaints speak at the same time, the language of affliction and veneration.

If, however, it shall happen by an unfortunate course of affairs, that our applications to his Majesty and the parliament for the redress, prove ineffectual, let us then take another step, by witholding from Great-Britain, all the advantages she has been used to receive from us. Then let us try, if our ingenuity, industry, and frugality, will not give weight to our remonstrances. Let us all be united with one spirit in one cause. Let us invent; let us work; let us save; let us at the same time, keep up our claims, and unceasingly repeat our complaints; but above all, let us implore the protection of that infinite good and gracious Being, "by whom kings reign and princes decree justice."

"Nil desperandum."

Nothing is to be despaired of.

40. "MASCULINE" RUM VERSUS "FEMININE" TEA*

After 1773, the British empire in North America disintegrated over the issue of taxing tea, a beverage consumed mostly by women. No comparable crisis ever arose over the taxation of molasses, which produced far more revenue than tea. About half of the molasses imported into the colonies was distilled into rum, a beverage consumed mostly by men. As this 1753 letter by Prudence Goodwife (obviously a pseudonym) indicates, contemporaries fully understood this distinction. Men also realized that a nonimportation movement targeted at molasses would have proven futile because almost all the molasses consumed in the British colonies was produced on French sugar islands, where the sufferings of the planters from any boycott would hardly prompt the British Parliament to repeal any legislation. Still, at times, women must have resented a strategy of resistance that demanded greater sacrifices from them, even though they were excluded from politics, than from the men who actually made the political decisions.

MR. PARKER,

As I understand you are a Native of *New-Jersey*, I doubt not therefore you are a Lover of your Country; and as such a One I now address you, and pray you to give this a Place in your Paper, which will not only oblige me but all the Good-Wives that have the Misfortune to have bad Husbands in this Province.

You must understand, Sir, that I have for some Years past borne, with uncommon Patience, the Lashes of an ill-natur'd Husband, who constantly made it a Practice, to stay at a Slop-Shop till he had drowned his Senses in Rum, his Darling Delight, and then poor I must stand clear; for the merciless Wretch wou'd spare neither my Tea Cups or Saucers to throw at my Head, besides whipping of me; but I must do him the Justice to acknowledge, that he always had Compassion on the

*From *The New York Gazette or the Weekly Post Boy*, December 31, 1753, reprinted in *Documents Relating to the Colonial History of the State of New Jersey*, ed. William Nelson (Paterson, New Jersey: The Press Printing and Publishing Co., 1897), vol. XIX, III:324–27.

Rum Glasses, which stood close by them; and tho' we have had but two of those Glasses for these Eight or Ten Years, yet they have liv'd to see as many Dozen of Tea Cups and Saucers broke over my Head; for he says if I can't drink my Tea out of those Glasses, I shall go without; which I had rather do; for I shou'd imagine I was drinking Rum instead of Tea, and I think he need not be so hard upon me, for they never cost him a Penny; but his destroying of 'em has brought me so low, that I have no more Apparel than I at present have on, and I will have Tea Cups and Saucers if I pawn my very Shift; for I must own I love Tea as well as he loves Rum.

Besides, Sir, I have two little Children, a Girl and a Boy, who while their Father was whip-ping of me, were frightened to such a Degree (for fear of losing their dear Mother) as wou'd make them fall into Fits in each others little Arms, while I could not afford them the least Assistance, and they might then have died before he would have given them any: Was not this hard, Sir; Ah! cruel hard, not only to use me so inhumanly, but to be so void of Bowels to those little Ones, that derived their Existence from him! and he would tell me, when I dar'd to complain, that Man had the government given him over the Woman; but I don't imagine his Authority was so extensive as to impower him, to beat her Brains out without Rhime or reason; and as often as I read my Bible (my greatest Delight) I never yet found that Adam ever whipped his Wife; tho' I must confess she justly dèserved it.

My Case being happily nois'd abroad, induced several generous young Men to discipline him. These young Persons do stile, or are stiled, REGULATORS; and so they are with Propriety; for they have regulated my dear Husband, and the rest of the bad Ones hereabouts, that they are afraid of using such Barbarity; and I must with Pleasure acknowledge, that since my Husband has felt what whipping was, he has entirely left off whipping me, and promises faithfully he will never begin again; which I have reason to believe; for there never was a better Harmony subsisting between Man and Wife, than there is at present betwixt us, and we are as happy as we were in our Courting Days; and He does with Pleasure own (as well as my self) that he is under infinite Obli-gations to those Persons before hinted of, and is so generous as to say, that if they had not done what they did, he might unhappily in his Anger whipp'd me into Eternity.

I doubt not all the World will agree with me, (especially those of my Sex, and those that have any Regard for 'em,) that it is a most Brutal Action for a Man, who Nature has endow'd with supe-rior Strength to a Woman, to exercise such Severity over her: While I say brutal, I do Injustice to the Brute Creation; for they shew more Compassion and Tenderness than such Monsters do.

Tho' there are some that are afraid of whipping their Wives, for fear of dancing the same Jigg; yet I understand, they are not afraid of making Application, in order to have those dear REGULA-TORS indicted; and if they should, it might discourage them for the future, to appear to the Assis-tance of the Innocent and Helpless; and then poor Wives who have the unhappiness to be lockt in Wedlock with bad Husbands, take Care of your tender Hides; for you may depend upon being bang'd without Mercy.

I am, Sir, your most Humble Servant,
Prudence Goodwife.

New-Jersey, December 7, 1753.

41. DECLARATION OF RIGHTS AND GRIEVANCES, 1774*

*M*ost colonists in 1774 could not imagine independence from Britain, and delegates to the First Continental Con-gress devoted much of their efforts to defining their rights—now as Americans rather than simply as English-

*American Archives: Fourth Series. Containing a Documentary History of the English Colonies in North America, from the King's Message to Parliament, of March 7, 1774, to the Declaration of Independence by the United States, 9 vols., comp. Peter Force (Washington, D.C.: M. St. Claire and Peter Force, 1837–1853), I:910–12.

men. Events of the previous ten years had shown that substantive differences existed between Great Britain and the colonies, and Congress struggled to find the best means of expressing the grievances that they believed endangered their liberties. The following document, addressed to King George III because representatives no longer recognized parliamentary authority as legitimate in the colonies, revealed the complexity of the concerns that Americans had and the bitterness of their feelings toward England.

Whereas, since the close of the last war, the *British* Parliament, claiming a power of right to bind the people of *America*, by statute, in all cases whatsoever, both, in some Acts, expressly imposed taxes on them, and in others, under various pretences, but in fact for the purpose of raising a revenue, hath imposed rates and duties payable in these Colonies, established a Board of Commissioners, with unconstitutional powers, and extended the jurisdiction of Courts of Admiralty, not only for collecting the said duties, but for the trial of causes merely arising within the body of a County:

And whereas, in consequence of other Statutes, Judges, who before held only estates at will in their offices, have been made dependent on the Crown alone for their salaries, and Standing Armies kept in times of Peace: And it has lately been resolved in Parliament, that by force of a Statute, made in the thirty-fifth year of the reign of King *Henry*, the Eighth, Colonists may be transported to England, and tried there upon accusations of treason, and misprisions, or concealments of treason committed in the Colonies, and by a late Statute, such trials have been directed in cases therein mentioned:

And whereas, in the last session of Parliament, three Statutes were made, one entitled, "An Act to discontinue, in such manner, and for such time, as are therein mentioned, the landing and discharging, lading or shipping of Goods, Wares, and Merchandise, at the Town, and within the Harbour of *Boston*, in the Province of *Massachusetts Bay*, in *North America;*" another, entitled, "An Act for the better regulating the Government of the Province of *Massachusetts Bay*, in *New England;*" and another, entitled "An Act for the impartial administration of Justice in the cases of persons questioned for any act done by them in the execution of the law, or for the suppression of riots and tumults in the Province of *Massachusetts Bay*, in *New England;*" and another Statute was then made "for making more effectual provision of the Government of the Province of *Quebec*," &c. All which statutes are impolitick, unjust, and cruel, as well as unconstitutional, and most dangerous and destructive of *American* rights:

And whereas, Assemblies have been frequently dissolved, contrary to the rights of the people, when they attempted to deliberate on grievances; and their dutiful, humble, loyal, and reasonable Petitions to the Crown for redress, have been repeatedly treated with contempt by his Majesty's Ministers of State:

The good people of the several Colonies of *New-Hampshire, Massachusetts Bay, Rhode-Island and Providence Plantations, Connecticut, New-York, New-Jersey, Pennsylvania, New-Castle, Kent,* and *Suzzex,* on *Delaware, Maryland, Virginia, North Carolina,* and *South Carolina,* justly alarmed at these arbitrary proceedings of Parliament and Administration, have severally elected, constituted, and appointed Deputies to meet and sit in General Congress, in the City of *Philadelphia*, in order to obtain and establish as that their religion, laws, and liberties may not be subverted; Whereupon the Deputies so appointed being now assembled, in a full and free representation of these Colonies, taking into their most serious consideration the best means of attaining the ends aforesaid, do, in the first place, as *Englishmen*, their ancestors in like cases have usually done, for asserting and vindicating their rights and liberties, *declare,*

That the inhabitants of the *English* Colonies in *North America*, by the immutable laws of nature, the principles of the *English* Constitution, and the several Charters or Compacts, have the following *Rights:*

Resolved, . . . 1. That they are entitled to life, liberty, and property, and they have never ceded to any sovereign power whatever a right to dispose of either without their consent.

Resolved, . . . 2. That our ancestors, who first settled these Colonies, were at the time of their emigration from the mother country, entitled to all the rights, liberties, and immunities of free and natural born subjects, within the Realm of England.

Resolved, . . . 3. That by such emigration they by no means forfeited, surrendered, or lost any of those rights, but that they were, and their descendants now are, entitled to the exercise and enjoyment of all such of them, as their local and other circumstances enable them to exercise and enjoy.

Resolved, 4. That the foundations of *English* Liberty, and of all free Government, is a right in the people to participate in their Legislative Council: and as the *English* Colonists are not represented, and from their local and other circumstances cannot be properly represented in the *British* Parliament, they are entitled to a free and exclusive power of legislation in their several Provincial Legislatures, where their right of Representation can alone be preserved, in all cases of taxation and internal polity, subject only to the negative of their Sovereign, in such manner as has been heretofore used and accustomed. But, from the necessity of the case, and a regard to the mutual interest of both Countries, we cheerfully consent to the operation of such Acts of the *British* Parliament, as are, *bona fide*, restrained to the regulation of our external commerce, for the purpose of securing the commercial advantages of the whole Empire to the mother country, and the commercial benefits of its respective members; excluding every idea of Taxation, internal or external, for raising a revenue on the subjects in *America*, without their consent.

Resolved, . . . 5. That the respective Colonies are entitled to the common law of *England*, and more especially to the great and inestimate privilege of being tried by their peers of the vicinage, according to the course of that law.

Resolved, 6. That they are entitled to the benefit of such of the English statutes as existed at the time of their Colonization; and which they have, by experience, respectively found to be applicable to their several local and other circumstances.

Resolved, . . . 7. That these, his Majesty's Colonies, are likewise entitled to all the immunities and privileges granted and confirmed to them by Royal Charters, or secured by their several codes of Provincial Laws.

Resolved, . . . 8. That they have a right peacefully to assemble, consider of their grievances, and Petition the King; and that all prosecutions, prohibitory Proclamations, and commitments of the same, are illegal.

Resolved, . . . 9. That the keeping a Standing Army in these Colonies, in times of peace, without the consent of the Legislatures of that Colony, in which such Army is kept, is against law.

Resolved, . . . 10. It is indespensably necessary to good Government, and rendered essential by the English Constitution, that the constituent branches of the Legislature be independent of each other; that; therefore, the exercise of Legislative power in several Colonies, by a Council appointed, during pleasure, by the Crown, is unconstitutional, dangerous, and destructive to the freedom of *American* legislation.

All and each of which aforesaid Deputies, in behalf of themselves and their constituents, do claim, demand, and insist on, as their indubitable rights and liberties; which cannot be legally taken from them, altered or abridged by any power whatever, without their own consent, by their Representatives in the several Provincial Legislatures.

In the course of our injury we find many infringements and violations of the foregoing Rights, which from an ardent desire, the harmony and mutual intercourse of affection and interest may be restored, we pass over for the present, and proceed to state such Acts and measures as have been adopted since the last war, which demonstrate a system formed to enslave *America*.

Resolved, . . . That the following Acts of Parliament are infringements and violations of the rights of the Colonists; and that the repeal of them is essentially necessary in order to restore harmony between *Great Britain* and the *American Colonies*, viz: . . .

[the list of objectionable statutes includes the Sugar Act, the Declaratory Act, the Revenue Act of 1766, the Townshend Revenue Act, the Tea Act, the Coercive Acts, the Quebec Act, and several others]

To these grevious Acts and measures Americans cannot submit, but in hopes that their fellow-subjects in *Great Britain* will, on a revision of them, restore us to that state in which both countries found happiness and prosperity, we have for the present only resolved to pursue the following peaceable measures: 1. To enter into a Non-Importation, Non-Consumption, and Non-Exportation Agreement or Association. 2. To prepare an Address to the People of **Great** *Britain*, and a Memorial to the Inhabitants of *British America*; and 3. To prepare a loyal Address to his Majesty, agreeable to Resolutions already entered into.

42. THE "OLIVE BRANCH PETITION," 1775*

*T*he following petition to King George III showed how moderate the Continental Congress remained, even after fighting had begun. This document summarized the Patriot interpretation of the events that had occurred following 1763, but it did not blame the king for the difficulties in the colonies. Instead, it called on him to find a peaceful resolution to the crisis that could ensure a lasting reconciliation between the colonies and the crown. George III refused to receive the petition; he declared the colonies in rebellion on August 23, 1775. Conflicts between British power and American liberties had become a full-scale war.

MOST GRACIOUS SOVEREIGN: We, your Majesty's faithful subjects, . . . in behalf of our-selves and the inhabitants of these Colonies, who have deputed us to represent them in General Congress, entreat your Majesty's gracious attention to this our humble petition.

The union between our Mother Country and these Colonies, and the energy of mild and just Government, produced benefits so remarkably important, and afforded such an assurance of their permanency and increase, that the wonder and envy of other nations were excited, while they beheld *Great Britain* rising to a power the most extraordinary the world had ever known.

Her rivals, observing that there was no probability of this happy connexion being broken by civil dissensions, and apprehending its future effects if left any longer undisturbed, resolved to prevent her receiving such continual and formidable accessions of wealth and strength, by checking the growth of those settlements from which they were to be deprived.

In the prosecution of this attempt, events so unfavorable to the design took place, that every friend to the interest of *Great Britain* and these Colonies, entertained pleasing and reasonable expectations of seeing an additional force and exertion immediately given to the operations of the union hitherto experienced, by an enlargement of the dominion of the Crown, and the removal of ancient and warlike enemies to greater distance.

At the conclusion, therefore, of the late war, the most glorious and advantageous that ever had been carried on by *British* arms, your loyal Colonists having contributed to its success by such repeated and strenuous exertions as frequently procured them the distinguished approbation of your Majesty, of the late King, and of Parliament, doubted not but that they should be permitted, with the rest of the Empire, to share in the blessings of peace, and the emoluments of victory and conquest.

While these recent and honourable acknowledgments of their merits remained on record on the Journals and acts of that august Legislature, the Parliament, undefaced by the imputation or even suspicion of any offence, they were alarmed by a new system of statutes and regulations

*American Archives: Fourth Series. Containing a Documentary History of the English Colonies in North America, from the King's Message to Parliament, of March 7, 1774, to the Declaration of Independence by the United States, 9 vols., comp. Peter Force (Washington, D.C.: M. St. Claire and Peter Force, 1837–1853), I:1870–72.

adopted for the administration of the Colonies, that filled their minds with the most painful fears and jealousies; and, to their inexpressible astonishment, perceived the danger of a foreign quarrel quickly succeeded by domestick danger, in their judgment of a more dreadful kind.

Nor were these anxieties alleviated by any tendency in this system to promote the welfare of their Mother country. For though its effects were more immediately felt by them, yet its influence appeared to be injurious to the commerce and prosperity of *Great Britain*.

We shall decline the ungrateful task of describing the irksome variety of artifices practised by many of your Majesty's Ministers, the delusive pretences, fruitless terrours, and unavailing severities, that have from time to time, been dealt out by them, in their attempts to execute this impolitick plan, or of tracing through a series of years past the progress of the unhappy differences between *Great Britain* and these Colonies, that have flowed from this fatal source.

Your Majesty's Ministers, persevering in their measures, and proceeding to open hostilities for enforcing them, have compelled us to arm in our own defence, and have engaged us in a controversy so peculiarly abhorrent to the affections of your still faithful Colonists, that when we consider whom we must oppose in this contest, and if it continues, what may be the consequences, our own particular misfortunes are accounted by us only as parts of our distress.

Knowing to what violent resentments and incurable animosities civil discords are apt to exasperate and inflame the contending parties, we think ourselves required by indispensable obligations to *Almighty God*, to your Majesty, to our fellow-subjects, and to ourselves, immediately to use all the means in our power, not incompatible with our safety, for stopping the further effusion of blood, and for averting the impending calamities that threaten the *British* Empire.

Thus called upon to address your Majesty on Affairs of such moment to *America*, and probably to all your Dominions, we are earnestly desirous of performing this office with the utmost deference to your Majesty; and we therefore pray, that your Majesty's royal magnanimity and benevolence may make the most favorable constructions of our expressions on so uncommon an occasion. Could we represent in their full force the sentiments that agitate the minds of us your dutiful subjects, we are persuaded your Majesty would ascribe any seeming deviation from reverence in our language, and even in our conduct, not to any reprehensible intention, but to the impossibility of reconciling the unusual appearances of respect with a just attention to our own preservation against those artful and cruel enemies who abuse your royal confidence and authority, for the purpose of effecting our destruction.

Attached to your Majesty's person, family, and Government, with all devotion that principle and affection can inspire; connected with *Great Britain* by the strongest ties that can unite societies, and deploring every event that tends in any degree to weaken them, we solemnly assure your Majesty, that we not only most ardently desire the former harmony between her and these Colonies may be restored, but that a concord may be established between them upon so firm a basis as to perpetuate its blessings, uninterrupted by any future dissensions, to succeeding generations in both countries, and to transmit your Majesty's name to posterity, adorned with that signal and lasting glory that has attended the memory of those illustrious personages, whose virtues and abilities have extricated states from dangerous convulsions, and, by securing happiness to others, have erected the most noble and durable monuments to their own fame.

We beg leave further to assure your Majesty, that notwithstanding the sufferings of your loyal Colonists during the course of this present controversy, our breasts retain too tender a regard for the kingdom from which we derive our origin, to request such a reconciliation as might, in any manner, be inconsistent with her dignity or her welfare. These, related as we are to her, honour and duty, as well as inclination, induce us to support and advance; and the apprehension that now oppress our hearts with unspeakable grief, being once removed, your Majesty will find your faithful subjects on this Continent, ready and willing at all times, as they have ever been, with their lives and fortunes, to assert and maintain the rights and interests of your Majesty, and of our Mother Country.

We therefore beseech your Majesty, that your royal authority and influence may be graciously interposed to procure us relief from our afflicting fears and jealousies, occasioned by the system before-mentioned, and to settle peace through every part of our Dominions, with all humility submitting to your Majesty's wise consideration, whether it may not be expedient, for facilitating those important purposes, that your Majesty be pleased to direct some mode, by which the united applications of your faithful Colonists to the Throne, in pursuance of their common counsels, may be improved into a happy and permanent reconciliation; and that, in the mean time, measures may be taken for preventing the further destruction of the lives of your Majesty's subjects; and that such statutes as more immediately distress any of your Majesty's Colonies, may be repealed. For such arrangements as your Majesty's wisdom can form for collecting the united sense of your *American* people, we are convinced your Majesty would receive such satisfactory proofs of the disposition of the Colonists toward their Sovereign and Parent State, that the wished for opportunity would soon be restored to them, of envincing the sincerity of their professions, by every testimony of devotion becoming the most dutiful subjects, and the most affectionate Colonists.

That your Majesty may enjoy a long and prosperous reign, and that your descendants may govern your Dominions with honour to themselves and happiness to their subjects, is our sincere prayer.

43. THOMAS PAINE ATTACKS GEORGE III AND THE INSTITUTION OF THE MONARCHY, 1776*

*U*ntil the Revolutionary War began, most colonists viewed their primary quarrel as directed against Parliament, not George III or the institution of the monarchy itself. Thus, the "Olive Branch Petition" respectfully urged the King to redress grievances attributed to parliamentary legislation and ministerial excess. Thomas Paine's pamphlet, Common Sense, published in January, 1776, redirected colonial anger at the king himself and successfully popularized the call for independence. With persuasive clarity, Paine denounced monarchy as an inherently corrupt institution and insisted that any policy of reconciliation could lead only to ruin.

OF MONARCHY AND HEREDITARY SUCCESSION

Mankind being originally equals in the order of creation, the equality could only be destroyed by some subsequent circumstance; the distinctions of rich, and poor, may in a great measure be accounted for, and that without having recourse to the harsh, ill-sounding names of oppression and avarice. Oppression is often the *consequence*, but seldom or never the *means* of riches; and though avarice will preserve a man from being necessitously poor, it generally makes him too timorous to be wealthy.

But there is another and greater distinction for which no truly natural or religious reason can be assigned, and that is, the distinction of men into KINGS and SUBJECTS. Male and female are the distinctions of nature, good and bad the distinctions of heaven; but how a race of men came into the world so exalted above the rest, and distinguished like some new species, is worth inquiring into, and whether they are the means of happiness or of misery to mankind. . . .

Government by kings was first introduced into the world by the Heathens, from whom the children of Israel copied the custom. It was the most prosperous invention the Devil ever set on foot for

---

*Thomas Paine, *Common Sense, Addressed to the Inhabitants of America* (Philadelphia, 1776) in *Life and Writings of Thomas Paine*, 10 vols., ed. Daniel Edwin Wheeler (New York: Vincent Parke and Company, 1915), II:12–14, 19–22, 26–28, 36–37, 43–45.

the promotion of idolatry. The Heathens paid divine honours to their deceased kings, and the Christian world hath improved on the plan by doing the same to their living ones. How impious is the title of *sacred majesty* applied to a worm, who in the midst of his splendour is crumbling into dust.

As the exalting one man so greatly above the rest cannot be justified on the equal rights of nature, so neither can it be defended on the authority of scripture; for the will of the Almighty, as declared by Gideon and the prophet Samuel, expressly disapproves of government by kings. All anti-monarchial parts of scripture have been very smoothly glossed over in monarchial governments, but they undoubtedly merit the attention of countries which have their governments yet to form. *'Render unto Caesar the things which are Caesar's'* is the scriptural doctrine of courts, yet it is no support of monarchial government, for the Jews at that time were without a king, and in a state of vassalage to the Romans. . . .

To the evil of monarchy we have added that of hereditary succession; and as the first is a degradation and lessening of ourselves, so the second, claimed as a matter of right, is an insult and an imposition on posterity. For all men being originally equals, no *one* by *birth* could have a right to set up his own family in perpetual preference to all others for ever, and though himself might deserve *some* decent degree of honours of his contemporaries, yet his descendants might be far too unworthy to inherit them. One of the strongest *natural* proofs of the folly of hereditary right in kings, is, that nature disapproves it, otherwise she would not so frequently turn it into ridicule by giving mankind an *ass for a lion*.

Secondly, as no man at first could possess any other public honours than were bestowed upon him, so the givers of those honours could have no power to give away the right of posterity, and though they might say 'We choose you for *our* head', they could not, without manifest injustice to their children, say 'that your children and your children's children shall reign over *ours* for ever'. Because such an unwise, unjust, unnatural compact might (perhaps) in the next succession put them under the government of a rogue or a fool. Most wise men, in their private sentiments, have ever treated hereditary right with contempt; yet it is one of those evils, which when once established is not easily removed; many submit from fear, others from superstition, and the more powerful part shares with the king the plunder of the rest.

This is supposing the present race of the kings in the world to have had an honourable origin; whereas it is more than probable, that could we take off the dark covering of antiquity, and trace them to their first rise, that we should find the first of them nothing better than the principal ruffian of some restless gang, whose savage manners or pre-eminence in subtlety obtained him the title of chief among plunderers; and who by increasing in power, and extending his depredations, over-awed the quiet and defenceless to purchase their safety by frequent contributions. Yet his electors could have no idea of giving hereditary right to his descendants, because such a perpetual exclusion of themselves was incompatible with the free and unrestrained principles they professed to live by. Wherefore, hereditary succession in the early ages of monarchy could not take place as a matter of claim, but as something casual or complimental; but as few or no records were extant in those days, and traditionary history stuffed with fables, it was very easy, after the lapse of a few generations, to trump up some superstitious tale, conveniently timed, Mahomet like, to cram hereditary right down the throats of the vulgar. Perhaps the disorders which threatened, or seemed to threaten on the decease of a leader and the choice of a new one (for elections among ruffians could not be very orderly) induced many at first to favour hereditary pretensions; by which means it happened, as it hath happened since, that what at first was submitted to as a convenience, was afterwards claimed as a right. . . .

In short, monarchy and succession have laid (not this or that kingdom only) but the world in blood and ashes. 'Tis a form of government which the word of God bears testimony against, and blood with attend it.

If we inquire into the business of a king, we shall find that in some countries they have none; and after sauntering away their lives without pleasure to themselves or advantage to the nation, withdraw from the scene, and leave their successors to tread the same idle round. In absolute monarchies the whole weight of business civil and military, lies on the king; the children of Israel in their request for a king, urged this plea 'that he may judge us, and go out before us and fight our battles'. But in countries where he is neither a judge nor a general, as in E—d, a man would be puzzled to know what **is** his business.

The nearer any government approaches to a republic the less business there is for a king. It is somewhat difficult to find a proper name for the government of E—. Sir William Meredith calls it a republic; but in its present state it is unworthy of the name, because the corrupt influence of the crown, by having all the places in its disposal, hath so effectually swallowed up the power, and eaten out the virtue of the house of commons (the republican part in the constitution) that the government of England is nearly as monarchical as that of France or Spain. Men fall out with names without understanding them. For it is the republican and not the monarchical part of the constitution of England with Englishmen glory in, viz. the liberty of choosing an house of commons from out of their own body—and it is easy to see that when the republican virtue fails, slavery ensues. Why is the constitution of E—d sickly, but because monarchy hath poisoned the republic, the crown hath engrossed the commons?

In England a king hath little more to do than to make war and give away places; which in plain terms, is to impoverish the nation and set it together by the ears. A pretty business indeed for a man to be allowed eight hundred thousand sterling a year for, and worshipped into the bargain! Of more worth is one honest man to society, and in the sight of God, than all the crowned ruffians that ever lived. . . .

I challenge the warmest advocate for reconciliation, to shew, a single advantage that this continent can reap, by being connected with Great Britain. I repeat the challenge, not a single advantage is derived. Our corn will fetch its price in any market in Europe, and our imported goods must be paid for buy them where we will.

But the injuries and disadvantages we sustain by that connection, are without number; and our duty to mankind at large, as well as to ourselves, instruct us to renounce the alliance: Because, any submission to, or dependence on Great Britain, tends directly to involve this continent in European wars and quarrels; and sets us at variance with nations, who would otherwise seek our friendship, and against whom, we have neither anger nor complaint. As Europe is our market for trade, we ought to form no partial connection with any part of it. It is the true interest of America to steer clear of European contentions, which she never can do, while by her dependence on Britain, she is made the make-weight in the scale of British politics.

Europe is too thickly planted with kingdoms to be long at peace, and whenever a war breaks out between England and any foreign power, the trade of America goes to ruin, *because of her connection with Britain.* The next war may not turn out like the last, and should it not, the advocates for reconciliation now will be wishing for separation then, because, neutrality in that case, would be a safer convoy than a man of war. Every thing that is right or natural pleads for separation. The blood of the slain, the weeping voice of nature cries, 'TIS TIME TO PART. Even the distance at which the Almighty hath placed England and America, is a strong and natural proof, that the authority of the one, over the other, was never the design of Heaven. . . .

Small islands not capable of protecting themselves, are the proper objects for kingdoms to take under their care; but there is something very absurd, in supposing a continent to be perpetually governed by an island. In no instance hath nature made the satellite larger than its primary planet, and as England and America, with respect to each other, reverses the common order of nature, it is evident they belong to different systems: England to Europe, America to itself.

I am not induced by motives of pride, party, or resentment to espouse the doctrine of separation and independence; I am clearly, positively, and conscientiously persuaded that it is the true interest of this continent to be so; that every thing short of *that* is mere patchwork, that it can afford no lasting felicity,—that it is leaving the sword to our children, and shrinking back at a time, when, a little more, a little farther, would have rendered this continent the glory of the earth.

As Britain hath not manifested the least inclination towards a compromise, we may be assured that no terms can be obtained worthy the acceptance of the continent, or any ways equal to the expense of blood and treasure we have been already put to. . . .

No man was a warmer wisher for reconciliation than myself, before the fatal nineteenth of April 1775,[1] but the moment the event of that day was made known, I rejected the hardened, sullen tempered Pharaoh of—for ever; and disdain the wretch, that with the pretended title of FATHER OF HIS PEOPLE can unfeelingly hear of their slaughter, and composedly sleep with their blood upon his soul. . . .

Discussion

1.   In what ways do the Proclamation of 1763 and the defense of imperial reform express royal power? Are there ways in which those two documents express or defend English liberties?

2.   Between 1765 and 1775 sharp conflicts over parliamentary power developed between Britain and the colonies. What do the documents reveal about efforts to resolve those conflicts? Do the selections suggest options other than rebellion that might have been pursued?

3.   Colonists had long claimed the rights of Englishmen. According to the documents, what did Americans think constituted those rights in the mid-eighteenth century? Are those rights the same liberties revealed in the documents from previous chapters?

4.   What differences, if any, exist between the Stamp Act resolution and the Declaration of Rights and Grievances and the "Olive Branch Petition" and *Common Sense*? What influence did the events of 1765–1775 have on the way Americans articulated their concerns over British power?

5.   How do the documents demonstrate shifting colonial attitudes toward royal authority? How was the publication of *Common Sense* a turning point in this shift of attitudes?

6.   According to the Pontiac document, what motivated the formation of the Native American alliance against the English?

---

[1]Massacre at Lexington.—Paine.

CHAPTER 6

The Revolutionary Republic

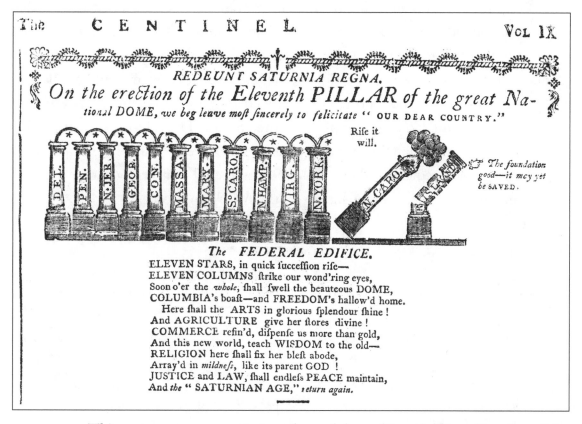

The CENTINEL.   **Vol IX**

REDEUNT SATURNIA REGNA.

On the erection of the Eleventh PILLAR of the great National DOME, we beg leave most sincerely to felicitate " OUR DEAR COUNTRY."

Rise it will.

☞ The foundation good—it may yet be SAVED.

The FEDERAL EDIFICE.

ELEVEN STARS, in quick succession rise—
ELEVEN COLUMNS strike our wond'ring eyes,
Soon o'er the *whole*, shall swell the beauteous DOME,
COLUMBIA's boast—and FREEDOM's hallow'd home.
  Here shall the ARTS in glorious splendour shine !
And AGRICULTURE give her stores divine !
COMMERCE refin'd, dispense us more than gold,
And this new world, teach WISDOM to the old—
RELIGION here shall fix her blest abode,
Array'd in *mildness*, like its parent GOD !
JUSTICE and LAW, shall endless PEACE maintain,
And *the* " SATURNIAN AGE," *return again.*

This cartoon was commissioned to celebrate New York's ratification of the new Constitution and to encourage North Carolina to do the same. The shattered pillar is Rhode Island, which refused to participate in the Philadelphia convention or to hold a ratifying convention in 1788. Rhode Island resisted ratification until May 1790.

A mericans faced an enormous task as they challenged the power of the world's greatest empire. The Revolution, however, involved more than merely overturning British authority in order to guarantee American liberties. Patriots enjoyed the opportunity to engage in an experiment in republicanism. As they wrote constitutions to create the new states, they established balanced and limited governments dedicated to protecting the rights of all citizens—that is, free adult males. In 1787, delegates applied those principles to the creation of a new central government established under the Constitution of the United States. The rhetoric of the Revolution had, on the other hand, insisted that all men are created equal. That ideal eventually made issues of equality, along with the traditional concerns over power and liberty, an important theme in the history of the American people.

44. THE BATTLE OF TRENTON, 1776*

American rebels faced the monumental task of defeating the British military—a challenge that took eight years of bloody warfare to accomplish. A critical event early in the Revolution came in December of 1776, when George Washington's army defeated a garrison of Hessian mercenaries at Trenton, New Jersey. This stunning victory, along with another at Princeton a week later, had important implications for the course of the War for Independence. British strategy in the immediate aftermath of these battles shifted from the offensive to the defensive, which gave Washington the opportunity to keep his army intact. More importantly, victory gave the Americans a crucial boost in morale as the soldiers, along with their commander in chief, realized that they could engage and defeat the enemy. In a brief letter to the Continental Congress, General Washington described that turning point in the war. The document serves as a reminder of the extreme hardships and severe dangers that soldiers faced in order to win independence.

Head-Quarters, Newtown, 27 December, 1776

Sir,

I have the pleasure of congratulating you upon the success of an enterprise, which I had formed against a detachment of the enemy lying in Trenton, and which was executed yesterday morning. The evening of the 25th I ordered the troops intended for this service to parade back of McKonkey's Ferry, that they might begin to pass as soon as it grew dark, imagining we should be able to throw them all over, with the necessary artillery, by twelve, o'clock, and that we might easily arrive at Trenton by five in the morning, the distance being about nine miles. But the quantity of ice, made that night, impeded the passage of the boats so much, that it was three o'clock before the artillery could all be got over; and near four, before the troops took up the line of march. This made me despair of surprising the town, as well I knew we could not reach it before the day was fairly broke. But as I was certain there was no making a retreat without being discovered and harassed on repassing the river, I formed my detachment into two divisions, one to march by the

*From Jared Sparks, *The Writings of George Washington, Being His Correspondence, Addresses, Messages, and Other Papers, Official and Private, Selected and Published from the Original Manuscripts; with a Life of the Author,* 12 vols. (Boston: Little, Brown, and Company, 1855), IV:246–49.

lower or river road, the other by the upper or Pennington road. As the divisions had nearly the same distance of march, I ordered each of them, immediately upon forcing the out-guards, to push directly into the town, that they might charge the enemy before they had time to form.

The upper division arrived at the enemy's advanced post exactly at eight o'clock; and in three minutes after, I found from the fire on the lower road, that that diversion had also got up. The out-guards made but small opposition, though, for their numbers, they behaved very well, keeping up a constant retreating fire from behind houses. We presently saw their main body formed; but, from their motions, they seemed undetermined how to act. Being hard pressed by our troops, who had already got possession of their artillery, they attempted to file off by a road on their right, leading to Princeton. But, perceiving their intention, I threw a body of troops in their way, which immediately checked them. Finding from our disposition, that they were surrounded, and that they must inevitably be cut to pieces if they made any further resistance, they agreed to lay down their arms. The number that submitted in this manner was twenty-three officers, and eight hundred and eighty-six men. Colonel Rahl, the commanding officer, and seven others were found wounded in the town. I do not exactly know how many were killed; but I fancy not above twenty or thirty, as they never made any regular stand. Our loss was trifling indeed, only two officers and one or two privates wounded.

I find that the detachment of the enemy consisted of three Hessian regiments of Anspach, Knyphausen, and Rahl, amounting to about fifteen hundred men, and a troop of British lighthorse; but, immediately upon the beginning of the attack, all those, who were not killed or taken, pushed directly down the road towards Bordentown. These would likewise have fallen into our hands, could my plan have been completely carried into execution. General Ewing was to have crossed before day at Trenton Ferry, and taken possession of the bridge leading out of town; but the quantity of ice was so great, that, though he did every thing in his power to effect it, he could not get over. This difficulty also hindered General Cadwalader from crossing with the Pennsylvania militia from Bristol. He got part of his foot over; but, finding it impossible to embark his artillery, he was obliged to desist. I am fully confident, that, could the troops under Generals Ewing and Cadwalader have passed the river, I should have been able with their assistance to drive the enemy from all their posts below Trenton. But the numbers I had with me being inferior to theirs below me, and a strong battalion of light infantry being at Princeton above me, I thought it most prudent to return the same evening with the prisoners and artillery we had taken. We found no stores of any consequence in the town.

In justice to the officers and men, I must add, that their behaviour upon this occasion reflects the highest honor upon them. The difficulty of passing the river in a very severe night, and their march through a violent storm of snow and hail, did not in the least abate their ardor; but, when they came to the charge, each seemed to vie with the other in pressing forward; and were I to give a preference to any particular corps, I should do great injustice to the others. Colonel Baylor, my first aid-de-camp, will have the honor of delivering this to you; and from him you may be made acquainted with many other particulars. His spirited behaviour upon every occasion requires me to recommend him to your particular notice. . . .

45. THE VIRGINIA BILL OF RIGHTS, 1776*

*E*stablishing constitutions for new state governments was one of the first steps taken by Americans experimenting with republicanism. Virginia representatives began their effort by preparing a declaration of rights, indicating

---

*From the *Constitution of Virginia, 1776,* in *The Federal and State Constitutions, Colonial Charters, and Other Organic Laws of the State Territories, and Colonies Now or Heretofore Forming the United States of America,* 7 vols., ed. Francis N. Thorpe (Washington, D.C.: U.S. Government Printing Office, 1909), VII:3812–14.

the importance that they placed on a written guarantee of liberty. The following document, drafted mostly by George Mason, served as a model for numerous bills of rights, including that of the national constitution. It enumerated the rights and liberties that Americans held most dear and for which they had proven willing to fight.

A declaration of rights made by the representatives of the good people of Virginia, assembled in full and free convention; which rights do pertain to them and their posterity, as the basis and foundation of government.

SECTION 1. That all men are by nature equally free and independent, and have certain inherent rights, of which, when they enter into a state of society, they cannot, by any compact, deprive or divest their posterity; namely, the enjoyment of life and liberty, with the means of acquiring and possessing property, and pursuing and obtaining happiness and safety.

Sec. 2. That all power is vested in, and consequently derived from, the people; that all magistrates are their trustees and servants, and at all times amenable to them.

Sec. 3. That government is, or ought to be, instituted for the common benefit, protection, and security of the people, nation, or community; of all the various modes and forms of government, that is best which is capable of producing the greatest degree of happiness and safety, and is most effectually secured against the danger of maladministration; and that, when any government shall be found inadequate or contrary to these purposes, a majority of the community hath an indubitable, inalienable, and indefeasible right to reform, alter, or abolish it, in such manner as shall be judged most conducive to the public weal.

Sec. 4. That no man, or set of men, are entitled to exclusive or separate emoluments or privileges from the community, but in consideration of public services; which, not being descendible, neither ought the offices magistrate, legislator, or judge to be hereditary.

Sec. 5. That the legislative and executive powers of the State should be separate and distinct from the judiciary; and that the members of the two first may be restrained from oppression, by feeling and participating the burdens of the people, they should, at fixed periods, be reduced to a private station, return into that body from which they were originally taken, and the vacancies be supplied by frequent, certain, and regular elections, in which all, or any part of the former members, to be again eligible, or ineligible, as the laws shall direct.

Sec. 6. That elections of members to serve as representatives of the people, in assembly, ought to be free; and that all men, having sufficient evidence of permanent common interest with, and attachment to, the community, have the right of suffrage, and cannot be taxed or deprived of their property for public uses, without their own consent, or that of their representatives so elected, nor bound by any law to which they have not, in like manner, assembled, for the public good.

Sec. 7. That all power of suspending laws, or the execution of laws, by any authority, without consent of the representatives of the people, is injurious to their rights, and ought not to be exercised.

Sec. 8. That in all capital or criminal prosecutions a man hath a right to demand the cause and the nature of his accusation, to be confronted with the accusers and witnesses, to call for evidence in his favor, and to a speedy trial by an impartial jury of twelve men of his vicinage, without whose unanimous consent he cannot be found guilty; nor can he be compelled to give evidence against himself; that no man be deprived of his liberty, except by the law of the land or the judgment of his peers.

Sec. 9. That excessive bail ought not to be required, nor excessive fines imposed, nor cruel and unusual punishment be inflicted.

Sec. 10. That general warrants, whereby an officer or messenger may be commanded to search suspected places without evidence of a fact committed, or to seize any person or persons, not named, or whose offence is not particularly described and supported by evidence, are grievous and oppressive, and ought not to be granted.

Sec. 11. That in controversies respecting property, and in suit between man and man, the ancient trial by jury is preferable to any other, and ought to be held sacred.

Sec. 12. That the freedom of the press is one of the great bulwarks of liberty, and can never be restrained but by despotic governments.

Sec. 13. That a well-regulated militia, composed of the body of the people, trained to arms, is the proper, natural, and safe defence of a free State; that standing armies, in time of peace, should be avoided, as dangerous to liberty; and that in all cases the military should be under strict subordination to, and governed by, the civil power.

Sec. 14. That the people have a right to uniform government; and, therefore, that no government separate from, or independent of the government of Virginia, ought to be erected or established within the limits thereof.

Sec. 15. That no free government, or the blessings of liberty, can be preserved to any people, but by a firm adherence to justice, moderation, temperance, frugality, and virtue, and by frequent recurrence to fundamental principles.

Sec. 16. That religion, or the duty which we owe to our Creator, and the manner of discharging it, can be directed only by reason and conviction, not by force or violence; and, therefore all men are equally entitled to the free exercise of religion, according to the dictates of conscience; and that it is the mutual duty of all to practise Christian forbearance, love, and charity towards each other.

46. "REMEMBER THE LADIES," 1776*

The American Revolution grew out of the conflict between British power and American liberties, but the movement for independence institutionalized the ideal of equality in the United States. Over the past two centuries, consequently, egalitarianism has become a major force in the nation's history. During the revolutionary era, artisans and yeomen worked to enhance their status, while many Americans urged the abolition of slavery. Women, too, hoped to improve their lot. In the following letters to her husband, Abigail Adams revealed her revolutionary understanding of the place of women in a republican society. Abigail and John Adams enjoyed a refreshingly forthright communication in their correspondence, and the documents reveal the powerful personality and incisive intellect of the future First Lady.

Braintree, 31 March, 1776

I wish you would ever write me a letter half as long as I write you, and tell me, if you may, where your fleet are gone; what sort of defense Virginia can make against our common enemy; whether it is so situated as to make an able defense. Are not the gentry lords, and the common people vassals? Are they not like the uncivilized vassals Britain represents us to be? I hope their riflemen, who have shown themselves very savage and even blood-thirsty, are not a specimen of the generality of the people. I am willing to allow the colony great merit for having produced a Washington; but they have been shamefully duped by a Dunmore.

I have sometimes been ready to think that the passion for liberty cannot be equally strong in the breasts of those who have been accustomed to deprive their fellow creatures of theirs. Of this I am certain, that it is not founded upon the generous and Christian principle of doing to others as we would that others should do unto us.

Do not you want to see Boston? I am fearful of the small-pox, or I should have been in before this time. I got Mr. Crane to go to our house and see what state it was in. I find it has been occupied

*From Charles Francis Adams, *Familiar Letters of John Adams and His Wife Abigail Adams, during the Revolution. With a Memoir of Mrs. Adams* (New York: Hurd and Houghton, 1876), 148–50, 212–14.

by one of the doctors of a regiment; very dirty, but no other damage has been done to it. The few things which were left in it are all gone. I look upon it as a new acquisition of property—a property which one month ago I did not value at a single shilling, and would with pleasure have seen it in flames.

The town in general is left in a better state than we expected; more owing to the precipitate flight than any regard to the inhabitants; though some individuals discovered a sense of honor and justice, and have left the rent of the houses in which they were, for the owners, and the furniture unhurt, or, if damaged, sufficient to make it good. Others have committed abominable ravages. The mansion-house of your President is safe, and the furniture unhurt; while the house and furniture of the Solicitor General have fallen a prey to their own merciless party. Surely the very fiends feel a reverential awe for virtue and patriotism, whilst they detest the patricide and traitor.

I feel very differently at the approach of spring from what I did a month ago. We knew not then whether we could plant or sow with safety, whether where we had tilled we could reap the fruits of our own industry, whether we could rest in our own cottages or whether we should be driven from the seacoast to seek shelter in the wilderness; but now we feel a temporary peace, and the poor fugitives are returning to their deserted habitations.

Though we felicitate ourselves, we sympathize with those who are trembling lest the lot of Boston should be theirs. But they cannot be in similar circumstances unless pusillanimity and cowardice should take possession of them. They have time and warning given them to see the evil and shun it.

I long to hear that you have declared an independency. And, by the way, in the code of laws which I suppose it will be necessary for you to make, I desire you would remember the ladies and be more generous and favorable to them than your ancestors. Do not put such unlimited power into the hands of the husbands. Remember, all men would be tyrants if they could. If particular care and attention is not paid to the ladies, we are determined to foment a rebellion, and will not hold ourselves bound by any laws in which we have no voice or representation.

That your sex are naturally tyrannical is a truth so thoroughly established as to admit of no dispute; but such of you as wish to be happy willingly give up the harsh title of master for the more tender and endearing one of friend. Why, then, not put it out of the power of the vicious and the lawless to use us with cruelty and indignity with impunity? Men of sense in all ages abhor those customs which treat us only as the vassals of your sex; regard us then as being placed by Providence under your protection, and in imitation of the Supreme Being make use of that power only for our happiness. . . .

————

14 August, 1776

Your letter of August 3 came by this day's post. I find it very convenient to be so handy. I can receive a letter at night, sit down and reply to it, and send it off in the morning.

You remark upon the deficiency of education in your countrymen. It never, I believe, was in a worse state, at least for many years. The college is not in the state one could wish. The scholars complain that their professor in philosophy is taken off by public business, to their great detriment. In this town I never saw so great a neglect of education. The poorer sort of children are wholly neglected, and left to range the streets, without schools, without business, given up to all evil. There is either too much business left upon the hands of a few, or too little care to do it. We daily see the necessity of a regular government.

You speak of our worthy brother. I often lament it, that a man so peculiarly formed for the education of youth, and so well qualified as he is in many branches of literature, excelling in philosophy and the mathematics, should not be employed in some public station. I know not the person who would make half so good a successor to Dr. Winthrop. He has a peculiar, easy manner if communicating his ideas to youth; and the goodness of his heart and the purity of his morals, without an affected austerity, must have a happy effect upon the minds of pupils.

If you complain of neglect of education in sons, what shall I say with regard to daughters, who every day experience the want of it? With regard to the education of my own children, I find myself soon out of my depth, destitute and deficient in every part of education.

I most sincerely wish that some more liberal plan might be laid and executed for the benefit of the rising generation, and that our new Constitution may be distinguished for encouraging learning and virtue. If we mean to have heroes, statesmen, and philosophers, we should have learned women. The world perhaps would laugh at me and accuse me of vanity, but you, I know, have a mind too enlarged and liberal to disregard the sentiment. If much depends, as is allowed, upon the early education of youth, and the first principles which are instilled take the deepest root, great benefit must arise from literary accomplishments in women.

Excuse me. My pen has run away with me. I have no thought of coming to Philadelphia. The length of time I have and shall be detained here would have prevented me, even if you had no thoughts of returning till December; but I live in daily expectation of seeing you here. Your health, I think, requires your immediate return. I expected Mr. G_____ would have set off before now, but he perhaps finds it very hard to leave his mistress. I won't say harder than some do to leave their wives. Mr. Gerry stood very high in my esteem. What is meat for one is not for another. No accounting for fancy. She is a queer dame and leads people [on?] wild dances.

But hush! Post, don't betray your trust and lose my letter.

47. AN ACT FOR ESTABLISHING RELIGIOUS FREEDOM, 1786*

The American Revolution rendered the Anglican Church, with George III as its "supreme head," vulnerable. Most Anglican clergy had supported independence or remained neutral, but a vocal loyalist minority had angered many patriots. By the end of the war every southern state had disestablished the Anglican Church and had deprived it of its tax support and other privileges. In 1779 Thomas Jefferson proposed a bill to enact religious freedom in Virginia, and the state assembly finally passed it in 1786. The act eloquently declared that "God hath created the mind free" and that efforts to use coercion in matters of religion "tend only to beget habits of hypocrisy and meanness."

Well aware that Almighty God hath created the mind free; that all attempts to influence it by temporal punishments or burdens, or by civil incapacitations, tend only to beget habits of hypocrisy and meanness, and are a departure from the plan of the Holy Author of our religion, who being Lord both of body and mind, yet chose not to propagate it by coercions on either, as was in his Almighty power to do; that the impious presumption of legislators and rulers, civil as well as ecclesiastical, who, being themselves but fallible and uninspired men, have assumed dominion over the faith of others, setting up their own opinions and modes of thinking as the only true and infallible, and as such endeavoring to impose them on others, hath established and maintained false religions over the greatest part of the world, and through all time; that to compel a man to furnish contributions of money for the propagation of opinions which he disbelieves, is sinful and tyrannical; that even the forcing him to support this or that teacher of his own religious persuasion, is depriving him of the comfortable liberty of giving his contributions to the particular pastor whose morals he would make his pattern, and whose powers he feels most persuasive to righteousness, and is withdrawing from the ministry those temporal rewards, which proceeding from an approbation of their personal conduct, are an additional incitement to earnest and unremitting labors for the instruction of mankind; that our civil rights have no dependence on our religious opinions, more than our opinions in

*From *The Writings of Thomas Jefferson*, 20 vols., ed. Albert E. Bergh (Washington, D.C.: The Thomas Jefferson Memorial Association, 1904–1905), II:300–03.

physics or geometry; that, therefore, the proscribing any citizen as unworthy the public confidence by laying upon him an incapacity of being called to the offices of trust and emolument, unless he profess or renounce this or that religious opinion, is depriving him injuriously of those privileges and advantages to which in common with his fellow citizens he has a natural right; that it tends also to corrupt the principles of that very religion it is meant to encourage, by bribing, with a monopoly of worldly honors and emoluments, those who will externally profess and conform to it; that though indeed these are criminal who do not withstand such temptation, yet neither are those innocent who lay the bait in their way; that to suffer the civil magistrate to intrude his powers into the field of opinion and to restrain the profession or propagation of principles, on the supposition of their ill tendency, is a dangerous fallacy, which at once destroys all religious liberty, because he being of course judge of that tendency, will make his opinions the rule of judgment, and approve or condemn the sentiments of others only as they shall square with or differ from his own; that it is time enough for the rightful purposes of civil government, for its officers to interfere when principles break out into overt acts against peace and good order; and finally, that truth is great and will prevail if left to herself, that she is the proper and sufficient antagonist to error, and has nothing to fear from the conflict, unless by human interposition disarmed of her natural weapons, free argument and debate, errors ceasing to be dangerous when it is permitted freely to contradict them.

Be it therefore enacted by the General Assembly, That no man shall be compelled to frequent or support any religious worship, place, or ministry whatsoever, nor shall be enforced, restrained, molested, or burdened in his body or goods, nor shall otherwise suffer on account of his religious opinions or belief; but that all men shall be free to profess, and by argument to maintain, their opinions in matters of religion, and that the same shall in nowise diminish, enlarge, or affect their civil capacities.

And though we well know this Assembly, elected by the people for the ordinary purposes of legislation only, have no powers equal to our own and that therefore to declare this act irrevocable would be of no effect in law, yet we are free to declare, and do declare, that the rights hereby asserted are of the natural rights of mankind, and that if any act shall be hereafter passed to repeal the present or to narrow its operation, such act will be an infringement of natural right.

48. *FEDERALIST* NUMBER NINE, 1787*

In the fall of 1787 supporters of the Constitution anticipated a bitter ratification fight at the New York convention slated for the following summer. Over the next several months Alexander Hamilton, along with John Jay and James Madison, published a series of newspaper articles in defense of the Constitution. Immediately collected in book form as The Federalist, *these essays were used extensively in other states and still, today, serve as a remarkable commentary on the basic principles embodied in the Constitution. The following essay, written by Hamilton, addressed the fear that domestic factions and local insurrections (such as Shays's Rebellion) could endanger the liberty of the union. To him, expanding the sphere of government would enable the confederation to suppress any threatening factions.*

A firm Union will be of the utmost moment to the peace and liberty of the States, as a barrier against domestic faction and insurrection. It is impossible to read the history of the petty republics of Greece and Italy without feeling sensations of horror and disgust at the distractions with which they were continually agitated, and at the rapid succession of revolutions, by which they were kept in a state of perpetual vibration, between the extremes of tyranny and anarchy. If they exhibit occa-

---

*From *The Federalist: A Collection of Essays by Alexander Hamilton, John Jay, and James Madison* (New York: P. F. Collier & Son, 1901), 38–43.

sional calms, these only serve as short-lived contrasts to the furious storms that are to succeed. . . . If momentary rays of glory break forth from the gloom, while they dazzle us with a transient and fleeting brilliancy, they at the same time admonish us to lament that the vices of government should pervert the direction and tarnish the lustre of those bright talents and exalted endowments for which the favored soils that produced them have been so justly celebrated.

From the disorders that disfigure the annals of those republics the advocates of despotism have drawn arguments, not only against the forms of republican government, but against the very principles of civil liberty. They have decried all free government as inconsistent with the order of society, and have indulged themselves in malicious exultation over its friends and partisans. Happily for mankind, stupendous fabrics reared on the basis of liberty, which have flourished for ages, have, in a few glorious instances, refuted their gloomy sophisms. And, I trust, America will be the broad and solid foundation of other edifices, not less magnificent, which will be equally permanent monuments of their errors.

But it is not to be denied that the portraits they have sketched of republican government were too just copies of the originals from which they were taken. If it had been found impracticable to have devised models of a more perfect structure, the enlightened friends to liberty would have been obliged to abandon the cause of that species of government as indefensible. The science of politics, however, like most other sciences, has received great improvement. The efficacy of various principles is now well understood, which were either not known at all or imperfectly known to the ancients. The regular distribution of power into distinct departments; the introduction of legislative balances and checks; the institution of courts composed of judges holding their offices during good behavior; the representation of the people in the legislature, by deputies of their own election—these are either wholly new discoveries or have made their principal progress toward perfection in modern times. They are means, and powerful means, by which the excellences of republican government may be retained. . . .

The utility of a confederacy, as well to suppress faction, and to guard the internal tranquillity of States, as to increase their external force and security, is in reality not a new idea. It has been practised upon, in different countries and ages, and has received the sanction of the most approved writers on the subjects of politics. The opponents of the plan proposed, have, with great assiduity, cited and circulated the observations of Montesquieu on the necessity of a contracted territory for a republican government. But they seem not to have been apprised of the sentiments of that great man, expressed in another part of his work, nor to have adverted to the consequences of the principle, to which they subscribe with such ready acquiescence. . . .

So far are the suggestion of Montesquieu from standing in opposition to a general Union of the States, that he explicitly treats of a confederate republic as the expedient for extending the sphere of popular government, and reconciling the advantages of monarchy with those of republicanism.

"It is very probable," says he,[1] "that mankind would have been obliged, at length, to live constantly under the Government of a single person, had they not contrived a kind of Constitution, that has all the internal advantages of a Republican, together with the external force of a Monarchical Government. I mean a Confederate Republic.

"This form of Government is a Convention by which several smaller States agreed to become members of a larger one, which they intend to form. It is a kind of assemblage of societies, that constitute a new one, capable of increasing by means of new associations, till they arrive to such a degree of power, as to be able to provide for the security of the united body.

"A Republic of this kind, able to withstand an external force, may support itself without any internal corruptions. The form of this society prevents all manner of inconveniences.

---

[1] *"Spirit of Laws,"* Vol. I, bk. IX. Chap. I.

"If a single member should attempt to usurp the supreme authority, he could not be supposed to have an equal authority and credit in all the Confederate States. Were he to have too great influence over one, this would alarm the rest. Were he to subdue a part, that which would still remain free might oppose him with forces, independent of those which he had usurped, and overpower him before he could be settled in his usurpation.

"Should a popular insurrection happen in one of the Confederate States, the others are able to quell it. Should abuses creep into one part, they are reformed by those that remain sound. The State may be destroyed on one side, and not on the other; the Confederacy may be dissolved, and the Confederates preserve their Sovereignty.

"As this Government is composed of small Republics, it enjoys the internal happiness of each; and with respect to its external situation, it is possessed, by means of the Association, of all the advantages of large Monarchies."

I have thought it proper to quote at length these interesting passages, because they contain a luminous abridgment of the principal arguments in favor of the Union, and must effectually remove the false impressions, which a misapplication of other parts of the work was calculated to make. They have, at the same time, an intimate connection with the more immediate design of this paper which is, to illustrate the tendency of the Union to repress domestic faction and insurrection.

A distinction, more subtle than accurate, has been raised between a confederacy and a consolidation of the States. The essential characteristic of the first is said to be, the restriction of its authority to the members in their collective capacities, without reaching to the individuals of whom they are composed. It is contended that the national council ought to have no concern with any object of internal administration. An exact equality of suffrage between the members has also been insisted upon as a leading feature of a confederate government. These positions are, in the main, arbitrary; they are supported neither by principle nor precedent. It has, indeed, happened that governments of this kind have generally operated in the manner which the distinction, taken notice of, supposes to be inherent in their nature; but there have been in most of them extensive exceptions to the practice, which serve to prove, as far as example will go, that there is no absolute rule on the subject. And it will be clearly shown, in the course of this investigation, that as far as the principle contended for has prevailed, it has been the cause of incurable disorder and imbecility in the government.

The definition of a confederate republic seems simply to be, "an assemblage of societies," or an association of two or more States into one State. The extent, modifications, and objects of the federal authority are mere matters of discretion. So long as the separate organization of the members be not abolished; so long as it exists, by a constitutional necessity, for local purposes; though it should be in perfect subordination to the general authority of the Union, it would still be, in fact and in theory, an association of States, or a confederacy. The proposed Constitution, so far from implying an abolition of the State governments, makes them constituent parts of the national sovereignty, by allowing them a direct representation in the Senate, and leaves in their possession certain exclusive and very important portions of sovereign power. This fully corresponds, in every rational import of the terms, with the idea of a federal government. . . .

49. *Federalist* Number Ten, 1787*

James Madison, in the following essay, addressed the antifederalist fear that a large republic would be inherently unstable and that factions posed a dire threat to all republics. He contended that in a large and diverse

---

*From *The Federalist: A Collection of Essays by Alexander Hamilton, John Jay, and James Madison* (New York: P. F. Collier & Son, 1901), 41–51.

nation like the United States no group or coalition would ever be able to attain the power that could destroy liberty. To him, expanding the sphere of government would neutralize or defuse any such peril.

Among the numerous advantages promised by a well-constructed union, none deserves to be more accurately developed than its tendency to break and control the violence of faction. The friend of popular governments never finds himself so much alarmed for their character and fate as when he contemplates their propensity to this dangerous vice. He will not fail, therefore, to set a due value on any plan which, without violating the principles to which he is attached, provides a proper cure for it. The instability, injustice, and confusion introduced into the public councils have, in truth, been the mortal diseases under which popular government have everywhere perished; as they continue to be the favorite and fruitful topics from which the adversaries to liberty derive their most specious declamations. The valuable improvements made by the American constitutions on the popular models, both ancient and modern, cannot certainly be too much admired; but it would be an unwarrantable partiality, to contend that they have as effectually obviated the danger on this side as was wished and expected. Complaints are everywhere heard from our most considerable and virtuous citizens, equally the friends of public and private faith and of public and personal liberty, that our governments are too unstable; that the public good is disregarded in the conflict of rival parties; and that measures are too often decided, not according to the rules of justice, and the rights of the minor party, but the superior force of an interested and overbearing majority. However anxiously we may wish that these complaints had no foundation, the evidence of known facts will not permit us to deny that they are in some degree true. It will be found, indeed, on a candid review of our situation, that some of the distresses under which we labor have been erroneously charged on the operation of our governments; but it will be found, at the same time, that other causes will not alone account for many of our heaviest misfortunes; and particularly, for that preling and increasing distrust of public engagements, and alarm for private rights, which are echoed from one end of the continent to the other. These must be chiefly, if not wholly, effects of the unsteadiness and injustice with which a factious spirit has tainted our public administrations.

By a faction, I understand a number of citizens, whether amounting to a majority or a minority of the whole, who are united and actuated by some common impulse of passion, or of interest, adverse to the rights of other citizens or to the permanent and aggregate interests of the community.

There are two methods of curing the mischiefs of faction: the one, by removing its cause; the other, by controlling its effects.

There are again two methods of removing the causes of faction: the one, by destroying the liberty which is essential to its existence; the other, by giving to every citizen the same opinions, the same passions, and the same interests.

It could never be more truly said than of the first remedy, that it is worse than the disease. Liberty is to faction what air is to fire, an [element] without which it instantly expires. But it could not be less folly to abolish liberty, which is essential to political life, because it nourished faction, than it would be to wish the annihilation of air, which is essential to animal life, because it imparts to fire its destructive agency.

The second expedient is as impracticable as the first would be unwise. As long as the reason of man continues fallible, and he is at liberty to exercise it, different opinions will be formed. As long as the connection subsists between his reason and his self-love, his opinions and his passions will have a reciprocal influence on each other; and the former will be objects to which the latter will attach themselves. The diversity in the faculties of men, from which the rights of property originate, is not less an insuperable obstacle to a uniformity, of interests. The protection of these faculties is the first object of government. From the protection of different and unequal faculties of acquiring property, the possession of different degrees and kinds of property immediately results;

and from the influence of these on the sentiments and views of the respective proprietors, ensues a division of the society into different interests and parties.

The latent causes of faction are thus sown in the nature of man; and we see them everywhere brought into different degrees of activity, according to the different circumstances of civil society. A zeal for different opinions concerning religion, concerning government and many other points, as well of speculation as of practice; an attachment to different leaders ambitiously contending for pre-eminence and power, or to persons of other descriptions whose fortunes have been interesting to the human passions, have, in turn, divided mankind into parties, inflamed them with mutual animosity, and rendered them much more disposed to vex and oppress each other, than to co-operate for their common good. So strong is this propensity of mankind to fall into mutual animosities, that where no substantial occasion presents itself, the most frivolous and fanciful distinctions have been sufficient to kindle their unfriendly passions and excite their most violent conflicts. But the most common and durable source of factions has been the various and unequal distribution of property. Those who are creditors and those who are debtors fall under a like discrimination. A landed interest, a manufacturing interest, a mercantile interest, a moneyed interest, with many lesser interests, grow up of necessity in civilized nations, and divide them into different classes, actuated by different sentiments and views. The regulation of these various and interfering interests forms the principle task of modern legislation, and involves the spirit of party and faction in the necessary and ordinary operations of the government.

No man is allowed to be a judge in his own cause; because his interest would certainly bias his judgment and, not improbably, corrupt his integrity. With equal, nay, with greater reason, a body of men are unfit to be both judges and parties at the same time; yet what are many of the most important acts of legislation, but so many judicial determinations, not indeed concerning the rights of single persons, but concerning the rights of large bodies of citizens. and what are the different classes of legislators, but advocates and parties to the causes which they determine? Is a law proposed concerning private debts?—it is a question to which the creditors are parties on one side, and the debtors on the other. Justice ought to hold the balance between them. Yet the parties are, and must be, themselves the judges; and the most numerous party, or, in other words, the most powerful faction, must be expected to prevail. Shall domestic manufacturing be encouraged, and in what degree, by restrictions on foreign manufactures? are questions which would be differently decided by the landed and the manufacturing classes, and probably neither with a sole regard to justice and the public good. The apportionment of taxes on the various descriptions of property is an act which seems to require the most exact impartiality; yet there is, perhaps, no legislative act in which greater opportunity and temptation are given to a predominant party, to trample on the rules of justice. Every shilling with which they overburden the inferior number is a shilling saved to their own pockets.

It is vain to say that enlightened statesmen will be able to adjust these clashing interests and render them all subservient to the public good. Enlightened statesmen will not always be at the helm; nor, in many cases, can such an adjustment be made at all, without taking into view indirect and remote considerations, which will rarely prevail over the immediate interest which one party may find in disregarding the rights of another or the good of the whole.

The inference to which we are brought is that the causes of faction cannot be removed, and that relief is only to be sought in the means of controlling its effects.

If a faction consist of less than a majority, relief is supplied by the republican principle, which enables the majority to defeat its sinister views by regular vote. It may clog the administration, it may convulse the society; but it will be unable to execute and mask its violence under the forms of the Constitution. When a majority is included in a faction, the form of popular government, on the other hand, enables it to sacrifice to its ruling passion of interest both the public good and the rights of other citizens. To secure the public good, and private rights, against the danger of such a faction, and at the same time to preserve the spirit and the form of popular government, is then the great object to which our inquiries are directed. Let me add that it is the great desideratum, by which alone this form of government can be rescued for the opprobrium under which it has too long labored, and be recommended to the esteem and the adoption of mankind.

By what means is this object attainable? Evidently by one of two only. Either the existence of the same passions or interest in a majority, at the same time, must be prevented; or the majority, having such coexistent passion or interest, must be rendered, by their number and local situation, unable to concert and carry into effect schemes of oppression. If the impulse and the opportunity be suffered to coincide, we well know that neither moral nor religious motives can be relied on as an adequate control. They are not found to be such on the injustice and violence of individuals, and lose their efficacy in proportion to the number combined together; that is, in proportion as their efficacy becomes needful.

From this view of the subject it may be concluded that a pure democracy, by which I mean a society consisting of a small number of citizens, who assemble and administer the government in person, can admit of no cure for the mischiefs of faction. A common passion or interest will, in almost every case, be felt by a majority of the whole; a communication and concert results from the form of government itself; and there is nothing to check the inducements to sacrifice the weaker party or an obnoxious individual. Hence it is that such democracies have ever been spectacles of turbulence and contention; have ever been found incompatible with personal security, or the rights of property, and have in general been as short in their lives as they have been violent in their deaths. Theocratic politicians, who have patronized this species of government, have erroneously supposed that by reducing mankind to a perfect equality in their political rights, they would at the same time be perfectly equalized and assimilated in their possessions, their opinions, and their passions.

A republic, by which I mean a government in which the scheme of representation takes place, opens a different prospect, and promises the cure for which we are seeking. Let us examine the points in which it varies from pure democracy, and we shall comprehend both the nature of the cure and the efficacy which it must derive from the union.

The two great points of difference between a democracy and a republic are: First, the delegation of the government, in the latter, to a small number of citizens elected by the rest; secondly, the greater number of citizens, and greater sphere of country, over which the latter may be extended.

The effect of the first difference is, on the one hand, to refine and enlarge the public views, by passing them through the medium of a chosen body of citizens, whose wisdom may best discern the true interest of their country, and whose patriotism and love of justice will be least likely to sacrifice it to temporary or partial considerations. Under such a regulation, it may well happen that the public voice, pronounced by the representatives of all the people, will be more consonant to the public good than if pronounced by the people themselves, convened for that purpose. On the other hand, the effect may be inverted. Men of factious tempers, of local prejudices, or the sinister designs, may by intrigue, by corruption, or by other means, first obtain the suffrages, and then betray the interests of the people. The question resulting is, whether small or extensive republics are most favorable to the election of proper guardians of the public weal; and it is clearly decided in favor of the latter by two obvious considerations.

In the first place, it is to be remarked that, however small the republic may be, the representatives must be raised to a certain number, in order to guard against the cabals of a few; and that, however large it may be, they must be limited to a certain number, in order to guard against the confusion of a multitude. Hence, the number of representatives in the two cases not being in proportion to that of the constituents, and being proportionally greatest in the small republic, it follows that if the proportion of fit characters be not less in the large than in the small republic, the former will present a greater option, and consequently a greater probability of a fit choice.

In the next place, as each representative will be chosen by a greater number of citizens in the large than in the small republic, it will be more difficult for unworthy candidates to practise with success the vicious arts, by which elections are too often carried; and the suffrages of the people, being more free, will be more likely to centre in men who possess the most attractive merits and the most diffusive and established characters.

It must be confessed that in this as in most other cases, there is a mean, on both sides of which inconveniences will be found to lie. By enlarging too much the number of electors, you render the representative too little acquainted with all their local circumstances and lesser interests; as by reducing it too much, you render him unduly attached to these, and too little fit to comprehend and pursue great and national objects. The federal Constitution forms a happy combination in this respect; the great and aggregate interests being referred to the national, the local and particular to the State, legislatures.

The other point of difference is, the greater number of citizens and extent of territory which may be brought within the compass of republican than of democratic government; and it is this circumstance principally which renders factious combinations less to be dreaded in the former, than in the latter. The smaller the society, the fewer probably will be the distinct parties and interests composing it; the fewer the distinct parties and interests, the more frequently will a majority be found of the same party; and the smaller the number of individuals composing a majority, and the smaller the compass within which they are placed, the more easily will they concert and execute their plans of oppression. Extend the sphere, and you take in a greater variety of parties and interests; you make it less probable that a majority of the whole will have a common motive to invade the rights of other citizens; or if such a common motive exists, it will be more difficult for all who feel it to discover their own strength, and to act in unison with each other. Besides other impediments, it may be remarked that where there is a consciousness of unjust or dishonorable purposes, communication is always checked by distrust, in proportion to the number whose concurrence is necessary.

Hence it clearly appears that the same advantage which a republic has over a democracy, in controlling the effects of faction, is enjoyed by a large over a small republic—is enjoyed by the Union over the States composing it. Does the advantage consist in the substitution of representatives, whose enlightened views and virtuous sentiments render them superior to local prejudices, and to schemes of injustice? It will not be denied that the representation of the Union will be most likely to possess these requisite endowments. Does it consist in the greater security afforded by a greater variety of parties, against the event of any one party being able to outnumber and oppress the rest? In an equal degree does the increased variety of parties, comprised within the Union, increase this security? Does it, in fine, consist in the greater obstacles opposed to the concert and accomplishment of the secret wishes of an unjust and interested majority? Here, again, the extent of the Union gives it the most palpable advantage.

The influence of factious leaders may kindle a flame within their particular States, but it will be unable to spread a general conflagration through the other States. A religious sect may degenerate into a political faction in a part of the confederacy; but the variety of sects dispersed over the entire face of it must secure the national councils against any danger from that source. A rage for paper money, for an abolition of debts, for an equal division of property, or for any other improper or wicked project will be less apt to pervade the whole body of the Union than a particular member of it; in the same proportion as such a malady is more likely to taint a particular country or district than an entire State.

In the extent and proper structure of the Union, therefore, we behold a republican remedy for the diseases most incident to republican government. And according to the degree of pleasure and pride we feel in being republicans, ought to be our zeal in cherishing the spirit and supporting the character of federalists.

Discussion

1. To gain independence, Americans had to defeat a major military power. What does George Washington's letter suggest about his ability to meet that task? Does the document reveal any of Washington's leadership qualities? Does the selection indicate something about Washington's attitudes toward liberty or equality?

2. How does the Virginia Bill of Rights address issues of liberty, equality, and power? What liberties did Americans hold dear, and how did they propose to protect them?

3. In her call for her husband to "remember the ladies," do you think Abigail Adams was advocating gender equality? What liberties does she seem to think women deserve? What do her letters suggest about issues of power within American families at the time of the Revolution?

4. Both selections from *The Federalist* addressed antifederalist concerns about factions. Do you think that the authors approached those fears in the same manner? Did they view liberty and power in the same way? If not, how did they differ?

5. How does Thomas Jefferson's religious freedom act address issues of liberty, equality, and power? Do you think that religious freedom is important? Is the United States a religious nation? If so, in what way?

CHAPTER 7

The Democratic Republic, 1790–1820

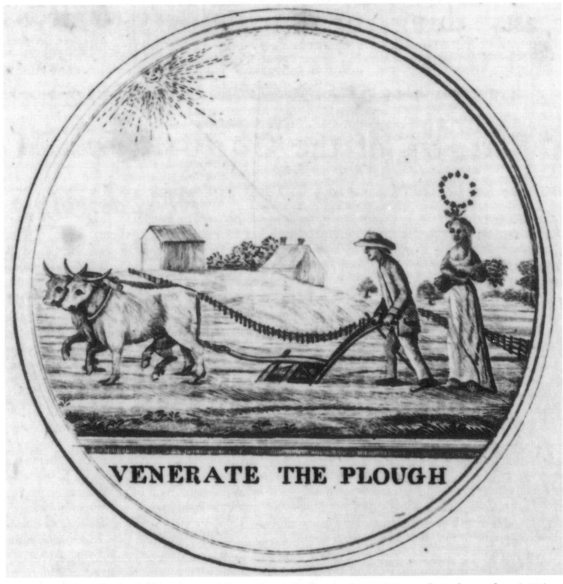

VENERATE THE PLOUGH

The ideal of the yeoman farmer, an independent citizen free from domination by business or government, has been popular since Jefferson's time, when most Americans had independent family farms. This plate links the farmer with a female America figure who combines mythical ideas of Mother Earth, husbandry, and the thirteen stars of the original states, suggesting that the yeoman farmer is the strength of the republic.

During the thirty years following ratification of the Constitution of the United States, Americans created a vibrant economy and a dynamic society. The United States remained largely rural, with farmers and frontiersmen often claiming a special status in the agrarian democratic republic, but in the young nation, all property-owning white fathers enjoyed power and liberty, along with a certain degree of equality. Their position, however, was based on the dependent condition of women and children and the subordinate roles of Indians and slaves. These disfranchised Americans held little or no power, they often did not share in the blessings of liberty, and they never obtained equality.

50. WHAT IS AN AMERICAN, 1782*

French-born J. Hector St. John de Crèvecoeur considered America a heaven compared to Europe, and for many property-holding males like Crèvecoeur the young country did indeed seem to be utopia. The essay below offered some of the reasons he believed in the inherent superiority of the agrarian republic. His description of the United States affirmed the notion that liberty had made equality possible, and that this new breed—these American people—need not suffer the abuses of power that burdened Europeans.

I wish I could be acquainted with the feelings and thoughts which must agitate the heart and present themselves to the mind of an enlightened Englishman, when he first lands on this continent. He must greatly rejoice that he lived at a time to see this fair country discovered and settled; he must necessarily feel a share of national pride, when he views the chain of settlements which embellishes these extended shores. When he says to himself, this is the work of my countrymen, who, when convulsed by factions, afflicted by a variety of miseries and wants, restless and impatient, took refuge here. They brought along with them their national genius, to which they principally owe what liberty they enjoy, and what substance they possess. Here he sees the industry of his native country displayed in a new manner, and traces in their works the embryos of all the arts, sciences, and ingenuity which flourish in Europe. Here he beholds fair cities, substantial villages, extensive fields, an immense country filled with decent houses, good roads, orchards, meadows, and bridges, where an hundred years ago all was wild, woody, and uncultivated! What a train of pleasing ideas this fair spectacle must suggest; it is a prospect which must inspire a good citizen with the most heartfelt pleasure. The difficulty consists in the manner of viewing so extensive a scene. He is arrived on a new continent; a modern society offers itself to his contemplation, different from what he had hitherto seen. It is not composed, as in Europe, of great lords who possess everything, and of a herd of people who have nothing. Here are no aristocratical families, no courts, no kings, no bishops, no ecclesiastical dominion, no invisible power given to a few very visible one[s]; no great manufacturers employing thousands, no great refinements of luxury. The rich and the poor are not so removed from each other as they are in Europe. Some few towns excepted, we are all tillers of the earth, from Nova Scotia to West Florida. We are a people of cultivators, sc[a]ttered over an immense territory, communicating with each other by means of good roads and navigable rivers, united by the silken

---

*From J. Hector St. John de Crèvecoeur, *Letter from an American Farmer* (New York: E. P. Dutton & Company, 1912), 39–41, 56–58.

bands of mild government, all respecting the laws, without dreading their power, because they are equitable. We are all animated with the spirit of industry, which is unfettered and unrestrained, because each person works for himself. If he travels through our rural district he views not the hostile castle, and the haughty mansion, contrasted with the clay-built and miserable cabin, where cattle and men help to keep each other warm, and dwell in meanness, smoke, and indigence. A pleasing uniformity of decent competence appears throughout our habitations. The meanest of our loghouses is a dry and comfortable habitation. Lawyer or merchant are the fairest titles our towns afford; that of a farmer is the only appellation of the rural inhabitants of our country. It must take some time ere he can reconcile himself to our dictionary, which is but short in words of dignity, and names of honour. There, on a Sunday, he sees a congregation of respectable farmers and their wives, all clad in neat homespun, well mounted, or riding in their own humble waggons. There is not among them an esquire, saving the unlettered magistrate. There he sees a parson as simple as his flock, a farmer who does not rot on the labour of others. We have no princes, for whom we toil, starve, and bleed: we are the most perfect society now existing in the world. Here man is as free as he ought to be; nor is this pleasing equality so transitory as many others are. Many ages will not see the shores of our great lakes replenished with inland nations, nor the unknown bounds of North America entirely peopled. Who can tell the millions of men whom it will feed and contain? for no European foot has yet travelled half the extent of this mighty continent. . . .

There is no wonder that this country has so many charms, and presents to Europeans so many temptations to remain in it. A traveller in Europe becomes a stranger as soon as he quits his own kingdom; but it is otherwise here. We know, properly speaking, no strangers; this is every person's country; the variety of our soils, situations, climates, governments, and produce, hath something which must please everybody. No sooner does an European arrive, no matter of what condition, than his eyes are opened upon the fair prospect; he hears his language spoke, he retraces many of his own country manners, he perpetually hears the names of families and towns with which he is acquainted; he sees happiness and prosperity in all places disseminated; he meets with hospitality, kindness, and plenty everywhere; he beholds hardly any poor, he seldom hears of punishments and executions; and he wonders at the elegance of our towns those miracles of industry and freedom. He cannot admire enough our rural districts, our convenient roads, good taverns, and our many accommodations; he involuntarily loves a country where everything is so lovely. When in England, he was a mere Englishman; here he stands on larger portion of the globe, not less than its fourth part, and may see the production of the north, in iron and naval stores; the provisions of Ireland, the grain of Egypt, the indigo, the rice of China. He does not find, as in Europe, a crowded society, where every place is over-stocked; he does not feel the perpetual collision of parties, that difficulty of beginning, that contention which oversets so many. There is room for everybody in America; has he any particular talent of industry? he exerts it in order to procure a livelihood, and it succeeds. Is he a merchant? the avenues of trade are infinite; is he eminent in any respect? he will be employed and respected. Does he love a country life? pleasant farms present themselves; he may purchase what he wants, and thereby become an American farmer. Is he a labourer, sober and industrius? he need not go many miles, nor receive many informations before he will be hired, well fed at the table of his employer, and paid four or five times more than he can get in Europe. Does he want uncultivated lands? thousands of acres present themselves, which he may purchase cheap. W[h]atever be his talents or inclinations, if they are moderate he may satisfy them. I do not mean that every one who comes here will grow rich in a little time; no, but he may procure an easy, decent maintenance, by his industry. Instead of starving, he will be fed, instead of being idle he will have employment; and these are riches enough for such men as come over here. The rich stay in Europe, it is only the middling and the poor that emigrate. Would you wish to travel in independent idleness, from north to south, you will find easy access, and the most cheerful reception at every house; society without ostentation, good cheer without pride, and every decent diversion which the country affords, with little expense. It is no wonder that the European who has lived here a few years, is desirous to remain; Europe with all its pomp, is not to be compared with this continent, for men of middle stations, or labourers.

An European, when he first arrives, seems limited in his intentions, as well as in his views; but he very suddenly alters his scale; two hundred miles formerly appeared a very great distance, it is now but a trifle; he no sooner breathes our air than he forms schemes, and embarks in designs he never would thought of in his own country. There the plenitude of society confines many useful ideas, and often extinguishes the most laudable schemes which here ripen into maturity. Thus Europeans become Americans. . . .

51. ON MOTHERHOOD*

*T*he patriarchal society of the early nineteenth century assigned very specific roles to women. This so-called cult of domesticity increasingly insisted that women should remain at home and that raising children should be their primary responsibility. Mothers bore a special obligation toward sons. Young men needed to know how to empower themselves and how to preserve liberty in order for the nation to survive. As time passed and the United States embraced egalitarianism, women taught their sons to consider themselves the equals of all other men. For the most part, however, these republican mothers could not empower themselves, economically or socially. Ironically, although they played a key part in ensuring that liberty flourished in America, women were not equal to men. The following selection summarizes the thinking of John Abbott, one of the more influential advocates of the ideals that so profoundly shaped the lives of women in the democratic republic.

Mothers have as powerful an influence over the welfare of future generations as all other causes combined.—Thus far the history of the world has been composed of the narrations of oppression and blood. War has scattered its unnumbered woes. The cry of the oppressed has unceasingly ascended to heaven. Where are we to look for the influence which shall change this scene, and fill the earth with the fruits of peace and benevolence? It is to Christianity as taught from a mother's lips. In nine cases out of ten, the first six or seven years decide the character of the man. If a boy leaves the paternal roof uncontrolled, turbulent and vicious, he will, in all probability, rush on in the mad career of self-indulgence. There are exceptions. But these exceptions are rare. If, on the other hand, your son goes from home accustomed to control himself, he will most undoubtedly retain that habit through life. If he has been taught to make sacrifices of his own enjoyment, that he may promote the happiness of those around him, he will continue to practise benevolence, and consequently he will be respected and useful and happy. If he has adopted firm resolutions to be faithful in all the relations of life, he in all probability will be a virtuous man, and an estimable citizen, and a benefactor of his race.

When our land is filled with virtuous and patriotic mothers, then will it be filled with virtuous and patriotic men. She who was first in the transgression, must be yet the principal earthly instrument in the restoration. Other causes may greatly aid. Other influences must be ready to receive the mind as it comes from the mother's hand, and carry it onward in its improvement. But the mothers of our race must be the chief instruments in its redemption. The brightest rays of the millennial morn must come from the cradle. This sentiment will bear examining; and the more it is examined the more manifestly true will it appear. It is alike the dictate of philosophy and experience. The mother who is neglecting personal effort, and relying upon other influences for the formation of virtuous character in her children, will find, when it is too late, that she has fatally erred. The patriot who hopes that schools, and lyceums, and the general diffusion of knowledge, will promote the

---

*From John S. C. Abbott, *The Mother at Home; or, The Principles of Maternal Duty*, revised and corrected by Daniel Walton (London: John Mason, 1834), 165–67, 182–84.

good order and happiness of the community, while family government is neglected, will find that he is attempting to purify the streams which are flowing from a corrupt fountain. It is maternal influence, after all, which must be the great agent, in the hands of God, in bringing back our guilty race to duty and happiness. O that mothers could feel this responsibility as they ought! then would the world assume a different aspect. Then should we less frequently behold unhappy families and brokenhearted parents. A new race of men would enter upon the busy scene of life, and cruelty and crime would pass away. O mothers! reflect upon the power your Maker has placed in your hands. There is no earthly influence to be compared with yours. There is no combination of causes so powerful, in promoting the happiness of the misery of our race, as the instructions of home. In a most particular sense, God has constituted you the guardians and the controllers of the human family. . . .

There is an impression upon the minds of many, that skill in governing must be instinctive; that it is an original and native talent, and not to be acquired by information or thought. But look at those parents who have been most successful in family government, and they will be found to be those who have most diligently and uniformly attended to the subject. You may go into the family of some man of celebrity in one of the learned professions, and, as you look upon his lawless children, you are perhaps discouraged. You say, If this man, with his powerful and highly-cultivated mind, cannot succeed in family government, how can I expect success? But a little observation will satisfy you that this man is giving his time and attention to other pursuits. He is neglecting his children; and they are forming precisely those characters we should expect from the influences to which they are exposed.

There is no absolute certainty that any procedure will result in the piety of the child. But if we go on in our attempts to govern without system or thought, or care, we shall undoubtedly reap most bitter consequences. The mother must study her duty. She must carefully observe the effect produced by her mode of discipline. There is but little advantage to be derived from books, unless we revolve their contents in our minds. Others may suggest the most valuable ideas. But we must take those ideas and dwell upon them, and trace out their effects, and incorporate them into our minds, by associating them with others of our own. We must accustom ourselves to investigation and thought. The mother who will do this will most certainly grow in wisdom. She will daily perceive that she is acquiring more facility in forming her children the character she desires. And the increasing obedience and affection she will receive will be her constant reward. Care and labour are necessary in training up a family. But no other cares are rewarded with so rich a recompence; no other labours ensure such permanent and real enjoyment. You, O mothers, have immortal souls entrusted to your keeping. Their destiny is in a great degree in your hands. Your ignorance or unfaithfulness may sink them to the world of woe: your fidelity, under the divine blessing, which will not be withheld, may elevate them to the mansions of heaven.

52. TREATY WITH THE WYANDOT, ETC., 1795*

Indian Relations

*W*omen held a dependent role in America, but at least they had a place in the young republic. Indians, on the other hand, did not. Consequently, the history of Indian relations in the United States is generally one of assertions of power that deprived Native Americans of their lands, their freedom, and their culture. This document and the one that follows it offer two examples of treaties between the federal government and various Indian tribes. The first, the Treaty of Greenville, followed the victory of troops under General "Mad" Anthony Wayne at the Battle of Fallen Timbers in 1794. This treaty opened up much of the Northwest Territory for American

*From *Indian Affairs, Laws, and Treaties*, 7 vols., comp. and ed. Charles J. Kappler (Washington, D.C.: U.S. Government Printing Office, 1904–1979), II:36–43.

settlement. The second treaty resulted from General Andrew Jackson's success at the Battle of Horseshoe Bend. The Creek Treaty made available millions of acres that became the southern "Cotton Belt." Both documents, then, helped make possible the agrarian society that served as a foundation for the rapid growth of the new nation.

A treaty of peace between the United States of America and the Tribes of Indians, called the Wyandots, Delawares, Shawnees, Ottawas, Chipewas, Putawatimes, Miamis, Eel-River, Weea's Kickapoos, Piankashaws, and Kaskaskias.

To put an end to a destructive war, to settle all controversies, and to restore harmony and a friendly intercourse between the said United States, and Indian tribes; Anthony Wayne, major-general, commanding the army of the United States, and sole commissioner for the good purposes above-mentioned, and the said tribes of Indians, by their Sachems, chiefs, and warriors, met together at Greenville, the head quarters of the said army, have agreed on the following articles, which, when ratified by the President, with the advice and consent of the Senate of the United States, shall be binding on them and the said Indian tribes.

ARTICLE I.

Henceforth all hostilities shall cease; peace is hereby established, and shall be perpetual; and a friendly intercourse shall take place, between the said United States and Indian tribes.

ARTICLE II.

All prisoners on both sides shall be restored. The Indians, prisoners to the United States, shall be immediately set at liberty. The people of the United States, still remaining prisoners among the Indians, shall be delivered up in ninety days, . . . and ten chiefs of the said tribes shall remain at Greenville as hostages, until the delivery of the prisoners shall be effected.

ARTICLE III.

The general boundary lines between the United States, and the lands of the . . . tribes, shall begin at the Cayahoga River, and run thence up the same to the portage between that and the Tus-carawas branch of the Muskingum; thence down that branch to the crossing place above Fort Lawrence; thence westerly to a fork of that branch of the great Miami River running into the Ohio, at or near which fork stood Loromie's store, and whence commences the portage between the Miami and Ohio, and St. Mary's river, which is a branch of the Miami, which runs into Lake Erie; thence a westerly course to Fort Recovery, which stands on a branch of the Wabash; then south-westerly in a direct line to the Ohio, so as to intersect that river opposite the mouth of the Ken-tucke or Cuttawa river. And in consideration of the peace now established; of the goods formerly received from the United States; of those now to be delivered, and of the yearly delivery of goods . . . to be made hereafter, and to indemnify the United States of the injuries and expenses they have sustained during the war; the . . . tribes do hereby cede and relinquish forever, all their claims to the lands lying eastwardly and southwardly of the general boundary line now described; and these lands, or any part of them, shall never hereafter be made a cause or pretence, on part of the said tribes . . . , of war or injury to the United States. . . .

And for the same considerations, and as an evidence of the returning friendship of the . . . tribes, . . . [they] do also cede to the United States the following pieces of land; to-wit. [Eleven specific pieces of land totaling 408 square miles, plus] . . . (12.) The post of Detroit and all the land to the north, the west, and south of it, of which the Indian title has been extinguished by gifts or grants to the French or English governments; and so much more of the land to be annexed to the district of Detroit as shall be comprehended between the river Rosine on the south, lake St. Clair on the north, and a line . . . six miles distant from the west end of lake Erie, and Detroit river. (13.) The post of Michillimackinac, and all the land on the island, on which that post stands, and the main land adjacent . . . ; and a piece of land on the main to the north of the island, to measure six miles on lake Huron, of the strait between lakes Huron and Michigan, and to extend three miles back from the water of the lake or strait, and also the island De Bois Blanc, being an extra and voluntary gift of the Chipewa nation. (14.) One piece of land six miles square at the mouth of the Chikago river, emptying into the south-west end of Lake Michigan. . . . (15.) One piece twelve miles square at or near the mouth of the Illinois river, emptying into the Mississippi. (16.) One piece six miles square at the old Piorias fort and village, near the south end of the Illinois lake on said Illinois river: And whenever the United States shall think proper to survey and mark the boundaries of the land hereby ceded to them, they shall give timely notice thereof to the . . . Indians, that they may appoint some of their wise chiefs to attend and see that the lines are run according to the terms of this treaty.

And the . . . tribes will allow the people of the United States a free passage by land and by water . . . through their country, along the chain of posts herein before mentioned. . . . And the . . . tribes will also allow to the people of the United States the free use of the harbors and mouths of the rivers along the lakes adjoining Indian lands, for sheltering vessels and boats, and liberty to land their cargoes where necessary for their safety.

ARTICLE IV.

In consideration of the peace now established . . . , and to manifest the liberality of the United States, as the great means of rendering this peace strong and perpetual; the United States relinquish their claims to all other Indian lands northward of the river Ohio, eastward of the Mississippi, and westward and southward of the Great Lakes and the waters uniting them, according to the boundary line agreed on by the United States and the king of Great-Britain, in the treaty of peace made between them in the year 1783. But from this relinquishment by the United States, the following tracts of land, are explicitly excepted. 1st. The tract of one hundred and fifty thousand acres near the rapids of the river Ohio, which has been assigned to General Clark. . . . 2d. The post of St. Vincennes on the river Wabash, and the lands adjacent, of which the Indian title has been extinguished. 3d. The lands at all other places in possession of the French people and other white settlers among them, of which the Indian title has been extinguished. . . ; and 4th. The post of fort Massac towards the mouth of the Ohio. . . .

And for the same considerations and with the same views as above mentioned, the United States now deliver to the . . . tribes a quantity of goods to the value of twenty thousand dollars . . . ; and henceforth every year forever the United States will deliver . . . like useful goods, suited to the circumstances of the Indians, of the value of nine thousand five hundred dollars. . . .

Provided, That if either of the said tribes shall hereafter . . . desire that a part of their annuity should be furnished in domestic animals, implements of husbandry, and other utensils convenient for them, . . . and [to] be employed for their benefit, the same shall at the subsequent annual deliveries be furnished accordingly.

ARTICLE V.

To prevent any misunderstanding about the Indian land relinquished by the United States . . . , it is now explicitly declared, that the meaning of relinquishment is this: The Indian tribes who have a right to those lands, are quietly to enjoy them, hunting, planting, and dwelling thereon as long as they please, without any molestation from the United States; but when those tribes . . . shall be disposed to sell their lands . . . they are to be sold only to the United States; and until such sale, the United States will protect all the . . . tribes. . . . And the . . . tribes again acknowledge themselves to be under the protection of the said United States and no other power whatever.

ARTICLE VI.

If any citizen of the United States, or any other white person or persons, shall presume to settle upon lands now relinquished by the United States, such . . . person shall be out of the protection of the United States; and the Indian tribe, on whose lands the settlement shall be made, may drive off the settler, or punish him in such manner as they shall think fit; and . . . the United States shall be at liberty to . . . remove and punish the settlers as they shall think proper, and so effect the protection of the Indian lands herein before stipulated.

ARTICLE VII.

The . . . Indians, parties to this treaty, shall be at liberty to hunt within the territory . . . they have now ceded to the United States, without hindrance or molestation, so long as they demean themselves peaceably, and offer no injury to the people of the United States.

ARTICLE VIII.

Trade shall be opened with the . . . tribes; and they do hereby respectfully engage to afford protection to such persons . . . as shall be duly licensed to reside among them for the purpose of trade . . . ; but no person shall be permitted to reside at any of their towns or hunting camps as a trader, who is not furnished with a license for that purpose. . . . And if any licensed trader shall abuse his privilege by unfair dealing, upon complaint and proof thereof, his license shall be taken away from him, and he shall be further punished according to the laws of the United States. . . . And to prevent impositions by forged licenses, the said Indians shall at least once a year give information to the superintendent or his deputies, of the names of the traders residing among them.

ARTICLE IX.

Lest the firm peace and friendship now established should be interrupted by the misconduct of individuals, the United States, and the . . . tribes agree, that for injuries done by individuals on either side, no private revenge or retaliation shall take place; but instead thereof, complaint shall be made by the party injured, to the other . . . : and such prudent measures shall then be pursued as shall be necessary to preserve the said peace and friendship. . . . Should any Indian tribes mediate a war against the United States or either of them, and the same shall come to the attention of the . . . tribes, . . . they do hereby engage to give immediate notice thereof to the . . . officer commanding the troops of the United States, at the nearest post. . . . In like manner, the United States shall give notice to the . . . tribes of any harm that may be meditated against them . . . ; and do all in their power to hinder and prevent the same. . . .

ARTICLE X.

All other treaties heretofore made between the United States and the . . . tribes . . . since the treaty of 1783, between the United States and Great Britain, that come within the purview of this treaty, shall henceforth cease and become void.

53. TREATY WITH THE CREEKS, 1814*

*S*ee headnote for preceding document.

Articles of agreement and capitulation, made and concluded this ninth day of August, one thousand eight hundred and fourteen, between major general Andrew Jackson, on behalf of the President of the United States of America, and the chiefs, deputies, and warriors of the Creek Nation.

WHEREAS an unprovoked, inhuman, and sanguinary war, waged by the hostile Creeks against the United States, hath been repelled, prosecuted, and determined, successfully, on the part of the said States, in conformity with principles of national justice and honorable warfare—And whereas consideration is due to the rectitude of proceeding dictated by instructions relating to the re-establishment of peace: be it remembered, that prior to the conquest of that part of the Creek nation hostile to the United States, numberless aggressions had been committed against the peace, property, and the lives of citizens of the United States, and those of the Creek nation in amity with her, at the mouth of Duck river, Fort Mimms, and elsewhere, contrary to national faith, and the

*From *Indian Affairs, Laws, and Treaties*, 7 vols., comp. and ed. Charles J. Kappler (Washington, D.C.: U.S. Government Printing Office, 1904–1979), II:107–09.

regard due to an article of the treaty concluded at New-York, in the year seventeen hundred ninety, between the two nations: That the United States, previously to the perpetration of such outrages did, in order to ensure future amity and concord between the Creek nation and the said states, in conformity with the stipulations of former treaties, fulfil, with punctuality and good faith, her engagements to the said nation: that more than two-thirds of the whole number of chiefs and warriors of the Creek nation, disregarding the genuine spirit of existing treaties, suffered themselves to be instigated to violations of their national honor, and the respect due to a part of their own nation faithful to the United States and the principles of humanity, by impostures [impostors,] denominating themselves Prophets, and by the duplicity and misrepresentations of foreign emissaries, whose governments are at war, open and understood, with the United States. Wherefore,

1st—The United States demand an equivalent for all expenses incurred in prosecuting the war to its termination, by a cession of all the territory belonging to the Creek nation within the territories of the United States, lying west, south, and south-eastwardly, of a line to be run and described by persons duly authorized by the President of the United States—Beginning at a point on the eastern bank of the Coosa river, where the south boundary line of the Cherokee nation crosses the same; running from thence . . . to a point one mile above the mouth of Cedar creek, at Fort Williams, thence . . . to a point opposite the upper end of the great falls, (called by the natives Woetumka,) thence east . . . to a point due north of the mouth of Ofucshee, thence south . . . to the mouth of Ofucshee on the south side of the Tallapoosa river, thence up the same . . . to a point where a direct course will cross the same at the distance of ten miles from the mouth thereof, thence a direct line to the mouth of Summochico creek, . . . thence east . . . to a point which shall intersect the line now dividing the lands claimed by the said Creek nation from those owned and claimed by the state of Georgia; Provided, nevertheless, that where any possession of any chief or warrior of the Creek nation, who shall have been friendly to the United States during the war, and taken an active part therein, shall be within the territory ceded by these articles to the United States, every person shall be entitled to a reservation of land within the said territory of one mile square, to include his improvements as near the centre thereof as may be, which shall inure to the said chief or warrior, and his descendants, so long as he or they shall continue to occupy the same, who shall be protected by and subject to the laws of the United States; but upon the voluntary abandonment thereof . . . the right of occupancy or possession of said lands shall devolve to the United States. . . .

2nd—The United States will guarantee to the Creek nation, the integrity of all their territory eastwardly and northwardly of the said line to be run and described as mentioned in the first article.

3d—The United States demand, that the Creek nation abandon all communication, and cease to hold any intercourse with any British or Spanish post, garrison, or town; and that they shall not admit among them, any agent or trader, who shall not derive authority to hold commercial, or other intercourse with them, by licence from the President or authorized agent of the United States.

4th—The United States demand an acknowledgment of the right to establish military posts and trading houses, and to open roads within the territory, guaranteed to the Creek nation by the second article, and a right to free navigation of all its waters.

5th—The United States demand, that a surrender be immediately made, of all the persons and property taken from the citizens of the United States, the friendly part of the Creek nation, the Cherokee, Chickasaw, and Choctaw nations, to the respective owners; and the United States will cause to be immediately restored to the formerly hostile Creeks, all the property taken from them since their submission, either by the United States, or by any Indian nation in amity with the United States, together with all the prisoners taken from them during the war.

6th—The United States demand the caption and surrender of all the prophets and instigators of the war, whether foreigners or natives, who have not submitted to the arms of the United States, and become party to these articles of capitulation, if ever they shall be found within the territory guaranteed to the Creek nation. . . .

7th—The Creek nation being reduced to extreme want, and not at present having the means of subsistence, the United States, from motives of humanity, will continue to furnish gratuitously the necessaries of life, until the crops of corn can be considered competent to yield the nation a supply, and will establish trading houses in the nation . . . to enable the nation, by industry and economy, to procure clothing.

8th—A permanent peace shall ensue from the date of these presents forever, between the Creek nation and the United States, and between the Creek nation and the Cherokee, Chickasaw, and Choctaw nations. . . .

The parties to these presents, after due consideration, for themselves and their constituents, agree to ratify and confirm the preceding articles, and constitute the basis of a permanent peace between the two nations. . . .

54. TECUMSEH STANDS AGAINST WHITE ENCROACHMENT 1810*

The flood of American settlers after the American Revolution into the trans-Appalachian region alarmed many Native Americans. Visionaries arose within Indian society who sought to regenerate native society and expel all whites from traditional tribal lands. After 1805 the Shawnee prophet Tenskwatawa preached a religious message of unity and a return to the old ways, establishing Prophetstown (Tippecanoe) in what is now Indiana. By 1810 Tecumseh had joined his brother Tenskwatawa and had created an Indian alliance to stop further encroachment by whites. Tecumseh declared himself to be the sole representative of the Indians north of the Ohio River; any land cessions not authorized by him were invalid. Tenskwatawa's prophecy of regeneration coupled with Tecumseh's political leadership united the Indians in the Old Northwest in an unprecedented stance against the rising tide of American settlement. In the following excerpt, Tecumseh outlines the various grievances that Indians had about the encroachment of whites.

You ought to know that after we agreed to bury the Tomahawk at Greenville we then found their new fathers in the Americans who told us they would treat us well, not like the British who gave us but a small piece of pork every day. I want now to remind you of the promises of the white people. . . .

Brother. Since the peace was made you have kill'd some of the Shawanese, Winebagoes Delawares and Miamies and you have taken our lands from us and I do not see how we can remain at peace with you if you continue to do so. You have given goods to the Kickapoos for the sale of their lands to you which has been the cause of many deaths amongst them. You have promised us assistance but I do not see that you have given us any.

You try to force the red people to do some injury. It is you that is pushing them on to do mischief. You endeavour to make destructions, you wish to prevent the Indians to do as we wish them to unite and let them consider their land as the common property of the whole you take tribes aside and advise them not to come into this measure and untill our design is accomplished we do not wish to accept of your invitation to go and visit the President.

The reason I tell you this is—You want by your distinctions of Indian tribes in allotting to each a particular track of land to make them to war with each other. You never see an Indian come and endeavour to make the white people do so. You are continually driving the red people when at last you will drive them into the great lake where they can't either stand or work.

Brother. You ought to know what you are doing with the Indians. Perhaps it is by direction of the President to make those distinctions. It is a very bad thing and we do not like it. Since my residence at Tippecanoe we have endeavoured to level all distinctions to destroy village chiefs by

*From *Governors' Messages and Papers*, ed. Logan B. Esarey, Indiana Historical Collections (Indianapolis: Indiana Historical Commission, 1922), VII:463–67.

whom all mischief is done; it is they who sell our land to the Americans our object is to let all our affairs be transacted by Warriors.

Brother. This land that was sold and the goods that was given for it was only done by a few. The treaty was afterwards brought here and the Weas were induced to give their consent because of their small numbers. The treaty at Fort Wayne was made through the threats of Winamac but in future we are prepared to punish those chiefs who may come forward to propose to sell their land. If you continue to purchase of them it will produce war among the different tribes and at last I do not know what will be the consequences to the white people.

Brother. I was glad to hear your speech you said if we could show that the land was sold by persons that had no right to sell you would restore it, that that did sell did not own it was me. These tribes set up a claim but the tribes with me will not agree to their claim, if the land is not restored to us you will soon see when we return to our homes how it will be settled. We shall have a great council at which all the tribes shall be present when we will show to those who sold that they had no right to see the claim they set up and we will know what will be done with those Chiefs that did sell the land to you. I am not alone in this determination it is the determination of all the warriors and red people that listen to me.

I now wish you to listen to me. If you do not it will appear as if you wished me to kill all the chiefs that sold you this land. I tell you so because I am authorised by all the tribes to do so. I am at the head of them all. I am a Warrior and all the Warriors will meet together in two or three moons from this. Then I will call for those chiefs that sold you that land and shall know what to do with them. If you do not restore the land you will have a hand in killing them.

Brother. Do not believe that I came here to get presents from you if you offer us anything we will not take it. By taking goods from you you will hereafter say that with them you purchased another piece of land from us. If we want anything we are able to buy it, from your traders. Since the land was sold to you no traders come among us. I now wish you would clear all the roads and let the traders come among us. Then perhaps some of our young men will occasionally call upon you to get their guns repaired. This is all the assistance we ask of you. . . .

Brother. It has been the object of both myself and brother from the beginning to prevent the lands being sold should you not return the land, it will occasion us to call a great council that will meet at the Huron Village where the council fire has already been lighted. At which those who sold the land shall be call'd and shall suffer for their conduct.

Brother. I wish you would take pity on all the red people and do what I have requested. If you will not give up the land and do cross the boundary of your present settlement it will be very hard and produce great troubles among us. How can we have confidence in the white people when Jesus Christ came upon the earth you kill'd and nail'd him on a cross, you thought he was dead but you were mistaken. You have shaken among you and you laugh and make light of their worship. . . .

55. DAVY CROCKETT*

*D*avid Crockett was a frontier entrepreneur who served as a scout during the Creek campaign and sat in the Tennessee legislature as well as the national Congress before his death at the Battle of the Alamo immortalized him as an American hero. Early in his career, Crockett had created an alter ego—"Davy"—that helped ensure his fame. Davy Crockett epitomized that archetypical rugged individualist who helped make egalitarianism a key theme in American history. The following selection, taken from his autobiography, shows how he created

*From *Life of Col. David Crockett, Written by Himself. Comprising His Early Life, Hunting Adventures, Services Under General Jackson in the Creek War, Electioneering Speeches, Career in Congress, Triumphal Tour in the Northern States, and Services in the Texan War. To Which is Added An Account of Colonel Crockett's Glorious Death at the Alamo, While Fighting in Defense of Texan Independence. By the Editor* (Philadelphia: G. G. Evans, 1859), 125–29, 135–37.

his image as a dauntless frontiersman and as a simple populist representative of the people. A dedicated husband and father who could meet extraordinary challenges, a fearless man who refused to suffer defeat, and an intrepid hunter who could "grin a bear out of a tree," Crockett was also an astute observer who understood well the nature of politics in a democratic society.

I gathered my corn, and then set out for my Fall's hunt. This was in the last of October 1822. I found bear very plenty, and, indeed, all sorts of game and wild varments, except buffalo. There was none of them. I hunted on till Christmas, having supplied my family very well all along with wild meat, at which time my powder gave out; and I had none either to fire Christmas guns, which is very common in that country, or to hunt with. I had a brother-in-law who had now moved out and settled about six miles west of me, on the opposite side of Rutherford's fork of the Obion river, and he had brought me a keg of powder, but I had never gotten it home. There had just been another of Noah's freshes, and the low grounds were flooded all over with water. I know'd the stream was at least a mile wide which I would have to cross, as the water was from hill to hill, and yet I determined to go on over in some way or another, so as to get my powder. I told this to my wife, and she immediately opposed it with all her might. I still insisted, telling her that we had no powder for Christmas, and, worse than all, we were out of meat. She said, we had as well starve as for me to freeze to death or to get drowned, and one or the other was certain if I attempted to go.

But I didn't believe the half of this; and so I took my woolen wrappers, and a pair of moccasins, and put them on, and tied up some dry clothes, and a pair of shoes and stockings, and started. But I didn't before know how much anybody could suffer and not die. This, and some of my other experiments in water, learned me something about it, and I therefore relate them.

The snow was about four inches deep when I started; and when I got to water, which was only about a quarter of a mile off, it looked like an ocean. I put in, and waded on till I come to the channel, where I crossed that on a high log. I then took water again, having my gun and all my hunting tools along, and waded till I came to a deep slough, that was wider than the river itself. I had crossed it often on a log; but behold, when I got there, no log was to be seen. . . . I then felt my way along with my feet, in the water, about waist deep, but it was a mighty ticklish business. However, I got over, and by this time I had very little feeling in my feet and legs, as I had been all the time in the water. . . .

I went but a short distance before I came to another slough, over which there was a log, and it was floating on the water. I thought I could walk it, and so I mounted on it; but when I had got about the middle of the deep water, somehow or somehow else, it turned over, and in I went up to my head. I waded out of this deep water, and went ahead until I came to a highland, where I stopp'd to pull of my wet clothes, and put on the others, which I had held up with my gun, above the water, when I fell in. I got them on, but my flesh had no feeling in it, I was so cold. I tied up the wet ones, and hung them up in a bush. I now thought I would run, so as to warm myself a little, but I couldn't raise a trot for some time; indeed, I couldn't step more than half the length of my foot. After awhile I got better, and went on five miles to the house of my brother-in-law, having not even smelt fire from the time I started. I got there late in the evening, and he was much astonished at seeing me at such a time. I staid all night, and the next morning was most piercing cold, and so they persuaded me not to go home that day. I agreed, and turned out and killed him two deer; but the weather still got worse and colder, instead of better. I staid that night, and in the morning they still insisted I couldn't get home. I knowed the water would be frozen over, but not hard enough to bear me, and so I agreed to stay that day. I went out hunting again, and pursued a big he-bear all day, but didn't kill him. The next morning was bitter cold, but I knowed my family was without meat, and I determined to get home to them, or die a-trying.

I took my keg of powder, and all my hunting tools, and cut out. When I got to the water, it was a sheet of ice as far as I could see. I put on to it, but hadn't got far before it broke through with me;

and so I took out my tomahawk, and broke my way along before me for a considerable distance. At last I got to where the ice would bear me for a short distance, and I mounted on it, and went ahead; but it soon broke again, and I had to wade on. . . . By this time I was nearly frozen to death, but I saw all along before me, where the ice had been fresh broke, and I thought it might be a bear straggling about in the water. I, therefore, fresh primed my gun, and, cold as I was, I was determined to make war on him, if we met. But I followed the trail till it led me home, and I then found it had been made by a young man that lived with me, who had been sent out by my distressed wife to see, if he could, what had become of me, for they all believed that I was dead. When I got home, I wasn't quite dead, but mighty nigh it; but had my powder, and that was what I went for. . . .

I had on hand a great many skins, and so, in the month of February, I packed a horse with them, and taking my eldest son with me, cut out for a little town called Jackson, situated about forty miles off. We got there well enough, and I sold my skins, and bought me some coffee, and sugar, powder, lead, and salt. I packed them all up in readiness for a start, which I intended to make early the next morning. Morning came, but I concluded, before I started, I would go and take a horn with some of my old fellow-soldiers that I had met with at Jackson.

I did so; and while we were engaged in this, I met with three candidates for the Legislature. A Doctor Butler, who was, by marriage, a nephew to General Jackson, a Major Lynn, and a Mr. McEver, all first-rate men. We all took a horn together, and some person present said to me, "Crockett, you must offer for the Legislature." I told him I lived at least forty miles from any white settlement; and had no thought of becoming a candidate at that time. So we all parted, and I and my little boy went on home.

It was about a week or two after this, that a man came to my house, and told me I was a candidate. I told him not so. But he took out a newspaper from his pocket, and showed me where I was announced. I said to my wife that this was all a burlesque on me, but I was determined to make it cost the man who had put it at least the value of the printing, and of the fun he wanted at my expense. So I hired a young man to work in my place on the farm, and turned out myself electioneering. I hadn't been out long, before I found the people began to talk very much about the bear hunter, the man from the cane; and the three gentlemen, who I have already named, soon found it necessary to enter into an agreement to have a sort of caucus at their March court, to determine which of them was the strongest, and the other two was to withdraw and support him. As the court came on, each one of them spread himself, to secure the nomination; but it fell on Dr. Butler, and the rest backed out. The doctor was a clever fellow, and I have often said he was the most talented man I ever run against for any office. His being related to General Jackson also helped him on very much; but I was in for it, and I was determined to push ahead and go through, or stick. Their meeting was held in Madison county, which was the strongest in the representative district, which was composed of eleven counties, and they seemed bent on having the member from there.

At the time Colonel Alexander was a candidate for Congress, and attending one of his public meetings one day, I walked to where he was treating the people, and he gave me an introduction to several of his acquaintances, and informed them that I was out electioneering. In a little time my competitor, Doctor Butler, came along; he passed by without noticing me, and I supposed, he did not recognize me. But I hailed him, as I was for all sorts of fun; and when he turned to me, I said to him, "Well, doctor, I suppose they have weighed you out to me; but I should like to know why they fixed your election for **March** instead of **August**? This is," said I, "a branfire new way of doing business, if a caucus is to make a representative of the people!" He now discovered who I was, and cried out, "D____n it, Crockett, is that you?" "Be sure it is," said I, "but I don't want it understood that I have come electioneering. I have just crept out of the cane, to see what discoveries I could make among the white folks." I told him that when I set out electioneering, I would go prepared to put every man on as good a footing as when I found him on. I would therefore have me a large buckskin hunting-shirt made, with a couple of pockets holding about a peck each; and that in one I would carry a great big twist of tobacco, and in the other my bottle of liquor; for I knowed when I met a man and offered him a dram, he would throw out his quid of tobacco to take one, and after he had taken his horn, I would out with my twist, and give him another chew. And in this way he would not be worse off than when I found him; and I would be sure to leave him in a first-rate good humor. He said I could beat him electioneering all hollow. I told him I would give him better evidence of that before August, notwithstanding he had many advantages over me, and particularly in the way of money; but I told him I would go on the products of the country; that I had industrious children, and the best of coondogs; and they would hunt every night till midnight to suport my election; and when the coon fur wasn't good, I would myself go a wolfing, and shoot down a wolf, and skin his head, and his scalp would be good to me for three dollars, in our State Treasury money; and in this way I would get along on the big string. He stood like he was both amused and astonished, and the whole crowd was in a roar of laughter. From this place I returned home, leaving the people in a first-rate way, and I was sure I would do a good business among them. At any rate, I was determined to stand up to my lick-log, salt or no salt.

In a short time there came out two other candidates, a Mr. Shaw and a Mr. Brown. We all ran the race through; and when the election was over, it turned that I had beat them all by a majority of two hundred and forty-seven votes, and was again returned as a member of the Legislature from a new region of the country, without losing a session. This reminded me of the old saw—"A fool for luck, and a poor man for children."

56. THE SLAVE TRADE, 1817*

Slavery in the United States was always a complex concern. A nation founded on liberty, and one becoming more dedicated to equality, enslaved millions of African Americans. That paradox caused intense debates over slavery, in both the North and the South. The following document, originally published in a New Orleans newspaper and reproduced in a leading national periodical, revealed that the slave trade, like many elements of the peculiar institution, did not enjoy unmitigated support in the slave states.

SLAVE TRADE—The legislatures of several of the southern states have passed very severe laws to check the late infamous trade that has been carried on in negroes. Of that enacted by *Georgia*, the Journal observes—"A section of our new penal code interdicts, under very severe penalties, the introduction of slaves into this state by negro traders for speculation—subjecting to a fine of a thousand dollars and to five years imprisonment in the penitentiary, the person who shall bring into the state a slave, and sell or offer for sale, *such slave within one year thereafter*, with the exception only of emigrants from the other states, who are allowed to bring with them, and dispose of as they think proper, slaves who are their *bona fide* property. It will be observed, that the section above alluded to, does not prevent residents of this state or others, from bringing negroes into it *for their own use*, but subjects them to the severe penalties of the act, *if they sell or offer them for sale within a specified time*."

By the law of *South Carolina*, it is made felony to introduce a slave into the state except by express permission of the legislature. This will seriously interfere with the business of many a scoundrel kidnapper and dealer in Maryland and elsewhere.

An increased vigilance is also manifested in *North Carolina*—some kidnappers have been caught there and imprisoned, we hope for life.

Louisiana appears alarmed at being made the depot of the very worst class of slaves, vomitings of the jails and penitentiaries and the refuse of all the rest of the states; and seems about to take measures to check the trade.

---

*From *Niles' Weekly Register* (Baltimore: H. Niles, 1817), XI:399–400.

This business of negro slavery is much easier deprecated than removed, even if all were consenting to it. It is to the praise of the American people that slaves were originally introduced against their consent and that they, first of all, enacted laws to abolish the trade. It is a great grievance—and how we are to be relieved of it has never yet been satisfactorily proposed—except in the gradual amelioration of their condition, preparatory to gradual emancipation. In the first stage of this mighty work, we are happy to believe that very considerable progress is making.

Negro convicts.—Some inhuman speculator at New York, has disburthened the prisons of that city of seventy or eighty negroes, by procuring their imprisonment to be committed for transportation, and shipping them for this place—where they arrived a few days ago. But he has been disappointed in his expectation of profit, and we doubt if he will clear even the freight of his cargo. The corporation has very properly ordered the vessel containing this gang of thieves and ruffians, to proceed without the limits of the city. We hope their exertions will not stop here: but that they will endeavour to bring to signal punishment every person concerned in this most villainous traffic.

[From] *New Orleans paper.*

Discussion

1. Based on the documents, how might various members of American society, such as male farmers, women, Indians, and slaves, have viewed liberty, equality, and power between 1790 and 1820?

2. The selection by J. Hector St. John de Crèvecoeur is different from many of the previously presented documents because he discusses neither power nor liberty. Why are these topics not discussed? How does his description of the early republic show the growing importance of equality to Americans?

3. Compare the preface and opening paragraph of the Treaty of Greenville with that of the Treaty with the Creeks. What do the two documents suggest about the nature of national power in 1795 and in 1814? What do they suggest about perceptions of power by the people who wrote the treaties? Is there anything in the selections that indicates prospects of liberty or equality for the Indians? If so, what? If not, why?

4. Based on the passage from Davy Crockett's autobiography, what might you conclude that Crockett thought about equality? Did he consider himself the equal of others? Did he embrace political egalitarianism? Were liberty and power important matters to him?

5. How do you think Mrs. Crockett might have reacted to the advice John Abbott gave to mothers? How might the women who read Abbott's books and frontier wives like Crockett have differed or been similar in their views of liberty, equality, and power?

6. What do you think led to the laws that curtailed the slave trade in different southern states? Does the document reveal concern for the liberties or equality of slaves? Does it deal with issues of power, and if so, whose?

7. Based on the Tecumseh document, what motivated the Native Americans to unite against white encroachment? What does this document reveal about Tecumseh's views about power? How do you think he was received by U.S. officials?

CHAPTER 8

Completing the Revolution, 1789–1815

Disagreements between Federalists and Republicans took many forms. Newspapers practiced character assassination, opposing factions fought in the streets, and violence spread to the hallowed floor of the House of Representatives. The pictured fight took place on February 15, 1798, between Republican Matthew Lyon (with the fire tongs) and Federalist Roger Griswold.

War gained America its independence, and the Constitution created a government for the new republic, but the country still faced tremendous challenges. Domestic programs had to be enacted and a vision for the nation articulated. Moreover, foreign powers seemed to dismiss the United States, and many Americans believed that they had to gain the respect of Europe before the Revolution would be complete. Between 1790 and 1815, the executive branch of the government played a critical role in accomplishing those tasks. Although coequal with the legislature and the judiciary, the president and the cabinet took a dynamic part in defining the relationship of liberty, equality, and power in the United States. Alexander Hamilton and George Washington proved to be particularly important in the development of the nation, but Jeffersonians believed that the Federalists assumed too much authority and that the policies they established imperiled liberty and equality. Beginning with Jefferson's election to the presidency in 1800, consequently, Republicans worked to dismantle state power in order to preserve revolutionary ideals. They found, however, that the agrarian republic they so admired was undergoing a transformation—one that in some ways would be as significant as the changes that occurred between 1775 and 1790.

57. MANUFACTURES, 1791*

Alexander Hamilton, who as secretary of the treasury ensured the financial strength of the nation, often advanced almost prerevolutionary attitudes toward power and liberty. He viewed property rights, especially as they related to commerce and manufacturing, as the fundamental source of liberty. He also believed that governments had to exercise power in order to protect and expand those essential rights. Many of his policies, therefore, dealt with matters of economic power and with the nature of the government's ability to deal with such issues. His 1791 Report on Manufactures revealed his economic insight, and it profoundly defined the debate over financial programs in the early years of the republic. In addition, his principles have continued to influence national policy for more than two hundred years. The following selection suggested ways in which the government might use its authority to encourage the growth of industry.

The expediency of encouraging manufactures in the United States, which was not long since deemed very questionable, appears at this time to be pretty generally admitted. The embarrassments which have obstructed the progress of our external trade, have led to serious reflections on the necessity of enlarging the sphere of our domestic commerce. The restrictive regulations, which, in foreign markets, abridge the vent of the increasing surplus of our agricultural produce, serve to beget an earnest desire that a more extensive demand for that surplus may be created at

---

*From *The Works of Alexander Hamilton*, 12 vols., ed. Henry Cabot Lodge (New York: G. P. Putnam's Sons, 1904), IV:70–71, 138–59.

home; and the complete success which has rewarded manufacturing enterprise in some valuable branches, conspiring with the promising symptoms which attend some less mature essays in others, justify a hope that the obstacles to the growth of the species of industry are less formidable than they were apprehended to be, and that it is not difficult to find, in its further extension, a full indemnification for any external disadvantages, which are or may be experienced, as well as an accession of resources, favorable to national independence and safety. . . .

It is not uncommon to meet with an opinion, that, though the promoting of manufactures may be the interest of a part of the Union, it is contrary to that of another part. The Northern and Southern regions are sometimes represented as having adverse interests in this respect. Those are called manufacturing, these agricultural States; and a species of opposition is imagined to subsist between the manufacturing and agricultural interests.

The idea of an opposition between those two interests is the common error of the early periods of every country; but experience gradually dissipates it. Indeed, they are perceived so often to succor and befriend each other, that they come at length to be considered as one—a supposition which has been frequently abused, and is not universally true. Particular encouragements of particular manufactures may be of a nature to sacrifice the interests of landholders to those of manufacturers; but it is nevertheless a maxim, well established by experience, and generally acknowledged, where there has been sufficient experience, that the aggregate prosperity of manufactures and the aggregate prosperity of agriculture are intimately connected. . . .

Ideas of a contrariety of interests between the Northern and Southern regions of the Union are, in the main, as unfounded as they are mischievous. The diversity of circumstances, on which such contrariety is usually predicated, authorizes a directly contrary conclusion. Mutual wants constitute one of the strongest links of political connection; and the extent of these bears a natural proportion to the diversity in the means of mutual supply. . . .

In proportion as the mind is accustomed to trace the intimate connection of interest which subsists between all the parts of a society united under the same government, the infinite variety of channels will serve to circulate the prosperity of each, to and through the rest,—in that proportion will be little apt to be disturbed by solicitudes and apprehensions which originate in local discriminations. . . .

But there are more particular considerations which serve to fortify the idea that the encouragement of manufactures is the interest of all parts of the Union. If the Northern and Middle States should be the principal scenes of such establishments, they would immediately benefit the more Southern, by creating a demand for productions, some of which they have in common with the other States, and others, which are either peculiar to them, or more abundant, or of better quality, than elsewhere. . . .

If, then, it satisfactorily appears, that it is the interest of the United States, generally, to encourage manufactures, it merits particular attention, that there are circumstances which render the present a critical moment for entering, with zeal, upon the important business. The effort cannot fail to be materially seconded by a considerable and increasing influx of money, in consequence of foreign speculations in the funds, and by the disorders which exist in different parts of Europe. . . .

There is, at the present juncture, a certain fermentation of mind, a certain activity of [foreign] speculation which, if properly directed, may be made subservient to useful purposes; but which, if left entirely to itself, may be attended with pernicious effects.

The disturbed state of Europe inclining its citizens to emigration, the requisite workmen will be more easily acquired than at another time; and the effect of multiplying the opportunities of employment to those who emigrate, may be an increase of the number and extent of valuable acquisitions to the population, arts, and industry of the country.

To find pleasure in the calamities of other nations should be criminal; but to benefit ourselves, by opening an asylum to these who suffer in consequence of them, is as justifiable as it is politic. . . .

[I]t is proper . . . to consider the means by which [the promotion of manufactures] may be effected, as introductory to a specification of the objects, which, in the present state of things, appear the most fit to be encouraged, and of the particular measures which it may be advisable to adopt, in respect to each.

In order to a better judgment of the means proper to be resorted to by the United States, it will be of use to advert to those which have been enjoyed with success in other countries. The principal of these are:

1. *Protecting duties—or duties on those foreign articles which are the rivals of the domestic ones intended to be encouraged*

    Duties of this nature evidently amount to a virtual bounty on the domestic fabrics; since, by enhancing the charges of foreign articles, they enable the national manufactures to undersell all their foreign competitors. . . . [I]t has the additional recommendation of being a source of revenue. Indeed, all the duties imposed on imported articles, have . . . a beneficent aspect toward the manufactures of the country.

2. *Prohibitions of rival articles, or duties equivalent to prohibitions*

    This is another and an efficacious mean of encouraging national manufactures; but, in general, it is only fit to be employed when a manufacture has made such progress, and is in so many hands, as to insure a due competition, and an adequate supply on reasonable terms. . . .

    Considering a monopoly of the domestic market to its own manufactures as the reigning policy of manufacturing nations, a similar policy, on the part of the United States, in every proper instance, is dictated, it might almost be said, by the principles of distributive justice; certainly, by the duty if endeavoring to secure to their own citizens a reciprocity of advantages.

3. *Prohibitions of the exportation of the materials of manufacture*

    The desire of securing a cheap and plentiful supply for the national workmen, and where the article is either peculiar to the country, or of a peculiar quality there, the jealousy of enabling foreign workmen to rival those of the nation with its own materials, are the leading motives to this species of regulation. It ought not to be affirmed that it is no instance proper; but is, certainly, one that ought to be adopted with great circumspection, and only in very plain cases. It is seen at once, that its immediate operation is to abridge the demand, and keep down the price of the produce of some other branch of industry—generally speaking, of agriculture—to the prejudice of those who carry it on; and . . . prudence seems to dictate that the expedient in question ought to be indulged with a sparing hand.

4. *Pecuniary bounties*

    This has been found one of the most efficacious means of encouraging manufactures, and is, in some views, the best. Though it has not yet been practised upon by the Government of the United States . . . , and though it is less favored by public opinion than some other modes, its advantages are these:

    1. It is a species of encouragement more positive and direct than any other, and, for that very reason, has a more immediate tendency to stimulate and uphold new enterprises. . . .
    2. It avoids the inconvenience of a temporary augmentation of price, which is incident to some other modes; or it produces it to a less degree, either by making no addition to the charges of the rival foreign articles, as is the case of protecting duties, or by making a smaller addition. . . . Indeed the bounty . . . is calculated to promote a reduction of price; because without laying any new charge on the foreign article, it serves to introduce a competition with it, and to increase the total quantity of the article in the market.
    3. Bounties have not, like high protecting duties, a tendency to produce scarcity. . . .

4. Bounties are, sometimes, not only the best but the only proper expedient for uniting the encouragement of a new object of agriculture with that of a new object of manufacture. . . .

Except the simple and ordinary kinds of household manufacture or those for which there are very commanding local advantages, pecuniary bounties are, in most cases, indispensable to the introduction of a new branch. A stimulus and a support, not less powerful and direct, is, generally speaking, essential to the overcoming of the obstacles which arise from the competitions of a superior skills and maturity elsewhere. . . .

The continuance of bounties on manufactures long established must always be of questionable policy; because a presumption would arise, in every such case, that there were natural and inherent impediments to success. But, in new undertakings, they are justifiable as they are oftentimes necessary. . . .

5. *Premiums*

These are of a nature allied to bounties, though distinguishable from them in some important features.

Bounties are applicable to the whole quantity of an article produced, or manufactured, or exported, and involve a correspondent expense. Premiums serve to reward some particular excellence or superiority, some extraordinary exertion or skill, and are dispensed only in a small number of cases. But their effect is to stimulate general effort. . . . They are, accordingly, a very economical means of exciting the enterprise of a whole community. . . .

6. *The exemption of the materials of manufactures from duty*

The policy of that exemption, . . . particularly in reference to new establishments, is obvious. It can hardly ever be advisable to add the obstructions of fiscal burthens to the difficulties which naturally embarrass a new manufacture; and where it is matured, in condition to become an object of revenue, it is . . . better that the fabric, than the material, should be the subject of taxation. . . .

7. *Drawbacks of the duties which are imposed on the materials of manufactures*

It has already been observed, as a general rule, that duties on those materials ought, with certain exceptions, to be forborne. Of these exceptions, three cases occur, which may serve as examples. One, where the material is itself an object of general or extensive consumption, and a fit and productive source of revenue. Another, where a manufacture of a simpler kind, the competition of which, with a like domestic article, is desired to be restrained, partakes of the nature of the raw material, from being capable, by a further process, to be converted into a manufacture of a different kind, the introduction or growth of which is desired to be encouraged. A third, where the material itself is a production of the country, and in sufficient abundance to furnish a cheap and plentiful supply to the national manufactures. . . .

8. *The encouragement of new inventions and discoveries at home, and of the introduction into the United States of such as may have been made in other countries; particularly those that relate to machinery*

This is among the most useful and unexceptionable of the aids which can be given to manufactures. The usual means of that encouragement are pecuniary rewards, and, for a time, exclusive privileges. . . . But it is desirable, in regard to improvements, and secrets of extraordinary value, to be able to extend the same benefits to introducers, as well as authors and inventors; a policy which has been practised with advantage in other countries. . . .

9. *Judicious regulations for the inspection of manufactured commodities*

This is not among the least important of the means by which prosperity of manufactures may be promoted. It is, indeed, in many cases, one of the most essential. Contributing to prevent frauds upon consumers at home and exporters to foreign countries, to improve the quality and preserve the character of the national manufactures, it cannot fail to aid the expeditious and advantageous sale of them, and to serve as a guard against successful competition from other quarters.

10. *The facilitating of pecuniary remittances from place to place—*

It is a point of considerable moment to trade in general, and to manufactures in particular, by rendering more easy the purchase of raw materials and provisions, and the payment for manufacturing supplies. A general circulation of bank money, which is to be expected from the institution lately established, will be a most valuable means to this end. But much good would also accrue from some additional provisions regarding inland bills of exchange. If those drawn in one State, payable in another, were made negotiable everywhere, . . . it would greatly promote negotiations between the citizens of different States, by rendering them more secure, and with it the convenience and advantage of the merchants and manufacturers of each.

11. *The facilitating of transportation of commodities*

Improvements favoring this object intimately concern all the domestic interests of a community; but they may, without impropriety, be mentioned as having an important relation to manufactures. There is, perhaps, scarcely anything which has been better calculated to assist the manufacturers of Great Britain than the melioration of the public roads of that kingdom, and the great progress which has been made of late in opening canals. Of the former, the United States stand much in need; for the latter, they present uncommon facilities.

The symptoms of attention to the improvement of inland navigation which have lately appeared in some quarters . . . must fill with pleasure every breast warmed with a true zeal for the prosperity of the country. These examples, it is to be hoped, will stimulate the exertions of the government and citizens of every State. There can certainly be no object more worthy of the cares of the local administration; and it were to be wished there was no doubt of the power of the National Government to lend its direct aid on a comprehensive plan. This is one of those improvements which could be prosecuted with more efficacy by the whole than by any part or parts of the Union. . . .

58. THE WHISKEY REBELLION, 1794*

In a direct challenge to federal authority, western farmers refused to pay Alexander Hamilton's hated 1791 excise tax on distilled spirits. By 1794 western Pennsylvania had emerged as the center of discontent; mobs tarred tax collectors and burned the property of distillers who complied with the law. In July 1794, nearly 6,000 angry "whiskey rebels" threatened to attack Pittsburgh. In September President George Washington called out the militia of four states to quell the insurrection. By the time they arrived at Pittsburgh, armed resistance had melted away. Nevertheless, the federal government had demonstrated that it retained the authority—and coercive power—to compel citizens to obey federal law. In the following selection, Secretary of the Treasury Hamilton sends instructions on behalf of President Washington to the Governor of Pennsylvania, detailing how the federalized militia should handle the "Whiskey Rebellion."

*From Hugh H. Brackenridge, *Incidents of the Insurrection in the Western Parts of Pennsylvania, in the Year 1794*, 3 vols. (Philadelphia: John M'Culloch, 1795), II:65–67.

To Henry Lee

Bedford [Pennsylvania] 20th October 1794

Sir,

I have it in special instruction from the President of the United States, now at this place, to convey to you on his behalf, the following instructions for the general direction of your conduct in the command of the Militia army, with which you are charged.

The objects for which the Militia have been called forth are

1. To suppress the combinations I which exist in some of the western counties in Pennsylvania in opposition to the laws laying duties upon spirits distilled within the United States and upon Stills.
2. To cause the laws to be executed.

These objects are to be effected in two ways

1. By military force.
2. By judiciary process, and other civil proceedings.

The objects of the Military force are twofold.

1. To overcome any armed opposition which may exist.
2. To countenance and support the civil officers in the means of executing, the laws.

With a view to the first of these two objects, you will proceed as speedily as may be, with the army under your command, into the insurgent counties to attack, and as far as shall be in your power subdue, all persons whom you may find in arms, in opposition to the laws above mentioned. You will march your army in two columns, from the places where they are now assembled, by the most convenient routes, having regard to the nature of the roads, the convenience of supply, and the facility of co-operation and union; and bearing in mind, that you ought to act, till the contrary shall be fully develloped, on the general principle of having to contend with the whole force of the Counties of Fayette, Westmoreland, Washington and Alleghany, and of that part of Bedford which lies westward of the town of Bedford; and that you are to put as little as possible to hazard. The approximation, therefore, of your columns, is to be sought, and the subdivision of them, so as to place the parts out of mutual supporting distance, to be avoided as far as local circumstances will permit. Parkinson's Ferry appears to be a proper point, towards which to direct the march of the column for the purpose of ulterior measures.

When arrived within the insurgent Country, if an armed opposition appear, it may be proper to publish a proclamation, inviting all good citizens, friends of the Constitution and laws, to join the standard of the United States. If no armed opposition exist—it may still be proper to publish a proclamation, exhorting to a peaceable and dutiful demeanour, and giving assurances of performing, with good faith and liberality, whatsoever may have been promised by the Commissioners I to those who have complied with the conditions prescribed by them, and who have not forfeited their title by subsequent misconduct.

Of those persons in arms, if any, whom you may make prisoners; leaders, including all persons in command, are to be delivered up to the civil magistrate: the rest to be disarmed, admonished and sent home (except such as may have been particularly violent and also influential) causing their own recognizances for their good behaviour to be taken, in the cases in which it may be deemed expedient.

With a view to the second point, namely, "the countenance and support of the civil officers, in the means of executing the laws," you will make such dispositions as shall appear proper to countenance and protect, and, if necessary and required by them, to support and aid the civil officers in the execution of their respective duties; for bringing offenders and delinquents to justice; for seizing the stills of delinquent distillers, as far as the same shall be deemed eligible by the supervisor of the Revenue, or chief-officer of Inspection; and also for conveying to places of safe custody. such persons as may be apprehended and not admitted to bail.

The objects of judiciary process and other civil proceedings, will be,

1. To bring offenders to justice.
2. To enforce penalties on delinquent distillers by suit.
3. To enforce the penalty of forfeiture on the same persons by seizure of their stills and spirits.

The better to effect these purposes, the Judge of the District, Richard Peters Esquire, and the Attorney of the district, William Rawle Esquire, accompany the army.

You are aware that the judge cannot be controuled in his functions. But I count on his disposition to cooperate in such a general plan as shall appear to you consistent with the policy of the case. But your method of giving a direction to legal proceedings, according to your general plan, will be by instruction to the District Attorney.

He ought particularly to be instructed, (with due regard to time and circumstance)—1st to procure to be arrested, all influential actors in riots and unlawful assemblies, relating to the insurrection, and combinations to resist the laws; or having for object to abet that insurrection, and those combinations; and who shall not have complied with the terms offered by the Commisioners; or manifested their repentance in some other way, which you may deem satisfactory. 2dly. To cause process to issue for enforcing penalties on delinquent distillers. 3d. To cause *offenders*, who may be arrested, to be conveyed to gaols[jails] where there will be no danger of rescue: those for misdemeanors to the gaols of York and Lancaster; those for capital offences to the gaol of Philadelphia, as more secure than the others. 4th. To prosecute indictable offences in the Courts of the United States—those for penalties on delinquents, under the laws beforementioned, in the courts of Pennsylvania.

As a guide in the case, the District Attorney has with him a list of the persons who have availed themselves of the offers of the Commissioners on the day appointed.

The seizure of Stills is the province of the Supervisor and other officers of Inspection. It is difficult to chalk out the precise line concerning it. There are opposite considerations which will require to be nicely balanced, and which must be judged of by those officers on the spot. It may be found useful to confine the seizures to stills of the most leading and refactory distillers. It may be adviseable to extend them far in the most refractory County.

When the insurrection is subdued, and the requisite means have been put in execution to secure obedience to the laws, so as to render it proper for the army to retire (an event which you will accelerate as much as shall be consistent with the object) you will endeavour to make an arrangement for detaching such a force as you deem adequate; to be stationed within the disaffected Country, in such manner as best to afford protection to well-disposed Citizens, and to the officers of the revenue, and to repress by their presence, the spirit of riot & opposition to the laws.

But before you withdraw the army, you will promise on behalf of the President a general pardon to all such as shall not have been arrested, with such exceptions as you shall deem proper. The promise must be so guarded as not to affect pecuniary claims under the revenue laws. In this measure, it is adviseable there should be a cooperation with the Governor of Pennsylvania.

On the return of the army, you will adopt some convenient and certain arrangement for restoring to the public magazines the arms, accoutrements, military stores, tents & other articles of camp equipage, and entrenching tools which have been furnished & shall not have been consumed or lost.

You are to exert yourself by all possible means to preserve discipline among the troops, particularly a scrupulous regard to the rights of persons and property and a respect for the authority of the civil magistrate; taking especial care to inculcate and cause to be observed this principle, that the duties of the army are confined to the attacking and subduing of armed opponents of the laws, and to the supporting and aiding of the civil officers in the execution of their functions.

It has been settled that the Governor of Pennsylvania will be second, the Governor of New Jersey third in command; and that the troops of the several States in line, on the march and upon detachment, are to be posted according to the rule which prevailed in the army during the late war—namely—in moving towards the seaboard, the most Southern troops will take the right—in moving westward, the most Northern will take the right.

These general instructions, however, are to be considered as liable to such alterations and deviations in the detail as from local and other causes may be found necessary the better to effect the main object upon the general principles which have been indicated.

With great respect I have the honor to be Sir, Your Obedt. Servt.
Alex. Hamilton

59. WASHINGTON'S FAREWELL ADDRESS, 1796*

President George Washington used his Farewell Address to share with the nation his vision of, and concerns for, the United States. Like many citizens, he feared the danger that partisanship posed to liberty, and he sternly warned against the perils that might occur with the rise of the new political parties. As a former general, Washington also felt grave concern for the threat that foreign struggles might present to the country; in his speech he advised the American people on how the United States might best meet its responsibilities as an international power.

. . . I have already intimated to you the dangers of parties in the state, with particular reference to the founding of them on geographical discriminations. Let me now take a more comprehensive view, and warn you in the most solemn manner against the baneful effects of the spirit of party, generally.

This spirit, unfortunately, is inseparable from our nature, having its root on the strongest passion of the human mind. It exists under different shapes in all governments, more or less stifled, controlled, or repressed; but, in those of the popular form, it is seen in its greatest rankness, and is truly their worst enemies.

The alternate domination of one faction over another, sharpened by the spirit of revenge, natural to party dissension, which in different ages and countries has perpetrated the most horrid enormities, is itself a frightful despotism. The disorders and miseries, which result, gradually incline the minds of men to seek security and repose in the absolute power of an individual; and sooner or later the chief of some prevailing faction, more able or more fortuitous than his competitors, turns this disposition to the purposes of his own elevation, and the ruins of Public Liberty.

Without looking forward to an extremity of this kind (which nevertheless ought not to be entirely out of sight,) the common and continual mischiefs of the spirit of party are sufficient to make the interest and the duty of a wise people to discourage and restrain it. . . .

There is an opinion, that parties in free countries are useful checks upon the administration of the Government, and serve to keep alive the spirit of Liberty. This within certain limits is probably true; and in Government of a Monarchical cast, Patriotism may look with indulgence, if not with favor, upon the spirit of party. But in those of the popular character, in Governments purely elective, it is a spirit not to be encouraged. From their natural tendency, it is certain there will always be enough of that spirit for every salutary purpose. And, there being constant danger of excess, the effort ought to be, by force of public opinion, to mitigate and assuage it. A fire not to be quenched,

*From *Messages of the Presidents of the United States*, comp. Jonathan Phillips (Columbus, Ohio: Jonathan Phillips, 1841), 74–79.

it demands a uniform vigilance to prevent it bursting into a flame, lest, instead of warming, it should consume.

It is important, likewise, that the habits of thinking in a free country should caution, in those intrusted with its administration, to confine themselves within their respective constitutional spheres, avoiding in the exercise of the powers of one department to encroach upon another. The spirit of encroachment tends to consolidate the powers of all the departments in one, and thus to create, whatever the form of government, a real despotism. A just estimate of the love of power, and proneness to abuse it, which predominates in the human heart, is sufficient to satisfy us of the truth of this position. . . .

Of all the dispositions and habits which lead to political prosperity, religion and morality are indispensable supports. In vain would that man claim the tribute of patriotism, who should labor to subvert these great pillars of human happiness—these finest props of the duties of men and citizens. . . . And let us with caution indulge the supposition, that morality can be maintained without religion. Whatever may be conceded to the influence of refined education on minds of peculiar structure, reason and experience both, forbid us to expect that national morality can prevail in exclusion of religious principle.

It is substantially true, that virtue or morality is a necessary spring of popular government. The rule indeed extends with more or less force to every species of free government. Who, that is a sincere friend to it, can look with indifference upon attempts to shake the foundations of the fabric?

Promote, then, as an object of primary importance, institutions for the general diffusion of knowledge. In proportion as the structure of a government gives force to public opinion, it is essential that public opinion should be enlightened.

As a very important source of strength and security, cherish public credit. One method of preserving it is to use it as sparingly as possible; avoiding occasions of expense, by cultivating peace, but remembering also that timely disbursements to prepare for danger, frequently prevent much greater disbursements to repel it; avoiding, likewise, the accumulation of debt; not only by shunning occasions of expense, but by vigorous exertions, in time of peace, to discharge the debts which unavoidable wars may have occasioned, not ungenerously throwing upon posterity the burthen which we ourselves ought to bear. The execution of these maxims belongs to your representatives, but it is necessary that public opinion should co-operate. To facilitate to them the performance of their duty, it is essential that you should practically bear in mind, that, towards the payment of debt, there must be revenue; that to have revenue, there must be taxes; that no taxes can be devised which are not more or less inconvenient and unpleasant. . . .

Observe good faith and justice towards all nations; cultivate peace and harmony with all. Religion and morality enjoin this conduct; and can it be that good policy does not equally enjoin it? It will be worthy of a free, enlightened, and, at no distant period, a great nation, to give to mankind the magnanimous and too novel example of a people always guided by an exalted justice and benevolence. . . .

In the execution of such a plan, nothing is more essential than that permanent inveterate antipathies against particular nations, and passionate attachments for others should be excluded; and that in place of them, just and amicable feelings towards all should be cultivated. The nation which indulges towards another an habitual hatred, or an habitual fondness, is, in some degree, a slave. . . .

Excessive partiality for one foreign nation, and excessive dislike of another, cause those whom they actuate to see danger only on one side, and serve to veil and even second the arts of influence on the other. Real patriots, who may resist the intrigues of the favorite, are liable to become suspected and odious, while its tools and dues usurp the applause and confidence of the people, to surrender their interests.

The great rule of conduct for us, in regard to foreign nations, is, in extending our commercial relations, to have with them as little *political* connexion as possible. So far as we have already formed engagements, let them be fulfilled with perfect good faith. Here let us stop.

Europe has a set of primary interests, which to us have none, or a very remote relation. Hence she must be engaged in frequent controversies, the causes of which are essentially foreign to our concerns. Hence, therefore, it must be unwise in us to implicate ourselves, by artificial ties, in the ordinary vicissitudes of her politics, or the ordinary combinations and collisions of her friendships or enmities.

Our detached and distant situation invites and enables us to pursue a different course. If we remain one people, under an efficient government, the period is not far off, when we may defy material injury from external annoyance; when we may take such an attitude as will cause the neutrality, we may at any time resolve upon, to be scrupulously respected; when belligerent nations, under the impossibility of making acquisitions upon us, will not lightly hazard the giving us provocation; when we may choose peace or war, as our interest, guided by justice, shall counsel. . . .

It is our true policy to steer clear of permanent alliances with any portion of the foreign world; so far, I mean, as we are now at liberty to do it; for let me not be understood as capable of patronizing infidelity of existing engagements. I hold the maxim no less applicable to public than to private affairs, that honesty is always the best policy. I repeat, therefore, let those engagements be observed in their genuine sense. But, in my opinion, it is unnecessary, and would be unwise to extend them.

Taking care always to keep ourselves, by suitable establishments, on a respectable defensive posture, we may safely trust to temporary alliances for extraordinary emergencies. . . .

In offering to you, my countrymen, these counsels of an old and affectionate friend, I dare not hope they will make the strong and lasting impression I could wish; that they will control the usual current of the passions, or prevent any nation from running the course, which hitherto has marked the destiny of nations. But, if I may even flatter myself, that they may be productive of some partial benefit, some occasional good; that they may now and then recur to moderate the fury of party spirit, to warn against the mischiefs of foreign intrigue, to guard against the impostures of pretended patriots; this hope will be a full recompense for the solicitude for your welfare, by which they have been dictated. . . .

60. JEFFERSON'S FIRST INAUGURAL ADDRESS, 1801*

*T*homas Jefferson emphasized egalitarian ideals throughout his life, and he understood how vulnerable liberty could be. He viewed the Federalists, particularly President John Adams, as tyrannical advocates of power, and Jefferson recognized the "Revolution of 1800" as an opportunity to restore liberty and equality to the United States. In his first inaugural address, he called for a reconciliation between the two parties, but he also used the speech to define his understanding of the emerging agrarian republic that would ensure equality for all men.

Called upon to undertake the duties of the first executive office of our country, I avail myself of the presence of that portion of my fellow-citizens which is here assembled to express my grateful thanks for the favor with which they have been pleased to look toward me, to declare a sincere consciousness that the task is above my talents, and that I approach it with those anxious and awful presentiments which the greatness of the charge and the weakness of my powers to justly inspire. A rising nation, spread over a wide and fruitful land, traversing all the seas with the rich productions of their industry, engaged in commerce with nations who feel power and forget right, advancing rapidly to destinies beyond the reach of mortal eye—when I contemplate these transcendent objects, and see the honor, the happiness, and the hopes of this beloved country committed to the issue and auspices of the day, I shrink from the contemplation, and humble myself before the magnitude of the undertaking. Utterly,

*From *A Compilation of the Messages and Papers of the Presidents, 1789–1897*, 10 vols., comp. James D. Richardson (Washington, D.C.: U.S. Government Printing Office, 1896–1899), I:321–24.

indeed, should I despair did not the presence of many whom I here see remind me that in the other high authorities provided by our Constitution shall I find resources of wisdom, of virtue, and of zeal on which to rely under all difficulties. . . .

During the contest of opinion through which we have passed the animation of discussions and of exertions has sometimes worn an aspect which might impose on strangers unused to think freely and to speak and to write what they think; but this being now decided by the voice of the nation, announced according to the rules of the Constitution, all will, of course, arrange themselves under the will of the law, and unite in common effort for the common good. All, too, will bear in mind this sacred principle, that though the will of the majority is in all cases to prevail, that will to be rightful must be reasonable; that the minority possess their equal rights, which equal law must protect, and to violate would be oppression. Let us, then, fellow-citizens, unite with one heart and one mind. Let us restore to social intercourse the harmony and affection without which liberty and even life itself are but dreary things. And let us reflect that, having banished from our land that religious intolerance under which mankind so long bled and suffered, we have yet gained little if we countenance a political intolerance as despotic, as wicked, and capable of as bitter and bloody persecutions. . . . But every difference of opinion is not a difference of principle. We have called by different names brethren of the same principle. We are all Republicans, we are all Federalists. If there is any among us who would wish to dissolve this Union or to change its republican form, let them stand undisturbed as monuments to the safety with which error of opinion may be tolerated where reason is left free to combat it. I know, indeed, that some honest men fear that a republican government can not be strong, that this Government is not strong enough; but would the honest patriot, in the full tide of successful experiment, abandon a government which has so far kept us free and firm on the theoretic and visionary fear that this Government, the world's best hope, may by possibility want energy to preserve itself? I trust not. I believe this, on the contrary, the strongest Government of earth. I believe it the only one where every man, at the call of the law would fly to the standard of the law, and would meet invasions of the public order as his own personal concern. . . .

Let us, then, with courage and confidence pursue our own Federal and Republican principles, our attachment to union and representative government. Kindly separated by nature and a wide ocean from the exterminating havoc of one quarter of the globe; too high-minded to endure the degradations of the others; possessing a chosen country, with room enough for our descendants to the thousandth and thousandth generation; entertaining a due sense of our equal right to the use of our own faculties, to the acquisitions of our own industry, to honor and confidence from our fellow-citizens, resulting not from birth, but from our actions and their sense of them; enlightened by a benign religion, professed, indeed, and practiced in various forms, yet all of them inculcating honesty, truth, temperance, gratitude, and the love of man; acknowledging and adoring an overruling Providence, which by all its dispensations proves that it delights in the happiness of man here and his greater happiness hereafter—with all these blessings, what more is necessary to make us a happy and a prosperous people? Still one thing more, fellow-citizens—a wise and frugal Government, which shall restrain men from injuring one another, shall leave them otherwise free to regulate their own pursuits of industry and improvement, and shall not take from the mouth of labor bread it has earned. This is the sum of good government. . . .

About to enter, fellow-citizens, on the exercise of duties which comprehend everything dear and valuable to you, it is proper you should understand what I deem the essential principles of our Government, and consequently those which ought to shape its Administration. . . . Equal and exact justice to all men, of whatever state or persuasion, religious or political; peace, commerce, and honest friendship with all nations, entangling alliances with none; the support of the State governments in all their rights, as the most competent administrations of our domestic concerns and the surest bulwarks against antirepublican tendencies; the preservation of the General Government in its whole constitutional vigor, as the sheet anchor of our peace at home and safety abroad; a jealous care of the right of election by the people—a mild and safe corrective of abuses which are lopped by the sword of revolution when peaceable remedies are unprovided; absolute acquiescence in the decisions of the majority, the vital principle of republics, from which is no appeal but to force, the vital principle and immediate parent of despotism; a well-disciplined militia, our best reliance in peace and for the first moments of war, till regulars may relieve them; the supremacy of the civil over the military authority; economy in the public expense, that labor may be lightly burthened; the honest payment of our debts and sacred preservation of the public faith; encouragement of agriculture, and of commerce as its handmaid; the diffusion of information and arraignment of all abuses at the bar of the public reason; freedom of religion; freedom of the press, and freedom of person under the protection of the habeas corpus, and trial by juries impartially selected. These principles form the bright constellation which has gone before us and guided our steps through an age of revolution and reformation. . . .

Relying, then, on the patronage of your good will, I advance with obedience to the work, ready to retire from it whenever you become sensible how much better choice it is in your power to make. And may the Infinite Power which rules the destinies of the universe lead our councils to what is best, and give them a favorable issue for your peace and prosperity.

61. JAMES MADISON'S WAR MESSAGE, 1812*

*T*he War of 1812 broke out for numerous reasons. To many people, however, English arrogance and disdain for American rights stood as the critical issues. In his war message to Congress, President James Madison emphasized the importance of British maritime policies in forcing the United States to fight. In a sense, the conflict was a continuation of the American Revolution. That War for Independence, which had erupted because Americans believed that Great Britain wanted to curtail their liberties, resulted in the removal of British power and a guarantee of those rights. Yet, until the English recognized the United States as an international power and respected its rights as one, the Revolution remained unfinished.

Without going back beyond the renewal in 1803 of the war in which Great Britain is engaged, and omitting unrepaired wrongs of inferior magnitude, the conduct of her Government presents a series of acts hostile to the United States as an independent and neutral nation.

British cruisers have been in the continued practice of violating the American flag on the great highway of nations, and of seizing and carrying off persons sailing under it, not in the exercise of a belligerent right founded on the law of nations against an enemy, but of a municipal prerogative over British subjects. British jurisdiction is thus extended to neutral vessels in a situation where no laws can operate but the law of nations and the laws of the country to which the vessels belong, and a self-redress is assumed, which if British subjects were wrongfully detained and alone concerned, is that substitution of force . . . which falls within the definition of war. Could the seizure of British subjects in such cases be regarded as within the exercise of a belligerent right, the acknowledged laws of war . . . would imperiously demand the fairest trial where the sacred rights of persons were at issue. In place of such a trial these rights are subjected to the will of every petty commander.

The practice, hence, is so far from affecting British subjects alone that, under the pretext of searching for these, thousands of American citizens, under the safeguard of public law and of their national flag, have been torn away from everything dear to them; have been dragged on board ships of war of a foreign nation and exposed, under the severities of their discipline, to be exiled to the

*From *A Compilation of the Messages and Papers of the Presidents, 1789–1897*, 10 vols., comp. James D. Richardson (Washington, D.C.: U.S. Government Printing Office, 1896–1899), I:499–505.

most distant and deadly climes, to risk their lives in the battles of their oppressors, and to be the melancholy instruments of taking away those of their own brethren.

Against this crying enormity, which Great Britain would be so prompt to avenge if committed against herself, the United States have in vain exhausted remonstrances and expostulations, and that no proof might be wanting of their conciliatory dispositions, and no pretext left for a continuance of the practice, the British Government was formally assured of the readiness of the United States to enter into arrangements such as could not be rejected if the recovery of British subjects were the real and sole object. The communication passed without effect.

British cruisers have been in practice also of violating the rights and the peace of our coasts. They hover over and harass our entering and departing commerce. To the most insulting pretensions they have added the most lawless proceedings in our very harbors, and have wantonly spilt American blood within the sanctuary of our territorial jurisdiction. The principles and rules enforced by that nation, when a neutral nation, against armed vessels of belligerents hovering near coasts and disturbing her commerce are well known. When called on, nevertheless, by the United States to punish the greater offenses committed by her own vessels, her Government has bestowed on their commanders additional marks of honor and confidence.

Under pretended blockades, without the presence of an adequate force and sometimes without the practicability of applying one, our commerce has been plundered in every sea, the great staples of our country have been cut off from their legitimate markets, and a destructive blow aimed at our agricultural and maritime interests. . . .

Not content with these occasional expedients for laying waste our neutral trade, the cabinet of Britain resorted at length to the sweeping system of blockades, under the name of orders in council, which has been molded and managed as might best suit its political views, its commercial jealousies, or the avidity of British cruisers.

To our remonstrances against the complicated and transcendent injustice of this innovation the first reply was that the orders were reluctantly adopted by Great Britain as a necessary retaliation on decrees of her enemy proclaiming a general blockade of the British Isles at a time when the naval force of that enemy dared not issue from his own ports. She was reminded without effect that her own prior blockades, unsupported by an adequate naval force actually applied and continued, were a bar to this plea; that executed edicts against millions of our property could not be retaliation on edicts confessedly impossible to be executed; that retaliation, to be just, should fall on the party setting the guilty example, not on an innocent party which was not even chargeable with an acquiescence in it.

When deprived of this flimsy veil for a prohibition of our trade with her enemy by the repeal of his prohibition of our trade with Great Britain, her cabinet, instead of a corresponding repeal or a practical discontinuance of its orders, formally avowed a determination to persist in them against the United States until the markets of her enemy should be laid open to British products, thus . . . contradicting her own practice toward all nations, in peace as well as war, and betraying the insincerity of those professions which inculcated a belief that, having resorted to her orders with regret, she was anxious to find an occasion for putting an end to them.

Abandoning still more all respect for the neutral rights of the United States and for its own constituency, the British Government now demands as prerequisites to a repeal of its orders as they relate to the United States that a formality should be observed in the repeal of the French decrees . . . and that the French repeal . . . should not be a single and special repeal in relations to the United States, but should be extended to whatever other neutral nations unconnected with them may be affected by those decrees. And as an additional insult, they are called on for a formal disavowal of conditions and pretensions advanced by the French Government for which the United States are so far from having made themselves responsible that . . . such a responsibility was explicitly and emphatically disclaimed.

It has become, indeed, sufficiently certain that the commerce of the United States is to be sacrificed, not as interfering with the belligerent rights of Great Britain; not as supplying the wants of her enemies, which she herself supplies; but as interfering with the monopoly which she covets for her own commerce and navigation. . . .

Anxious to make every experiment short of the last resort of injured nations, the United States have withheld from Great Britain . . . the benefits of a free intercourse with their market. . . . And to entitle these experiments to the more favorable consideration they were so framed as to enable her to place her adversary under the exclusive operation of them. To these appeals her Government has been equally inflexible, as if willing to make sacrifices of every sort rather than yield to the claims of justice or renounce the errors of a false pride. Nay, so far were the attempts carried to overcome the attachment of the British cabinet to its unjust edicts that it received every encouragement within the competency of the executive branch of our Government to expect that a repeal of them would be followed by a war between the United States and France, unless the French edicts should be repealed. Even this communication . . . received no attention. . . .

There was a period when a favorable change in the policy of the British cabinet was justly considered as established. The minister plenipotentiary of His Britannic Majesty here proposed an adjustment of the differences more immediately endangering the harmony of the two countries. The proposition was accepted with the promptitude and cordiality corresponding with the invariable professions of this Government. A foundation appeared to be laid for a sincere and a lasting reconciliation. The prospect, however, quickly vanished. The whole proceeding was disavowed by the British Government, without any explanations which could at that time repress the belief that the disavowal proceeded from a spirit of hostility to the commercial rights and prosperity of the United States; and . . . at the very moment when the public minister was holding the language of friendship and inspiring confidence in the sincerity of the negotiations with which he was charged a secret agent of his Government was employed in intrigues having for their object a subversion of our Government and a dismemberment of our happy union.

In reviewing the conduct of Great Britain towards the United States our attention is necessarily drawn to the warfare just renewed by the savages on one of our extensive frontiers—a warfare which is known to spare neither age nor sex and to be distinguished by features peculiarly shocking to humanity. It is difficult to account for the activity and combinations which have for some time been developing themselves among tribes in constant intercourse with British traders and garrisons without connecting their hostility with that influence and without recollecting the authenticated examples of such interpositions heretofore furnished by the officers and agents of that Government.

Such is the spectacle of injuries and indignities which have been heaped on our country. . . . It might have least been expected that an enlightened nation . . . would have found in its true interest alone a sufficient motive to respect [the] rights [of the United States] and their tranquillity on the high seas; that an enlarged policy would have favored that free and general circulation of commerce in which the British nation is at all times interested, and which in times of war is the best alleviation of its calamities to herself. . . .

Other counsels have prevailed. Our moderation and conciliation have had no other effect than to encourage perseverance and to enlarge pretensions. We behold our seafaring citizens still the daily victims of lawless violence, committed on the great common and highway of nations, even within sight of the country which owes them protection. We behold our vessels, freighted with the products of our soil and industry, or returning with the honest proceeds of them, wrested from their lawful destinations, confiscated by prize courts no longer the organs of public law but the instruments of arbitrary edicts, and their unfortunate crews dispersed and lost, or forced or inveigled in British ports into British fleets. . . .

We behold, in fine, on the side of Great Britain a state of war against the United States, and on the side of the United States a state of peace toward Great Britain.

Whether the United States shall continue passive under these progressive usurpations and these accumulating wrongs, or, opposing force to force in defense of their natural rights, shall commit a just cause into the hands of the Almighty Disposer of Events, avoiding all connections which might entangle it in the contest or views of other powers, and preserving a constant readiness to concur in an honorable reestablishment of peace and friendship, is a solemn question which the Constitution wisely confides to the legislative department of the Government. In recommending it to their early deliberations I am happy in the assurance that the decision will be worthy the enlightened and patriotic councils of a virtuous, a free, and a powerful nation. . . .

62. *MARBURY V. MADISON, 1803**

*I*n 1803 Supreme Court Chief Justice John Marshall's decision in the case of Marbury v. Madison *laid the basis for the practice of judicial review—the Supreme Court's authority to rule on the constitutionality of acts of Congress. In arguing that Congress could not alter the jurisdiction of the Supreme Court, Marshall asserted that the Constitution is the "fundamental and paramount law of the nation" and it is "emphatically the province and duty of the judicial department to say what law is." Marbury v. Madison helped establish the independence of the judiciary as well as affirm the balance of powers outlined in the Constitution.*

. . .The question, whether an act, repugnant to the constitution, can become the law of the land, is a question deeply interesting to the United States; but, happily, not of an intricacy proportioned to its interest. It seems only necessary to recognize certain principles, supposed to have been long and well established, to decide it.

That the people have an original right to establish, for their future government, such principles, as, in their opinion, shall most conduce to their own happiness is the basis on which the whole American fabric has been erected. The exercise of this original right is a very great exertion; nor can it, nor ought it, to be frequently repeated. The principles, therefore, so established, are deemed fundamental. And as the authority from which they proceed is supreme, and can seldom act, they are designed to be permanent.

This original and supreme will organizes the government and assigns to different departments their respective powers. It may either stop here, or establish certain limits not to be transcended by those departments.

The government of the United States is of the latter description. The powers of the legislature are defined and limited; and that those limits may not be mistaken, or forgotten, the constitution is written. To what purpose are powers limited, and to what purpose is that limitation committed to writing, if those limits may, at any time, be passed by those intended to be restrained? The distinction between a government with limited and unlimited powers is abolished, if those limits do not confine the persons on whom they are imposed, and if acts prohibited and acts allowed, are of equal obligation. It is a proposition too plain to be contested, that the constitution controls any legislative act repugnant to it; or, that the legislature may alter the constitution by an ordinary act.

Between these alternatives there is no middle ground. The constitution is either a superior paramount law, unchangeable by ordinary means, or it is on a level with ordinary legislative acts, and, like other acts, is alterable when the legislature shall please to alter it.

If the former part of the alternative be true, then a legislative act contrary to the constitution is not law; if the latter part be true, then written constitutions are absurd attempts, on the part of the people, to limit a power in its own nature illimitable.

*From "Marbury v. Madison," in *The Constitutional Decisions of John Marshall*, 2 vols., ed. Joseph P. Cotton, Jr. (New York: G. P. Putnam's Sons, 1905), I:37–43.

Certainly all those who have framed written constitutions contemplate them as forming the fundamental and paramount law of the nation, and, consequently, the theory of every such government must be, that an act of the legislature, repugnant to the constitution, is void.

This theory is essentialy attached to a written constitution, and, is consequently, to be considered, by this court, as one of the fundamentals of our society. It is not therefore to be lost sight of in the further consideration of this subject.

If an act of the legislature, repugnant to the constitution, is void, does it notwithstanding its invalidity, bind the courts, and oblige them to give it effect? Or, in other words, though it be not law, does it constitute a rule as operative as if it was a law? This would be to overthrow in fact what was established in theory; and would seem, at first view, an absurdity too gross to be insisted on. It shall, however, receive a more attentive consideration.

It is emphatically the province and duty of the judicial department to say what the law is. Those who apply the rule to particular cases, must of necessity expound and interpret that rule. If two laws conflict with each other, the courts must decide on the operation of each.

So if a law in opposition to the constitution; if both the law and the constitution apply to a particular case, so that the court must either decide that case conformably to the law, disregarding the constitution; or conformably to the constitution, disregarding the law; the court must determine which of these conflicting rules governs the case. This is of the very essence of judicial duty.

If, then, the courts are to regard the constitution, and the constitution is superior to any ordinary act of the legislature, the constitution, and not such ordinary act, must govern the case to which they both apply.

Those, then, who controvert the principle that the constitution is to be considered, in court, as a paramount law, are reduced to the necessity of maintaining that courts must close their eyes on the constitution, and see only the law.

This doctrine would subvert the very foundation of all written constitutions. It would declare than an act which, according to the principles and theory of our government, is entirely void, is yet, in practice, completely obligatory. It would declare that if the legislature shall do what is expressly forbidden, such act, notwithstanding the express prohibition, is in reality effectual. It would be giving to the legislature a practical and real omnipotence, with the same breath which professes to restrict their powers within narrow limits. It is prescribing limits, and declaring that those limits may be passed at pleasure.

That it thus reduces to nothing what we have deemed the greatest improvement on political institutions, a written constitution, would of itself be sufficient, in America, where written constitutions have been viewed with so much reverence, for rejecting the construction. But the peculiar expressions of the constitution of the United States furnish additional arguments in favour of its rejection.

The judicial power of the United States is extended to all cases arising under the constitution.

Could it be the intention of those who gave this power, to say that in using it the constitution should not be looked into? That a case arising under the constitution should be decided without examining the instrument under which it arises?

This is too extravagant to be maintained.

In some cases, then, the constitution must be looked into by the judges. And if they can open it at all, what part of it are they forbidden to read or to obey?

There are many other parts of the constitution which serve to illustrate this subject.

It is declared that "no tax or duty shall be laid on articles exported for any state." Suppose a duty on the export of cotton, of tobacco, or of flour; and a suit instituted to recover it. Ought a judgment to be rendered in such a case? ought the judges to close their eyes on the constitution, and only see the law?

The constitution declares "that no bill of attainder or ex post facto law shall be passed."

If, however, such a bill should be passed, and a person should be prosecuted under it; must the court condemn to death those victims whom the constitution endeavours to preserve?

"No person," says the constitution, "shall be convicted of treason unless on the testimony of two witnesses to the same overt act, or on confession in open court."

Here the language of the constitution is addressed especially to the courts. It prescribes, directly for them, a rule of evidence not to be departed from. If the legislature should change that rule, and declare one witness, or a confession out of court, sufficient for conviction, must the constitutional principle yield to the legislative act?

From these, and many other selections which might be made, it is apparent, that the framers of the constitution contemplated that instrument as a rule for the government of courts, as well as of the legislature.

Why otherwise does it direct the judges to take an oath to support it? This oath certainly applies in an especial manner, to their conduct in their official character. How immoral to impose it on them, if they were to be used as the instruments, and the knowing instruments, for violating what they swear to support!

The oath of office, too, imposed by the legislature, is completely demonstrative of the legislative opinion on this subject. It is in these words: "I do solemnly swear that I will administer justice without respect to persons, and do equal right to the poor and to the rich; and that I will faithfully and impartially discharge all the duties incumbent on me as ———, according to the best of my abilities and understanding, agreeably to the constitution and laws of the United States."

Why does a judge swear to discharge his duties agreeably to the constitution of the United States, if that constitution forms no rule for his government—if it is closed upon him, and cannot be inspected by him?

If such be the real state of things, this is worse than solemn mockery. To prescribe, or to take this oath, becomes equally a crime.

It is not entirely unworthy of observation, that in declaring what shall be the supreme law of the land, the constitution itself is first mentioned; and not the laws of the United States generally, but those only which shall be made in pursuance of the constitution, have that rank.

Thus, the particular phraseology of the constitution of the United States confirms and strengthens the principle, supposed to be essential to all written constitutions, that a law repugnant to the constitution is void; and that courts, as well as other departments, are bound by that instrument.

63. THE HARTFORD CONVENTION, 1814–1815*

By the fall of 1814 Federalist New Englanders had become increasingly bitter about continued war with England. Some extremists advocated secession and making a separate peace with Britain. In December 1814, disaffected delegates from throughout the region met at Hartford, Connecticut, to discuss their grievances. Moderates dominated the proceedings and proposed a series of amendments to the Constitution that would curb Republican power, protect their sectional interests, and halt their eroding national power. In January, 1815, convention leaders traveled to Washington to present their resolutions only to hear news about both the peace treaty at Ghent and the stunning British defeat at New Orleans. As a result, their proposals, summarized in the following document, were seen as selfish and unpatriotic—even treasonous. The Federalist party, stigmatized by such labels, never recovered.

---

*From Theodore Dwight, *History of the Hartford Convention: With a Review of the Policy of the United States Government, Which Led to the War of 1812* (New York: N. & J. White, 1833), 368–70, 376–78.

. . . While Europe reposes from the convulsions that had shaken down her ancient institutions, she beholds with amazement this remote country, once so happy and so envied, involved in a ruinous war, and excluded from intercourse with the rest of the world.

"To investigate and explain the means whereby this fatal reverse has been effected, would require a voluminous discussion. Nothing more can be attempted in this report than a general allusion to the principal outlines of the policy which has produced this vicissitude. Among these may be enumerated—

"*First.*—A deliberate and extensive system for effecting a combination among certain states, by exciting local jealousies and ambition, so as to secure to popular leaders in one section of the Union, the controul of public affairs in perpetual succession. To which primary object most other characteristics of the system may be reconciled.

"*Secondly.*—The political intolerance displayed and avowed in excluding from office men of unexceptionable merit, for want of adherence to the executive creed.

"*Thirdly.*—The infraction of the judiciary authority and rights, by depriving judges of their offices in violation of the constitution.

"*Fourthly.*—The abolition of existing taxes, requisite to prepare the country for those changes to which nations are always exposed, with a view to the acquisition of popular favour.

"*Fifthly.*—The influence of patronage in the distribution of offices, which in these states has been almost invariably made among men the least entitled to such distinction, and who have sold themselves as ready instruments for distracting public opinion, and encouraging administration to hold in contempt the wishes and remonstrances of a people thus apparently divided.

"*Sixthly.*—The admission of new states into the Union formed at pleasure in the western region, has destroyed the balance of power which existed among the original States, and deeply affected their interest.

"*Seventhly.*—The easy admission of naturalized foreigners, to places of trust, honour or profit, operating as an inducement to the malcontent subjects of the old world to come to these States, in quest of executive patronage, and to repay it by an abject devotion to executive measures.

"*Eighthly.*—Hostility to Great Britain, and partiality to the late government of France, adopted as coincident with popular prejudice, and subservient to the main object, party power. Connected with these must be ranked erroneous and distorted estimates of the power and resources of those nations, of the probable results of their controversies, and of our political relations to them respectively.

"*Lastly and principally.*—A visionary and superficial theory in regard to commerce, accompanied by a real hatred but a feigned regard to its interests, and a ruinous perseverance in efforts to render it an instrument of coercion and war.

"But it is not conceivable that the obliquity of any administration could, in so short a period, have so nearly consummated the work of national ruin, unless favoured by defects in the constitution.

"To enumerate all the improvements of which that instrument is susceptible, and to propose such amendments as might render it in all respects perfect, would be a task which this convention has not thought proper to assume. They have confined their attention to such as experience has demonstrated to be essential, and even among these, some are considered entitled to a more serious attention than others. They are suggested without any intentional disrespect to other states, and are meant to be such as all shall find an interest in promoting. Their object is to strengthen, and if possible to perpetuate, the union of the states, by removing the grounds of existing jealousies, and providing for a fair and equal representation, and a limitation of powers, which have been misused. . . .

[An analysis of the proposed amendments follows.]

"THEREFORE RESOLVED,

"That it be and hereby is recommended to the legislatures of the several states represented in this Convention, to adopt all such measures as may be necessary effectually to protect the citizens of said states from the operation and effects of all acts which have been or may be passed by the Congress of the United States, which shall contain provisions, subjecting the militia or other citizens to forcible drafts, conscriptions, or impressments, not authorised by the constitution of the United States.

"*Resolved*, That it be and hereby is recommended to the said Legislatures, to authorize an immediate and earnest application to be made to the government of the United States, requesting their consent to some arrangement, whereby the said states may, separately or in concert, be empowered to assume upon themselves the defence of their territory against the enemy; and a reasonable portion of the taxes, collected within said States, may be paid into the respective treasuries thereof, and appropriated to the payment of the balance due said states, and to the future defence of the same. The amount so paid into the said treasuries to be credited, and the disbursements made as aforesaid to be charged to the United States.

"*Resolved*, That it be, and hereby is, recommended to the legislatures of the aforesaid states, to pass laws (where it has not already been done) authorizing the governors or commanders-in-chief of their militia to make detachments from the same, or to form voluntary corps, as shall be most convenient and conformable to their constitutions, and to cause the same to be well armed, equipped, and disciplined, and held in readiness for service; and upon the request of the governor of either of the other states to employ the whole of such detachment or corps, as well as the regular forces of the state, or such part thereof as may be required and can be spared consistently with the safety of the state, in assisting the state, making such request to repel any invasion thereof which shall be made or attempted by the public enemy.

"*Resolved*, That the following amendments of the constitution of the United States be recommended to the states represented as aforesaid, to be proposed by them for adoption by the state legislatures, and in such cases as may be deemed expedient by a convention chosen by the people of each state.

"And it is further recommended, that the said states shall persevere in their efforts to obtain such amendments, until the same shall be effected.

"*First*. Representatives and direct taxes shall be apportioned among the several states which may be included within this Union, according to their respective numbers of free persons, including those bound to serve for a term of years, and excluding Indians not taxed, and all other persons.

"*Second*. No new state shall be admitted into the Union by Congress, in virtue of the power granted by the constitution, without the concurrence of two thirds of both houses.

"*Third*. Congress shall not have power to lay any embargo on the ships or vessels of the citizens of the United States, in the ports or harbours thereof, for more than sixty days.

"*Fourth*. Congress shall not have power, without the concurrence of two thirds of both houses, to interdict the commercial intercourse between the United States and any foreign nation, or the dependencies thereof.

"*Fifth*. Congress shall not make or declare war, or authorize acts of hostility against any foreign nation, without the concurrence of two thirds of both houses, except such acts of hostility be in defence of the territories of the United States when actually invaded.

"*Sixth*. No persons who shall hereafter be naturalized, shall be eligible as a member of the senate or house of representatives of the United States, nor capable of holding any civil office under the authority of the United States.

"*Seventh*. The same person shall not be elected president of the United States a second time; nor shall the president be elected from the same state two terms in succession.

"*Resolved*, That if the application of these states to the government of the United States, recommended in a foregoing resolution, should be unsuccessful, and peace should not be concluded, and the defence of these states should be neglected, as it has been since the commencement of the war, it will, in the opinion of this convention, be expedient for the legislatures of the several states to appoint delegates to another convention, to meet at Boston . . . with such powers and instructions as the exigency of a crisis so momentous may require.

Discussion

1. The first five documents presented in this chapter all had a significant influence on the early history of the United States, and they all emanated from the executive branch. What does this suggest about political power between 1790 and 1815? What does it reveal about the power of the government? Are there any implications about the long-term power of the presidency?

2. Based on Alexander Hamilton's Report on Manufactures, what elements of society would gain power through his policies? Who would lose power? Is there anything in the document to suggest that Hamilton believed in liberty or equality?

3. Based on George Washington's Farewell Address, what do you think Washington feared posed the gravest threat to liberty? What do you think he believed were the best ways to preserve liberty? Are there any issues of equality in the speech? If so, what; if not, why not?

4. After reading Jefferson's inaugural address, how do you think Jefferson viewed liberty, equality, and power? How would you compare Jefferson's principles as he expressed them in the speech to the ideals Hamilton presented in his report?

5. In his war message, how does President Madison describe assertions of British power and English threats to American liberties? Exactly what liberties did the English endanger? Does anything about the speech suggest Madison viewed the War of 1812 as an extension or continuation of the Revolution? How did the war relate to issues of liberty, equality, and power?

6. Based on the grievances expressed and the resolutions passed at the Hartford Convention, how did the delegates plan to restore their power and protect their liberties? Under their proposals, who would gain and who would lose power?

7. According to Chief Justice Marshall in *Marybury* v. *Madison*, on what grounds did the judiciary have the power to rule on the constitutionality of acts of Congress? What do you think Marshall believed posed the greatest threat to the Constitution? Why was this decision significant?

CHAPTER 9

The Market Revolution, 1815–1860

Part of the Lowell appeal for young New England women was the mill owners' claim that the women could improve themselves. *The Lowell Offering*, originally sponsored by a local minister, published work by members of a working woman's self-improvement society. This title page from the 1845 collection shows the supposed glamour of mill life.

period of unprecedented development followed the War of 1812 as the United States experienced yet another revolution—this one economic. Between 1815 and 1860 the United States changed from a society based primarily on subsistence agricultural households to a large, expanding market economy. This transition had important implications for families and the organization of labor, but the shift also rearranged the distribution of economic power and altered concepts of liberty. The advent of the market economy, for example, raised issues concerning the government's authority to increase tariffs and to fund internal improvements. The market revolution also posed concerns for the role of workers and the liberties they would enjoy in an emerging factory system. By 1860, much of the economic growth had occurred in the North, exacerbating questions of sectional power that had existed from the earliest years of the republic. Although the South remained mostly agrarian, increased cotton production played a crucial role in the growth of the American economy. Ironically, a tremendous amount of the wealth in the United States was drawn from the labor of slaves who had no power, liberty, or equality.

64. IN DEFENCE OF THE AMERICAN SYSTEM, 1832*

Henry Clay of Kentucky, in what he referred to as the "American system," advanced many of the principles that Alexander Hamilton had proposed. In the following excerpt from one of his speeches, Clay defends the use of protective tariffs to ensure a vibrant economy. Such tariffs posed several questions of power. For one thing, they helped increase the profits of American manufacturers, giving them economic strength that could be translated into political and social influence. In addition, increased revenues from high tariffs enhanced the power of the national government. In the following selection, Clay raised still another concern by addressing the increasing sectional fears associated with the tariff question.

. . . I stand here as the humble but zealous advocate, not of the interests of one state, or of seven states only, but of the whole union. And never before have I felt, more intensely, the overpowering weight of that share of responsibility which belongs to me in these deliberations. Never before have I had more occasion than I now have, to lament my want of those intellectual powers, the possession of which might enable me to unfold to this senate and to illustrate to this people great truths, intimately connected with the lasting welfare of my country. I should, indeed, sink overwhelmed and subdued beneath the appalling magnitude of the task which lies before me, if I did not feel myself sustained and fortified by a thorough consciousness of the justness of the cause which I have espoused, and by a persuasion, I hope not presumptuous, that it has the approbation of that Providence who has so often smiled upon these United States.

*From *The Life and Speeches of the Honorable Henry Clay*, 2 vols., ed. Daniel Mallory (Hartford: Silas Andrus & Son, 1855), II:6–9, 13, 17–18, 23–24, 27–31, 37–38, 41–43, 46.

Eight years ago, it was my painful duty to present to the other house of congress an unexaggerated picture of the general distress pervading the whole land. We must all yet remember some of its frightful features. We all know that the people were then oppressed, and borne down by an enormous load of debt; that the value of property was at the lowest point of depression; that ruinous sales and sacrifices were every where made of real estate; that stop laws, and relief laws, and paper money were adopted, to save the people from impending destruction; that a deficit in the public revenue existed, which compelled government to seize upon, and divert from its legitimate object, the appropriations to the sinking fund, to redeem the national debt; and that our commerce and navigation were threatened with a complete paralysis. In short, sir, if I were to select any term of seven years since the adoption of the present constitution which exhibited a scene of the most wide-spread dismay and destruction, it would be exactly that term of seven years which immediately preceded the establishment of the tariff of 1824.

I have now to perform the more pleasing task of exhibiting an imperfect sketch of the existing state of the unparalleled prosperity of the country. On a general survey, we behold cultivation extended, the arts flourishing, the face of the country improved, our people fully and profitably employed, and the public countenance exhibiting tranquillity, contentment, and happiness. And if we descend into particulars, we have the agreeable contemplation of a people out of debt; land rising slowly in value, but in a secure and salutary degree; a ready though not extravagant market for all the surplus productions of our industry; innumerable flocks and herds browsing and gamboling on ten thousand hills and plains, covered with rich and verdant grasses; our cities expanded, and whole villages springing up, as it were, by enchantment; our exports and imports increased and increasing; our tonnage, foreign and coastwise, swelling and fully occupied; the rivers of our interior animated by the perpetual thunder and lightening of countless steamboats; the currency sound and abundant; the public debt of two wars nearly redeemed; and, to crown all, the public treasury overflowing, embarrassing congress, not to find subjects of taxation, but to select the objects which shall be liberated from the impost. If the term of seven years were to be selected, of the greatest prosperity which this people have enjoyed since the establishment of their present constitution, it would be exactly that period of seven years which immediately followed the passage of the tariff of 1824. . . .

It is now proposed to abolish the system, to which we owe so much of the public prosperity. . . .

If the system of protection be founded on principle erroneous in theory, pernicious in practice, above all, if it be unconstitutional, as is alleged, it ought to be forthwith abolished, and not a vestige of it suffered to remain. But, before we sanction this sweeping denunciation, let us look a little at this system, its magnitude, its ramifications, its duration, and the high authorities which have sustained it. . . . Why, sir, there is scarcely an interest, scarcely a vocation in society, which is not embraced by the beneficence of this system. . . .

The question, therefore, which we are now called upon to determine, is . . . whether we shall break down and destroy a long established system, patiently and carefully built up and sanctioned, during a series of years, again and again, by the nation and by its highest and most revered authorities. . . .

When gentlemen have succeeded in their design of an immediate or gradual destruction of the American system, what is their substitute? Free trade! Free trade! The call for free trade is as unavailing, as the cry of a spoiled child in its nurse's arms, for the moon, or the stars that glitter in the firmament of heaven. It never has existed, it never will exist. Trade implies at least two parties. To be free, it should be fair, equal, and reciprocal. But if we throw our ports wide open to the admission of foreign productions, free of all duty, what ports of any other foreign nation shall we find to be open to the free admission of our surplus produce? We may break down all barriers to free trade on our part, but the work will not be complete, until foreign powers shall have removed theirs. There would be freedom on one side, and restrictions, prohibitions, and exclusions on the other. . . .

Gentlemen deceive themselves. It is not free trade that they are recommending to our acceptance. It is, in effect, the British colonial system that we are invited to adopt; and, if their policy prevail, it will lead substantially to the recolonization of these states, under the commercial dominion of Great Britain. . . .

I will now . . . proceed to a more particular consideration of the arguments urged against the protective system, and an inquiry into its practical operation, especially on the cotton-growing industry. . . . It is alleged, that the system operates prejudicially to the cotton planter, by diminishing the foreign demand for his staple; that we cannot sell to Great Britain unless we buy from her; that the import duty is equivalent to an export duty, and falls upon the cotton grower; that South Carolina pays a disproportionate quota of the public revenue, that an abandonment of the protective policy would lead to an augmentation of our exports . . . ; and, finally, that the south cannot partake of the advantages of manufacturing, if there be any. Let us examine these various propositions in detail. First, that the foreign demand for cotton is diminished, and we cannot sell to Great Britain unless we buy from her. The demand of both our great foreign customers is constantly and annually increasing. It is true, that the ratio of the increase may not be equal to that of production; but this is owing to the fact, that the power of producing the raw material is much greater, and is, therefore, constantly in advance of the power of consumption. . . .

Second, that the import duty is equivalent to an export duty, and falls on the producer of cotton.

The framers of our constitution, by granting the power to congress to lay imports, and prohibiting that of laying an export duty, manifested that they did not regard them as equivalent. Nor does the common sense of mankind. An export duty fastens upon, and incorporates itself with, the article on which it is laid. The article cannot escape from it—it pursues and follows it, wherever the article goes; and if, in the foreign market, the supply is above or just equal to the demand, the amount of the export duty will be a clear deduction to the exporter from the price of the article. But an import duty on a foreign article leaves the exporter of the domestic article free, first to import specie; secondly, goods which are free from the protecting duty; or, thirdly, such goods as, being chargeable with the protecting duty, he can still sell at home, and throw the duty on the consumer. . . .

Third. The next objection to the American system is, that it subjects South Carolina to the payment of an undue proportion of the public revenue. The basis of this objection is the assumption, shown to have been erroneous, that the producer of the exports from this country pays the duty on its imports, instead of the consumer of those imports. . . .

Fourth. An abandonment of the American system, it is urged, would lead to an addition to our export of one hundred and fifty millions of dollars. The amount of one hundred and fifty millions of cotton in the raw state, would produce four hundred and fifty millions in the manufactured state. . . . Now . . . , where would markets be found for this vast addition to the supply? Not in the United States, certainly, nor in any other quarter of the globe, England having already everywhere pressed her cotton manufactures to the utmost point of repletion. We must look for new worlds, seek for a new and unknown race of mortals, to consume this immense increase of cotton fabrics. . . .

Fifth. But it is contended, in the last place, that the south cannot, from physical and other causes, engage in the manufacturing arts. I deny the premises, and I deny the conclusion. I deny the fact of inability; and, if it existed, I deny the conclusion, that we must, therefore break down our manufactures, and nourish those of foreign countries. The south possesses in an extraordinary degree, two of the most important elements of manufacturing industry—water-power and labor. The former gives to our whole country a decided advantage over Great Britain. But a single experiment . . . in which a faithless slave put the torch to a manufacturing establishment, has discouraged similar enterprises. We have in Kentucky the same description of population, and we employ them almost exclusively, in many of our hemp manufactories. A neighbor of mine, one of our most opulent and respectable citizens, has had one, two, if not three, manufactories burnt by incendiaries; but he persevered, and his perseverance has been rewarded with wealth. . . .

I pass . . . from this . . . topic, to two general propositions which cover the entire ground of debate. The first is, that, under the operation of the American system, the objects which it protects and fosters are brought to the consumer at cheaper prices, than they commanded prior to its introduction, or, than they would command if it did not exist. . . .

This brings me to consider what I apprehend to be the most efficient of all causes in the reduction of the prices of manufactured articles, and that is COMPETITION. By competition, the total amount of the supply is increased, and by increase of the supply, a competition in the sale ensues, and this enables the consumer to buy at lower rates. . . .

The great law of *price* is determined by supply and demand. Whatever affects either, affects the price. If the supply is increased, the demand remaining the same, the price declines; if the demand is increased, the supply remaining the same, the price advances; if both supply and demand are undiminished, the price is stationary, and the price is influenced exactly in proportion to the degree of the disturbance to the demand or supply. It is, therefore, a great error to suppose that an existing or new duty *necessarily* becomes a component element to its exact amount of price. If the proportions of demand and supply are varied by the duty, either in augmenting the supply, or diminishing the demand, or *vice versa*, price is affected to the extent of that variation. But the duty never becomes an integral part of the price, except in the instances where the demand and the supply remain after the duty is imposed, precisely what they were before, or the demand is increased, and the supply remains stationary.

Competition, therefore, wherever existing, whether at home or abroad, is the parent cause of cheapness. If a high duty excites production at home, and the quantity of the domestic article exceeds the amount which had been previously imported, the price will fall. . . .

I have now to consider the remaining of the two propositions which I have already announced. That is,

Second, that under the operation of the American system, the products of our agriculture command a higher price than they would do without it, by the creation of a home market; and by the augmentation of wealth produced by manufacturing industry, which enlarges our powers of consumption both of domestic and foreign articles. The importance of the home market is among the established maxims which are universally recognized by all writers and all men. . . .

What would be the condition of the farming country of the United States . . . if a home market did not exist for this immense amount of agricultural produce? Without that market, where could it be sold? In foreign markets? If their restrictive laws did not exist, their capacity would not enable them to purchase and consume this vast addition to their present supplies, which must be thrown in, or thrown away, but for the home market. . . .

I conclude this part of the argument with the hope that my humble exertions have not been altogether unsuccessful in showing,

First, that the policy which we have been considering ought to continue to be regarded as the genuine American system.

Secondly, that the free trade system, which is proposed as its substitute, ought really to be considered as the British colonial system.

Thirdly, that the American system is beneficial to all parts of the union, and absolutely necessary to much the larger portion.

Fourthly, that the price of the great staple cotton, and of all our chief productions of agriculture, has been sustained and upheld, and a decline averted, by the protective system.

Fifthly, that if the foreign demand for cotton has been at all diminished, by the operation of that system, the diminution has been more than compensated, in the additional demand created at home.

Sixthly, that the constant tendency of the system, by creating competition among ourselves, and between American and European industry, reciprocally acting upon each other, is to reduce prices of manufactured objects.

Seventhly, that, in point of fact, objects within the scope of the policy of protection, have greatly fallen in price. . . .

65. PRESIDENT JAMES MONROE VETOES THE NATIONAL ROAD, 1822*

A viable market economy depended on the transportation revolution that made possible the large-scale movement of people and commodities. The need for good roads attracted strong popular support for what were called "internal improvements," President James Monroe believed that a federal role in building highways violated the Constitution. He presented his opinions on the matter in a veto message delivered in 1822. The document raises two interesting points regarding power. One of those points involved the authority of the national government to construct roads, which Madison clearly rejected. The second significant point involves the use of presidential power in the early republic. Presidents initially believed that the veto power could be exercised only over questions of constitutional authority, as Madison does here. Later presidents assumed a different power, often rejecting acts of Congress for partisan or political, rather than for constitutional, reasons.

Having duly considered the bill entitled "An act for the preservation and repair of the Cumberland road," it is with deep regret, approving as I do the policy, that I am compelled to object to its passage and to return the bill to the House of Representatives, in which it originated, under a conviction that Congress do not possess the power under the Constitution to pass such a law.

A power to establish turnpikes with gates and tolls, and to enforce the collection of tolls by penalties, implies a power to adopt and execute a complete system of internal improvement. A right to impose duties to be paid by all persons passing a certain road, and on horses and carriages, as is done by this bill, involves the right to take the land from the proprietor on a valuation and pass laws for the protection of the road from injuries, and if it exists as to one road it exists as to any other, and to as many roads as Congress may think proper to establish. A right to legislate for one of these purposes is a right to legislate for the others. It is a complete right of jurisdiction and sovereignty for all the purposes of internal improvement, and not merely the right of applying money under the power vested in Congress to make appropriations, under which power, with the consent of the States through which the road passes, the work was originally commenced, and has been so far executed. I am of opinion that Congress do not possess this power; that the States individually can not grant it, for although they may assent to the appropriation of money within their limits for such purposes, they can grant no power of jurisdiction or sovereignty by special compacts with the United States. This power can be granted only by an amendment to the Constitution and in the mode prescribed by it.

If the power exist, it must be either because it has been specifically granted to the United States or that it is incidental to some power which has been specifically granted. If we examine the specific grants of power we do not find it among them, nor is it incidental to any power which has been specifically granted.

It has never been contended that the power was specifically granted. It is claimed only as being incidental to some one or more of the powers which are specifically granted. The following are powers from which it is said to be derived:

First, from the right to establish post-offices and post-roads; second, from the right to declare war; third, to regulate commerce; fourth, to pay debts and provide for the common defense and

*From *A Compilation of the Messages and Papers of the Presidents, 1789–1897*, 10 vols., comp. James D. Richardson (Washington, D.C.: U.S. Goverment Printing Office, 1896–1899), II:142–43.

general welfare; fifth, from the power to make all laws necessary and proper for carrying into execution all the powers vested by the Constitution in the Government of the United States or in any department or officer thereof; sixth and lastly, from the power to dispose of and make all needful rules and regulations respecting the territory and other property of the United States.

According to my judgment it can not be derived from either of those powers, nor from all of them united, and in consequence it does not exist.

Having stated my objections to the bill, I should now cheerfully communicate at large the reasons on which they are founded if I had time to reduce them to such form as to include them in this paper. The advanced stage of the session renders that impossible. Having at the commencement of my service in this high trust considered it a duty to express the opinion that the United States do not possess the power in question, and to suggest for the consideration of Congress the propriety of recommending to the States an amendment to the Constitution to vest the power in the United States, my attention has been often drawn to the subject since, in consequence whereof I have occasionally committed my sentiments to paper respecting it. The form which this exposition has assumed is not such as I would have given it had it been intended for Congress, nor is it included. Nevertheless, as it contains my views on this subject, being one which I deem of very high importance, and which in many of its bearings has now become peculiarly urgent, I will communicate it to Congress, if in my power, in the course of the day, or certainly on Monday next.

66. THE IMPACT OF THE ERIE CANAL, 1852*

*T*he Erie Canal, completed in 1825, represents a classic example of how dramatic improvements in transportation assisted the United States to become a market-oriented society. The following report, issued by the Secretary of Treasury in 1852, analyzes how the canal reduced the cost of bulk shipping, affected neglected regions of New York and other states bordering the Great Lakes, and established New York City as the primary gateway to the northwestern interior.

Previous to the construction of the [Erie] canal, the cost of transportation from Lake Erie to tide-water was such as nearly to prevent all movement of merchandise. A report of the committee of the [New York state] legislature, . . . dated March 17, 1817, states that at that time the cost of transportation *from* Buffalo to Montreal was $30 per ton, and the *returning* transportation from $60 to $75. The expense of transportation from Buffalo to New York was stated at $100 per ton, and the ordinary length of passage *twenty days;* so that, upon the very route through which the heaviest and cheapest products of the West were now sent to market, the cost of transportation was nearly *three* times the market value of wheat in New York; *six* times the value of the corn; *twelve* times the value of oats; and far exceeded the value of most kinds of cured provisions. These facts afford a striking illustration of the value of internal improvements to a country like the United States. . . .

Although the rates of transportation over the Erie canal, at its opening, were nearly double the present charges—which ranged from $3 to $7 per ton, according to the character of the freight—it immediately became the convenient and favorite route for a large portion of the produce of the northwestern States, and secured to the city of New York the position which she now holds as the emporium of the Confederacy. Previous to the opening of the canal, the trade of the West was

*From "Communication From the Secretary of the Treasury in Compliance with a Resolution of the Senate on March 8, 1851, Report of Israel D. Andrews, Consul of the United States for Canada and New Brunswick on the Trade and Commerce of the British North American Colonies and upon the Trade of the Great Lakes and Rivers," August 19, 1852, *Senate Executive Documents*, No. 112 (Washington, D.C.: Robert Armstrong, 1853), 278–79.

chiefly carried on through the cities of Baltimore and Philadelphia, particularly the latter, which was at that time the first city of the United States in population and wealth, and in the amount of its internal commerce.

As soon as the [great] lakes were reached, the line of navigable water was extended through them nearly one thousand miles farther into the interior. The western States immediately commenced the construction of similar works, for the purpose of opening a communication from the more remote portions of their territories, with this great water-line. All these works took their direction and character from the Erie canal, which in this manner became the outlet for almost the greater part of the West.

It is difficult to estimate the influence which this canal has exerted upon the commerce, growth and prosperity of the whole country, for it is impossible to imagine what would have been the state of things without it. But for this work, the West would have held out few inducements to the settler, who would have been without a market for his most important products, and consequently without the means of supplying many of his most essential wants. That portion of the country would have remained comparatively unsettled up to the present time; and, where now exist rich and populous communities, we should find an uncultivated wilderness. The East would have been equally without the elements of growth. The canal has supplied it with cheap food, and has opened an outlet and created a market for the products of its manufactures and commerce. The increase in commerce, and the growth of the country, have been very accurately measured by the growth of the business of the canal. It has been one great bond of strength, infusing life and vigor into the whole. Commercially and politically, it has secured and maintained to the United States the characteristics of a homogenous people.

67. CHICAGO IN THE MID-1830s*

*T*he completion of the Erie Canal in 1825 brought the Great Lakes within reach of the metropolitan New York market, thus opening up the economically neglected northern regions of Ohio, Indiana, and Illinois to a swiftly expanding market-oriented society. More canals, better roads, and finally railroads transformed once-sleepy frontier towns into rapidly growing cities. During the mid-1830s, English traveler Harriet Martineau, visited Chicago, a vibrant young community on the verge of such a transformation. She correctly predicted that it would become one of the "thriving lake and river ports of America."

Chicago looks raw and bare, standing on the high prairie above the lake-shore. The houses appeared all insignificant, and run up in various directions, without any principle at all. A friend of mine who resides there had told me that we should find the inns intolerable, at the period of the great land sales, which bring a concourse of speculators to the place. It was even so. The very sight of them was intolerable; and there was not room for our party among them all. I do not know what we should have done, (unless to betake ourselves to the vessels in the harbour,) if our coming had not been foreknown, and most kindly provided for. We were divided between three families, who had the art of removing all our scruples about intruding on perfect strangers. None of us will lose the lively and pleasant associations with the place, which were caused by the hospitalities of its inhabitants.

I never saw a busier place than Chicago was at the time of our arrival. The streets were crowded with land speculators, hurrying from one sale to another. A negro, dressed up in scarlet, bearing a scarlet flag, and riding a white horse with housings of scarlet, announced the times of sale. At every street-corner where he stopped, the crowd flocked round him; and it seemed as if

---

*Harriet Martineau, *Society in America*, 3 vols. (London: Saunders and Otley, 1837), I:349–53.

some prevalent mania infected the whole people. The rage for speculation might fairly be so regarded. As the gentlemen of our party walked the streets, store-keepers hailed them from their doors, with offers of farms, and all manner of land-lots, advising them to speculate before the price of land rose higher. A young lawyer, of my acquaintance there, had realised five hundred dollars per day, the five preceding days, by merely making out titles to land. Another friend had realised, in two years, ten times as much money as he had before fixed upon as a competence for life. Of course, this rapid money-making is a merely temporary evil. A bursting of the bubble must come soon. Tbe absurdity of the speculation is so striking, that the wonder is that the fever should have attained such a height as I witnessed. The immediate occasion of the bustle which prevailed, the week we were at Chicago, was the sale of lots, to the value of two millions of dollars, along the course of a projected canal; and of another set, immediately behind these. Persons not intending to game, and not infected with mania, would endeavour to form some reasonable conjecture as to the ultimate value of the lots, by calculating the cost of the canal, the risks from accident, from the possible competition from other places, &c., and, finally, the possible profits, under the most favourable circumstances, within so many years' purchase. Such a calculation would serve as some sort of guide as to the amount of purchase-money to be risked. Whereas, wild land on the banks of a canal, not yet even marked out, was selling at Cbicago for more than rich land, well improved, in the finest part of the valley of the Mohawk, on the banks of a canal which is already the medium of an almost inestimable amount of traffic. If sharpers and gamblers were to be the sufferers by the impending crash at Chicago, no one would feel much concerned: but they, unfortunately, are the people who encourage the delusion, in order to profit by it. Many a high-spirited, but inexperienced, young man; many a simple settler, will be ruined for the advantage of knaves.

Others, besides lawyers and speculators by trade, make a fortune in such extraordinary times. A poor man at Chicago had a pre-emption right to some land, for which he paid in the morning one hundred and fifty dollars. In the afternoon, he sold it to a friend of mine for five thousand dollars. A poor Frenchman, married to a squaw, had a suit pending, when I was there, which he was likely to gain, for the right of purchasing some land by the lake for one hundred dollars, which would immediately become worth one million dollars.

There was much gaiety going on at Chicago, as well as business. On the evening of our arrival a fancy fair took place. As I was too much fatigued to go, the ladies sent me a bouquet of prairie flowers. There is some allowable pride in the place about its society. It is a remarkable thing to meet such an assemblage of educated, refined, and wealthy persons as may be found there, living in small, inconvenient houses on the edge of a wild prairie. There is a mixture, of course. I heard of a family of half-breeds setting up a carriage, and wearing fine jewellery. When the present intoxication of prosperity passes away, some of the inhabitants will go back to the eastward; there will be an accession of settlers from the mechanic classes; good houses will have been built for the richer families, and the singularity of the place will subside. It will be like all the other new and thriving lake and river ports of America. Meantime, I am glad to have seen it in its strange early days.

68. MORAL POLICE*

The Lowell System

*T*he growth of factories created the need for an industrial working class, a prospect that alarmed many people who feared that a permanent proletariat would create class differences dangerous to American liberties and equality. The Lowell system hoped to avert that threat by using unmarried young women as workers who after temporary employment in the factories would return to their homes to establish their own families. This document

*Henry A. Miles, *Lowell, As It Was, And As It Is*, 2nd ed. (Lowell: Merrill & Heywood, 1846), 128–46.

and the one following it provide some insight into the lives of those "factory girls." In the first selection, a male observer gives a favorable view of several of the key elements that characterized the Lowell system. The second selection, from the memoirs of a former employee, offers an additional perspective on working in the factories.

. . . The productiveness of these works depends on one primary and indispensable condition—the existence of an industrious, sober, orderly, and moral class of operatives. Without this, the mills in Lowell would be worthless. Profits would be absorbed by cases of irregularity, carelessness, and neglect; while the existence of any great moral exposure in Lowell would cut off the supply of help from the virtuous homesteads of the country. Public morals and private interests, identical in all places, are here to be linked together in an indissoluble connection. Accordingly, the sagacity of self-interest, as well as more disinterested considerations, has led to the adoption of a strict system of moral police.

Before we proceed to notice the details of this system, there is one consideration bearing upon the character of the operatives, which must be all the while borne in mind. *We have no permanent factory population.* This is the wide gulf which separates the English manufacturing town from Lowell. Only a very few of our operatives have their homes in this city. The most of them come from the distant interior of the country. . . .

To the general fact, here noticed, should be added another, of scarcely less importance to a just comprehension of this subject,—*the female operatives in Lowell do not work, on average, more than four and a half years in the factories.* They then return to their homes, and their places are taken by their sisters, or other female friends from their neighborhood. . . .

Here, then, we have two important elements of the difference between English and American operatives. The former are resident operatives, and are operatives for life, and constitute a permanent, dependent factory caste. The latter comes from distant homes, to which in a few years they return, to be the wives of the farmers and the mechanics of the country towns and villages. The English visitor to Lowell, when he finds it so hard to understand why American operatives are so superior to those of Leeds and Manchester, will do well to remember what a different class of females we have here to *begin* with—girls well educated in virtuous rural homes; nor must the Lowell manufacturer forget, that we forfeit the distinction, from that moment, when we cease to obtain such girls as the operatives of the city.

To obtain this constant importation of female hands from the country, it is necessary to secure *the moral protection of their characters while they are resident in Lowell.* This, therefore, is the chief object of that moral police referred to, some details of which will now be given.

It should be stated, in the outset, that no persons are employed on the Corporations who are addicted to intemperance, or who are known to be guilty of any immoralities of conduct. As the parent of all other vices, intemperance is most carefully excluded. Absolute freedom from intoxicating liquors is understood, throughout the city, to be a prerequisite to obtaining employment in the mills, and any person known to be addicted to their use is at once dismissed. This point has not received the attention, from writers upon the moral conditions of Lowell, which it deserves; and we are surprised that the English traveler and divine, Dr. Scoresby, in his recent book upon Lowell, has given no more notice to this subject. A more strictly and universally temperate class of persons cannot be found, than the nine thousand operatives of this city; and the fact is well known to all others living here, as it is of some honest pride among themselves. In relation to other immoralities, it may be stated, that the suspicion of criminal conduct, association with suspected persons, and general and habitual light behavior and conversation, are regarded as sufficient reasons for dismissions, and for which delinquent operatives are discharged.

In respect to discharged operatives, there is a system observed, of such an effectual and salutary operation, that it deserves to be minutely described.

Any person wishing to leave a mill, is at liberty to do so, at any time, after giving a fortnight's notice. The operative so leaving, if of good character, and having worked a year, is entitled, as a matter of right, to an honorable discharge, made out after a printed form, with which every counting-room is supplied. . . .

This letter of discharge is a letter of recommendation to any other mill in the city, and not without its influence in procuring employment in any other mill in New England. A record of all such discharges is made in each counting-room, in a book kept for that purpose.

So much for honorable discharges. Those dishonorable have another treatment. The names of all persons dismissed for bad conduct, or who leave the mill irregularly, are also entered in a book kept for that purpose, and these names are sent to all counting-rooms of the city, and are there entered upon *their* books. Such persons obtain no more employment throughout the city. The question is put to each applicant, "Have you worked before in the city, and if so, where is your discharge? If no discharge be presented, an inquiry of the applicant's name will enable the superintendent to know whether that name stands on his book of dishonorable discharges, and he is thus saved from taking in a corrupt or unworthy hand. This system, which has been in operation in Lowell from the beginning, is of great important effect in driving unworthy persons from our city, and in preserving the high character of our operatives. . . .

Any description of the moral care, studied by the Corporations, would be defective if it omitted a reference to the overseers. Every room in every mill has its first and second overseers. The former, or, in his absence, the latter, has the entire care of the room, taking in such operatives as he wants for the work of the room, assigning them to their employment, superintending each process, directing the repairs of disordered machinery, giving answers to questions of advice, and granting permissions of absence. At his small desk, near the door, where he can see all who go out or come in, the overseer may generally be found; and he is held responsible for the good order, propriety of conduct, and attention to business, of the operatives of that room. Hence, this is a post of most importance, and the good management of the mill is almost wholly dependent upon the character of the overseers. It is for this reason that peculiar care is exercised in their appointment. Raw hands, and of unknown characters, are never placed in this office. It is attained only by those who have either served a regular apprenticeship as machinists in the Repair Shop, or have become well known and well tried, as third hands, and assistant overseers. It is a post for which there are always many applicants, the pay being two dollars a day, with a good house, owned by the company, and rented at . . . reduced charge. . . . The overseers are almost universally married men, with families; and as a body, numbering about one hundred and eighty, in all, are among the most permanent residents, and most trustworthy and valuable citizens of the place. A large number of them are members of our churches, and are often chosen as council men in the city government, and representatives in the State legislature. The guiding and salutary influence which they exert over the operatives, is one of the most essential parts of the moral machinery of the mills. . . .

Still another source of trust which a Corporation has, for the good character of its operatives, is the moral control which they have over one another. Of course this control would be nothing among a generally corrupt and degraded class. But among virtuous and high-minded young women, who feel that they have the keeping of their characters, and that any stain upon their associates brings reproach upon themselves, the power of opinion becomes an ever-present, and ever-active restraint. A girl, *suspected* of immoralities, or serious improprieties of conduct, at once loses caste. Her fellow-boarders will at once leave the house, if the keeper does not dismiss the offender. In self-protection, therefore, the matron is obliged to put the offender away. Nor will her former companions walk with, or work with, her; till at length, finding herself everywhere talked about, and pointed at, and shunned, she is obliged to relieve her fellow-operatives of a presence which they feel brings disgrace. From this power of opinion, there is no appeal; and as long as it is exerted in favor of propriety of behavior and purity of life, it is one of the most active and effective safeguards of character.

It may not be out of place to present here the regulations, which are observed alike on all the Corporations, which are given to the operatives when they are first employed, and are posted up conspicuously in all the mills. They are as follows:—

"*Regulations to be observed by all persons employed by the* _____ *Manufacturing Company, in the Factories.*

Every overseer is required to be punctual himself, and to see that those employed under him are so.

The overseers may, at their discretion, grant leave of absence to those employed under them, when there are sufficient spare hands in the room to supply their place; but when there are not sufficient spare hands, they are not allowed to grant leave of absence unless in cases of absolute necessity.

All persons are required to observe the regulations of the room in which they are employed. They are not allowed to be absent from their work without the consent of their overseer, except in the case of sickness, and then they are required to send him word for the cause of their absence.

All persons are required to board in one of the boarding houses belonging to the company, and conform to the regulations of the house in which they board.

All persons are required to be constant in attendance on public worship, at one of the regular places of worship in this place.

Persons who do not comply with the above regulations will not be employed by the company.

Persons entering the employment of the company, are considered as engaging to work one year.

All persons intending to leave the employment of the company, are required to give notice of the same to their overseer, at least two weeks previous to the time of leaving.

Any one who shall take from the mills, or the yard, any yarn, cloth, or other article belonging to the company, will be considered guilty of STEALING—and prosecuted accordingly.

The above regulations are considered part of the contract with all persons entering the employment of the _____ MANUFACTURING COMPANY. All persons who shall have complied with them, on leaving the company, shall be entitled to an honorable discharge, which will serve as a recommendation to any of the factories in Lowell. No one who shall not have complied to them will be entitled to such a discharge."

69. LUCY LARCOM REMEMBERS THE MILLS*

See the headnote for the preceding document.

. . . The printed regulations forbade us to bring books into the mill, so I made my window-seat into a small library of poetry, pasting its side all over with newspaper clippings. In those days we had only weekly papers, and they had always a "poet's corner," where standard writers were well represented, with anonymous ones also. . . . I chose my verses for their sentiment, and because I wanted to commit them to memory. . . .

Some of the girls could not believe that the Bible was meant to be counted among forbidden books. We all thought that the Scriptures had a right to go wherever we went, and that if we needed them anywhere, it was at our work. I evaded the law by carrying some leaves from a torn Testament in my pocket.

The overseer, caring more for the law than gospel, confiscated all he found. He had his desk full of Bibles. It sounded oddly to hear him say to the most religious girl in the room, when he took

*Lucy Larcom, *A New England Girlhood, Outlined from Memory* (Boston: Houghton Mifflin Company, 1889), 175–76, 180–83, 201–02, 233.

hers away, "I always did think you had more conscience than to bring that book here." But we had some close ethical questions to settle in those days. It was a rigid code of morality under which we lived. Nobody complained of it, however, and we were doubtless better off for its strictness, in the end. . . .

I do not believe that any Lowell mill-girl was ever absurd enough to wish to be known as a "factory-lady," although most of them knew that "factory-girl" did not represent a high type of womanhood in the Old World. But they themselves belonged to the New World, not to the Old; and they were making their own traditions, to hand down to their Republican descendants,—one of which was and is that honest work has no need to assert itself or to humble itself in a nation like ours, but simply to take its place as one of the foundation stones of the Republic.

The young women who worked at Lowell had the advantage of living in a community where character alone commanded respect. They never, at their work or away from it, heard themselves contemptuously spoken of on account of their occupation, except by the ignorant or weak-minded, whose comments they were of course too sensible to heed. . . .

We were allowed to have books in the cloth-room. The absence of machinery permitted that privilege. Our superintendent, who was a man of culture and a Christian gentleman of the Puritan-school, dignified and reserved, used often to stop at my desk in his daily round to see what book I was reading. . . . It was a satisfaction to have a superintendent like him, whose granite principles, emphasized by his stately figure and bearing, made him a strength in the church and in the community. He kept a silent, kindly, rigid watch over the corporation life of which he was the head; and only those of us who were incidentally admitted to his confidence knew how carefully we were guarded. . . .

70. THE COTTON SOUTH, 1835*

Harriet Martineau, a visitor from England, traveled extensively through the United States early in the 1830s, and she wrote an excellent account of life in America. Martineau made the following comments based on a visit to the booming "cotton belt" of Alabama. Although southerners often mistrusted industrialization, and although they came to fear the growing power of the manufacturing North, Martineau's comments left little doubt that cotton growers were as attracted as Yankee factory owners to the wealth of the market economy. The Englishwoman's observations, in addition, touched briefly on the conditions of the slaves who served as the labor foundation for the cotton economy.

We saw to-day, the common sight of companies of slaves travelling westwards; and the very uncommon one of a party returning to South Carolina. When we overtook such a company proceeding westwards, and esked where they were going, the answer commonly given by the slaves was, "Into Yellibama."—Sometimes these poor creatures were encamped, under the care of a slave-trader, on the banks of a clear stream, to spend a day in washing their clothes. Sometimes they were loitering along the road; the old folks and infants mounted on top of a wagon-load of luggage; the able-bodied, on foot, perhaps silent, perhaps laughing; the prettier of the girls, perhaps with a flower in her hair, and a lover's arm around her shoulder. There were wide differences in the air and gait of these people. It is usual to call the most depressed of them brutish in appearance. In some sense, they are so; but I never saw in any brute an expression of countenance so low, so lost, as in the most degraded class of negroes. There is some life and intelligence in the countenance of every animal; even in that of the "silly sheep," nothing so dead as the vacant, unheeding look of the

*Harriet Martineau, *Society in America*, 3 vols. (London: Saunders and Otley, 1837), I: 291–92, 297–98, 300–01, 307–09.

depressed slaves is to be seen. To-day there was a spectacle by the roadside which showed that this has nothing to do with negro nature; though no such proof is needed by those who have seen negroes in favorable circumstances, and know how pleasant an aspect those grotesque features may wear. To-day we passed, in the Creek Territory, an establishment of Indians who held slaves. Negroes are anxious to be sold to Indians, who give them moderate work, and accommodations as good as their own. Those seen today among the Indians, were sleek, intelligent, and cheerful-looking, like the most favoured house-slaves, or free servants of colour, where the prejudice is least strong. . . .

Our friends, now residing seven miles from Montgomery, were from South Carolina; and the lady, at least, does not relish living in Alabama. It was delightful to me to be a guest in such an abode as theirs. They were about to build a good house: meantime, they were in one which I liked exceedingly: a log-house, with the usual open passage in the middle. Roses and honeysuckles, to which humming-birds resort, grew before the door. Abundance of books, and handsome furniture and plate, were within the house, while daylight was to be seen through its walls. In my well furnished chamber, I could see through the chinks between the logs. During the summer, I should be sorry to change this primitive kind of abode for a better.

It is not difficult to procure the necessaries and comforts of life. Most articles are provided on the plantation. Wine and groceries are obtained from Mobile or New Orleans; and clothing and furniture come from the north. Tea is twenty shillings English per lb.; brown sugar, threepence-halfpenny; white sugar, sixpence-halfpenny. A gentlemen's family, where there are children to be educated, cannot live for less than from seven hundred pounds to one thousands pounds per annum. The sons take land and buy slaves very early; and the daughters marry almost in childhood; so that education is less thought of, and sooner ended, than in almost any part of the world. The pioneers of civilisation, as the settlers in these new districts may be regarded, care for other things more than for education; or they would not come. They are, from whatever motive, money-getters; and few but money-getting qualification are to be looked for in them. It was partly amusing, and partly sad, to observe the young people of these regions; some, fit for a better mode of life, discontented; some youths pedantic, some maidens romantic, to a degree which makes the stranger almost doubt the reality of the scenes and personages before his eyes. The few better educated who come to get money, see the absurdity, and feel the wearisomeness of this kind of literary cultivation; but the being in such society is the tax they must pay for making haste to be rich.

I heard in Montgomery of a wealthy old planter in the neighborhood, who has amassed millions of dollars, while his children can scarcely write their names. Becoming aware of their deficiencies, as the place began to be peopled from the eastward, he sent a son of sixteen to school, and a younger one to college; but they proved "such gawks," that they were unable to learn, or even to remain in the society of others who were learning; and their old father has bought land in Missouri, whither he was about to take his children, to remove them from the contempt of their neighbors. They are doomed to the lowest office of social beings; to be the mechanical, unintelligent pioneers of man in the wilderness. Surely such a warning as this should strike awe into the whole region, lest they should also perish to all the best purposes of life, by getting to consider money, not as a means, but an end. . . .

We saw several plantations while we were in this neighborhood. Nothing can be richer than the soil of one to which we went, to take a lesson in cotton-growing. It will never want more than to have the cotton seed returned to it. We saw the plough, which is very shallow. Two throw up a ridge, which is wrought by hand into little mounds. After these are drilled, the seed is put in by hand. This plantation consists of nine hundred and fifty acres, and is flourishing in every way. The air is healthy, as the situation is high prairie land. The water is generally good; but, after rain, so impregnated with lime, as to be disagreeable to the smell and taste. . . . Another grievance is, that no trees can be allowed to grow near the house for fear of mosquitoes. Everything else is done for coolness; there are wide piazzas on both sides of the house; the rooms are lofty, and amply provided with green blinds; but all this does not compensate to the eye for the want of the shade of trees. . . . But the plague of mosquitoes is a sufficient warrant for the pleasures of the eye; for they allow but little enjoyment of anything in their presence. . . .

The profits of cotton-growing, when I was in Alabama, were thirty-five per cent. One planter whom I knew had bought fifteen thousand dollars worth of land within two years, which he could then have sold for sixty-five thousand dollars. He expected to make, that season, fifty or sixty thousand dollars of his growing crop. It is certainly the place to become rich in; but the state of society is fearful. One of my hosts, a man of great good-nature, as he shows in the treatment of his slaves, and in his family relations, had been stabbed in the back in the reading-room of the town, two years before, and no prosecution was instituted. Another of my hosts carried loaded pistols . . . knowing that he was lain in wait for by persons against whose illegal practices he had given information to a magistrate. . . . It will be understood that I describe this region as presenting an extreme case of the material advantages and moral evils of a new settlement, under the institution of slavery. The most prominent relief is the hospitality,—the virtue of a young society. It is so remarkable, and to the stranger so grateful, that there is danger of its blinding him to the real state of affairs. In the drawing-rooms, the piazza, the barouche, all is so gay and friendly, there is such a prevailing hilarity and kindness, that it seems positively ungrateful and unjust to pronounce, even in one's heart, that all this way of life is full of wrong and peril. . . .

Discussion

1. How might the policies that Henry Clay defended have influenced the distribution of economic powers in the United States? How do you think Clay perceived liberty and equality? How do the policies he advanced compare to those outlined in Hamilton's Report on Manufactures in Chapter 9? How does Clay's vision of the United States compare to that of Thomas Jefferson as expressed in his first inaugural address?

2. What does President Madison's veto message suggest about his understanding of national power? Why do you think Madison considered subsidizing roads to be unconstitutional? What does the message reveal about the nature of presidential power?

3. Based on the documents describing the Lowell system, how do you think that factory girls might have understood liberty, equality, and power? To what degree did the Lowell workers enjoy power? Did they have any liberties? If so, what; if not, why not? How does the Lowell system relate to the American faith in equality?

4. Would you describe Harriet Martineau as being sympathetic toward or critical of the American South? Who held power in the South, and how was that power manifested? Did southerners believe in equality or liberty?

5. How might a factory girl or a white southerner have responded to Henry Clay's proposals?

6. How did the Erie Canal help transform the Northeast into a center of economic power?

7. Would you describe Harriet Martineau as being impressed with the city of Chicago? How would you compare her views of the South with her impressions of Chicago?

CHAPTER 10

Toward an American Culture

Blacks resisted slavery in many ways, from destroying equipment and work slowdowns to the extreme of slave revolts. Running away was another extreme, but seldom successful, response to the system. Notice in this 1849 handbill the detailed descriptions of the runaways, as well as the size of the reward— $600 was more than most workers earned in a year.

Attitudes toward liberty, equality, and power shaped the politics as well as the economics of the early republic, but those three forces also profoundly influenced the development of an American culture. In the years following the War of 1812, the nation underwent a religious and intellectual transformation that affected all sectional, social, and racial groups. Certain groups came to hold power in the United States, and since that concentration of power had deep implications for liberty and equality, cultural differences became apparent. On one hand, "core" groups of middle-class northerners and commercially minded southerners generally supported the traditional American ideals of republicanism and capitalism promoted by men such as Alexander Hamilton and Henry Clay. On the other hand, poorer and more marginal Americans advanced a different vision of popular government and property by insisting on a democratic society that stressed equality—especially for white male adults.

71. AMERICAN REVIVALISM, 1835*

Charles G. Finney played a critical role in the religious experience known as the Second Great Awakening, and in the following selection he summarized his views on revivals. In the selection, taken from an introduction to a book, he stressed the dynamic part that human beings should assume in carrying out God's will. Finney placed a strong emphasis on individuals, because each person had the opportunity to choose between good and evil. That egalitarianism reflected the growing democratic character of the nation. His message of "free agency," which called for active human intervention to improve the moral universe, also fit nicely with the emerging middle-class values of material progress built upon sobriety and industriousness. Finney's theology, then, helped provide a moral imperative to the economic and political power that many Americans were gaining as a result of the market revolution, and his ideas served as a foundation for the middle-class culture that emerged in the 1830s.

1. Revivals were formerly regarded as miracles. And it has been so by some even in our day. And others have ideas on the subject so loose and unsatisfactory, that if they would only *think*, they would see their absurdity. For a long time, it was supposed by the church, that a revival was a miracle, an interposition of Divine power which they had nothing to do with, and which they had no more agency in producing, than they had in producing thunder, or a storm of hail, or an earthquake. It is only within a few years that ministers generally have supposed revivals were to be *promoted*, by the use of means designed and adapted specially to that object. Even in New England, it has been supposed that revivals came just as showers do, sometimes in one town, and sometimes in another, and that ministers and churches could do nothing more to produce them, than they could to make showers of rain come on their own town, when they are falling on a neighboring town.

It used to be supposed that a revival would come about once in fifteen years, and all would be converted that God intended to save, and then they must wait until another crop came forward on the stage of life. Finally, the time got shortened down to five years, and they supposed there might be a revival about as often as that.

---

*Charles G. Finney, "What a Revival of Religion Is," in *Lectures on Revivals of Religion* (New York: Leavitt, Lord & Company, 1835), 17–20.

I have heard a fact in relation to one of these pastors, who supposed revival might come about once in five years. There had been a revival in his congregation. The next year, there was a revival in a neighboring town, and he went there to preach, and staid several days, till he got his soul all engaged in the work. He returned home on Saturday, and went into his study to prepare for the Sabbath. And his soul was in an agony. He thought how many adult persons there were in his congregation at enmity with God—so many still unconverted—so many persons *die* yearly—such a portion of them unconverted—if a revival does not come under five years, so many adult heads of families will be in hell. He put down his calculations on paper, and embodied them in his sermon for the next day, with his heart bleeding at the dreadful picture. As I understood it, he did not do this with any expectation of a revival, but he felt deeply, and poured out his heart to his people. And that sermon awakened *forty heads of families*, and a powerful revival followed; and so his theory about a revival once in five years was all exploded.

Thus God has overthrown, generally, the theory that revivals are miracles.

2. Mistaken notions concerning the sovereignty of God, have greatly hindered revivals. Many people have supposed God's sovereignty to be something very different from what it is. They have supposed it to be such an arbitrary disposal of events, and particularly of the gift of his Spirit, as precluded a rational employment of means for promoting a revival of religion. But there is no evidence from the Bible, that God exercises any such sovereignty as that. There are no facts to prove it. But every thing goes to show, that God has connected means with the end through all the departments of his government—in nature and in grace. There is no *natural* event in which his own agency is not concerned. He has not built the creation like a vast machine, that will go on alone without his further care. He has not retired from the universe, to let it work for itself. This is mere atheism. He exercises a universal superintendence and control. And yet every event in nature has been brought about by means. He neither administers providence nor grace with that sort of sovereignty, that dispenses with the use of means. There is no more sovereignty in one than in the other.

And yet some people are terribly alarmed at all direct efforts to promote a revival, and they cry out, "you are trying to get up a revival in your own strength. Take care, you are interfering with the sovereignty of God. Better keep along in the usual course, and let God give a revival when he thinks it is best. God is a sovereign, and it is very wrong for you to attempt to get up a revival, just because *you think* a revival is needed." This is just such preaching as the devil wants. And men cannot do the devil's work more effectually, than by preaching up the sovereignty of God, as a reason why we should not put forth efforts to produce a revival.

3. You see the error of those who are beginning to think that religion can be better promoted in the world without revivals, and who are disposed to give up all efforts to produce religious excitements. Because there are evils arising in some instances out of great excitements on the subject of religion, they are of an opinion that it is best to dispense with them altogether. This cannot, and must not be. True, there is danger of abuses. In cases of great *religious* as well as other excitements, more or less incidental evils may be expected of course. But this is no reason why they should be given up. The best things are always liable to abuses. Great and manifold evils have originated in the providential and moral government of God. But these *foreseen* perversions and evils were not considered a sufficient reason for giving them up. For the establishment of these governments was on the whole the best that could be done for the production of the greatest amount of happiness. So in revivals of religion, it is found by experience, that in the present state of the world, religion cannot be promoted to any considerable extent without them. The evils which are sometimes complained of, when they are real, are incidental, and of small importance when compared with the amount of good produced by revivals. The sentiment should not be admitted by the church for a moment, that revivals may be given up. It is fraught with all that is dangerous to the interests of Zion, is death to the cause of missions, and brings in its train the damnation of the world.

FINALLY—I have a proposal to make to you who are here present. I have not commenced this course of Lectures on Revivals to get up a curious theory of my own on the subject. I would not spend my time and strength merely to give you instructions, to gratify your curiosity, and furnish you something to talk about. I have no idea preaching *about* revivals. It is not my design to preach so as to have you able to say at the close, "We *understand* all about revivals now," while you do *nothing*. But I wish to ask you a question. What do you hear lectures on revivals for? Do you mean that whenever you are convinced what your duty is in promoting a revival, you will go to work and practise it?

Will you follow the instructions I shall give you from the word of God, and put them in practice in your own hearts? Will you bring them to bear upon your families, your acquaintance, neighbors, and through the city? Or will you spend the winter in learning *about* revivals, and do nothing *for* them? I want you, as fast as you learn anything on the subject of revivals, to put it in practice, and go to work and see if you cannot promote a revival among sinners here. If you will not do this, I wish you to let me know at the beginning, so that I need not waste my strength. You ought to decide *now* whether you will do this or not. You know that we call sinners to decide on the spot whether they will obey the gospel. And we have no more authority to let you take time to deliberate whether *you* will obey God, than we have to let sinners do so. We call on you to unite now in a solemn pledge to God, that you will do your duty as fast as you learn what it is and to pray that He will pour out his Spirit upon this church and upon all the city this winter.

72. A VISIT TO AN INDIANA CAMP MEETING, 1828*

The camp-meeting revivals of the early 19th century continued throughout the antebellum years, but became increasingly respectable. The inclusive, ecstatic meetings of the past evolved into events held by single denominations and conducted with more decorum. Still, the meetings sometimes shocked unfriendly observers. One such visitor, Englishwoman Frances Trollope (1780-1863), attended an Indiana Methodist camp meeting in 1828. Although demonstrating her Anglican distaste for Methodist preaching and religious emotionalism, Trollope provides a detailed and sharply witty account of one such spiritual celebration.

It was in the course of this summer that I found the opportunity I had long wished for, of attending a camp-meeting, and I gladly accepted the invitation of an English lady and gentleman to accompany them in their carriage to the spot where it is held; this was in a wild district on the confines of Indiana.

The prospect of passing a night in the back-woods of Indiana was by no means agreeable, but I screwed my courage to the proper pitch, and set forth determined to see with my own eyes, and hear with my own ears, what a camp-meeting really was. I had heard it said that being at a camp-meeting was like standing at the gate of heaven, and seeing it opening before you; I had heard it said, that being at a camp-meeting was like finding yourself within the gates of hell; in either case there must be something to gratify curiosity, and compensate one for the fatigue of a long rumbling ride and a sleepless night.

We reached the ground about an hour before midnight, and the approach to it was highly picturesque. The spot chosen was the verge of an unbroken forest, where a space of about twenty acres appeared to have been partially cleared for the purpose. Tents of different sizes were pitched very near together in a circle round the cleared space; behind them were ranged an exterior circle of carriages of every description, and at the back of each were fastened the horses which had drawn them thither. Through this triple circle of defence we distinguished numerous fires burning brightly within it; and still more numerous lights flickering from the trees that were left in the enclosure. The moon was in meridian splendour above our heads.

---

*From Frances Trollope, *Domestic Manners of the Americans* (London: Whittaker, Treacher, & Company, 1832), 139–44.

We left the carriage to the care of a servant . . . and entered the inner circle. The first glance reminded me of Vauxhall, from the effect of the lights among the trees, and the moving crowd below them; but the second showed a scene totally unlike any thing I had ever witnessed. Four high frames, constructed in the form of altars, were placed at the four corners of the inclosure; on these were supported layers of earth and sod, on which burned immense fires of blazing pine-wood. On one side a rude platform was erected to accommodate the preachers, fifteen of whom attended this meeting, and with very short intervals for necessary refreshment and private devotion, preached in rotation, day and night, from Tuesday to Saturday.

When we arrived, the preachers were silent; but we heard issuing from nearly every tent mingled sounds of praying, preaching, singing, and lamentation. The curtains in front of each tent were dropped, and the faint light that gleamed through the white drapery, backed as it was by the dark forest, had a beautitul and mysterious effect, that set the imagination at work; and had the sounds which vibrated around us been less discordant, harsh, and unnatural, I should have enjoyed it; but listening at the corner of a tent, which poured forth more than its proportion of clamour, in a few moments chased every feeling derived from imagination, and furnished realities that could neither be mistaken nor forgotten.

Great numbers of persons were walking about the ground, who appeared like ourselves to be present only as spectators; some of these very unceremoniously contrived to raise the drapery of this tent at one corner, so as to afford us a perfect view of the interior.

The floor was covered with straw, which round the sides was heaped in masses, that might serve as seats, but which at that moment were used to support the heads and the arms of the close-packed circle of men nnd women who kneeled on the floor.

Out of about thirty persons thus placed, perhaps half a dozen were men. One of these, a handsome-looking youth of eighteen or twenty, kneeled just below the opening through which I looked. His arm was encircling the neck of a young girl who knelt beside him, with her hair hanging dishevelled upon her shoulders, and her features working with the most violent agitation; soon after they both fell forward on the straw, as if unable to endure in any other attitude the burning eloquence of a tall grim figure in black, who, standing erect in the centre, was uttering with incredible vehemence an oration that seemed to hover between praying and preaching; his arms hung stiff and immoveable by his side, and he looked like an ill-constructed machine, set in action by a movement so violent as to threaten its own destruction, so jerkingly, painfully, yet rapidly, did his words tumble out; the kneeling circle ceasing not to call, in every variety of tone, on the name of Jesus; accompanied with sobs, groans, and a sort of low howling inexpressibly painful to listen to. . . .

We made the circuit of the tents, pausing where attention was particularly excited by sounds more vehement than ordinary. We contrived to look into many; all were strewed with straw, and the distorted figures that we saw kneeling, sitting, and lying among it, joined to the woful and convulsive cries, gave to each the air of a cell in Bedlam.

One tent was occupied exclusively by Negroes. They were all full-dressed, and looked exactly as if they were performing a scene on the stage. One woman wore a dress of pink gauze trimmed with silver lace; another was dressed in pale yellow silk; one or two had splendid turbans; and all wore a profusion of ornaments. The men were in snow white pantaloons, with gay coloured linen jackets. One of these, a youth of coal-black comeliness, was preaching with the most violent gesticulations, frequently springing high from the ground, and clapping his hands over his head. Could our missionary societies have heard the trash he uttered, by way of an address to the Deity, they might perhaps have doubted whether his conversion had much enlightened his mind.

At midnight, a horn sounded through the camp, which, we were told, was to call the people from private to public worship; and we presently saw them flocking from all sides to the front of the preachers' stand. . . . There were about two thousand persons assembled.

One of the preachers began in a low nasal tone, and, like all other Methodist preachers, assured us of the enormous depravity of man as he comes from the hands of his Maker, and of his perfect sanctification after he had wrestled sufficiently with the Lord to get hold of him, *et cetera*. The admiration of the crowd was evinced by almost constant cries of "Amen! Amen!" "Jesus! Jesus !" "Glory! Glory !" and, the like. But this comparative tranquillity did not last long: the preacher told them that "this night was the time fixed upon for anxious sinners to wrestle with the Lord;" that he and his brethren "were at hand to help them," and that such as needed their help were to come forward into the "pen." . . . immediately below the preachers' stand; we were therefore placed on the edge of it, and were enabled to see and hear all that took place in the very centre of this extraordinary exhibition.

The crowd fell back at the mention of the *pen*, and for some minutes there was a vacant space before us. The preachers came down from their stand, and placed themselves in the midst of it, beginning to sing a hymn, calling upon the penitents to come forth. As they sung they kept turning themselves round to every part of the crowd, and, by degrees, the voices of the whole multitude joined in chorus. This was the only moment at which I perceived any thing like the solemn and beautiful effect which I had heard ascribed to this woodland worship. It is certain that the combined voices of such a multitude, heard at dead of night, from the depths of their eternal forests, the many fair young faces turned upward, and looking paler and lovelier as they met the moonbeams, the dark figures of the officials in the middle of the circle, the lurid glare thrown by the altar fires on the woods beyond, did altogether produce a fine and solemn effect, that I shall not easily forget; but ere I had well enjoyed it, the scene changed, and sublimity gave place to horror and disgust.

The exhortation nearly resembled that which I had heard at "the revival," but the result was very different; for, instead of the few hysterical women who had distinguished themselves on that occasion, above a hundred persons, nearly all females, came forward, uttering howlings and groans so terrible that I shall never cease to shudder when I recall them. They appeared to drag each other forward, and on the word being given, "let us pray," they all fell on their knees; but this posture was soon changed for others that permitted greater scope for the convulsive movements of their limbs; and they were soon all lying on the ground in an indescribable confusion of heads and legs. They threw about their limbs with such incessant and violent motion, that I was every instant expecting some serious accident to occur.

But how am I to describe the sounds that proceeded from this strange mass of human beings? I know no words which can convey an idea of it. Hysterical sobbings, convulsive groans, shrieks and screams the most appalling, burst forth on all sides. I felt sick with horror. As if their hoarse and overstrained voices failed to make noise enough, they soon began to clap their hands violently. . . .

73. THE EMPIRE OF WOMAN, 1845*

After 1815 the market revolution produced a growing distinction between male and female work in middle-class America. Evangelical preachers and magazines aimed at middle-class women encouraged this division of labor; women reigned over a "sphere of domesticity" while men worked in the public world. In the following selection, Sarah Josepha Hale, editor of the mass-circulated Godey's Lady's Book, *reinforces this idea in her 1845 poem, "The Empire of Woman."*

THE EMPIRE OF WOMAN.

1.

Woman's Empire defined.

THE outward World, for rugged Toil design'd,

Where Evil from true Good the crown hath riven,
Has been to Man's dominion ever given;

---

*From Sarah Josepha Hale, "The Empire of Woman," *Godey's Lady's Book* 31 (July, 1845), 12.

But Woman's empire, holier, more refin'd,
Moulds, moves and sways the fall'n but God-
    breath'd mind,
    Lifting the earth-crushed heart to hope and
      heaven:
As plants put forth to Summer's gentle wind,
    And 'neath the sweet, soft light of starry even,
Those treasures which the tyrant Winter's sway
    Could never wrest from Nature,—so the soul
Will Woman's sweet and gentle power obey—
    Thus doth her summer smile its strength control;
Her love sow flowers along life's thorny way;
    Her star-bright faith lead up toward heaven's
      goal.

2.

The Daughter.

The iron cares that load and press men down
    A father can, like school-boy tasks, lay by,
    When gazing in his Daughter's loving eye,
Her soft arm like a spell around him thrown:
The passions that, like Upas' leaves, have grown
    Most deadly in dark places, which defy
Earth, heaven and human will, even these were
      shown
    All powerless to resist the pleading cry
Which pierced a savage but a father's ear,
    And shook a soul where pity's pulse seemed
      dead:
When Pocahontas, heeding not the fear
    That daunted boldest warriors, laid her head
Beside the doomed! Now with our country's fame,
Sweet forest* Daughter, we have blent thy name.

3.

The Sister.

Wild as a colt, o'er prairies bounding free,
    The wakened spirit of the Boy doth spring,
    Spurning the rein authority would fling,
And striving with his peers for mastery;
But in the household gathering let him see
    His Sister's winning smile, and it will bring
A change o'er all his nature; patiently,
    As cagéd bird, that never used its wing,

He turns him to the tasks that she doth share—
    His better feelings kindle by her side—
Visions of angel beauty fill the air,—
    And she may summon such to be his guide:—
Our Saviour listened to a Sister's prayer,
    When, "Lazarus, from the tomb come forth!"
      he cried.

4.

The Wife.

The Daughter from her father's bosom goes—
    The Sister drops her brother's clasping hand—
    For God himself ordained a holier band
Than kindred blood on human minds bestows:
That stronger, deeper, dearer tie she knows.
    The heart-wed Wife; as heaven by rainbow
      spann'd
Thus bright with hope life's path before her
      glows—
    Proves it like mirage on the desert's sand?
Still in her soul the light divine remains—
    And if her husband's strength be overborne
By sorrow, sickness, or the felon's chains,—
    Such as by England's noblest son* were worn—
    Unheeding how her own poor heart is torn,
She, angel-like, his sinking soul sustains.

5.

The Mother.

Earth held no symbol, had no living sign
    To image forth the Mother's deathless love;
    And so the tender care the righteous prove
Beneath the ever-watching eye divine,
Was given a type to show how pure that shrine.
    The Mother's heart, was hallowed from above.
And how her mortal hopes must intertwine
    With hopes immortal,—and she may not move
From this high station which her Saviour sealed.
When in maternal arms he lay revealed.
    Oh! wondrous power, how little understood.
Entrusted to the Mother's mind alone,
    To fashion genius, form the soul for good.
Inspire a West,[†] or train a Washington!

---

*See the splendid painting, "Baptism of Pocahontas," at the Capitol.

*Lord William Russell.
[†]"My mother's kiss made me a painter," was the testimony of this great artist.

74. UNCLE TOM'S CABIN, 1852*

Uncle Tom's Cabin was an incredibly popular novel, and in the following passage there occurred one of the most dramatic moments in 19th-century American literature—the death of Little Eva St. Clare. The melodrama that Harriet Beecher Stowe described in her novel certainly revealed the sentimentalism of the mid-1800s. The story also stressed the importance of evangelical religion, and it is striking in its presentation of a female as the moral agent of Christianity. In addition, the book dealt with some of the issues of power and liberty that marked the era. The dependent status of the slaves is apparent, and Stowe clearly hoped to attract attention to the plight of the people she referred to as the "lowly." She addressed gender relations as well, with three women providing the most powerful characters in the scene presented here. Like most cultural works, then, Uncle Tom's Cabin *reflected much of the society out of which it emerged.*

Eva lay back on her pillows; her hair hanging loosely about her face, her crimson cheeks contrasting painfully with the intense whiteness of her complexion and the thin contour of her limbs and features, and her large soul-like eyes fixed earnestly on every one.

The servants were struck with a sudden emotion. The spiritual face, the long locks of hair cut off and lying by her, her father's averted face, and Marie's sobs, struck at once upon feelings of a sensitive and impressible race; and as they came in, they looked at one another, sighed, and shook their heads. There was a deep silence, like that of a funeral.

Eva raised herself, and looked long and earnestly round at every one. All looked sad and apprehensive. Many of the women hid their faces in their aprons.

"I sent for you all, my dear friends," said Eva, "because I love you. I love you all; and I have something to say to you, which I want you always to remember. . . . I am going to leave you. In a few more weeks, you will see me no more—"

Here the child was interrupted by bursts of groans, sobs, and lamentations, which broke from all present, and in which her slender voice was lost entirely. She waited a moment, and then, speaking in a tone that checked the sobs of all, she said

"If you love me, you must not interrupt me so. Listen to what I say. I want to speak to you about your souls. . . . Many of you, I am afraid, are very careless. You are thinking only about this world. I want you to remember that there is a beautiful world, where Jesus is. I am going there, and you can go there. It is for you, as much as me. But, if you want to go there, you must not live idle, careless, thoughtless lives. You must be Christians. You must remember that each one of you can become angels and be angels forever. . . . If you want to be Christians, Jesus will help you. You must pray to him; you must read—"

The child checked herself, looked piteously at them, and said, sorrowfully,

"O, dear! you *can't* read,—poor souls!" and she hid her face in the pillow and sobbed, while many a smothered sob from those she was addressing, who were kneeling on the floor, aroused her.

"Never mind," she said, raising her face and smiling brightly through her tears, "I have prayed for you; and I know Jesus will help you, even if you can't read. Try all to do the best you can; pray every day; ask Him to help you, and get the Bible read to you whenever you can; and I think I shall see you all in heaven."

"Amen," was the murmured response from the lips of Tom and Mammy, and some of the elder ones, who belonged to the Methodist church. The younger and more thoughtless ones, for the time completely overcome, were sobbing, with their heads bowed upon their knees.

"I know" said Eva, "you all love me."

"Yes; oh, yes! indeed we do! Lord bless her!" was the involuntary answer of all.

---

*From Harriet Beecher Stowe, *Uncle Tom's Cabin, or, Life Among the Lowly*, 2 vols. (Boston: J. P. Jewett, 1852), II:102–05, 107–08, 110–13.

"Yes, I know you do! There is n't one of you that has n't always been very kind to me; and I want to give you something that, when you look at, you shall always remember. I'm going to give all of you a curl of my hair; and when you look at it, think that I loved you and am gone to heaven, and that I want to see all of you there."

It is impossible to describe the scene, as, with tears and sobs, they gathered round the little creature, and took from her hands what seemed to them a last mark of her love. They fell on their knees; they sobbed, and prayed, and kissed the hem of her garment; and the elder ones poured forth words of endearment, mingled in prayers and blessings, after the manner of their susceptible race.

As each one took their gift, Miss Ophelia, who was apprehensive for the effect of the excitement on her little patient, signed to each one to pass out of the apartment.

At last, all were gone but Tom and Mammy.

"Here, Uncle Tom," said Eva, "is a beautiful one for you. O, I am so happy, Uncle Tom, to think I shall see you in heaven,—for I'm sure I shall; and Mammy, —dear, good, kind Mammy!" she said, fondly throwing her arms round her old nurse,—"I know you'll be there, too."

"O, Miss Eva, don't see how I can live without ye, no how!" said the faithful creature. "'Pears like it's just taking everything off the place to oncet" and Mammy gave way to a passion of grief.

Miss Ophelia pushed her and Tom gently from the apartment. . . .

Eva, after this, declined rapidly; there was no more any doubt of the event; the fondest hope could not be blinded. Her beautiful room was avowedly a sick room; and Miss Ophelia day and night performed the duties of a nurse,—and never did her friends appreciate her value more than in that capacity. With so well-trained a hand and eye, such perfect adroitness and practice in every art which could promote neatness and comfort, and keep out of sight every disagreeable incident of sickness,—with such a perfect sense of time, such a clear, untroubled head, such exact accuracy in remembering every prescription and direction of the doctors,—she was everything to him. They who had shrugged their shoulders at her little peculiarities and setnesses, so unlike the careless freedom of southern manners, acknowledged that now she was the exact person that was wanted.

Uncle Tom was much in Eva's room. The child suffered much from nervous restlessness, and it was a relief to her to be carried; and it was Tom's greatest delight to carry her little frail form in his arms, resting on a pillow, now up and down her room, now out into the verandah; and when the fresh sea-breezes blew from the lake,—and the child felt freshest in the morning,—he would sometimes walk with her under the orange-trees in the garden, or, sitting down in some of their old seats, sing to her their favorite old hymns.

Her father often did the same thing; but his frame was slighter, and when he was weary, Eva would say to him,

"O, papa, let Tom take me. Poor fellow! it pleases him; and you know it's all he can do for now, and he wants to do something!"

"So do I, Eva!" said her father.

"Well, papa, you can do everything, and are everything to me. You read to me,—you sit up nights,—and Tom has only this one thing, and his singing; and I know, too, he does it easier than you can. He carries me so strong!"

. . . Eva had been unusually bright and cheerful, that afternoon, and had sat raised in her bed, and looked all over her little trinkets and precious things, and designated the friends to whom she would have them given; and her manner was more animated, and her voice more natural, than they had known it for weeks. Her father had been in, in the evening, and had said that Eva appeared more like her former self than ever she had done since her sickness; and when he kissed her for the night, he said to Miss Ophelia,—"Cousin, we may keep her with us, after all; she is certainly better;" and he had retired with a lighter heart in his bosom than he had had there for weeks.

But at midnight,—strange, mystic hour!—when the veil between the frail present and the eternal future grows thin,—then came the messenger!

There was a sound in that chamber, first of one who stepped quickly. It was Miss Ophelia, who had resolved to sit up all night with her little charge, and who, at the turn of the night, had discerned what experienced nurses significantly call "a change." The outer door was quickly opened, and Tom, who was watching outside, was on the alert, in a moment.

"Go for the doctor, Tom! lose not a moment," said Miss Ophelia. . . .

On the face of the child, however, there was no ghastly imprint,—only a high and almost sublime expression,—the overshadowing presence of spiritual natures, the drawing of immortal life in that childish soul.

They stood there so still, gazing upon her, that even the ticking of the watch seemed too loud. In a few moments, Tom returned, with the doctor. He entered, gave one look, and stood silent as the rest.

"When did this change take place?" said he, in a low whisper, to Miss Ophelia.

"About the turn of night," was the reply.

Marie, roused by the entrance of the doctor, appeared, hurriedly, from the next room.

"Augustine! Cousin!—O!—what!" she hurriedly began.

"Hush!" said St. Clare, hoarsely; "*she is dying!*"

Mammy heard the words, and flew to awaken the servants. The house was soon roused,—lights were seen, footsteps heard, anxious faces thronged the verandah, and looked tearfully through the glass doors; but St. Clare heard and said nothing,—he saw only *that look* on the face of the little sleeper.

"O, if she would only wake, and speak once more!" he said; and, stooping over her, he spoke in her ear,—"Eva, darling!"

The large blue eyes unclosed,—a smile passed over her face;—she tried to raise her head, and to speak.

"Do you know me, Eva?"

"Dear papa," said the child, with a last effort, throwing her arms about his neck. In a moment they dropped again; and, as St. Clare raised his head, he saw a spasm of mortal agony pass over the face,—she struggled for breath, and threw up her little hands.

"O, God, this is dreadful!" he said, turning away in agony, and wringing Tom's hand, scarce conscious what he was doing. "O, Tom, my boy, it is killing me!"

Tom had his master's hands between his own; and, with tears streaming down his dark cheeks, looked up for help where he had always been used to look.

"Pray that this may be cut short!" said St. Clare,—"this wrings my heart."

"O, bless the Lord! it's over.—it's over, dear Master!" said Tom; "look at her."

The child lay panting on her pillows, as one exhausted,—the large clear eyes rolled up and fixed. Ah, what said those eyes, that spoke so much of heaven? Earth was past, and earthly pain; but so solemn, so mysterious, was the triumphant brightness of that face, that it checked even the sobs of sorrow. They pressed around her, in breathless stillness.

"Eva," said St. Clare, gently.

She did not hear.

"O, Eva, tell us what you see! What is it?" said her father.

A bright, a glorious smile passed over her face, and she said brokenly.—"O! love,—joy,—peace!" gave one sigh, and passed from death unto life!

"Farewell, beloved child! the bright, eternal doors have closed after thee; we shall see thy sweet face no more. O, woe for them who watched the entrance into heaven, when they shall wake and find only the cold gray sky of daily life, and thou gone forever!"

75. HENRY DAVID THOREAU, 1854*

In Walden, *Henry David Thoreau espoused the lessons to be taken from living close to nature. In the selection presented below, he warned against the conventional belief that wealth created power and happiness. Thoreau insisted instead that real power, and hence true liberty and equality, came from an internal moral wealth rather than from any profits that might be made in the market economy. Consequently, much of what Thoreau learned during his sojourn at Walden Pond appeared out of step with the middle-class values that influenced many of his contemporaries. For numerous people, however, especially those outside the mainstream, his reflections have become an integral part of their American culture.*

I left the woods for as good a reason as I went there. Perhaps it seemed to me that I had several more lives to live, and could not spare any more time for that one. It is remarkable how easily and insensibly we fall into a particular route, and make a beaten track for ourselves. I had not lived there for a week before my feet wore a path from my door to the pond-side; and though it is five or six years since I trod it, it is still quite distinct. It is true, I fear that others may have fallen into it, and so helped to keep it open. The surface of the earth is soft and impressible by the feet of men; and so with the paths which the mind travels. How worn and dusty, then, must the highways of the world, how deep the ruts of tradition and conformity! I did not wish to take a cabin passage, but rather to go before the mast and on the deck of the world, for there I could best see the moonlight amid the mountains. I do not wish to go below now.

I learned this, at least, by my experiment: that if one advances confidently in the direction of his dreams, and endeavors to live the life which he has imagined, he will meet with a success unexpected in the common hours. He will put some things behind, will pass on an invisible boundary; new, universal, and more liberal laws will begin to establish themselves around and within him; or the old laws be expanded, and interpreted in his favor in a more liberal sense, and he will live with the license of a higher order of beings. In proportion as he simplifies his life, the laws of the universe will appear less complex, and solitude will not be solitude, nor poverty poverty, nor weakness weakness. If you have built castles in the air, your work need not be lost; that is where they should be. Now put the foundations under them. . . .

Some are dinning in our ears that we Americans, and moderns generally, are intellectual dwarfs compared with ancients, or even the Elizabethan men. But what is that to the purpose? A living dog is better than a dead lion. Shall a man go and hang himself because he belongs to the race of pygmies, and not be the biggest pygmy that he can? Let every one mind his own business, and endeavor to be what he was made.

Why should we be in such desperate haste to succeed, and in such desperate enterprises? If a man does not keep pace with his companions, perhaps it is because he hears a different drummer. Let him step to the music which he hears, however measured or far away. It is not important that he should mature as soon as an apple tree or an oak. Shall he turn his spring into summer? If the condition of things which we were made for is not yet, what were any reality which we can substitute? We will not be shipwrecked on a vain reality. Shall we with pains erect a heaven of blue grass over ourselves, though when it is done we shall be sure to gaze still at the true ethereal heaven far above, as if the former were not? . . .

However mean your life is, meet it and live it; do not shun it and call it hard names. It is not so bad as you are. It looks poorest when you are richest. The faultfinder will find faults even in paradise. Love your life, poor as it is. You may perhaps have some pleasant, thrilling, glorious hours, even in a poorhouse. The setting sun is reflected from the windows of the almshouse as brightly as

---

*From Henry David Thoreau, *Walden* (New York: Grosset & Dunlap, 1910), 426–27, 430, 433–34.

from the rich man's abode; the snow melts before its door as early in the spring. I do not see but a quiet mind may live as contentedly there, and have as cheering thoughts, as in a palace. The town's poor seem to me often to live the most independent life of any. Maybe they are simply great enough to receive without misgiving. Most think that they are above being supported by the town; but it oftener happens that they are not above supporting themselves by dishonest means, which should be more disreputable. Cultivate poverty like a garden herb, like sage. Do not trouble yourself much to get new things, whether clothes or friends. Turn the old; return to them. Things do not change; we change. Sell your clothes and keep your thoughts. God will see that you do not want society. If I were confined to a corner of a garret all my days, like a spider, the world would be just as large to me while I had my thoughts about me. The philosopher said: "From an army of three divisions one can take away its general, and put it in disorder; from the man the most abject and vulgar one cannot take away his thought." Do not seek so anxiously to be developed, to subject yourselves to so many influences to be on; it is all dissipation. Humility like darkness reveals the heavenly lights. The shadows of poverty and meanness gather around us, "and lo! creation widens to our view." We are often reminded that if there were bestowed on us the wealth of Croesus, our aims must still be the same, and our means essentially the same. Moreover, if you are restricted in your range by poverty, if you cannot buy books and newspapers, for instance, you are but confined to the most significant and vital experiences; you are compelled to deal with the material which yields the most sugar and the most starch. It is life near the bone where it is sweetest. You are defended from being a trifler. No man loses ever on a lower level by magnanimity on a higher. Superfluous wealth can buy superfluities only. Money is not required to buy one necessary of the soul. . . .

76. ASTOR PLACE RIOT, 1849*

As the United States grew and the market economy expanded, some poorer Americans came to believe that an unequal distribution of wealth threatened their liberty as surely as the British had threatened the rights of an earlier generation. Such powerful social tensions led to a number of violent urban demonstrations, including the famous Astor Place Riot. That disturbance, sparked by a theatrical performance by English actor William Charles Macready, revealed the depth of the anger that many people felt toward the wealthy aristocracy that they believed endangered the egalitarian principles of the democratic republic. The following material provided one of the first accounts of the brutal incident that took place in New York City in 1849.

[May 16, 1849] RIOT IN NEW YORK.—The city of New York has become the scene of a terrible riot, arising from a private quarrel between two actors, Forrest and Macready. The details of it are too voluminous for our columns, and we confine ourselves to some leading particulars. On Monday, 7th inst. Macready, who is an Englishman, attempted to play, but the disturbance was so great that it was impossible to proceed. At the advice of leading play-goers he attempted it again on Thursday, the 10th inst. at the Aster Place Opera House. A mob soon assembled, and a strong police force was assembled to preserve the peace. The national guards were called out to aid the police. At the commencement of the performance rioters inside of the house raised a disturbance, and were immediately seized by the police.

The leading rioters having been taken out, a mob outside—about five thousand persons having gathered around the house—commenced throwing stones at the windows. Some of these missiles, weighing from one to three pounds, passed into the building, and fell among the audience, knocking off hats and inflicting injuries. Nobody was seriously hurt.

*Niles' National Register, LXXV (1849), 319, 368.

During these proceedings, a number of policemen, headed by their chief, remained inside, picking out the rioters from the various parts of the building, while outside a troop of cavalry and a body of police were kept at bay by the mob.

The cavalry, from some cause or other, did not arrive on the ground until near 9 o'clock, when the police conquered the rioters inside.

All the doors were guarded by police and strongly barred inside, which prevented the mob from breaking in, although some uneasiness prevailed, lest an attempt be made to fire the building.

Between eight and nine o'clock the mob outside was increasing each moment in numbers and ferocity. Several of the policemen had been brought in severely wounded, one or two of the entrances were forced, and as imminent danger was apprehended, Mayor Woodhall, who was present, gave orders to Gen. Sanford to bring the military into the melee. The order was promptly obeyed, and in a few minutes several companies of the National Guard were placed in position around the theatre.

They were at first greeted with hisses and groans, but in a short time, just after the curtain fell on Macbeth, the paving-stones began to be hurled at them, and many of them were very severely, if not fatally injured. They stood this pelting, however, like veterans, nearly half an hour, only removing their comrades inside the theatre, as fast as they were struck down. At the solicitation of the Chief of Police, Mr. Recorder Tallmadge, amid a shower of missiles ventured his life to warn them off. The caution was unheeded, and the Mayor and Sheriff Westervelt being called to the scene, the order was finally given to *fire!*

A platoon of the National Guard instantly answered the summons! a number of the mob fell, and among them a noted convict from the State Prison. The rioters then retreated in confusion, but soon rallying, they came on more determined than ever, and it was only until three more volleys had been discharged into the crowd, that they were induced to retire. Probably two hundred balls were fired, of which twenty took effect.

The whole number killed and who have since died of their wounds, *is twenty-one;* and the number of wounded, including the military, is *thirty-three.* Several persons were killed and wounded who were attracted to the scene by mere foolish curiosity. The city was in a high state of excitement; many citizens approving of the course adopted by the authorities to suppress the mob, and others condemning it. Attempts by the lawless and reckless have happily failed to renew the scenes of violence; many arrests have been made, and the law has regained supremacy. Thus a whole community has been inflamed, and blood has been profusely shed, and all about a couple of worthless players. The coroner's inquest on the dead is awaited with some anxiety and supprehension.

The Coroner's jury have brought in a verdict in relation to those killed in the late riot, "that *the circumstances existing at the time justified the authorities in giving the order to fire upon the mob.* We further believe that if a larger number of the police had been ordered out, the necessity of a resort to the use of the military might have been avoided."

[May 30, 1849] DAMAGES BY THE ASTER PLACE RIOTS.—Mr. Hackett, Manager of the Astor Place Theatre, has presented to the city of New York, a claim of $5,005.20, for the damages sustained during the late riot. The bill for meals and refreshments to the police is $754.50; and the aggregate will be about $6,000.

77. CONCERNING SLAVES, 1842*

Charles Colcock Jones, who encouraged the religious instruction of slaves, hoped to bring Christianity to them—unquestionably to ensure their salvation but also to obtain absolute obedience to their masters. The

---

*Charles C. Jones, *The Religious Instruction of the Negroes in the United States* (Savannah: Thomas Purse, 1842), 112–19.

government and economy of the United States empowered many people, but the presence of millions of slaves posed a dilemma for American society. A republic founded on concepts of freedom and equality denied all hope of liberty to a vast segment of its population. As the country matured, therefore, questions concerning the "peculiar institution" took on increasing significance, and the place of African Americans in the national culture became one of the important themes in the history of the American people. In the passage below, Jones, who was not a "typical" southerner, leveled sharp criticisms at slaveowners. At the same time, his description of the slaves mirrored many of the white attitudes toward African Americans during the antebellum period.

The character of a people may be gathered from their circumstances. A consideration therefore of the circumstances in which we find our Negro population, is a necessary and preparatory step to the inquiry we have in hand.

1. *The circumstances of the Slave Population.*

As habits of virtue and vice are formed, and character shaped, at a very early age, I shall begin with—

The Negro in his Childhood.—The formation of good character depends upon family government and training; upon religious instruction, private and public; access to the Scriptures and other sources of intellectual and moral improvement; the character of associates; modesty of clothing, and general mode of living.

If we take the mass of the slave population, properly speaking, we shall find but little *family government,* and for the reason that parents are not qualified, neither are they so circumstanced as to fulfil perfectly the duties devolving upon them as such.

In the more intellectual and pious families, the children are taught to say their prayers, to go to church on the Sabbath, to attend evening prayers on the plantation, and a few simple rules of good conduct and manners. The majority of church members, come short of this. The moral training of their children forms but a small part of their effort in the family. There is not one family in a thousand in which family prayer is observed morning and evening. Prayers are held in some families morning and evening on the Sabbath day; in others in the evening of every day. But a general meeting of all the members of the church as well as of worldly persons, for prayer in the evening on the plantations, conducted by some prominent person among them, takes the place of family worship—the plantation is considered one large family. To this meeting children are required to come or not, as the case may be. The hour is usually so late that most of the children have retired for the night. If such is the state of religious families what must be the state of those who are irreligious? In multitudes of families, both by precept and example, the children are trained up in iniquity; taught by their parents to steal, to lie, to deceive; nor can the rod of correction induce a confession or revelation of their clearly ascertained transgressions. Virtue is not cherished nor protected in them. Parents put their children to use as early as it is possible, and their discipline mainly respects omissions of duty in the household; moral delinquencies are passed by; and that discipline owes its chief efficiency to excited passion, and consequently exists in the extreme of laxity or severity. They ofttimes when under no restraint, beat their children unmercifully.

As to the direct *religious instruction,* we have seen that the amount communicated in *families* is small. The Negroes on plantations sometimes appoint one of their number, commonly the old woman who minds the children during the day, to teach them to say prayers, repeat a little catechism and a few hymns, every evening. The instances are however not frequent, and it is the only approximation I have ever known to systematic instruction for their children, adopted by the Negroes themselves.

But how much religious instruction do the young Negroes receive from their *Masters,* who sustain very much the relation of parents to them? What is the number of planters who have established plantation schools? In other words, who have commenced a system of regular instruction for their Negro children; conducting themselves that instruction daily or weekly, or engaging the services of members of their own families, or even going to the expense of employing missionaries for the purpose?

Push the inquiry still further. How may *ministers* assemble at stated seasons, the colored children of their congregations for catechetical instruction, exhortation, and prayer? How many *churches* have established Sabbath schools at convenient stations in the country, or in towns and villages for colored children and youth, and do maintain them from year to year? To all of these questions, it must in candor be replied that the numbers are small compared to the whole.

Shall we speak of *public instruction* such as is communicated by a *preached* Gospel? Negro children do not enjoy the advantages of a preached Gospel; for the custom is, where no effort is made to alter it, for the children to remain at home on the Sabbath. Multitudes never having been taught to "remember the Sabbath day to keep it holy," consider it in the light, purely, of a holyday;—a day of rest, of sports, and plays. The distance to the house of worship is frequently considerable, too considerable for the attendance of small children; and, in short, should the children accompany them, the service being conducted for the most part for the special benefit of masters, do them no good, being above not only their comprehension, but even that of their parents.

Shall we speak of *access to the Scriptures?* The *statutes* of our respective slave States forbid all knowledge of letters to the Negroes; and where the statutes do not *custom does*. It is impossible to form an estimate of the number of Negroes that *read*. My belief is that the proportion would be expressed by an almost inconceivable fraction. The greatest number of readers is found in and about towns and cities, and among the free Negro population, some two or three generations removed from servitude. There are perhaps in all of the larger cities in the South, schools for the education of colored children, supported chiefly by the *free* Negroes, and kept generally in the shade. On the one hand, therefore, the Negro children cannot be "hearers of the law," for oral instruction is but sparingly afforded to the mass of them; and on the other, they cannot "search the Scriptures," for a knowledge of letters they have not, and legally, they cannot obtain.

With whom is the young Negro *associated?* With children no better instructed and disciplined than himself, and the whole subjected to the pernicious examples of the adults. They are favored with no association calculated to elevate and refine.

Negroes, especially the children, are exceedingly inattentive to the preservation of their *clothing*. The habits, in the particular of dress, of their forefathers from Africa still cleave to them, especially in the warmer seasons of the year, when they are left to themselves. This very improvidence on the part of the Negroes presents an increase of expenditure on the part of owners for clothing. The waste is great. And indeed, once for all, I will here say, that the wastes of the system are so great, as well as the fluctuations in the price of staple articles for market, that it is difficult, nay, impossible, to indulge in large expenditures on plantations and make them savingly profitable.

Their general *mode of living* is coarse and vulgar. Many Negro houses are small, low to the ground, blackened with smoke, often with dirt floors, and the furniture of the plainest kind. On some estates the houses are framed, weather-boarded, neatly white-washed, and made sufficiently large and comfortable in every respect. The improvements in the size, material, and finish of Negro houses is extending. Occasionally they may be found constructed of tabby or brick.

A room is partitioned off for a sleeping apartment and store-room, though houses are found destitute of the convenience. In such dwellings privacy is impossible, and we may in a manner say that families live, sleep, and grow up together; their habits and manners being coarse and rude. Some owners make additions to the house according to the number and age of the children of families.

Having now considered the circumstances of the Negro during his childhood, we may proceed and consider the circumstances of—

The Negro at Adult Age.—he lives in a house similar to the ones in which he passed his childhood and youth. He has the necessary and annual provision made for his wants; associates with fellow-servants of like character to his own. The seeds of virtue or vice sown in his youth, now blossom and bear fruit. He marries and settles in life, his children grow up around him and tread in his footsteps, as he did in the footsteps of his father before him.

The remarks on the *religious instruction of children* apply with equal correctness to *adults*. Religious instruction of adults *on plantations*, communicated by masters, ministers, or missionaries employed for the purpose, taking the slave States together, is not of frequent occurrence. The chief privilege enjoyed by thousands on plantations is *evening prayers*, conducted by themselves. If the individuals upon whom the conduct of the evening meeting devolves are able to *read*, a chapter in the Bible is read; a hymn is read and given out and sung; followed with prayer. If they cannot read, then a brief exhortation in place of the Scriptures founded, it may be, on some remembered passage, then a hymn from memory and prayer. There are thousands also, who, although freely allowed the privilege, do not embrace it, either from want of inclination, or of suitable persons to conduct the meetings. It is a matter of thankfulness that the owners are few in number, indeed, who forbid religious meetings on their plantations, held either by their servants themselves, or by competent and approved white instructors or ministers. "All men have not faith." I have never known servants forbidden to attend the worship of God *on the Sabbath day*, except as a restraint temporarily laid, for some flagrant misconduct.

On special occasions, such as fast days, communion seasons, and protracted meetings, a day or more is allowed servants by many masters. Throughout the slave-holding States the rest of the Sabbath is secured to the Negroes, and on this day they have extensive opportunities of attending divine worship, in town and country. But it is well known to those who have attentively observed the habits of this people, that large numbers of adults remain at home or spend the day in visiting or in ways still more exceptionable. Various causes conspire to produce the effect. For instance; it is their day of rest; the distance which they must walk to church is considerable; the accommodations for seats, in certain cases, are limited; the services of the sanctuary are too elevated for them; they are not required or encouraged to go; they have no exalted ideas of the importance of religion, and in common with all men, are naturally disinclined to it; and other causes which might be mentioned. Many, in settlements that are and that are not supplied with Gospel ministrations, live and die without an adequate knowledge of the way of salvation.

Nor can the adult Negro acquaint himself with duty and the way of salvation *through the reading of the Scriptures*, any more than can the child. Of those that do read, but few read well enough for the edification of the hearers. Not all the colored *preachers* read.

Two other circumstances which have considerable bearing on the moral and religious character of the Negro deserve attention. The first is that the *marriage state is not protected by law*. Whatever of protection it enjoys is to be attributed to custom, to the conscientious efforts of owners, and the discipline and doctrines of the churches; and also the correct principle and virtue of the contracting parties. But the relation is liable to disruption in a variety of forms, for some of which there is no remedy. The second is that *the government* to which they are subjected is *too much physical* in its nature. To discard an appeal to the principle of fear—the fear of punishment of *the person* of the transgressor in some form or other, would be running contrary to all governments in existence, both human and divine. While the necessity is admitted, yet the appeal should be made as seldom as possible and in the mildest form consistent with the due support of authority and the reformation of the transgressor. Man has a *spiritual* as well as an animal nature, and corrective influences, should be brought to bear upon that *directly* and in the *first instance*, as soon as he is able to discern between good and evil.

Such then are the circumstances of the slave population, which have an unfavorable influence upon their moral and religious condition. These circumstances only have been referred to which prominently assist us in our inquiry. In conclusion it may be added that servants have neither intellectual nor moral intercourse with their masters generally, sufficient to redeem them from the adverse influence of the circumstances alluded to; for the two classes are distinct in their association, and it cannot well be otherwise. Nor have servants any redeeming intercourse with any other persons. On the contrary in certain situations there is intercourse had with them, and many temptations laid before them against they have little or no defence, and the effect is deplorable. . . .

78. THE NAT TURNER REVOLT, 1831*

In August, 1831, Nat Turner, a Baptist lay preacher, led a slave rebellion in southeastern Virginia. Before the state militia could put down the uprising, Turner and his followers murdered 55 white men, women, and children. The chilling event sent fear through the white South and led to tighter controls over the slave population. While awaiting execution, Turner dictated his "Confessions" to local attorney Thomas R. Gray. In the following excerpt, Turner explains the background and motives of the insurrection.

SIR,-You have asked me to give a history of the motives which induced me to undertake the late insurrection as you call it—To do so I must go back to the days of my infancy, and even before I was born. I was thirty-one years of age the 2d of October last, and born the property of Benj. Turner, of this county. In my childhood a circumstance occurred which made an indelible impression on my mind, and laid the ground work of that enthusiasm, which has terminated so fatally to many, both white and black, and for which I am about to atone at the gallows. It is here necessary to relate this circumstance—trifling as it may seem, it was the commencement of that belief which has grown with time, and even now, sir, in this dungeon, helpless and forsaken as I am, I cannot divest myself of. Being at play with other children, when three or four years old, I was telling them something, which my mother overhearing, said it had happened before I was born—I stuck to my story, however, and related somethings which went, in her opinion, to confirm it—others being called on were greatly astonished, knowing that these things had happened, and caused them to say in my hearing, I surely would be a prophet, as the Lord had shewn me things that had happened before my birth. And my father and mother strengthened me in this my first impression, saying in my presence, I was intended for some great purpose. . . . My grandmother, who was very religious, and to whom I was much attached—my master, who belonged to the church, and other religious persons who visited the house, and whom I often saw at prayers, noticing the singularity of my manners, I suppose, and my uncommon intelligence for a child, remarked I had too much sense to be raised, and if I was, I would never be of any service to any one as a slave—To a mind like mine, restless, inquisitive and observant of every thing that was passing, it is easy to suppose that religion was the subject to which it would be directed, and although this subject principally occupied my thoughts—there was nothing that I saw or heard of to which my attention was not directed—The manner in which I learned to read and write, not only had great influence on my own mind, as I acquired it with the most perfect ease, so much so, that I have no recollection whatever of learning the alphabet—but to the astonishment of the family, one day, when a book was shewn me to keep me from crying, I began spelling the names of different objects—this was a source of wonder to all in the neighborhood, particularly the blacks—and this learning [w]as constantly improved at all opportunities—when I got large enough to go to work, while employed, I was reflecting on many things that would present themselves to my imagination, and whenever an opportunity occurred of looking at a book, when the school children were getting their lessons, I would find many things that the fertility of my own imagination had depicted to me before; all my time, not devoted to my master's service, was spent either in prayer, or in making experiments in casting different things in moulds made of earth, in attempting to make paper, gun-powder, and many other experiments, that although I could not perfect, yet convinced me of its practicability if I had the means. I was not

*From *The Confessions of Nat Turner* (Baltimore: Thomas R. Gray, 1831).

addicted to stealing in my youth, nor have ever been—Yet such was the confidence of the negroes in the neighborhood, even at this early period of my life, in my superior judgment, that they would often carry me with them when they were going on any roguery, to plan for them. Growing up among them, with this confidence in my superior judgment, and when this, in their opinions, was perfected by Divine inspiration, from the circumstances already alluded to in my infancy, and which belief was ever afterwards zealously inculcated by the austerity of my life and manners, which became the subject of remark by white and black. Having soon discovered to be great, I must appear so, and therefore studiously avoided mixing in society, and wrapped myself in mystery, devoting my time to fasting and prayer—By this time, having arrived to man's estate, and hearing the scriptures commented on at meetings, I was struck with that particular passage which says: "Seek ye the kingdom of Heaven and all things shall be added unto you." I reflected much on this passage, and prayed daily for light on this subject—As I was praying one day at my plough, the spirit spoke to me, saying "Seek ye the kingdom of heaven and all things shall be added unto you."

QUESTION: what do you mean by the Spirit. ANSWER: The Spirit that spoke to the prophets in former days—and I was greatly astonished, and for two years prayed continually, whenever my duty would permit—and then again I had the same revelation, which fully confirmed me in the impression that I was ordained for some great purpose in the hands of the Almighty.

Several years rolled round, in which many events occurred to strengthen me in this my belief. At this time I reverted in my mind to the remarks made of me in my childhood, and the things that had been shown me—and as it had been said of me in my childhood by those by whom I had been taught to pray, both white and black, and in whom I had the greatest confidence, that I had too much sense to be raised, and if I was, I would never be of any use to any one as a slave. Now finding I had arrived to man's estate, and was a slave, and these revelations being made known to me, I began to direct my attention to this great object, to fulfil the purpose for which, by this time, I felt assured I was intended. Knowing the influence I had obtained over the minds of my fellow servants, (not by the means of conjuring and such like tricks—for to them I always spoke of such things with contempt) but by the communions of the Spirit whose revelations I often communicated to them, and they believed and said my wisdom came from God. I now began to prepare them for my purpose, by telling them something was about to happen that would terminate in fulfilling the great promise that had been made to me. About this time I was placed under an overseer, from whom I ran away— and after remaining in the woods thirty days, I returned, to the astonishment of the Negroes on the plantation, who thought I had made my escape to some other part of the country, as my father had done before. But the reason of my return was, that the Spirit appeared to me and said I had my wishes directed to the things of this world, and not to the kingdom of Heaven, and that I should return to the service of my earthly master—"For he who knoweth his Master's will, and doeth it not, shall be beaten with many stripes, and thus have I chastened you." And the negroes found fault, and murmured against me saying that if they had my sense they would not serve any master in the world. And about this time I had a vision—and I saw white spirits and black spirits engaged in battle, and the sun was darkened—the thunder rolled in the Heavens, and blood flowed in streams—and I heard a voice saying, "Such is your luck, such you are called to see, and let it come rough or smooth, you must surely bare it." I now withdrew myself as much as my situation would permit, from the intercourse of my fellow servants, for the avowed purpose of serving the Spirit more fully—and it appeared to me, and reminded me of the things it had already shown me, and that it would then reveal to me the knowledge of the elements, the revolution of the planets, the operation of tides, and changes of the seasons. After this revelation in the year 1825, and the knowledge of the elements being made known to me, I sought more than ever to obtain true holiness before the great day of judgment should appear, and then I began to receive the true knowledge of faith. And from the first steps of righteousness until the last, was I made perfect; and the Holy Ghost was with me, and said, "Behold me as I stand in the Heavens"—and I looked and saw the forms of men in different attitudes and there were lights in the sky to which the children of darkness gave other names than what they really were—for they were the lights of the Saviour's hands, stretched forth from east to west, even as they were extended on the cross on Calvary for the redemption of sinners. And I wondered greatly at these miracles, and prayed to be informed of a certainty of the meaning thereof—and shortly afterwards, while laboring in the field, I discovered drops of blood on the corn as though it were dew from heaven—and I communicated it to many, both white and black, in the neighborhood—and I then found on the leaves in the woods hieroglyphic characters, and numbers, with the forms of men in different attitudes, portrayed in blood, and representing the figures I had seen before in the heavens. And now the Holy Ghost had revealed itself to me, and made plain the miracles it had shown me—For as the blood of Christ had been shed on this earth, and had ascended to heaven for the salvation of sinners, and was now returning to earth again in the form of dew—and as the leaves on the trees bore the impression of the figures I had seen in the heavens, it was plain to me that the Saviour was about to lay down the yoke he had borne for the sins of men, and the great day of judgment was at hand. . . . [A]nd the Spirit appeared to me again, and said, as the Saviour had been baptised so should we be also—and when the white people would not let us be baptised by the church, we went down into the water together, in the sight of many who reviled us, and were baptised by the Spirit—After this I rejoiced greatly, and gave thanks to God. And on the 12th of May, 1828, I heard a loud noise in the heavens, and the Spirit instantly appeared to me and said the Serpent was loosened, and Christ had laid down the yoke he had borne for the sins of men, and that I should take it on and fight against the Serpent, for the time was fast approaching when the first should be last and the last should be first.

QUESTION: Do you not find yourself mistaken now? ANSWER: Was not Christ crucified.

And by signs in the heavens that it would make known to me when I should commence the great work—and until the first sign appeared, I should conceal it from the knowledge of men—And on the appearance of the sign, (the eclipse of the sun last February) I should arise and prepare myself, and slay my enemies with their own weapons. And immediately on the sign appearing in the heavens, the seal was removed from my lips, and I communicated the great work laid out for me to do, to four in whom I had the greatest confidence (Henry, Hark, Nelson, and Sam)—it was intended by us to have begun the work of death on the 4th July last—Many were the plans formed and rejected by us, and it affected my mind to such a degree, that I fell sick, and the time passed without our coming to any determination how to commence—Still forming new schemes and rejecting them, when the sign appeared again, which determined me not to wait longer. Since the commencement of 1830, I had been living with Mr. Joseph Travis, who was to me a kind master, and placed the greatest confidence in me; in fact, I had no cause to complain of his treatment to me. On Saturday evening, the 20th of August, it was agreed between Henry, Hark and myself, to prepare a dinner the next day for the men we expected, and then to concert a plan, as we had not yet determined on any. Hark, on the following morning, brought a pig, and Henry brandy, and being joined by Sam, Nelson, Will and Jack, they prepared in the woods a dinner, where, about three o'clock, I joined them. . . .

I saluted them on coming up, and asked Will how came he there, he answered, his life was worth no more than others, and his liberty as dear to him. I asked him if he thought to obtain it? He said he would or loose his life. This was enough to put him in full confidence. Jack, I knew, was only a tool in the hands of Hark, it was quickly agreed we should commence at home (Mr. J. Travis') on that night, and until we had armed and equipped ourselves, and gathered sufficient force, neither age nor sex was to be spared, (which was invariably adhered to). We remained at the feast, until about two hours in the night, when we went to the house and found Austin; they all went to the cider press and drank, except myself. On returning to the house, Hark went to the door with an axe, for the purpose of breaking it open, as we knew we were strong enough to murder the family, if they were awaked by the noise; but reflecting that it might create an alarm in the neighborhood, we determined to enter the house secretly, and murder them whilst sleeping. Hark got a ladder and set it against the chimney, on which I ascended, and hoisting a window, entered and came down stairs, unbarred the door, and removed the guns from their places. It was then observed that I must spill the first blood. . . .

Discussion

1. In the documents by Charles G. Finney, Harriet Beecher Stowe, Henry David Thoreau, and Charles Colcock Jones, who do you think the authors believed held power in the United States? Which of the documents discuss liberty, and how do they do so? Which of the selections raise issues of equality, and how are they presented?

2. Why do you think Charles G. Finney expressed so much excitement over the conversions of heads of households? What does his enthusiasm over their conversion suggest about American culture in the 1830s? Do his comments have any significance regarding gender relations during the era?

3. Both Harriet Beecher Stowe and Charles Colcock Jones stress the illiteracy of slaves. What are the implications concerning power when one social group refuses to allow another group to read? What are the implications for liberty and for equality?

4. Compare the ideas that Henry David Thoreau expressed with the selection from the previous chapter on Moral Police. How do the two documents reveal different understandings of power and liberty in the United States? How do you think Thoreau would have reacted to the rules the mill owners imposed?

5. How do you think that different people in the United States might have responded to the Astor Place Riot? What groups might have feared the demonstrations? What groups might have seen the riots as an expression of patriotism? How do you think Charles G. Finney or Charles Colcock Jones might have reacted to the report on the riot?

6. What does the poem, "The Empire of Woman," reveal about middle-class attitudes toward liberty, equality, and power for women in the mid-19th century?

7. How would you describe Frances Trollope's attitude about her experience at the Indiana camp meeting?

8. Based on the excerpt from Nat Turner's "Confessions," how did he address the issues of liberty, equality, and power?

CHAPTER 11

Society, Culture, and Politics, 1820s–1840s

Temperance supporters wished to save the family, promote industry, create a reliable
workforce, and "Americanize" Irish and German immigrants.
Using easily understood, vividly illustrated texts, they spread their message of the
personal demise and family ruin caused by drink.

During the antebellum period, intense moral fervor spawned a widespread reform movement in the United States. Whigs, showing the influence of the Christian evangelicalism of the period, wanted to use the power of the government to ensure moral progress as well as economic opportunity. These crusaders turned their attention to a variety of causes, including the plight of criminals, the care of the mentally ill, the fate of alcoholics, the suffering of slaves, and the place of women. Democrats, who clung to the traditional faith that power destroyed liberty, often resisted such reform efforts because they endangered the status and equality of adult white males. In addition to shaping politics by creating a new party system, then, differences between Democrats and Whigs also had significant ramifications for American culture and society.

79. HORACE MANN PROMOTES EDUCATION, 1842*

In 1837 Massachusetts Senate leader Horace Mann recognized the need for school reform and helped create a state board of education. Subsequently, he resigned from politics to head this new board and during the next decade emerged as the nation's leading educational reformer. His achievements were substantial. Despite state monetary problems, Mann built better facilities, banished cruel and harsh punishments, established "normal" schools to educate teachers, lengthened the school term, revised the curriculum by adding such subjects as art and music, doubled appropriations for public schools, and increased teacher salaries. His efforts to improve the quality of the public school system in Massachusetts set the standard for other reform-minded states; his annual education reports were widely circulated. In the following excerpt from his fifth report (covering 1841), Mann eloquently presents the benefits of education for laboring people, business, and the greater nation.

So where there are different kinds of labor, some simple, others complicated, and, of course, requiring different degrees of intelligence and skill, it is easy to observe what class of persons rise from a lower to a higher grade of employment.

This, too, is not to be forgotten,—that in a manufacturing or mechanical establishment, or among a set of hands engaged in filling up a valley or cutting down a hill, where scores of people are working together, the absurd and adventitious distinctions of society do not intrude. The capitalist and his agents are looking for the greatest amount of labor, or the largest income in money from their investments; and they do not promote a dunce to a station where he will destroy raw material, or slacken industry, because of his name or birth or family connections. The obscurest and humblest person has an open and fair field for competition. That he proves himself capable of earning more money for his employer is a testimonial better than a diploma from all the colleges.

Now, many of the most intelligent and valuable men in our community, in compliance with my request,—for which I tender them my public and grateful acknowledgments,—have examined their books for a series of years, and have ascertained both the quality and the amount of work performed by persons in their employment; and the result of the investigation is a most astonishing

*From Horace Mann, "Fifth Annual Report of the Secretary of the Board of Education," *Fifth Annual Report of the Board of Education, Together With the Fifth Annual Report of the Secretary of the Board* (Boston: Dutton and Wentworth, 1842), 84–86, 99–101.

superiority, in productive power, on the part of the educated over the uneducated laborer. The hand is found to be another hand when guided by an intelligent mind. Processes are performed, not only more rapidly, but better, when faculties which have been exercised in early life furnish their assistance. Individuals who, without the aid of knowledge, would have been condemned to perpetual inferiority of condition, and subjected to all the evils of want and poverty, rise to competence and independence by the uplifting power of education. In great establishments, and among large bodies of laboring men, where all services are rated according to their pecuniary value; where there are no extrinsic circumstances to bind a man down to a fixed position, after he has shown a capacity to rise above it; where, indeed, men pass by each other, ascending or descending in their grades of labor, just as easily and certainly as particles of water of different degrees of temperature glide by each other,—there it is found as an almost invariable fact, other things being equal, that those who have been blessed with a good common-school education rise to a higher and a higher point in the kinds of labor performed, and also in the rate of wages paid, while the ignorant sink like dregs, and are always found at the bottom.

I now proceed to lay before the Board some portions of the evidence I have obtained, first inserting my Circular Letter, in answer to which, communications have been made.

* * *

EXTRACTS FROM A LETTER OF JONATHAN CRANE, ESQ., FOR SEVERAL YEARS A LARGE CONTRACTOR ON THE RAILROADS IN MASSACHUSETTS

My principal business, for about ten years past, has been grading railroads. During that time, the number of men employed has varied from fifty to three hundred and fifty, nearly all Irishmen, with the exception of superintendents. Some facts have been so apparent, that my superintendents and myself could not but notice them: these I will freely give you. I should say that not less than three thousand different men have been, more or less, in my employment during the before-mentioned period, and that the number that could read and write intelligibly was about one to eight. Independently of their natural endowments, those who could read and write, and had some knowledge of the first principles of arithmetic, have almost invariably manifested a readiness to apprehend what was required of them, and skill in performing it, and have more readily and frequently devised new modes by which the same amount of work could be better done. Some of these men we have selected for superintendents, and they are now contractors. With regard to the morals of the two classes, we have seen very little difference; but the better-educated class are more cleanly in their persons and their households, and generally discover more refinement in their manners, and practise a more economical mode in their living. Their families are better brought up, and they are more anxious to send their children to school. In regard to their standing and respectability among co-laborers, neighbors, and fellow-citizens, the more educated are much more respected; and in settling minor controversies, they are more commonly applied to as arbitrators. With regard to the morals of the two classes before mentioned, permit me to remark, that it furnishes an illustration of the truth of a common saying, that merely cultivating the understanding, without improving the heart, does not make a man better. The more extensively knowledge and virtue prevail in our country, the greater security have we that our institutions will not be overthrown. Our common-school system, connected as it is, or ought to be, with the inculcation of sound and practical morality, is the most vigilant and efficient police for the protection of persons, property, and character, that could be devised; and is it not gratifying that men of wealth are beginning to see, that, if they would protect their property and persons, a portion of that property should be expended for the education of the poorer classes? Merely selfish considerations would lead any man of wealth to do this, if he would only view the subject in its true light. Nowhere is this subject better understood than in Massachusetts; and the free discussions which have of late been held, in county and town meetings, have had the effect to call the attention of the public to it; and I trust the time is not far distant, when, at least in Massachusetts, the common-school system will accomplish all the good which it is capable of producing. Why do we not in these United States have a revolution, almost annually, as in the republics of South America? Ignorance and vice always have invited, and always will invite, such characters as Shakespeare's Jack Cade to rule over them. And may we not feel an assurance, that in proportion as the nation shall recover from the baneful influence of intemperance, so will its attention be directed preeminently to the promotion of virtue and knowledge, and nowhere in our country will an incompetent or intemperate common-school teacher be intrusted with the education of our children?

These are a fair specimen, and no more than a fair specimen, of a mass of facts which I have obtained from the most authentic sources. They seem to prove incontestably that education is not only a moral renovator, and a multiplier of intellectual power, but that it is also the most prolific parent of material riches. It has a right, therefore, not only to be included in the grand inventory of a nation's resources, but to be placed at the very head of that inventory. It is not only the most honest and honorable, but the surest means of amassing property. A trespasser or a knave may forcibly or fraudulently appropriate the earnings of others to himself; but education has the prerogative of originating or generating property more certainly and more rapidly than it was ever accumulated by force or fraud.

80. PRISONS, 1838*

*R*eformers, beginning in the 1820s, sought ways to impose the authority of the state against criminals while still preserving the ideals of freedom and equality. Penitentiaries, where convicts could reflect on the errors of their ways and grow penitent, seemed to offer an effective means of reconciling power and liberty. New York established a prison at Auburn that relied on solitary confinement at night and strictly controlled labor during the day to create an environment in which prisoners could be rehabilitated. The "Auburn system" attracted international attention, and in the following selection Englishwoman Harriet Martineau discussed the relative merits of "congregate" incarceration as practiced at the Auburn Prison and the solitary confinement employed in Pennsylvania.

I have shown in my account of Society in America that, after visiting several prisons in the United States, I was convinced that the system of solitary confinement at Philadelphia is the best that has yet been adopted. So much has been heard in England of the Auburn prison, its details look so complete and satisfactory on paper, and it is so much a better system than the English have been accustomed to see followed at home, that it has a high reputation among us. But I think a careful survey of the institution on the spot must lessen the admiration entertained for this mode of punishment.

The convicts are, almost without exception, pale and haggard. As their work is done either in the open air or in well-ventilated shops, and their diet is good, their unhealthy appearance is no doubt owing to the bad construction of their night-cells. These cells are small and ill-ventilated, and do not even answer the purpose of placing the prisoners in solitude during the night. The convicts converse with nearly as much ease, through the air-pipes or otherwise, at night, as they do by speaking behind their teeth, without moving the lips, while at work in the day. In both cases they feel that they are transgressing the laws of the prison by doing an otherwise innocent and almost necessary act; a knowledge and feeling most unfavourable to reformation; and destructive of any conscientiousness which retribution may be generating in them. Their anxious and haggard looks may easily be accounted for. They are denied the forgetfulness of themselves and their miseries which they might enjoy in free conversation; and also the repose and the shelter from shame which

---

*From Harriet Martineau, *Retrospect of Western Travel*, 2 vols. (London: Saunders and Otley, 1838), I:123–39.

are the privileges of solitary confinement. Every movement reminds them that they are in disgrace; a multitude of eyes (the eyes of the wicked, too) is ever upon them; they can live neither to themselves nor to society, and self-respect is rendered next to impossible. A man must be either hardened, or restless and wretched under such circumstance; and the faces at Auburn are no mystery.

The finishing of the day's work and the housing for the night are sights barely endurable. The governor saw my disgust, and explained that he utterly disapproved of strangers being allowed to be present at all this; but that the free Americans would not be debarred from beholding the operation of anything which they have decreed. This is right enough; the evil is in there being such a spectacle to behold. The prisoners are ranged in companies for the march from the workshops into the prison. Each fills his pail and carries it, and takes up the can with his supper as he passes the kitchen; and, when I was there, this was done in the presence of staring and amused strangers, who looked down smiling from the portico. Some of the prisoners turned their heads every possible way to avoid meeting our eyes, and were in an agony of shame. . . .

The arrangements for the women were extremely bad at that time; but the governor needed no convincing of this, and hoped for a speedy rectification. The women were all in one large room, sewing. The attempt to enforce silence was soon given up as hopeless; and the gabble of tongues among the few who were there was enough to paralyze any matron. . . . There was an engine in sight which made me doubt the evidence of my own eyes; stocks of a terrible construction; a chair, with a fastening for the head and for all of the limbs. Any lunatic asylum ought to be ashamed of such an instrument. The governor liked it no better that we; but he pleaded that it was his only means of keeping his refractory female prisoners quiet while he was allowed only one room to put them all into. I hope these stocks have been used for firewood before this.

The first principle in the management of the guilty seems to me to be to treat them as men and women; which they were before they were guilty, and will always be when they are no longer so; and which they are in the midst of all of it. Their humanity is the principal thing about them; their guilt is a temporary state. The insane are first men, and secondarily diseased men; and in a due consideration of this order of things lies the main secret of the successful treatment of such. The drunkard is first a man, and secondarily a man with a peculiar weakness. The convict is, in like manner, first a man, and then a sinner. Now, there is something in the isolation of the convict which tends to keep this order of consideration right in the mind of his guardians. The warden and his prisoner converse like two men when they are face to face; but when the keeper watches a hundred men herded together in virtue of the one common characteristic of their being criminals, the guilt becomes the prominent circumstance, and there is an end of the brotherly faith in each, to which each must mainly owe his cure. This, in our human weakness, is the great evil attendant upon the good of collecting together sufferers under any particular physical or moral evil. Visitors are shy of the blind, the deaf and dumb, and insane, when they see them all together, while they would feel little or nothing of this shyness if they met each sufferer in the bosom of his own family. In the one case, the infirmity, defying sympathy, is the prominent circumstance; in the other, not. It follows from this, that such an association of prisoners as that at Auburn must be more difficult to reform, more difficult to do the state's duty by, than any number or kind of criminals who are classed by some other characteristic, or not classed at all. . . .

The greatest advantage of solitary confinement is that it presents the best part of a prisoner's mind to be acted upon by his guardians; and the next is, that the prisoner is preserved from the evil influences of vicious companionship, of shame within the prison walls, and of degradation when he comes out. I am persuaded that no system of secondary punishment has yet been devised that can be compared with this. I need not, at this time of day, explain that I mean solitary confinement with labour, and with frequent visits from the guardians of the prisoner. Without labour, the punishment is too horrible and unjust to be thought of. The reflective man would go mad, and the clown would sleep away his term, and none of the purposes of human existence could be answered. Work is, in prison as out of it, the grand equalizer, stimulus, composer, and rectifier; the prime obligation and the prime privilege. It is delightful to see how soon its character is recognized there. In the Philadelphia penitentiary work is forbidden to the criminal for two days subsequent to his entrance; he petitions for it before the two days are out, however doggedly he may have declared that he will never work. . . .

On his entrance the convict is taken to the bathroom, where he is well cleansed, and his state of health examined into and recorded by the physician and warden. A hood is then put over his head, and he is led to his apartment. I never met with one who could in the least tell what the form of the central part of the prison was, or which of the radii his cell was placed in, though they make very accurate observances of the times at which the sun shines in. At the end of two days, during which the convict has neither book nor work, the warden visits him, and has a conversation with him about the mode of life in the institution. If he asks for work, he is offered a choice of three or four kinds, of which weaving and shoemaking are the chief. He is told that if he does a certain amount of work, he will have the full diet provided for hard labourers; if less, he will have what is sufficient for a moderate worker; if more, the price of it will be laid by to accumulate, and paid over to him on his leaving the prison. He is furnished with a Bible; and other books, provided by the friends to the institution, circulate among the convicts. Some who have books at home are allowed to have them brought. . . .

As the system of imprisonment gains ground, I trust that the practice of prison-visiting will gain ground too. It is most desirable that it should not be left wholly in the hands of proselyting religionists, but be shared by those who better understand human nature and command a greater variety of influences. For the sake of religion itself this is desirable, to rescue it from becoming a mere prison solace; an excitement seized when no other can be had, and to be laid aside when old pursuits offer themselves for resumption. Kind-hearted persons will have an opportunity of doing extensive and unquestionable good by keeping up the social affections of the prisoners, giving them new ideas, making them cheerful, and investing with pleasant associations whatever things are honest, pure, lovely, and of good report.

In other prisons much might thus be done, though not, I think, with such extraordinary affect as under the system of solitary confinement. I was struck with something I saw at the Charlestown prison (Massachusetts). Several convicts, black and white, who had behaved well, were practising singing, which is allowed as an indulgence. It seemed strange to hear "The heavens are telling" from such lips; but I listened to it with more pleasure than in some finer places. Any kind person who can introduce a new innocent pursuit into a prison as a solace to its inmates cannot fail to be doing an important good. . . .

I saw at the Charlesto[w]n prison a sight more impressive to me than all else that the walls contained; a man of might, but whose power has taken a wrong direction; his hand being against every man, and every man's against him. He is a prison-breaker so formidable as to be regarded and treated as if he were of Satanic race, and not as made up of flesh and blood, and emotions that may be roused, and affections subject to touch. He seems, indeed, to have become somewhat of the Satanic kind, for now he is piqued to do all the harm he can. His pride is in for it; his reputation stands upon it. I was shown an enormous block of stone which he had displaced by the aid of a "gentleman" outside, who, for fear of the prison-breaker's blabbing, committed suicide on his recapture. The strong man was heavily fettered, confined in a different cell every night, and conducted to it by a procession of turnkeys. As we stood aside in the echoing passage to let the array go by, there was something really grand in the air of a man who had virtually said to himself, "Evil, be thou my good!" He stepped slowly, clanking his chains, and looking us full in the face as he passed. He cannot but have a calm sense of power when he nightly sees the irons, the bars and locks, and the six fellow-men, all in requisition to keep him from working his will. As we saw him slowly turn into his cell, and heard lock after lock shot behind him, I could not help thinking that there was much true monarchical feeling within those four narrow walls. . . .

81. CARING FOR THE MENTALLY ILL, 1843*

In March, 1841, Dorothea Dix, a Boston schoolteacher, visited a local prison and was appalled at the horrid living conditions of the insane who were housed there. The experience transformed her into an ardent advocate for the mentally ill; for most of the next two years she toured Massachusetts jails and almshouses, collecting information about their treatment. In January, 1843, she petitioned the state legislature, calling for extensive reforms. Her report, excerpted in the following document, led to additional appropriations for the care of the insane in Massachusetts. Dix, using similar methodology in other states with much success, continued her crusade for more humane asylums until her death in 1887.

I RESPECTFULLY ask to present this Memorial, believing that the *cause*, which actuates to and sanctions so unusual as movement, presents no equivocal claim to public consideration and sympathy. Surrendering to calm and deep convictions of duty my habitual views of what is womanly and becoming, I proceed briefly to explain what has conducted me before you unsolicited and unsustained, trusting, while I do so, that the memorialist will be speedily forgotten in the memorial.

About two years since leisure afforded opportunity, and duty prompted me to visit several prisons and alms-houses in the vicinity of this metropolis. I found, near Boston, in the Jails and Asylums for the poor, a numerous class brought into unsuitable connexion with criminals and the general mass of Paupers. I refer to Idiots and Insane persons, dwelling in circumstances not only adverse to their own physical and moral improvement, but productive of extreme disadvantages to all other persons brought into association with them. I applied myself diligently to trace the causes of these evils, and sought to supply remedies. As one obstacle was surmounted, fresh difficulties appeared. Every new investigation has given depth to the conviction that it is only by decided, prompt, and vigorous legislation the evils to which I refer, and which I shall proceed more fully to illustrate, can be remedied. I shall be obliged to speak with great plainness, and to reveal many things revolting to the taste, and from which my woman's nature shrinks with peculiar sensitiveness. But truth is the highest consideration. *I tell what I have seen*—"painful and shocking" as the details often are—that from them you may feel more deeply the imperative obligation which lies upon you to prevent the possibility of a repetition or continuance of such outrages upon humanity. If I inflict pain upon you, and move you to horror, it is to acquaint you with sufferings which you have the power to alleviate, and make you hasten to the relief of the victims of legalized barbarity.

I come to present the strong claims of suffering humanity. I come to place before the Legislature of Massachusetts the condition of the miserable, the desolate, the outcast. I come as the advocate of helpless, forgotten, insane and idiotic men and women; of beings sunk to a condition from which the most unconcerned would start with real horror; of beings wretched in our Prisons, and more wretched in our Alms-Houses. . . .

I must confine myself to few examples, but am ready to furnish other and more complete details, if required. If my pictures are displeasing, coarse, and severe, my subjects, it must be recollected, offer no tranquil, refined, or composing features. The condition of human beings, reduced to the extremest states of degradation and misery, cannot be exhibited in softened language, or adorn a polished page.

I proceed, Gentlemen, briefly to call your attention to the *present* state of Insane Persons confined within this Commonwealth, in *cages, closets, cellars, stalls, pens! Chained, naked, beaten with rods*, and *lashed* into obedience! . . .

It is the Commonwealth, not its integral parts, that is accountable for most of the abuses which have lately, and do still exist. I repeat it, it is defective legislation which perpetuates and multiplies these abuses.

---

*From Dorothea L. Dix, *Memorial to the Legislature of Massachusetts* (Boston: Munroe & Francis, 1843), 3–6, 16, 24–26, 28–32.

In illustration of my subject, I offer the following extracts from my Note-Book and Journal:—
Springfield.   In the jail, one lunatic woman, furiously mad, a state pauper, improperly situated, both in regard to the prisoners, the keepers, and herself. It is a case of extreme self-forgetfulness and oblivion to all the decencies of life; to describe which, would be to repeat only the grossest scenes. She is much worse since leaving Worcester. In the almshouse of the same town is a woman apparently only needing judicious care, and some well-chosen employment, to make it unnecessary to confine her in solitude, in a dreary unfurnished room. Her appeals for employment and companionship are most touching, but the mistress replied, 'she had no time to attend to her.' . . .

Charlemont.	One man caged.
Savoy.	One man caged.
Lenox.	Two in the jail; against whose unfit condition there, the jailor protests.
Dedham.	The insane disadvantageously placed in the jail. In the almshouse, two females in stalls, situated in the main building; lie in wooden bunks filled with straw; always shut up. One of these subjects is supposed curable. The overseers of the poor have declined giving her a trial at the hospital, as I was informed, on account of expense.
Franklin.	One man chained; decent.
Taunton.	One woman caged.
Plymouth.	One man stall-caged, from Worcester hospital.
Scituate.	One man and one woman stall-caged.
Bridgewater.	Three idiots; never removed from one room.
Barnstable.	Four females in pens and stalls; two chained certainly, I think all. Jail, one idiot.
Welfleet.	Three insane; one man and one woman chained, the latter in a bad condition. . . .

Besides the above, I have seen many who, part of the year, are chained or caged. The use of cages all but universal; hardly a town but can refer to some not distant period of using them: chains are less common: negligences frequent: wilful abuse less frequent than sufferings proceeding from ignorance, or want of consideration. I encountered during the last three months many poor creatures wandering reckless and unprotected through the country. . . .

Wayland.   Visited the almshouse. There, as in Sudbury, caged in a wood-shed, and also *fully exposed* upon the *public* road, was seen a man at that time less violent, but equally debased by exposure and irritation. He then wore a portion of clothing, though the mistress remarked that he was "more likely to be naked than not"; and added that he was "less noisy than usual." I spoke to him, but received no answer; a wild, strange gaze, and impatient movement of the hand, motioned his head a torn coverlet; want of accommodations for the imperative calls of nature had converted the cage into a place of utter offence. "My husband cleans him out once a week or so; but it's a hard matter to master him sometimes. He does better since the last time he was broken in." I learnt that the confinement and cold together, had so affected his limbs that he was often powerless to rise; "you see him" said my conductress, "in his best state." *His best state!* what then was the *worst?*

Of the dangers and mischiefs sometimes following the location of insane persons in our almhouses, I will record but one more example. In Worcester, has for several years resided a young woman, a lunatic pauper of decent life and respectable family. I have seen her as she usually appeared, listless and silent, almost or quite sunk into a state of dementia, sitting one amidst the family, 'but of them.' A few weeks since, revisiting that almshouse, judge my horror and amazement to see her negligently bearing in her arms a young infant, of which I was told she was the unconscious parent! Who was the father, none could or would declare. Disqualified for the perfor-

mance of maternal cares and duties, regarding the helpless little creature with a perplexed, or indifferent gaze, she sat a silent, but O how eloquent, a pleader for the protection of others of her
neglected and outraged sex! Details of that black story would not strengthen the cause; needs it a
weightier plea, than the sight of that forlorn creature and her wailing infant? Poor little child, more
than orphan from birth, in this unfriendly world! a demented Mother—a Father, on whom the sun
might blush or refuse to shine!

Men of Massachusetts, I beg, I implore, I demand, pity and protection, for these of my suffering, outraged sex!—Fathers, Husbands, Brothers, I would supplicate you for this boon—but what
do I say? I dishonor you, divest you at once of christianity and humanity—does this appeal imply
distrust. If it comes burthened with a doubt of your righteousness in this Legislation, then blot it
out; while I declare confidence in your honor, not less than your humanity. Here you will put away
the cold, calculating spirit of selfishness and self-seeking; lay off the armor of local strife and political opposition; here and now, for once, forgetful of the earthly and perishable, come up to these
halls and consecrate them with one heart and one mind to works of righteousness and just judgment. Become the benefactors of your race, the just guardians of the solemn rights you hold in
trust. Raise up the fallen; succor the desolate; restore the outcast; defend the helpless; and for your
eternal and great reward, receive the benediction. . . . "Well done, good and faithful servants,
become rulers over many things!" . . .

This crying evil and abuse of institutions, is not confined to our almshouses. The warden of a
populous prison near this metropolis, populous, not with criminals only, but with the insane in
almost every stage of insanity, and the idiotic in descending states from silly and simple, to helpless
and speechless, has declared that: "the prison has often more resembled the infernal regions than
any place on earth!"

I have the verbal and written testimony of many officers of this Commonwealth . . . that the
occupation of prisons for the detention of lunatics and of idiots is, under all circumstances, an evil,
subversive alike of good order, strict discipline, and good morals. I transcribe a few passages which
will place this mischief in its true light. . . .

A letter from the surgeon and physicians of the Prison Hospital at Cambridge, . . .

"*Injustice* is also done to the convicts; it is certainly very wrong that they should be doomed day
after day, and night after night, to listen to the ravings of madmen and madwomen. This is a kind
of punishment, that is not recognised by our statutes; and is what the criminal ought not to be
called upon to undergo. The confinement of the criminal and of the insane in the same building is
subversive of that good order and discipline which should be observed in every well-regulated
prison. I do most sincerely hope that more permanent provision will be made for the Pauper
Insane by the state, either to restore Worcester Insane Asylum to what it was originally designed to
be, or else make some just appropriation for the benefit of this very unfortunate class of our 'fellow
beings'." . . .

From the Sheriff of Dukes county I have testimony. . . .

"With proper care and attention, lunatics may not only be made comfortable, but in many
instances restored again to society with sound minds. But this care and attention cannot be
expected from those who have charge of prisons, worthy men though many of them be; it requires
a union of qualifications rarely found in one individual, to manage successfully those from whom,
that which chiefly distinguishes man from the brute creation, is taken away.

"I conclude with expressing the hope that the wisdom of our Legislature may devise a remedy
for the evils now attending the unfortunate pauper lunatic and idiot." . . .

It is not few but many, it is not a part but the whole, who bear unqualified testimony to this evil.
A voice strong and deep comes up from every almshouse and prison in Massachusetts where the
insane are or have been, protesting against such evils as have been illustrated in the preceding pages.

Gentlemen, I commit to you this sacred cause. Your action upon this subject will affect the present and future condition of hundreds and of thousands.

In this legislation, as in all things, may you exercise that "wisdom which is the breath of the power of God."

82. REFLECTIONS ON PROHIBITION, 1852*

The use of alcohol has been one of the most widely discussed social concerns in the history of the United States. In the antebellum period, Democrats and Whigs often had substantial differences of opinion over the issue. As time passed and Americans continued to drink, reformers came to believe that they would have to use the power of the government to compel individuals to behave properly. Democrats, for the most part, feared that such coercion threatened American liberties. The Democratic attitudes are clearly evident in the following document, an editorial condemning the Maine Law of 1851 that was the first comprehensive effort to prohibit the manufacture and sale of liquor.

Intemperance is an evil; but for a free government to violate, for any cause, the plainest, most vital and fundamental principles of civil liberty, is also an evil, and one with which the first may not at all be compared.

A majority of the people of Maine, not liking, themselves, to drink, have forbidden the minority to do so. Our downeast friends have discovered, that the old theory of the fall of man, and the true plan of his redemption, was a gross error. According to them, the way of it was thus: when the first pair bit the first apple, they sucked the juice, and thereby acquired a relish for cider, which, transmitted to their progeny, became a taste for wine, and finally, in later times and colder climates, grew into a thirst for downright rum. This, they say, is original sin, the veritable, original article specified in Genesis. And the deduction they draw is, that the salvation of the race is to be found neither in sacramental wine nor sprinkled water, but in stringent anti-liquor laws, and internal applications of the baptismal fluid; a plan which, to their minds, loses not a whit of its plausibility from having never been so much as dreamed of by the leaders, prophets, and judges of Israel, the Savior and his apostles, the bishops, priests, and deacons of the church, all of whom came eating and drinking—and, of course, all signally failed.

This new sect, pursuing their idea with the zeal common to all such propagandists, and urging their measures through thousands of affiliated organizations, whose special business it has been to disseminate fallacies, which, however unsound, it has been no one's particular vocation to refute, and politic enough to scorn none of the tricks of the stump, none of the arts of lobbying, "log rolling," and electioneering intrigue, have succeeded at length, in one state, to get their theory of morals and dietetics actualized in the form of a statute law, which, though it does not honestly and boldly prohibit *buying* or *drinking*, puts its penalty upon *selling* or *keeping to sell*, "flogging the demon of intemperance" round the rum barrel, as it were, in the fashion of the most noted despot of the season, who, not venturing to prohibit the mere **use** of printing-presses, makes it penal to sell them except for special uses. And now, flushed with this success, the same sort of means and meanness are being put into play to extend this law into other states.

We claim to be a free people, and are accustomed to find the sanction for the continuance of our liberties, not in the chance good-will or unguided discretion of our rulers, but in those fundamental principles which every commonwealth in the true confederacy has adopted, as well for the enlightenment of legislators as the protection of the undelegated or unprescriptable rights of the citizen. But really such doings as this admonish us that those principles are either not comprehen-

*From "The Maine Liquor Law," *The Democratic Review* 30 (March, 1852), 271–73.

sible, or else are a miserably insufficient shield against the strong arm of a rampant majority, and render a short explanation of the meaning of free principles not all impertinent.

It is to be hoped that the greater number of our people will accuse us of uttering a self-evident proposition, when we say, that a free government is something more than a despotism administered by a benevolent despot; something more than a constitution under which the majority rules, for it may rule with a rod of iron; something more than an equal government, for their [sic] may be equality in slavery. A state can be called free only while the power of the rulers is restrained, and their judgment controlled, by certain well-understood, constantly referred to, and inviolably kept, *principles;* broad enough for all circumstances, and superior to all expediency; guarantying to the citizen that freedom which, coming from any other source, is accidental and precarious, and unworthy the acceptance of an intelligent people.

And what is freedom? The only definition which does not define away all meaning is, that *it is the absence of restraint.* The right to make laws, results solely from necessity. "The best government is that which governs least." And since even the most arbitrary rulers usually permit all such actions as *they* conceive to be right, we aver that the only criterion for knowing how far a government is free, is the extent to which bad actions are allowed, and that civil liberty may be termed the constitutional right to do wrong. What is the freedom of the press—but the power to punish wicked and pernicious doctrines? or freedom of speech, but the power to speak them? What is religious freedom, but the power to follow a false worship—freedom of locomotion, but the power to go to the wrong place—freedom of occupation but the power to choose the wrong trade? And yet the proposition remains true, that the right to do wrong in all these, and as many other respects as possible, is the essential condition of all true development, real happiness, and healthful progress.

Let it not, however, be thought important, that a very wide definition of civil liberty need be laid down, in order to show the grossness of a Maine liquor law. There are few governments, even of those the most arbitrary in their constitution, which do not recognize principles, with which such legislation as this is utterly inconsistent. Narrow down the word "freedom" to its scantiest limit, and it still retains a meaning that forbids a thing like this, for it is the very centre and core of it that is now attacked: it is the liberty of the person that is here struck down, and the contents of its inward parts to which these notion-mongers apply their chemical test.

It may not be easy precisely to define the limits of the law-making power. A wide range of human activity must ever remain guarded only by the best discretion of the legislature. But political philosophy has been able to set up, here and there, a few positive land-marks, and it must be true, that in the very nature and fitness of things, there does somewhere exist a sphere of right, quite apart and distinct from the limits of legislation, within which the individual may repose, unmolested by civil law.

The power wielded in the passage of the law we are considering, is so tremendous, that it is difficult to conceive it. Legislation, so overwhelming upon private action, is startling to the minds of the best balance, and the most favorably disposed towards the needed restraints of law.

Nothing could be more cheering to the mind, than the prospect of society redeemed from vice of every kind. But like children, brought up under the rod only, we shall find that prohibitory enactments, acting upon ill-regulated character, only lead to evasion and deceit. The frightful relief of opium will be sought by many who see their external independence thus abruptly checked, while, notwithstanding, the fires of uncontrolled license are burning within. It is known that the effects of indulgence in this drug, are more debasing mentally and physically, than even those of drunkenness from liquor, revolting as they are. Unhappily, this experience begins to obtain even in respectable families, and—pale be the ink that writes it—among women, refined and cultivated!

We believe, then, that moral means, which have lately, we are sorry to say, come to be sneered at, will, in the end, as they have progressively, heretofore, prove to be the true corrective. It is unjust to the efforts of that respectable class of our citizens, who have been so long and so faithfully presenting this subject to the moral consideration of mankind, to say that their efforts have had no effect. Every one who reflects, knows better. We do not wish to see the cause injured by substituting physical force for moral influence. Without this immense reach of legislation, means more justifiable, more profitable, more wholesome, and really effective may be discovered and applied.

We do not wish the community to stand still, or go back on this, any more than on any other great measure; but we desire to see it go forward well. We want the step to be an advance, and not a retrogression.

With this in view, we say, then, that we condemn the principle involved in this measure, as regards its expediency. We have, moreover, no faith in its final moral success, and we are constrained to declare unconstitutional the attempt thus to lay the iron hand of a gigantic governmental control upon the conscience and habits of a whole people. This last objection with us is final.

On the *policy* of entire restraint, apart from other considerations, we will say that we are in favor of the use of light wines. The experience of Europe is favorable as to the temperance of those nations, with whom wine is a daily beverage. Our own country promises most favorably for the cultivation of the vine, and we anticipate its success with hope and pleasure; believing that this itself will be a powerful auxiliary aid in the suppression of the gross taste for coarse and strong drink. We are opposed, however, to the negative policy of all kinds; we admit also that when a scheme has been proposed for the accomplishment of a great good, and those who oppose it should feel themselves in justice bound to suggest at least the elements of some substitute.

We propose, then, that stringent laws be put into practical effect against drunkenness. That it should be punished as a crime—as it is.

A man found drunk upon the street should be regarded as having forfeited his personal liberty, in having invaded the safety of society. The police should be required to seize, fine, and imprison him.

An habitual drunkard, having surrendered his reason, may justly be deprived of the dignity of a citizen, and should not be allowed to vote.

The carrying of a secret weapon is forbidden by law—not the sale of them, however; and this is a fair parallel. The public sense is against the carrying of private weapons, the law is against it, and they are seldom carried. We think the same good effect will result from public decision in the other case, especially joined with stringent laws which will be in accordance with the Federal Constitution, and will attack the evil in the right place.

83. THE TEMPERANCE MOVEMENT MANIFESTO, 1826*

By the 1820s the national consumption of hard liquor reached an all-time high. Social critics, especially evangelical reformers, linked alcohol to a variety of societal problems: domestic discord, public rowdiness, waning productivity of laborers, and the rising cost of public welfare. The temperance crusade began in earnest in 1826 with the establishment of what soon became the American Temperance Society. The movement's manifesto was Lyman Beecher's Six Sermons on the Nature, Occasions, Signs, Evils, and Remedy of Intemperance *(1826). Targeting the churchgoing middle class, Beecher declared alcohol an addictive drug and warned that even moderate drinkers risked becoming hopeless drunks. Although Beecher promoted self-discipline, he pushed middle-class abstainers to spread reform through both example and coercion.*

No sin has fewer apologies than intemperance. The suffrage of the world is against it; and yet there is no sin so naked in its character, and whose commencement and progress is indicated by so

---

*From Lyman Beecher, "Lectures on Intemperance," in *Lectures on Political Atheism and Kindred Subjects; Together with Six Lectures on Intemperance* (Boston: John P. Jewett and Company, 1852), 348–51, 356–57, 360, 376–78.

many signs, concerning which there is among mankind such profound ignorance. All reprobate drunkenness; and yet, not one of the thousands who fall into it, dreams of danger when he enters the way that leads to it.

The soldier, approaching the deadly breach, and seeing rank after rank of those who preceded him swept away, hesitates sometimes and recoils from certain death. But men behold the effects upon others . . .—they see them begin, advance, and end, in confirmed intemperance,—and unappalled rush heedlessly upon the same ruin.

A part of this heedlessness arises from the undefined nature of the crime in its early stages, and the ignorance of men, concerning what may be termed the experimental indications of its approach. Theft and falsehood are definite actions. But intemperance is a state of internal sensation, and the indications may exist long, and multiply, and the subject of them not be aware that they are the signs of intemperance. It is not unfrequent, that men become irreclaimable in their habits, without suspicion of danger. . . .

Intemperance is the sin of our land, and, with our boundless prosperity, is coming in upon us like a flood; and if anything shall defeat the hopes of the world, which hang upon our experiment of civil liberty, it is that river of fire, which is rolling through the land, destroying the vital air, and extending around an atmosphere of death. . . .

It is a matter of undoubted certainty, that habitual tippling is worse than periodical drunkenness. The poor Indian, who, once a month, drinks himself *dead* all but simple breathing, will outlive for years the man who drinks little and often, and is not, perhaps, suspected of intemperance. The use of ardent spirits daily, as ministering to cheerfulness or bodily vigor, ought to be regarded as intemperance. No person, probably, ever did or ever will, receive ardent spirits into his system once a day, and fortify his constitution against its deleterious effects, or exercise such discretion and self-government, as that the quantity will not be increased, and bodily infirmities and mental imbecility be the result, and, in more than half the instances, inebriation. Nature may hold out long against this sapping and mining of the constitution, which daily tippling is carrying on; but, first or last, this foe of life will bring to the assault enemies of its own formation, before whose power the feeble and the mighty will be alike unable to stand. . . .

Ardent spirits, given as a matter of hospitality, are not unfrequently the occasion of intemperance. In this case the temptation is a stated inmate of the family. The utensils are present, and the occasions for their use are not unfrequent. And when there is no guest, the sight of the liquor, the state of the health, or even lassitude of spirits, may indicate the propriety of the "prudent use;" until the "prudent use" becomes, by repetition, habitual use, and habitual use becomes irreclaimable intemperance. In this manner, doubtless, has many a father, and mother, and son, and daughter, been ruined forever.

Of the guests, also, who partake of this family hospitality, the number is not small who become ensnared; especially among those whose profession calls them to visit families often, and many on the same day. Instead of being regarded, therefore, as an act of hospitality, and a token of friendship, to invite our friends to drink, it ought to be regarded as an act of incivility to place ourselves and them in circumstances of such high temptation. . . .

The use of ardent spirits to invigorate the intellect, or restore exhausted nature under severe study, is often a fatal experiment. Mighty men have been cast down in this manner, never to rise. The quickened circulation does, for a time, invigorate intellect, and restore exhausted nature. But, for the adventitious energy imparted, it exhausts the native energy of the soul, and induces that faintness of heart and flagging of the spirits which cry incessantly, "Give, give," and never, but with expiring breath, say "It is enough." . . .

There is no remedy for intemperance but the cessation of it. Nature must be released from the unnatural war which is made upon her, and be allowed to rest, and then nutrition, and sleep, and exercise, will perform the work of restoration. Gradually the spring of life will recover tone, appetite will return, digestion become efficient, sleep sweet, and the muscular system vigorous, until the elastic heart, with every beat, shall send health through the system, and joy through the soul. . . .

Are there then set times, days, and places, when you calculate always to indulge yourselves in drinking ardent spirits? Do you stop often to take something at the tavern when you travel, and always when you come to the village, town, or city? This frequency of drinking will plant in your system, before you are aware of it, the seeds of the most terrific disease which afflicts humanity. Have you any friends or companions whose presence, when you meet them, awakens the thought and the desire of drinking? Both of you have entered on a course in which there is neither safety nor hope but from instant retreat.

Do any of you love to avail yourselves of every little catch and circumstance among your companions, to bring out "a treat"? "Alas, my lord, there is death in the pot!"

Do you find the desire of strong drink returning daily, and at stated hours? Unless you intend to travel all the length of the highway of intemperance, it is time to stop. Unless you intend soon to resign your liberty forever, and come under a despotism of the most cruel and inexorable character, you must abandon the morning bitters, the noontide stimulant, and the evening bowl.

Do any of you drink in secret, because you are unwilling your friends or the world should know how much you drink? You might as well cut loose in a frail boat before a hurricane, and expect safety: you are gone, gone irretrievably, if you do not stop. . . .

84. SCIENTIFIC RACISM, 1861*

Prior to the 1850s, most white Americans believed that historical and environmental circumstances accounted for the differences between the various human races. New ways of thinking, however, insisted that biological forces had made Africans a subhuman race; to the most extreme proponents of this view, Africans were members of an inferior species. John Van Evrie, a doctor and leading advocate of this "scientific" racism, summarized his opinions in the introduction and conclusion to a book he published in 1861. Those opinions, presented in the following document, influenced countless Americans and had grave implications for the liberty of slaves and the equality of blacks and other minorities well into the 20th century.

TO THE WHITE MEN OF AMERICA—

There are now thirty millions of white men, twelve millions of negroes, and perhaps twelve millions of Indians or Aborigines, in America.

God has made these white men, Indians, and negroes just what we see they are—just what our senses, as well as our instincts and our reason show us they are—different creatures, different *species* of men, with different bodies, and different minds, and different natures, exactly as we witness all about us in all other forms of life. Why, or when, or how the Creator saw fit, in His infinite wisdom and almighty power, to thus order things, we can never know, nor need to know, any thing further or beyond the fixed and indestructible *facts* thus presented to us. And it certainly needs but a moment's reflection to convince any *American* mind that a universal equality or affiliation with these Indians and negroes would, of necessity, result in the universal degradation and destruction of the white blood of America, with the consequent overthrow of republican institutions, and, indeed, the civilization and Christianity of the New World. The great men of the Revolutionary era, therefore, with a wise instinct and that lofty perception of the superiority of their race which always distinguishes the true America,

---

*From J. H. Van Evrie, *Negroes and Negro "Slavery": The First an Inferior Race: The Latter Its Normal Condition* (New York: Van Evrie, Horton & Company, 1861), v–vii, 336–39.

laid the foundations of a white republic, and organized a government of white men, which, as they declared in the preamble to the Constitution, should secure the blessings of liberty to *themselves* and *their* posterity forever.

The enemies of this glorious fabric of freedom, unable to beat it down by the strong hand of physical force, have resorted to fraud, and originated an imposture—the most disgusting, the most impious, the most irrational—and yet strange indeed, the most extensive and powerful that has ever stultified the reason or perverted the moral instincts of the race. They set up the dogma or assumption of a single human species—that the negro had the same nature, and therefore was naturally entitled to the same liberty or rights as the white man—and the governments of Europe, with American dependencies, have labored together, and constantly, for more than half a century past, to apply this monstrous assumption to the unfortunate people subject to their rule.

England alone has expended five hundred millions, and mortgaged the bodies and souls of unborn generations of white men and women at home, to abolish the natural supremacy of the white man over the negro in America—to blot out the distinctions of nature and equalize races—to thrust aside the Almighty and make those equal He has eternally decreed shall remain unequal. This monstrous policy is now applied to the whole of tropical America save Cuba, and is designed to pen up our negro population within its present limits, when, with free negroism in front, backed by European governments, and as they hope an "anti-slavery" party in our midst in its rear, the ultimate result must be the abolition of white supremacy, as in Jamaica, etc., with the consequent affiliation with negroes.

The time, therefore, has come when the truth must be laid before the people, and the millions at the North made to understand that this "anti-slavery" policy which, in their blindness they have regarded as philanthropy, is treason to themselves, to their posterity, to their country, and to American civilization.

The author has attempted to perform this great work for the benefit of his countrymen, and indeed, for the civilized and master race of America; and if the time and labor, patient investigation, and unfaltering devotion to truth, and the cause of real freedom deserve success, then he shall have succeeded. And, indeed, however much he may fail, from want of ability, to do justice to a subject so vast, and involving such stupendous consequences, and which no one hitherto has ever ventured to discuss from the stand-point of scientific fact, he can not be mistaken or doubt for a moment the final triumph of the great fundamental truths embodied in the title of this work, for while the first of these traits is fixed forever by the hand of God himself, the latter is an unavoidable induction that can no longer be disregarded without involving the destruction of our institutions, and, finally the ruin of our civilization.

In conclusion, the author begs to say to those who have read the introductory chapter of this work, published several years ago in pamphlet form, that the publication of the entire work has been protracted by unavoidable consequences; but however much it may be regretted in some respects, it has given the author time and reflection to thoroughly examine the facts at its basis, and to test the soundness of his own reasonings on this great subject, while the wide-spread excitement and fearful danger now impending over the country may perhaps induce some to inquire into it who at another time, and under other circumstances, might remain indifferent. . . .

It has been shown in the foregoing pages of this work how that providential arrangement of human affairs, in which the negro is placed in natural juxtaposition with the white man, has resulted in the freedom of the latter and the general well-being of both. It has been seen how a subordinate and widely different social element in Virginia and other States, naturally gave origin to new ideas and new modes of thought, which, thrusting aside the mental habits and political notions brought from the Old World, naturally culminated in the grand idea of 1776, and the establishment of a new political existence, based on the natural, organic, and everlasting equality of the race. It has been seen, moreover, how the great civil revolution of 1800, which, under the lead of Mr. Jefferson, restored the purity and simplicity of republican principles, saved the Northern laboring and producing classes from the rule of an oligarchy, otherwise unavoidable, however it might have been disguised by republican formulas.

It is scarcely necessary to appeal to the political history of the country since 1800 to demonstrate the vital importance—indeed, the measureless benefit—of what, by an absurd perversion of terms, has been called negro slavery, to the freedom, progress, and posterity of the laboring classes of the North, and indeed, to all mankind. It is seen that the existence of an inferior race—the presence of a natural substratum in the political society of the New World—has resulted in the creation of a new political and social order, and relieved the producing classes from that abject dependence on capital which in Europe, and especially in England, renders them mere beasts of burthen to a fraction of their brethren. The simple but transcendent fact, that capital and labor are united at the South—that the planter, or so-called slaveholder, is, **per se** and of necessity, the defender of the rights of the producing classes—this simple fact is the key to our political history, and the hinging-point of our party politics for half a century past.

The Southern planter and the Northern farmer—the producing classes—a Southern majority and a Northern minority—have governed the country, fought all its battles, acquired all its territories, and conducted the nation step by step to its present position of strength, power, and grandeur. Just as steadily a Northern majority and a Southern minority have opposed this progress, and labored blindly, doubtless, to return to the system of the federalists, indeed to the European idea of class distinctions, and to render the government an instrument for the benefit of the few at the expense of the many.

They have sought to create national banks; demanded favors for those engaged in manufactures; for others engaged in Northern fisheries; for the benefit of bands of jobbers and speculators, under pretence of internal improvements; in short, the Northern majority have labored continually to render the government, as in England, an instrument for benefiting classes at the expense of the great body of people.

All these efforts, however, have been defeated by the union of Northern and Southern producers, and mainly by the latter. A large majority of the votes in Congress against special legislation and schemes of corruption have been those of so-called slaveholders; and in those extraordinary instances when Northern representatives of agricultural constituencies have proved faithless, and those schemes "worked" through Congress, "slaveholders" in the Presidential chair have interposed the veto, and saved the laboring and producing classes from this dangerous legislation, and the government from being perverted into an instrument of mischief.

Such has been our political and current party history, and from the nature and necessity of things, every "extension of slavery," or every expansion of territory, must in the future, as it has in the past, strengthen the cause of the producing classes, and give greater scope and power to the American idea of government.

The acquisition of Louisiana, of Florida, of Texas, etc., of those great producing States on the Gulf Coast, has nearly overwhelmed the anti-republican tendencies of the North, and rendered almost powerless those combinations of capital and speculation which have always endangered the purity and simplicity of our republican system, and thus the rights and safety of the laboring and producing millions everywhere.

Indeed, it is a truth, a simple fact, that can not be too often repeated, that in precise proportion to the amount or extent so-called "slaveholding"—of the number of negroes in their normal condition—is freedom rendered secure to the white millions of the North. And when in the progress of time Cuba and Central America, and the whole tropical center of the continent is added to the Union, and placed in the same relation to New York and Ohio that Mississippi, Alabama, etc., are now, then it is evident that the democratic or American idea of government will be securely established forever, and the rights and interests of the producing millions who ask nothing from government but its protection, will be no longer endangered by those anti-republican tendencies which in the North have so long conflicted with the natural development of our system, and struggled so long and fiercely against its existence.

If this freedom and prosperity of the white man rested on wrong or oppression of the negro, then it would be valueless, for the Almighty has evidently designed that all His creatures should be permitted to live out the life to which He has adapted them. But when all the facts are considered, and the negro population of the South contrasted with any similar number of their race now or at any other time in human experience, then it is seen that, relatively considered, they are, perhaps, benefited to even a greater extent than the white population themselves.

The efforts, as it has been shown, to reverse the natural order of things—to force the negro into the position of the white man—are not merely failures, but frightful cruelties—cruelties that among ourselves end in the extinction of those poor creatures, while in the tropics it destroys the white man and impels the negro into barbarian.

In conclusion, therefore, it is clear, or will be clear to every mind that grasps the facts of this great question, with the inductive facts, of the unavoidable inferences that belong to them, that any American citizen, party, sect, or class among us, so blinded, bewildered, and besotted by foreign theories and false mental habits as to labor for negro "freedom"—to drag down their own race, or to thrust the negro from his normal condition, is alike the enemy of both, a traitor to his blood and at war with the decrees of the Eternal.

85. IMMEDIATE EMANCIPATION, 1831*

Not all Americans accepted the inherent inferiority of blacks that Van Evrie believed he had proven. Abolitionists insisted that slaves were human beings who deserved to be free, and the more radical members of the movement championed full equality for African Americans. Among the most vocal of the abolitionists was William Lloyd Garrison. Disenchanted with the failure to end slavery through gradual emancipation, he began publishing The Liberator *in 1831 to demand immediate abolition. His efforts helped impassion the debate over the slavery issue, and he played a critical part in turning the effort to free the slaves into an overwhelming crusade. In his introductory editorial, presented here, he displayed the fervor that characterized his efforts to destroy slavery in the United States.*

In the month of August, I issued proposals for publishing "THE LIBERATOR" in Washington City; but the enterprise, though hailed in different sections of the country, was palsied by public indifference. Since that time, the removal of the *Genius of Universal Emancipation* to the seat of government has rendered less imperious the establishment of a similar periodical in that quarter.

During my recent tour for the purpose of exciting the minds of the people by a series of discourses on the subject of slavery, every place that I visited gave fresh evidence of the fact, that a greater revolution in public sentiment was to be effected in the free States—*and particularly in New-England*—than at the South. I found contempt more bitter, opposition more active, detraction more relentless, prejudice more stubborn, and apathy more frozen, than among the slave-owners themselves. Of course, there were individual exceptions to the contrary. This state of things afflicted, but did not dishearten me. I determined, at every hazard, to lift up the standard of emancipation in the eyes of the nation, *within sight of Bunker Hill and in the birthplace of liberty*. That standard is now unfurled; and long may it float, unhurt by the spoliations of time or the missiles of a desperate foe—yea, till every chain be broken, and every bondsman set free! Let Southern oppressors tremble—let their secret abettors tremble—let their Northern apologists tremble—let all the enemies of the persecuted blacks tremble.

---

*From Wendell Phillips Garrison, *William Lloyd Garrison, 1805–1879: The Story of His Life, Told by His Children*, 4 vols. (New York: The Century Company, 1885–1892), I:224–25.

I deem the publication of my original Prospectus unnecessary, as it has obtained a wide circulation. The principles therein inculcated will be steadily pursued in this paper, excepting that I shall not array myself as the political partisan of any man. In defending the great cause of human rights, I wish to derive the assistance of all religions and of all parties.

Assenting to the "self-evident truth" maintained in the American Declaration of Independence, "that all men are created equal, and endowed by their Creator with certain inalienable rights—among which are life, liberty and the pursuit of happiness," I shall strenuously contend for the immediate enfranchisement of our slave population. In Park-Street Church, on the Fourth of July, 1829, in an address on slavery, I unreflectingly assented to the popular but pernicious doctrine of *gradual* emancipation. I seize this opportunity to make a full and unequivocal recantation, and thus publicly to ask pardon of my God, of my country, and of my brethren the poor slaves, for having uttered a sentiment so full of timidity, injustice, and absurdity. A similar recantation, from my pen, was published in the *Genius of Universal Emancipation* at Baltimore, in September, 1829. My conscience is now satisfied.

I am aware that many object to the severity of my language; but is there not cause for severity? I *will be* as harsh as truth, and as uncompromising as justice. On this subject, I do not wish to think, or speak, or write, with moderation. No! no! Tell a man whose house is on fire to give a moderate alarm; tell him to moderately rescue his wife from the hands of the ravisher; tell the mother to gradually extricate her babe from the fire into which it has fallen;—but urge me not to use moderation in a cause like the present. I am in earnest—I will not equivocate—I will not excuse—I will not retreat a single inch—AND I WILL BE HEARD. The apathy of the people is enough to make every statue leap from his pedestal, and to hasten the resurrection of the dead.

It is pretended, that I am retarding the cause of emancipation by the coarseness of my invective and the precipitancy of my measures. *The charge is not true.* On this question my influence,—humble as it is,—is felt at this moment to a considerable extent, and shall be felt in coming years—not perniciously, but beneficially—not as a curse, but as a blessing; and posterity will bear witness that I was right. I desire to thank God, that he enables me to disregard "the fear of man which bringeth a snare," and to speak his truth in its simplicity and power. . . .

86. DECLARATION OF SENTIMENTS AND RESOLUTIONS, SENECA FALLS, 1848*

By the 1830s many middle-class women in the North worked for moral reforms, participating, for instance, in the temperance movement and the struggle to end slavery. Relegated by their gender to subordinate status, some began to clamor for equality. The refusal of London organizers at the 1840 World Anti-Slavery Convention to seat several female American delegates because of their gender served as a catalyst for future action. In July, 1848, Lucretia Mott and Elizabeth Cady Stanton (two of the rejected London delegates) organized a convention at Seneca Falls, New York—the first formal meeting for women's rights. The following selection includes the convention's "Declaration of Sentiments" (written by Stanton who used the Declaration of Independence as a model) and a series of adopted resolutions demanding equal rights for women.

DECLARATION OF SENTIMENTS.

When, in the course of human events, it becomes necessary for one portion of the family of man to assume among the people of the earth a position different from that which they have hitherto occupied, but one to which the laws of nature and of nature's God entitle them, a decent respect to the

*From *History of Woman Suffrage*, 3 vols., eds. Susan B. Anthony, Elizabeth Cady Stanton and Matilda Joslyn Gage (Rochester, New York: Charles Mann, 1889), I:70–73.

opinions of mankind requires that they should declare the causes that impel them to such a course. We hold these truths to be self-evident: that all men and women are created equal; that they are endowed by their Creator with certain inalienable rights; that among these are life, liberty, and the pursuit of happiness; that to secure these rights governments are instituted, deriving their just powers from the consent of the governed. Whenever any form of government becomes destructive of these ends, it is the right of those who suffer from it to refuse allegiance to it, and to insist upon the institution of a new government, laying its foundation on such principles, and organizing its powers in such form, as to them shall seem most likely to effect their safety and happiness. Prudence, indeed, will dictate that governments long established should not be changed for light and transient causes; and accordingly all experience hath shown that mankind are more disposed to suffer, while evils are sufferable, than to right themselves by abolishing the forms to which they were accustomed. But when a long train of abuses and usurpations, pursuing invariably the same object evinces a design to reduce them under absolute despotism, it is their duty to throw off such government, and to provide new guards for their future security. Such has been the patient sufferance of the women under this government, and such is now the necessity which constrains them to demand the equal station to which they are entitled.

The history of mankind is a history of repeated injuries and usurpations on the part of man toward woman, having in direct object the establishment of an absolute tyranny over her. To prove this, let facts be submitted to a candid world.

He has never permitted her to exercise her inalienable right to the elective franchise.

He has compelled her to submit to laws, in the formation of which she had no voice.

He has withheld from her rights which are given to the most ignorant and degraded men— both natives and foreigners.

Having deprived her of this first right of a citizen, the elective franchise, thereby leaving her without representation in the halls of legislation, he has oppressed her on all sides.

He has made her, if married, in the eye of the law, civilly dead.

He has taken from her all right in property, even to the wages she earns.

He has made her, morally, an irresponsible being, as she can commit many crimes with impunity, provided they be done in the presence of her husband. In the covenant of marriage, she is compelled to promise obedience to her husband, he becoming, to all intents and purposes, her master—the law giving him power to deprive her of her liberty, and to administer chastisement.

He has so framed the laws of divorce, as to what shall be the proper causes, and in case of separation, to whom the guardianship of the children shall be given, as to be wholly regardless of the happiness of women—the law, in all cases, going upon a false supposition of the supremacy of man, and giving all power into his hands.

After depriving her of all rights as a married woman, if single, and the owner of property, he has taxed her to support a government which recognizes her only when her property can be made profitable to it.

He has monopolized nearly all the profitable employments, and from those she is permitted to follow, she receives but a scanty remuneration. He closes against her all the avenues to wealth and distinction which he considers most honorable to himself. As a teacher of theology, medicine, or law, she is not known.

He has denied her the facilities for obtaining a thorough education, all colleges being closed against her.

He allows her in Church, as well as State, but a subordinate position, claiming Apostolic authority for her exclusion from the ministry, and, with some exceptions, from any public participation in the affairs of the Church.

He has created a false public sentiment by giving to the world a different code of morals for men and women, by which moral delinquencies which exclude women from society, are not only tolerated, but deemed of little account in man.

He has usurped the prerogative of Jehovah himself, claiming it as his right to assign for her a sphere of action, when that belongs to her conscience and to her God.

He has endeavored, in every way that he could, to destroy her confidence in her own powers, to lessen her self-respect, and to make her willing to lead a dependent and abject life.

Now, in view of this entire disfranchisement of one-half the people of this country, their social and religious degradation—in view of the unjust laws above mentioned, and because women do feel themselves aggrieved, oppressed, and fraudulently deprived of their most sacred rights, we insist that they have immediate admission to all the rights and privileges which belong to them as citizens of the United States.

In entering upon the great work before us, we anticipate no small amount of misconception, misrepresentation, and ridicule; but we shall use every instrumentality within our power to effect our object. We shall employ agents, circulate tracts, petition the State and National legislatures, and endeavor to enlist the pulpit and the press in our behalf. We hope this Convention will be followed by a series of Conventions embracing every part of the country.

RESOLUTIONS

WHEREAS, The great percept of nature is conceded to be, that "man shall pursue his own true and substantial happiness." Blackstone in his Commentaries remarks, that this law of Nature being coeval with mankind, and dictated by God himself, is of course superior in obligation to any other. It is binding over all the globe, in all countries and at all times; no human laws are of any validity if contrary to this, and such of them as are valid, derive all their force, and all their validity, and all their authority, mediately and immediately, from this original; therefore,

Resolved, That such laws as conflict, in any way, with the true and substantial happiness of woman, are contrary to the great percept of nature and of no validity, for this is "superior in obligation to any other."

Resolved, That all laws which prevent woman from occupying such a station in society as her conscience shall dictate, or which place her in a position inferior to that of man, are contrary to the great percept of nature, and therefore of no force or authority.

Resolved, That woman is man's equal—was intended to be so by the Creator, and the highest good of the race demands that she should be recognized as such.

Resolved, That the women of this country ought to be enlightened in regard to the laws under which they live, that they may no longer publish their degradation by declaring themselves satisfied with their present position, nor their ignorance, by asserting that they have all the rights they want.

Resolved, That inasmuch as man, while claiming for himself intellectual superiority, does accord to woman moral superiority, it is pre-eminently his duty to encourage her to speak and teach, as she has an opportunity, in all religious assemblies.

Resolved, That the same amount of virtue, delicacy, and refinement of behavior that is required of woman in the social state, should also be required of man, and the same transgressions should be visited with equal severity on both man and woman.

Resolved, That the objection of indelicacy and impropriety, which is so often brought against woman when she addresses a public audience, comes with a very ill-grace from those who encourage, by their attendance, her appearance on the stage, in the concert, or in feats of the circus.

Resolved, That woman has too long rested satisfied in the circumscribed limits which corrupt customs and a perverted application of the Scriptures have marked out for her, and that it is time she should move in the enlarged sphere which her great Creator has assigned her.

Resolved, That it is the duty of the women of this country to secure to themselves their sacred right to the elective franchise.

Resolved, That the equality of human rights results necessarily from the fact of the identity of the race in capabilities and responsibilities. . . .

Resolved, That the speedy success of our cause depends upon the zealous and untiring efforts of both men and women, for the overthrow of the monopoly of the pulpit, and for the securing to woman an equal participation with men in the various trades, professions, and commerce. . . .

Resolved, therefore, That, being invested by the Creator with the same capabilities, and the same consciousness of responsibility for their exercise, it is demonstrably the right and duty of woman, equally with man, to promote every righteous cause by every righteous means; and especially in regard to the great subjects of morals and religion, it is self-evidently her right to participate with her brother in teaching them, both in private and in public, by writing and by speaking, by any instrumentalities proper to be used, and in any assemblies proper to be held; and this being a self-evident truth growing out of the divinely implanted principles of human nature, any custom or authority adverse to it, whether modern or wearing the hoary sanction of antiquity, is to be regarded as a self-evident falsehood, and at war with mankind.

Discussion

1. Harriet Martineau stressed equality throughout her essay. What are some examples of her focus, and what do they suggest about the relationship of criminal justice and liberty? Do prisoners deserve to be treated as equals, and do they deserve the blessings of liberty? What do you think of Martineau's assertion that prisons can empower convicts?

2. What do you think motivated Dorothea Dix to investigate the living conditions of the mentally ill? Why were her techniques successful? Why were the insane mistreated? Why did Dix believe that they should not be housed in prisons or jails?

3. Based on the editorial on the Maine Law and Lyman Beecher's call for temperance, what do both documents reveal about liberty, equality, and power? How do the Democrats differ from the Whig reformers? Do you agree that liberty is the "right to do wrong"? If so, why; if not, why not?

4. Who do you think John Van Evrie believed held power in the United States? Do you think that Van Evrie believed that all white people were equal? Why or why not? If not, who is superior? How does Van Evrie argue that slavery had guaranteed liberty in the United States?

5. Who do you think William Lloyd Garrison believed held power in the United States? Why might northerners and New Englanders have been more opposed to Garrison than the slaveowners? What are the implications in the editorial for the liberty of slaves and the equality of African Americans?

6. How did the Seneca Falls delegates express their beliefs about liberty, equality, and power? In their view, what were the sources of inequality? How do you think the writer of "Empire of Woman" (see Chapter 10) would have reacted to the convention?

7. According to Horace Mann, why was education beneficial to American society? How is education related to the issues of liberty, equality, and power today?

CHAPTER 12

Jacksonian Democracy

Calhoun was roundly criticized for his nullification doctrine. Here he steps from nullification, past treason and civil war, to despotism, as both the Constitution and the Union lie dead where he slew them. Off to the right, President Jackson restrains one of Calhoun's supporters and threatens to hang them all.

The years from 1819 to 1840 marked a time of growing interest in politics, and consequently the period is often regarded as the beginning of American democracy. Concern over important issues, such as slavery and monetary policy, helped spark the high voter turnout that accompanied the creation of a new party system in the United States. Those Americans who hoped to use government power to establish an integrated commercial republic became known as Whigs, a name they adopted because of their opposition to what they saw as the reign of King Andrew Jackson. Jackson's supporters, the Democrats, argued that the Whigs' concept of government threatened liberty and the equality of adult white males. As a result of those party differences, the new power relationships that had developed with the rise of the market economy profoundly influenced American political institutions.

87. Thomas Jefferson Sends Instructions to Lewis and Clark, 1803*

In June, 1803, President Thomas Jefferson sent the following instructions to Meriwether Lewis. He outlined the official objectives for the expedition which reflected government expectations as well as his own personal interests. The directives emphasized commercial development, peaceful relations with Indians, and scientific inquiry.

. . . The object of your mission is to explore the Missouri river, and such principal stream of it, as, by its course and communication with the waters of the Pacific Ocean, may offer the most direct and practicable water communication across this continent, for the purposes of commerce.

Beginning at the mouth of the Missouri, you will take observations of latitude and longitude, at all remarkable points on the river, and especially at the mouths of rivers, at rapids, at islands and other places and objects distinguished by such natural marks and characters of a durable kind, as that they may with certainty be recognized hereafter. The courses of the river between these points of observation may be supplied by the compass, the log-line and by time, corrected by the observations themselves. The variations of the compass too, in different places, should be noticed.

The interesting points of portage between the heads of the Missouri and the water offering the best communication with the Pacific Ocean should also be fixed by observation, and the course of that water to the ocean, in the same manner as that of the Missouri.

Your observations are to be taken with great pains and accuracy, to be entered distinctly, and intelligibly for others as well as yourself, to comprehend all the elements necessary, with the aid of the usual tables, to fix the latitude and longitude of the places at which they were taken, & are to be rendered to the War Office, for the purpose of having the calculations made concurrently by proper persons within the United States. . . .

*From *The Writings of Thomas Jefferson*, 20 vols., ed. Albert E. Bergh (Washington, D.C.: The Thomas Jefferson Memorial Association, 1904–1905), XVIII:145–57.

The commerce which may be carried on with the people inhabiting the line you will pursue, renders a knowlege of these people important. You will therefore endeavor to make yourself acquainted, as far as a diligent pursuit of your journey shall admit,

with the names of the nations and their numbers;
the extent and limits of their possessions;
their relations with other tribes or nations;
their language, traditions, monuments;
their ordinary occupations in agriculture, fishing, hunting, war, arts, and the
    implements for these;
their food, clothing, and domestic accom[m]odations;
the diseases prevalent among them, and the remedies they use;
moral and physical circumstances which distinguish them from the tribes we know;
peculiarities in their laws, customs and dispositions;
and articles of commerce they may need or furnish, and to what extent;

And, considering the interest which every nation has in extending and strengthening the authority of reason and justice among the people around them, it will be useful to acquire what knowledge you can of the state of morality, religion and information among them, as it may better enable those who endeavor to civilize and instruct them, to adapt their measures to the existing notions and practises of those on whom they are to operate.

Other object worthy of notice will be,
the soil and face of the country, its growth and vegetable productions, especially those
    not of the United States;
the animals of the country generally, and especially those not known in the United States;
the remains and accounts of any which may deemed rare or extinct;
the mineral productions of every kind; but more particularly metals, limestone, pit coal
    and salpetre; salines and mineral waters, noting the temperature of the last, and
    such circumstances as may indicate their character.
volcanic appearances.
climate as characterized by the thermometer, by the proportion of rainy, cloudy and
    clear days, by lightning, hail, snow, ice, by the access and recess of frost, by the
    winds prevailing at different seasons, the dates
at which particular plants put forth or lose their flowers, or leaf, times of appearance
    of particular birds, reptiles or insects.

Although your route will be along the channel of the Missouri, yet you will endeavor to inform yourself, by inquiry, of the character and extent of the country watered by its branches, and especially on its southern side. The North river or Rio Bravo, which runs into the Gulf of Mexico, and the North river, or Rio Colorado, which runs into the Gulf of California, are understood to be the principal streams heading opposite to the waters of the Missouri, and running Southwardly. Whether the dividing grounds between the Missouri and them are mountains or flatlands, what are their distance from the Missouri, the character of the intermediate country, and the people inhabiting it, are worthy of particular enquiry. The Northern waters of the Missouri are less to be enquired after, because they have been ascertained to a considerable degree, and are still in a course of ascertainment by English traders and travellers, but if you can learn anything certain of the most Northern source of the Mississippi, and of its position relative to the Lake of the Woods, it will be interesting to us. Some account, too, of the path of the Canadian traders from the Mississippi, at the mouth of the Ouisconsing to where it strikes the Missouri, and of the soil and rivers in its course, is desirable.

In all your intercourse with the natives treat them in the most friendly and conciliatory manner which their own conduct will admit; allay all jealousies as to the object of your journey, satisfy them of its innocence, make them acquainted with the position, extent, character, peaceable and commercial dispositions of the United States of our wish to be neighborly, friendly and useful to them, and of our dispositions to a commercial intercourse with them; confer with them on the points most convenient as mutual emporiums, and the articles of most desirable interchange for them and us. If a few of their influential chiefs, within practicable distance, wish to visit us, arrange such a visit with them, and furnish them with authority to call on our officers, on their entering the United States to have them conveyed to this place at public expence. If any of them should wish to have some of their young people brought up with us, and taught such arts as may be useful to them, we will receive, instruct and take care of them. Such a mission, whether of influential chiefs, or of young people, would give some security to your own party. Carry with you some matter of the kine-pox, inform those of them with whom you may be of its efficacy as a preservative from the small-pox; and instruct and encourage them in the use of it. This may be especially done wherever you winter.

As it is impossible for us to foresee in what manner you will be received by those people, whether with hospitality or hostility, so is it impossible to prescribe the exact degree of perseverance with which you are to pursue your journey. We value too much the lives of citizens to offer them to probably destruction. Your numbers will be sufficient to secure you against the unauthorized opposition of individuals, or of small parties: but if a superior force, authorized or not authorized by a nation, should be arrayed against your further passage, and inflexibly determined to arrest it, you must decline its further pursuit, and return. In the loss of yourselves, we should lose also the information you will have acquired. By returning safely with that, you may enable us to renew the essay with better calculated means. To your own discretion therefore must be left the degree of danger you may risk, and the point at which you should decline, only saying we wish you to err on the side of your safety, and bring back your party safe, even if it be with less information.

Should you reach the Pacific ocean inform yourself of the circumstances which may decide whether the furs of those parts may not be collected as advantageously at the head of the Missouri (convenient as is supposed to the waters of the Colorado & Oregon or Columbia) as at Nootka Sound or any other point of that coast; and that trade be consequently conducted through the Missouri and United States more beneficially than by the circumnavigation now practised. . . .

On your arrival on that coast, endeavor to learn if there be any port within your reach frequented by the sea vessels of any nation, and to send two of your trusty people back by sea, in such way as shall appear practicable, with a copy of your notes; and should you be of opinion that the return of your party by the way they went will be eminently dangerous, then ship the whole, and return by sea by way of Cape Horn or the Cape of Good Hope, as you shall be able. . . .

Should you find it safe to return by the way you go, after sending two of your party round by sea, or with your whole party, if no conveyance by sea can be found, do so; making such observations on your return as may serve to supply, correct or confirm those made on your outward journey.

On re-entering the United States and reaching a place of safety, discharge any of your attendants who may desire and deserve it, procuring for them immediate paiment of all arrears of pay and clothing which may have incurred since their departure; and assure them that they shall be recommended to the liberality of the legislature for the grant of a soldier's portion of land each, as proposed in my message to Congress and repair yourself with your papers to the seat of government. . . .

Given under my hand at the city of Washington, this 20th day of June 1803

Thomas Jefferson
President of the United States of America

88. THE MISSOURI QUESTION, 1819*

Virulent debate over Missouri statehood in 1819 focused attention on the expansion of slavery—a matter that assumed increasing importance during the subsequent decades. The issue raised few concerns over equality, since most white Americans had little interest in, or compassion for, the status of African Americans. The Missouri question did, however, raise grave concerns over power. Admitting another slave state to the Union would increase southern strength in the national government, while, to southerners, prohibiting slavery would be an assertion of power that threatened their liberty. When New York Congressman James Tallmadge, Jr., proposed eliminating slavery in Missouri gradually, he was surprised at the vicious attacks the proposal brought. In the following speech, he responded to those attacks and defended his proposal to limit slavery in the new state. His comments touched on some of the important topics that shaped the argument over slavery; they also revealed the bitterness that the matter generated and that so terrorized Thomas Jefferson and many other Americans.

Mr. Tallmadge, of New York, rose.—Sir, said he, it has been my desire and my intention to avoid any debate on the present painful and unpleasant subject. When I had the honor to submit to this House the amendment now under consideration, I accompanied it with a declaration, that it was intended to confine its operation to the newly acquired territory across the Mississippi; and I then expressly declared that I would in no manner intermeddle with the slaveholding States, nor attempt manumission in any of the original States in the Union. Sir, I even went further, and stated that I was aware of the delicacy of the subject, and that I had learned from Southern gentlemen the difficulties and the dangers of having free blacks intermingle with slaves; and, on that account, and with a view to the safety of the white population of the adjoining States, I would not even advocate the prohibition of slavery in the Alabama Territory; because, surrounded as it was by slaveholding States, and with only imaginary lines of division, the intercourse between slaves and free blacks could not be prevented, and a *servile* war might be the result. While we deprecate and mourn over the evil of slavery, humanity and good morals require us to wish its abolition, under circumstances consistent with the safety of the white population. Willingly, therefore, will I submit to an evil which we cannot safely remedy. I admitted all that had been said of the danger of having free blacks visible to slaves, and therefore did not hesitate to pledge myself that I would neither advise nor attempt coercive manumission. But, sir, all these reasons cease when we cross the banks of the Mississippi, a newly acquired territory, never contemplated in the formation of our Government, not included within the compromise or mutual pledge in the adoption of our Constitution, a new territory acquired by our common fund, and ought justly to be subject to our common legislation.

Sir, when I submitted the amendment now under consideration, accompanied with these explanations, and with these avowals of my intentions and my motives, I did expect that gentlemen who might differ from me in opinion would appreciate the liberality of my views, and would meet with moderation, as upon a fair subject for general legislation. Sir, I did expect at least that the frank declaration of my views would protect me from harsh expressions, and from the unfriendly imputations which have been cast out on this occasion. But, sir, such has been the character and the violence of this debate, and expressions of so much intemperance, and of an aspect so threatening have been used, that continued silence on my part would ill become me, who had submitted to this House the original proposition. While this subject was under debate before the Committee of the Whole, I did not take the floor, and I avail myself of this occasion to acknowledge my obligations to my friends, (Mssrs. Taylor and Mills,) for the manner in which they supported my amendment, at a time when I was unable to partake in the debate. I had only on that day returned from a journey long in its extent, and painful in its occasion; and, from an affection of my breast, I could not then speak; I cannot yet hope to do justice to the subject; but I do hope to say enough to assure my

---

*From *Annals of the Congress of the United States . . .*, 15th Congress, 2nd Session, vol. I (1818–1819), 1203–05.

friends that I have not left them in the controversy, and to convince the opponents of the measure, that their violence has not driven me from the debate. . . .

Sir, if a dissolution of the Union must take place, let it be so! If civil war, which gentlemen so much threaten, must come, I can only say, let it come! My hold on life is probably as frail as that of any man who now hears me; but, while that hold lasts, it shall be devoted to the service of my country—to the freedom of man. If blood is necessary to extinguish any fire which I have assisted to kindle, I can assure gentlemen, while I regret the necessity, I shall nor forbear to contribute my mite. Sir, the violence to which gentlemen have resorted on this subject will not move my purpose, nor drive me from my place. I have the fortune and the honor to stand here as the representative of freemen, who possess intelligence to know their rights, who have the spirit to maintain them. Whatever might be my own private sentiments on this subject, standing here as the representatives of others, no choice is left me. I know the will of my constituents, and, regardless of consequences, I will avow it; as their representative, I will proclaim their hatred to slavery in every shape; as their representative, here will I hold my stand, until this floor, with the Constitution of my country which supports it, shall sink beneath me. If I am doomed to fall, I shall at least have the painful consolation to believe that I fall, as a fragment, in the ruins of my country. . . .

89. A CONGRESSMAN OPPOSES LIMITING SLAVERY IN MISSOURI, 1820*

In February 1820, Representative Charles Pinckney of South Carolina, former governor and United States Senator from South Carolina as well as one of the few surviving members of the 1787 Philadelphia Constitutional Convention, spoke out forcefully against restricting slavery in Missouri. In the following speech, Pinckney defended the institution of slavery and warned his fellow congressmen that any limitations could result in dire consequences for the Union. Despite Pinckney's rhetoric, a compromise was worked out. Still, the debates had revealed the bitterness that the matter generated and the deepening fissures between North and South.

A great deal has been said on the subject of slavery—that it is an infamous stain and blot on the States that hold them; not only degrading the slave, but the master, and making him unfit for republican government; that it is contrary to religion and the law of God; and that Congress ought to do every thing in their power to prevent its extension among the new States.

Now, sir, I should be glad to know how any man is acquainted with what is the will or the law of God on this subject. Has it ever been imparted either to the old or new world? Is there a single line in the Old or New Testament, either censuring or forbidding it? I answer without hesitation, no. But there are hundreds speaking of and recognising it. Hagar, from whom millions sprang, was an African slave, bought out of Egypt by Abraham, the father of the faithful and the beloved servant of the Most High; and he had, besides, three hundred and eighteen male slaves. The Jews, in the time of the theocracy, and the Greeks and Romans, had all slaves; at that time there was no nation without them. If we are to believe that this world was formed by a great and omnipotent Being; that nothing is permited to exist here but by his will, and then throw our eyes throughout the whole of it, we should form an opinion very different indeed from that asserted, that slavery was against the law of God. . . .

. . .

From the opinions expressed respecting the Southern States and the slaves there, it appears to me most clear, that the members on the opposite side know nothing of the Southern States, their lands, products, or slaves.

. . .

*From *Annals of the Congress of the United States*, 16th Congress, 1st session, vol. II (1819–1820), 1323–25, 1327–28.

It will not be a matter of surprise to any one, that so much anxiety should be shown by the slaveholding States, when it is known that the alarm, given by this attempt to legislate on slavery, has led to the opinion, that the very foundations of that kind of property are shaken; that the establishment of the precedent is a measure of the most alarming nature; for, should succeeding Congresses continue to push it, there is no knowing to what length it may be carried.

Have the Northern States any idea of the value of our slaves? At least, sir, six hundred millions of dollars. If, we lose them, the value of the lands they cultivate will be diminished in all cases one half, and, in many, they will become wholly useless, and an annual income of at least forty millions of dollars will be lost to your citizens; the loss of which will not alone be felt by the non-slaveholding States, but by the whole Union; for, to whom, at present, do the Eastern States, most particularly, and the Eastern and Northern, generally, look for the employment of their shipping, in transporting our bulky and valuable products, and bringing us the manufactures and merchandises of Europe? Another thing, in case of these losses being brought on us, and our being forced into a division of the Union, what becomes of your public debt? Who are to pay this, and how will it be paid? In a pecuniary view of this subject, therefore, it must ever be the policy of the Eastern and Northern States to continue connected with us. But, sir, there is an infinitely greater call upon them, and this is the call of justice, of affection, and humanity. Reposing at a great distance, in safety, in the full enjoyment of all their Federal and State rights, unattacked in either, or in their individual rights, can they, with indifference, or ought they to risk, in the remotest degree, the consequences which this measure may produce. These may be the division of this Union, and a civil war. Knowing that whatever is said here, must get into the public prints, I am unwilling, for obvious reasons, to go into the description of the horrors which such a war must produce, and ardently pray that none of us may ever live to witness such an event. . . .

I cannot, on any ground, think of agreeing to a compromise on this subject. However we all may wish to see Missouri admitted, as she ought, on equal terms with the other States, this is a very unimportant object to her, compared with keeping the Constitution inviolate—with keeping the hands of Congress from touching the question of slavery. On the subject of the Constitution, no compromise ought ever to be made. Neither can any be made on the national faith, so seriously involved in the treaty which gives to all Louisiana, to every part of it, a right to be incorporated into the Union on equal terms with the other States.

90. THE NATIONALISM OF JOHN QUINCY ADAMS, 1825*

In his first annual address to Congress, President John Quincy Adams argued that the "progressive improvement of the condition of the governed" was the "great object of the institution of government." His broad vision included not only canals and roads, but such "moral, political, intellectual improvements" as a national university and a national astronomical observatory. Adams' view of energetic government, however, was rapidly falling into popular disfavor. And his assertion that Congress should not be "palsied by the will of our constituents" only incited further suspicions that he was an opponent of democracy.

. . . Upon this first occasion of addressing the Legislature of the Union, with which I have been honored, in presenting to their view the execution so far as it has been effected of the measures sanctioned by them for promoting the internal improvement of our country, I can not close the communication without recommending to their calm and persevering consideration the general principle in a more enlarged extent. The great object of the institution of civil government is the

*From *A Compilation of the Messages and Papers of the Presidents, 1789–1897*, 10 vols., comp. James D. Richardson (Washington, D.C.: Government Printing Office, 1896–1899), II:311–14, 316–17.

improvement of the condition of those who are parties to the social compact, and no government, in whatever form constituted, can accomplish the lawful ends of its institution but in proportion as it improves the condition of those over whom it is established. Roads and canals, by multiplying and facilitating the communications and intercourse between distant regions and multitudes of men, are among the most important means of improvement. But moral, political, intellectual improvement are duties assigned by the Author of Our Existence to social no less than to individual man. For the fulfillment of those duties governments are invested with power, and to the attainment of the end—the progressive improvement of the condition of the governed—the exercise of delegated powers is a duty as sacred and indispensable as the usurpation of powers not granted is criminal and odious. Among the first, perhaps the very first, instrument for the improvement of the condition of men is knowledge, and to the acquisition of much of the knowledge adapted to the wants, the comforts, and enjoyments of human life public institutions and seminaries of learning are essential. So convinced of this was the first of my predecessors in this office, now first in the memory, as, living, he was first in the hearts, of our countrymen, that once and again in his addresses to the Congresses with whom he cooperated in the public service he earnestly recommended the establishment of seminaries of learning, to prepare for all the emergencies of peace and war—a national university and a military academy. With respect to the later, had he lived to the present day, in turning his eyes to the institution at West Point he would have enjoyed the gratification of his most earnest wishes; but in surveying the city which has been honored with his name he would have seen the spot of earth which he had destined and bequeathed to the use and benefit of his country as the site for an university still bare and barren.

In assuming her station among the civilized nations of the earth it would seem that our country had contracted the engagement to contribute her share of mind, of labor, and of expense to the improvement of those parts of knowledge which lie beyond the reach of individual acquisition, and particularly to geographical and astronomical science. Looking back to the history only of the half century since the declaration of our independence, and observing the generous emulation with which the Governments of France, Great Britain, and Russia have devoted the genius, the intelligence, the treasures of their respective nations to the common improvement of the species in these branches of science, is it not incumbent upon us to inquire whether we are not bound by obligations of a high and honorable character to contribute our portion of energy and exertion to the common stock? . . .

In inviting the attention of Congress to the subject of internal improvements upon a view thus enlarged it is not my design to recommend the equipment of an expedition for circumnavigating the globe for purposes of scientific research and inquiry. We have objects of useful investigation nearer home, and to which our cares may be more beneficially applied. The interior of our own territories has yet been very imperfectly explored. Our coasts along many degrees of latitude upon the shores of the Pacific Ocean, though much frequented by our spirited commercial navigators, have been barely visited by our public ships. The River of the West, first fully discovered and navigated by a countryman of our own, still bears, the name of the ship in which he ascended its waters, and claims the protection of our armed national flag at its mouth. With the establishment of a military post there or at some point of that coast, recommended by my predecessor and already matured in the deliberations of the last Congress, I would suggest the expediency of connecting the equipment of a public ship for the exploration of the whole northwest coast of this continent. . . .

Connected with the establishment of an university, or separate from it, might be undertaken the erection of an astronomical observatory, with provision for the support of an astronomer, to be in constant attendance of observation upon the phenomena of the heavens, and for the periodical publication of his observations. It is with no feeling of pride as an American that the remark may be made that on the comparatively small territorial surface of Europe there are existing upward of 130 of these light-houses of the skies, while throughout the whole American hemisphere there is not one. If we reflect a moment upon the discoveries which in the last four centuries have been made in the physical constitution of the universe by the means of these buildings and of observers stationed in them, shall we doubt of their usefulness to every nation? And while scarcely a year passes over our heads without bringing some new astronomical discovery to light, which we must fain receive at second hand from Europe, are we not cutting ourselves off from the means of returning light for light while we have neither observatory nor observer upon our half of the globe and the earth revolves in perpetual darkness to our unsearching eyes? . . .

The spirit of improvement is abroad upon the earth. It stimulates the hearts and sharpens the faculties not of our fellow-citizens alone, but of the nations of Europe and of their rulers. While dwelling with pleasing satisfaction upon the superior excellence of our political institutions, let us not be unmindful that liberty is power; that the nation blessed with the largest portion of liberty must in proportion to its numbers be the most powerful nation upon earth, and that the tenure of power by man is, in the moral purposes of his Creator, upon condition that it shall be exercised to ends of beneficence, to improve the condition of himself and his fellowmen. While foreign nations less blessed with that freedom which is power than ourselves are advancing with gigantic strides in the career of public improvement, were we to slumber in indolence or fold up our arms and proclaim to the world that we are palsied by the will of our constituents, would it not be to cast away the bounties of Providence and doom ourselves to perpetual inferiority? In the course of the year now drawing to its close we have beheld, under the auspices and at the expense of one State of this Union, a new university unfolding its portals to the sons of science and holding up the torch of human improvement to eyes that seek the light. We have seen under the persevering and enlightened enterprise of another State the waters of our Western lakes mingle with those of the ocean. If undertakings like these have been accomplished in the compass of a few years by the authority of single members of our Confederation, can we, the representative authorities of the whole Union, fall behind our fellow-servants in the exercise of the trust committed to us for the benefit of our common sovereign by the accomplishment of works important to the whole and to which neither the authority nor the resources of any one State can be adequate?

Finally, fellow-citizens, I shall await with cheering hope and faithful cooperation the result of your deliberations, assured that, without encroaching upon the powers reserved to the authorities of the respective States or to the people, you will, with a due sense of your obligations to your country and of the high responsibilities weighing upon yourselves, give efficacy to the means committed to you for the common good. . . .

91. THE CHEROKEE NATION ADDRESSES THE PEOPLE OF THE UNITED STATES, 1830*

*M*any land-hungry white Americans in the Old Southwest coveted Indian lands. Late in the 1820s the Cherokee nation, despite treaty commitments from the United States and a reputation as a "civilized tribe," faced eviction from their ancestral lands in northwestern Georgia. They had sought to protect their rights peacefully, even petitioning the Supreme Court for an injunction against attempts to remove them. But the state of Georgia asserted its authority over the Cherokees and prepared to seize their lands. In July, 1830, the Cherokee nation appealed to the American people to permit them to remain in their "beloved country," but to no avail. Despite sympathy from some northeastern humanitarians and the support of two Supreme Court decisions, the 18,000 Cherokees who remained in Georgia were forced to leave for Oklahoma in 1838; 4,000 died on this "Trail of Tears."

*From Address of the "Committee and Council of the Cherokee Nation, in General Council Convened," to the People of the United States (Chester County, Pennsylvania: privately printed, 1830), 6–9.

. . . The people of the United States will have the fairness to reflect, that all the treaties between them and the Cherokees were made, at the solicitation, and for the benefit, of the whites; that valuable considerations were given for every stipulation, on the part of the United States; that it is impossible to reinstate the parties in their former situation; there are now hundreds of thousands of citizens of the United States residing upon lands ceded by the Cherokees in these very treaties; and that our people have trusted their country to the guaranty of the United States: If this guaranty fails them, in what can they trust, and where can they look for protection?

We are aware, that some persons suppose it will be for our advantage to remove beyond the Mississippi. We think otherwise. Our people universally think otherwise. Thinking that it would be fatal to their interests, they have almost to a man sent their memorial to Congress, deprecating the necessity of a removal. This question was distinctly before their minds when they signed their memorial. Not an adult person can be found, who has not an opinion on the subject, and if the people were to understand distinctly, that they could be protected against the laws of the neighboring States, there is probably not an adult person in the nation who would think it best to remove; though possibly a few might emigrate individually. There are doubtless many, who would flee to an unknown country, however beset with dangers, privations and sufferings, rather than be sentenced to spend six years in a Georgia prison for advising one of their neighbors not to betray his country. And there are others who could not think of living as outlaws in their native land, exposed to numberless vexations, and excluded from being parties or witnesses in a court of justice. It is incredible that Georgia should ever have enacted the oppressive laws, to which reference is here made, unless she had supposed that something extremely terrific in its character was necessary in order to make the Cherokees willing to remove. We are not willing to remove, and if we could be brought to this extremity, it would be not by argument, not because our judgment was satisfied, not because our disposition will be improved; but only because we cannot endure to be deprived of our national and individual rights and subjected to a process of intolerable oppression.

We wish to remain on the land of our fathers. We have a perfect and original right to claim without interruption or molestation. The treaties with us, and laws of the United States made in pursuance of treaties, guaranty our residence, and our privileges, and secure us against intruders. Our only request is, that these treaties may be fulfilled, and these laws executed.

But if we are compelled to leave our country, we see nothing but ruin before us. The country west of the Arkansas territ[or]y is unknown to us. From what we can learn of it we have no prepossessions in its favor. All the inviting parts of it as we believe, are preoccupied by various Indians or nations, to which it has been assigned. They would regard us as intruders, and look upon us with an evil eye. The far greater part of that region is beyond all controversy, badly supplied with wood and water; and no Indian tribe can live as agriculturists, without these articles. All our neighbours, in case of our removal though crowded into our near vicinity, would speak a language totally different from ours, and practice different customs. The orginal possessors of that region are now wandering savages, lurking for prey in the neighborhood. They have always been at war, and would be easily tempted to turn their arms against peaceful emigrants. Were the country to which we are urged much better than it is represented to be, and were it free from the objections which we have made to it, still it is not the land of our birth, nor of our affections. It contains neither the scenes of our childhood, nor the graves of our fathers.

The removal of families to a new country, even under the most favorable auspices, and when the spirits are sustained by pleasing visions of the future, is attended with much depression of mind and sinking of heart. This is the case, when the removal is a matter of decided preference, and when the persons concerned are in early youth or vigorous manhood. Judge, then, what must be the circumstances of a removal, when a whole community, embracing persons of all classes and every description, from the infant to the man of extreme old age, the sick, the blind, the lame, the improvident, the reckless, the desperate, as well as the prudent,—the considerate, the industrious, are compelled to remove by odious and intolerable vexations and persecutions, brought upon them in the forms of law, when all will agree only in this, that they have been cruelly robbed of their country, in violation of the most solemn compacts which it is possible for communities to form with each other; and that, if they should make themselves comfortable in their residence, they have nothing to expect hereafter but to be the victims of a future legalized robbery!

Such we deem, and are absolutely certain, will be the feelings of the whole Cherokee people, if they are forcibly compelled by the laws of Georgia to remove; and with these feelings, how is it possible that we should pursue our present course of improvement, or avoid sinking into utter despondency? We have been called a poor, ignorant, and degraded people. We certainly are not rich; nor have we ever boasted of our knowledge, or our moral or intellectual elevation. But there is not a man within our limits so ignorant as not to know that he has a right to live on the land of his fathers, in the possession of his immemorial privileges, and that this right has been acknowledged and guaranteed by the United States; nor is there a man so degraded as not to feel a keen sense of injury, on being deprived of this right and driven into exile.

It is under a sense of the most pungent feelings that we make this, perhaps our last appeal to the good people of the United States. It cannot be that the community we are addressing, remarkable for its intelligence and religious sensibilities, and pre-eminent for its devotion to the rights of man, will lay aside this appeal, without considering that we stand in need of its sympathy and commiseration. . . . In our own land, on our own soil, and in our own dwellings, which we reared for our wives and for our little ones, when there was peace on our mountains and in our valleys, we are encountering troubles which cannot but try our very souls. But shall we on account of these troubles, forsake our beloved country? Shall we be compelled, by a civilized and Christian people, with whom we have lived in perfect peace for the last forty years, and for whom we have willingly bled in war, to bid a final adieu to our homes, our farms, our streams, and our beautiful forests? No. We are still firm. We intend still to cling, with our wonted affection, to the land which gave us birth, and which, every day of our lives, brings to us new and stronger ties of attachment. We appeal to the judge of all the earth, who will finally award us justice, and to the good sense of the American people, whether we are intruders upon the land of others. Our consciences bear us witness that we are the invaders of no man's rights—we have robbed no man of his territory—we have usurped no man's authority, nor have we deprived any one of his unalienable privileges. How then shall we indirectly confess the right of another people to our land by leaving it forever? On the soil which contains the ashes of our beloved men we wish to live—on this soil we wish to die. . . .

92. JACKSON DEFENDS INDIAN REMOVAL POLICY, 1829*

*I*n his first annual message to Congress, President Andrew Jackson refused to challenge the actions of Georgia and other southern states which had extended their authority over Indian lands. He maintained that the federal government lacked the jurisdiction to defend any claims of Indian sovereignty within the various states. Rather, Jackson argued, the tribes should be encouraged to move to federal land west of the Mississippi, where they could reside peacefully—far away from any land coveted by white Americans.

. . . The condition and ulterior destiny of the Indian tribes within the limits of some of our States have become objects of much interest and importance. It has long been the policy of Government to introduce among them the arts of civilization, in the hope of gradually reclaiming them

---

*From *A Compilation of the Messages and Papers of the Presidents, 1789–1897*, 10 vols., comp. James D. Richardson (Washington, D.C.: Government Printing Office, 1896–1899), II:456–59.

from a wandering life. This policy has, however, been coupled with another wholly incompatible with its success. Professing a desire to civilize and settle them, we have at the same time lost no opportunity to purchase their lands and thrust them farther into the wilderness. By this means they have not only been kept in a wandering state, but been led to look upon us as unjust and indifferent to their fate. Thus, though lavish in its expenditures upon the subject, Government has constantly defeated its own policy, and the Indians in general, receding farther and farther to the west, have retained their savage habits. A portion, however, of the Southern tribes, having mingled much with the whites and made some progress in the arts of civilized life, have lately attempted to erect an independent government within the limits of Georgia and Alabama. These States, claiming to be the only sovereigns within their territories, extended their laws over the Indians, which induced the latter to call upon the United States for protection.

Under these circumstances the question presented was whether the General Government had a right to sustain those people in their pretensions. The Constitution declares that "no new State shall be formed or erected within the jurisdiction of any other State" without the consent of its legislature. . . . There is no constitutional, conventional, or legal provision which allows them less power over the Indians within their borders than is possessed by Maine or New York. . . .

. . . Actuated by this view of the subject, I informed the Indians inhabiting parts of Georgia and Alabama that their attempt to establish an independent government would not be countenanced by the Executive of the United States, and advised them to emigrate beyond the Mississippi or submit to the laws of those States.

Our conduct toward these people is deeply interesting to our national character. Their present condition, contrasted with what they once were, makes a most powerful appeal to our sympathies. Our ancestors found them the uncontrolled possessors of these vast regions. By persuasion and force they have been made to retire from river to river and from mountain to mountain, until some of the tribes have become extinct and others have left but remnants to preserve for awhile their once terrible names. Surrounded by the whites with their arts of civilization, which by destroying the resources of the savage doom him to weakness and decay, the fate of the Mohegan, the Narragansett, and the Delaware is fast overtaking the Choctaw, the Cherokee, and the Creek. That this fate surely awaits them if they remain within the limits of the States does not admit of a doubt. Humanity and national honor demand that every effort should be made to avert so great a calamity. . . .

As a means of effecting this end I suggest for your consideration the propriety of setting apart an ample district west of the Mississippi, and without the limits of any State or Territory now formed, to be guaranteed to the Indian tribes as long as they shall occupy it, each tribe having a distinct control over the portion designated for its use. There they may be secured in the enjoyment of governments of their own choice, subject to no other control from the United States than such as may be necessary to preserve peace on the frontier and between the several tribes. There the benevolent may endeavor to teach them the arts of civilization, and, by promoting union and harmony among them, to raise up an interesting commonwealth, destined to perpetuate the race and to attest the humanity and justice of this Government.

This emigration should be voluntary, for it would be as cruel as unjust to compel the aborigines to abandon the graves of their fathers and seek a home in a distant land. But they should be distinctly informed that if they remain within the limits of the States they must be subject to their laws. In return for their obedience as individuals they will without doubt be protected in the enjoyment of those possessions which they have improved by their industry. But it seems to me visionary to suppose that in this state of things claims can be allowed on tracts of country on which they have neither dwelt nor made improvements, merely because they have seen them from the mountain or passed them in the chase. Submitting to the laws of the States, and receiving, like other citizens, protection in their persons and property, they will ere long become merged in the mass of our population. . . .

93. SOUTH CAROLINA PROTESTS THE TARIFF OF 1828*

After the settlement of the Missouri slavery question in 1820, the tariff issue emerged as the next great sectional struggle. In an effort to win Andrew Jackson votes in the 1828 election, congressional supporters, already assured of southern support, cobbled together a tariff bill that pleased northern and western farmers, but alienated many southerners. South Carolina, guided by Vice President John C. Calhoun, led southern opposition to the Tariff of 1828. In response to this "tariff of abominations," Calhoun anonymously published an essay entitled "Exposition and Protest" in which he outlined his compact theory of government and asserted the right of states to nullify federal law. In December, 1828, the South Carolina legislature published Calhoun's essay (without identifying the author) as the "South Carolina Exposition and Protest," accompanied by the following resolutions which condemned the tariff.

THE TARIFF. SOUTH CAROLINA. PROTEST

The Senate and House of Representatives of South Carolina, now met, and sitting in General Assembly, through the Hon. William Smith and the Hon. Robert Y. Hayne, their representatives in the Senate of the United States, do, in the name and on behalf of the good people of the said commonwealth, solemnly *PROTEST* against the system of protecting duties, lately adopted by the federal government, for the following reasons : —

1st. *Because* the good people of this commonwealth believe that the powers of Congress were delegated to it in trust for the accomplishment of certain specified objects which limit and control them, and that every exercise of them for any other purposes, is a violation of the Constitution as unwarrantable as the undisguised assumption of substantive, independent powers not granted or expressly withheld.

2d. *Because* the power to lay duties on imports is, and in its very nature can be, only a means of effecting objects specified by the Constitution; since no free government, and least of all a government of enumerated powers, can of right impose any tax, any more than a penalty, which is not at once justified by public necessity, and clearly within the scope and purview of the social compact; and since the right of confining appropriations of the public money to such legitimate and constitutional objects is as essential to the liberties of the people as their unquestionable privilege to be taxed only by their own consent.

3d. *Because* they believe that the tariff law passed by Congress at its last session, and all other acts of which the principal object is the protection of manufactures, or any other branch of domestic industry, if they be considered as the exercise of a power in Congress to tax the people at its own good will and pleasure, and to apply the money raised to objects not specified in the Constitution, is a violation of these fundamental principles, a breach of a well-defined trust, and a perversion of the high powers vested in the federal government for federal purposes only.

4th. *Because* such acts, considered in the light of a regulation of commerce, are equally liable to objection; since, although the power to regulate commerce may, like other powers, be exercised so as to protect domestic manufactures, yet it is clearly distinguishable from a power to do so *eo nomine*, both in the nature of the thing and in the common acceptation of the terms; and because the confounding of them would lead to the most extravagant results, since the encouragement of domestic industry implies an absolute control over all the interests, resources, and pursuits of a people, and is inconsistent with the idea of any other than a simple, consolidated government.

---

*From *The Debates in the Several State Conventions on the Adoption of the Federal Constitution, as Recommended by the General Convention at Philadelphia in 1787; Together with the Journal of the Federal Convention, Luther Martin's Letter, Yates's Minutes, Congressional Opinions, Virginia and Kentucky Resolutions of 98–99 and Other Illustrations of the Constitution*, 5 vols., comp. and ed. Jonathan Elliot (Philadelphia: J. B. Lippincott Company, 1836), Iv: 580–82.

5th. *Because*, from the contemporaneous exposition of the Constitution in the numbers of the Federalist, (which is cited only because the Supreme Court has recognized its authority,) it is clear that the power to regulate commerce was considered by the Convention as only incidentally connected with the encouragement of agriculture and manufactures; and because the power of laying imposts and duties on imports was not understood to justify, in any case, a prohibition of foreign commodities, except as a means of extending commerce, by coercing foreign nations to a fair reciprocity in their intercourse with us, or for some other *bona fide* commercial purpose.

6th. *Because*, whilst the power to protect manufactures is nowhere expressly granted to Congress, nor can be considered as necessary and proper to carry into effect any specified power, it seems to be expressly reserved to the states, by the 10th section of the 1st article of the Constitution.

7th. *Because*, even admitting Congress to have a constitutional right to protect manufactures by the imposition of duties, or by regulations of commerce, designed principally for that purpose, yet a tariff of which the operation is grossly unequal and oppressive, is such an abuse of power as is incompatible with the principles of a free government and the great ends of civil society, justice, and equality of rights and protection.

8th. *Finally*, because South Carolina, from her climate, situation, and peculiar institutions, is, and must ever continue to be, wholly dependent upon agriculture and commerce, not only for her prosperity, but for her very existence as a state; because the valuable products of her soil—the blessings by which Divine Providence seems to have designed to compensate for the great disadvantages under which she suffers in other respects—are among the very few that can be cultivated with any profit by slave labor; and if, by the loss of her foreign commerce, these products should be confined to an inadequate market, the fate of this fertile state would be poverty and utter desolation; her citizens, in despair, would emigrate to more fortunate regions, and the whole frame and constitution of her civil polity be impaired and deranged, if not dissolved entirely.

Deeply impressed with these considerations, the representatives of the good people of this commonwealth, anxiously desiring to live in peace with their fellow-citizens, and to do all that in them lies to preserve and perpetuate the union of the states, and liberties of which it is the surest pledge, but feeling it to be their bounden duty to expose and resist all encroachments upon the true spirit of the Constitution, lest an apparent acquiescence in the system of protecting duties should be drawn into precedent—do, in the name of the commonwealth of South Carolina, claim to enter upon the Journal of the Senate their *protest* against it as unconstitutional, oppressive, and unjust.

94. JACKSON RESPONDS TO SOUTH CAROLINA'S ORDINANCE OF NULLIFICATION, 1832*

*M*any South Carolinians viewed the Tariff of 1832 with only slightly less antipathy than the "abominable" Tariff of 1828. To them, the hated principle of protectionism only hurt the South. By 1832, southern extremists, empowered by John C. Calhoun's anonymously published 1828 essay "Exposition and Protest," firmly believed that a state could nullify a federal law. In November, 1832, a state convention called by the South Carolina legislature nullified the tariffs of 1828 and 1832, declaring both acts unconstitutional. In the following selection, President Andrew Jackson responded to such defiance with a ringing denouncement of nullification and secession; to him, disunion was unthinkable.

---

*From *A Compilation of the Messages and Papers of the Presidents, 1789–1897*, 10 vols., comp. James D. Richardson (Washington, D.C.: Government Printing Office, 1896–1899), II:652, 654–56.

. . . This, then, is the position in which we stand: A small majority of the citizens of one State in the Union have elected delegates to a State convention; that convention has ordained that all the revenue laws of the United States must be repealed, or that they are no longer a member of the Union. The governor of that State has recommended to the legislature the raising of an army to carry the secession into effect, and that he may be empowered to give clearances to vessels in the name of the State. No act of violent opposition to the laws has yet been committed, but such a state of things is hourly apprehended. And it is the intent of this instrument to *proclaim*, not only that the duty imposed on me by the Constitution "to take care that the laws be faithfully executed" shall be performed to the extent of the powers already vested in me by law, or of such others as the wisdom of Congress shall devise and intrust to me for that purpose, but to warn the citizens of South Carolina who have been deluded into an opposition to the laws of the danger they will incur by obedience to the illegal and disorganizing ordinance of the convention; to exhort those who have refused to support it to persevere in their determination to uphold the Constitution and laws of their country; and to point out to all the perilous situation into which the good people of that State have been led, and that the course they are urged to pursue is one of ruin and disgrace to the very State whose rights they affect to support. . . .

For what would you exchange your share in the advantages and honor of the Union? For the dream of a separate independence—a dream interrupted by bloody conflicts with your neighbors and a vile dependence on a foreign power. If your leaders could succeed in establishing a separation, what would be your situation? Are you united at home? Are you free from the apprehension of civil discord, with all its fearful consequences? Do our neighboring republics, every day suffering some new revolution or contending with some new insurrection, do they excite your envy? But the dictates of a high duty oblige me solemnly to announce that you can not succeed. The laws of the United States must be executed. I have no discretionary power on the subject; my duty is emphatically pronounced in the Constitution. Those who told you that you might peaceably prevent their execution deceived you; they could not have been deceived themselves. They know that a forcible opposition could alone prevent the execution of the laws, and they know that such opposition must be repelled. Their object is disunion. But be not deceived by names. Disunion by armed force is *treason*. Are you really ready to incur its guilt? If you are, on the heads of the instigators of the act be the dreadful consequences; on their heads be the dishonor, but on yours may fall the punishment. On your unhappy State will inevitably fall all the evils of the conflict you force upon the Government of your country. It can not accede to the mad project of disunion, of which you would be the first victims. Its First Magistrate can not, if he would, avoid the performance of his duty. The consequence must be fearful for you, distressing to your fellow-citizens here and to the friends of good government throughout the world. Its enemies have beheld our prosperity with a vexation they could not conceal; it was a standing refutation of their slavish doctrines, and they will point to our discord with the triumph of malignant joy. It is yet in your power to disappoint them. . . .

Fellow-citizens of the United States, the threat of unhallowed disunion, the names of those once respected by whom it is uttered, the array of military force to support it, denote the approach of a crisis in our affairs on which the continuance of our unexampled prosperity, our political existence, and perhaps that of all free governments may depend. The conjuncture demanded a free, a full, and explicit enunciation, not only of my intentions, but of my principles of action; and as the claim was asserted of a right by a State to annul the laws of the Union, and even to secede from it at pleasure, a frank exposition of my opinions in relation to the origin and form of our Government and the construction I give to the instrument by which it was created seemed to be proper. Having the fullest confidence in the justness of the legal and constitutional opinion of my duties which has been expressed, I rely with equal confidence on your undivided support in my determination to execute the laws, to preserve the Union by all constitutional means, to arrest, if possible, by moderate and firm measures the necessity of a recourse to force; and if it be the will of Heaven that the recurrence of its primeval curse on man for the shedding of a brother's blood should fall upon our land, that it be not called down by any offensive act on the part of the United States. . . .

Discussion

1. Based on the two opposing speeches on slavery in Missouri, what issues of power were at stake? What does the tone of the addresses and the threats of civil war they contain suggest about political power struggles in the United States during this era?

2. What were John Quincy Adams' attitudes toward the power of government, and what were those powers? How do you think such ideas about energetic government were viewed by Jackson supporters, and why?

3. On the issue of Indian removal, how did members of the Cherokee nation and President Andrew Jackson differ in their views of liberty, equality, and power? Which side had a more persuasive argument, and why?

4. What arguments did President Jackson use in his attempt to persuade the citizens of South Carolina that disunion was unacceptable? In his view, how were the liberties of the people and the power of the Union threatened by the state action?

5. How did President Jefferson's instructions to Lewis and Clark reflect the issues of liberty, equality, and power? What were the objectives of the expedition, and how do they reflect Jefferson's political ambitions and the broad interests of the Enlightenment?

6. How would the authors of the South Carolina resolutions against the tariff differ with the views of President Jackson on the issues of power and liberty? What are the fundamental differences of the two viewpoints?

CHAPTER 13

Manifest Destiny:
An Empire for Liberty—or Slavery?

"This is the house that Polk built." This c. 1846 anti-Polk cartoon protests his expansionist goals and the Mexican War. Polk sits on a nest hatching his plans under the walls of territorial expansion and tariff reduction. His flimsy house of cards cannot last.

During the 1830s and 1840s, the national faith that the United States should expand across the continent became more and more apparent. This Manifest Destiny, which in many ways was the legacy of John Winthrop's hope for creating a "city upon a hill," encouraged emigration to western states and sparked interest in gaining additional territories. By 1850, the nation reached to the Pacific Ocean and stretched from Canada to the southwestern deserts. American power, and American concepts of liberty and equality, spread from sea to sea. Expansion, however, deepened the already existing sectional differences over slavery. The debate over Texas statehood, for instance, brought into sharp focus the growing animosity between northerners and southerners. War with Mexico only served to exacerbate the problem, because the status of slavery in newly acquired territory became an overriding, and extremely divisive, political issue. To northerners, expanding slavery threatened the economic prospects and the equality of white men. Southerners feared just as strongly that limiting slavery endangered their rights and liberties. Ironically, just as the United States seemed to have achieved an unprecedented power, it appeared that questions of liberty and equality might destroy the Union.

95. OVERLAND TRAILS, 1859*

In the years prior to the Civil War, thousands of Americans headed west hoping to find new and better prospects. Those pioneers, motivated by a variety of personal reasons, carried across the continent with them the republican principles of the nation. Most of the emigrants had never been to the West, and they had not experienced the rigors of the overland trails. For help, they turned to the many available guidebooks that offered advice and suggestions to travelers. Randolph B. Marcy, who explored vast regions of the American West as an officer in the United States Army, wrote one of the most popular of the emigrant's guides. In his book he outlined a method for governing overland expeditions—a system that underscored the cooperative and democratic nature of westward expansion. His essay also pointed out some of the hardships and dangers the settlers might face on their journey west.

After a particular route has been selected to make the journey across the plains, and the requisite number have arrived at the eastern terminus, their first business should be to organize themselves into a company and elect a commander. The company should be of sufficient magnitude to herd and guard animals, and for protection against Indians.

From 50 to 70 men, properly armed and equipped, will be enough for these purposes, and any greater number only makes the movements of the party more cumbersome and tardy.

In the selection of a captain, good judgment, integrity of purpose, and practical experience are the essential requisites, and these are indispensable to the harmony and consolidation of the association.

*From Randolph B. Marcy, *A Hand-book for Overland Expeditions, with Maps, Illustrations, and Itineraries of the Principal Routes between the Mississippi and the Pacific* (New York: Harper & Brothers, 1859), 22–25, 46–54.

His duty should be to direct the order of march, the time of starting and halting, to select the camps, detail and give orders, and, indeed, to control and superintend all the movements of the company.

An obligation should then be drawn up and signed by all the members of the association, wherein each one should bind himself to abide in all cases by the orders and decisions of the captain, and to aid him by every means in his power in the execution of his duties; and they should also obligate themselves to aid each other, so as to make the individual interest of each member the common concern of the whole company. To insure this, a fund should be raised for the purchase of extra animals to supply the places of those which may give out or die on the road; and if the wagons or team of a particular member should fail and have to be abandoned, the company should obligate themselves to transport his luggage, and the captain should see that he has his share of transportation equal with any other member. Thus it will be made the interest of every member of the company to watch over and protect the property of others as well as his own.

In case of failure on the part of any one to comply with the obligations imposed by the articles of agreement after they have been duly executed, the company should of course have the power to punish the delinquent member, and, if necessary, to exclude him from all the benefits of the association.

On such a journey as this, there is much to interest and amuse one who is fond of picturesque scenery, and of wild life in its most primitive aspect, yet no one should attempt it without anticipating many rough knocks and much hard labor; every man must expect to do his share of any duty faithfully and without a murmur.

On long and arduous expeditions men are apt to become irritable and ill-natured, and oftentimes fancy they have more labor imposed on them than their comrades, and that person who directs the march is partial to his favorites, etc. That man who exercises the greatest forbearance under such circumstances, who is cheerful, slow to take up quarrels, and endeavors to reconcile difficulties among his companions, is deserving of all praise, and will, without doubt, contribute largely to the success and comfort of an expedition.

The advantages of an association such as I have mentioned are manifestly numerous. The animals can be herded and guarded by the different members of the company in rotation, thereby securing to all the opportunities of sleep and rest. Besides this, this is the only way to resist depredations of the Indians, and to prevent their stampeding and driving off animals; and much more efficiency is secured in every respect., especially in crossing streams, repairing roads, etc., etc.

Unless a systematic organization be adopted, it is impossible for a party of any magnitude to travel in company for any great length of time, and for all the members to agree upon the same arrangements in marching, camping, etc. I have several times observed, where this has been attempted, that discords and dissensions sooner or later arose which invariably resulted in breaking up and separating the company.

When a captain has once been chosen, he should be sustained in all his decisions unless he commit some manifest outrage, when a majority of the company can always remove him, and put a more competent man in his place. Sometimes men may be selected who, upon trial, do not come up to the anticipations of those who have placed him in power, and other men will exhibit, during the course of the march, more capacity. Under these circumstances it will not be unwise to make a change, the first election having been distinctly provisional. . . .

The scarcity of water upon some of the routes across the plains occasionally exposes the traveler to intense suffering, and renders it a matter of much importance for him to learn the best methods of guarding against the disasters liable to occur to men and animals in the absence of this most necessary element.

In mountainous districts water can generally be found either in springs, the dry beds of streams, or in holes in the rocks, where they are sheltered from rapid evaporation. . . .

During a season of the year when there are occasional showers, water will generally be found in low places where there is a substratum of clay, but after the dry season has set in these pools evaporate, and it is necessary to dig wells. The lowest spots should be selected for this purpose when the grass is green and the surface earth moist.

In searching for water along the dry sandy beds of streams, it is well to try the earth with a stick or ramrod, and if this indicates moisture water will generally be obtained by excavation. Streams often sink in light and porous sand, and sometimes make their appearance again lower down, where the bed is more tenacious; but it is a rule with prairie travelers, in searching for water in a sandy country, to ascend the streams, and the nearer their sources are approached the more water will be found in a dry season.

When it becomes necessary to sink a well in a stream bed of which is quicksand, a flour-barrel, perforated with small holes, should be used as a curb, to prevent the sand from caving in. The barrel must be forced down as the sand is removed; and when, as is often the case, there is an undercurrent through the sand, the well will be continually filled with water. . . .

The use of water is a matter of habit, very much within our control, as by practice we may discipline ourselves so as to require but a small amount. Some persons, for example, who place no restraint upon their appetites, will, if they can get it, drink water twenty times a day, while others will not perhaps drink more than once or twice during the same time. I have found a very effectual preventative to thirst by drinking a large quantity of water before breakfast, and, on feeling thirsty on the march, chewing a small green twig or leaf.

Water taken from stagnant pools, charged with putrid vegetable matter and animalculae, would be very likely to generate fevers and dysentaries [sic] if taken into the stomach without purification. It should therefore be thoroughly boiled, and all the scum removed from the surface as it rises; this clarifies it, and by mixing powdered charcoal with it the disinfecting process is perfected. Water may also be purified by placing a piece of alum in the end of a stick that has been split, and stirring it around in a bucket of water. Charcoal and the leaves of the prickly pear are also used for the same purpose. . . . Water may be partially filtered in a muddy pond by taking a barrel and boring the lower half full of holes, then filling it up with grass or moss above the upper holes, after which it is placed in the pond with the top above the surface. The water filters through the grass or moss, and rises in the barrel to a level with the pond. Travelers often drink muddy water by placing a cloth or handkerchief over the mouth of a cup to catch the larger particles of dirt and animalculae.

Water may be cooled so as to be quite palatable by wrapping cloths around the vessels containing it, wetting them and hanging them in the air, where rapid evaporation will be produced. Some of the frontier-men use a leathern sack for carrying water: this is porous, and allows the necessary evaporation without wetting.

No expedition should ever set out into the plains without being supplied with the means of carrying water, especially in an unknown region. If wooden kegs are used they must frequently be looked after, and soaked, in order that they may not shrink and fall to pieces. Men, in marching in a hot climate, throw off a great amount of perspiration from the skin, and require a corresponding quantity of water to supply the deficiency, and unless they get this they suffer greatly. When a party makes an expedition into a desert section, where there is a probability of finding no water, and intend to return over the same track, it is well to carry water as far as convenient, and bury it in the ground for use on the return trip. . . .

In some localities 50 or 60 miles, and even greater distances, are frequently traversed without water; these long stretches are called by the Mexicans "*journadas,*" [*jornadas*]or day's journey. There is one in New Mexico called *Journada*[*Jornada*] *del Muerto* ["Journey of Death"], which is 78 1/2 miles in length, where, in a dry season, there is not a drop of water; yet, with proper care, this drive can be made with ox or mule teams, and without loss or injury to the animals. . . .

96. THE DONNER PARTY TRAGEDY, 1846*

*O*verland emigrants faced harsh conditions and untold dangers as they crossed plains and mountains. The Donner party, numbering ninety people, struck out from Independence, Missouri, and headed for California late in spring 1846. Various delays resulted in reaching the Sierra Nevada Mountains in October. Early snows trapped them with diminishing supplies. Forced to spend the winter in makeshift shelters, the miserable pioneers struggled to survive. Many died and some resorted to cannibalism before their eventual rescue. Nearly half of the original party perished during the long ordeal. In 1879 Charles F. McGlashan published History of the Donnner Party, a well-researched narrative of this tragic story. Although the style seems sentimental by contemporary standards, the author's account remains convincing. In the following excerpt, news of the stranded Donner party arrives west of the Sierras, the first relief party embarks, and these first rescuers encounter the stranded emigrants.

By making abridgements from valuable manuscript contributed by George W. Tucker, of Calistoga, this narrative may be appropriately continued. Mr. Tucker's father and relatives had reached Johnson's Ranch on the 25th of October, 1846. They had been with the Donner Party until Fort Bridger was reached, and then took the Fort Hall road. Their journey had been full of dangers and difficulties, and reaching Johnson's Ranch, the first settlement on the west side of the Sierras, they determined to remain during the Winter.

One evening, about the last of January, Mr. Tucker says a man was seen coming down Bear River, accompanied by an Indian. His haggard, forlorn look showed he was in great distress. When he reached us he said he was of the Donner Party. He told briefly how the train had been caught in the snow east of the mountains, and was unable to get back or forward. He told how the fifteen had started, and that six beside himself were still alive. That the six were back in the mountains, almost starved. R. P. Tucker and three other men started at once with provisions, the Indian acting as guide. They reached them, fifteen miles back, some time during the night, and brought them in next day. . . . It had been thirty-two days since they left Donner Lake!

At Johnson's Ranch there were only three or four families of poor emigrants. Nothing could be done toward relieving those at Donner Lake until help could arrive from Sutter's Fort. A rainy Winter had flooded Bear River, and rendered the Sacramento plains a vast quagmire. Yet one man volunteered to go to Sacramento with the tale of horror, and get men and provisions. This man was John Rhodes. Lashing two pine logs together with rawhides, and forming a raft, John Rhodes was ferried over Bear River. Taking his shoes in his hands, and rolling his pants up above his knees, he started on foot through water that frequently was from one to three feet deep. Some time during the night he reached the Fort.

A train in the mountains! Men, women and children starving! It was enough to make one's blood curdle to think of it! Captain Sutter, generous old soul, and Alcalde Sinclair, who lived at Norris' Ranch, two and a half miles from the Fort, offered provisions, and five or six men volunteered to carry them over the mountains. In about a week, six men, fully provided with supplies, reached Johnson's Ranch. Meantime the Tuckers and their neighbors had slaughtered five or six fat cattle, and had dried or "jerked" the meat. The country was scoured for horses and mules, and for saddles and pack-saddles, but at last, in ten or twelve days, they were ready to start. Alcalde Sinclair had come up from the Fort, and when all were ready to begin their march, he made them a thrilling little address. They were, he said, starting out upon a hazardous journey. Nothing could justify them in attempting so perilous an undertaking except the obligations due to their suffering fellow men. He urged them to do all in their power without sacrificing their lives, to save the perishing emigrants from starvation and death. He then appointed Reasin P. Tucker, the father of our

---

*From Charles F. McGlashan, *History of the Donner Party, A Tragedy of the Sierras* (Truckee, CA: Crowley & McGlashan, 1879), 90–92, 106–11.

informant, Captain of the company. With a pencil he carefully wrote down the name of each man in the relief party. . . . Thus the first relief party [consisting of thirteen men] started.

*   *   *

On the morning of the 19th of February, 1847, the relief party of Captain R. P. Tucker began the descent of the gorge leading to Donner Lake.

Let us glance ahead at the picture soon to be unfolded to their gaze. The mid-winter snows had almost concealed the cabins. The inmates lived subterranean lives. Steps cut in the icy snow led up from the doorways to the surface. Deep despair had settled upon all hearts. The dead were lying all around, some even unburied, and nearly all with only a covering of snow. So weak and powerless had the emigrants become, that it was hardly possible for them to lift the dead bodies up the steps out of the cabins. All were reduced to mere skeletons. They had lived on pieces of raw-hide, or on old cast-away bones which were boiled or burned until they could be eaten, and they were so reduced that it seemed as if only a dry, shriveled skin covered their emaciated frames. The eyes were sunken deep in their sockets, and had a fierce, ghastly, demoniacal look. The faces were haggard, woe-begone, and sepulchral. One seldom heard the sound of a voice, and when heard, it was weak, tremulous, pitiful. Sometimes a child would moan and sob for a mouthful of food, and the poor, helpless mothers, with breaking hearts, would have to soothe them, as best they could, with kind words and tender caresses. Food, there was none. Oh! what words can fitly frame a tribute for those noble mothers! When strong men gave up, and passively awaited the delirium of death, the mothers were actively administering to the wants of the dying, and striving to cheer and comfort the living. Marble monuments never bore more heroic names than those of Margaret W. Reed, Lavina Murphy, Elizabeth Graves, Margaret Breen, Tamsen Donner, and Elizabeth Donner. Their charity, fortitude, and self-sacrifice failed not in the darkest hour. Death came so often now, that little notice was taken of his approach save by these mothers. A dreadful want of consciousness precedes starvation. The actual death is not so terrible. The delirious would rave of feasts, and rich viands, and bountiful stores of food. As the shadows of death more closely enveloped the poor creatures, the mutterings grew unintelligible, and were interrupted now and then by startled cries of phrensy[frenzy], which gradually grew fainter until the victims finally slumbered. From this slumber there was no awakening. The breathing became feebler and more irregular, and finally ceased. It was not so terrible to the unconscious dying, as to weeping mother who watched by the sufferer's side.

*   *   *

As time wore wearily on, another and more severe trial awaited Mrs. Reed. Her daughter Virginia was dying. The innutritious raw-hide was not sufficient to sustain life in the poor famished body of the delicate child. Indeed, toward the last, her system became so debilitated that she found it impossible to eat the loathsome, gluelike preparation which formed their only food. Silently she had endured her sufferings, until she was at the very portals of death. This beautiful girl was a great favorite of Mrs. Breen's. Oftentimes during the days of horror and despair, this good Irish mother had managed, unobserved, to slip an extra piece of meat or morsel of food to Virginia. Mrs. Breen was the first to discover that the mark of death was visible upon the girl's brow. In order to break the news to Mrs. Reed, without giving those in the cabin a shock which might prove fatal, Mrs. Breen asked the mother up out of the cabin on the crisp white snow.

It was the evening of the 19th of February, 1847. The sun was setting, and his rays, in long lance-like lines sifted through the darkening forests. Far to the eastward, the summits of the Washoe mountains lay bathed in golden sun-light, while the deep gorges at their feet were purpling into night. The gentle breeze which crept over the bosom of the ice-bound lake softly wafted from the treetops a muffled dirge for the dying girl. Ere another day dawned over the expanse of snow, her spirit would pass to a haven of peace, where the demons of famine could never enter.

In the desolate cabin, all was silence. Living under the snow, passing an underground life as it were, seldom visiting each other, or leaving the cabins, these poor prisoners learned to listen, rather than look for relief. During the first days they watched hour after hour the upper end of the lake where the "fifteen" had disappeared. With aching eyes and weary hearts, they always turned back to their subterranean abodes disappointed. Hope finally deserted the strongest hearts. The brave mothers had constantly encouraged the despondent by speaking of the promised relief, yet this was prompted more by the necessities of the situation than from any belief that help would arrive. It was human nature, however, to glance toward the towering summits whenever they ascended to the surface of the snow, and to listen at all times for an unfamiliar sound or footstep. So delicate became their sense of hearing, that every noise of the wind, every visitor's tread, every sound that ordinarily occurred above their heads, was known and instantly detected.

On this evening, as the two women were sobbing despairingly upon the snow, the silence of the twilight was broken by a shout from near Donner Lake! In an instant every person forgot weakness and infirmity, and clambered up the stairway! It was a 'strange['] voice, and in the distance they discovered strange forms approaching. The Reed and the Breen children thought, at first, that it was a band of Indians, but Patrick Breen, the good old father, soon declared that the strangers were white men. Captain Tucker and his men had found the wide expanse of snow covering forest and valley, and had shouted to attract attention, if any of the emigrants yet survived. Oh! what joy! There were tears in other eyes than those of the little children. The strongest men in the relief party sat down on the snow and wept with the rest. It is related of one or two mothers, and can readily be believed, that their first act was to fall upon their knees, and with faces turned to God, to pour out their gratitude to Him for having brought assistance to their dying children. Virginia Reed did not die. . . .

97. FEMALE LIFE AMONG THE MORMONS, 1855*

*A*lthough most pioneers headed west as individuals, single families, or small groups, the Church of Jesus Christ of Latter-Day Saints organized a massive immigration of thousands of people from Illinois to the Great Basin. The Mormons had suffered violent persecution—especially for their practice of polygamy—and they moved west to find a haven far from the Gentile animosity they had faced in the past. Their efforts were successful for many reasons, including the powerful leadership of Brigham Young. Maria Ward, the wife of a church elder, wrote a memoir in which she expressed strong admiration for founder Joseph Smith but showed less devotion to Brigham Young. The following selection, noticeably critical, presented one woman's view of Mormon polygamy. She also discussed the pervasive influence that Young had on church members.

It is scarcely necessary to remark that with the demise of Smith, Mormonism took a new aspect in many particulars. This is chiefly to be attributed to the differences in the characters of the leaders. B_____m, though professing to believe in miracles, rarely attempted the exhibition of them, and finally, ceased to talk of any such thing. Smith had introduced spiritual-wifery, under the pretence of a pure platonic, or rather spiritual affection; B_____m openly advocated polygamy; and, in order that his precepts and practices might coincide, he espoused three wives in one day. Before the demise of Smith, however, polygamy was slowly coming into practice, though the sentiments of the ladies were divided on the subject. It was decided by the latter to be not simply a privilege, but a duty, and the virtues of the believers were estimated very much by the numbers of their wives. During the journey, however, they had little time for marrying, or giving in marriage. . . .

---

*From Maria Ward, *Female Life Among the Mormons; A Narrative of Many Years' Personal Experience* (New York: G. H. Wooten, 1855), 165, 318–19, 321–22.

It was the general policy of B_____m to encourage preaching mostly, in those who were well off in temporal affairs. This obviated any necessity of assistance on the part of the Church. The rich men likewise monopolized the women, to a great extent, consequently, while one man enjoyed the honor of being a preacher and a rich man, with a house full of women, all loveable and lovely, waiting to do his bidding, another, quite as good, or better probably better in mind and heart, though with less of this world's goods, was doomed to the cold and joyless trials of celibacy.

In this respect, however, it cannot be denied that some of the women were culpable, and that their conduct contributed, in a small degree, to the continuance of polygamy. Not a few preferred a rich man, with a dozen wives, to a poor without any, and, though repentance might inevitably ensue, it would be too late. The Prophet encouraged this state of things, for various reasons; indeed, he seemed to consider poverty as little short of crime, whose punishment consisted in the deprivation of social and domestic comforts.

It seemed the policy of B_____m, to give the Mormon creed a consistency, or rather a systematized form, such as it had never taken under the administration of Smith. Besides the wonders of millennial glory, on which the preachers loved to descant, they were fond of expatiating on spiritual life. They professed to believe, and they certainly taught, that God had constantly on a hand a multitude of little spirits, who want to come, and whom he has ordained shall come, and assume mortal bodies, and sojourn on earth for a time; human bodies being earthly tabernacles, temporary dwelling-houses for spirits. Yet, conjugal intercourse is necessary to accomplish the work, and hence, as God is very anxious that these spirits should be provided with bodies, and as the spirits themselves are very anxious to get down here, it became the duty of all true believers to lend their aid and produce the bodies as fast as possible. . . .

As the principles of Mormonism developed, it became evident that the females were to be regarded as an inferior order of beings. One by one the rights to which they had been accustomed, as well as the courtesies generally conceded to them were taken away. When the husband died, his property reverted to the church, instead of going to support his bereaved family, a regulation which occasioned an infinite amount of trouble and difficulty. However, if the husband and father was particularly interested in making provision of the future support of his family, he could do so, by paying the church during his life-time a certain extra stipend, which would release its claim.

Many widows were thus actually necessitated to take husbands on the first opportunity, and many young girls, not exceeding the ages of twelve and fourteen years, became the wives of men old enough to be their grandfathers, to save them from the streets.

No family in Utah ever hires household service. Some few have slaves, but generally speaking when one wife is insufficient to perform the labor, another is taken, perhaps a third, or fourth, and so on, for the number is only limited by the discretion and desire of the husband.

In all cases where the father was living, his consent was necessary to the marriage of a daughter, even though that daughter was a widow and a mother. In the case of his death, the head of the church acted in the capacity of guardian, and his consent was indispensable. The fathers, from the instruction they constantly received, and other causes, paid little attention to the inclinations of their children, but were greatly influenced by the size of the nominal gift. . . . These bargains were not unfrequently the subjects of much chicanery and intrigue, as if the object for sale was a horse, and the contracting parties two regular jockies. . . .

98. AN ANTI-SLAVERY PROTEST, 1837*

*W*hen the new Republic of Texas petitioned to join the Union, the request initiated a long, bitter national debate that became known as the "Texas question." Concern centered on the addition of such a large slave

*From *American History Told by Contemporaries*, 5 vols., ed. Albert Bushnell Hart (New York: The Macmillan Company, 1914), IV:642–45.

territory to the Union, particularly since Texas would have the right to divide into as many as five states. Unitarian Reverend William E. Channing wrote a powerful statement of opposition to annexation, and his essay mirrored many of the contemporary attitudes. He began his essay with a discussion of the political power the South would gain with the addition of Texas—the traditional argument against expanding slavery. He next advanced a relatively new contention that slave labor threatened the rights of free labor. Finally, he made clear his belief that slavery was an evil that had to be, and would be, destroyed. Channing, like William Lloyd Garrison, helped turn the issue into a moral concern that gained intensity over the following two decades. Beginning with the Texas question, issues of liberty, power, and equality in the United States increasingly involved the matter of slavery.

. . . I proceed now to a consideration of what is to me the strongest argument against annexing Texas to the United States. This measure will extend and perpetuate slavery. . . .

. . . On this point there can be no doubt. As far back as the year 1829, the annexation of Texas was agitated in the Southern and Western States; and it was urged on the ground of the strength and extension it would give to the slaveholding interest. In a series of essays ascribed to a gentleman, now a senator in Congress, it was maintained, that five or six slaveholding states by this measure could be added to the Union; and he even intimated that as many as nine states as large as Kentucky might be formed within the limits of Texas. In Virginia, about the same time, calculations were made as to the increased value which would thus be given to slaves, and it was said, that this acquisition would raise the price fifty per cent. Of late the language on this subject is most explicit. The great argument for annexing Texas, that it will strengthen "the peculiar institution" of the South and open a new and vast field for slavery.

By this act, slavery will spread over regions to which it is now impossible to set limits. Texas, I repeat it, is but the first step of aggressions. I trust, indeed, that Providence will beat back and humble our cupidity and ambition. But one guilty success is often suffered to be crowned, as men call it, with greater; in order that a more awful retribution may at length vindicate the justice of God, and the rights of the oppressed. Texas, smitten with slavery, will spread the infection beyond herself. We know that the tropical regions have been found most propitious to this pestilence; nor can we promise ourselves, that its expulsion from them for a season for-bids its return. By annexing Texas, we may send this scourge to a distance, which, if now revealed, would appal us, and through these vast regions every cry of the injured will invoke wrath on our heads.

By this act, slavery will be perpetuated in the old states as well as spread over new. It is well known, that the soil of some of the old states have become exhausted by slave cultivation. Their neighborhood to communities, which are flourishing under free labor, forces on them perpetual arguments for adopting the better system. They now adhere to slavery, not on account of the wealth which it extracts from the soil, but because it furnishes men and women to be sold in newly settled and more southern districts. It is by slave breeding and slave selling that these states subsist. Take away from them a foreign market, and slavery would die. Of consequence, by opening a new market, it is prolonged and invigorated. By annexing Texas, we shall not only create it where it does not exist, but breathe new life into it, where its end seemed to be near. States, which might and ought to throw it off, will make the multiplication of slaves their great aim and chief resource.

Nor is the worst told. As I have before intimated, and it cannot be too often repeated, we shall not only quicken the domestic slave trade; we shall give new impulse to the foreign. This indeed we have pronounced in our laws to be felony; but we make our laws cobwebs, when we offer to rapacious men strong motives for their violation. Open a market for slaves in an unsettled country, with a sweep of sea-coast, and at such distance from the seat of government that laws may be evaded with immunity, and how can you exclude slaves from Africa? It is well known that cargoes have been landed in Louisiana. What is to drive them from Texas? In incorporating this region with the Union to make it a slave country, we send the kidnapper to prowl through the jungles, and to dart, like a beast of prey, on the defenceless villages of Africa. We chain the helpless despairing victims;

crowd them into the fetid, pestilential slave ship; expose them to the unutterable cruelties of the middle passage, and, if they survive it, crush them with perpetual bondage.

I now ask, whether as a people, we are prepared to seize on a neighboring territory for the end of extending slavery? I ask, whether, as a people, we can stand forth in the sight of God, in the sight of the nations, and adopt this atrocious policy? Sooner perish! Sooner be our name blotted out from the record of nations! . . .

Whoever studies modern history with any care, must discern in it a steady growing movement towards one most interesting result, I mean, towards the elevation of the laboring class of society. . . .

It is the great mission of this country, to forward this revolution, and never was a sublimer work committed to a nation. Our mission is to elevate society through all its conditions, to secure every human being the means of progress, to substitute the government of equal laws for that of irresponsible individuals, to prove that, under popular institutions, the people may be carried forward, that the multitude who toil are capable of enjoying the noblest blessings of the social state. The prejudice, that labor is a degradation, one of the worst prejudices handed down from barbarous ages, is to receive here, a practical refutation. The power of liberty to raise up the whole people, this is the great Idea, on which our institutions rest, and which is to be wrought out in our history. Shall a nation having such a mission abjure it, and even fight against the progress which it is specially called to promote?

The annexation of Texas, if it should be accomplished, would do much to determine the future history and character of this country. It is one of those measures, which call a nation to pause, reflect, look forward, because their force is not soon exhausted. . . . The chief interest of a people lies in measures, which, making, perhaps little noise, go far to fix its character, to determine its policy for ages, to decide its rank among other nations. A fearful responsibility rests on those who originate or control these pregnant acts. The destiny of millions is in their hands. The execration of millions may fall on their heads. Long after present excitements have passed away, long after they and their generation shall have vanished from the earth, the fruits of their agency will be reaped. Such is a measure that of which I now write. It will commit us to a degrading policy, the issues of which lie beyond human foresight. In opening to ourselves vast regions, through which we may spread slavery, and in spreading it for this, among other ends, that the slaveholding states may bear rule in the national councils, we make slavery the predominant interest of the state. We make it the basis of power, the spring or guide of public measures, the object for which revenues, strength, and wealth of the country, are to be exhausted. Slavery will be branded on our front, as the great Idea, the prominent feature of the country. We shall renounce our high calling as a people, and accomplish the lowest destiny to which a nation can be bound.

And are we prepared for this degradation? Are we prepared to couple with the name of our country the infamy of deliberately spreading slavery? and especially of spreading it through regions from which the wise and humane legislation of a neighboring republic had excluded it? We call Mexico a semi-barbarous people; and yet we talk of planting slavery where Mexico would not suffer it to live. What American will not blush to lift his head in Europe, if this disgrace shall be fastened on his country? Let other calamities, if God so will, come on us. Let us be steeped in poverty. Let pestilence stalk through our land. Let famine thin our population. Let the world join hands against free institutions, and deluge our shores with blood. All this can be endured. A few years of industry and peace will recruit our wasted numbers, and spread fruitfulness over our desolated fields. But a nation devoting itself to the work of spreading and perpetuating slavery, stamps itself with a guilt and shame, which generations will not be able to efface. The plea on which we have rested, that slavery was not our choice, but a sad necessity bequeathed to us by our fathers, will avail us no longer. The whole guilt will be assumed by ourselves.

It is very lamentable, that among the distinguished men of the South, any should be found so wanting to their own fame, as to become advocates of slavery. . . . Have they nothing of that prophetic instinct, by which truly great men read the future? Can they learn nothing from the sentence now passed on men, who fifty years ago, defended the slave trade? . . .

I have expressed my fears, that by the annexation of Texas, slavery is to be continued and extended. But I wish not to be understood, as having the slightest doubt as to the approaching fall of the institution. It may be prolonged to our reproach and greater ultimate suffering. But fall it will and must. . . . Moral laws are as irresistible as physical. In the most enlightened countries of Europe, a man would forfeit his place in society, by vindicating slavery. The slaveholder must not imagine, that he has nothing to do but fight with a few societies. These, of themselves, are nothing. He should not waste on them one fear. They are strong, only as representing the spirit of the Christian and civilized world. His battle is with the laws of human nature and the irresistible tendency of human affairs. These are not to be withstood by artful strokes of policy, or by daring crimes. The world is against him, and the world's Maker. Every day the sympathies of the world are forsaking him. Can he hope to sustain slavery against the moral feeling, the solemn sentence of the human race?

99. PRESIDENT POLK ON TEXAS AND OREGON, 1845*

*D*espite the strong resistance to Texas statehood that forced the Lone Star Republic to remain independent for almost ten years, Manifest Destiny proved too alluring for most Americans. The dream of national expansion outweighed the fear of a slaveowners' conspiracy, especially since the free Oregon territory could counterbalance Texas. In 1844, Democratic presidential candidate James K. Polk won the election with a platform to re-annex Texas, which many people felt already belonged to the United States as part of the Louisiana Purchase, and the acquisition of Oregon. President Polk used his inaugural address to set forth his reasons for claiming vast new holdings for the Republic. The United States would have its continental empire; it remained to be determined whether it would be an empire for liberty or an empire for slavery.

The Republic of Texas has made known her desire to come into our Union, to form a part of our Confederacy and enjoy with us the blessings of liberty secured and guaranteed by our Constitution. Texas was once a part of our country—was unwisely ceded away to a foreign power—is now independent, and possesses an undoubted right to dispose of a part of the whole of her territory and to merge her sovereignty as a separate and independent state in ours. I congratulate my country that by an act of the late Congress of the United States the assent of this government has been given to the reunion, and it only remains for the two countries to agree upon terms to consummate an object so important to both.

I regard the question of annexation as belonging exclusively to the United States and Texas. They are independent powers competent to contract, and foreign nations have no right to interfere with them or to take exceptions to their reunion. Foreign powers do not seem to appreciate the true character of our Government. Our Union is a confederation of independent States, whose policy is peace with each other and all the world. To enlarge its limits is to extend the dominions of peace over additional territories and increasing millions. The world has nothing to fear from military ambition in our Government. While the Chief Magistrate and the popular branch of Congress are elected for short terms by the suffrages of those millions who must in their own persons bear all the burdens and miseries of war, our Government can not be otherwise than pacific. Foreign powers should therefore look on the annexation of Texas to the United States not as the conquest of a nation seeking to extend her dominions by arms and violence, but as the peaceful acquisitions of a

---

*From *A Compilation of the Messages and Papers of the Presidents, 1789–1897*, 10 vols., comp. James D. Richardson (Washington, D.C.: U.S. Government Printing Office, 1896–1899), IV:379–81.

territory once her own, by adding another member to our confederation, with the consent of that member, thereby diminishing the chances of war and opening to them new and ever-increasing markets for their products.

To Texas the reunion is important, because the strong protecting arm of our Government would be extended over her, and the vast resources of her fertile soil and genial climate would be speedily developed, while the safety of New Orleans and our whole southwestern frontier against hostile aggression, as well as the interests of the whole Union, would be promoted by it. . . .

None can fail to see the danger to our safety and future peace if Texas remains an independent state or becomes an ally or dependency of some foreign nation more powerful than herself. . . . Whatever is good or evil in the local institutions of Texas will remain her own whether annexed to the United States or not. None of the present States will be responsible for them any more than they are the local institutions of each other. They have confederated together for certain specified objects. Upon the same principle that they would refuse to form a perpetual union with Texas because of her local institutions our forefathers would have been prevented from forming our present Union. Perceiving no valid objection to the measure and many reasons for its adoption vitally affecting the peace, the safety, and the prosperity of both countries, I shall on the broad principle which formed the basis and produced the adoption of our Constitution, and not in any narrow spirit of sectional policy, endeavor all constitutional, honorable, and appropriate means to consummate the expressed will of the people and Government of the United States by the reannexation of Texas to our Union at the earliest practicable period.

Nor will it become in a less degree my duty to assert and maintain by all constitutional means the right of the Untied States to that portion of our territory which lies beyond the Rocky Mountains. Our title to the country of the Oregon is "clear and unquestionable," and already are our people preparing to perfect that title by occupying it with their wives and children. But eighty years ago our population was confined on the west by the ridge of the Alleghanies. Within that period—within the lifetime, I might say, of some of my hearers—our people, increasing to many millions, have filled the eastern valley of the Mississippi, adventurously ascended the Missouri to its headsprings, and are already engaged in establishing the blessings of self-government in valleys of which the rivers flow to the Pacific. The world beholds the peaceful triumphs of the industry of our emigrants. To us belongs the duty of protecting them adequately wherever they may be upon our soil. The jurisdiction of our laws and the benefits of our republican institutions should be extended over them in the distant regions which they have selected for their homes. The increasing facilities of intercourse will easily bring the States, of which the formation in that part of our territory can not be long delayed, within the sphere of our federative Union. In the meantime, every obligation imposed by treaty or conventional stipulations should be sacredly respected. . . .

100. DAVID WILMOT OPPOSES THE EXTENSION OF SLAVERY, 1847*

While war raged between the United States and Mexico, Representative David Wilmot of Pennsylvania proposed prohibiting the expansion of slavery into any territory taken during the conflict. In the following speech, he elaborated on his position. His statements clearly revealed the growing northern conviction that since the founding of the country, national power had been used to expand slavery. He also touched upon the immorality of the institution, and he suggested the inherent superiority of a free society to a slave culture. The Pennsylvania congressman articulated the feelings of many northerners, and the Wilmot Proviso became the focal point of

*From *Appendix to the Congressional Globe*, 29th Congress, 2nd Session (1847), 315, 317, 318.

the debate over slavery for the next fifteen years. Wilmot was prescient indeed when he recognized that the issue posed a "difficult and dangerous problem" for the nation.

. . . Sir, the issue now presented is not whether slavery shall exist unmolested where it now is, but whether it shall be carried to new and distant regions, now free, where the footprint of a slave cannot be found. This, sir, is the issue. Upon it I take my stand, and from it I cannot be frightened or driven by idle charges of abolitionism. I demand that this Government preserve the integrity of *free territory* against the aggressions of slavery—against its wrongful usurpations. Sir, I was in favor of the annexation of Texas. I supported it with my whole influence and strength. I was willing to take Texas as she was. I sought not to change the character of her institutions. Slavery existed in Texas—planted there, it is true, in defiance of law; still it existed. It gave character to the country. True, it was held out to the North, that at least two of the five States to be formed out of Texas would be free. Yet, sir, the whole of Texas has been given up to slavery. The Democracy of the North, almost to a man, went for annexation. Yes, sir, here was an empire larger than France given up to slavery. Shall further concessions be made by the North? Shall we give up free territory, the inheritance of free labor? Must we yield this also? Never, sir, never, until we ourselves are fit to be slaves. The North may be betrayed by her Representatives, but upon this great question she will be true to herself—true to posterity. Defeat! Sir, there can be no defeat. Defeat to-day will but arouse the teeming millions of the North, and lead to a more decisive and triumphant victory to-morrow.

But, sir, we are told, that the joint blood and treasure of the whole country being extended in this acquisition, therefore it should be divided, and slavery allowed to take its share. Sir, the South has her share already; the instalment for slavery was paid in advance. We are fighting this war for Texas and for the South. I affirm it—every intelligent man knows it—Texas is the primary cause of the war. For this, sir, northern treasure is being exhausted, and northern blood poured out upon the plains of Mexico. We are fighting this war cheerfully, not reluctantly—cheerfully fighting this war for Texas; and yet we seek not to change the character of her institutions. Slavery is there; there let it remain. Sir, the whole history of this question is a history of concessions on the part of the North. The money of the North was expended in the purchase of Louisiana, two-thirds of which was given up to slavery. Again, in the purchase of Florida, did slavery gain new acquisitions. Slavery acquired an empire in the annexation of Texas. Three slave states have been admitted out of the Louisiana purchase. The slave State of Florida has been received into the Union; and Texas annexed, with the privilege of making five States out of her territory. What has the North obtained from these vast acquisitions, purchased by the joint treasure and defended by the common blood of the Union? One State, sir—one: young Iowa, just admitted to the Union, and not yet represented on the floor of the Senate. This, sir, is a history of our acquisitions since we became a nation. A history of northern concessions—of southern triumphs. . . .

Sir, I have said before, that I have no morbid sympathies upon the subject of slavery; still, I regard it as a great social and political evil—a blight and deadly mildew upon any country or State in which it exists. I regard it as the most difficult and dangerous problem which we will have to work out in this free Government. If we go back to the period of the establishment of the Constitution, we find there were six slave and seven free States; the slave States containing an area of some fifty thousand square miles more than the free, with about an equal population. Now, these free States have doubled the population of the slave. Why is this? In the Revolution, Massachusetts furnished more men for carrying on the war than the entire slave States. How happened this? Not from any want of patriotism on the part of the South, but from the want of ability, growing out of this institution. Where the men who labor are slaves, you cannot place arms in their hands; and it is the free laboring man who constitutes the strength and defence of his country on the field of battle. If this war continues, Pennsylvania will, if permitted, I believe, send more men into the field than the original six slave States. Not that Pennsylvania would be more forward than they in the vindication of the honor of the country, but because she has the men; and, owing to this peculiar institution of the South, they have them not. Their laborers cannot take up arms; indeed, they dare not form them into military organizations, and teach them the use of the weapons of war. Why is it that Virginia, the "mother of States"—that State which has ever been foremost in the vindication of the rights of the States, and of the liberties of the people—why is it that the sun of the glorious "Old Dominion" is not still in the ascendant? She stood first—before New York, before Pennsylvania—and now she is out-stripped by States that have grown up within the memory of the present generation. Why is it? Can any doubt that slavery is the cause? . . .

Viewing slavery as I do, I must resist its further extension and propagation on the North American continent. It is an evil, the magnitude and the end of which, no man can see. . . .

101. JOHN C. CALHOUN APPEALS FOR UNION ON SOUTHERN TERMS, 1850*

By 1850, the problems confronting the nation dictated the need for compromise. Unless sectional grievances were addressed, the Union faced dissolution. Henry Clay provided the blueprint for compromise, but the details were negotiated in the Senate chamber. On March 4, 1850, John C. Calhoun, in one notable speech, spoke for the South. After tracing the sources of sectional hostility, Calhoun reasoned that the Union could be saved only if the North ceased agitation over the slavery question, granted southerners equal rights in the territories, returned fugitive slaves, and restored lost power to the South through constitutional amendment. If such a settlement could be reached, the South "could remain honorably and safely in the Union."

I have, Senators, believed from the first that the agitation of the subject of slavery would, if not prevented by some timely and effective measure, end in disunion. Entertaining this opinion, I have, on all proper occasions, endeavored to call the attention of each of the two great parties which divide the country to adopt some measure to prevent so great a disaster, but without success. The agitation has been permitted to proceed, with almost no attempt to resist it, until it has reached a period when it can no longer be disguised or denied that the Union is in danger. You have thus had forced upon you the greatest and the gravest question that can ever come under your consideration: How can the Union be preserved? . . .

. . . the North has acquired a decided ascendency over every department of this Government, and through it a control over all the powers of the system. A single section, governed by the will of the numerical majority, has now, in fact, the control of the Government and the entire powers of the system. What was once a constitutional Federal Republic is now converted, in reality, into one as absolute as that of the Autocrat of Russia, and as despotic in its tendency as any absolute Government that ever existed.

As, then, the North has the absolute control over the Government, it is manifest that on all questions between it and the South, where there is a diversity of interests, the interests of the latter will be sacrificed to the former, however oppressive the effects may be, as the South possesses no means by which it can resist through the action of the Government. . . . There is a question of vital importance to the southern section, in reference to which the views and feelings of the two sections are as opposite and hostile as they can possibly be.

I refer to the relation between the two races in the southern section, which constitutes a vital portion of her social organization. Every portion of the North entertains views and feelings more or less hostile to it. . . .

*From *Congressional Globe*, 31st Congress, 1st Session, vol. XXII, pt. 1 (1850), 451–53, 455.

This hostile feeling . . . long lay dormant, but it only required some cause to act on those who felt most intensely that they were responsible for its continuance, to call it into action. The increasing power of the Government, and of the control of the northern section over all its departments, furnished the cause. It was this which made an impression on the minds of many that there was little or no restraint to prevent the Government from doing whatever it might choose to do. This was sufficient of itself to put the most fanatical portion of the North in action for the purpose of destroying the existing relation between the two races in the South.

The first organized movement towards it commenced in 1835. Then, for the first time, societies were organized, presses established, lecturers sent forth to excite the people of the North, and incendiary publications scattered over the whole South, through the mail. The South was thoroughly aroused. Meetings were held everywhere, and resolutions adopted, calling upon the North to apply a remedy to arrest the threatened evil, and pledging themselves to adopt measures for their own protection if it was not arrested. At the meeting of Congress, petitions poured in from the North, calling upon Congress to abolish slavery in the District of Columbia, and to prohibit what they called the internal slave trade between the States, announcing at the same time that their ultimate object was to abolish slavery, not only in the District, but in the States and throughout the Union. . . .

With the increase of their influence, they extended the sphere of their action. In a short time after the commencement of their first movement, they had acquired sufficient influence to induce the Legislatures of most of the northern States to pass acts which in effect abrogated the provision of the Constitution that provides for the delivery up of fugitive slaves. Not long after, petitions followed to abolish slavery in forts, magazines, and dock-yards, and all other places where Congress had exclusive power of legislation. This was followed by the petitions and resolutions of Legislatures of the northern States and popular meetings, to exclude the southern States from all territories acquired or to be acquired, and to prevent the admission of any State hereafter into the Union which, by its constitution, does not prohibit slavery. And Congress is invoked to do all this expressly with the view to the final abolition of slavery in the States. That has been avowed to be the ultimate object from the beginning of the agitation until the present time; and yet the great body of both parties of the North, with the full knowledge of the fact, although disavowing the abolitionists, have cooperated with them in almost all their measures. . . .

. . .

I return to the question with which I commenced, How can the Union be saved? There is but one way by which it can with any certainty; and that is, by a full and final settlement, on the principle of justice, of all the questions at issue between the two sections. The South asks for justice, simple justice, and less she ought not to take. She has no compromise to offer but the Constitution, and no concession or surrender to make. She has already surrendered so much that she has little left to surrender. Such a settlement would go to the root of the evil, and remove all cause of discontent, by satisfying the South she could remain honorably and safely in the Union, and thereby restore the harmony and fraternal feelings between the sections which existed anterior to the Missouri agitation. Nothing else can, with any certainty, finally and forever settle the questions at issue, terminate agitation, and save the Union.

But can this be done? Yes, easily; not by the weaker party, for it can of itself do nothing—not even protect itself—but by the stronger. The North has only to will it to accomplish it—to do justice by conceding to the South an equal right in the acquired territory, and to do her duty by causing the stipulations relative to fugitive slaves to be faithfully fulfilled—to cease the agitation of the slave question, and to provide for the insertion of a provision in the Constitution, by an amendment, which will restore to the South in substance the power she possessed of protecting herself, before the equilibrium between the sections was destroyed by the action of this Government. There will be no difficulty in devising such a provision—one that will protect the South, and which at the same time will improve and strengthen the Government, instead of impairing and weakening it.

But will the North agree to do this? It is for her to answer this question. But, I will say, she cannot refuse, if she has half the love of the Union which she professes to have, or without justly exposing herself to the charge that her love of power and aggrandizement is far greater than her love of the Union. At all events, the responsibility of saving the Union rests on the North, and not the South. The South cannot save it by any act of hers, and the North may save it without any sacrifice whatever, unless to do justice, and to perform her duties under the Constitution, should be regarded by her as a sacrifice.

It is time, Senators, that there should be an open and manly avowal on all sides, as to what is intended to be done. If the question is not now settled, it is uncertain whether it ever can hereafter be; and we, as the representatives of the States of this Union, regarded as governments, should come to a distinct understanding as to our respective views, in order to ascertain whether the great questions at issue can be settled or not. If you, who represent the stronger portion, cannot agree to settle them on the broad principle of justice and duty, say so; and let the States we both represent agree to separate and part in peace. If you are unwilling we should part in peace, tell us so, and we shall know what to do, when you reduce the question to submission or resistance. . . .

102. DANIEL WEBSTER DEFENDS COMPROMISE TO PRESERVE THE UNION, 1850*

On March 7, 1850, Senator Daniel Webster responded to Calhoun and endorsed compromise, speaking for moderation and union. In the following speech, he recognized that the South had legitimate grievances. He criticized abolitionist agitation and conceded that the fugitive slave laws should be better enforced. But he also maintained that the territories of New Mexico and California were not conducive to a slave economy; the law of nature would exclude slavery. Finally, Webster sharply repudiated Calhoun's threat of secession. To him, "the idea of the separation of these States . . . [was] a moral impossibility."

Mr. President, I wish to speak to-day, not as a Massachusetts man, nor as a northern man, but as an American, and a member of the Senate of the United States. It is fortunate that there is a Senate of the United States; a body not yet moved from its propriety, not lost to a just sense of its own dignity, and its own high responsibilities, and a body to which the country looks with confidence, for wise, moderate, patriotic, and healing counsels. It is not to be denied that we live in the midst of strong agitations, and are surrounded by very considerable dangers to our institutions of government. The imprisoned winds are let loose. The East, the West, the North, and the stormy South, all combine to throw the whole ocean into commotion, to toss its billows to the skies, and to disclose its profoundest depths. I do not affect to regard myself, Mr. President, as holding, or as fit to hold, the helm in this combat of the political elements; but I have a duty to perform, and I mean to perform it with fidelity—not without a sense of surrounding dangers, but not without hope. I have a part to act, not for my own security or safety, for I am looking out for no fragment upon which to float away from the wreck, if wreck there must be, but for the good of the whole, and the preservation of the whole; and there is that which will keep me to my duty during this struggle, whether the sun and the stars shall appear, or shall not appear, for many days. I speak to-day for the preservation of the Union. "Hear me for my cause." I speak to-day, out of a solicitous and anxious heart, for the restoration to the country of that quiet and that harmony which make the blessings of this Union

*From *Appendix to the Congressional Globe*, 31st Congress, 1st Session, vol. XXII, pt. 1 (1850), 269, 274–76.

so rich and so dear to us all. These are the topics that I propose to myself to discuss; these are the motives, and the sole motives, that influence me in the wish to communicate my opinions to the Senate and the country; and if I can do anything, however little, for the promotion of these ends, I shall have accomplished all that I desire. . . .

Now, as to California and New Mexico, I hold slavery to be excluded from those territories by a law even superior to that which admits and sanctions it in Texas—I mean the law of nature—of physical geography—the law of the formation of the earth. That law settles forever, with a strength beyond all terms of human enactment, that slavery cannot exist in California or New Mexico. Understand me, sir—I mean slavery as we regard it; slaves in gross, of the colored race, transferable by sale and delivery, like other property. . . .

California and New Mexico are Asiatic, in their formation and scenery. They are composed of vast ridges of mountains of enormous height, with broken ridges and deep valleys. The sides of these mountains are barren—entirely barren—their tops capped by perennial snow. There may be in California, now made free by its constitution—and no doubt there are—some tracts of valuable land. But it is not so in New Mexico. . . . What is there in New Mexico that could by any possibility induce anybody to go there with slaves? There are some narrow strips of tillable land on the borders of the rivers; but the rivers themselves dry up before mid-summer is gone. All that the people can do, is to raise some little articles—some little wheat for their tortillas—and all that by irrigation. And who expects to see a hundred black men cultivating tobacco, corn, cotton, rice, or anything else, on lands in New Mexico, made fertile only by irrigation? I look upon it, therefore, as a fixed fact, to use an expression current at this day, that both California and New Mexico are destined to be free, so far as they are settled at all, which I believe, especially in regard to New Mexico, will be very little for a great length of time—free by the arrangement of things by the Power above us. I have therefore to say, in this respect also, that this country is fixed for freedom, to as many persons as shall ever live there, by as irrepealable and a more irrepealable law, than the law that attaches to the right of holding slaves in Texas; and I will say further, that if a resolution, or a law, were now before us, to provide a territorial government for New Mexico, I would not vote to put any prohibition into it whatever. The use of such a prohibition would be idle, as it respects any effect it would have upon the territory; and I would not take pains to reaffirm an ordinance of nature, nor to reenact the will of God. And I would put in no Wilmot proviso, for the purpose of a taunt or a reproach. I would put into it no evidence of the votes of superior power, to wound the pride, even whether a just pride, a rational pride, or an irrational pride—to wound the pride of the gentlemen who belong to the southern States. . . .

Sir, wherever there is a particular good to be done—wherever there is a foot of land to be staid back from becoming slave territory—I am ready to assert the principle of the exclusion of slavery. I am pledged to it from the year 1837; I have been pledged to it again and again; and I will perform those pledges; but I will not do a thing unnecessary, that wounds the feelings of others, or that does disgrace to my own understanding.

Mr. President, in the excited times in which we live, there is found to exist a state of crimination and recrimination between the North and the South. There are lists of grievances produced by each; and those grievances, real or supposed, alienate the minds of one portion of the country from the other, exasperate the feelings, subdue the sense of fraternal connection, and patriotic love, and mutual regard. I shall bestow a little attention, sir, upon these various grievances, produced on the one side and on the other. I begin with the complaints of the South: I will not answer, farther than I have, the general statements of the honorable Senator from South Carolina, that the North has grown upon the South in consequence of the manner of administering this Government, in the collecting of its revenues, and so forth. These are disputed topics, and I have no inclination to enter into them. But I will state these complaints, especially one complaint of the South, which has in my opinion just foundation; and that is, that there has been found at the North, among individuals and among the Legislatures of the North, a disinclination to perform, fully, their constitutional duties, in regard to the return of persons bound to service, who have escaped into the free States. In that respect, it is my judgement that the South is right, and the North is wrong. Every member of every northern Legislature is bound, by oath, like every other officer in the country, to support the Constitution of the United States; and this article of the Constitution, which says to these States, they shall deliver up fugitives from service, is as binding in honor and conscience as any other article. No man fulfills his duty in any Legislature who sets himself to find excuses, evasions, escapes from this constitutional obligation. . . .

Therefore, I repeat, sir, that here is a ground of complaint against the North, well founded, which ought to be removed—which it is now in the power of the different departments of this Government to remove—which calls for the enactment of proper laws, authorizing the judicature of this Government, in the several States, to do all that is necessary for the recapture of fugitive slaves, and for the restoration of them to those who claim them. Wherever I go, and whenever I speak on the subject—and when I speak here, I desire to speak to the whole North—I say that the South has been injured in this respect, and has a right to complain; and the North has been too careless of what I think the Constitution peremptorily and emphatically enjoins upon it as a duty. . . .

Then, sir, there are those abolition societies, of which I am unwilling to speak, but in regard to which I have very clear notions and opinions. I do not think them useful. I think their operations for the last twenty years have produced nothing good or valuable. At the same time, I know thousands of them are honest and good men; perfectly well-meaning men. They have excited feelings; they think they must do something for the cause of liberty; and in their sphere of action, they do not see what else they can do, than to contribute to an abolition press, or an abolition society, or to pay an abolition lecturer. I do not mean to impute gross motives even to the leaders of these societies, but I am not blind to the consequences. I cannot but see what mischiefs their interference with the South has produced. And is it not plain to every man? . . .

We all know the fact, and we all know the cause, and everything that this agitating people have done, has been, not to enlarge, but to restrain, not to set free, but to bind faster, the slave population of the South. That is my judgment. . . .

There can be no such thing a peaceable secession. Peaceable secession is an utter impossibility. Is the great Constitution under which we live here—covering this whole country—is it to be thawed and melted away by secession, as the snows on the mountain melt under the influence of a vernal sun—disappear almost unobserved, and die off? No, sir! no, sir! I will not state what might produce the disruption of the States; but, sir, I see it as plainly as I see the sun in heaven—I see that disruption must produce such a war as I will not describe, in its twofold characters.

Peaceable secession! peaceable secession! The concurrent agreement of all the members of this great Republic to separate! A voluntary separation, with alimony on one side and on the other. . . .

I know, although the idea has not been stated distinctly, there is to be a southern Confederacy. I do not mean, when I allude to this statement, that any one seriously contemplates such a state of things. I do not mean to say that it is true, but I have heard it suggested elsewhere, that that idea has originated in a design to separate. I am sorry, sir, that it has ever been thought of, talked of, or dreamed of, in the wildest flights of human imagination. But the idea must be of a separation, including the slave States upon one side, and the free States on the other. Sir, there is not—I may express myself too strongly perhaps—but some things, some moral things, are almost as impossible, as other natural or physical things; and I hold the idea of a separation of these States—those that are free to form one government, and those that are slaveholding to form another—as a moral impossibility. We could not separate the States by any such line, if we were to draw it. We could not sit down here to-day, and draw a line of separation, that would satisfy any five men in the country. There are natural causes that would keep and tie us together, and there are social and domestic relations which we could not break, if we would, and which we should not, if we could. . . .

103. WILLIAM H. SEWARD DEPLORES COMPROMISE, 1850*

On March 11, 1850, William H. Seward of New York, in a Senate speech that enhanced his reputation in the North, defended the antislavery viewpoint toward the issues of 1850. To Seward, compromise over slavery was "radically wrong and essentially vicious." He denounced the fugitive slave law as "unjust, unconstitutional, and immoral." He also refused to accept the expansion of slavery as the price for the admission of California. And he dismissed Calhoun's arguments that the Constitution protected slavery in the territories by appealing to a "higher law than the Constitution"—the law of God. As for the institution itself, Seward insisted that emancipation was "inevitable and . . . near"; southerners could not "roll back the tide of social progress."

I AM OPPOSED TO ANY SUCH COMPROMISE, IN ANY AND ALL THE FORMS IN WHICH IT HAS BEEN PROPOSED, because, while admitting the purity and the patriotism of all from whom it is my misfortune to differ, I think all legislative compromises radically wrong and essentially vicious. They involve the surrender of the exercise of judgment and conscience on distinct and separate questions, at distinct and separate times, with the indispensable advantages it affords for ascertaining truth. They involve a relinquishment of the right to reconsider in future the decisions of the present, on questions prematurely anticipated; and they are a usurpation as to future questions of the province of future legislators. . . .

. . .

But, sir, if I could overcome my repugnance to compromises in general, I should object to this one, on the ground of the *inequality* and *incongruity* of the interests to be compromised. Why, sir, according to the views I have submitted, California ought to come in, and must come in, whether slavery stands or falls in the District of Columbia, whether slavery stands or falls in New Mexico and Eastern California, and even whether slavery stands or falls in the slave States. California ought to come in, being a free State, and under the circumstances of her conquest, her compact, her abandonment, her justifiable and necessary establishment of a constitution, and the inevitable dismemberment of the empire consequent upon her rejection. I should have voted for her admission, even if she had come as a slave State. California ought to come in, and must come in, at all events. It is, then, an independent—a paramount question. What, then, are these questions arising out of slavery, thus interposed, but collateral questions? They are unnecessary and incongruous, and therefore false issues, not introduced designedly, indeed, to defeat that great policy, yet unavoidably tending to that end. . . .

. . .

We deem the principle of the law for the recapture of fugitives, therefore unjust, unconstitutional, and immoral; and thus, while patriotism withholds its approbation, the consciences of our people condemn it.

You will say that these convictions of ours are disloyal. Grant it for the sake of argument. They are, nevertheless, honest; and the law is to be executed among us, not among you; not by us, but by the Federal authority. Has any Government ever succeeded in changing the moral convictions of its subjects by force? But these convictions imply no disloyalty. We reverence the Constitution, although we perceive this defect, just as we acknowledge the splendor and the power of the sun, although its surface is tarnished with here and there an opaque spot.

Your Constitution and laws convert hospitality to the refugee, from the most degrading oppression on earth, into a crime, but all mankind except you esteem that hospitality a virtue. The

---

*From *Appendix to the Congressional Globe*, 31st Congress, 1st Session, vol. XXII, pt. 1 (1850), 262–63, 265–66, 268.

right of extradition of a fugitive from justice, is not admitted by the law of nature and of nations, but rests in voluntary compacts. . . .

. . .

The law of nations disavows such compacts; the law of nature, written on the hearts and consciences of freemen, repudiates them. Armed power could not enforce them, because there is no public conscience to sustain them. I know that there are laws of various sorts which regulate the conduct of men. There are constitutions and statutes, codes mercantile and codes civil; but when we are legislating for States, especially when we are founding States, all these laws must be brought to the standard of the laws of God, and must be tried by that standard, and must stand or fall by it. . . .

. . .

To conclude on this point: We are not slaveholders. We cannot, in our judgment, be either true Christians or real freemen, if we impose on another a chain that we defy all human power to fasten on ourselves. You believe and think otherwise, and doubtlessly with equal sincerity. We judge you not, and He alone who ordained the conscience of man and its laws of action, can judge us. Do we, then, in this conflict, demand of you an unreasonable thing in asking that, since you will have property that can and will exercise human powers to effect its escape, you shall be your own police, and in acting among us as such, you shall conform to principles indispensable to the security of admitted rights of freemen? If you will have this law executed, you must alleviate, not increase, its rigors. . . .

There is another aspect of the principle of compromise, which deserves consideration. It assumes that slavery, if not the only institution in a slave State, is at least a ruling institution, and that this characteristic is recognized by the Constitution. But *slavery* is only *one* of many institutions there—freedom is equally an institution there. Slavery is only a temporary, accidental, partial, and incongruous one; freedom, on the contrary, is a perpetual, organic, universal one, in harmony with the Constitution of the United States. The slaveholder himself stands under the protection of the latter, in common with all the free citizens of the State; but it is, moreover, an indispensable institution. You may separate slavery from South Carolina, and the State will still remain; but if you subvert freedom there, the State will cease to exist. But the principle of this compromise gives complete ascendency in the slave State, and in the Constitution of the United States, to the subordinate, accidental, and incongruous institution over its paramount antagonist. To reduce this claim for slavery, to an absurdity, it is only necessary to add, that there are only two States in which slaves are a majority, and not one in which the slaveholders are not a very disproportionate minority.

But there is yet another aspect in which this principle must be examined. It regards the domain only as a possession, to be enjoyed, either in common or by partition, by the citizens of the old States. It is true, indeed, that the national domain is ours; it is true, it was acquired by the valor and with the wealth of the whole nation; but we hold, nevertheless, no arbitrary power over it. We hold no arbitrary authority over anything, whether acquired lawfully, or seized by usurpation. The Constitution regulates our stewardship; the Constitution devotes the domain to union, to justice, to defence, to welfare, and to liberty.

But there is a higher law than the Constitution, which regulates our authority over the domain, and devotes it to the same noble purposes. The territory is a part—no inconsiderable part—of the common heritage of mankind, bestowed upon them by the Creator of the universe. We are his stewards, and must so discharge our trust as to secure, in the highest attainable degree, their happiness. . . .

. . .

I cannot stop to debate long with those who maintain that slavery is itself practically economical and humane. I might be content with saying, that there are some axioms in political science that a statesman or a founder of States may adopt, especially in the Congress of the United States, and that among those axioms are these: that all men are created equal, and have inalienable rights of life, liberty, and the choice of pursuits of happiness; that knowledge promotes virtue, and righteousness exalteth a nation; that freedom is preferable to slavery; and that democratic governments, where they can be maintained by acquiescence, without force, are preferable to institutions exercising arbitrary and irresponsible power.

It remains only to remark, that our own experience has proved the dangerous influence and tendency of slavery. All our apprehensions of dangers, present and future, begin and end with slavery. If slavery, limited as it yet is, now threatens to subvert the Constitution, how can we, as wise, and prudent statesmen, enlarge its boundaries and increase its influence, and thus increase already impending dangers? Whether, then, I regard merely the welfare of the future inhabitants of the new territories, or the security and welfare of the whole people of the United States, or the welfare of the whole family of mankind, I cannot consent to introduce slavery into any part of this continent which is now exempt from what seems to me so great an evil. These are my reasons for declining to compromise the question relating to slavery as a condition of the admission of California. . . .

. . .

Sir, there is no climate uncongenial to slavery. It is true, it is less productive than free labor in many northern countries; but so it is less productive than free white labor in even tropical climates. Labor is in demand quick in all new countries. Slave labor is cheaper than free labor, and it would go first into new regions; and wherever it goes, it brings labor into dishonor, and therefore, free white labor avoids competition with it. Sir, I might rely on climate if I had not been born in a land where slavery existed—and this land was all of it north of the 40th parallel of latitude—and if I did not know the struggle it has cost, and which is yet going on, to get complete relief from the institution and its baleful consequences. I desire to propound this question to those who are now in favor of dispensing with the Wilmot proviso, Was the ordinance of 1787 necessary or not? Necessary, we all agree. It has received too many eulogisms to be now decried as an idle and superfluous thing. And yet that ordinance extended the inhibition of slavery from the 37th to the 40th parallel of north latitude; and now we are told that the inhibition named is unnecessary anywhere north of 36°30'! We are also told that we may rely upon the laws of God, which prohibit slave labor north of that line, and that it is absurd to reënact the laws of God. Sir, there is no human enactment which is just, that is not a reënactment of the law of God. The Constitution of the United States, and the constitutions of all the States, are full of such reënactments. Wherever I find a law of God or a law of nature disregarded, or in danger of being disregarded, there I shall vote to reaffirm it, with all the sanction of the civil authority. But I find no authority for the position, that climate prevents slavery anywhere. It is the indolence of mankind, in any climate, and not the natural necessity, that introduces slavery in any climate. . . .

. . .

When this answer shall be given, it will appear that the question of dissolving the Union is a complex question; that it embraces the fearful issue whether the Union shall stand, and slavery, under the steady, peaceful action of moral, social, and political causes, be removed by gradual, voluntary effort, and with compensation, or whether the Union shall be dissolved, and civil wars ensue, bringing on violent but complete and immediate emancipation. We are now arrived at that stage of our national progress when that crisis can be foreseen—when we must foresee it. It is directly before us. Its shadow is upon us. It darkens the legislative halls, the temples of worship, and the home and the hearth. Every question, political, civil, or ecclesiastical—however foreign to the subject of slavery—brings up slavery as an incident; and the incident supplants the principal question. We hear of nothing but slavery, and we can talk of nothing but slavery. And now, it seems to me that all our difficulties, embarrassments, and dangers, arise, not out of unlawful perversions of the question of slavery, as some suppose, but from the want of moral courage to meet this question of emancipation as we ought. Consequently, we hear on one side demands—absurd, indeed, but yet unceasing—for an immediate and unconditional abolition of slavery; as if any power, except the people of the slave States, could abolish it, and as if they could be moved to abolish it by merely sounding the trumpet violently and proclaiming emancipation, where the institution is interwoven with all their social and political interests, constitutions and customs.

On the other hand, our statesmen say that "slavery has always existed, and, for aught they know or can do, it always must exist. God permitted it, and he alone can indicate the way to remove it." . . .

Here, then, is the point of my separation from both of these parties. I feel assured that slavery must give way, and will give way, to the salutary instructions of economy, and to the ripening influences of humanity; that emancipation is inevitable, and is near; that it may be hastened or hindered; and that, whether it be peaceful or violent, depends upon the question, whether it be hastened or hindered—that all measures which fortify slavery, or extend it, tend to the consummation of violence—all that check its extension and abate its strength, tend to its peaceful extirpation. But I will adopt none but lawful, constitutional, and peaceful means, to secure even that end; and none such can I or will I forego. Nor do I know any important or responsible body that proposes to do more than this. No free State claims to extend its legislation into a slave State. None claims that Congress shall usurp power to abolish slavery in the slave States. None claims that any violent, unconstitutional, or unlawful measures shall be embraced. And, on the other hand, if we offer no scheme or plan for the adoption of the slave States, with the assent and coöperation of Congress, it is only because the slave States are unwilling, as yet, to receive such suggestions, or even to entertain the question of emancipation in any form. . . .

. . .

I have thus endeavored to show that there is not now, and there is not likely to occur, and adequate cause for revolution in regard to slavery. But you reply that, nevertheless, you must have guaranties; and the first one is for the surrender of fugitives from labor. That guaranty you cannot have, as I have already shown, because you cannot roll back the tide of social progress. You must be content with what you have. If you wage war against us, you can, at most, only conquer us, and then all you can get will be a treaty, and that you have already.

But you insist on a guaranty against the abolition of slavery in the District of Columbia, or war. Well, when you shall have declared war against us, what shall hinder us from immediately decreeing that slavery shall cease within the national capital?

You say that you will not submit to the exclusion of slaves from the new territories. What will you gain by resistance? Liberty follows the sword, although her sway is one of peace and beneficence. Can you propagate slavery, then, by the sword?

You insist that you cannot submit to the freedom with which slavery is discussed in the free States. Will war—a war for slavery—arrest, or even moderate, that discussion? No, sir; that discussion will not cease; war would only inflame it to a greater height. It is a part of the eternal conflict between truth and error—between mind and physical force—the conflict of man against the obstacles which oppose his way to an ultimate and glorious destiny. It will go on until you shall terminate it in the only way in which any State or nation has ever terminated it—by yielding to it—yielding in your own time, and in your own manner, indeed, but nevertheless yielding to the progress of emancipation. You will do this, sooner or later, whatever may be your opinion now; because nations which were prudent, and humane, and wise, as you are, have done so already. . . .

104. MASSACHUSETTS PERSONAL LIBERTY ACT, 1855*

The Compromise of 1850 called for a tougher fugitive slave law. In response, several northern states enacted so-called "personal liberty" laws to impede the new federal requirements; various procedural devices helped protect runaway slaves and created difficulties for slaveowners to prove their cases in court. In 1855 the Massachusetts legislature passed its personal liberty act in response to the public outcry after the forced return of a runaway slave to Virginia. A key provision of the act called for the removal of any state official who aided in the return of fugitive slaves. As a result, Massachusetts joined other northern states in defiantly obstructing federal law, thus further alienating many southerners.

MASSACHUSETTS PERSONAL LIBERTY ACT (1855)

. . . Sec. 2. The meaning of the one hundred and eleventh chapter of the Revised Statutes is hereby declared to be, that every person imprisoned or restrained of his liberty is entitled, as of right and of course, to the writ of habeas corpus, except in the cases mentioned in the second section of that chapter.

Sec. 3. The writ of habeas corpus may be issued by the supreme judicial court, the court of common pleas, by any justice's court or police court of any town or city, by any court of record, or by any justice of either of said courts, or by any judge of probate; and it may be issued by any justice of the peace, if no magistrate above named is known to said justice of the peace to be within five miles of the place where the party is imprisoned or restrained, and it shall be returnable before the supreme judicial court, or any one of the justices thereof, whether the court may be in session or not, and in term time or vacation. . . .

Sec. 6. If any claimant shall appear to demand the custody or possession of the person for whose benefit such writ is sued out, such claimant shall state in writing the facts on which he relies, with precision and certainty; and neither the claimant of the alleged fugitive, nor any person interested in his alleged obligation to service or labor, nor the alleged fugitive, shall be permitted to testify at the trial of the issue; and no confessions, admissions or declarations of the alleged fugitive against himself shall be given in evidence. Upon every question of fact involved in the issue, the burden of proof shall be on the claimant, and the facts alleged and necessary to be established, must be proved by the testimony of at least two credible witnesses, or other legal evidence equivalent thereto, and by the rules of evidence known and secured by the common law; and no ex parte deposition or affidavit shall be received in proof in behalf of the claimant, and no presumption shall arise in favor of the claimant from any proof that the alleged fugitive or any of his ancestors had actually been held as a slave, without proof that such holding was legal.

Sec. 7. If any person shall remove from the limits of this Commonwealth, or shall assist in removing therefrom, or shall come into the Commonwealth with the intention of removing or of assisting in the removing therefrom, or shall procure or assist in procuring to be so removed, any person being in the place thereof who is not "held to service or labor" by the "party" making "claim," or who has not "escaped" from the "party" making "claim," within the meaning of those words in the constitution of the United States, on the pretence that such person is so held or has so escaped, or that his "service or labor" is so "due," or with the intent to subject him to such "service or labor," he shall be punished by a fine of not less than one thousand, nor more than five thousand dollars, and by imprisonment in the State Prison not less than one, nor more than five years. . . .

---

*From "Massachusetts Personal Liberty Act (1855)," with source as *Massachusetts, Acts, and Resolves* (1855), 924, accessed May 1, 2001; available from http://usinfo.state.gov/usa/infousa/facts/democrac/20.htm; Internet

Sec. 9. No person, while holding any office of honor, trust, or emolument, under the laws of this Commonwealth, shall, in any capacity, issue any warrant or other process, or grant any certificate, under or by virtue of an act of congress . . . or shall in any capacity, serve any such warrant or other process.

Sec. 10. Any person who shall grant any certificate under or by virtue of the acts of congress, mentioned in the preceding section, shall be deemed to have resigned any commission from the Commonwealth which he may possess, his office shall be deemed vacant, and he shall be forever thereafter ineligible to any office of trust, honor or emolument under the laws of this Commonwealth.

Sec. 11. Any person who shall act as counsel or attorney for any claimant of any alleged fugitive from service or labor, under or by virtue of the acts of congress mentioned in the ninth section of this act, shall be deemed to have resigned any commission from the Commonwealth that he may possess, and he shall be thereafter incapacitated from appearing as counsel or attorney in the courts of this Commonwealth. . . .

Sec. 14. Any person holding any judicial office under the constitution or laws of this Commonwealth, who shall continue, for ten days after the passage of this act, to hold the office of United States commissioner, or any office . . . which qualifies him to issue any warrant or other process . . . under the [Fugitive Slave Acts] shall be deemed to have violated good behavior, to have given reason for the loss of public confidence, and furnished sufficient ground either for impeachment or for removal by address.

Sec. 15. Any sheriff, deputy sheriff, jailer, coroner, constable, or other officer of this Commonwealth, or the police of any city or town, or any district, county, city or town officer, or any officer or other member of the volunteer militia of this Commonwealth, who shall hereafter arrest . . . any person for the reason that he is claimed or adjudged to be a fugitive from service or labor, shall be punished by fine . . . and by imprisonment. . . .

Sec. 16. The volunteer militia of the Commonwealth shall not act in any manner in the seizure . . . of any person for the reason that he is claimed or adjudged to be a fugitive from service or labor. . . .

Sec. 19. No jail, prison, or other place of confinement belonging to, or used by, either the Commonwealth of Massachusetts or any county therein, shall be used for the detention or imprisonment of any person accused or convicted of any offence created by [the Federal Fugitive Slave Acts] . . . or accused or convicted of obstructing or resisting any process, warrant, or order issued under either of said acts, or of rescuing, or attempting to rescue, any person arrested or detained under any of the provisions of either of the said acts.

Discussion

1. The document by Randolph B. Marcy reveals the strong democratic feelings he held. What are some of the expressions of liberty and equality in the selection? Why might an army officer suggest that expeditions elect their leaders?

2. Why do you think Maria Ward is so critical of the power of the church? Do you think the situation she described was particularly unique to the Mormons?

3. Who do you think William E. Channing believed held power in the United States? Whose liberty did he think slavery threatened, and why? Does Channing seem very concerned with equality? If so, whose and how?

4. The address by President James Polk presented his reasons for wanting to gain Texas and Oregon for the United States. What do you think about his arguments? Was it the Manifest Destiny of the United States to acquire territory across the entire continent? Why or why not? What does his message imply about the power of the nation? Are there any implications for the principles of liberty and equality?

5. Who do you think David Wilmot believed held power in the United States? How do his comments compare to those of William Channing? What do the differences or similarities between the two passages suggest about the slave question in the 1830s and 1840s? What concerns does Wilmot express for liberty or equality?

6. In the three Senate speeches regarding the Compromise of 1850, how did each speaker address the issues of the time, in terms of liberty, equality, and power? To each, who was responsible for the sectional tensions over slavery? In each senator's view, how could the Union be saved?

7. Based on the Donner party selection, how do you think you would react in such circumstances?

8. How would each of the following—John C. Calhoun, Daniel Webster, and William Seward—react to the Massachusetts Personal Liberty Act, and why? Would they agree or disagree?

The Gathering Tempest, 1853–1860

SOUTHERN CHIVALRY — ARGUMENT VERSUS CLUB'S.

The violence of "Bleeding Kansas" spread to the halls of Congress in 1856. This famous political drawing by an antislavery northerner shows South Carolina Representative Preston Brooks beating Senator Charles Sumner of Massachusetts in the Senate chamber on May 22, 1856. The incident made Brooks a hero in the South and Sumner a martyr in the North.

Most Americans hoped that the Compromise of 1850 had resolved the slavery issue, but sectional differences grew even more pronounced during the subsequent years. Those differences, especially as manifested in Kansas, led to the creation of the Republican party and further hardening of the divisions between the North and the South. The Republicans established an antislavery coalition made up of several northern factions that stood adamantly against the expansion of slavery, and they hoped to gain enough power in Congress to implement the Wilmot Proviso. Proslavery forces obviously insisted on the right to extend slavery, and they gained the support of the Supreme Court when it ruled that Congress could not exclude the institution from any territory. The Dred Scott decision only helped fan the passions on both sides, and as the decade ended almost every national issue was tied to the slavery question. By the time John Brown was executed in 1859 for his attack on Harpers Ferry, emotions ran so high and bitterness so deep that, in effect, the nation had already divided.

105. NATIVISM, 1835*

Samuel F. B. Morse, who gained fame as the inventor of the telegraph, wrote a series of nativist essays in the 1830s just as a new wave of immigration to the United States began. In the following selection, Morse revealed the virulent anti-Catholicism that characterized the nativist movement. Hatred of Catholics had a long tradition in America, and in some ways Morse was merely repeating centuries-old feelings. Fears of conspiratorial threats to liberty were also a part of the nation's heritage, and Morse directed his anger toward the Pope and the Jesuits in much the same manner that an earlier generation had attacked King George III and the British Redcoats. In the 1850s, Republicans increased their political strength by channeling northerners' anxieties about immigrants into a campaign against the power of the slave aristocracy in the South. Consequently, many people came to believe that the gravest danger to freedom and equality was not a foreign state or a religious leader. The threat came from fellow Americans.

I have shown that a Society, (the "St. Leopold Foundation") is organized in a Foreign Absolute government, having its central direction in the capital of that government in Vienna, under the patronage of the Emperor of Austria, and the other Despotic Rulers,—a Society for the purpose of spreading Popery in this country. Of this fact there is no doubt. This "St. Leopold Foundation" has its ramifications through the whole of the Austria empire. It is not a small private association, but a great and extensive combination. It embraces in its extent, as shown by their own documents, not merely the wide Austrian Empire, Hungary, and Italy, but it includes Piedmont, Savoy, and Catholic France; it embodies the civil and ecclesiastical authorities of all these countries. And is such an extensive combination in foreign countries for the avowed purpose of operating in this country, (no matter for what purpose,) so trivial an affair, that we may safely dismiss it with a sneer?

---

*From Samuel F. B. Morse, *Imminent Dangers to the Free Institutions of the United States through Foreign Immigration, and the Present State of the Naturalization Laws* (New York: E. B. Clayton, 1835), 9–11.

Have these foreign Rulers so much sympathy with our system of government, that we may trust them safely to meddle with it, in any way? Are they so impotent in combination as to excite in us no alarm? May they send money, and agents, and a system of government wholly at variance with our own, and spread it through all our borders with impunity from our search, because it is nick-named Religion? There was a time when American sensibilities were quick on the subject of foreign interference. What has recently deadened them?

Let us examine the operation of this Austrian Society, for it is hard at work all around us; yes, here in this country, from one end to the other, at our very doors, in this city. From a machinery of such a character and power, we shall doubtless be able to see already some effect. With its headquarters at Vienna, under the immediate direction and inspection of Metternich, the well-known great managing general of the diplomacy of Europe, it makes itself already felt through the republic. Its emissaries are here. And who are these enemies? They are JESUITS. The society of men, after exerting their tyranny for upwards of 200 years, at length became so formidable to the world, threatening the entire subversion of all social order, that even the Pope, whose devoted subjects they are, and must be, by the vow of their society, was compelled to dissolve them. They had not been suppressed, however, for 50 years, before the waning influence of Popery and Despotism required their useful labours, to resist the spreading light of Democratic liberty, and the Pope, (Pius VII,) simultaneously with the formation of the Holy Alliance, revived the order of the Jesuits in all their power. From the vow of "unqualified submission to the Sovereign Pontiff," they have been appropriately called the Pope's body guard. It should be known, that Austrian influence elected the present Pope; his body guard are therefore at the service of Austria, and these are the soldiers that the Leopold Society has sent to this country, and they are agents of this society, to execute its designs, whatever these designs may be. And do Americans need to be told what Jesuits are? If any are ignorant, let them inform themselves of their history without delay; no time is to be lost: their workings are before you in every day's events: they are a secret society, a sort of Masonic order, with superadded features of most revolting odiousness, and a thousand times more dangerous. They are not confined to one class in society; they are not merely priests, or priest of one religious creed, they are merchants, and lawyers, and editors, and men of any profession. and no profession, having no outward badge, (in this country,) by which to be recognized; they are about in all your society. They can assume any character, that of angels of light, of ministers of darkness, to accomplish their one great end, the service upon which they are sent, whatever that service may be. "They are all educated men, prepared, and sworn to start at any moment, in any direction, and for any service, commanded by the general of their order, bound to no family, to community, or country, by the ordinary ties which bind men; and sold for life to the cause of the Roman Pontiff."

These are the men at this moment ordered to America. And can they do nothing, Americans, to derange the free workings of your democratic institutions? Can they not, and do they not fan the slightest embers of discontent into a flame, those thousand little differences which must perpetually occur in any society, into riot, and quell its excess among their own people as it suits their policy and the establishment of their own control? Yes, they can be the aggressors, and contrive to be the aggrieved. They can do the mischief, and manage to be publicly lauded for their praiseworthy forbearance and their suffering patience. They can persecute, and turn away from the popular indignation, ever roused by the cry of persecution from themselves, and make it fall upon their victim. They can control the press in a thousand secret ways. They can write under the signature of "Whig," to-day, and if it suits their turn, "Tory," to-morrow. They can be Democrat to-day, and Aristocrat to-morrow. They can out-American Americans in admiration of American institutions to-day, and "condemn them as unfit for any people" to-morrow. These are the men that Austria has sent here, that she supplies with money, with whom she keeps up an active correspondence, and whose officers (the Bishops) are passing back and forth between Europe and America, doubtless to impart that information orally which not be so safe committed to writing.

Is there no danger to the Democracy of the country from such formidable foes arrayed against it? Is Metternich its friend? Is the Pope its friend? Are his official documents, now daily put forth, Democratic in their character?

O there is no danger to the Democracy; for those most devoted to the Pope, the Roman Catholics, especially the Irish Catholics, are all on the side of Democracy. Yes; to be sure they are on the side of Democracy. They are just where I should look for them. Judas Iscariot joined with the true disciples. Jesuits are not fools. They would not startle our slumbering fears, by bolting out their monarchical designs, directly in our teeth, and by joining the opposing ranks, except so far as to cover their designs. This is a Democratic country, and the Democratic party is and ever must be the strongest party, unless ruined by traitors and Jesuits in the camp. Yes; it is in the ranks of Democracy I should expect to find them, and for no good purpose be assured. Every measure of Democratic policy in the least exciting will be pushed to ultraism, so soon as it is introduced for discussion. Let every real Democrat guard against this common Jesuitical artifice of tyrants, an artifice which there is much evidence to believe is practicing against them at this moment, an artifice which if not heeded will surely be the ruin of Democracy: it is founded on the well-known principle that "extremes meet." The writer has seen it pass under his own eyes in Europe, in more than one instance. When in despotic governments popular discontent, arising from the intolerable oppressions of the tyrants of the people, has manifested itself by popular outbreakings, to such a degree as to endanger the throne, and the people seemed prepared to shove their masters from their horses, and are likely to mount, and seize the reins themselves; then, the popular movement, unmanageable any longer by resistance, is pushed to the extreme. The passions of the ignorant and vicious are excited to outrage by pretended friends of the people. Anarchy ensues; and then the mass of the people, who are always lovers of order and quiet, unite at once in support of the strong arm of force for protection; and despotism, perhaps, in another, but preconcerted shape, resumesits iron reign. Italy and Germany are furnishing examples every day. If an illustration is wanted on a larger scale, look at France in her late Republican revolution, and in her present relapse into despotism.

He who would prevent you from mounting his horse, has two ways of thwarting your design. If he finds your efforts to rise too strong for his resistance, he has but to add a little more impulse to them, and he shoves you over on the other side. In either case you are on the ground.

106. THE CRIME AGAINST KANSAS, 1856*

In 1856, Congressman Preston Brooks walked into the Senate chamber and soundly whipped Senator Charles Sumner of Massachusetts. The violence that had plagued Kansas was replayed on the Senate floor. Perhaps no single incident revealed the intensity of the slavery issue as vividly as the Brooks-Sumner Affair. Sumner had attracted wide attention with a speech on conditions in Kansas. In the opening portion of his lengthy address, he harshly criticized Senators Andrew Butler of South Carolina and Stephen Douglas of Illinois. Representative Preston Brooks of South Carolina took exception to the comments regarding Butler, who was a cousin, and he replied with vigor. The portion of the Sumner speech presented here includes the comments that infuriated Brooks.

Mr. President, you are now called to redress a great transgression. Seldom in the history of nations has such a question been presented. Tariffs, Army bills, Navy bills, Land bills, are important, and justly occupy your care; but these all belong to the course of ordinary legislation. As means and instruments only, they are necessarily subordinate to the conservation of Government itself. Grant them or deny them, in greater or less degree, and you will inflict no shock. The machinery of Government will continue to move. The State will not cease to exist. For otherwise it

---

*From *Appendix to the Congressional Globe*, 34th Congress, 1st Session (1856), 529–31.

is with the eminent question now before you, involving, as it does, Liberty in a broad Territory, and also involving the peace of the whole country with our good name in history for evermore. . . .

But, before entering upon the argument, I must say something of a general character, particularly in response to what has fallen from Senators who have raised themselves to eminence on this floor in championing human wrongs; I mean the Senator from South Carolina, [Mr. Butler,] and the Senator form Illinois, [Mr. Douglas,] who, though unlike as Don Quixote and Sancho Panza, yet, like this couple, sally forth together in the same adventure. I regret much to miss the elder Senator from his seat; but the cause, against which he has run a tilt, with such activity of animosity, demands that the opportunity of exposing him should not be lost; and it is for the cause that I speak. The Senator from South Carolina has read many books of chivalry, and believes himself a chivalrous knight, with sentiments of honor and courage. Of course he has chosen a mistress to whom he has made his vows, and who, though ugly to others, is always lovely to him; though polluted in the sight of the world, is chaste in his sight—I mean the harlot, Slavery. For her, his tongue is always profuse in words. Let her be impeached in character, or any proposition made to shut her out from the extension of her wantonness, and no extravagance of manner or hardihood of assertion is then too great for this Senator. The frenzy of Don Quixote, in behalf of his wench, Dulcinea del Toboso, is all surpassed. The asserted rights of slavery, which shock equality of all kinds, are cloaked by a fantastic claim of equality. If the slave States cannot enjoy what, in a mockery of the great fathers of this Republic, he misnames equality under the Constitution—in other words, the full power in the National Territories to compel fellow-men to unpaid toil, to separate husband and wife, and to sell little children at the auction block—then, sir, the chivalric Senator will conduct the State of South Carolina out of the Union! Heroic knight! Exalted Senator! A second Moses come for a second exodus!

But not content with this poor menace, . . . the Senator, in the unrestrained chivalry of his nature, has undertaken to apply opprobrious words to those who differ from him on this floor. He calls them "sectional and fanatical;" and opposition to the usurpation in Kansas he denounces as "an uncalculating fanaticism." To be sure, those charges lack all grace of originality, and all sentiment of truth; but the adventurous Senator does not hesitate. He is the uncompromising, the unblushing representative on this floor of a flagrant sectionalism, which now dominates over the Republic, and yet with a ludicrous ignorance of his own position—unable to see himself as others see him—or with an effrontery which even his white head ought not to protect from rebuke, he applies to those here who resist his sectionalism the very epithet which designates himself. The men who strive to bring back the Government to its original policy, when Freedom and not Slavery was national, while Slavery and not Freedom was sectional, he arraigns as sectional. This will not do. It involves too great a perversion of terms. I tell that Senator, that it is to himself, and to the "organization" of which he is the "committed advocate," that his epithet belongs. I now fasten it upon them. For myself, I care little for names; but since the question has been raised here, I affirm that the Republican party of the Union is in no just sense sectional, but, more than any other party, national, and that it now goes forth to dislodge from the high places of the Government the tyrannical sectionalism of which the Senator from South Carolina is one of the maddest zealots.

To the charge of fanaticism I also reply. Sir, fanaticism is found in an enthusiasm or exaggeration of opinions, particularly on religious subjects; but there may be a fanaticism for evil as well as good. Now, I will not deny, that there are persons among us loving Liberty too well for their own personal good, in a selfish generation. Such there may be, and, for the sake of their example, would that there were more! In calling them "fanatics," you cast contumely upon the noble army of martyrs, from the earliest day down to this hour; upon the great tribunes of human rights, by whom life, liberty, and happiness on earth, have been secured; upon the long line of devoted patriots, who, throughout history, have truly loved their country; and, upon all, who, in noble aspirations for the general good and in forgetfulness of self, have stood out before their age, and gathered into their generous bosoms the shafts of tyranny and wrong, in order to make a pathway for Truth. . . . But I tell the Senator, that there are characters badly eminent, of whose fanaticism there can be no question. Such were the ancient Egyptians, who worshipped divinities in brutish forms; the Druids, who darkened the forests of oak, in which they lived, by sacrificing blood; the Mexicans, who surrendered countless victims to the propritiations of their obscene idols. . . . And in this same dreary catalogue faithful history must record all who now, in an enlightened age and in a land of boasted Freedom, stand up, in perversion of the Constitution and in denial of immortal truth, to fasten a new shackle upon their fellow-man. If the Senator wishes to see fanatics, let him look round among his own associates; let him look at himself. . . .

As the Senator from South Carolina is the Don Quixote, the Senator from Illinois [Mr. Douglas] is the squire of Slavery, its very Sancho Panza, ready to do all its humiliating offices. . . . Standing on this floor, the Senator issued his rescript, requiring submission to the Usurped Power of Kansas; and this was accompanied by a manner—all his own—such as befits the tyrannical threat. Very well. Let the Senator try. I tell him now that he cannot enforce any such submission. The Senator, with the Slave Power at his back, is strong, but he is not strong enough for this purpose. He is bold. He shrinks from nothing. . . . The Senator copies the British officer, who, with boastful swagger, said that with the hilt of his sword he would cram the "stamps" down the throat of the American people, and he will meet a similar failure. He may convulse this country with civil feud. Like the ancient madman, he may set fire to this Temple of Constitutional Liberty, grander than the Ephesian dome; but he cannot enforce obedience to that tyrannical Usurpation.

The Senator dreams that he can subdue the North. He disclaims the open threat, but his conduct still implies it. How little that Senator knows himself or the strength of the cause which he persecutes! He is but a mortal man; against him is an immortal principle. With finite power he wrestles with the infinite, and he must fall. Against him are stronger battalions than any marshaled by mortal arm—the inborn, ineradicable, invincible sentiments of the human heart; against him is nature in all her subtle forces; against him is God. Let him try to subdue these. . . .

107. PRESTON BROOKS RESIGNS HIS SEAT IN THE HOUSE, 1856*

At the request of the Senate, the House of Representatives voted to censure Representative Brooks. He responded to that condemnation with the following remarks. Brooks offered an explanation for his attack on Charles Sumner and freely admitted that he had staged the assault. He insisted, however, that the House lacked authority to censure him for actions taken in the Senate chamber. Like many of the events in the United States during the 1850s, this incident, which clearly resulted from the slavery issue, was expanded to include a multitude of constitutional questions and a variety of concerns over liberty and power. Following his resignation, the voters of his district voted overwhelmingly to return Brooks to Congress. Sumner, on the other hand, did not return to his Senate seat for more than three years—an absence that convinced his constituents of the brutality of the South.

Until this moment I have felt that there was a propriety in my remaining silent, and in trusting my defense to friends who are abler and more learned than myself. I have heretofore felt that other and higher interests than any which affect me personally were involved in the proceedings of this case. The interests of my constituents, of the House, and of all, indeed, who are concerned in the Constitution itself, in my view, have been intimately and inseparably complicated. . . .

I have been content, therefore, to meet personally and in silence all the consequences of these proceedings.

*From *Appendix to the Congressional Globe*, 34th Congress, 1st Session (1856), 831–33.

Some time since a Senator from Massachusetts allowed himself, in an elaborately prepared speech, to offer a great insult to my State and to a venerable friend, who is my State representative, and who was absent at the time.

Not content with that, he published to the world, and circulated extensively, this uncalled for libel on my State and my blood. Whatever insults my State insults me. Her history and character have commanded my pious veneration; and in her defense I hope I shall always be prepared humbly and modestly, to perform the duty of a son. I should have forfeited my own self-respect, and perhaps the good opinion of my countrymen, if I had failed to resent such an injury by calling the offender in question to a personal account. It was a personal affair, and in taking redress into my own hands I meant no disrespect to the Senate of the United States or to this House. Nor, sir, did I design insult or disrespect to the State of Massachusetts. I was aware of the personal responsibilities I incurred, and was willing to meet them. I know, too, that I was amenable to the laws of the country, which afford the same protection to all, whether they be members of Congress or private citizens. I did not, and do not now, believe that I could be properly punished, not only in a court of law, but here also, at the pleasure and discretion of the House. I did not then, and do not now, believe that the spirit of American freemen would tolerate slander in high places, and permit a member of Congress to publish and circulate a libel on another, and then call upon either House to protect him against the personal responsibilities which he had thus incurred.

But if I had committed a breach of privilege, it was the privilege of the Senate, and not of this House, which was violated. I was answerable there, and not here. They had no right, as it seems to me, to prosecute me in these Halls, nor have you the right in law or under the Constitution, as I respectfully submit, to take jurisdiction over offenses committed against them. The Constitution does not justify them in making such a request, nor this House in granting it. . . .

Matters may go smoothly enough when one House asks the other to punish a member who is offensive to a majority of its own body; but how will it be when, upon a pretense of insulted dignity, demands are made of this House to expel a member who happens to run counter to its party predilections, or other demands which may not be so agreeable to grant? It could never have been designed by the Constitution of the United States to expose the two Houses to such temptations to collision, or to extend so far the discretionary power which was given to either House to punish its own members for the violation of its rules and orders. Discretion has been said to be the law of the tyrant, and when exercised under the color of the law, and under the influence of party dictation, it may and will become a terrible and insufferable despotism. . . .

So far as public interests and constitutional rights are involved, I have now exhausted my means of defense. I may, then, be allowed to take a more personal view of the question at issue. . . .

Sir, I cannot, on my own account, assume the responsibility, in the face of the American people, of commencing a line of conduct which in my heart of hearts I believe would result in subverting the foundations of this Government, and in drenching this Hall in blood. No act of mine, and on my personal account, shall inaugurate revolution; but when you, Mr. Speaker, return to your home, and hear the people of the great North—and they are a great people—speak of me as a bad man, you will do me the justice to say that a blow struck by me at this time would be followed by revolution—and this I know. . . .

At the same time, Mr. Speaker, I am not willing to see the Constitution wounded through me; nor will I submit voluntarily to a wrong if I can avoid it. I will not voluntarily give my name to countenance parliamentary misrule or constitutional aggression. If I am to be tried again for the matter now before us, I will choose my own tribunal. I will appeal from this House to my own constituents. If an expression of public opinion is to be invoked in my case, let my constituents and my fellow-citizens pronounce upon it. From that verdict I will not appeal. The temper of the times is not favorable for a calm and dispassionate judgment of the case; and if, by any act of mine, I can save the majority of this House from the consequences of a rash decision, the time may come when the good men who are pursuing me—and I believe there are such in the Opposition—will admit that I deserve their thanks for the deed. The ax that is uplifted to strike me may fall upon others, and fall upon them after they have parted with the shield of the Constitution to protect them.

For myself I have only to say that, if I cannot preserve my self-respect and constitutional rights, together with a seat in this body, I must renounce the last rather than the former.

I have no desire, sir, to continue an argument which my friends have exhausted. The determination of the majority is fixed, and it is vain to resist it. I will make no appeal to a packed jury, but I protest against its inconsistencies and usurpations. . . . At the first session of the last Congress a member leaped from his seat, and, while the Speaker was in his chair, he passed over several tables toward his antagonist, who drew a weapon in defense, and neither gentleman was subject to the censure of this House. . . .

And yet, sir, the vote which has just been taken transmits me to prosperity as a man unworthy, in the judgment of a majority of my peers, of a seat in this Hall. And for what? The member from New Jersey, [Mr. Pennington]—the prosecuting member . . . says it was for making a "murderous" assault with a "bludgeon;" and he, forsooth, would have the House and the country believe, with an intent to kill. Now, sir, I see that a very respectable and excellent gentleman from Massachusetts has in his hand a cane of the ordinary size for a gentleman of his age, and I beg him to raise it for inspection of the member from New Jersey. . . . Now, sir, I ask that member to answer as a gentleman—I beg his pardon, that is a word which he cannot comprehend—but as a man on the witness-stand, is not that cane double the weight and thickness of the one used by me, and which you have impudently and falsely called a "bludgeon"? . . .

If I desired to kill the Senator, why did not I do it? You all admit that I had him in my power. Let me tell the member from New Jersey that it was expressly to avoid taking life that I used an ordinary cane. . . . I went to work very deliberately, as I am charged—and this is admitted—and speculated somewhat as to whether I should employ a horsewhip or a cowhide; but knowing that the Senator was my superior in strength, it occurred to me that he might wrest it from my hand, and then—for I never attempt anything I do not perform—I might have been compelled to do that which I would have regretted the balance of my natural life.

The question has been asked in certain newspapers, why did I not invite the Senator to personal combat in the mode usually adopted. Well, sir, as I desire the whole truth to be known about the matter, I will for once notice as newspaper article on the floor of the House, and answer here.

My answer is, that I knew the Senator would not accept a message, and having formed an unalterable determination to punish him, I believed that the offense of "sending a hostile message," superadded to the indictment for assault and battery, would subject me to legal penalties more severe than would be imposed for a simple assault and battery. . . .

For this act, which the Senate, with a solitary exception . . . , have pronounced me guilty of a breach of its privileges—for this act I am complained of by that body to this House. Your committee have declared, and this House has now concurred in the opinion, that my offense is to the Senate, and that no rule or order of this body is violated. . . .

Now, Mr. Speaker, I have nearly finished what I intended to say. If my opponents, who have pursued me with an unparalleled bitterness, are satisfied with the present condition of this affair, I am. I return my thanks to my friends, and especially to those who are from non-slaveowning States, who have magnanimously sustained me, and felt that it was a higher honor to themselves to be just in their judgment of a gentleman than to be a member of Congress for life. In taking my leave, I feel that it is proper that I should say that I believe some of the votes which have been cast against me have been extorted by an outside pressure at home, and that their votes do not express the feelings or opinions of the members who gave them.

To such of these as have given their votes and made their speeches on the constitutional principles involved, and without indulging in personal vilification, I owe my respect. But, sir, they have written me down upon the history of the country as worthy of expulsion, and in no unkindness I must tell them that for all future time my self-respect requires that I shall pass them as strangers.

And now, Mr. Speaker, I announce to you and to this House, that I am no longer a member of the Thirty-Fourth Congress.

108. THE DRED SCOTT CASE, 1857*

*M*any Americans—on both sides of the slavery issue—hoped that the Dred Scott case would finally settle the controversial question of slavery in the territories. On March 6, 1857, Chief Justice Roger B. Taney spoke for the Court, his chief arguments summarized in the following selection. In short, the Court ruled that Congress could not keep slavery out of the territories, because slaves were considered property and the Constitution prohibited Congress from depriving citizens of their property without due process of law. Thus, the Missouri Compromise was unconstitutional. Many southerners exalted in the outcome. But critics refused to accept Taney's "majority" opinion, some advocating a new reading of the Constitution based on the dissenting views of Justices Curtis and McLean, others vowing to use the presidential ballot box to change the sectional and political composition of the Supreme Court. Far from resolving the slavery controversy, the Dred Scott decision only exacerbated intersectional tensions.*

The question is simply this: Can a negro, whose ancestors were imported into this country, and sold as slaves, become a member of the political community formed and brought into existence by the Constitution of the United States, and as such become entitled to all the rights, and privileges, and immunities, guarantied by that instrument to the citizen? One of which rights is the privilege of suing in a court of the United States in the cases specified in the Constitution.

It will be observed, that the plea applies to that class of persons only whose ancestors were negroes of the African race, and imported into this country, and sold and held as slaves. The only matter in issue before the court, therefore, is, whether the descendants of such slaves, when they shall be emancipated, or who are born of parents who had become free before their birth, are citizens of a State, in the sense in which the word citizen is used in the Constitution of the United States. And this being the only matter in dispute on the pleadings, the court must be understood as speaking in this opinion of that class only, that is, of those persons who are the descendants of Africans who were imported into this country, and sold as slaves. . . .

We proceed to examine the case as presented by the pleadings.

The words "people of the United States" and "citizens" are synonymous terms, and mean the same thing. They both describe the political body who, according to our republican institutions, form the sovereignty, and who hold the power and conduct the Government through their representatives. They are what we familiarly call the "sovereign people," and every citizen is one of this people, and a constituent member of this sovereignty. The question before us is, whether the class of persons described in the plea in abatement compose a portion of this people, and are constituent members of the sovereignty? We think they are not, and that they are not included, and were not intended to be included, under the word "citizens" in the Constitution, and can therefore claim none of the rights and privileges which that instrument provides for and secures to citizens of the United States. On the contrary, they were at that time considered as a subordinate and inferior class of beings, who had been subjugated by the dominant race, and, whether emancipated or not, yet remained subject to their authority, and had no rights or privileges but such as those who held the power and the Government might choose to grant them.

---

*From *Dred Scott* v. *Sandford*, 19 *United States Reports*, 403–10, 426–27, 430, 432, 439–40, 449–52, 454.

It is not the province of the court to decide upon the justice or injustice, the policy or impolicy, of these laws. The decision of that question belonged to the political or law-making power; to those who formed the sovereignty and framed the Constitution. The duty of the court is, to interpret the instrument they have framed, with the best lights we can obtain on the subject, and to administer it as we find it, according to its true intent and meaning when it was adopted.

In discussing this question, we must not confound the rights of citizenship which a State may confer within its own limits, and the rights of citizenship as a member of the Union. It does not by any means follow, because he has all the rights and privileges of a citizen of a State, that he must be a citizen of the United States. He may have all of the rights and privileges of the citizen of a State, and yet not be entitled to the rights and privileges of a citizen in any other State. . . .

It is very clear, therefore, that no State can, by any act or law of its own, passed since the adoption of the Constitution, introduce a new member into the political community created by the Constitution of the United States. It cannot make him a member of this community by making him a member of its own. And for the same reason it cannot introduce any person, or description of persons, who were not intended to be embraced in this new political family, which the Constitution brought into existence, but were intended to be excluded from it.

The question then arises, whether the provisions of the Constitution, in relation to the personal rights and privileges to which the citizen of a State should be entitled, embraced the negro African race, at that time in this country, or who might afterwards be imported, who had then or should afterwards be made free in any State; and to put it in the power of a single State to make him a citizen of the United States, and endue him with the full rights of citizenship in every other State without their consent? Does the Constitution of the United States act upon him whenever he shall be made free under the laws of a State, and raised there to be the rank of a citizen, and immediately clothe him with all the privileges of a citizen in every other State, and in its own courts?

The court think the affirmative of these propositions cannot be maintained. And if it cannot, the plaintiff in error could not be a citizen of the State of Missouri, within the meaning of the Constitution of the United States, and, consequently, was not entitled to sue in its courts.

It is true, every person, and every class and description of persons, who were at the time of the adoption of the Constitution recognised as citizens in the several States, became also citizens of this new political body; but none other; it was formed by them, and for them and their posterity, but for no one else. . . .

In the opinion of the court, the legislation and histories of the times, and the language used in the Declaration of Independence, show, that neither the class of persons who had been imported as slaves, nor their descendants, whether they had become free or not, were then acknowledged as a part of the people, nor intended to be included in the general words used in that memorable instrument.

It is difficult at this day to realize the state of public opinion in relation to that unfortunate race, which prevailed in the civilized and enlightened portions of the world at the time of the Declaration of Independence, and when the Constitution of the United States was framed and adopted. . . .

They had for more than a century before been regarded as beings of an inferior order, and altogether unfit to associate with the white race, either in social or political relations; and so far inferior, that they had no rights which the white man was bound to respect; and that the negro might justly and lawfully be reduced to slavery for his benefit. He was bought and sold, and treated as an ordinary article of merchandise and traffic, whenever a profit could be made by it. This opinion was at that time fixed and universal in the civilized portion of the white race. It was regarded as an axiom in morals as well as in politics, which on one thought of disputing, or supposed to be open to dispute; and men in every grade and position in society daily and habitually acted upon it in their private pursuits, as well as in matters of public concern, without doubting for a moment the correctness of this opinion. . . .

The legislation of the different colonies furnishes positive and indisputable proof of this fact. . . .
The language of the Declaration of Independence is equally conclusive. . . .

This state of public opinion had undergone no change when the Constitution was adopted, as is equally evident from its provisions and language. . . .

No one, we presume, supposes that any change in public opinion or feeling, in relation to this unfortunate race, in the civilized nations of Europe or in this country, should induce the court to give to the words of the Constitution a more liberal construction in their favor than they were intended to bear when the instrument was framed and adopted. Such an argument would be altogether inadmissible in any tribunal called on to interpret it. If any of its provisions are deemed unjust, there is a mode prescribed in the instrument itself by which it may be amended; but while it remains unaltered, it must be construed now as it was understood at the time of its adoption. It is not only the same in words, but the same in meaning, and delegates the same powers to the Government, and reserves and secures the same rights and privileges to the citizen; and as long as it continues to exist in its present form, it speaks not only in the same words, but with the same meaning and intent with which it spoke when it came from the hands of its framers, and was voted on and adopted by the people of the United States. Any other rule of construction would abrogate the judicial character of this court, and make it the mere reflex of the popular opinion or passion of the day. This court was not created by the Constitution for such purposes. Higher and graver trusts have been confided to it, and it must not falter in the path of duty.

What the construction was at that time, we think can hardly admit of doubt. We have the language of the Declaration of Independence and of the Articles of Confederation, in addition to the plain words of the Constitution itself; we have the legislation of the different States, before, about the time, and since, the Constitution was adopted; we have the legislation of Congress, from the time of its adoption to a recent period; and we have the constant and uniform action of the Executive Department, all concurring together, and leading to the same result. And if anything in relation to the construction of the Constitution can be regarded as settled, it is that which we now give to the word "citizen" and the word "people."

And upon a full and careful consideration of the subject, the court is of opinion, that, upon the facts stated in the plea in abatement, Dred Scott was not a citizen of Missouri within the meaning of the Constitution of the United States, and not entitled as such to sue in its courts; and, consequently, that the Circuit Court had no jurisdiction of the case, and that the judgment on the plea in abatement is erroneous. . . .

We proceed, therefore, to inquire whether the facts relied on by the plaintiff entitled him to his freedom. . . .

The act of Congress, upon which the plaintiff relies, declares that slavery and involuntary servitude, except as a punishment for crime, shall be forever prohibited in all that part of the territory ceded by France, under the name of Louisiana, which lies north of thirty-six degrees thirty minutes north latitude, and not included within the limits of Missouri. And the difficulty which meets us at the threshold of this part of the inquiry is, whether Congress was authorized to pass this law under any of the powers granted to it by the Constitution; for if the authority is not given by that instrument, it is the duty of this court to declare it void and inoperative, and incapable of conferring freedom upon any one who is held as a slave under the laws of any one of the States.

The counsel for the plaintiff has laid much stress upon that article in the Constitution which confers on Congress the power "to dispose of and make all needful rules and regulations respecting the territory or other property belonging to the United States;" but, in the judgment of the court, that provision has no bearing on the present controversy, and the power there given, whatever it may be, is confined, and was intended to be confined, to the territory which at that time belonged to, or was claimed by, the United States, and was within their boundaries as settled by the treaty with Great Britain, and can have no influence upon a territory afterwards acquired from a foreign

Government. It was a special provision for a known and particular territory, and to meet a present emergency, and nothing more. . . .

But if this clause is construed to extend to territory acquired by the present Government from a foreign nation, outside of the limits of any charter from the British Government to a colony, it would be difficult to say, why it was deemed necessary to give the Government the power to sell any vacant lands belonging to the sovereignty which might be found within it; and if this was necessary, why the grant of this power should precede the power to legislate over it and establish a Government there; and still more difficult to say, why it was deemed necessary so specially and particularly to grant the power to make needful rules and regulations in relation to any personal or movable property it might acquire there. For the words, *other property* necessarily, by every known rule of interpretation, must mean property of a different description from territory or land. And the difficulty would perhaps be insurmountable in endeavoring to account for the last member of the sentence, which provides that "nothing in this Constitution shall be so construed as to prejudice any claims of the United States or any particular State," or to say how any particular State could have claims in or to a territory ceded by a foreign Government, or to account for associating this provision with the preceding provisions of the clause, with which it would appear to have no connection. . . .

But the power of Congress over the person or property of a citizen can never be a mere discretionary power under our Constitution and form of Government. The powers of the Government and the rights and privileges of the citizen are regulated and plainly defined by the Constitution itself. And when the Territory becomes a part of the United States, the Federal Government enters into possession in the character impressed upon it by those who created it. It enters upon it with its powers over the citizen strictly defined, and limited by the Constitution, from which it derives its own existence, and by virtue of which alone it continues to exist and act as Government and sovereignty. It has no power of any kind beyond it; and it cannot, when it enters a Territory of the United States, put off its character, and assume discretionary or despotic powers which the Constitution has denied to it. It cannot create for itself a new character separated from the citizens of the United States, and the duties it owes them under the provisions of the Constitution. The Territory being a part of the United States, the Government and the citizen both enter it under the authority of the Constitution, with their respective rights defined and marked out; and the Federal Government can exercise no power over his person or property, beyond what that instrument confers, nor lawfully deny any right which it has reserved. . . .

The rights of private property have been guarded with equal care. Thus the rights of property are united with the rights of person, and placed on the same ground by the fifth amendment to the Constitution, which provides that no person shall be deprived of life, liberty, and property, without due process of law. And an act of Congress which deprives a citizen of the United States of his liberty or property, merely because he came himself or brought his property into a particular Territory of the United States, and who had committed no offence against the laws, could hardly be dignified with the name of due process of law. . . .

The powers over person and property of which we speak are not only not granted to Congress, but are in express terms denied, and they are forbidden to exercise them. And this prohibition is not confined to the States, but the words are general, and extend to the whole territory over which the Constitution gives it power to legislate, including those portions of it remaining under Territorial Government, as well as that covered by States. It is a total absence of power everywhere within the dominion of the United States, and places the citizens of a Territory, so far as these rights are concerned, on the same footing with citizens of the States, and guards them as firmly and plainly against any inroads which the General Government might attempt, under the plea of implied or incidental powers. And if Congress itself cannot do this—if it is beyond the powers conferred on the Federal Government—it will be admitted, we presume, that it could not authorize a Territorial

Government to exercise them. It could confer no power on any local Government, established by its authority, to violate the provisions of the Constitution.

It seems, however, to be supposed, that there is a difference between property in a slave and other property, and that different rules may be applied to it in expounding the Constitution of the United States. And the laws and usages of nations, and the writings of eminent jurists upon the relation of master and slave and their mutual rights and duties, and the powers which Governments may exercise over it, have been dwelt upon in the argument. . . .

Now . . . the right of property in a slave is distinctly and expressly affirmed in the Constitution. The right to traffic in it, like an ordinary article of merchandise and property, was guarantied to the citizens of the United States, in every State that might desire it, for twenty years. And the Government in express terms is pledged to protect it in all future time, if the slave escapes from his owner. This is done in plain words—too plain to be misunderstood. And no word can be found in the Constitution which gives Congress a greater power over slave property, or which entitles property of that kind to less protection than property of any other description. The only power conferred is the power coupled with the duty of guarding and protecting the owner in his rights.

Upon these considerations, it is the opinion of the court that the act of Congress which prohibited a citizen from holding and owning property of this kind in the territory of the United States north of the line therein mentioned, is not warranted by the Constitution, and is therefore void; and that neither Dred Scott himself, nor any of his family, were made free by being carried into this territory; even if they had been carried there by the owner, with the intention of becoming a permanent resident. . . .

Upon the whole, therefore, it is the judgment of this court, that it appears by the record before us that the plaintiff in error is not a citizen of Missouri, in the sense in which that word is used in the Constitution; and that the Circuit Court of the United States, for that reason, had no jurisdiction in the case, and could give no judgment in it. Its judgment for the defendant must, consequently, be reversed, and a mandate issued, directing the suit to be dismissed for want of jurisdiction.

109. *CANNIBALS ALL! OR, SLAVES WITHOUT MASTERS*, 1857*

During the 1850s many southerners aggressively defended the institution of slavery. They insisted that the black slaves of the South were better off than the white "wage slaves" in northern factories. In 1857 George Fitzhugh (1806-1881), a Virginia farmer-lawyer, fully developed this argument in Cannibals All! or, Slaves Without Masters. *He accused the North of using liberty as a deception for reducing white laborers to "slaves without masters." And he asserted that slaves in the South were "the happiest, and, in some sense, the freest people in the world."*

We are, all, North and South, engaged in the White Slave Trade, and he who succeeds best, is esteemed most respectable. It is far more cruel than the Black Slave Trade, because it exacts more of its slaves, and neither protects nor governs them. We boast, that it exacts more, when we say, "that the profits made from employing free labor are greater than those from slave labor." The profits, made from free labor, are the amount of the products of such labor, which the employer, by means of the command which capital or skill gives him, takes away, exacts or "exploitates" from the free laborer. The profits of slave labor are that portion of the products of such labor which the power of the master enables him to appropriate. These profits are less, because the master allows the slave to retain a larger share of the results of his own labor, than do the employers of free labor. But we not only boast that the

*From George Fitzhugh, *Cannibals All! or, Slaves Without Masters* (Richmond: A. Morris, 1857), 25–32.

White Slave Trade is more exacting and fraudulent (in fact, though not in intention,) than Black Slavery; but we also boast, that it is more cruel, in leaving the laborer to take care of himself and family out of the pittance which skill or capital have allowed him to retain. When the day's labor is ended, he is free, but is overburdened with the cares of family and household, which make his freedom an empty and delusive mockery. But his employer is really free, and may enjoy the profits made by others' labor, without a care, or a trouble, as to their well-being. The negro slave is free, too, when the labors of the day are over, and free in mind as well as body; for the master provides food, raiment, house, fuel, and everything else necessary to the physical well-being of himself and family. The master's labors commence just when the slave's end. No wonder men should prefer white slavery to capital, to negro slavery, since it is more profitable, and is free from all the cares and labors of black slave-holding.

Now, reader, if you wish to know yourself—to "descant on your own deformity"—read on. But if you would cherish self-conceit, self-esteem, or self-appreciation, throw down our book; for we will dispel illusions which have promoted your happiness, and shew you that what you have considered and practiced as virtue, is little better than moral Cannibalism. But you will find yourself in numerous and respectable company; for all good and respectable people are "Cannibals all," who do not labor, or who are successfully trying to live without labor, on the unrequited labor of other people: Whilst low, bad, and disreputable people, are those who labor to support themselves, and to support said respectable people besides. Throwing the negro slaves out of the account, and society is divided in Christendom into four classes: The rich, or independent respectable people, who live well and labor not at all; the professional and skillful respectable people, who do a little light work, for enormous wages; the poor hard-working people, who support every body, and starve themselves; and the poor thieves, swindlers and sturdy beggars, who live like gentlemen, without labor, on the labor of other people. The gentlemen exploitate, which being done on a large scale, and requiring a great many victims, is highly respectable—whilst the rogues and beggars take so little from others, that they fare little better than those who labor.

But, reader, we do not wish to fire into the flock. "Thou art the man!" You are a Cannibal! and if a successful one, pride yourself on the number of your victims, quite as much as any Feejee chieftain, who breakfasts, dines and sups on human flesh. And your conscience smites you, if you have failed to succeed, quite as much as his, when he returns from an unsuccessful foray.

Probably, you are a lawyer, or a merchant, or a doctor, who have made by your business fifty thousand dollars, and retired to live on your capital. But, mark not to spend your capital. That would be vulgar, disreputable, criminal. That would be, to live by your own labor; for your capital is your amassed labor. That would be, to do as common working men do; for they take the pittance which their employers leave them, to live on. They live by labor; for they exchange the results of their own labor for the products of other people's labor. It is, no doubt, an honest, vulgar way of living; but not at all a respectable way. The respectable way of living is, to make other people work for you, and to pay them nothing for so doing—and to have no concern about them after their work is done. Hence, white slave-holding is much more respectable than negro slavery—for the master works nearly as hard for the negro, as he for the master. But you, my virtuous, respectable reader, exact three thousand dollars per annum from white labor, (for your income is the product of white labor,) and make not one cent of return in any form. You retain your capital, and never labor, and yet live in luxury on the labor of others. Capital commands labor, as the master does the slave. Neither pays for labor; but the master permits the slave to retain a larger allowance from the proceeds of his own labor, and hence "free labor is cheaper than slave labor." You, with the command over labor which your capital gives you, are a slave owner—a master, without the obligations of a master. They who work for you, who create your income, are slaves, without the rights of slaves. Slaves without a master! Whilst you were engaged in amassing your capital, in seeking to become independent, you were in the White Slave Trade. To become independent, is to be able to make other people support you, without being obliged to labor for them. Now, what man in society is not seeking to attain this situation? He who attains it, is a slave owner, in the worst sense. He who is in pursuit of it, is engaged in the slave trade. You, reader, belong to the one or other class. The men without property, in free society, are theoretically in a worse condition than slaves. Practically, their condition corresponds with this theory, as history and statistics every where demonstrate. The capitalists, in free society, live in ten times the luxury and show that Southern masters do, because the slaves to capital work harder and cost less, than negro slaves.

The negro slaves of the South are the happiest, and, in some sense, the freest people in the world. The children and the aged and infirm work not at all, and yet have all the comforts and necessaries of life provided for them. They enjoy liberty, because they are oppressed neither by care nor labor. The women do little hard work, and are protected from the despotism of their husbands by their masters. The negro men and stout boys work, on the average, in good weather, not more than nine hours a day. The balance of their time is spent in perfect abandon. Besides, they have their Sabbaths and holidays. White men, with so much of license and liberty, would die of ennui; but negroes luxuriate in corporeal and mental repose. With their faces upturned to the sun, they can sleep at any hour; and quiet sleep is the greatest of human enjoyments. "Blessed be the man who invented sleep." 'Tis happiness in itself—and results from contentment with the present, and confident assurance of the future. We do not know whether free laborers ever sleep. They are fools to do so; for, whilst they sleep, the wily and watchful capitalist is devising means to ensnare and exploitate them. The free laborer must work or starve. He is more of a slave than the negro, because he works longer and harder for less allowance than the slave, and has no holiday, because the cares of life with him begin when its labors end. He has no liberty, and not a single right. . . .

Free laborers have not a thousandth part of the rights and liberties of negro slaves. Indeed, they have not a single right or a single liberty, unless it be the right or liberty to die. But the reader may think that he and other capitalists and employers are freer than negro slaves. Your capital would soon vanish, if you dared indulge in the liberty and abandon of negroes. You hold your wealth and position by the tenure of constant watchfulness, care and circumspection. You never labor; but you are never free.

Where a few own the soil, they have unlimited power over the balance of society, until domestic slavery comes in, to compel them to permit this balance of society to draw a sufficient and comfortable living from "terra mater." Free society, asserts the right of a few to the earth—slavery, maintains that it belongs, in different degrees, to all.

But, reader, well may you follow the slave trade. It is the only trade worth following, and slaves the only property worth owning. All other is worthless, a mere *caput mortuum*, except in so far as it vests the owner with the power to command the labors of others—to enslave them. Give you a palace, ten thousand acres of land, sumptuous clothes, equipage and every other luxury; and with your artificial wants, you are poorer than Robinson Crusoe, or the lowest working man, if you have no slaves to capital, or domestic slaves. Your capital will not bring you an income of a cent, nor supply one of your wants, without labor. Labor is indispensable to give value to property, and if you owned every thing else, and did not own labor, you would be poor. But fifty thousand dollars means, and is, fifty thousand dollars worth of slaves. You can command, without touching on that capital, three thousand dollars' worth of labor per annum. You could do no more were you to buy slaves with it, and then you would be cumbered with the cares of governing and providing for them. You are a slaveholder now, to the amount of fifty thousand dollars, with all the advantages, and none of the cares and responsibilities of a master.

"Property in man" is what all are struggling to obtain. Why should they not be obliged to take care of man, their property, as they do of their horses and their hounds, their cattle and their sheep. Now, under the delusive name of liberty, you work him, "from morn to dewy eve"—from infancy to old age—then turn him out to starve. You treat your horses and hounds better. Capital is a cruel master. The free slave trade, the commonest, yet the cruellest of trades. . . .

110. *THE IMPENDING CRISIS OF THE SOUTH, 1857**

The non-slaveholding majority of Southern whites generally aligned themselves with the slavery interest and acquiesced to the political leadership of the planter elite. In 1857 North Carolina author Hinton Rowan Helper (1829–1909), a self-appointed spokesmen for his region of small farms and few slaves, assaulted this alignment from within Southern society in an incendiary book entitled The Impending Crisis of the South. *Helper attacked the dominance of the slaveowning aristocracy whose actions, he believed, retarded the economic and social development of the South. He contrasted the more successful North with a dismal picture of his own region, claiming that "slavery lies at the root of all the shame, poverty, ignorance, tyranny, and imbecility of the South." He encouraged non-slaveholding farmers to liberate themselves from "this entire system of oligarchical despotism" and assert their own economic interests. Although Helper proposed abolition, he held little sympathy for African Americans, slave or free. Nevertheless, his book was virtually banned in the South but found an audience among Northerners who embraced Helper's condemnation of slavery and advocacy of free labor.*

And now that we have come to the very heart and soul of our subject, we feel no disposition to mince matters, but mean to speak plainly, and to the point, without any equivocation, mental reservation, or secret evasion whatever. The son of a venerated parent, who, while he lived, was a considerate and merciful slaveholder, a native of the South, born and bred in North Carolina, of a family whose home has been in the valley of the Yadkin for nearly a century and a half, a Southerner by instinct and by all the influences of thought, habits, and kindred, and with the desire and fixed purpose to reside permanently within the limits of the South, and with the expectation of dying there also, we feel that we have the right to express our opinion, however humble or unimportant it may be, on any and every question that affects the public good; and, so help us God, "sink or swim, live or die, survive or perish," we are determined to exercise that right with manly firmness, and without fear, favor or affection.

And now to the point. In our opinion, an opinion which has been formed from data obtained by assiduous researches, and comparisons, from laborious investigation, logical reasoning, and earnest reflection, the causes which have impeded the progress and prosperity of the South, which have dwindled our commerce, and other similar pursuits, into the most contemptible insignificance; sunk a large majority of our people in galling poverty and ignorance, rendered a small minority conceited and tyrannical, and driven the rest away from their homes; entailed upon us a humiliating dependence on the Free States; disgraced us in the recesses of our own souls, and brought us under reproach in the eyes of all civilized and enlightened nations—may all be traced to one common source, and there find solution in the most hateful and horrible word, that was ever incorporated into the vocabulary of human economy—Slavery !

Reared amidst the institution of slavery, believing it to be wrong both in principle and in practice, and having seen and felt its evil influences upon individuals, communities and states, we deem it a duty, no less than a privilege, to enter our protest against it, and to use our most strenuous efforts to overturn and abolish it! Then we are an abolitionist? Yes! not merely a freesoiler, but an abolitionist, in the fullest sense of the term. We are not only in favor of keeping slavery out of the territories, but, carrying our opposition to the institution a step further, we here unhesitatingly declare ourself in favor of its immediate and unconditional abolition, in every state in this confederacy, where it now exists! Patriotism makes us a freesoiler; state pride makes us an emancipationist; a profound sense of duty to the South makes us an abolitionist; a reasonable degree of fellow

---

*From Hinton Rowan Helper, *The Impending Crisis of the South: How to Meet It* (New York: A. B. Burdick, 1860), 24–28, 42–45, 128–29.

feeling for the negro, makes us a colonizationist. With the free state men in Kansas and Nebraska, we sympathize with all our heart. We love the whole country, the great family of states and territories, one and inseparable, and would have the word Liberty engraved as an appropriate and truthful motto, on the escutcheon of every member of the confederacy. We love freedom, we hate slavery, and rather than give up the one or submit to the other, we will forfeit the pound of flesh nearest our heart. Is this sufficiently explicit and categorical? If not, we hold ourself in readiness at all times, to return a prompt reply to any properquestion that may be propounded.

Our repugnance to the institution of slavery, springs from no one-sided idea, or sickly sentimentality. We have not been hasty in making up our mind on the subject; we have jumped at no conclusions; we have acted with perfect calmness and deliberation; we have carefully considered, and examined the reasons for and against the institution, and have also taken into account the propable consequences of our decision. The more we investigate the matter, the deeper becomes the conviction that we are right; and with this to impel and sustain us, we pursue our labor with love, with hope, and with constantly renewing vigor.

That we shall encounter opposition we consider as certain; perhaps we may even be subjected to insult and violence. From the conceited and cruel oligarchy, of the South, we could look for nothing less. But we shall shrink from no responsibility, and do nothing unbecoming a man; we know how to repel indignity, and if assaulted, shall not fail to make the blow recoil upon the aggressor's head. The road we have to travel may be a rough one, but no impediment shall cause us to falter in out course. The line of our duty is clearly defined, and it is our intention to follow it faithfully, or die in the attempt.

But, thanks to heaven, we have no ominous forebodings of the result of the contest now pending between Liberty and Slavery in this confederacy. Though neither a prophet nor the son of a prophet, our vision is sufficiently penetrative to divine the future so far as to be able to see that the "peculiar institution" has but a short, and, as heretofore, inglorious existence before it. Time, the righter of every wrong, is ripening events for the desired consummation of our labors and the fulfillment of our cherished hopes. Each revolving year brings nearer the inevitable crisis. The sooner it comes the better; may heaven, through our humble efforts, hasten its advent.

The first and most sacred duty of every Southerner, who has the honor and the interest of his country at heart, is to declare himself an unqualified and uncompromising abolitionist. No conditional or half-way declaration will avail; no mere threatening demonstration will succeed. With those who desire to be instrumental in bringing about the triumph of liberty over slavery, there should be neither evasion, vacillation, nor equivocation. We should listen to no modifying terms or compromises that may be proposed by the proprietors of the unprofitable and ungodly institution. Nothing short of the complete abolition of slavery can save the South from falling into the vortex of utter ruin. Too long have we yielded a submissive obedience to the tyrannical domination of an inflated oligarchy; too long have we tolerated their arrogance and self-conceit; too long have we submitted to their unjust and savage exactions. Let us now wrest from them the sceptre of power, establish liberty and equal rights throughout the land, and henceforth and forever guard our legislative halls from the pollutions and usurpations of proslavery demagogues.

*   *   *

. . . Thus our disappointment gives way to a feeling of intense mortification, and our soul involuntarily, but justly, we believe, cries out for retribution against the treacherous, slavedriving legislators, who have so basely and unpatriotically neglected the interests of their poor white constituents and bargained away the rights of posterity. Notwithstanding the fact that the white nonslaveholders of the South, are in the majority, as five to one, they have never yet had any part or lot in framing the laws under which they live. There is no legislation except for the benefit of slavery, and slaveholders. As a general rule, poor white persons are regarded with less esteem and attention than negroes, and though the condition of the latter is wretched beyond description, vast numbers of the former are infinitely worse off. A cunningly devised mockery of freedom is guarantied to them, and that is all. To all intents and purposes they are disfranchised, and outlawed, and the only privilege extended to them, is a shallow and circumscribed participation in the political movements that usher slaveholders into office.

We have not breathed away seven and twenty years in the South, without becoming acquainted with the demagogical manoeuverings of the oligarchy. Their intrigues and tricks of leg-erdemain are as familiar to us as household words; in vain might the world be ransacked for a more precious junto of flatterers and cajolers, It is amusing to ignorance, amazing to credulity, and insulting to intelligence, to hear them in their blattering efforts to mystify and pervert the sacred principles of liberty, and turn the curse of slavery into a blessing. To the illiterate poor whites—made poor and ignorant by the system of slavery—they hold out the idea that slavery is the very bulwark of our liberties, and the foundation of American independence! For hours at a time, day after day, will they expatiate upon the inexpressible beauties and excellencies of this great, *free* and *independent* nation; and finally, with the most extravagant gesticulations and rhetorical flourishes, conclude their nonsensical ravings, by attributing all the glory and prosperity of the country, from Maine to Texas, and from Georgia to California, to the "invaluable institutions of the South!" With what patience we could command, we have frequently listened to the incoherent and truth-murdering declamations of these champions of slavery, and, in the absence of a more politic method of giving vent to our disgust and indignation, have involuntarily bit our lips into blisters.

The lords of the lash are not only absolute masters of the blacks, who are bought and sold, and driven about like so many cattle, but they are also the oracles and arbiters of all non-slaveholding whites, whose freedom is merely nominal, and whose unparalleled illiteracy and degradation is purposely and fiendishly perpetuated. How little the "poor white trash," the great majority of the Southern people, know of the real condition of the country is, indeed, sadly astonishing. The truth is, they know nothing of public measures, and little of private affairs, except what their imperious masters, the slave-drivers, descend to tell, and that is but precious little, and even that little, always garbled and one-sided, is never told except in public harangues; for the haughty cavaliers of shack-les and handcuffs will not degrade themselves by holding private converse with those who have neither dimes nor hereditary rights in human flesh.

Whenever it pleases, and to the extent it pleases, a slaveholder to become communicative, poor whites may hear with fear and trembling, but not speak. They must be as mum as dumb brutes, and stand in awe of their august superiors, or be crushed with stern rebukes, cruel oppressions, or downright violence. If they dare to think for themselves, their thoughts must be forever concealed. The expression of any sentiment at all conflicting with the gospel of slavery, dooms them at once in the community in which they live, and then, whether willing or unwilling, they are obliged to become heroes, martyrs, or exiles. They may thirst for knowledge, but there is no Moses among them to smite it out of the rocks of Horeb. The black veil, through whose almost impenetrable meshes light seldom gleams, has long been pendent over their eyes, and there, with fiendish jeal-ousy, the slave-driving ruffians sedulously guard it. Non-slaveholdors are not only kept in igno-rance of what is transpiring at the North, but they are continually misinformed of what is going on even in the South. Never were the poorer classes of a people, and those classes so largely in the majority, and all inhabiting the same country, so basely duped, so adroitly swindled, or so damnably outraged.

It is expected that the stupid and sequacious masses, the white victims of slavery, will believe, and, as a general thing, they do believe, whatever the slaveholders tell them; and thus it is that they are cajoled into the notion that they are the freest, happiest and most intelligent people in the world, and are taught to look with prejudice and disapprobation upon every new principle or progressive movement. Thus it is that the South, woefully inert and inventionless, has lagged behind the North, and is now weltering in the cesspool of ignorance and degradation.

. . . You can goad us no further; you shall oppress us no longer; heretofore, earnestly but submissively, we have asked you to redress the more atrocious outrages which you have perpetrated against us; but what has been the invariable fate of our petitions? With scarcely a perusal, with a degree of contempt that added insult to injury, you have laid them on the table, and from thence they have been swept into the furnance of oblivion. Henceforth, Sirs, we are demandants, not suppli[c]ants. We demand our rights, nothing more, nothing less. It is for you to decide whether we are to have justice peaceably or by violence, for whatever consequences may follow, we are determined to have it one way or the other. Do you aspire to become the victims of white non-slaveholding vengeance by day, and of barbarous massacre by the negroes at night? Would you be instrumental in bringing upon yourselves, your wives, and your children, a fate too horrible to contemplate? Shall history cease to cite, as an instance of unexampled cruelty, the Massacre of St. Bartholomew, because the World—the South—shall have furnished a more direful scene of atrocity and carnage? Sirs, we would not wantonly pluck a single hair from your heads but we have endured long, we have endured much; slaves only of the most despicable class would endure more. An enumeration or classification of all the abuses, insults, wrongs, injuries, usurpations, and oppressions, to which you have subjected us, would fill a larger volume than this; it is our purpose, therefore, to speak only of those that affect us most deeply. Out of our effects your have long since overpaid yourselves for your negroes; and now, Sirs, you must emancipate them—speedily emancipate them, or we will emancipate them for you! Every non-slaveholder in the South is, or ought to be, and will be, against you. You yourselves ought to join us at once in our laudable crusade against "the mother of harlots." Slavery has polluted and impoverished your lands; freedom will restore them to their virgin purity. . . .

111. THE LINCOLN-DOUGLAS DEBATES, 1858*

In the summer and fall of 1858, incumbent Senator Stephen A. Douglas joined rival candidate Abraham Lincoln in a series of seven debates during the Illinois senatorial campaign. On October 15, 1858, they appeared for their final debate at Alton, Illinois. In his opening speech, Douglas made a stirring appeal for "popular sovereignty" as the only alternative to civil war. Lincoln, in his reply, insisted that the real issue was whether slavery was right or wrong. Believing that bondage was unacceptable, Lincoln contended that his generation must prevent the additional spread of slavery, contain the institution within its present boundaries, and eventually bring about the "ultimate extinction" of slavery. In the aftermath of the debates, Douglas won the election, but Lincoln had enhanced his national reputation as an appealing moderate Republican.

Stephen A. Douglas at Alton

It is now nearly four months since the canvass between Mr. Lincoln and myself commenced. On the 16th of June the Republican Convention assembled at Springfield and nominated Mr. Lincoln as their candidate for the United States Senate, and he, on that occasion, delivered a speech in which he laid down what he understood to be the Republican creed, and the platform on which he proposed to stand during the contest.

The principal points in the speech of Mr. Lincoln's were: First, that this Government could not endure permanently divided into Free and Slave States, as our fathers made it; that they must

*From Edwin Erle Sparks, ed., *The Lincoln-Douglas Debates of 1858*, Collections of the Illinois State Historical Library, vol. III, Lincoln Series, vol. I (Springfield: Illinois State Historical Library, 1908), 451–53, 461–65, 482–87.

all become Free or all become Slave; all become one thing, or all become the other,—otherwise this Union could not continue to exist. I give you his opinions almost in the identical language he used. His second proposition was a crusade against the Supreme Court of the United States because of the Dred Scott decision, urging as an especial reason for his opposition to that decision that it deprived the negroes of the rights and benefits of that clause in the Constitution of the United States which guarantees to the citizens of each State all the rights, privileges, and immunities of the citizens of the several States.

On the . . . 11th of July, Mr. Lincoln replied to me at Chicago, explaining at some length and reaffirming the positions which he had taken in his Springfield speech. In that Chicago speech he even went further than he had before, and uttered sentiments in regard to the negro being on an equality with the white man. ["That's so."] He adopted in support of this position the argument which Lovejoy and Codding and other Abolition lecturers had made familiar in the northern and central portions of the State; to-wit, that the Declaration of Independence having declared all men free and equal, by divine law, also that negro equality was an inalienable right, of which they could not be deprived. He insisted, in that speech, that the Declaration of Independence included the negro in the clause asserting that all men were created equal, and went so far as to say that if one man was allowed to take the position that it did not include the negro, others might take the position that it did not include other men. He said that all these distinctions between this man and that man, this race and the other race must be discarded, and we must all stand by the Declaration of Independence, declaring that all men were created equal.

The issue thus being made up between Mr. Lincoln and myself on three points, we went before the people of the State. . . .

I took up Mr. Lincoln's three propositions in my several speeches, analyzed them, and pointed out what I believed to be the radical errors contained in them. First, in regard to his doctrine that this Government was in violation of the law of God, which says that a house divided against itself cannot stand, I repudiated it as a slander upon the immortal framers of our Constitution. I then said, I have often repeated, and now again assert, that in my opinion our Government can endure forever, ["Good."] divided into Free and Slave States as our fathers made it,—each State having the right to prohibit, abolish, or sustain slavery, just as it pleases. ["Good;" "right;" and cheers.]

This Government was made upon the great basis of the sovereignty of the States, the right of each State to regulate its own domestic institutions to suit itself; and that right was conferred with the understanding and expectation that inasmuch as each locality had separate interests, each locality must have different and distinct local and domestic institutions, corresponding to its wants and interests. Our fathers knew when they made the Government that the laws and institutions which were well adapted to the Green Mountains of Vermont were unsuited to the rice plantations of South Carolina. They knew then, as well as we know now, that the laws and institutions which would be well adapted to the beautiful prairies of Illinois would not be suited to the mining regions of California. They knew that in a Republic as broad as this, having such a variety of soil, climate, and interest, there must necessarily be a corresponding variety of local laws,— the policy and institutions of each State adapted to its condition and wants. For this reason this Union was established on the right of each State to do as it pleased on the question of slavery, and every other question; and the various States were not allowed to complain of, much less interfere with, the policy of their neighbors. . . .

My friends, there never was a time when it was as important for the Democratic party, for all national men, to rally and stand together, as it is to-day. We find all sectional men giving up past differences and uniting[1] on the one question of slavery; and when we find sectional men thus uniting, we should unite to resist them and their treasonable designs. . . . It was so in 1850, when Aboli-

---

[1]Reads: "continuing" for "uniting."

tionism had even so far divided this country, North and South, as to endanger the peace of the Union; Whigs and Democrats united in establishing the Compromise Measures of that year, and restoring tranquility and good feeling. These measures passed on the joint action of the two parties. They rested on the great principle that the people of each State and each Territory should be left perfectly free to form and regulate their domestic institutions to suit themselves. You Whigs and we Democrats justified them in that principle. In 1854, when it became necessary to organize the Territories of Kansas and Nebraska, I brought forward the bill on the same principle. In the Kansas-Nebraska bill you find it declared to be the true intent and meaning of the Act not to legislate slavery into any State or Territory, nor to exclude it therefrom, but to leave the people thereof perfectly free to form and regulate their domestic institutions in their own way. ["That's so," and cheers.] I stand on that same platform in 1858 that I did in 1850, 1854, and 1856. . . .

I answer specifically if you want a further answer, and say that while under the decision of the Supreme Court, as recorded in the opinion of Chief Justice Taney slaves are property like all other property, and can be carried into any Territory of the United States the same as any other description of property, yet when you get them there they are subject to the local law of the Territory just like all other property. . . .

The whole South is rallying to the support of the doctrine that if the people of a Territory want slavery they have a right to have it, and if they do not want it, that no power on earth can force it upon them. I hold that there is no principle on earth more sacred to all the friends of freedom than that which says that no institution, no law, no constitution, should be forced on an unwilling people contrary to their wishes; and I assert that the Kansas and Nebraska bill contains that principle. It is the great principle contained in that bill. . . . I have defended it against the North and the South, and I will defend it against whoever assails it, and I will follow it wherever its logical conclusions lead me. ["So will we all," "Hurrah for Douglas."] I say to you that there is but one hope, one safety for this country, and that is to stand immovably by that principle which declares the right of each State and each Territory to decide these questions for themselves. ["Hear him, hear him."] This Government was founded on that principle, and must be administered in the same sense in which it was founded.

But the Abolition party really think that under the Declaration of Independence the negro is equal to the white man, and that negro equality is an inalienable right conferred by the Almighty, and hence that all human laws in violation of it are null and void. With such men it is no use for me to argue. I hold that the signers of the Declaration of Independence had no reference to negroes at all when they declared all men to be created equal. They did not mean negroes, nor the savage Indians, not the Fiji Islanders, nor any other barbarous race. They were speaking of white men. ["It's so," "it's so," and cheers.] They alluded to men of European birth and European descent,—to white men, and to none others,—when they declared that doctrine. ["That's the truth."] I hold that this Government was established on the white basis. It was established by white men for the benefit of white men and their posterity forever, and should be administered by white men, and none others.

But it does not follow, by any means, that merely because the negro is not a citizen, and merely because he is not our equal, that, therefore, he should be a slave. On the contrary, it does follow that we ought to extend to the negro race, and to all other dependent races, all the rights, all the privileges, and all the immunities which they can exercise consistently with the safety of society. Humanity requires that we should give them all these privileges; Christianity commands that we should extend those privileges to them. The question then arises, What are those privileges, and what is the nature and extent of them? My answer is that that is a question which each State must answer for itself. We in Illinois have decided it for ourselves. We tried slavery, kept it up for twelve years, and finding that it was not profitable, we abolished it for that reason, and became a Free State. We adopted in its stead the policy that a negro in this State shall not be a slave and shall not be a citizen. We have a right to adopt that policy. For my part, I think it is a wise and sound policy for us. You in Missouri must judge for yourselves whether it is a wise policy for you. If you choose to follow our example, very good; if you reject it, still well,—it is your business, not ours. So with Kentucky. Let Kentucky adopt a policy to suit herself. If we do not like it we will keep away from it; and if she does not like ours, let her stay at home, mind her own business, and let us alone. If the people of all the States will act on that great principle, and each State mind its own business, attend to its own affairs, take care of its own negroes, and not meddle with its neighbors, then there will be peace between the North and the South, the East and the West, throughout the whole Union. [Cheers.] . . .

Abraham Lincoln at Alton

. . . I have stated upon former occasions, and I may as well state again, what I understand to be the real issue in this controversy between Judge Douglas and myself. On the point of my wanting to make war between the Free and the Slave States, there has been no issue between us. So, too, when he assumes that I am in favor of introducing a perfect social and political equality between the white and black races. These are false issues, upon which Judge Douglas has tried to force the controversy. There is no foundation in truth for the charge that I maintain either of these propositions. The real issue in this controversy—the one pressing upon every mind—is the sentiment on the part of one class that looks upon the institution of slavery as a wrong, and of another class that does not look upon it as a wrong.

The sentiment that contemplates the institution of slavery in this country as a wrong is the sentiment of the Republican party. It is the sentiment around which all their actions, all their arguments, circle, from which all their propositions radiate. They look upon it as being a moral, social, and political wrong; and while they contemplate it as such, they nevertheless have due regard for its actual existence among us, and the difficulties of getting rid of it in any satisfactory way, and to all the constitutional obligations thrown about it. Yet, having a due regard for these, they desire a policy in regard to it that looks to its not creating any more danger. They insist that it should, as[2] far as may be, *be treated* as a wrong; and one of the methods of treating it as a wrong is to *make provision that it shall grow no larger.* [Loud applause.] They also desire a policy that looks to a peaceful end of slavery at some time, as being wrong.

These are the views they entertain in regard to it as I understand them; and all their sentiments, all their arguments and propositions, are brought into this range. I have said, and I repeat it here, that if there be a man amongst us who does not think that the institution of slavery is wrong in any one of the aspects of which I have spoken, he is misplaced, and ought not to be with us. And if there be a man amongst us who is so impatient of it as a wrong as to disregard its actual presence among us and the difficulty of getting rid of it suddenly in a satisfactory way, and to disregard the constitutional obligations thrown about it, that man is misplaced if he is on our platform. We disclaim sympathy with him in practical action. He is not placed properly with us.

On this subject of treating it as a wrong, and limiting its spread, let me say a word. Has anything ever threatened the existence of this Union save and except this very institution of slavery? What is it that we hold most dear amongst us? Our own liberty and prosperity. What has ever threatened our liberty and prosperity, save and except this institution of slavery? If this is true, how do you propose to improve the condition of things by enlarging slavery,—by spreading it out and making it bigger? You can have a wen or cancer upon your person, and not be able to cut it out, lest you bleed to death; but surely it is no way to cure it, to engraft it and spread it over your whole body. That is no proper way of treating what you regard a wrong. You see this peaceful way of dealing with it as a wrong,—restricting the spread of it, and not allowing it to go into new countries

---

[2]Reads: "so" for "as."

where it has not already existed. That is the peaceful way, the old-fashioned way, the way in which the fathers themselves set us the example.

On the other hand, I have said there is a sentiment which treats it as **not** being wrong. That is the Democratic sentiment of this day. I do not mean to say that every man who stands within that range positively asserts that it is right. That class will include all who positively assert that it is right, and all who, like Judge Douglas, treat it as indifferent and do not say it is either right or wrong. These two classes of men fall within the general class of those who do not look upon it as a wrong. . . . The Democratic policy in regard to that institution will not tolerate the merest breath, the slightest hint, of the least degree of wrong about it.

Try it by some of Judge Douglas's arguments. He says he "don't care whether it is voted up or voted down" in the Territories. I do not care myself, in dealing with that expression, whether it is intended to be expressive of his individual sentiments on the subject, or only of the national policy he desires to have established. It is alike valuable for my purpose. Any man can say that, who does not see anything wrong in slavery; but no man can logically say it who does see a wrong in it, because no man can logically say he don't care whether a wrong is voted up or voted down. He may say he don't care whether an indifferent thing is voted up or down; but he must logically have a choice between a right thing and a wrong thing. He contends that whatever community wants slaves has [a] right to have them. So they have, if it is not a wrong. But if it is a wrong, he cannot say people have a right to do wrong. He says that upon the score of equality, slaves should be allowed to go into a new Territory, like other property. This is strictly logical if there is no difference between it and other property. If it and other property are equal, his argument is entirely logical. But if you insist that one is wrong and the other right, there is no use to institute a comparison between right and wrong. You may turn over everything in the Democratic policy from beginning to end, whether in the shape it takes on the statute book, in the shape it takes in the Dred Scott decision, in the shape it takes in conversation, or the shape it takes in short maxim-like arguments,—it everywhere carefully excludes the idea that there is anything wrong in it.

That is the real issue. That is the issue that will continue in this country when these poor tongues of Judge Douglas and myself shall be silent. It is the eternal struggle between these two principles—right and wrong—throughout the world. They are the two principles that have stood face to face from the beginning of time, and will ever continue to struggle. The one is the common right of humanity, and the other the "divine right of kings." It is the same principle in whatever shape it develops itself. It is the same spirit that says, "You work and toil and earn bread, and I'll eat it." [Loud applause.] No matter in what shape it comes, whether from the mouth of a king who seeks to bestride the people of his own nation and live by the fruit of their labor, or from one race of men as an apology for enslaving another race, it is the same tyrannical principle. . . .

I was glad to express my gratitude at Quincy, and I re-express it here to Judge Douglas,—*that he looks to no end of the institution of slavery.* That will help the people to see where the struggle really is. It will hereafter place with us all men who really do wish the wrong may have an end. And whenever we can get rid of the fog which obscures the real question, when we can get Judge Douglas and his friends to avow a policy looking to its perpetuation,—we can get them out from among that class of men and bring them to the side of those who treat it as a wrong. Then there will soon be an end of it, and that distinctly made, and all extraneous matter thrown out so that men can fairly see the real difference between the parties, this controversy will soon be settled, and it will be done peaceably too. There will be no war, no violence. . . .

I understand I have ten minutes yet. I will employ it in saying something about this argument Judge Douglas uses, while he sustains the Dred Scott decision, that the people of the Territories can still somehow exclude slavery. The first thing I ask attention to is the fact that Judge Douglas constantly said, before the decision, that whether they could or not, *was a question for the Supreme Court.* [Cheers.] But after the court has made the decision he virtually says it is **not** a question for the Supreme Court, but for the people. [Renewed applause.] And how is it he tells us they can exclude it? He says it needs "police regulations," and that admits of "unfriendly legislation." Although it is a right established by the Constitution of the United States to take a slave into a Territory of the United States and hold him as property, yet unless the Territorial Legislature will give friendly legislation, and, more especially, if they adopt unfriendly legislation, they can practically exclude him.

Now, without meeting this proposition as a matter of fact, I pass to consider the real constitutional obligation. Let me take the gentleman who looks me in the face before me, and let us suppose that he is a member of the Territorial Legislature. The first thing he will do will be to swear that he will support the Constitution of the United States. [Great applause.] His neighbor by his side in the Territory has slaves and needs Territorial legislation to enable him to enjoy that constitutional right. Can he withhold the legislation which his neighbor needs for the enjoyment of a right which is fixed in his favor in the Constitution of the United States which he has sworn to support? Can he withhold it without violating his oath? And more especially, can he pass unfriendly legislation to violate his oath?

Why, this is a *monstrous* sort of talk about the Constitution of the United States! [Great applause.] *There has never been as outlandish or lawless a doctrine from the mouth of any respectable man on earth.* [Tremendous cheers.] I do not believe it is a constitutional right to hold slaves in a Territory of the United States. I believe the decision was improperly made and I go for reversing it. Judge Douglas is furious against those who go for reversing a decision. But he is for legislating it out of all force while the law itself stands. I repeat that there has never been so monstrous a doctrine uttered from the mouth of a respectable man. [Loud cheers.] . . .

112. JOHN BROWN'S STATEMENT TO THE COURT, 1859*

The North and the South moved further and further apart during the 1850s, and John Brown's raid on Harpers Ferry provided an alarming end to the violent decade. Brown apparently planned to obtain weapons that could be used in an insurrection that would destroy slavery. He failed. Federal troops captured him, authorities put him on trial for treason, and the judge sentenced him to be hanged. In an eloquent statement to the court, presented below, Brown explained his mission. Northerners embraced the remarks as a martyr's final, compassionate words. Southerners viewed Brown differently, and he symbolized the threat that northern power posed to southern liberties. Throughout the 1850s, emotions had been inflamed, blood had been spilled, lives had been lost. Americans would elect a president in 1860 hoping that the crisis could be averted, but fearing that it could not.

I have, may it please the Court, a few words to say. In the first place, I deny everything but what I have all along admitted, of a design on my part to free slaves. I intended certainly to have made a clean thing of that matter, as I did last winter when I went into Missouri, and there took slaves without the snapping of a gun on either side, moving them through the country, and finally leaving them in Canada. I designed to have done the same thing again on a larger scale. That was all I intended to do. I never did intend murder or treason, or the destruction of property, or to excite or incite the slaves to rebellion, or to make insurrection. I have another objection, and that is that it is unjust that I should suffer such a penalty. Had I interfered in the manner which I admit, and which I admit has been fairly proved—for I admire the truthfulness and candor of the greater portion of the witnesses who have testified in this case—had I so interfered in behalf of the rich, the powerful, the intelligent, the so-called great, or in behalf of any of their friends, either father,

*From *The Life, Trial, and Execution of Captain John Brown* (New York: Robert M. De Witt, 1859), 94–95.

mother, brother, sister, wife, children, or any of that class, and suffered and sacrificed what I have in this interference, it would have been all right, and every man in this Court would have deemed it an act worthy of reward rather than punishment. This Court acknowledges, too, as I suppose, the validity of the law of God. I see a book kissed, which I suppose to be the Bible, or at least the New Testament, which teaches me that all things whatsoever I would that men should do to me, I should do even so to them. I endeavored to act up to that instruction. I say I am yet too young to understand that God is any respecter of persons. I believe to have interfered as I have done, as I have always freely admitted I have done in behalf of His despised poor, is no wrong, but right. Now, if it is deemed necessary that I should forfeit my life for the furtherance of the ends of justice, and mingle my blood further with the blood of my children, and with the blood of millions in this slave country whose rights are disregarded by wicked, cruel, and unjust enactments, I say let it be done. Let me say one word further. I feel entirely satisfied with the treatment I have received on my trial. Considering all the circumstances, it has been more generous than I expected. But I feel no consciousness of guilt. I have stated from the first what is my intention, and what was not. I never had any design against the liberty of any person, nor any disposition to commit treason or excite slaves to rebel or make any general insurrection. I never encouraged any man to do so, but always discouraged any idea of that kind. Let me say also in regard to the statements by some of those who were connected with me, I fear it has been stated by some of them that I have induced them to join me, but the contrary is true. I do not say this to injure them, but as regretting their weakness. Not one but joind me of his own accord, and the greater part at their own expense. A number of them I never saw, and never had a word of conversation with till the day they came to me, and that was for the purpose I have stated. Now I am done.

Discussion

1. Why do you think Samuel Morse expressed such fear of the power of the Pope, the Jesuits, and the St. Leopold Foundation? How and why do you think he saw them as a threat to liberty and equality? How are his fears similar to or different from the rhetoric of revolutionary Americans? How might Republicans have appealed to anti-Catholic nativists to turn their anger against southerners?

2. What did Charles Sumner say that made Preston Brooks so angry? How might Brooks have justified his attack on Sumner? Do you agree with Brooks' contention that the House of Representatives did not have the power to punish him? Why or why not? How might each of the two men have argued that the other threatened liberty?

3. How did Chief Justice Roger B. Taney express concepts of liberty and equality in his Supreme Court opinion concerning Dred Scott? What do you think he believed about the power of the national government? How might the Republicans have dismissed his comments and insisted the decision was really a pro-slavery statement?

4. Based on the Lincoln-Douglas debates selection, how did each speaker view the concepts of liberty and equality, the Dred Scott case, the expansion and morality of slavery, and the future of slavery?

5. John Brown insisted that he did not feel any guilt for his raid on Harpers Ferry. Why might he have felt that way? What are the implications for power and liberty of such a stance? The power of the state executed John Brown, but southerners still feared for their liberties. Why do you think they believed that the government could not or would not protect slavery?

6. How do the selections by Hinton Helper and George Fitzhugh address issues of liberty, equality, and power?

CHAPTER 15

Secession and Civil War, 1860–1862

This cartoon, drawn by a John Bell supporter, graphically illustrates the feared dissolution of the Union. On the left, Lincoln and Douglas fight over the United States. In the center Breckinridge rips away the South, while Bell tries futilely to paste the nation together again.

With the election of 1860, the acrimonious debate over slavery became a bitter war over states' rights and secession. The fundamental question was the nature of the Union under the Constitution. The South claimed that the compact allowed states to secede as an expression of their sovereignty, and, despite the reluctance of many southerners to leave the Union, seven states withdrew by the time Abraham Lincoln became president in March of 1861. Lincoln insisted that no such right of secession existed, and his commitment to the Union led to a crisis at Fort Sumter that brought on war. Once the fighting began, he used the full force of the government to preserve the nation. Southerners, too, fought with all their will. Ironically, each side declared that the other threatened liberty. The South feared that an assertion of federal power would overturn slavery and thereby destroy the one institution that guaranteed equality for white Americans. Lincoln insisted that liberty could only be preserved by a republican government that represented the will of the people. If the southern states left the Union because of discontent with an election, the American experiment in self-government would have failed and liberty would be denied to all.

113. A SOUTHERNER SPEAKS AGAINST SECESSION, 1861*

In the following speech presented to the Georgia Secession Convention, Alexander H. Stephens urged delegates to move slowly on a decision so monumental as disunion. Like many southerners, however, Stephens swore to support secession wholeheartedly if his state withdrew from the Union. Georgia rejected his counsel and seceded. Stephens honored his promise by becoming the vice president of the Confederacy.

It is well known that my judgment is against secession for existing causes. I have not lost hope of securing our rights in the Union and under the Constitution. My judgment on this point is as unshaken as it was when the Convention was called. I do not now intend to go into my arguments on the subject. No good could be effected by it. That was fully considered in the late canvass, and I doubt not every delegate's mind is made up on the question. I have thought, and still think, that we should not take this extreme step before some positive aggression upon our rights by the General Government, which may never occur; or until we fail, after effort made, to get a faithful performance of their Constitutional obligations, on the part of those Confederate States which now stand so derelict in their plighted faith. I have been, and am still opposed to Secession as a remedy against anticipated aggressions on the part of the Federal Executive, or Congress. I have held, and do now hold, that the point of resistance should be the point of aggression.

Pardon me, Mr. President, for trespassing on your time but for a moment longer. I have ever believed, and do now believe, that it is to the interest of all the States to be and remain united

*From Alexander H. Stephens, *A Constitutional View of the Late War Between the States . . .*, 2 vols. (Philadelphia: National Publishing Company, 1870), II:305–07.

under the Constitution of the United States, with a faithful performance by each of all its constitutional obligations. If the Union could be maintained on this basis, and on these principles, I think it would be the best for the security, the liberty, happiness, and common prosperity of all. I do further feel confident, if Georgia would now stand firm, and unite with the Border States, as they are called, in an effort to obtain a redress of these grievances on the part of some of their Northern Confederates, whereof they have such just cause to complain, that complete success would be granted. In this opinion I may be mistaken, but I feel almost as confident of it as I do of my existence. Hence, if upon this test vote, which I trust will be made on the motion pending, to refer both the propositions before us to a committee of twenty-one, a majority shall vote to commit them, then I shall do all I can to perfect the plan of a united Southern co-operation, submitted by the honorable delegate from Jefferson, and put it in such a shape as will, in the opinion of the Convention, best secure its object. That object, as I understand it, does not look to Secession by the 16th of February, or the 4th of March, if redress should not be obtained by that time. In my opinion, it cannot be obtained by the 16th of February, or even the 4th of March. But by the 16th of February we can see whether the Border States and other non-seceding Southern States will respond to our call for the proposed Congress or Convention at Atlanta. If they do, as I trust they may, then that body, so composed of representatives, or delegates, or commissioners as contemplated, from the whole of the slaveholding States, could, and would I doubt not, adopt either our plan or some other, which would fully secure our rights with ample guarantees, and thus preserve and maintain the ultimate peace and Union of the States. Whatever plan of peaceful adjustment might be adopted by such a Congress, I feel confident would be acceded to by the people of every Northern State. This would not be done in a month, or two months, or perhaps short of twelve months, or even longer. Time would necessarily have to be allowed for a consideration of the question submitted to the people of the Northern States, and for their deliberate action on them in view of all their interests, present, and future. How long a time should be allowed, would be a proper question for that Congress to determine. Meanwhile, this Convention could continue its existence, by adjourning over to hear and decide upon the ultimate result of this patriotic effort.

My judgment, as is well known, is against the policy of immediate Secession for any existing causes. It cannot receive the sanction of my vote; but if the judgment of a majority of this Convention, embodying as it does the Sovereignty of Georgia, be against mine; if a majority of the delegates in this Convention shall, by their votes, dissolve the Compact of the Union which has now connected her so long with her Confederate States, and to which I have been so ardently attached, and have made such efforts to continue and perpetuate upon the principles on which it was founded, I shall bow in submission to that decision.

114. A SOUTHERNER SPEAKS FOR SECESSION, 1861*

*O*pponents to secession, such as Alexander Stephens, could only advise moderation and offer vague promises of a resolution. Many southerners believed that by 1861 they had already shown abundant patience. They understood, as had their forefathers, that power often threatened liberty. They, too, feared the forces that could conspire to destroy their rights, and they saw the Republican electoral victory as such a conspiracy. In a speech to his colleagues, U.S. Senator from Georgia Robert Toombs presented the concerns that he and other secessionists had. Despite the Dred Scott case, President Lincoln and Republican Congressmen had vowed to prohibit the expansion of slavery. To Toombs, the Republican insistence on ignoring the Supreme Court decision was an unconstitutional usurpation of power that justified leaving the Union.

---

*From *The Congressional Globe*, 36th Congress, 2nd Session, vol. XXX, pt. 2 (1861), 269.

Senators, the Constitution is a compact. It contains all our obligations and duties of the Federal Government. I am content, and have ever been content, to sustain it. While I doubt its perfection; while I do not believe it was a good compact; and while I never saw the day that I would have voted for it as a proposition *de novo*, yet I am bound to it by oath and by that common prudence which would induce men to abide by established forms, rather than to rush into unknown dangers. I have given to it, and intend to give to it, unfaltering support and allegiance; but I choose to put that allegiance on the true ground, not on the false idea that anybody's blood was shed for it. I say that the Constitution is the whole compact. All the obligations, all the chains that fetter the limbs of my people, are nominated in the bond, and they wisely excluded any conclusion against them, by declaring that the powers not granted by the Constitution to the United States, or forbidden by it to the States, belonged to the States respectively or the people. Now I will try it by that standard; I will subject it to that test. The law of nature, the law of justice, would say—and it is so expounded by the publicists—that equal rights in the common property shall be enjoyed. Even in a monarchy the king cannot prevent the subjects from enjoying equality in the disposition of the public property. Even in a despotic Government this principle is recognized. It was the blood and money of the whole people (says the learned Grotius, and say all the publicists) which acquired the public property, and therefore it is not the property of the sovereign. This right of equality being, then, according to justice and natural equity, a right belonging to all States, when did we give it up? You say Congress has a right to pass rules and regulations concerning the Territory and other property of the United States. Very well. Does that exclude those whose blood and money paid for it? Does "dispose of" mean to rob the rightful owners? You must show a better title than that, or a better sword than we have.

But, you say, try the right. I agree to it. But how? By our judgment? No, not until the last resort. What then; by yours? No, not until the same time. How then try it? The South has always said by the Supreme Court. But that is in our favor, and Lincoln says he will not stand that judgment. Then each much judge for himself of the mode and manner of redress. But you deny us that privilege, and finally reduce us to accepting your judgment. We decline it. You say you will enforce it by executing laws; that means your judgment of what the laws ought to be. Perhaps you will have a good time of executing that judgment. The Senator from Kentucky comes to your aid, and says he can find no constitutional right of secession. Perhaps not; but the Constitution is not the place to look for State rights. If that right belongs to the independent States, and they did not cede it to the Federal Government, it is reserved to the States, or to the people. Ask your new commander where he gets your right to judge for us. Is it in the bond?

The northern doctrine was, many years ago, that the Supreme Court was the judge. That was the doctrine in 1800. They denounced Madison for the report of 1799, on the Virginia resolutions; they denounced Jefferson for framing the Kentucky resolutions, because they were presumed to impugn the decisions of the Supreme Court of the United States; and they declared that that court was made, by the Constitution, the ultimate and supreme arbiter. That was the universal judgment—the declaration of every free State in this Union, in answer to the Virginia resolutions of 1798, or of all who did answer, even including the State of Delaware, then under Federal control.

The Supreme Court have decided that, by the Constitution, we have a right to go to the Territories and be protected there with our property. You say, we cannot decide the compact for ourselves. Well, can the Supreme Court decide it for us? Mr. Lincoln says he does not care what the Supreme Court decides, he will turn us out anyway. He says this in the debate with the honorable Senator from Illinois, [Mr. Douglas.] [.] I have it before me. He said he would vote against the decision of the Supreme Court. Then you do not accept the arbiter. You will not take my construction; you will not take the Supreme Court as an arbiter; you will not take the treaties under Jefferson and Madison; you will not take the opinion of Madison upon the very question of prohibition in 1820. You will take nothing but your own judgment; that is, you not only judge for yourselves, not only discard the court, discard our construction, discard the practice of the Government, but you will drive us out, simply because you will it. Come and do it! You have sapped the foundations of society; you have destroyed almost all hope of peace. In a compact where there is no common arbiter, where the parties finally decide for themselves, the sword alone at last becomes the real, if not the constitutional, arbiter. Your party says that you will not take the decision of the Supreme Court. You said so at Chicago; you said so in committee; every man of you in both Houses says so. What are you going to do? You say **we shall submit to your construction.** We shall do it, if you can make us; but not otherwise, or in any other manner. That is settled. You may call it secession, or you may call it revolution; but there is a big fact standing before you—that fact is, freemen with arms in their hands. The cry of the Union will not disperse them; we have passed that point; they demand equal rights; you had better heed the demand. . . .

115. TEXANS ISSUE A DECLARATION OF THE CAUSES FOR SECESSION, 1861*

*T*he 1860 election of Abraham Lincoln to the presidency led many Southern "fire-eaters" to call for secession. Before Lincoln's inauguration on March 4, 1861, seven southern states withdrew from the United States. In Texas, secessionists overcame the strong opposition of Governor Sam Houston and called for a convention that met in Austin on January 28, 1861. Within a few days delegates voted decisively—166 to 8—for secession, but left final approval to a referendum scheduled on February 23. To outline their reasoning and to build public support for their actions, the convention passed the following declaration on February 2, 1861.

A declaration of the causes which impel the State of Texas to secede from the Federal Union.

The government of the United States, by certain joint resolutions, bearing date the 1st day of March, in the year A. D. 1845, proposed to the Republic of Texas, then *a free, sovereign and independent nation*, the annexation of the latter to the former, as one of the co-equal States thereof,

The people of Texas, by deputies in convention assembled, on the fourth day of July of the same year, assented to and accepted said proposals and formed a constitution for the proposed State, upon which on the 29th day of December in the same year, said State was formally admitted into the Confederated Union.

Texas abandoned her separate national existence and consented to become one of the Confederated States to promote her welfare, insure domestic tranquility and secure more substantially the blessings of peace and liberty to her people. She was received into the confederacy with her own constitution, under the guarantee of the federal constitution and the compact of annexation, that she should enjoy these blessings. She was received as a commonwealth holding, maintaining and protecting the institution known as negro slavery—the servitude of the African to the white race within her limits—a relation that had existed from the first settlement of her wilderness by the white race, and which her people intended should exist in all future time. Her institutions and geographical position established the strongest ties between her and other slave-holding States of the confederacy. Those ties have been strengthened by association. But what has been the course of the government of the United States, and of the people and authorities of the non-slave-holding States, since our connection with them?

---

*From *Journal of the Secession Convention of Texas, 1861*, ed. Ernest W. Winkler (Austin: Austin Printing Company, 1912), 61–65.

The controlling majority of the Federal Government, under various pretences and disguises, has so administered the same as to exclude the citizens of the Southern States, unless under odious and unconstitutional restrictions, from all the immense territory owned in common by all the States on the Pacific Ocean, for the avowed purpose of acquiring sufficient power in the common government to use it as a means of destroying the institutions of Texas and her sister slaveholding States.

By the disloyalty of the Northern States and their citizens and the imbecility of the Federal Government, infamous combinations of incendiaries and outlaws have been permitted in those States and the common territory of Kansas to trample upon the federal laws, to war upon the lives and property of Southern citizens in that territory, and finally, by violence and mob law, to usurp the possession of the same as exclusively the property of the Northern States.

The Federal Government, while but partially under the control of these our unnatural and sectional enemies, has for years almost entirely failed to protect the lives and property of the people of Texas against the Indian savages on our border, and more recently against the murderous forays of banditti from the neighboring territory of Mexico; and when our State government has expended large amounts for such purpose, the Federal Government has refused reimbursement therefor, thus rendering our condition more insecure and harrassing than it was during the existence of the Republic of Texas.

These and other wrongs we have patiently borne in the vain hope that a returning sense of justice and humanity would induce a different course of administration.

When we advert to the course of individual non-slave-holding States, and that a majority of their citizens, our grievances assume far greater magnitude.

The States of Maine, Vermont, New Hampshire, Connecticut, Rhode Island, Massachusetts, New York, Pennsylvania, Ohio, Wisconsin, Michigan and Iowa, by solemn legislative enactments, have deliberately, directly or indirectly violated the 3rd clause of the 2nd section of the 4th article of the federal constitution, and laws passed inpursuance thereof; thereby annulling a material provision of the compact, designed by its framers to perpetuate amity between the members of the confederacy and to secure the rights of the slave-holding States in their domestic institutions—a provision founded in justice and wisdom, and without the enforcement of which the compact fails to accomplish the object of its creation. Some of those States have imposed high fines and degrading penalties upon any of their citizens or officers who may carry out in good faith that provision of the compact, or the federal laws enacted in accordance therewith.

In all the non-slave-holding States, in violation of that good faith and comity which should exist between entirely distinct nations, the people have formed themselves into a great sectional party, now strong enough in numbers to control the affairs of each of those States, based upon the unnatural feeling of hostility to these Southern States and their beneficent and patriarchal system of African slavery, proclaiming the debasing doctrine of the equality of all men, irrespective of race or color—a doctrine at war with nature, in opposition to the experience of mankind, and in violation of the plainest revelations of the Divine Law. They demand the abolition of negro slavery throughout the confederacy, the recognition of political equality between the white and the negro races, and avow their determination to press on their crusade against us, so long as a negro slave remains in these States.

For years past this abolition organization has been actively sowing the seeds of discord through the Union, and has rendered the federal congress the arena for spreading firebrands and hatred between the slave-holding and non-slave-holding States.

By consolidating their strength, they have placed the slave-holding, States in a hopeless minority in the federal congress, and rendered representation of no avail in protecting Southern rights against their exactions and encroachments.

They have proclaimed, and at the ballot box sustained, the revolutionary doctrine that there is a "higher law" than the constitution and laws of our Federal Union, and virtually that they will disregard their oaths and trample upon our rights.

They have for years past encouraged and sustained lawless organizations to steal our slaves and prevent their recapture, and have repeatedly murdered Southern citizens while lawfully seeking their rendition.

They have invaded Southern soil and murdered unoffending citizens, and through the press their leading men and a fanatical pulpit have bestowed praise upon the actors and assassins in these crimes, while the governors of several of their States have refused to deliver parties implicated and indicted for participation in such offences, upon the legal demands of the States aggrieved.

They have, through the mails and hired emissaries, sent seditious pamphlets and papers among us to stir up servile insurrection and bring blood and carnage to our firesides.

They have sent hired emissaries among us to burn our towns and distribute arms and poison to our slaves for the same purpose.

They have impoverished the slave-holding States by unequal and partial legislation, thereby enriching themselves by draining our substance.

They have refused to vote appropriations for protecting Texas against ruthless savages, for the sole reason that she is a slave-holding State.

And, finally, by the combined sectional vote of the seventeen nonslave-holding States, they have elected as president and vice-president of the whole confederacy two men whose chief claims to such high positions are their approval of these long continued wrongs, and their pledges to continue them to the final consummation of these schemes for the ruin of the slave-holding States.

In view of these and many other facts, it is meet that our own views should be distinctly proclaimed.

We hold as undeniable truths that the governments of the various States, and of the confederacy itself, were established exclusively by the white race, for themselves and their posterity; that the African race had no agency in their establishment; that they were rightfully held, and regarded as an inferior and dependent race, and in that condition only could their existence in this country be rendered beneficial or tolerable.

That in this free government *all white men are and of right ought to be entitled to equal civil and political rights;* that the servitude of the African race, as existing in these States, is mutually beneficial to both bond and free, and is abundantly authorized and justified by the experience of mankind, and the revealed will of the Almighty Creator, as recognized by all Christian nations; while the destruction of the existing relations between the two races, as advocated by our sectional enemies, would bring inevitable calamities upon both and desolation upon the fifteen slave-holding States.

By the secession of six of the slave-holding States, and the certainty that others will speedily do likewise, Texas has no alternative but remain in an isolated connection with the North, or unite her destinies with the South.

For these and other reasons, solemnly asserting that the federal constitution has been violated and virtually abrogated by the several States named, seeing that the federal government is now passing under the control of our enemies to be diverted from the exalted objects of its creation to those of oppression and wrong, and realizing that our own State can no longer look for protection, but to God and her own sons—We the delegates of the people of Texas, in Convention assembled, have passed an ordinance dissolving all political connection with the government of the United States of America and the people thereof and confidently appeal to the intelligence and patriotism of the freemen of Texas to ratify the same at the ballot box, on the 23rd day of the present month.

Adapoted in Convention on the 2nd day of Feby, in the year of our Lord one thousand eight hundred and sixty-one and of the independence of Texas the twenty-fifth.

116. THE SUMTER CRISIS, 1861*

Upon his inauguration, Abraham Lincoln faced the difficult task of determining the fate of Fort Sumter. He asked the advice of his cabinet members, and most of them, like Secretary of the Navy Gideon Welles, urged the president not to reinforce or resupply the post. The majority of the administration proved reluctant to use the power of the government in a way that would turn secession into war. Lincoln, as became typical of his leadership, listened to the various viewpoints and then made his own decision.

In answer to your inquiry of this date, I take it for granted that Fort Sumter cannot be provisioned except by force, and assuming that it is possible to be done by force, is it wise to make the attempt?

The question has two aspects—one military, the other political. The military gentlemen who have been consulted, as well as the officers at the fort, represent that it would be unwise to attempt to succor the garrison under existing circumstance, and I am not disposed to controvert their opinions.

But a plan has been submitted by a gentleman of undoubted courage and intelligence,—not of the army or navy,—to run in supplies by steam tugs, to be chartered in New York. It is admitted to be a hazardous scheme, which, if successful, is likely to be attended with some loss of life and the total destruction of the boats. The force which would constitute the expedition, if undertaken, as well as the officer in command, would not, if I rightly understand the proposition, be of the army or navy. It is proposed to aid and carry out the enterprise by an armed ship at the mouth of the harbor and beyond the range of the shore batteries, which is to drive in the armed boats of the enemy beyond Fort Sumter. But suppose these armed boats of the enemy refuse to go into the inner harbor, as I think they will refuse, and shall station themselves between Sumter and the ship for the express purpose of intercepting your boats, how can you prevent them from taking that station and capturing the tugs? There can be but one way, and that is by opening fire upon them from Sumter, or the ship, or perhaps both. If this is done, will it not be claimed that aggressive war has been commenced by us upon the State and its citizens in their own harbor? It may be possible to provision Fort Sumter by the volunteer expedition, aided by the guns of Sumter and the ship—the military gentlemen admit its possibility, but they question the wisdom of the enterprise in its military aspect, and I would not impeach their conclusion.

In a political view I entertain doubts of the wisdom of the measure, when the condition of the public mind in different sections of the country, and the peculiar exigency of affairs, are considered. Notwithstanding the hostile attitude of South Carolina, and her long and expensive preparations, there is a prevailing belief that there will be no actual collision. An impression has gone abroad that Sumter is to be evacuated, and the shock caused by that announcement has done its work. The public mind is becoming tranquilized under it, and will become fully reconciled to it when the causes which have led to that necessity shall have been made public and are rightly understood. They are attributable to no act of those who now administer the government.

By sending or attempting to send provisions into Sumter, will not war be precipitated? It may be impossible to escape it under any course of policy that may be pursued, but I am not prepared to advise a course that would provoke hostilities. It does not appear to me that the dignity, strength, or character of the government will be promoted by an attempt to provision Sumter in the manner proposed, even should it succeed, while a failure would be attended with untold disaster.

I do not, therefore, under all the circumstances, think it wise to attempt to provision Fort Sumter.

---

*From Gideon Welles to Abraham Lincoln, March 15, 1861, in *Complete Works of Abraham Lincoln*, ed. John G. Nicolay and John Hay, 12 vols. (New York: Lamb Publishing Company, 1905), vi:208–10.

117. FORT SUMTER UNDER ATTACK, 1861*

On April 6, 1861, President Lincoln notified the South Carolina governor of his intention to resupply Fort Sumter "with provisions only"; no reinforcements or ammunition would be sent in unless Confederate forces attacked the unarmed relief ships. With this statement, he had adroitly shifted the decision for peace or war to Confederate officials. Early on April 12, before any supply ships could reach the isolated outpost, booming Charleston shore batteries signaled the response—the South would fight for their liberty. In the following diary excerpt, Mary Boykin Chesnut, wife of a prominent South Carolina politician, describes Charleston society in the days surrounding the attack on Fort Sumter.

. . . [April 8th] To-day things seem to have settled down a little. One can but hope still. Lincoln, or Seward, has made such silly advances and then far sillier drawings back. There may be a chance for peace after all. Things are happening so fast. . . .

Three hours ago we were quickly packing to go home. The Convention has adjourned. Now [my husband] tells me the attack on Fort Sumter may begin to-night; depends upon Anderson and the fleet outside. . . .

To-day at dinner there was no allusion to things as they stand in the Charleston Harbor. There was an undercurrent of intense excitement. There could not have been a more brilliant circle. In addition to our usual quartette (Judge Withers, Langdon, Cheves, and Trescott), our two ex-Governors dined with us, Means and Manning. These men all talked so delightfully. For once in my life I listened. That over, business began in earnest. Governor Means had rummaged a sword and red sash from somewhere and brought it for Colonel Chestnut, who had gone to demand the surrender of Fort Sumter. And now patience—we must wait.

Why did that green goose Anderson go into Fort Sumter? Then everything began to go wrong. Now they have intercepted a letter from him urging them to let him surrender. He paints the horrors likely to ensue if they will not. He ought to have thought of all that before he put his head in the hole.

April 12th.—Anderson will not capitulate. Yesterday's was the merriest, maddest dinner we have had yet. Men were audaciously wise and witty. We had an unspoken foreboding that it was to be our last pleasant meeting. Mr. Miles dined with us to-day. Mrs. Henry King rushed in saying, "The news, I come for the latest news. All the men of the King family are on the Island," of which fact she seemed proud.

While she was here our peace negotiator, or envoy, came in—that is, Mr. Chesnut returned. His interview with Colonel Anderson had been deeply interesting, but Mr. Chesnut was not inclined to be communicative. He wanted his dinner. He felt for Anderson and had telegraphed to President Davis for instructions—what answer to give Anderson, etc. He has now gone back to Fort Sumter with additional instructions. . . .

I do not pretend to go to sleep. How can I? If Anderson does not accept terms at four, the orders are, he shall be fired upon. I count four, St. Michael's bells chime out and I begin to hope. At half-past four the heavy booming of a cannon. I sprang out of bed, and on my knees prostrate I prayed as I never prayed before.

There was a sound of stir all over the house, pattering of feet in the corridors. All seemed hurrying one way. I put on my double-gown and a shawl and went, too. It was to the housetop. The shells were bursting. In the dark I heard a man say, "Waste of ammunition." I knew my husband was rowing about in a boat somewhere in that dark bay, and that the shells were roofing it over, bursting toward the fort. If Anderson was obstinate, Colonel Chesnut was to order the fort on one

---

*From Mary Boykin Chesnut, *A Diary from Dixie*, ed. by Isabella D. Martin and Myrta L. Avary (New York: D. Appleton & Company, 1905), 33–36, 38–40.

side to open fire. Certainly fire had begun. The regular roar of the cannon, there it was. And who could tell what each volley accomplished of death and destruction?

The women were wild there on the housetop. Prayers came from the women and imprecations from the men. And then a shell would light up the scene. To-night they say the forces are to attempt to land. We watched up there, and everybody wondered that Fort Sumter did not fire a shot. . . .

April 13th.—Nobody has been hurt after all. How gay we were last night. Reaction after the dread of all the slaughter we thought those dreadful cannon were making. Not even a battery the worse for wear. Fort Sumter has been on fire. Anderson has not yet silenced any of our guns. So the aides, still with swords and red sashes by way of uniform, tell us. But the sound of those guns makes regular meals impossible. None of us go to table. Tea-trays pervade the corridors going everywhere. Some of the anxious hearts lie on their beds and moan in solitary misery. Mrs. Wigfall and I solace ourselves with tea in my room. These women have all a satisfying faith. "God is on our side," they say. When we are shut in Mrs. Wigfall and I ask "Why?" "Of course, He hates the Yankees, we are told. You'll think that well of Him."

Not by one word or look can we detect any change in the demeanor of these negro servants. Lawrence sits at our door, sleepy and respectful, and profoundly indifferent. So are they all, but they carry it too far. You could not tell that they even heard the awful roar going on in the bay, though it has been dinning in their ears night and day. People talk before them as if they were chairs and tables. They make no sign. Are they stolidly stupid? or wiser than we are; silent and strong, biding their time?

April 15th.—I did not know that one could live such days of excitement. Some one called: "Come out! There is a crowd coming." A mob it was, indeed, but it was headed by Colonels Chesnut and Manning. The crowd was shouting and showing these two as messengers of good news. They were escorted to Beauregard's headquarters. Fort Sumter had surrendered! Those upon the housetops shouted to us "The fort is on fire." That had been the story once or twice before.

When we had calmed down, Colonel Chesnut, who had taken it all quietly enough, if anything more unruffled than usual in his serenity, told us how the surrender came about. Wigfall was with them on Morris Island when they saw the fire in the fort; he jumped in a little boat, and with his handkerchief as a white flag, rowed over. Wigfall went in through a porthole. When Colonel Chesnut arrived shortly after, and was received at the regular entrance, Colonel Anderson told him he had need to pick his way warily, for the place was all mined. As far as I can make out the fort surrendered to Wigfall. But it is all confusion. Our flag is flying there. Fire-engines have been sent for to put out the fire. Everybody tells you half of something and then rushes off to tell something else or to hear the last news.

In the afternoon, Mrs. Preston, Mrs. Joe Heyward, and I drove around the Battery. We were in an open carriage. What a changed scene—the very liveliest crowd I think I ever saw, everybody talking at once. All glasses were still turned on the grim old fort. . . .

118. JEFFERSON DAVIS JUSTIFIES SECESSION, 1861*

On April 29, 1861, President Jefferson Davis summoned the Confederate Congress into special session to respond to Lincoln's proclamation calling for 75,000 militiamen—a move the Confederacy considered a declaration of war. Davis asked the southern people to make all necessary measures for the "defense of the country" and outlined the events that had resulted in armed conflict. In the following excerpt, he justified southern action,

*From *A Compilation of the Messages and Papers of the Confederacy, Including the Diplomatic Correspondence*, 1861–1865, 2 vols., comp. James D. Richardson (Nashville: United States Publishing Company, 1905), I:63–70, 82.

holding the North responsible for the history of intersectional conflict. He also used constitutional arguments to affirm states' rights and the right of secession. The South, according to Davis, would "continue to struggle for . . . [their] right to freedom, independence, and self-government."

. . . The declaration of war made against this Confederacy by Abraham Lincoln, the President of the United States, in his proclamation issued on the 15th day of the present month, rendered it necessary, in my judgment, that you should convene at the earliest practicable moment to devise the measures necessary for the defense of the country. The occasion is indeed an extraordinary one. It justifies me in a brief review of the relations heretofore existing between us and the States which now unite in warfare against us and in a succinct statement of the events which have resulted in this warfare, to the end that mankind may pass intelligent and impartial judgment on its motives and objects. During the war waged against Great Britain by her colonies on this continent a common danger impelled them to a close alliance and to the formation of a Confederation, by the terms of which the colonies, styling themselves States, entered "*severally* into a firm league of friendship with each other for their common defense, the security of their liberties, and their mutual and general welfare, binding themselves to assist each other against all force offered to or attacks made upon them, or any of them, on account of religion, sovereignty, trade, or any other pretense whatever." In order to guard against any misconstruction of their compact, the several States made explicit declaration in a distinct article—that "*each* State *retains its* sovereignty, freedom, and independence, and every power, jurisdiction, and right which is not by this Confederation *expressly delegated* to the United States in Congress assembled."

Under this contract of alliance, the war of the Revolution was successfully waged, and resulted in the treaty of peace with Great Britain in 1783, by the terms of which the several States were *each by name* recognized to be independent. The Articles of Confederation contained a clause whereby all alterations were prohibited unless confirmed by the Legislatures of *every State* after being agreed to by the Congress; and in obedience to this provision, under the resolution of Congress of the 21st of February, 1787, the several States appointed delegates who attended a convention "for the *sole and express purpose* of revising the Articles of Confederation and reporting to Congress and the several Legislatures such alterations and provisions therein as shall, when agreed to in Congress *and confirmed by the States*, render the Federal Constitution adequate to the exigencies of Government and the preservation of the Union." It was by the delegates chosen by the *several States* under the resolution just quoted that the Constitution of the United States was framed in 1787 and submitted to the *several States* for ratification, as shown by the seventh article, which in these words: "The ratification of the *conventions of nine States* shall be sufficient for the establishment of this Constitution *between the States* so ratifying the same." I have italicized certain words in the quotations just made for the purpose of attracting attention to the singular and marked caution with which the States endeavored in every possible form to exclude the idea that the separate and independent sovereignty of each State was merged into one common government and nation, and the earnest desire they evinced to impress on the Constitution its true character—that of a *compact between* independent States. The Constitution of 1787, having, however, omitted the clause already recited from the Articles of Confederation, which provided in explicit terms that each State *retained* its sovereignty and independence, some alarm was felt in the States, when invited to ratify the Constitution, lest this omission should be construed into an abandonment of their cherished principle, and they refused to be satisfied until amendments were added to the Constitution placing beyond any pretense of doubt the reservation by the States of all their sovereign rights and powers not expressly delegated to the United States by the Constitution.

Strange, indeed, must it appear to the impartial observer, but it is none the less true that all these carefully worded clauses proved unavailing to prevent the rise and growth in the Northern States of a political school which has persistently claimed that the government thus formed was not [a] compact *between* States, but was in effect a national government, set up *above* and *over* the States. An organization created by the States to secure the blessings of liberty and independent against *foreign* aggression, has been gradually perverted into a machine for their control in their *domestic* affairs. The *creature* has been exalted above its *creators;* the *principals* have been made subordinate to the *agent* appointed by themselves. The people of the Southern States, whose almost exclusive occupation was agriculture, early perceived a tendency in the Northern States to render the common government subservient to their own purposes by imposing burdens on commerce as a protection to their manufacturing and shipping interests. . . . By degrees, as the Northern States gained preponderance in the National Congress, self-interest taught their people to yield ready assent to any plausible advocacy of their right as a majority to govern the minority without control. They learned to listen with impatience to the suggestion of any constitutional impediment to the exercise of their will, and so utterly have the principles of the Constitution been corrupted in the Northern mind that, in the inaugural address delivered by President Lincoln in March last, he asserts as an axiom, which he plainly deems to [be] undeniable, that the theory of the Constitution requires that in all cases the majority shall govern; . . . This is the lamentable and fundamental error on which rests the policy that has culminated in his declaration of war against these Confederate States. . . . [Davis defends slavery and outlines Northern aggression against the slaves states.]

. . . Finally a great party was organized for the purpose of obtaining the administration of the Government, with the avowed object of using its power for the total exclusion of the slave States from all participation in the benefits of the public domain acquired by all the States in common, whether by conquest or purchase; of surrounding them entirely by States in which slavery should be prohibited; of thus rendering the property in slaves so insecure as to be comparatively worthless, and thereby annihilating in effect property worth thousands of millions of dollars. This party, thus organized, succeeded in the month of November last in the election of its candidate for the Presidency of the United States.

. . . the people of the Southern States were driven by the conduct of the North to the adoption of some course of action to avert the danger with which they were openly menaced. With this view the Legislatures of the several States invited the people to select delegates to conventions to be held for the purpose of determining for themselves what measures were best adapted to meet so alarming a crisis in their history. Here it may be proper to observe that from a period as early as 1798 there had existed in *all* of the States of the Union a party almost uninterruptedly in the majority based upon the creed that each State was, in the last resort, the sole judge as well of its wrongs as of the mode and measure of redress. . . . In the exercise of a right so ancient, so well-established, and so necessary for self-preservation, the people of the Confederate States, in their conventions, determined that the wrongs which they had suffered and the evils with which they were menaced required that they should revoke the delegation of powers to the Federal Government which they had ratified in their several conventions. They consequently passed ordinances resuming all their rights as sovereign and independent States and dissolved their connection with the other States of the Union.

Having done this, they proceeded to form a new compact amongst themselves by new articles of confederation, which have been also ratified by the conventions of the several States with an approach to unanimity far exceeding that of the conventions which adopted the Constitution of 1787. They have organized their new Government in all its departments; the functions of the executive, legislative, and judicial magistrates are performed in accordance with the will of the people, as displayed not merely in a cheerful acquiescence, but in the enthusiastic support of the Government thus established by themselves; and but for the interference of the Government of the United States in this legitimate exercise of the right of a people to self-government, peace, happiness, and prosperity would now smile on our land. . . .

. . . We feel that our cause is just and holy; we protest solemnly in the face of mankind that we desire peace at any sacrifice save that of honor and independence; we seek no conquest, no aggrandizement, no concession of any kind from the States with which we were lately confederated; all we ask is to be let alone; that those who never held power over us shall not now attempt our subjugation by arms. This we will, this we must, resist to the direst extremity. The moment that this pretension is abandoned the sword will drop from our grasp, and we shall be ready to enter into treaties of amity and commerce that cannot but be mutually beneficial. So long as this pretension is maintained, with a firm reliance on that Divine Power which covers with its protection the just cause, we will continue to struggle for our inherent right to freedom, independence, and self-government.

119. PRESIDENT ABRAHAM LINCOLN ADDRESSES CONGRESS, 1861*

On July 4, 1861, President Abraham Lincoln addressed a special session of Congress and summarized the events surrounding the outbreak of war with the Confederacy. In the following selection, he offered his understanding of states' rights, the nature of the Constitution, and the responsibility of the national government. He clearly saw the war as an effort to save the Union and by so doing preserving liberty.

Having been convened on an extraordinary occasion, as authorized by the Constitution, your attention is not called to any ordinary subject of legislation.

At the beginning of the present Presidential term, four months ago, the functions of the Federal Government were found to be generally suspended within the several States of South Carolina, Georgia, Alabama, Mississippi, Louisiana, and Florida, excepting only those of the Post Office Department. . . .

The purpose to sever the Federal Union was openly avowed. In accordance with this purpose, an ordinance had been adopted in each of these States declaring the States respectively to be separated from the National Union. A formula for instituting a combined government of these States had been promulgated, and this illegal organization, in the character of Confederate States, was already invoking recognition, aid, and intervention from foreign powers.

Finding this condition of things and believing it to be an imperative duty upon the incoming Executive to prevent, if possible, the consummation of such attempt to destroy the Federal Union, a choice of means to that end became indispensable. This choice was made, and was declared in the inaugural address. The policy chosen looked to the exhaustion of all peaceful measures before a resort to any stronger ones. It sought only to hold the public places and property not already wrested from the Government and to collect the revenue, relying for the rest on time, discussion, and the ballot box. It promised a continuance of the mails at Government expense to the very people who were resisting the Government, and it gave repeated pledges against any disturbance to any of the people and any of their rights. Of all that which a President might constitutionally and justifiably do in such a case, everything was forborne without which it was believed possible to keep the Government on foot. . . .

And this issue embraces more than the fate of these United States. It presents to the whole family of man the question whether a constitutional republic, or democracy—a government of the

*From *A Compilation of the Messages and Papers of the Presidents, 1789–1897*, 10 vols., comp. James D. Richardson (Washington, D.C.: U.S. Government Printing Office, 1896–1899), VI:20–31.

people by the same people—can or can not maintain its territorial integrity against its own domestic foes. It presents the question whether discontented individuals, too few in numbers to control administration according to organic law in any case, can always, upon the pretenses made in this case, or on any other pretenses, or arbitrarily without any pretense, break up their government, and thus practically put an end to free government upon the earth. It forces us to ask, Is there in all republics this inherent and fatal weakness? Must a government of necessity be too *strong* for the liberties of its own people, or too *weak* to maintain its own existence?

So viewing the issue, no choice was left but to call out the war power of the Government and so to resist force employed for its destruction by force for its own preservation. . . .

It might seem at first thought to be of little difference whether the present movement at the South ought to be called "secession" or "rebellion." The movers, however, will understand the difference. At the beginning they knew they could never raise their treasons to any respectable magnitude by any name which implies *violation* of law. They knew their people possessed as much of moral sense, as much of devotion to law and order, and as much pride in and reverence for the history and Government of their common country as any other civilized and patriotic people. They could make no advancement directly in the teeth of these strong and noble sentiments. Accordingly, they commenced by an insidious debauching of the public mind. They invented an ingenious sophism, which, if conceded, was followed by perfectly logical steps through all the incidents to the complete destruction of the Union. The sophism itself is that any State of the Union may *consistently* with the national Constitution, and therefore *lawfully* and *peacefully*, withdraw from the Union without the consent of the Union or of any other State. The little disguise that the supposed right is to be exercised only for just cause, themselves to be the sole judge of its justice, is too thin to merit any notice.

With rebellion thus sugar coated they have been dragging the public mind of their section for more than thirty years, and until at length they have brought many good men to a willingness to take up arms against the Government the day *after* some assemblage of men have enacted the farcical pretense of taking their State out of the Union who could have been brought to do no such thing the day *before*.

This sophism derives much, perhaps the whole, of its currency from the assumption that there is some omnipotent and sacred supremacy pertaining to a *State*—to each State of our Federal Union. Our States have neither more nor less power than that reserved to them in the Union by the Constitution, no one of them ever having been a State *out* of the Union. The original ones passed into the Union even *before* they cast off their British colonial dependence, and the new ones each came into the Union directly from a condition of dependence, excepting Texas; and even Texas, in its temporary independence, was never designated a State. The new ones only took the designation of States on coming into the Union, while that name was first adopted for the old ones in and by the Declaration of Independence. Therein the "United Colonies" were declared to be "free and independent States;" but even then the object plainly was not to declare their independence of *one another* or of the *Union*, but directly the contrary, as their mutual pledge and their mutual action before, at the time, and afterwards abundantly show. The express plighting of faith by each and all of the original thirteen in the Articles of Confederation, two years later, that the Union shall be perpetual is most conclusive. Having never been States, either in substance or in name, *outside* of the Union, whence this magical omnipotence of "State rights," asserting a claim of power to lawfully destroy the Union itself? Much is said about the "sovereignty" of the States, but the word even is not in the National Constitution, nor, as is believed, in any of the State constitutions. What is "sovereignty" in the political sense of the term? Would it be far wrong to define it "a political community without political superior"? Tested by this, no one of our States, except Texas, ever was a sovereignty. . . The States have their status in the Union, and they have no other legal status. If they break from this, they can only do so against law and by revolution. The

Union, and not themselves separately, procured their independence and their liberty. By conquest or purchase the Union gave each of them whatever of independence and liberty it has. The Union is older than any of the States, and, in fact, it created them as States. Originally some dependent colonies made the Union, and in turn the Union threw off their old dependence for them and made them States, such as they are. Not one of them ever had a State constitution independent of the Union. Of course it is not forgotten that all the new States framed their constitutions before they entered the Union, nevertheless dependent upon and preparatory to coming into the Union. . . .

What is now combated is the position that secession is *consistent* with the Constitution—is *lawful* and *peaceful*. It is not contended that there is any express law for it, and nothing should ever be implied as law which leads to unjust or absurd consequences. . . .

The seceders insist that our Constitution admits of secession. They have assumed to make a national constitution of their own, in which of necessity they have either *discarded* or *retained* the right of secession, as they insist it exists in ours. If they have discarded it, they thereby admit that on principle it ought not to be in ours. If they have retained it, by their own construction of ours they show that to be consistent they must secede from one another whenever they shall find it the easiest way of settling their debts or effecting any other selfish or unjust object. The principle itself is one of disintegration, and upon which no government can possibly endure. . . .

It may well be questioned whether there is to-day a majority of the legally qualified voters of any State, except, perhaps, South Carolina, in favor of disunion. There is much reason to believe that the Union men are the majority in many, if not in every other one, of the so-called seceded States. The contrary has not been demonstrated in any one of them. It is ventured to affirm this even of Virginia and Tennessee; for the result of an election held in military camps, where the bayonets are all on one side of the question voted upon, can scarcely be considered as demonstrating popular sentiment. At such an election all that large class who are at once *for* the Union and *against* coercion would be coerced to vote against the Union. . . .

This is essentially a people's contest. On the side of the Union it is a struggle for maintaining in the world that form and substance of government whose leading object is to elevate the condition of men; to lift artificial weights from all shoulders; to clear the paths of laudable pursuit for all; to afford all an unfettered start and a fair chance in the race of life. Yielding to partial and temporary departures, from necessity, this is the leading object of the Government for whose existence we contend. . . .

Our popular Government has often been called an experiment. Two points in it our people have already settled—the successful *establishing* and the successful *administering* of it. One still remains—its successful *maintenance* against a formidable internal attempt to overthrow it. It is now for them to demonstrate to the world that those who can fairly carry an election can also suppress a rebellion; that ballots are the rightful and peaceful successors of bullets, and that when ballots have fairly and constitutionally decided there can be no successful appeal back to bullets; that there can be no successful appeal except to ballots themselves at succeeding elections. Such will be a great lesson of peace, teaching men that what they can not take by an election neither can they take it by a war; teaching all the folly of being the beginners of a war. . . .

The Constitution provides, and all the States have accepted the provision, that "the United States shall guarantee to every State in this Union a republican form of government." But if a State may lawfully go out of the Union, having done so it may also discard the republican form of government; so that to prevent its going out is an indispensable *means* to the *end* of maintaining the guaranty mentioned; and when an end is lawful and obligatory the indispensable means to it are also lawful and obligatory. . . .

And having thus chosen our course, without guile and with pure purpose, let us renew our trust in God and go forward without fear and with manly hearts.

120. THE BATTLE OF BULL RUN (MANASSAS), 1861*

*T*he hard fighting of the Civil War began on a sluggish stream called Bull Run, located just 25 miles southwest of Washington near the key northern Virginia rail town of Manassas. On July 21, 1861, federal troops forded the stream and attacked Confederate forces, driving them back. By the afternoon Federals seemed on the verge of victory. But Confederate reinforcements counterattacked and drove the exhausted and disorganized Yankees back across Bull Run in a retreat that turned into a rout. The following selection, in two parts, reveals how both sides characterized this first battle. The first excerpt, from the New York World, vividly describes the "shameful" retreat of Union forces. The second excerpt, from the New Orleans Picayune, revels in a "grand victory for the armies of the South."

NEW YORK "WORLD" NARRATIVE
WASHINGTON, Monday, July 22.

. . . All eyes were now directed to the distant hill-top, now the centre of the fight. All could see the enemy's infantry ranging darkly against the sky beyond, and the first lines of our men moving with fine determination up the steep slope. The cannonading upon our advance, the struggle upon the hill-top, the interchange of position between the contestants, were watched by us, and as new forces rushed in upon the enemy's side the scene was repeated over and over again. It must have been here, I think, that the Sixty-ninth took and lost a battery eight times in succession, and finally were compelled, totally exhausted, to resign the completion of their work to the Connecticut regiments, which had just come up. The Third Connecticut finally carried that summit, unfurled the Stars and Stripes above it, and paused from the fight to cheer for the Union cause.

Then the battle began to work down the hill, the returning half of the circle which the enemy, driven before the desperate charges of our troops, described during the day, until the very point where Tyler's advance commenced the action. Down the hill and into the valley thickets on the left, the Zouaves, the Connecticut, and New York regiments, with the unconquerable Rhode Islanders, drove the continually enlarging but always vanquished columns of the enemy. It was only to meet more batteries, earthwork succeeding earthwork, ambuscade after ambuscade. Our fellows were hot and weary; most had drunk no water during hours of dust, and smoke, and insufferable heat. No one knows what choking the battle atmosphere produces in a few moments, until he has personally experienced it. And so the conflict lulled for a little while. It was the middle of a blazing afternoon. Our regiments held the positions they had won, but the enemy kept receiving additions, and continued a flank movement towards our left—a dangerous movement for us, a movement which those in the rear perceived, and vainly endeavored to induce some general officer to guard against.

Here was the grand blunder, or misfortune of the battle. A misfortune, that we had no troops in reserve after the Ohio regiments were again sent forward, this time to assist in building a bridge across the run on the Warrenton road, by the side of the stone bridge known to be mined. A blunder, in that the last reserve was sent forward at all. It should have been retained to guard the rear of the left, and every other regiment on the field should have been promptly recalled over the route by which it had advanced, and ordered only to maintain such positions as rested on a supported, continuous line. Gen. Scott says, to-day, that our troops had accomplished three days' work, and should have rested long before. But McDowell tried to vanquish the South in a single struggle, and the sad result is before us.

. . . . The victory seemed ours. It was an hour sublime in unselfishness, and apparently glorious in its results!

---

*From *The Rebellion Record: A Diary of American Events, with Documents, Narratives, Illustrative Incidents, Poetry, Etc.*, 12 vols., ed. Frank Moore (New York: G. P. Putnam, 1861–1863; D. Van Nostrand, 1864–1868), II: 86–88, 110–11.

At this time, near four o'clock, I rode forward through the open plain to the creek where the abatis was being assailed by our engineers. . . . Where were our officers? Where was the foe? Who knew whether we bad won or lost?

The question was to be quickly decided for us. A sudden swoop, and a body of cavalry rushed down upon our columns near the bridge. They came from the woods on the left, and infantry poured out behind them. Tyler and his staff, with the reserve, were apparently cut off by the quick manoeuvre. I succeeded in gaining the position I had just left, there witnessed the capture of Carlisle's battery in the plain, and saw another force of cavalry and infantry, pouring into the road at the very spot where the battle commenced, and near which the South Carolinians, who manned the battery silenced in the morning, had doubtless all day been lying concealed. The ambulances and wagons had gradually advanced to this spot, and of course an instantaneous confusion and dismay resulted. Our own infantry broke ranks in the field, plunged into the woods to avoid the road, got up the hill as best they could, without leaders, every man saving himself in his own way.

The Flight from the Field.

By the time I reached the top of the hill, the retreat, the panic, the hideous headlong confusion, were now beyond a hope. I was near the rear of the movement, with the brave Capt. Alexander, who endeavored by the most gallant but unavailable exertions to check the onward tumult. It was difficult to believe in the reality of our sudden reverse. "What does it all mean?" I asked Alexander. "It means defeat," was his reply. "We are beaten; it is a shameful, a cowardly retreat! Hold up men !" he shouted, "don't be such infernal cowards!" and he rode backwards and forwards, placing his horse across the road and vainly trying to rally the running troops. . . . Mean time I saw officers with leaves and eagles on their shoulder-straps, majors and colonels, who had deserted their commands, pass me galloping as if for dear life. No enemy pursued just then; but, I suppose all were afraid that his guns would be trained down the long, narrow avenue, and mow the retreating thousands, and batter to pieces army wagons and every thing else which crowded it. . . .

But what a scene! and how terrific the onset of that tumultuous retreat. For three miles, hosts of Federal troops—all detached from their regiments, all mingled in one disorderly rout— were fleeing along the road, but mostly through the lots on either side. Army wagons, sutlers' teams, and private carriages, choked the passage, tumbling against each other, amid clouds of dust, and sickening sights and sounds. Hacks, containing unlucky spectators of the late affray, were smashed like glass, and the occupants were lost sight of in the debris. Horses, flying wildly from the battle-field, many of them in death agony, galloped at random forward, joining in the stampede. Those on foot who could catch them rode them bareback, as much to save themselves from being run over, as to make quicker time. Wounded men, lying along the banks—the few neither left on the field nor taken to the captured hospitals—appealed with raised hands to those who rode horses, begging to be lifted behind, but few regarded such petitions. Then the artillery, such as was saved, came thundering along, smashing and overpowering every thing. The regular cavalry, I record it to their shame, joined in the mêlée, adding to its terrors, for they rode down foot-men without mercy. . . . Who ever saw such a flight? Could the retreat at Borodino have exceeded it in confusion and tumult? I think not. It did not slack in the least until Centreville was reached. There the sight of the reserve—Miles's brigade—formed in order on the hill, seemed somewhat to reassure the van. But still the teams and foot-soldiers pushed on, passing their own camps and heading swiftly for the distant Potomac, until for ten miles the road over which the grand army had so lately passed southward, gay with unstained banners, and flushed with surety of strength, was covered with the fragments of its retreating forces, shattered and panic-stricken in a single day. From the branch route the trains attached to Hunter's division had caught the contagion of the flight, and poured into its already swollen current another turbid freshet of confusion and dismay. Who ever saw a more shameful abandonment of munitions gathered at such vast expense? The teamsters, many of them, cut the traces of their horses, and galloped from the wagons. Others threw out their loads to accelerate their flight, and grain, picks, and shovels, and provisions of every kind lay trampled in the dust for leagues. Thousands of muskets strewed the route, and when some of us succeeded in rallying a body of fugitives, and forming them in a line across the road hardly one but had thrown away his arms. If the enemy had brought up his artillery and served it upon the retreating train, or had intercepted our progress with five hundred of his cavalry, he might have captured enough supplies for a week's feast of thanksgiving. As it was, enough was left behind to tell the story of the panic. The rout of the Federal army seemed complete. . . .

N. Y. World, July 23.

* * *

The Southern Press Celebrate "A Grand Victory"

Our telegraphic despatches this morning tell a glorious tale for the South. It is not the bulletins of our friends alone which announce a grand victory for the armies of the South. It is confessed in all its greatness and completeness by the wailings which come to us from the city of Washington, the head-quarters of our enemies. It is told in the groans of the panic-stricken Unionists of tyranny, who are quaking behind their entrenchments with apprehension for the approach of the avenging soldiery of the South, driving before it the routed remnants of that magnificent army which they had prepared and sent forth with the boastful promise of an easy victory. From Richmond, on the contrary, come the glad signs of exceeding joy over a triumph of our arms, so great and overwhelming as though the God of Battles had fought visibly on our side, and smitten and scattered our enemies with a thunderbolt.

Such a rout of such an army—so large, so equipped, and so commanded—was never known before in the wars on this continent. Whole corps disorganized, regiments cut to pieces, artillery captured in whole batteries, and a mighty body of disciplined men converted into a panic-stricken mob—such things have not been read of, except on that smaller scale where the disciplined troops who bore Scott into Mexico encountered the races of semi-barbarians, who parted before him like sheep before a charge of cavalry. It is the same iron race which took Scott upon their shoulders, and carried him into the Capital of Mexico, which now bars his way to Richmond with a wall of steel and fire. The leaders may clamor for new and greater efforts for the straining of the resources of the people and the gathering of large armaments, to be precipitated upon the South in the desperate hope of retrieving the fortunes of a day so deplorably lost. We will not venture to say to what extent rage, disappointment, baffled cupidity, and thirst for revenge, may carry a deluded people; but the confidence of the South will rise high, that no continued and often repeated struggles can be entered upon in the face of such obstacles which have been found in the courage and constancy of the Confederate army, and the genius of its illustrious chief.

In every corner of this land, and at every capital in Europe, it will be received as the emphatic and exulting endorsement, by a young and unconquerable nation, of the lofty assurance President Davis spread before the world on the very eve of the battle, that the noble race of freemen who inherit these States will, what ever may be the proportions the war may assume, "renew their sacrifices and their services from year to year, until they have made good to the uttermost their right to self-government."

The day of battle shows how they redeemed this pledge for them, and in adversity as in victory, it is the undying pledge, of all.

New Orleans Picayune, July 23.

121. THE BATTLE OF SHILOH, 1862*

While politicians could theorize and debate the nature of republicanism and constitutional government, soldiers fought the war. Well over half a million of them died. When the conflict began, both sides confidently bragged that they could whip the other in just a few months. The Battle of Shiloh in the spring of 1862 was the bloodiest battle in American history up until that time, and it made clear that nothing would be settled within a matter of months. General Ulysses S. Grant filed the following preliminary report on the battle, a Union victory that guaranteed federal control of much of Tennessee and the western theater of operations. The casualty rates of the two days foretold the intensity of the combat that came to characterize the war, and Shiloh offered a portent of the incredible military power that would be required to save the Union. In his initial account of the fighting, however, Grant downplayed the number of casualties he had suffered.

CAPTAIN: It becomes my duty to report another battle fought between two great armies, one contending for the maintenance of the best government ever devised, the other for its destruction. It is pleasant to record the success of the army contending for the former principles.

On Sunday morning our pickets were attacked and driven in by the enemy. Immediately the five divisions stationed at this place were drawn up in line of battle, ready to meet them. The battle soon waxed warm on the left and center, varying at time[s] to all parts of the line. The most continuous firing of musketry and artillery ever heard on this continent was kept up until night-fall, the enemy having forced the entire line to fall back nearly half way from their camps to the Landing.

At a late hour in the afternoon a desperate effort was made by the enemy to turn our left and get possession of the Landing, transports, &c. This point was guarded by the gunboats Tyler and Lexington, Captains Gwin and Shirk, U. S. Navy, commanding, four 20-pounder Parrott guns and a battery of rifled guns. As there is a deep and impassable ravine for artillery or cavalry, and very difficult for infantry, at this point, no troops were stationed here, except the necessary artillerists and a small infantry force for their support. Just at this moment the advance of Major-General Buell's column (a part of the division under General Nelson) arrived, the two generals named both being present. An advance was immediately made upon the point of attack and [the] enemy soon driven back. In this repulse much is due to the presence of the gunboats Tyler and Lexington, and their able commanders, Captains Gwin and Shirk.

During the night the divisions under General Crittenden and McCook arrived. General Lewis Wallace, at Crump's Landing, 6 miles below, was ordered at an early hour in the morning to hold his division in readiness to be moved in any direction to which it might be ordered. At about 11 o'clock the order was delivered to move it up to Pittsburg, but owing to its being led by a circuitous route did not arrive in time to take part in Sunday's action.

During the night all was quiet, and feeling that a great moral advantage would be gained by becoming the attacking party, an advance was ordered as soon as day dawned. The result was a gradual repulse of the enemy at all parts of the line from the morning until probably 5 o'clock in the afternoon, when it became evident the enemy was retreating. Before the close of the action the advance of General T. J. Wood's division arrived in time to take part in the action.

My force was much too fatigued from two days' hard fighting and exposure in the open air to a drenching rain during the intervening night to pursue immediately.

Night closed in cloudy and with heavy rain, making the roads impracticable for artillery by the next morning. General Sherman, however, followed the enemy, finding that the main part of the army had retreated in good order.

---

*From Ulysses S. Grant to N. H. McLean, Adjutant General's Office, Department of the Mississippi, April 9, 1862, *The War of the Rebellion: A Compilation of the Official Records of the Union and Confederate Armies*, 128 vols. (Washington, D.C.: Government Printing Office, 1880–1901), series I, vol. X, part I: 108–11.

Hospitals of the enemy's wounded were found all along the road as far as a pursuit was made. Dead bodies of the enemy and many graves were also found. . . .

Of the part taken by each separate command I cannot take special notice in this report, but I will do so more fully when reports of division commanders are handed in.

General Buell, coming on the field with a distinct army long under his command, and which did such efficient service, commanded by himself in person on the field, will be much better able to notice those of his command who particularly distinguished themselves than I possibly can.

I feel it a duty, however, to a gallant and able officer, Brig. Gen. W. T. Sherman, to make a special mention. He not only was with his command during the entire two days' action, but displayed great judgment and skill in the management of his men. Although severely wounded in the hand the first day his place was never vacant. He was again wounded, and had three horses killed under him.

In making this mention of a gallant officer no disparagement is intended to other division commanders, Maj. Gens. John A. and Lewis Wallace, and Brig. Gens. S. A. Hurlbut, B. M. Prentiss, and W. H. L. Wallace, all of whom maintained their places with credit to themselves and the cause.

General Prentiss was taken prisoner in the first day's action, and General W. H. L. Wallace severely, probably mortally, wounded. His assistant adjutant general, Captain William McMichael, is missing; probably taken prisoner. . . .

The medical department, under the direction of Surgeon Hewitt, medical director, showed great energy in providing for the wounded and in getting them from the field regardless of the danger.

Colonel Webster was placed in special charge of all the artillery and was constantly upon the field. He displayed, as always heretobefore, both skill and bravery. At least in one instance he was the means of placing an entire regiment in a position of doing most valuable service, and where it would not have been but for his exertions.

Lieutenant-Colonel McPherson, attached to my staff as chief engineer, deserves more than a passing notice for his activity and courage. All the grounds beyond our camps for miles have been reconnoitered by him, and plats carefully prepared under his supervision give accurate information of the nature of the approaches to our lines. During the two days' battle he was constantly in the saddle, leading troops as they arrived to points where their services were required. During the engagement he had one horse shot under him.

The country will have to mourn the loss of many brave men who fell at the battle of Pittsburg, or Shiloh, more properly. The exact loss on killed and wounded will be known in a day or two. At present I can only give it approximately at 1,500 killed and 3,500 wounded.

The loss of artillery was great, many pieces being disabled by the enemy's shots and some losing all their horses and many men. There were probably not less than 200 horses killed.

The loss of the enemy in killed and left upon the field was greater than ours. In wounded the estimate cannot be made, as many of them must have been sent back to Corinth and other points.

The enemy suffered terribly from demoralization and desertion. . . .

122. THE BATTLE OF MALVERN HILL [1862], 1863*

*T*he Seven Days' Battles, June 25–July 1, 1862, successfully lifted the Union siege of Richmond, Virginia, but the price was staggering. The thirty thousand casualties during that one week equaled the number of

---

*From General Robert E. Lee to General Samuel Cooper, "General Lee's Report," March 6, 1863, in *Reports of the Operations of the Army of Northern Virginia, From June 1862 to and Including the Battle at Fredericksburg, Dec. 13, 1862,* 2 vols. (Richmond: R. M. Smith, 1864). I: 12–14.

killed and wounded in all the battles in the western theater of operations—including Shiloh—during the first six months of 1862. The losses for the Army of Northern Virginia totaled twenty thousand—almost a quarter of the army. In the following report written in March, 1863, General Robert E. Lee describes the last engagement of the bloody week, a frontal assault against fortified Union positions on Malvern Hill.

Battle of Malvern Hill

Early on the 1st of July, Jackson reached the battle field of the previous day, having succeeded in crossing White Oak swamp, where he captured a part of the enemy's artillery and a number of prisoners. He was directed to continue the pursuit down the Willis church road, and soon found that the enemy occupying a high range, extending obliquely across the road, in front of Malvern Hill. On this position, of great natural strength, he had concentrated his powerful artillery, supported by masses of infantry, partially protected by earthworks. His left rested near Crew's house, and his right near Binford's. Immediately in his front the ground was open, varying in width from a quarter to half a mile, and sloping gradually from the crest, was completely swept by the fire of his infantry and artillery. To reach this open ground, our troops had to advance through a broken and thickly wooded country, traversed, nearly throughout its whole extent, by a swamp passable at but few places, and difficult at those. The whole was within range of the batteries on the heights, and the gunboats in the river, under whose incessant fire, our movements had to be executed. Jackson formed his line with Whiting's division on his left and D. H. Hill's on his right, one of Ewell's brigades occupying the interval. . . . Owing to ignorance of the country, the dense forests impeding necessary communications, and the extreme difficulty of the ground, the whole line was not formed until a late hour in the afternoon. The obstacles presented by the woods and swamp made it impracticable to bring up a sufficient amount of artillery to oppose successfully, the extraordinary force of that arm employed by the enemy, while the field itself afforded us few positions favorable for its use, and none for its proper concentration.

Orders were issued for a general advance at a given signal, but the causes referred to prevented a proper concert of action among the troops. D. H. Hill pressed forward across the open field, and engaged the enemy gallantly, breaking and driving back his first line, but a simultaneous advance of the other troops not taking place, he found himself unable to maintain the ground he had gained against the overwhelming numbers and numerous batteries of the enemy. Jackson sent to his support his own division and that part of Ewell's which was in reserve, but owing to the increasing darkness and intricacy of the forest and swamp, they did not arrive in time to render the desired assistance. Hill was therefore compelled to abandon part of the ground he had gained, after suffering severe loss, and inflicting heavy damage upon the enemy. On the right, the attack was gallantly made by Huger's and Magruder's commands. Two brigades of the former commenced the action, the other two were subsequently sent to the support of Magruder and Hill. Several determined efforts were made to storm the hill at Crew's house. The brigades advanced bravely across the open field, raked by the fire of a hundred cannon, and the musketry of large bodies of infantry. Some were broken and gave way, others approached close to the guns, driving back the infantry, compelling the advanced batteries to retire to escape capture, and mingling their dead with those of the enemy. For want of concert among the attacking columns, their assaults were too weak to break the Federal line, and, after struggling gallantly, sustaining and inflicting great loss, they were compelled successively to retire. Night was approaching when the attack began, and it soon became difficult to distinguish friend from foe. The firing continued until after nine P.M., but no decided result was gained. Part of the troops were withdrawn to their original positions, others remained on the open field, and some rested within a hundred yards of the batteries that had been so bravely but vainly assailed. The general conduct of the troops was excellent; in some instances heroic. The lateness of the hour at which the attack necessarily began, gave the enemy the full advantage of his superior position and augmented the natural difficulties of our own. . . .

On the 2d of July, it was discovered that the enemy had withdrawn during the night, leaving the ground covered with his dead and wounded, and his route exhibiting abundant evidence of precipitate retreat. The pursuit was commenced, General Stuart with his cavalry in the advance, but a violent storm, which prevailed throughout the day, greatly retarded our progress. The enemy, harassed and closely followed by the cavalry, succeeded in gaining Westover, on James river, and the protection of his gunboats. He immediately began to fortify his position, which was one of great natural strength, flanked on each side by a creek, and the approach to his front commanded by the heavy guns of his shipping in addition to those mounted in his entrenchments. It was deemed inexpedient to attack him, and in view of the condition of our troops, who had been marching and fighting almost incessantly for seven days, under the most trying circumstances, it was determined to withdraw, in order to afford them the repose, of which they stood so much in need. . . .

Under ordinary circumstances the Federal army should have been destroyed. Its escape was due to the causes already stated. Prominent among these is the want of correct and timely information. This fact, attributable chiefly to the character of the country, enabled General McClellan skillfully to conceal his retreat and to add much to the obstructions with which nature had beset the way of our pursuing columns. But regret that more was not accomplished gives way to gratitude to the Sovereign Ruler of the Universe for the results achieved. The siege of Richmond was raised, and the object of a campaign, which had been prosecuted, after months of preparation, at an enormous expenditure of men and money, completely frustrated. More than ten thousand prisoners, including officers of rank, fifty-two pieces of artillery, and upwards of thirty-five thousand stand of small arms were captured. The stores and supplies of every description, which fell into our hands, were great in amount and value, but small in comparison with those destroyed by the enemy. . . .

Discussion

1. In his speech, Senator Robert Toombs criticized Republicans for ignoring the Dred Scott decision. Was the Republican stance on the decision legitimate or not? What are the implications for power and liberty of an administration that refuses to accept a court decision? How might the Republicans have justified their position?

2. Senator Robert Toombs insisted that the South wanted to have equal rights. Do you think that statement was sincere? How do you think Toombs, and other southerners, defined equality? Had the North and South ever been equal? Why or why not?

3. How did both Jefferson Davis and Abraham Lincoln express concepts of liberty and power in their speeches? How did each defend his actions? How did each view states' rights, the nature of government, and the right of secession?

4. After examining the selections by Stephens, Toombs, Davis, and Lincoln, do you think that the southern states had the right to secede? If so, why; if not, why not? Was the Constitution a voluntary compact of the states? Why or why not?

5. According to the Texas secession document, why did the convention delegates want to leave the United States? Do you think they had legitimate grievances? Why or why not? How would the authors of the declaration address the issues of liberty, equality, and power?

CHAPTER 16

A New Birth of Freedom, 1862–1865

PUNCH, OR THE LONDON CHARIVARI.— October 18, 1862.

ABE LINCOLN'S LAST CARD; OR, ROUGE-ET-NOIR.

Most English newspapers and illustrators were either hostile or indifferent to the Northern cause. Here a desperate Abraham Lincoln plays the black ace representing emancipation of the slaves. Jefferson Davis keeps his cards hidden from view.

The Civil War marked a true watershed in American history. Although the fighting began in an effort to save the Union, as a military measure President Lincoln emancipated some slaves in 1863 and the Thirteenth Amendment ended slavery altogether two years later. With the liberation of the slaves, the rights of African Americans became a major concern in the United States. Women played important roles in the war efforts of both the North and the South, and they too emerged from the crisis with increased expectations of equal rights. The conflict had additional implications for the nation. Republicans took advantage of their congressional power to pass a number of laws promoting economic growth, which set the stage for the rapid western settlement and industrial expansion that occurred after 1865. The Civil War, then, dramatically altered the nature of liberty, equality, and power in the United States. In a slightly different vein, the war also produced a hero of mythical proportion, and the words of Abraham Lincoln still serve to define the national character of the republic.

123. THE FRÉMONT INCIDENT, 1861*

The two documents that follow touch on several issues important during the early months of the war: the proper approach to the "Border States," civil versus military authority, and emancipation. General John C. Frémont, commander of the Union forces in Missouri, declared martial law in August 1861 to maintain control over that important Border State. In his declaration, Frémont threatened to shoot armed citizens and to free the slaves of Rebel sympathizers. President Lincoln, fearful of Confederate response to the first order and concerned about slave-owning Unionists' reaction to the second, countermanded Frémont. In so doing, Lincoln made clear that the objective of preserving the Union prevailed over freeing the slaves. The President's response also showed his willingness to direct military matters, a dynamic style that came to characterize Lincoln's approach to the war.

Circumstances, in my judgment, of sufficient urgency render it necessary that the commanding general of this department should assume the administrative powers of the State. Its disorganized condition, the helplessness of the civil authority, the total insecurity of life, and the devastation of property by bands of murderers and marauders, who infest nearly every county of the State, and avail themselves of the public misfortunes and the vicinity of a hostile force to gratify private and neighborhood vengeance, and who find an enemy wherever they find plunder, finally demand the severest measures to repress the daily-increasing crimes and outrages which are driving off the inhabitants and ruining the State.

In this condition the public safety and the success of our arms require unity of purpose, without let or hindrance to the prompt administration of affairs. In order, therefore, to suppress disorder, to maintain as far as practicable the public peace, and to give security and protection to the persons and property of loyal citizens, I do hereby extend and declare established martial law throughout the State of Missouri.

---

*From John C. Frémont, "Proclamation," August 30, 1861, and Abraham Lincoln to John C. Frémont, September 2, 1861, both in *The War of the Rebellion: A Compilation of the Official Records of the Union and Confederate Armies*, 128 vols. (Washington, D.C.: U.S. Government Printing Office, 1880–1901), series I, vol. III:466–67, 469–70.

The lines of the army of occupation in this State are for the present declared to extend from Leavenworth, by way of the posts of Jefferson City, Rolla, and Ironton, to Cape Girardeau, on the Mississippi River.

All persons who shall be taken with arms in their hands within these lines shall be tried by court-martial, and if found guilty will be shot.

The property, real and personal, of all persons in the State of Missouri who shall take up arms against the United States, or who shall be directly proven to have taken an active part with their enemies in the field, is declared to be confiscated to the public use, and their slaves, if any they have, are hereby declared freemen.

All persons who shall be proven to have destroyed, after the publication of this order, railroad tracks, bridges, or telegraphs shall suffer the extreme penalty of the law.

All persons engaged in treasonable correspondence, in giving or procuring aid to the enemies of the United States, in fomenting tumults, in disturbing the public tranquillity by creating and circulating false reports or incendiary documents, are in their own interests warned that they are exposing themselves to sudden and severe punishment.

All persons who have been led away from their allegiance are required to return to their homes forthwith. Any such absence, without sufficient cause, will be held to be presumptive evidence against them.

The object of this declaration is to place in the hands of the military authorities the power to give instantaneous effect to existing laws, and to supply such deficiencies as the conditions of war demand. But this is not intended to suspend the ordinary tribunals of the country, where the law will be administered by the civil officers in the usual manner, and with their customary authority, while the same can be peaceably exercised.

The commanding general will labor vigilantly for the public welfare, and in his efforts for their safety hopes to obtain not only the acquiescence but the active support of the loyal people of the country.

J. C. Frémont

Major-General Frémont:

MY DEAR SIR: Two points in your proclamation of August 30 give me some anxiety:

First, Should you shoot a man, according to the proclamation, the Confederates would very certainly shoot our best men in their hands in retaliation; and so, man for man, indefinitely. It is, therefore, my order that you allow no man to be shot under the proclamation without first having my approbation or consent.

Second, I think there is great danger that the closing paragraph, in relation to the confiscation of property and the liberating slaves of traitorous owners, will alarm our Southern Union friends and turn them against us; perhaps ruin our rather fair prospect for Kentucky. Allow me, therefore, to ask that you will, as of your own motion, modify that paragraph so as to conform to the first and fourth sections of the act of Congress entitled "An act to confiscate property used for insurrectionary purposes," approved August 6, 1861, and a copy of which act I herewith send you.

The letter is written in a spirit of caution and not of censure. I send it by special messenger, in order that it may certainly and speedily reach you. . . .

A. Lincoln

124. THE EMANCIPATION PROCLAMATION, 1863*

*A*braham Lincoln personally opposed slavery as a monstrous evil, but early in the war he feared that emancipation would hurt the federal effort to save the Union. By fall of 1862, however, he decided that freeing the slaves in the rebellious states would significantly improve the North's military situation. With the Union victory at Antietam in

---

*From Abraham Lincoln, "A Proclamation," January 1, 1863, *United States at Large*, XII:1268–69.

September, Lincoln announced that slaves in the Confederacy would be liberated on January 1, 1863. Although the decree could not take effect until the South had been defeated, few Executive Orders have had as significant and as long-lasting implications for the nation. The Emancipation Proclamation marked the birth of a new freedom for thousands of Americans, and it began a tremendous struggle to establish racial equality in the United States.

WHEREAS on the twenty-second day of September of the year of our Lord eighteen hundred and sixty-two, a proclamation was issued by the President of the United States, containing among other things, the following, to wit:

"That on the first day of January, in the year of our Lord eighteen hundred and sixty-three, all persons held as slaves within any state or designated part of a state the people whereof shall then be in rebellion against the United States shall be then, thenceforward, and forever free; and the Executive Government of the United States, including the military and naval authority thereof, will recognize and maintain the freedom of such persons, and will do no act or acts to repress such persons, or any of them, in any efforts they may make for their actual freedom."

"That the Executive will on the first day of January aforesaid, by proclamation, designate the states and parts of states, if any, in which the people thereof, respectively, shall then be in rebellion against the United States; and the fact that any state or the people thereof, shall on that day be in good faith represented in the Congress of the United States by members chosen thereto at elections wherein a majority of the qualified voters of such states shall have participated shall, in the absence of strong countervailing testimony, be deemed conclusive evidence that such state and the people thereof are not then in rebellion against the United States."

Now, therefore, I, ABRAHAM LINCOLN, President of the United States, by virtue of the power in me vested as commander in chief of the army and navy of the United States, in time of actual armed rebellion against the authority and Government of the United States, and as a fit and necessary war measure for suppressing said rebellion, do, on this first day of January, in the year of our Lord eighteen hundred and sixty-three, and in accordance with my purpose so to do, publicly proclaimed for the full period of one hundred days from the first day above mentioned, order and designate as the states and parts of states wherein the people thereof, respectively, are this day in rebellion against the United States the following, to wit:

Arkansas, Texas, Louisiana (except the parishes of St. Bernard, Plaquemines, Jefferson, St. John, St. Charles, St. James, Ascension, Assumption, Terre Bonne, Lafourche, St. Mary, St. Martin, and Orleans, including the city of New Orleans), Mississippi, Alabama, Florida, Georgia, South Carolina, North Carolina, and Virginia (except the forty-eight counties designated as West Virginia, and also the counties of Berkeley, Accomac, Northhampton, Elizabeth City, York, Princess Ann, and Norfolk, including the cities of Norfolk and Portsmouth), and which excepted parts are for the present left precisely as if this proclamation were not issued.

And by virtue of the power and for the purpose aforesaid, I do order and declare that all persons held as slaves within said designated states and parts of states are, and henceforward shall be free; and that the Executive Government of the United States, including the military and naval authorities thereof, will recognize and maintain the freedom of said persons.

And I hereby enjoin upon the so declared to be free to abstain from all violence, unless in necessary self-defense; and I recommend to them that, in all cases when allowed, they labor faithfully for reasonable wages.

And I further declare and make known that such persons of suitable condition, will be received into the armed service of the United States to garrison forts, positions, stations, and other places, and to man vessels of all sorts in said service.

And upon this act, sincerely believed to be an act of justice, warranted by the Constitution upon military necessity, I invoke the considerable judgment of mankind and the gracious favor of Almighty God. . . .

125. LIFE IN THE CIVIL WAR SOUTH, 1862–1865*

The Civil War, in addition to freeing millions of slaves, changed the lives of thousands of white women. During war, women assume tasks and responsibilities denied them in peacetime—a social phenomenon that can serve to erode or alter their traditional roles. Once peace returns, on the other hand, powerful cultural pressures are brought to bear on women to resume their "proper" place. Consequently, the changes in women's status that accompany war may be real and significant, but they are often subtle and limited. The following passage, taken from the memoirs of Victoria Virginia Clayton, wife of a prominent Alabaman, offered a view of the southern home front. The reminiscence may present a rather romantic picture of life in the Civil War South, but it does reveal some of the substantial domestic changes Southerners experienced between 1861 and 1865.

While my husband was at the front during active service, suffering fatigue, privations, and many ills attendant on a soldier's life, I was at home struggling to keep the family comfortable.

We were blockaded on every side, and could get nothing from without, so had to make everything at home; and having been heretofore only an agricultural people, it became necessary for every home to be supplied with spinning wheels and the old-fashioned loom, in order to manufacture clothing for the members of the family. This was no small undertaking. I knew nothing about spinning and weaving cloth. I had to learn myself, and then to teach the negroes. Fortunately for me, most of the negroes knew how to spin thread, the first step toward cloth making. Our work was hard and continuous. To this we did not object, but our hearts sorrowed for our loved ones in the field.

Our home was situated a mile from the town of Clayton. On going to town one day I discovered a small bridge over which we had to pass that needed repairing. It was almost impassable. I went home, called some of our men, and gave them instructions to get up the necessary articles and put the bridge in condition to be passed over safely. I was there giving instructions about the work, when an old gentleman, our Probate Judge, came along. He stopped to see what we were doing. When satisfied, he said to me:

"Madam, I think we will never be conquered, possessing such noble women as we do." . . .

There was no white person on the plantation beside myself and children, the oldest of whom was attending school at Eufaula, as our Clayton schools were closed, and my time was so occupied that it was impossible for me to teach my children. Four small children and myself constituted the white family at home.

I entrusted the planting and cultivation of the various crops to old Joe. He had been my husband's nurse in infancy, and we always loved and trusted him. I kept a gentle saddle horse, and occasionally, accompanied by Joe, would ride over the entire plantation on a tour of inspection. Each night, when the day's work was done, Joe came in to make a report of everything that had been done on the plantation that day. When Mr. Clayton was where he could receive my letters, I wrote him a letter every night before retiring, and in this way he, being kept informed about the work at home, could write and make suggestions about various things to help me manage successfully.

We made good crops every year, but after the second year we planted provision crops entirely, except enough cotton for home use.

All the coloring matter for cloth had to be gathered from the forest. We would get roots and herbs and experiment with them until we found the color desired, or a near approach to it. We also found out what would dye cotton and what woolen fabrics. We had about one hundred head of sheep; and the wool yielded by these sheep and the cotton grown in the fields furnished us the

*From "Home Life of a Southern Lady (1862–1865)," in *American History Told by Contemporaries*, 5 vols., ed. Albert Bushnell Hart (New York: The Macmillan Company, 1914), IV:244–47.

material for our looms. After much hard work and experience we learned to make very comfortable clothing, some of our cloth being really pretty.

Our ladies would attend services in the church of God, dressed in their home-spun goods, and felt well pleased with their appearances; indeed, better pleased than if they had been dressed in silk of the finest fabric.

We made good warm flannels and other articles of apparel for our soldiers, and every woman learned to knit socks and stockings for her household, and many of the former were sent to the army.

In these dark days the Southern matron, when we sat down at night feeling that the day's work was over, took her knitting in her hands as a pastime, instead of the fancy work which ladies so frequently indulge in now.

I kept one woman at the loom weaving, and several spinning all the time, but found that I could not get sufficient cloth made at home; consequently I gave employment to many a poor woman whose husband was far away. Many a time have I gone ten miles in the country with my buggy filled with thread, to get one of these ladies to weave a piece of cloth for me, and then in return for her labor sent her syrup, sugar, or any of our home produce she wished.

We always planted and raised large crops of wheat, rice, sugar cane, and potatoes. In fact, we grew almost everything that would make food for man or beast. Our land is particularly blessed in this respect. I venture to say there is no land under the sun that will grow a greater variety of products than the land in these Southern states.

Being blockaded, we were obliged to put our ingenuity to work to meet the demands on us as heads of families. Some things we could not raise; for instance, the accustomed necessary luxury of every home—coffee. So we went to work to hunt up a substitute. Various articles were tried, but the best of all was the sweet potato. The potatoes were peeled, sliced, and cut into pieces as large as a coffee bean, dried, and then roasted, just as we prepared coffee. The substitute, mixed with genuine coffee, makes a very palatable drink for breakfast. . . .

Another accustomed luxury of which we were deprived was white sugar. We had, however, a good substitute with which we soon became satisfied; our home-made brown sugar, from the sugar cane. It had the redeeming quality of being pure. . . .

We made many gallons of wine from the scuppernong and other grapes every year. One year I remember particularly. Sheets were spread under the long scuppernong arbors, little negro boys put in top to throw the grapes down, and grown men underneath to gather them in baskets as they fell. When brought to the house they measured thirty-two bushels, and made one hundred and twenty gallons of wine. I did not make so large a quantity from the other varieties of grapes. This wine was kept in the cellar and used for the common benefit. When the negroes would get caught out in the rain, and come to the house wet, they did not hesitate to say, "Missus, please give me a little wine to keep cold away;" and they always received it. There was never any ill result from the use of domestic wine. We were a temperate family and the use was invariably beneficial.

Closed in as we were on every side, with nearly every white man of proper age and health enlisted in the army, with the country filled with white women, children, and old, infirm men, with thousands of slaves to be controlled, and caused through their systematic labor to feed and clothe the people at home, and to provide for our army, I often wonder, as I contemplate those by-gone days of labor and sorrow, and recall how peacefully we moved on and accomplished what we did.

We were required to give one-tenth of all that was raised, to the government. There being no educated white person on the plantation except myself, it was necessary that I should attend to the gathering and measuring of every crop and the delivery of the tenth to the government authorities. This one-tenth we gave cheerfully and often wished we had more to give.

My duties . . . were numerous and often laborious; the family on the increase continually, and every one added increased labor and responsibility. And this was the case with the typical Southern woman.

126. THE HOMESTEAD ACT, 1862*

Republicans took advantage of their majority in Congress to pass several important laws in 1862. The Homestead Act provided "free" land to settlers and encouraged the development of the vast public domain. The law did not ensure the survival of yeoman farmers, but it helped stimulate the post-Civil War agricultural production that served as a foundation for incredible economic growth in the United States after 1865.

Be it enacted by . . . Congress . . ., That any person who is the head of a family, or who has arrived at the age of twenty-one years, and is a citizen of the United States, or who shall have filed his declaration of intention to become such, as required by the naturalization laws of the United States, and who has never borne arms against the United States Government or given aid and comfort to its enemies, shall, from and after the first of January, eighteen hundred and sixty-three, be entitled to enter one quarter-section or a less quantity of unappropriated public lands, upon which said person may have filed a preëmption claim, or which may, at the time the application is made, be subject to preëmption at one dollar and twenty-five cents, or less, per acre; or, eighty acres or less of such unappropriated lands at two dollars and fifty cents per acre, to be located in a body, in conformity to the legal subdivisions of the public lands, and after the same shall have been surveyed: Provided, That any person owning or residing on land may, under the provisions of this act, enter other land lying contiguous to his or her said land, which shall not, with the land so already owned and occupied, exceed in the aggregate one hundred and sixty acres.

SEC. 2. *And be it further enacted,* That the person applying for the benefit of this act shall upon application to the register of the land office in which he or she is about to make such entry, make affidavit before the said register or receiver that he or she is the head of a family, or is twenty-one or more years of age, or shall have performed service in the army or navy of the United States, and that he has never borne arms against the Government of the United States or given aid and comfort to its enemies, and that such application is made for his or her exclusive use and benefit, and that said entry is made for the purpose of actual settlement and cultivation, and not, either directly or indirectly, for the use or benefit of any other person or persons whomsoever; and upon filing the said affidavit with the register or receiver, and on payment of ten dollars, he or she shall thereupon be permitted to enter the quantity of land specified: *Provided, however,* That no certificate shall be given or patent issued therefor until the expiration of five years from the date of such entry; and if, at the expiration of such time, or at any time within two years thereafter, the person making such entry; or, if he be dead, his widow; or in case of her death, his heirs or devisee; or in case of a widow making such an entry, her heirs or devisee, in case of her death; shall prove by two credible witnesses that he, she, or they have resided upon or cultivated the same for the term of five years immediately succeeding the time of filing the affidavit aforesaid, and shall make affidavit that no part of said land has been alienated, and that he has borne true allegiance to the Government of the United States; then, in such case, he, she, or they, if at that time a citizen of the United States, shall be entitled to a patent, as in other cases provided for by law; *And provided, further,* That in case of the death of both father and mother, leaving an infant child or children under twenty-one years of age, the right and fee shall enure to the benefit of said infant child or children; and the executor, administrator, or guardian may, at any time within two years after the death of the surviving parent, and in accordance with the laws of the State in which such children for the time being have their domicile, sell said land for the benefit of the said infants, but for no other purpose; and the purchaser shall acquire the absolute title by the purchase, and be entitled to a patent from the United States, on payment of the office fees and sum of money herein specified.

SEC. 3. *And be it further enacted,* That the register of the land office shall note and such applications on the tract books and plats of his office and keep a register of all such entries. . . .

---

*From "An Act to secure homesteads to actual settlers on the public domian," May 20, 1862, *United States Statutes at Large,* XII:392–439.

SEC. 5. *And be it further enacted*, That if, at any time after the filing of the affidavit . . . and before the expiration of the five years aforesaid, it shall be proven, after due notice to the settler, . . . that the person having filed such affidavit shall have actually changed his or her residence, or abandoned the said land for more that six months at any time, then and in that event the land so entered shall revert to the government.

SEC. 6. And be it further enacted, That no individual shall be permitted to acquire title to more than one quarter section under the provisions of this act; and that the Commissioner of the General Land Office is hereby required to prepare and issue such rules and regulations, consistent with this act, as shall be necessary and proper to carry its provisions into effect . . . : *Provided, further*, That no person who has served, or may hereafter serve, for a period of not less than fourteen days in the army or navy of the United States, either regular or volunteer, under the laws thereof, during the existence of an actual war, domestic or foreign, shall be deprived of the benefits of this act on account of not having attained the age of twenty-one years. . . .

127. THE MORRILL ACT, 1862*

The Morrill Land-Grant College Act gave states the opportunity to support higher public education on an unprecedented scale by giving them federal land to subsidize agricultural and mechanical colleges. With the Republican policy, the wealth of the nation would be used to provide educational and economic opportunities for thousands of Americans. Approved on July 2, 1862, the bill made possible the creation of many of the major universities in the United States.

Be it enacted by . . . Congress . . . , That there be granted to the several States, for the purpose hereinafter mentioned, an amount of public land, to be appropriated to each State a quantity equal to thirty thousand acres for each senator and representative in Congress to which the States are respectively entitled by the apportionment under the census of eighteen hundred and sixty: Provided, That no mineral lands shall be selected or purchased under the provisions of this act.

SEC. 2. *And be it further enacted*, That the land aforesaid, after being surveyed, shall be apportioned to the several States in sections or subdivisions of sections, not less than one quarter of a section; and whenever there are public lands in a State subject to sale at private entry at one dollar and twenty-five cents per acre, the quantity to which said States shall be entitled shall be selected from such lands within the limits of said States, and the Secretary of the Interior is hereby directed to issue to each of the States in which there is not the quantity of public lands subject to sale at private entry at one dollar and twenty-five cents per acre, to which said State may be entitled under the provisions of this act, land scrip to the amount in acres for the deficiency of its distributive share: said scrip to be sold by said States and the proceeds thereof applied to the uses and purposes in this act, and for no other use or purpose whatsoever: Provided, That in no case shall any State in which land scrip may thus be issued be allowed to locate the same within any other State, or Territory . . . ; *And provided, further*, That not more than one million acres shall be located by . . . assignees in any one of the States: *And provided, further*, That no such location shall be made before one year from the passage of this act.

SEC. 4. *And be it further enacted*, That all moneys derived from the sale of the lands aforesaid by the States to which lands are apportioned, and from the sale of the land scrip hereinbefore provided for, shall be invested in stocks of the United States, or of the States, or some other safe stocks, yielding not less than five percentum upon the par value of said stocks; and that the moneys so invested shall constitute a perpetual fund, the capital of which shall remain forever undiminished, (except so

---

*"An Act donating Public Lands to the several States and Territories which may provide Colleges for the Benefit of Agriculture and the Mechanic Arts," July 2, 1862, *United States Statutes at Large*, XII:503–05.

far as may be provided in section fifth of this act,) and the interest of which shall be inviolably appropriated, by each State which may take and claim the benefit of this act, to the endowment, support, and maintenance of at least one college where the leading object shall be, without excluding other scientific and classical studies, and including military tactics, to teach such branches of learning as are related to agriculture and mechanic arts, in such manner as the legislatures of the States may respectively prescribe, in order to promote the liberal and practical education of the industrial classes in the several pursuits and professions of life.

SEC. 5. . . .[Paragraph Six]. No State while in a condition of rebellion or insurrection against the government of the United States shall be entitled to the benefits of this Act. . . .

128. A NORTHERN PEACE DEMOCRAT SPEAKS OUT AGAINST THE WAR, 1863*

During the "Winter of Discontent," 1862–1863, Union fortunes deteriorated. Defeat at Fredericksburg and stalemate in the campaign against Vicksburg produced gloom in Washington. Morale declined and desertions increased sharply among Union troops. In this climate, Northern "Copperhead" Democrats declared to a growing audience that the war was a failure and should be abandoned. Congressman Clement L. Vallandigham (1820–1871) of Ohio was among the most virulent Democratic critics of Lincoln's wartime administration. In the following excerpt from a January, 1863, speech to Congress, Vallandigham condemned the failed prosecution of the war, called for an end to all abolitionist efforts, and suggested a negotiated settlement to restore the Union—with slavery.

And now, sir, I recur to the state of the Union to-day. What is it? Sir, twenty months have elapsed, but the rebellion is not crushed out; its military power has not been broken; the insurgents have not dispersed. The Union is not restored; nor the Constitution maintained; nor the laws enforced. Twenty, sixty, ninety, three hundred, six hundred days have passed; a thousand millions been expended; and three hundred thousand lives lost or bodies mangled; and to-day the Confederate flag is still near the Potomac and the Ohio, and the Confederate Government stronger, many times, than at the beginning. Not a State has been restored, not any part of any State has voluntarily returned to the Union. And has any thing been wanting that Congress, or the States, or the people in their most generous enthusiasm, their most impassionate patriotism, could bestow? Was it power? And did the party of the Executive control the entire Federal Government, every State government, every county, every city, town and village in the North and West? Was it patronage? All belonged to it. Was it influence? What more? Did not the school, the college, the church, the press, the secret orders, the municipality, the corporation, railroads, telegraphs, express companies, the voluntary association, all, all yield it to the utmost? Was it unanimity? Never was an Administration so supported in England or America. Five men and half a score of newspapers made up the Opposition. Was it enthusiasm? The enthusiasm was fanatical. There has been nothing like it since the Crusades. Was it confidence? Sir, the faith of the people exceeded that of the patriarch. They gave up Constitution, law, right, liberty, all at your demand for arbitrary power that the rebellion might, as you promised, be crushed out in three months, and the Union restored. Was credit needed? You took control of a country, young, vigorous, and inexhaustible in wealth and resources, and of a Government almost free from public debt, and whose good faith had never been tarnished. Your great national loan bubble failed miserably, as it deserved to fail; but the bankers and merchants of Philadelphia, New York and Boston lent you more than their entire banking capital. And when that failed too, you forced credit by declaring your paper promises to pay, a legal tender for all debts. Was money wanted? You had all the revenues of the United States, diminished

---

*From *Appendix to the Congressional Globe*, 37th Congress, 2nd Session (1863), 54–55, 58–59.

indeed, but still in gold. The whole wealth of the country, to the last dollar, lay at your feet. Private individuals, municipal corporations, the State governments, all, in their frenzy, gave you money or the means with reckless prodigality. . . .

Money and credit, then, you have had in prodigal profusion. And were men wanted? More than a million rushed to arms! Seventy-five thousand first, (and the country stood aghast at the multitude,) then eighty-three thousand more were demanded; and three hundred and ten thousand responded to the call. The President next asked for four hundred thousand, and Congress, in their generous confidence, gave him five hundred thousand; and, not to be outdone, he took six hundred and thirty-seven thousand. Half of these melted away in their first campaign; and the President demanded three hundred thousand more for the war, and then drafted yet another three hundred thousand for nine months. The fabled hosts of Xerxes have been out-numbered. And yet victory, strangely, follows the standard of the foe. From Great Bethel to Vicksburg, the battle has not been to the strong. Yet every disaster, except the last, has been followed by a call for more troops, and every time, so far, they have been promptly furnished. From the beginning the war has been conducted like a political campaign, and it has been the folly of the party in power that they have assumed, that numbers alone would win the field in a contest not with ballots but with musket and sword. But numbers, you have had almost without number—the largest, best appointed, best armed, fed, and clad host of brave men, well organized and well disciplined, ever marshaled. A Navy, too, not the most formidable perhaps, but the most numerous and gallant, and the costliest in the world, and against a foe, almost without a navy at all. Thus, with twenty millions of people, and every element of strength and force at command— power, patronage, influence unanimity, enthusiasm, confidence, credit, money, men, an Army and a Navy the largest and the noblest ever set in the field, or afloat upon the sea; with the support, almost servile, of every State, county, and municipality in the North and West, with a Congress swift to do the bidding of the Executive; without opposition anywhere at home; and with an arbitrary power which neither the Czar of Russia, nor the Emperor of Austria dare exercise; yet after nearly two years of more vigorous prosecution of war than ever recorded in history; after more skirmishes, combats and battles than Alexander, Caesar, or the first Napoleon ever fought in any five years of their military career, you have utterly, signally, disastrously—I will not say ignominiously—failed to subdue ten millions of "rebels," whom you had taught the people of the North and West—not only to hate, but to despise. . . . Rebels certainly they are; but all the persistent and stupendous efforts of the most gigantic warfare of modern times have, through your incompetency and folly, availed nothing to crush them out, cut off though they have been, by your blockade, from all the world, and dependent only upon their own courage and resources. And yet, they were to be utterly conquered and subdued in six weeks, or three months! Sir, my judgment was made up, and expressed from the first. I learned it from Chatham: "My lords, you can not conquer America." And you have not conquered the South. You never will. It is not in the nature of things possible; much less under your auspices. But money you have expended without limit, and blood poured out like water. Defeat, debt, taxation, sepulchers, these are your trophies. In vain, the people gave you treasure; and the soldier yielded up his life. "Fight, tax, emancipate, let these," said the gentleman from Maine, [Mr.Pike] at the last session, "be the trinity of our salvation." Sir, they have become the trinity of your deep damnation. The war for the Union is, in your hands, a most bloody and costly failure. The President confessed it on the 22d of September, solemnly, officially, and under the broad seal of the United States. And he has now repeated the confession. The priests and rabbis of abolition taught him that God would not prosper such a cause. War for the Union was abandoned; war for the negro openly begun, and with stronger battalions than before. With what success? Let the dead at Fredericksburg and Vicksburg answer.

And now, sir, can this war continue? Whence the money to carry it on? Where the men? Can you borrow? From whom? Can you tax more? Will the people bear it? Wait till you have collected what is already levied. How many millions more of "legal tender"-to-day forty-seven per cent below the par of gold-can you float? Will men enlist now at any price? Ah, sir, it is easier to die at home. I beg pardon; but I trust I am not "discouraging enlistments." If I am, then first arrest Lincoln, Stanton, Halleck, and some of your other generals, and I will retract; yes, I will recant. . . .

. . . And now, Sir, after two years of persistent and most gigantic effort on part of this Administration to compel them to submit, but with utter and signal failure, the people of the free States are now, or are fast becoming, satisfied that the price of the Union is the utter suppression of Abolitionism or anti-slavery as a political element, and the complete subordination of the spirit of fanaticism and intermeddling which gave it birth. In any event, they are ready now, if I have not greatly misread the signs of the times, to return to the old Constitutional and actual basis of fifty years ago: three-fifths rule of representation, speedy rendition of fugitives from labor, equal rights in the Territories, no more slavery agitation anywhere, and transit and temporary sojourn with slaves, without molestation, in the free States. Without all these there could be neither peace nor permanence to a restored union of States "part slave and part free." With it, the South, in addition to all the other great and multiplied benefits of union, would be far more secure in her slave property, her domestic institutions, than under a separate government. Sir, let no man, North or West, tell me that this would perpetuate African slavery. I know it. But so does the Constitution. I repeat, Sir, it is the price of the Union. Whoever hates negro slavery more than he loves the Union must demand separation at last. I think that you can never abolish slavery by fighting. Certainly you never can till you have first destroyed the South, and then, in the language, first of Mr. Douglas and afterward of Mr. Seward, converted this Government into an imperial despotism. And, Sir, whenever I am forced to a choice between the loss, to my own country and race, of personal and political liberty, with all its blessings, and the involuntary domestic servitude of the negro, I shall not hesitate one moment to choose the latter alternative. The sole question, to-day, is between the Union, with slavery, or final disunion, and, I think, anarchy and despotism. I am for the Union. It was good enough for my fathers. It is good enough for us, and our children after us. . . .

129. NEW YORK CITY DRAFT RIOTS, 1863*

In March 1863, Congress passed a new conscription law, decreeing that all male citizens ages 20 to 45 must enroll for the draft. The law was intended to encourage volunteers to come forward, but instead it increased public discontent and eventually led to violence. Northern Democrats, who opposed conscription as well as emancipation, had nurtured a sense of class resentment tinged with racism. And the practice of hiring substitutes for the draft led to the cry of "rich man's war, poor man's fight" among northern workingmen. When the northern draft got under way in the summer of 1863, widespread violence erupted. The worst riot occurred in New York City on July 13 through 16, where huge mobs consisting mostly of Irish Americans demolished draft offices, lynched several blacks, and destroyed huge areas of the city. In the following excerpt, local U.S. Army observers describe the riots.

NEW YORK, July 13, 1863
(Received 12.10 p. m.)

SIR: What is represented as a serious riot is now taking place on Third avenue, at the provost-marshal's office. The office is said to have been burned, and the adjoining block to be on fire. Our

*From *The War of the Rebellion: A Compilation of the Official Records of the Union and Confederate Armies,* 128 vols. (Washington, D.C.: U.S. Government Printing Office, 1880–1901), series I, vol. XXVII, part 2:886–87, 903–04.

wires in that direction have all been torn down. A report just in says the regulars from Governor's Island have been ordered to the vicinity.

Respectfully,
E. S. SANFORD
Hon. E. M. Stanton

NEW YORK, July 13, 1863
(Received 2.30 p. m.)

SIR: The riot has assumed serious proportions, and is entirely beyond the control of the police. Superintendent Kennedy is badly injured. So far the rioters have everything their own way. They are estimated at from 30,000 to 40,000. I am inclined to think from 2,000 to 3,000 are actually engaged. Appearances indicate an organized attempt to take advantage of the absence of military force.

Respectfully,
E. S. SANFORD
Hon. E. M. Stanton

NEW YORK, July 13, 1863—9.30 p. m.
(Received 11.45 p. m.)

SIR: The situation is not improved since dark. The programme is diversified by small mobs chasing isolated negroes as hounds would chase a fox. I mention this to indicate to you that the spirit of mob is loose, and all parts of the city pervaded. The Tribune office has been attacked by a reconnoitering party, and partially sacked. A strong body of police repulsed the assailants, but another attack in force is threatened. The telegraph is especially sought for destruction. One office has been burned by the rioters, and several others compelled to close. . . .

In brief, the city of New York is to-night at the mercy of a mob, whether organized or improvised, I am unable to say. As far as I can learn, the fireman and military companies sympathize too closely with the draft resistance movement to be relied upon for the extinguishment of fires or the restoration of order. It is to be hoped that to-morrow will open upon a brighter prospect than is promised to-night.

Respectfully
E. S. SANFORD
Hon. E. M. Stanton

NEW YORK, July 18, 1863.

SIR: On the 16th instant I had the honor of informing you, by two separate communications, as to the state of affairs in this city and neighborhood, relative to the draft. Yesterday and to-day, up to the time of writing, this city has been comparatively quiet, but I cannot tell at what moment the riot may break out with redoubled violence.

The authorities in Washington do not seem able or willing to comprehend the magnitude of the opposition to the Government which exists in New York. There is no doubt but that most, if not all, of the Democratic politicians are at the bottom of this riot, and that the rioters themselves include not only the thieves and gamblers that infest this metropolis, but nearly every one of the vast Democratic majority, which has so constantly been thrown at every election against the Administration. When you consider the depraved and desperate character of those men, and their hostility to President Lincoln's Government, stimulated as it is by inflammatory harangues in the newspapers and on the public highways, and by the copious supply of liquor, you will easily appreciate the difficulties of enforcing the draft. As I said before, it will require at least 15,000 armed men to enforce it, and these men must be placed under the absolute control of some energetic and zealous officer. I do not hesitate to say that the moment the draft is resumed, more than one-half of the laboring portion of our population will rise in opposition against its execution, and that it will require an adequate force and a decisive executive to subdue them. No reliance can be placed upon the Governor of the State; very little on the militia, who are now returning home, and who are, ordered to report to Governor Seymour. Our only dependence must be on the regular army and the volunteers, who are independent of State control. Should any conflict between the Federal and State authorities occur, and it is not unlikely that it should, Seymour will most certainly side with the State, and would bring with him most of the militia. If I were permitted to offer a suggestion to the Executive, I would advise the proclamation of martial law, and the presence of an adequate force here, before any steps are taken to enforce the draft.

From what I have learned and from what I knew of Governor Seymour, as well as from the substance and tone of his speeches, I am convinced that little or no reliance can be placed on the loyalty of Governor Seymour, and I would caution the Administration against placing any reliance whatever on his professions.

If the New York mob is to be subdued and the law of the United States carried out, it must be done by Federal officers, and by means entirely under the direction of the General Government.

I am, sir, very respectfully, your obedient servant,
ROBERT NUGENT,
Colonel Sixty-ninth N.Y. Vols., and A. A. P. M. G.

Col. J. B. FRY, Provost-Marshal-General.

130. THE GETTYSBURG ADDRESS, 1863*

*I*n 1863, President Lincoln made a few comments at the dedication of a cemetery at Gettysburg. The most famous speech in the history of the United States, the Gettysburg Address offered an eloquent statement of American ideals. Lincoln used the opportunity to define the democratic principles for which the Union fought. The war that had begun to save the Union, and that had brought freedom to African Americans, would, prayed Lincoln, guarantee the survival of government by and for the people.

Fourscore and seven years ago our fathers brought forth on this continent, a new nation, conceived in liberty, and dedicated to the proposition that all men are created equal. Now we are engaged in a great civil war, testing whether that nation or any nation so conceived and so dedicated, can long endure. We are met on a great battle-field of that war. We have come to dedicate a portion of that field, as a final resting place for those who here gave their lives that that nation

---

*From Abraham Lincoln, "The Gettysburg Address," November 19, 1863, in *Select Orations Illustrating American Political History*, ed. Samuel B. Harding (Indianapolis: Hollenbeck Press, 1908), 416.

might live. It is altogether fitting and proper that we should do this. But, in a larger sense, we can not dedicate, we can not consecrate, we can not hallow, this ground. The brave men, living and dead, who struggled here, have consecrated it, far above our poor power to add or detract. The world will little note, nor long remember what we say here, but it can never forget what they did here. It is for us the living, rather, to be dedicated here to the unfinished work which they who fought here have thus far so nobly advanced. It is rather for us to be here dedicated to the great task remaining before us, that from these honored dead we take increased devotion to that cause for which they gave the last full measure of devotion; that we here highly resolve these dead shall not have died in vain; that this nation, under God, shall have a new birth of freedom, and that government of the people, by the people, and for the people, shall not perish from the earth.

131. THE FIRST SOUTH CAROLINA, U. S. C. T., 1862*

When the federal government established African American military regiments (designated as United States Colored Troops, or U. S. C. T.), white officers served in command. Blacks could fight, but they could not lead. The discriminatory policy prophesied the overwhelming difficulty former slaves would face in trying to gain equality in the United States. Nevertheless, many of the commanders proved quite sympathetic to the freedmen, as the following selections from one colonel's journal revealed. The excerpts were published in a national magazine, and they provided northerners with one of the earliest descriptions of emancipated slaves. The comments also mirrored many of the attitudes and perceptions that white Americans held about black Americans.

November 24, 1862

Yesterday afternoon we were steaming over a summer sea, the deck level as a parlor-floor, no land in sight, no sail, until at last appeared one light-house, said to be Cape Romaine, and then a line of trees and two distant vessels and nothing more. The sun set, a great illuminated bubble, emerged in one vast bank of rosy suffusion. . . . Towards morning the boat stopped, and when I came on deck, before six, . . .

Hilton Head lay on one side, the gunboats on the other; all that was raw and bare in the low buildings of the new settlement was softened into picturesqueness by the early light. Stars were still overhead, gulls wheeled and shrieked, and the broad river rippled duskily toward Beaufort.

The shores were low and wooded like any New-England shore; there were a few gunboats, twenty schooners, and some steamers, among them the "Planter," which Robert Small, the slave, presented to the nation. The river-banks were soft and graceful, though low, and as we steamed up to Beaufort, on the flood-tide this morning, it seemed almost as fair as the smooth and lovely canals which Stedman traversed to meet his negro soldiers in Surinam. The air was cool as at home, yet the foliage seemed green, glimpses of stiff tropical vegetation appeared along the banks, with great clumps of shrubs whose pale seed-vessels looked like tardy blossoms. Then we saw on a picturesque point an old plantation, with stately magnolia avenue, decaying house, and tiny church amid the woods, reminding me of Virginia; behind it stood a neat encampment of white tents, "and there," said my companion, "is your favorite regiment of negro soldiers."

Three miles farther brought us to the pretty town of Beaufort, with its stately houses amid Southern foliage. Reporting to General Saxton, I had the luck to encounter a company of my destined command, marched in to be mustered into the United States service. They were without arms, and all looked as thoroughly black as the most faithful philanthropist could desire; there did not seem to be so much as a mulatto among them. Their coloring suited me, all but the legs, which

---

*From "Leaves from an Officer's Journal," *The Atlantic Monthly* 14 (July–December, 1864), 522–27.

were clad in a lively scarlet, as intolerable to my eyes as if I had been a turkey. I saw them mustered; General Saxton talked to them a little, in his direct, manly way; they gave close attention, though their faces looked impenetrable. Then I conversed with some of them. The first to whom I spoke had been wounded in a small expedition after lumber, from which a party had just returned, and in which they had been under fire and done very well. I said, pointing to his lame arm,—

"Did you think that was more than you bargained for, my man?"

His answer came promptly and stoutly,—

"I been a-tinking, Mas'r, **dat's jess what I went for.**"

I thought this did well enough for my first interchange of dialogue with my recruits.

December 1, 1862

How absurd is the impression bequeathed by slavery in regard to these Southern blacks, that they are sluggish and inefficient in labor! Last night, after a hard day's work, (our guns and the remainder of our tents being just issued,) an order came from Beaufort that we should be ready in the evening to unload a steamboat's cargo of boards, being some of those captured by them a few weeks since, and now assigned for their use. I wondered if the men would grumble at the night-work; but the steamboat arrived by seven, and it was bright moonlight when they went at it. Never have I beheld such a jolly scene of labor. Tugging those wet and heavy boards over a bridge of boats ashore, then across the slimy beach at low tide, then up a steep bank, and all in one great uproar of merriment for two hours. Running most of the time, chattering all the time, snatching the boards from each other's back as if they were coveted treasure, getting up eager rivalries between different companies, pouring great choruses of ridicule on the heads of all shirkers, they made the whole scene so enlivening that I gladly stayed out in the moonlight for the whole time to watch it. And all this without any urging or any promised reward, but simply as the most natural way of doing the thing. The steamboat-captain declared that they unloaded the ten thousand feet of boards quicker than any white gang could have done it; and they felt it so little, that, when, later in the night, I reproached one whom I found sitting by a camp-fire, cooking a surreptitious opossum, telling him that he ought to sleep after such a job of work, he answered with the broadest grin,—

"Oh, no, Cunnel, da's no work at all, Cunnel; dat only jess enough **for stretch we.**"

December 2, 1862

I believe I have not yet enumerated the probable drawbacks to the success of this regiment, if any. We are exposed to no direct annoyance from the white regiments, being out of their way; and we have as yet no discomforts or privations which we do not share with them. I do not as yet see the slightest obstacle, in the nature of the blacks, to making them good soldiers,—but rather the contrary. They take readily to drill, and do not object to discipline; they are not especially dull or inattentive; they seem fully to understand the importance of the contest, and their share of it. They show no jealousy or suspicion towards their officers.

They do show those feelings, however, to the Government itself; and no one can wonder why. Here lies the drawback to rapid recruiting. Were this a wholly new regiment, it would have been full to overflowing, I am satisfied, ere now. The trouble is in the legacy of bitter distrust bequeathed by the abortive regiment of General Hunter,—into which they were driven like cattle, kept for several months in camp, and then turned off without a shilling, by order of the War Department. The formation of that regiment was on the whole a great injury to this one; and the men who came from it, though the best soldiers we have in other respects, are the least sanguine and cheerful; while those who now refuse to enlist have great influence in deterring others. Our soldiers are constantly twitted by their families and friends with the prospect of risking their lives in the service, and being paid nothing; and it is vain that we read them the instructions of the Secretary of War to General Saxton, promising them the full pay of soldiers.*

Another drawback is that some of the white soldiers delight in frightening the women on the plantations with doleful tales of plans for putting us in the front rank in all battles, and such silly talk,—the object being, perhaps, to prevent our being employed on active service at all. All these considerations they feel precisely as white men would,—no less, no more; and it is the comparative freedom from such unfavorable influences which makes the Florida men seem more bold and manly, as they undoubtedly do. To-day General Saxton has returned from Fernandina with seventy-six recruits, and the eagerness of the captains to secure them was a sight to me. Yet they cannot deny that some of the very best men in the regiment are South Carolinians.

December 3, 1862

What a life is this I lead! It is a dark, mild, drizzling evening, and as the foggy air breeds sand-flies, so it calls out melodies and strange antics from this mysterious race of grown-up children with whom my lot is cast. All over the camp the lights glimmer in the tents, and as I sit at my desk in the open doorway, there come mingled sounds of stir and glee. Boys laugh and shout,—a feeble flute stirs somewhere in some tent, not an officer's,—a drum throbs far away in another,—wild kildeer-plover flit and wail above us, like the haunting souls of dead slave-masters,—and from a neighboring cook-fire comes the monotonous sound of that strange festival, half powwow, half prayer-meeting, which they know only as a "shout." These fires are usually included in a little booth, made neatly of palm-leaves and covered in at top, a regular native African hut, in short, such as is pictured in books, and such as I once got up from dried palm-leaves, for a fair, at home. This hut is now crammed with men, singing at the top of their voices, in one of their quaint, monotonous, endless, negro-Methodist chants, with obscure syllables recurring constantly, and slight variations interwoven, all accompanied with a regular drumming of the feet and clapping of the hands, like castanets. Then the excitement spreads; inside and outside the inclosure men begin to quiver and dance, others join, a circle forms, winding monotonously round some one in the centre; some "heel and toe" tumultuously, others merely tremble and stagger on, others stoop and rise, others whirl, others caper sideways, all keep steadily circling like dervishes; spectators applaud special strokes of skill; my approach only enlivens the scene; the circle enlarges, louder grows the singing, rousing shouts of encouragement come in, half bacchanalian, half devout, "Wak 'em, brudder!" "Stan up to 'em, brudder!"—And still the ceaseless drumming and clapping, in perfect cadence, goes steadily on. Suddenly there comes a sort of snap, and the spell breaks, amid general sighing and laughter. And this not rarely and occasionally, but night after night,—while in other parts of the camp the soberest prayers and exhortations are proceeding sedately.

A simple and lovable people, whose graces seem to come by nature, and whose vices by training. Some of the best superintendents confirm the early tales of innocence, and Dr. Zachos told me last night that on his plantation, a sequestered one, "they had absolutely no vices." Nor have these men of mine shown any worth mentioning; since I took command I have heard of no man intoxicated, and there has been but one small quarrel. I suppose that scarcely a white regiment in the army shows so little swearing. Take the "Progressive Friends" and put them in red trousers, and I verily believe they would fill a guard-house sooner than these men. If camp-regulations are violated, it seems to be usually through heedlessness. They love passionately three things, besides their spiritual incantations,—namely, sugar, home, and tobacco. The last affection brings tears to their eyes, almost, when they speak of the urgent need of pay: they speak of their last-remembered

---

*With what utter humiliation were we, their officers, obliged to confess to them, eighteen months afterwards, that it was their distrust which was wise, and our faith in the pledges of the United States Government which was foolishness!

quid as if it were some deceased relative, too early lost, and to be mourned forever. As for sugar, no white man can drink coffee after they have sweetened it to their liking.

I see that the pride which military life creates may cause the plantation-trickeries to diminish. For instance, these men make the most admirable sentinels. It is far harder to pass the camp-lines at night than in the camp from which I just came; and I have seen none of that disposition to connive at the offences of members of one's own company which is so troublesome among white soldiers. Nor are they lazy, either about work or drill; in all respects they seem better material for soldiers than I had dared to hope.

There is one company in particular, all Florida men, which I certainly think the finest-looking company I ever saw, white or black; they range admirably in size, have remarkable erectness and ease of carriage, and really march splendidly. Not a visitor but notices them; yet they have been under drill only a fortnight, and part only two days. They have all been slaves, and very few are even mulattoes.

132. SHERMAN RESPONDS TO THE CITIZENS OF ATLANTA, 1864*

*O*n September 2, 1864, Federal troops, under the command of General William T. Sherman, occupied Atlanta—a city second only to Richmond in symbolic and substantive value to the Confederacy. When Sherman subsequently ordered the removal of all civilian inhabitants from the city, Atlanta officials pleaded for reconsideration. Believing that the will of the civilians who sustained the war must be crushed, Sherman refused to yield. He reminded city officials that "war is cruelty" and that "you might as well appeal against the thunderstorm as against these terrible hardships of war." On November 16, after burning one-third of the city, Sherman's army marched out of Atlanta and headed for the coast, determined to make "Georgia howl."

HEADQUARTERS MILITARY DIVISION OF THE MISSISSIPPI
IN THE FIELD, ATLANTA, GEORGIA, *September 12, 1864.*

JAMES M. CALHOUN, Mayor, E. E. RAWSON and S. C. WELLS, representing City Council of Atlanta.

GENTLEMEN: I have your letter of the 11th, in the nature of a petition to revoke my orders removing all the inhabitants from Atlanta. I have read it carefully, and give full credit to your statements of the distress that will be occasioned, and yet shall not revoke my orders, because they were not designed to meet the humanities of the case, but to prepare for the future struggles in which millions of good people outside of Atlanta have a deep interest. We must have peace, not only at Atlanta, but in all America. To secure this, we must stop the war that now desolates our once happy and favored country. To stop war, we must defeat the rebel armies which are arrayed against the laws and Constitution that all must respect and obey. To defeat those armies, we must prepare the way to reach them in their recesses, provided with the arms and instruments which enable us to accomplish our purpose. Now, I know the vindictive nature of our enemy, that we may have many years of military operations from this quarter; and, therefore, deem it wise and prudent to prepare in time. The use of Atlanta for warlike purposes

---

*From William T. Sherman, *Personal Memoirs of Gen. W. T. Sherman*, 2 vols., 4th ed. (New York: Charles L. Webster and Company, 1891), II: 125–27.

is inconsistent with its character as a home for families. There will be no manufactures, commerce, or agriculture here, for the maintenance of families, and sooner or later want will compel the inhabitants to go. Why not go now, when all the arrangements are completed for the transfer, instead of waiting till the plunging shot of contending armies will renew the scenes of the past month? Of course, I do not apprehend any such thing at this moment, but you do not suppose this army will be here until the war is over. I cannot discuss this subject with you fairly, because I cannot impart to you what we propose to do, but I assert that our military plans make it necessary for the inhabitants to go away, and I can only renew my offer of services to make their exodus in any direction as easy and comfortable as possible.

You cannot qualify war in harsher terms than I will. War is cruelty, and you cannot refine it; and those who brought war into our country deserve all the curses and maledictions a people can pour out. I know I had no hand in making this war, and I know I will make more sacrifices to-day than any of you to secure peace. But you cannot have peace and a division of our country. If the United States submits to a division now, it will not stop, but will go on until we reap the fate of Mexico, which is eternal war. The United States does and must assert its authority, wherever it once had power; for, if it relaxes one bit to pressure, it is gone, and I believe that such is the national feeling. This feeling assumes various shapes, but always comes back to that of Union. Once admit the Union, once more acknowledge the authority of the national Government, and, instead of devoting your houses and streets and roads to the dread uses of war, I and this army become at once your protectors and supporters, shielding you from danger, let it come from what quarter it may. I know that a few individuals cannot resist a torrent of error and passion, such as swept the South into rebellion, but you can point out, so that we may know those who desire a government, and those who insist on war and its desolation.

You might as well appeal against the thunder-storm as against these terrible hardships of war. They are inevitable, and the only way the people of Atlanta can hope once more to live in peace and quiet at home, is to stop the war, which can only be done by admitting that it began in error and is perpetuated in pride.

We don't want your negroes, or your horses, or your houses, or your lands, or any thing you have, but we do want and will have a just obedience to the laws of the United States. That we will have, and, if it involves the destruction of your improvements, we cannot help it.

You have heretofore read public sentiment in your newspapers, that live by falsehood and excitement; and the quicker you seek for truth in other quarters, the better. I repeat then that, by the original compact of Government, the United States had certain rights in Georgia, which have never been relinquished and never will be; that the South began war by seizing forts, arsenals, mints, custom-houses, etc., etc., long before Mr. Lincoln was installed, and before the South had one jot or tittle of provocation. I myself have seen in Missouri, Kentucky, Tennessee, and Mississippi, hundreds and thousands of women and children fleeing from your armies and desperadoes, hungry and with bleeding feet. In Memphis, Vicksburg, and Mississippi, we fed thousands upon thousands of the families of rebel soldiers left on our hands, and whom we could not see starve. Now that war comes home to you, you feel very different. You deprecate its horrors, but did not feel them when you sent car-loads of soldiers and ammunition, and moulded shells and shot, to carry war into Kentucky and Tennessee, to desolate the homes of hundreds and thousands of good people who only asked to live in peace at their old homes, and under the Government of their inheritance. But these comparisons are idle. I want peace, and believe it can only be reached through union and war, and I will ever conduct war with a view to perfect and early success.

But, my dear sirs, when peace does come, you may call on me for any thing. Then will I share with you the last cracker, and watch with you to shield your homes and families against danger from every quarter.

Now you must go, and take with you the old and feeble, feed and nurse them, and build for them, in more quiet places, proper habitations to shield them against the weather until the mad passions of men cool down, and allow the Union and peace once more to settle over your old homes at Atlanta. Yours in haste,

W. T. SHERMAN, Major-General commanding.

133. ABRAHAM LINCOLN'S SECOND INAUGURAL ADDRESS, 1865*

The war that Americans hoped would last no more than a few weeks dragged on for four years. During that time, it had become for northerners a campaign to make men free—a crusade that cost hundreds of thousands of lives. At his second inauguration, Abraham Lincoln underscored the moral cause the Union now so vigorously pursued. That purpose would be achieved no matter the expense, declared Lincoln, but he also held out hope that the United States would quickly recover from the devastation the conflict had caused.

FELLOW-COUNTRYMEN: At this second appearing to take the oath of the Presidential Office there is less occasion for an extended address than there was at the first. Then a statement somewhat in detail of a course to be pursued seemed fitting and proper. Now, at the expiration of four years, during which public declarations have been constantly called forth on every point and phase of the great contest which still absorbs the attention and engrosses the energies of the nation, little that is new could be presented. The progress of our arms, upon which all else chiefly depends, it is as well known to the public as to myself, and it is, I trust, reasonably satisfactory and encouraging to all. With high hope for the future, no prediction in regard to it is ventured.

On the occasion corresponding to this four years ago all thoughts were anxiously directed to an impending civil war. All dreaded it, all sought to avert it. While the inaugural address was being delivered from this place, devoted altogether to *saving* the Union without war, insurgent agents were in the city seeking to destroy it without war—seeking to dissolve the Union and divide effects by negotiation. Both parties deprecated war, but one of them would make war rather than let the nation survive, and the other would *accept* war rather than let it perish, and the war came.

One-eighth of the whole population were colored slaves, not distributed generally over the Union, but localized in the southern part of it. These slaves constituted a peculiar and powerful interest. All knew that this interest was somehow the cause of war. To strengthen, perpetuate, and extend this interest was the object for which the insurgents would rend the Union even by war, while the Government claimed no right to do more than to restrict the territorial enlargement of it. Neither party expected for the war the magnitude or the duration which it has already attained. Neither anticipated that the *cause* of the conflict might cease with or even before the conflict itself should cease. Each looked for an easier triumph, and a result less fundamental and astounding. Both read the same Bible and pray to the same God, and each invokes His aid against the other. It may seem strange that any men should dare to ask a just God's assistance in wringing their bread from the sweat of other men's faces, but let us judge not, that we

*From *A Compilation of the Messages and Papers of the Presidents, 1789–1897*, 10 vols., comp. James D. Richardson (Washington, D.C.: U.S. Government Printing Office, 1896–1899), VI:276–77.

be not judged. The prayers of both could not be answered. That of neither has been answered fully. The Almighty has His own purposes. "Woe unto the world because of offenses; for it must needs be that offenses come, but woe to that man by whom the offense cometh." If we shall suppose that American slavery is one of those offenses which, in the providence of God, must needs come, but which having continued through His appointed time, He now wills to remove, and that He gives to both North and South this terrible war as the woe due to those by whom the offense came, shall we discern therein any departure from those divine attributions which the believers in a living God always ascribe to Him? Fondly do we hope, fervently do we pray, that this mighty scourge of war may speedily pass away. Yet, if God wills that it continue until all the wealth piled by the bondsman's two hundred and fifty years of unrequited toil shall be sunk, and until every drop of blood drawn with the lash shall be paid by anther drawn with the sword, as was said three thousand years ago, so still it must be said "the judgments of the lord are true and righteous altogether."

With malice toward none, with charity for all, with firmness in the right as God gives us to see the right, let us strive on to finish the work we are in, to bind up the nation's wounds, to care for him who shall have borne the battle and for his widow and orphan, to do all which may achieve and cherish a just and lasting peace among ourselves and with all nations.

134. GRANT'S SURRENDER TERMS AT APPOMATTOX, 1865*

Early in April, 1865, Union troops had effectively trapped the exhausted and disintegrating Army of Northern Virginia. To General Grant, further bloodshed seemed senseless. In the following exchange of letters written over three days (April 7–9, 1865), Generals Grant and Lee negotiated surrender terms, demonstrating the civility between these opposing commanders. Their correspondence also revealed the generosity of the victor for the vanquished. The war was over.

April 7, 1865–5 p.m.

General R. E. Lee,
Commanding C. S. Army:

GENERAL: The result of the last week must convince you of the hopelessness of further resistance on the part of the Army of Northern Virginia in this struggle. I feel that it is so, and regard it as my duty to shift from myself the responsibility of any further effusion of blood by asking of you the surrender of that portion of the C. S. Army known as the Army of Northern Virginia.

Very respectfully, your obedient servant,
U.S. GRANT,
Lieutenant-General, Commanding Armies of the United States.

April 7, 1865.

Lieut. Gen. U.S. GRANT,
Commanding Armies of the United States:

GENERAL: I have received your note of this date. Though not entertaining the opinion you express of the hopelessness of further resistance on the part of the Army of Northern Virginia, I

---

*From *The War of the Rebellion: A Compilation of the Official Records of the Union and Confederate Armies*, 128 vols. (Washington, D.C.: U.S. Government Printing Office, 1880–1901), series I, vol. XLVI, part 3: 619, 641, 664–66.

reciprocate your desire to avoid useless effusion of blood, and therefore, before considering your proposition, ask the terms you will offer on condition of its surrender.

R. E. LEE
General.

April 8, 1865.

General R. E. Lee,
Commanding C. S. Army:
GENERAL: Your note of last evening, in reply to mine of same date, asking the condition on which I will accept the surrender of the Army of Northern Virginia, is just received. In reply I would say that, peace being my great desire, there is but one condition I would insist upon, viz, that the men and officers surrendered shall be disqualified for taking up arms again against the Government of the United States until properly exchanged. I will meet you, or will designate officers to meet any officers you may name for the same purpose, at any point agreeable to you, for the purpose of arranging definitely the terms upon which the surrender of the Army of Northern Virginia will be received.

Very respectfully, your obedient servant,
U. S. GRANT,
Commanding Armies of the United States.

April 8, 1865.

Lieutenant-General GRANT,
Commanding Armies of the United States:
GENERAL: I received at a late hour your note of to-day. In mine of yesterday I did not intend to propose the surrender of the Army of Northern Virginia, but to ask the terms of your proposition. To be frank, I do not think the emergency has arisen to call for the surrender of this army; but as the restoration of peace should be the sole object of all, I desired to know whether your proposals would lead to that end. I cannot, therefore, meet you with a view to surrender the Army of Northern Virginia; but as far as your proposal may affect the C. S. forces under my command, and tend to the restoration of peace, I should be pleased to meet you at 10 a.m. to-morrow, on the old stage road to Richmond, between the picket-lines of the two armies.

Very respectfully, your obedient servant,
R. E. LEE,
General.

April 9, 1865.

General R. E. Lee,
Commanding C. S. Army:
GENERAL: Your note of yesterday is received. As I have no authority to treat on the subject of peace the meeting proposed for 10 a. m. to-day could lead to no good. I will state, however, general, that I am equally anxious for peace with yourself, and the whole North entertain the same feeling. The terms upon which peace can be had are well understood. By the South laying down their arms they will hasten that most desirable event, save thousands of human lives, and hundreds of millions of property not yet destroyed. Sincerely hoping that all our difficulties may be settled without the loss of another life, I subscribe myself,

Very respectfully, your obedient servant,
U. S. GRANT,
Lieutenant-General, U. S. Army.

April 9, 1865.

Lieut. Gen. U. S. GRANT,
Commanding U. S. Armies:
GENERAL: I received your note of this morning on the picket-line, whither I had come to meet you and ascertain definitely what terms were embraced in your proposal of yesterday with reference to the surrender of this army. I now request an interview in accordance with the offer contained in your letter of yesterday for that purpose.

Very respectfully, your obedient servant,
R. E. LEE,
General.

April 9, 1865.

Lieut. Gen. U. S. GRANT,
Commanding U. S. Armies:
General: I ask a suspension of hostilities pending the adjustment of the terms of the surrender of this army, in the interview requested in my former communication to-day.

Very respectfully, your obedient servant,
R. E. LEE,
General.

April 9, 1865.

Lieut. Gen. U. S. GRANT,
Commanding U. S. Armies:
GENERAL: I sent a communication to you to-day from the picketline, whither I had gone in hopes of meeting you in pursuance of the request contained in my letter of yesterday. Major-General Meade informs me that it would probably expedite matters to send a duplicate through some other part of your lines. I therefore request an interview, at such time and place as you may designate, to discuss the terms of the surrender of this army in accordance with your offer to have such an interview, contained in your letter of yesterday.

Very respectfully, your obedient servant,
R. E. LEE,
General.

April 9, 1865.

General R. E. Lee,
Commanding C. S. Army:
Your note of this date is but this moment (11.50 a.m.) received. In consequence of my having passed from the Richmond and Lynchburg road to the Farmville and Lynchburg road I am at this writing about four miles west of Walker's Church, and will push forward to the front for the purpose of meeting you. Notice sent to me on this road where you wish the interview to take place will meet me.

Very respectfully, your obedient servant,
U. S. GRANT,
Lieutenant-General.

Appomottox Court-House, Va., April 9, 1865.

General R. E. Lee,
Commanding C. S. Army:

GENERAL: In accordance with the substance of my letter to you of the 8th instant, I propose to receive the surrender of the Army of Northern Virginia on the following terms, to wit: Rolls of all the officers and men to be made in duplicate—one copy to be given to an officer to be designated by me, the other to be retained by such officer or officers as you may designate; the officers to give their individual paroles not to take up arms against the Government of the United States until properly exchanged, and each company or regimental commander sign a like parole for the men of their commands. The arms, artillery, and public property to be parked and stacked, and turned over to the officers appointed by me to receive them. This will not embrace the side-arms of the officers, nor their private horses or baggage. This done, each officer and man will be allowed to return to their homes, not to be disturbed by United States authority so long as they observe their paroles and the laws in force where they may reside.

Very respectfully,
U. S. GRANT,
Lieutenant-General.

April 9, 1865.

Lieut. Gen. U. S. Grant,
Commanding Armies of the United States:

GENERAL: I have received your letter of this date containing the terms of surrender of the Army of Northern Virginia as proposed by you. As they are substantially the same as those expressed in your letter of the 8th instant, they are accepted. I will proceed to designate the proper officers to carry the stipulations into effect.

Very respectfully, your obedient servant,
R. E. LEE,
General.

. . .

135. LEE'S FAREWELL ADDRESS TO THE ARMY OF NORTHERN VIRGINIA, 1865*

After surrendering his army to Union forces, General Robert E. Lee returned to his anguished troops and tearfully told them: "Men, we have fought through the war together; I have done my best for you; my heart is too full to say more." On the next day, April 10, 1865, Lee issued his farewell address, the last general order published to the army.

Headquarters, Army of Northern Virginia,

April 10, 1865.

After four years' of arduous service, marked by unsurpassed courage and fortitude, the Army of Northern Virginia has been compelled to yield to overwhelming numbers and resources. I need

---

*From Robert Edward Lee, *Recollections and Letters of General Robert E. Lee, by his son, Captain Robert E. Lee* (New York: Doubleday, Page & Company, 1904), 153–54.

not tell the survivors of so many hard-fought battles, who have remained steadfast to the last, that I have consented to this result from no distrust of them; but, feeling that valour and devotion could accomplish nothing that could compensate for the loss that would have attended the continuation of the contest, I have determined to avoid the useless sacrifice of those whose past services have endeared them to their countrymen. By the terms of the agreement, officers and men can return to their homes and remain there until exchanged. You will take with you the satisfaction that proceeds from the consciousness of duty faithfully performed; and I earnestly pray that a merciful God will extend to you His blessing and protection. With an increasing admiration of your constancy and devotion to your country, and a grateful remembrance of your kind and generous consideration of myself, I bid you an affectionate farewell.

"R. E. Lee, General."

Discussion

1. Based on the four documents by Abraham Lincoln, how do you think Lincoln defined power in the United States? How are the documents in this chapter similar to or different from Lincoln's address to Congress in the previous chapter? How do you think Lincoln viewed liberty and equality?

2. What does the exchange between Lincoln and John C. Frémont imply about civilian versus military power in the United States?

3. Compare the memoirs of Victoria Clayton with the description of Alabama by Harriet Martineau in Chapter 9. Based on those two selections, how was life for southern women similar or different in the 1830s and the 1860s? Clayton expressed no concern that the slaves might revolt, even though so many of the white men were away from home. What power do you believe prevented massive slave insurrections during the Civil War? How do you react to Clayton's description of slavery and the apparent egalitarian treatment her slaves received?

4. How are the Homestead Act and the Morrill Act expressions of Republican faith in liberty and equality? Are the laws expressions of power; why or why not? In what ways do the laws reflect American traditions? In what ways are they innovative and modern? In his farewell address, George Washington encouraged support for "institutions for the general diffusion of knowledge." How do you think Washington might have responded to the Morrill Act? What might he have objected to about the law?

5. What are some of the possible reasons that the U.S. Army placed white officers in charge of black troops? What are the implications of that policy for power and equality? How might their experience as slaves have prepared the troops of the 1st South Carolina, U. S. C. T., for life in the army?

6. The Civil War marked a new birth of freedom and a new emphasis on liberty and equality in the United States. How do the various documents in this chapter support that thesis? Is there anything in the documents that casts doubt on that conclusion?

7. Based on the exchange of letters between Grant and Lee as well as Lee's farewell address, how do you react to the sentiments and attitudes expressed by both men?

8. How do you think Abraham Lincoln reacted to the criticisms of Congressman Vallandigham? Both men believed in the Union; how would both men view the Civil War in terms of liberty, equality, and power?

9. Do you think that General William T. Sherman was justified in his evacuation of Atlanta? Why or why not? Are his arguments valid? What was he trying to accomplish? How would Sherman address the issues of liberty, equality, and power?

CHAPTER 17

Reconstruction, 1863–1877

Staunchly Republican Thomas Nast refined the political cartoon into a modern art form. Postwar Republicans appealed to voters' heated emotions to gather votes. Here Nast equates Republicans with patriotism, as stereotyped Democrats (the Irish, Confederate veterans, and sell-out businessmen) stand over a black Union veteran and the national flag.

319

Having fought a deadly Civil War, Americans faced the difficult prospect of rebuilding the nation. President Abraham Lincoln began efforts to restore the former Confederate states to the Union while the fighting continued, and after the war Andrew Johnson attempted to enact a policy similar to that of Lincoln. Southern recalcitrance, on the other hand, led to a more extreme approach—the reconstructing of the South. Radical Republicans in Congress eventually gained control of Reconstruction, and they passed several laws to assist the freed slaves and to control the former Rebels. Republicans used federal power to ensure the liberty of slaves and to provide freedpeople some degree of opportunity and political equality. Consequently, southern bitterness over the war and Reconstruction, along with northern efforts to enforce the victory they had gained on the battlefield, strained relations between the North and South for more than ten years after Lee's surrender at Appomattox Courthouse. Despite the intense antagonism that Reconstruction caused in the former Confederacy, however, by the 1870s other issues gained importance. After decades of conflict over the slavery question, the United States slowly began to address other concerns.

136. ABRAHAM LINCOLN'S "TEN PERCENT PLAN," 1863*

President Lincoln hoped that a broad grant of amnesty would encourage Confederates to abandon the rebellion. Believing that a nucleus of loyal southerners could initiate a quick restoration of the states, Lincoln issued a proclamation offering to recognize governments established by a small percentage of pro-Union voters. Under Lincoln's policy, federal force would put down the insurrection, but he did not want to use the power of the government to punish unduly the majority of southerners. Tragically, Lincoln died before he could fully implement his plan, and his death ended the prospect for a magnanimous reconciliation between the North and South.

Whereas in and by the Constitution of the United States it is provided the President "shall have power to grant reprieves and pardons for offenses against the United States, except in cases of impeachment;" and

Whereas a rebellion now exists whereby the loyal State governments of several States have for a long time been subverted, and many persons have committed and are now guilty of treason against the United States; and,

Whereas, with reference to said rebellion and treason, laws have been enacted by Congress declaring forfeitures and confiscation of property and liberation of slaves, all upon terms and conditions therein stated, and also declaring that the President was thereby authorized at any time thereafter, by proclamation, to extend to persons who may have participated in the existing rebel-

*From *A Compilation of the Messages and Papers of the Presidents, 1789–1897*, 10 vols., comp. James D. Richardson (Washington, D.C.: U.S. Government Printing Office, 1896–1899), VI:213–15.

lion in any State or part thereof pardon and amnesty, with such exceptions and at such times and on such conditions as he may deem expedient for the public welfare; and

Whereas the Constitutional declaration for limited and conditional pardon accords with well-established judicial exposition of the pardoning power; and

Whereas, with reference to said rebellion, the President of the United States has issued several proclamations with provisions in regard to the liberation of slaves; and

Whereas it is now desired by some persons heretofore engaged in said rebellion to resume their allegiance to the United States and to reestablish loyal State governments within and for their respective States:

Therefore, I, Abraham Lincoln, President of the United States, do proclaim, declare, and make known to all persons who have, directly or by implication, participated in the existing rebellion, except as hereinafter excepted, that a full pardon is hereby granted to them and each of them, with restoration of all rights of property, except as in slaves and in property cases where rights of third parties shall have intervened, and upon the condition that every such person shall take and subscribe an oath and thenceforward keep and maintain said oath inviolate, and which oath shall be registered for permanent preservation and shall be of the tenor and effect following; to wit:

"I, _____ _____, do solemnly swear, in presence of Almighty God, that I will henceforth faithfully support, protect, and defend the Constitution of the United States and the Union of the States thereunder; and that I will in like manner abide by and faithfully support all acts of Congress passed during the existing rebellion with references to slaves, so long and so far as not repealed, modified, or held void by Congress or by decision of the Supreme Court; and that I will in like manner abide by and faithfully support all proclamations of the President made during the existing rebellion having reference to slaves, so long and so far as not modified or declared void by decision of the Supreme Court. So help me God."

The persons excepted from the benefits of the foregoing provisions are all who are or shall have been civil or diplomatic officers or agents of the so-called Confederate Government; all who have left judicial stations under the United States to aid the rebellion; all who are or who shall have been military or naval officers of the said so-called Confederate Government above the rank of colonel in the army or of lieutenant in the navy; all who left seats in the United States Congress to aid the rebellion; all who resigned commissions in the Army or Navy of the United States and afterwards aided the rebellion; and all who have engaged in any way in treating colored persons, or white persons in charge of such, otherwise than lawfully as prisoners of war, and which persons may have been found in the United States service as soldiers, seamen, or in any other capacity.

And I do further proclaim, declare, and make known that whenever, in any of the States of Arkansas, Texas, Louisiana, Mississippi, Tennessee, Alabama, Georgia, Florida, South Carolina, and North Carolina, a number of persons, not less than one-tenth in number of the votes cast in such State at the Presidential election of the year a.d. 1860, each having taken the oath aforesaid, and not having since violated it, and being a qualified voter by the election law of the State existing immediately before the so-called act of secession, and excluding all others, shall reestablish a State government which shall be recognized as the true government of the State, and the State shall receive thereunder the benefits of the constitutional provisions which declares that "the United States shall guarantee to every State in this Union a republican form of government and shall protect each of them against invasion, and, on application of the legislature, or the executive (when the legislature can not be convened), against domestic violence."

And I do further proclaim, declare, and make known that any provision which may be adopted by such State government in relation to the freed people of such State which shall recognize and declare their permanent freedom, provide for their education, and which may yet be consistent as a temporary arrangement with their present condition as a laboring, landless, and homeless class, will not be objected to by the national Executive.

And it is suggested as not improper that in constructing a loyal State government in any State the name of the State, the boundary, the subdivision, the constitution, and the general code of laws as before the rebellion be maintained, subject only to the modifications made necessary by the conditions hereinbefore stated, and such others, if any, not contravening said conditions and which may be deemed expedient by those framing the new State government.

To avoid misunderstanding, it may be proper to say that this proclamation, so far as it relates to States governments, has no reference to States wherein loyal State governments have all the while been maintained. And for the same reason it may be proper to further say that whether members sent to Congress from any State shall be admitted to seats conditionally rests exclusively with the respective Houses, and not to any extent with the Executive. And, still further, that this proclamation is intended to present the people of the States wherein the national authority has been suspended and loyal State governments have been subverted a mode in and by which the national authority and loyal State governments may be reestablished within said States or in any of them; and while the mode presented is the best the Executive can suggest, with his present impressions, it must not be understood that no other possible mode would be acceptable. . . .

137. PRESIDENT ANDREW JOHNSON'S AMNESTY PROCLAMATION*

When Andrew Johnson became president, he used the office much differently than had Lincoln. Johnson had long resented the influence of wealthy southerners, and he viewed Reconstruction as an opportunity to destroy the strength of what he viewed as an arrogant aristocracy. His Amnesty Proclamation, presented here, made clear his animosity by denying a general pardon to high-ranking Confederate officials and to any Confederate worth more than $20,000. At the same time, the decree gave him great discretion in granting special pardons, a practice that later angered many Republicans. That anger eventually became a full-scale power struggle between Congress and Johnson, a conflict with grave ramifications for the president and for the South.

Whereas the President of the United States, on the 8th day of December, A.D. 1863, and on the 26th day of March, A.D. 1864, did, with the object to suppress the existing rebellion, to induce all persons to return to their loyalty, and to restore the authority of the United States, issue proclamations offering amnesty and pardon to certain persons who had, directly or by implication, participated in the said rebellion; and

Whereas many persons who had so engaged in said rebellion have, since the issuance of said proclamations, failed or neglected to take the benefits offered thereby; and

Whereas many persons who have been justly deprived of all claim to amnesty and pardon thereunder by reason of their participation, directly or by implication, in said rebellion and continued hostility to the Government of the United States since the date of said proclamations now desire to apply for and obtain amnesty and pardon.

To the end, therefore, that the authority of the Government of the United States may be restored and that peace, order, and freedom may be established, I, Andrew Johnson, President of the United States, do proclaim and declare that I hereby grant to all persons who have, directly or indirectly, participated in the existing rebellion, except as hereinafter excepted, amnesty and pardon, with restoration of all rights of property, except as to slaves and except in cases where legal

*From *A Compilation of the Messages and Papers of the Presidents, 1789–1897*, 10 vols., comp. James D. Richardson (Washington, D.C.; U.S. Government Printing Office, 1896–1899), VI:310–12.

proceedings under the laws of the United States providing for the confiscation of property of persons engaged in rebellion have been instituted; but upon the condition, nevertheless, that every such person shall take and subscribe the following oath (or affirmation) and thence forward keep and maintain said oath inviolate, and which oath shall be registered for permanent preservation and shall be of the tenor and effect following, to wit:

"I _____ _____, do solemnly swear (or affirm) in the presence of Almighty God, that I will henceforth faithfully support, protect, and defend the Constitution of the United States and the Union of the States thereunder, and that I will in like manner abide by and faithfully support all laws and proclamations which have been made during the existing rebellion with references to the emancipation of slaves. So help me God."

The following classes of persons are excepted from the benefits of this proclamation:

First. All who are or shall have been pretended civil or diplomatic officers or otherwise domestic or foreign agents of the pretended Confederate government.

Second. All who left judicial stations under the United States to aid the rebellion.

Third. All who shall have been military or naval officers of said pretended Confederate government above the rank of colonel in the army or lieutenant in the navy.

Fourth. All who left seats in the Congress of the United States to aid the rebellion.

Fifth. All who resigned or tendered resignations of their commission in the Army or Navy of the United States to evade duty in resisting the rebellion.

Sixth. All who have engaged in any way treating otherwise than lawfully as prisoners of war persons found in the United States service as officers, soldiers, seamen, or in other capacities.

Seventh. All persons who have been or are absentees from the United States for purposes of aiding the rebellion.

Eighth. All military and naval officers in the rebel services who were educated by the Government in the Military Academy at West Point or the United States Naval Academy.

Ninth. All persons who held the pretended offices of governors of States in insurrection against the United States.

Tenth. All persons who left their homes within the jurisdiction and protection of the United States and passed beyond the Federal military lines into the pretended Confederate States for the purpose of aiding the rebellion.

Eleventh. All persons who have been engaged in the destruction of the commerce of the United States upon the high seas and all persons who have made raids into the United States from Canada or been engaged in destroying the commerce of the United States upon the lakes and rivers that separate the British Provinces from the United States.

Twelfth. All persons who, at the time when they seek to obtain the benefits hereof by taking the oath herein prescribed, are in military, naval, or civil confinement of custody, or under bonds of the civil, military, or naval authorities or agents of the United States as prisoners of war, or persons detained for offenses of any kind, either before or after conviction.

Thirteenth. All persons who have voluntarily participated in said rebellion and the estimated value of whose taxable property is over $20,000.

Fourteenth. All persons who have taken the oath of amnesty as prescribed in the President's proclamation of December 8, A.D. 1863, or an oath of allegiance to the Government of the United States since the date of said proclamation and who have not thenceforth kept and maintained the same inviolate.

Provided, That special application may be made to the President for pardon by any person belonging to the excepted classes, and such clemency will be liberally extended as may be consistent with the facts of the cases and the peace and dignity of the United States.

The Secretary of State will establish rules and regulations for administering and recording the said amnesty oath, as to insure its benefit to the people and guard the Government against fraud.

138. THE FREEDMEN'S BUREAU, 1865*

Concern for former slaves and other refugees led to the creation of the Bureau of Refugees, Freedmen, and Abandoned Lands just prior to the end of the war. The law creating the bureau provided for some immediate relief measures, but it made the commissioners responsible for most long-term efforts. The Freedmen's Bureau became the primary civilian agency for enforcing Reconstruction policy, and many white southerners despised it as an intrusion of federal power. To the freed slaves, who had their liberty and little else, the bureau offered at least some chance for equitable race relations and fair economic prospects.

Be it enacted by . . . Congress . . . , That there is hereby established in the War Department, to continue during the present war of rebellion, and for one year thereafter, a bureau of refugees, freedmen, and abandoned lands, to which shall be committed, as hereinafter provided, the supervision and management of all abandoned lands, and the control of all subjects relating to refugees and freedmen from rebel states, or from any district or county within the territory embraced in the operation of the army, under such rules and regulations as may be prescribed by the head of the bureau and approved by the President. The said bureau shall be under the management and control of a commissioner to be appointed by the President, by and with the advice and consent of the Senate, whose compensation shall be three thousand dollars per annum, and such number of clerks as may be assigned to him by the Secretary of War, not exceeding one chief clerk, two of the fourth class, two of the third class, and five of the first class. And the commissioner and all persons appointed under this act, shall, before entering upon their duties, take the oath of office prescribed in an act entitled "An act to prescribe an oath of office, and for other purposes, "approved July second, eighteen hundred and sixty-two, and the commissioner and the chief clerk shall, before entering upon their duties, give bonds to the treasurer of the United States, the former in the sum of fifty thousand dollars, and the latter in the sum of ten thousand dollars, conditioned for the faithful discharge of their duties respectively, with securities to be approved as sufficient by the Attorney-General, which bonds shall be filed in the office of the first comptroller of the treasury, to be by him put in suit for the benefit of any injured party upon any breach of the conditions thereof.

SEC. 2. And be it further enacted, That the Secretary of War may direct such issues of provisions, clothing, and fuel, as he may deem needful for the immediate and temporary shelter and supply of the destitute and suffering refugees and freedmen and their wives and children, under such rules and regulations as he may direct.

SEC. 3. And be it further enacted, That the President may, by and with the advice and consent of the Senate, appoint an assistant commissioner for each of the states declared to be in insurrection, not exceeding ten in number, who shall, under the direction of the commissioner, aid in the execution of the provisions of this act; and he shall give bond to the Treasurer of the United States, in the sum of twenty thousand dollars, in the form and manner prescribed in the first section of this act. Each of said commissioners shall receive an annual salary of two thousand five hundred dollars in full compensation for all services. And any military officer may be detailed and assigned to duty under this act without increase of pay or allowances. The commissioner shall, before the commencement of each regular session of congress, make full report of his proceedings with exhibits of the state of his accounts to the President, who shall communicate the same to congress, and shall also make special reports whenever required to do so by the President or either house of congress; and the assistant commissioner shall make quarterly reports of their proceedings to the commissioner, and also such other reports as from time to time may be required.

---

*"An Act to Establish a Bureau for the Relief of Freedmen and Refugees," March 3, 1865, *United States Statutes at Large*, XIII:507–09.

SEC. 4. And be it further enacted, That the commissioner, under the direction of the President, shall have authority to set apart, for the use of loyal refugees and freedmen, such tracts of land within the insurrectionary states as shall have been abandoned, or to which the United States shall have acquired title by confiscation or sale, or otherwise, and to every male citizen, whether refugee or freedman, as aforesaid, there shall be assigned not more than forty acres of such land, and the person to whom it was so assigned shall be protected in the use and enjoyment of the land for the term of three years at an annual rent not exceeding six per centum upon the value of such land, as it was appraised by the state authorities in the year eighteen hundred and sixty, for the purpose of taxation, and in case no such appraisal can be found, then the rental shall be based upon the estimated value of the land in said year, to be ascertained in such manner as the commissioner may by regulation prescribe. At the end of said term, or at any time during said term, the occupants of any parcels so assigned may purchase the land and receive such title thereto as the United States can convey, upon paying therefore the value of the land, as ascertained and fixed for the purpose of determining the annual rent aforesaid.

139. MISSISSIPPI BLACK CODE, 1865*

*I*n the aftermath of the Civil War, defiant southern state governments devoted to white supremacy moved to reduce freedpeople to a condition close to slavery. They passed laws, called "black codes," that created a second-class citizenship for African Americans, denying them the basic civil rights enjoyed by whites. In November 1865, the Mississippi legislature passed a harshly discriminatory series of laws that severely regulated the lives and labor of former slaves. This "black code," excerpted below, dealt with segregation on railroads, apprenticeship, vagrancy, civil rights, and disorderly conduct.

Railroad Segregation Law

Sec. 6. It shall be unlawful for any officer, station agent, collector, or employee on any railroad in this State, to allow any freedman, negro, or mulatto, to ride in any first class passenger cars, set apart, or used by, and for white persons; and any person offending against the provisions of this section, shall be deemed guilty of a misdemeanor; and on conviction thereof before the circuit court of the county in which said offence was committed, shall be fined not less than fifty dollars, nor more than five hundred dollars; and shall be imprisoned in the county jail, until such fine, and costs of prosecution are paid: *Provided,* That this section of this act, shall not apply, in the case of negroes or mulattoes, travelling with their mistress, in the capacity of maids.

Apprentice Law

Sec. 1. It shall be the duty of all sheriffs, justices of the peace, and other civil officers of the several counties in this State, to report to the probate courts of their respective counties semi-annually, at the January and July terms of said courts, all freedmen, free negroes, and mulattoes, under the age of eighteen, in their respective counties, beats, or districts, who are orphans, or whose parent or parents have not the means or who refuse to provide for and support said minors; and thereupon it shall be the duty of said probate court to order the clerk of said court to apprentice said minors to some competent and suitable person, on such terms as the court may direct, having a particular care to the interest of said minor: Provided, that the former owner of said minors shall

*From *Documentary History of Reconstruction*, 2 vols., ed. W. L. Fleming (Cleveland: The Arthur H. Clark Company, 1906), I: 281–90.

have the preference when, in the opinion of the court, he or she shall be a suitable person for that purpose.

Sec. 2. . . The said court shall be fully satisfied that the person or persons to whom said minor shall be apprenticed shall be a suitable person to have the charge and care of said minor, and fully to protect the interest of said minor. The said court shall require the said master or mistress to execute bond and security, payable to the State of Mississippi, conditioned that he or she shall furnish said minor with sufficient food and clothing; to treat said minor humanely; furnish medical attention in case of sickness; teach, or cause to be taught, him or her to read and write, if under fifteen years old, and will conform to any law that may be hereafter passed for the regulation of the duties and relation of master and apprentice. . . .

Sec. 3. . . in the management and control of said apprentices, said master or mistress shall have the power to inflict such moderate corporal chastisement as a father or guardian is allowed to inflict on his or her child or ward at common law: *Provided*, that in no case shall cruel or inhuman punishment be inflicted.

Sec. 4. . . if any apprentice shall leave the employment of his or her master or mistress, without his or her consent, said master or mistress may pursue and recapture said apprentice, and bring him or her before any justice of the peace of the county, whose duty it shall be to remand said apprentice to the service of his or her master or mistress; and in the event of a refusal on the part of said apprentice so to return, then said justice shall commit said apprentice to the jail of said county, on failure to give bond, to the next term of the county court; and it shall be the duty of said court at the first term thereafter to investigate said case, and if the court shall be of opinion that said apprentice left the employment of his or her master or mistress without good cause, to order him or her to be punished, as provided for the punishment of hired freedmen, as may be from time to time provided for by law for desertion, until he or she shall agree to return to the service of his or her master or mistress: . . if the court shall believe that said apprentice had good cause to quit his said master or mistress, the court shall discharge said apprentice from said indenture, and also enter a judgment against the master or mistress for not more than one hundred dollars, for the use and benefit of said apprentice. . . .

Sec. 5. . . if any person entice away any apprentice from his or her master or mistress, or shall knowingly employ an apprentice, or furnish him or her food or clothing without the written consent of his or her master or mistress, or shall sell or give said apprentice ardent spirits without such consent, said person so offending shall be deemed guilty of a high misdemeanor, and shall, upon conviction thereof before the county court, be punished as provided for the punishment of persons enticing from their employer hired freedmen, free negroes or mulattoes.

Vagrant Law

Sec. 1. Be it *enacted*, etc., . . That all rogues and vagabonds, idle and dissipated persons, beggars, jugglers, or persons practicing unlawful games or plays, runaways, common drunkards, common night-walkers, pilferers, lewd, wanton, or lascivious persons, in speech or behavior, common railers and brawlers, persons who neglect their calling or employment, misspend what they earn, or do not provide for the support of themselves or their families, or dependants, and all other idle and disorderly persons, including all who neglect all lawful business, habitually misspend their time by frequenting houses of illfame, gaming-houses, or tippling shops, shall be deemed and considered vagrants, under the provisions of this act, and upon conviction thereof shall be fined not exceeding one hundred dollars, with all accruing costs, and be imprisoned, at the discretion of the court, not exceeding ten days.

Sec. 2. . . All freedmen, free negroes and mulattoes in this State, over the age of eighteen years, found on the second Monday in January, 1866, or thereafter, with no lawful employment or business, or found unlawfully assembling themselves together, either in the day or night time, and all white persons so assembling themselves with freedmen, free negroes or mulattoes, or usually associating with freedmen, free negroes or mulattoes, on terms of equality, or living in adultery or fornication with a freed woman, free negro or mulatto, shall be deemed vagrants, and on conviction thereof shall be fined in a sum not exceeding, in the case of a freedman, free negro, or mulatto, fifty dollars, and a white man two hundred dollars, and imprisoned at the discretion of the court, the free negro not exceeding ten days, and the white man not exceeding six months.

Sec. 3. . . . All justices of the peace, mayors, and aldermen of incorporated towns and cities of the several counties in this State shall have jurisdiction to try all questions of vagrancy in their respective towns, counties, and cities, and it is hereby made their duty, whenever they shall ascertain that any person or persons in their respective towns, counties, and cities are violating any of the provisions of this act, to have said party or parties arrested, and brought before them, and immediately investigate said charge, and, on conviction, punish said party or parties, as provided for herein. . . .

Sec. 6. The same duties and liabilities existing among white persons of this State shall attach to freedmen, free negroes or mulattoes, to support their indigent families and all colored paupers; and that in order to secure a support for such indigent freedmen, free negroes, or mulattoes, it shall be lawful and is hereby made the duty of the county police of each county in this State, to levy a poll or capitation tax on each and every freedman, free negro, or mulatto, between the ages of eighteen and sixty years, not to exceed the sum of one dollar annually to each person so taxed, which tax, when collected, shall be paid into the county treasurer's hands, and constitute a fund to be called the Freedmen's Pauper Fund, which shall be applied by the commissioners of the poor for the mainte-nance of the poor of the freedmen, free negroes, and mulattoes of this State, under such regulations as may be established by the boards of county police in the respective counties of this State.

Sec. 7. . . . If any freedman, free negro, or mulatto shall fail or refuse to pay any tax levied according to the provisions of the sixth section of this act, it shall be *prima facie* evidence of vagrancy, and it shall be the duty of the sheriff to arrest such freedman, free negro, or mulatto or such person refusing or neglecting to pay such tax, and proceed at once to hire for the shortest time such delinquent tax-payer to any one who will pay the said tax, with accruing costs, giving prefer-ence to the employer, if there be one.

Civil Rights of Freedmen

[Prohibition against owning a farm]

Sec. 1. *Be it enacted*, That all freedmen, free negroes, and mulattoes may sue and be sued, implead and be impleaded, in all the courts of law and equity of this State, and may acquire per-sonal property, and choses in action, by descent or purchase, and may dispose of the same in the same manner and to the same extent that white persons may: *Provided*, That the provisions of this section shall not be so construed as to allow any freedman, free negro, or mulatto to rent or lease any lands or tenements except in incorporated cities or towns, in which places the corporate authorities shall control the same.

[On marriage]

Sec. 2. . . . All freedmen, free negroes, and mulattoes may intermarry with each other, in the same manner and under the same regulations that are provided by law for white persons: *Provided*, That the clerk of probate shall keep separate records of the same.

Sec. 3. . . . All freedmen, free negroes, or mulattoes who do now and have herebefore lived and cohabited together as husband and wife shall be taken and held in law as legally married, and the issue shall be taken and held as legitimate for all purposes; that it shall not be lawful for any freedman, free negro, or mulatto to intermarry with any white person; nor for any white person to intermarry with any freedman, free negro, or mulatto; and any person who shall so intermarry, shall be deemed guilty of felony, and on conviction thereof shall be confined in the State penitentiary for life; and those shall be deemed freedmen, free negroes, and mulattoes who are of pure negro blood, and those descended from a negro to the third generation, inclusive, though one ancestor in each generation may have been a white person.

[On labor relations]

Sec. 5. . . . Every freedman, free negro, and mulatto shall, on the second Monday of January, one thousand eight hundred and sixty-six and annually thereafter, have a lawful home or employment, and shall have written evidence thereof as follows, to-wit: if living in any incorporated city, town, or village, a license from the mayor thereof; and if living outside of an incorporated city, town, or village, from the member of the board of police of his beat, authorizing him or her to do irregular and job work; or a written contract, as provided in section six in this act; which licenses may be revoked for cause at any time by the authority granting the same.

Sec. 6. . . . All contracts for labor made with freedmen, free negroes, and mulattoes for a longer period than one month shall be in writing, and in duplicate, attested and read to said freedman, free negro, or mulatto by a beat, city or county officer, or two disinterested white persons of the county in which the labor is to be performed, of which each party shall have one; and said contracts shall be taken and held as entire contracts, and if the laborer shall quit the service of the employer before the expiration of his term of service, without good cause, he shall forfeit his wages for that year up to the time of quitting.

Sec. 7. Every civil officer shall, and every person may, arrest and carry back to his or her legal employer any freedman, free negro, or mulatto who shall have quit the service of his or her employer before the expiration of his or her term of service without good cause; and said officer and person shall be entitled to receive for arresting and carrying back every deserting employee aforesaid the sum of five dollars, and ten cents per mile from the place of arrest to the place of delivery; and the same shall be paid by the employer, and held as a set-off for so much against the wages of said deserting employee. . . .

Certain Offenses of Freedmen

[Prohibition against carrying weapons]

Sec. 1. *Be it enacted*, . . That no freedman, free negro or mulatto, not in the military service of the United States government, and not licensed so to do by the board of police of his or her county, shall keep or carry fire-arms of any kind, or any ammunition, dirk or bowie knife, and on conviction thereof in the county court shall be punished by fine, not exceeding ten dollars, and pay the costs of such proceedings, and all such arms or ammunition shall be forfeited to the informer; and it shall be the duty of every civil and military officer to arrest any freedman, free negro, or mulatto found with any such arms or ammunition, and cause him or her to be committed to trial in default of bail.

[Disorderly conduct]

Sec. 2. . . . Any freedman, free negro, or mulatto committing riots, routs, affrays, trespasses, malicious mischief, cruel treatment to animals, seditious speeches, insulting gestures, language, or acts, or assaults on any person, disturbance of the peace, exercising the function of a minister of the Gospel without a license from some regularly organized church, vending spirituous or intoxicating liquors, or committing any other misdemeanor, the punishment of which is not specifically provided for by law, shall, upon conviction thereof in the county court, be fined not less than ten dollars, and not more than one hundred dollars, and may be imprisoned at the discretion of the court, not exceeding thirty days.

Sec. 5. . . . If any freedman, free negro, or mulatto, convicted of any of the misdemeanors provided against in this act, shall fail or refuse for the space of five days, after conviction, to pay the fine and costs imposed, such person shall be hired out by the sheriff or other officer, at public outcry, to any white person who will pay said fine and all costs, and take said convict for the shortest time.

140. IN DEFENSE OF RADICAL RECONSTRUCTION, 1866*

In an Atlantic Monthly *article published in December 1866, Frederick Douglass, former slave and leading abolitionist, urged the incoming Congress to pursue a radical policy of reconstruction. In his view, the measures passed during the previous session had little impact on the "late rebellious States." The recent congressional elections, however, had given the Republicans a mandate to bypass a "defeated and treacherous" President Andrew Johnson and to seize control over the unrepentant southern states in order to safeguard the liberty and human rights of the freedmen. The South, Douglass argued, "must be opened to the light of law and liberty."*

The assembling of the Second Session of the Thirty-ninth Congress may very properly be made the occasion of a few earnest words on the already much-worn topic of reconstruction.

Seldom has any legislative body been the subject of a solicitude more intense, or of aspirations more sincere and ardent. There are the best of reasons for this profound interest. Questions of vast moment, left undecided by the last session of Congress, must be manfully grappled with by this. No political skirmishing will avail. The occasion demands statesmanship.

Whether the tremendous war so heroically fought and so victoriously ended shall pass into history a miserable failure, barren of permanent results,—a scandalous and shocking waste of blood and treasure,—a strife for empire, as Earl Russell characterized it, of no value to liberty or civilization,—an attempt to re-establish a Union by force, which must be the merest mockery of a Union,—an effort to bring under Federal authority States into which no loyal man from the North may safely enter, and to bring men into the national councils who deliberate with daggers and vote with revolvers, and who do not even conceal their deadly hate of the country that conquered them; or whether, on the other hand, we shall, as the rightful reward of victory over treason, have a solid nation, entirely delivered from all contradictions and social antagonisms, based upon loyalty, liberty, and equality, must be determined one way or the other by the present session of Congress. The last session really did nothing which can be considered final as to these questions. The Civil Rights Bill and the Freedmen's Bureau Bill and the proposed constitutional amendments, with the amendment already adopted and recognized as the law of the land, do not reach the difficulty, and cannot, unless the whole structure of the government is changed from a government by States to something like a despotic central government, with power to control even the municipal regulations of States, and to make them conform to its own despotic will. While there remains such an idea as the right of each State to control its own local affairs,—an idea, by the way, more deeply rooted in the minds of men of all sections of the country than perhaps any one other political idea,—no general assertion of human rights can be of any practical value. To change the character of the government at this point is neither

---

*From "Reconstruction," *Atlantic Monthly* 18 (December, 1866), 761–65.

possible nor desirable. All that is necessary to be done is to make the government consistent with itself, and render the rights of the States compatible with the sacred rights of human nature.

The arm of the Federal government is long, but it is far too short to protect the rights of individuals in the interior of distant States. They must have the power to protect themselves, or they will go unprotected, [in] spite of all the laws the Federal government can put upon the national statute-book.

Slavery, like all other great systems of wrong, founded in the depths of human selfishness, and existing for ages, has not neglected its own conservation. It has steadily exerted an influence upon all around it favorable to its own continuance. And to-day it is so strong that it could exist, not only without law, but even against law. Custom, manners, morals, religion, are all on its side everywhere in the South; and when you add the ignorance and servility of the ex-slave to the intelligence and accustomed authority of the master, you have the conditions, not out of which slavery will again grow, but under which it is impossible for the Federal government to wholly destroy it, unless the Federal government be armed with despotic power, to blot out State authority, and to station a Federal officer at every cross-road. This, of course, cannot be done, and ought not even if it could. The true way and the easiest way is to make our government entirely consistent with itself, and give to every loyal citizen the elective franchise,—a right and power which will be ever present, and will form a wall of fire for his protection.

One of the invaluable compensations of the late Rebellion is the highly instructive disclosure it made of the true source of danger to republican government. Whatever may be tolerated in monarchical and despotic governments, no republic is safe that tolerates a privileged class, or denies to any of its citizens equal rights and equal means to maintain them. What was theory before the war has been made fact by the war.

There is cause to be thankful even for rebellion. It is an impressive teacher, though a stern and terrible one. In both characters it has come to us, and it was perhaps needed in both. It is an instructor never a day before its time, for it comes only when all other means of progress and enlightenment have failed. Whether the oppressed and despairing bondman, no longer able to repress his deep yearnings for manhood, or the tyrant, in his pride and impatience, takes the initiative, and strikes the blow for a firmer hold and a longer lease of oppression, the result is the same,—society is instructed, or may be.

Such are the limitations of the common mind, and so thoroughly engrossing are the cares of common life, that only the few among men can discern through the glitter and dazzle of present prosperity the dark outlines of approaching disasters, even though they may have come up to our very gates, and are already within striking distance. The yawning seam and corroded bolt conceal their defects from the mariner until the storm calls all hands to the pumps. Prophets, indeed, were abundant before the war; but who cares for prophets while their predictions remain unfulfilled, and the calamities of which they tell are masked behind a blinding blaze of national prosperity?

It is asked, said Henry Clay, on a memorable occasion, Will slavery never come to an end? That question, said he, was asked fifty years ago, and it has been answered by fifty years of unprecedented prosperity. [In] Spite of the eloquence of the earnest Abolitionists,—poured out against slavery during thirty years,—even they must confess that, in all the probabilities of the case, that system of barbarism would have continued its horrors far beyond the limits of the nineteenth century but for the Rebellion, and perhaps only have disappeared at last in a fiery conflict, even more fierce and bloody than that which has now been suppressed.

It is no disparagement to truth, that it can only prevail where reason prevails. War begins where reason ends. The thing worse than rebellion is the thing that causes rebellion. What that thing is, we have been taught to our cost. It remains now to be seen whether we have the needed courage to have that cause entirely removed from the Republic. At any rate, to this grand work of national regeneration and entire purification Congress must now address itself, with full purpose that the work shall this time be thoroughly done. The deadly upas, root and branch, leaf and fibre, body and sap, must be utterly destroyed. The country is evidently not in a condition to listen patiently to pleas for postponement, however plausible, nor will it permit the responsibility to be shifted to other shoulders. Authority and power are here commensurate with the duty imposed. There are no cloudflung shadows to obscure the way. Truth shines with brighter light and intenser heat at every moment, and a country torn and rent and bleeding implores relief from its distress and agony.

If time was at first needed, Congress has now had time. All the requisite materials from which to form an intelligent judgment are now before it. Whether its members look at the origin, the progress, the termination of the war, or at the mockery of a peace now existing, they will find only one unbroken chain of argument in favor of a radical policy of reconstruction. For the omissions of the last session, some excuses may be allowed. A treacherous President stood in the way; and it can be easily seen how reluctant good men might be to admit an apostasy which involved so much of baseness and ingratitude. It was natural that they should seek to save him by bending to him even when he leaned to the side of terror. But all is changed now. Congress knows now that it must go on without his aid, and even against his machinations. The advantage of the present session over the last is immense. Where that investigated, this has the facts. Where that walked by faith, this may walk by sight. Where that halted, this must go forward, and where that failed, this must succeed, giving the country whole measures where that gave us half-measures, merely as a means of saving the elections in a few doubtful districts. That Congress saw what was right, but distrusted the enlightenment of the loyal masses; but what was forborne in distrust of the people must now be done with a full knowledge that the people expect and require it. The members go to Washington fresh from the inspiring presence of the people. In every considerable public meeting, and in almost every conceivable way, whether at court-house, school-house, or cross-roads, in doors and out, the subject has been discussed, and the people have emphatically pronounced in favor of a radical policy. Listening to the doctrines of expediency and compromise with pity, impatience, and disgust, they have everywhere broken into demonstrations of the wildest enthusiasm when a brave word has been spoken in favor of equal rights and impartial suffrage. Radicalism, so far from being odious, is now the popular passport to power. The men most bitterly charged with it go to Congress with the largest majorities, while the timid and doubtful are sent by lean majorities, or else left at home. The strange controversy between the President and Congress, at one time so threatening, is disposed of by the people. The high reconstructive powers which he so confidently, ostentatiously, and haughtily claimed, have been disallowed, denounced, and utterly repudiated; while those claimed by Congress have been confirmed.

Of the spirit and magnitude of the canvass nothing need be said. The appeal was to the people, and the verdict was worthy of the tribunal. Upon an occasion of his own selection, with the advice and approval of his astute Secretary, soon after the members of Congress had returned to their constituents, the President quitted the executive mansion, sandwiched himself between two recognized heroes,—men whom the whole country delighted to honor,—and, with all the advantage which such company could give him, stumped the country from the Atlantic to the Mississippi, advocating everywhere his policy as against that of Congress. It was a strange sight, and perhaps the most disgraceful exhibition ever made by any President; but, as no evil is entirely unmixed, good has come of this, as from many others. Ambitious, unscrupulous, energetic, indefatigable, voluble, and plausible,—a political gladiator, ready for a "set-to" in any crowd,—he is beaten in his own chosen field, and stands to-day before the country as a convicted usurper, a political criminal, guilty of a bold and persistent attempt to possess himself of the legislative powers solemnly secured to Congress by the Constitution. No vindication could be more complete, no condemnation could be more absolute and humiliating. Unless reopened by the sword, as recklessly threatened in some circles, this question is now closed for all time.

Without attempting to settle here the metaphysical and somewhat theological question (about which so much has already been said and written), whether once in the Union means always in the Union,—agreeably to the formula, Once in grace always in grace,—it is obvious to common sense that the rebellious States stand to-day, in point of law, precisely where they stood when, exhausted, beaten, conquered, they fell powerless at the feet of Federal authority. Their State governments were overthrown, and the lives and property of the leaders of the Rebellion were forfeited. In reconstructing the institutions of these shattered and overthrown States, Congress should begin with a clean slate, and make clean work of it. Let there be no hesitation. It would be a cowardly deference to a defeated and treacherous President, if any account were made of the illegitimate, one-sided, sham governments hurried into existence for a malign purpose in the absence of Congress. These pretended governments, which were never submitted to the people, and from participation in which four millions of the loyal people were excluded by Presidential order, should now be treated according to their true character, as shams and impositions, and supplanted by true and legitimate governments, in the formation of which loyal men, black and white, shall participate.

It is now, however, within the scope of this paper to point out the precise steps to be taken, and the means to be employed. The people are less concerned about these than the grand end to be attained. They demand such a reconstruction as shall put an end to the present anarchical state of things in the late rebellious States,—where frightful murders and wholesale massacres are perpetrated in the very presence of Federal soldiers. This horrible business they require shall cease. They want a reconstruction such as will protect loyal men, black and white, in their persons and property; such a one as will cause Northern industry, Northern capital, and Northern civilization to flow into the South, and make a man from New England as much at home in Carolina as elsewhere in the Republic. No Chinese wall can now be tolerated. The South must be opened to the light of law and liberty, and this session of Congress is relied upon to accomplish this important work.

The plain, common-sense way of doing this work, as intimated at the beginning, is simply to establish in the South one law, one government, one administration of justice, one condition to the exercise of the elective franchise, for men of all races and colors alike. This great measure is sought as earnestly by loyal white men as by loyal blacks, and is needed alike by both. Let sound political prescience but take the place of an unreasoning prejudice, and this will be done.

Men denounce the negro for his prominence in this discussion; but it is no fault of his that in peace as in war, that in conquering Rebel armies as in reconstructing the rebellious States, the right of the negro is the true solution of our national troubles. The stern logic of events, which goes directly to the point, disdaining all concern for the color or features of men, has determined the interests of men, has determined the interests of the country as identical with and inseparable from those of the negro.

The policy that emancipated and armed the negro—now seen to have been wise and proper by the dullest—was not certainly more sternly demanded than is now the policy of enfranchisement. If with the negro was success in war, and without him failure, so in peace it will be found that the nation must fall or flourish with the negro.

Fortunately, the Constitution of the United States knows no distinction between citizens on account of color. Neither does it know any difference between a citizen of a State and a citizen of the United States. Citizenship evidently includes all the rights of citizens, whether State or national. If the Constitution knows none, it is clearly no part of the duty of a Republican Congress now to institute one. The mistake of the last session was the attempt to do this very thing, by a renunciation of its power to secure political rights to any class of citizens, with the obvious purpose to allow the rebellious States to disfranchise, if they should see fit, their colored citizens. This unfortunate blunder must now be retrieved, and the emasculated citizenship given to the negro supplanted by that contemplated in the Constitution of the United States, which declares that the citizens of each State shall enjoy all the rights and immunities of citizens of the several States,—so that a legal voter in any State shall be a legal voter in all the States.

141. MILITARY RECONSTRUCTION, 1867*

The following law instituted military Reconstruction in the South, in effect turning most of the former Confederacy into an occupied territory. The great antebellum fear that federal power would end slavery, thereby destroying the liberties and equality of white people, had become an all-too-evident reality. Such a massive extension of government force that appeared designed simply to punish white southerners while helping elevate former slaves to positions of influence created an anger in the South that lasted well into the twentieth century.

WHEREAS no legal State governments or adequate protection for life and property now exists in the rebel States of Virginia, North Carolina, South Carolina, Georgia, Mississippi, Alabama, Louisiana, Florida, Texas, and Arkansas; and whereas it is necessary that peace and good order should be enforced in said States until loyal and republican State governments can be legally established: Therefore,

Be it enacted by . . . Congress . . . ,That said rebel States shall be divided into military districts and made subject to the military authority of the United States as hereinafter described, and for that purpose Virginia shall constitute the first district; North and South Carolina the second district; Georgia, Alabama, and Florida the third district; Mississippi and Arkansas the fourth district; and Louisiana and Texas the fifth district.

SEC. 2. And be it further enacted, That it shall be the duty of the President to assign to the command of each of said districts an officer of the army, not below the rank of brigadier-general, and to detail a sufficient military force to enable such officer to perform his duties and enforce his authority within the district to which he is assigned.

SEC. 3. And be it further enacted, That it shall be the duty of each officer assigned as aforesaid, to protect all persons in their rights of persons and property, to suppress insurrection, disorder, and violence, and to punish, or cause to be punished, all disturbers of the public peace and criminals; and to this end he may allow local civil tribunals to take jurisdiction of and to try offenders, or, when in his judgment it may be necessary for the trial of offenders, he shall have power to organize military commissions or tribunals for that purpose, and all interference under color of State authority when the exercise of military authority under this act, shall be null and void.

SEC. 4. And be it further enacted, That all persons put under military arrest by virtue of this act shall be tried without unnecessary delay, and no cruel or unusual punishment shall be inflicted, and no sentence of any military commission or tribunal hereby authorized, affecting the life or liberty of any person, shall be executed until it is approved by the officer in command of the district, and the laws and regulations for the government of the army shall not be affected by this act, except in so far as they conflict with its provisions; Provided, That no sentence of death under the provisions of this act shall be carried into effect without the approval of the President.

SEC. 5. And be it further enacted, That when the people of any one of said rebel States shall have formed a constitution of government in conformity with the Constitution of the United States in all respects, framed by a convention of delegates elected by the male citizens of said State, twenty-one years old and upward, of whatever race, color, or previous condition, who have been resident in said State for one year previous to the day of such election, except such as may be disfranchised for participation in the rebellion or for felony at common law, and when such constitution shall provide that the elective franchise shall be enjoyed by all such persons as have the qualifications herein stated for electors of delegates, and when such constitution shall be ratified by a majority of the persons voting on the question of ratification who are qualified as electors for delegates, and when such constitution shall have been submitted to Congress for examination and approval, and when Congress shall have approved the same,

---

*"An Act to Provide for the More Efficient Government of the Rebel States," March 2, 1867, *United States Statutes at Large*, XIV:428–30.

and when said State, by a vote of its legislature elected under said constitution, shall have adopted the amendment to the Constitution of the United States, proposed by the Thirty-ninth Congress, and known as article fourteen, and when said article shall become a part of the Constitution of the United States said State shall be declared entitled to representation on Congress, and senators and representatives shall be admitted therefrom on their taking the oath prescribed by law, and then and thereafter the preceding section of this act shall be inoperative in said State; Provided, That no person excluded from the privilege of holding office by said proposed amendment to the Constitution of the United States shall be eligible to election as a member of the convention to frame a constitution for any of said rebel States, nor shall any such person vote for members of such convention.

SEC. 6. And be it further enacted, That, until the people of said rebel States shall be by law admitted to representation in the Congress of the United States, any civil governments which may exist therein shall be deemed provisional only, and in all respects subject to the paramount authority of the United States at any time to abolish, modify, control, or supersede the same; and in all elections to any office under such provisional governments all persons shall be entitled to vote, and no others, who are entitled to vote, under the provisions of the fifth section of this act; and no persons shall be eligible to any office under any such provisional governments who would be disqualified from holding office under the provisions of the third article of said constitutional amendment.

142. THE ELECTION OF 1868*

*T*he election of 1868 was a referendum on Reconstruction policy. The Republicans nominated General Ulysses S. Grant, whom they believed would guarantee that the northern military victory would not be undone by former Confederates and their sympathizers. Democrats brazenly campaigned against Radical programs, and their untempered, obviously unreconstructed, rhetoric enraged many northerners. The following essay, by Thomas Wentworth Higginson, editor of the Atlantic Monthly magazine, revealed just how much rancor the campaign had generated.

The victory which the Republican party gained in the November election, after the most fiercely contested struggle recorded in our political history, is the crowning victory of the War of the Rebellion, and its real close. A war such as raged in this country between April, 1861 and April, 1865, is ended, not when the defeated party ceases to fight, but when it ceases to hope. The sentiments and principles which led to the Rebellion were overturned, not in 1865, but in 1868. After the exhaustion of physical power, which compelled the Rebels to lay down their arms, came the moral struggle which has resulted in compelling them to surrender their ideas. If these ideas had been on a level with a civilization of the age, or in advance of it; if the "Lost Cause" had been the cause of humanity and freedom, of reason and justice, of good morals and good sense,—such a catastrophe would be viewed by every right-minded man as a great calamity. But the Rebellion was essentially a revolt of tyrants for the privilege to oppress, and of bullies for the right to domineer. Its interpretation of the Constitution was an ingenious reversal of the purposes for which the Constitution was declared to be made, and its doctrine of State Rights was a mere cover for a comprehensive conspiracy against the rights of man. The success of such a "cause" could not have benefited even its defenders, for the worst government for the permanent welfare even of the governing classes is that in which the intelligent systematically prey upon the ignorant, and the strong mercilessly trample on the weak. In a large view, the South is better off to-day for the military defeat which dissipated its wild dream of insolent domination, and for the political defeat which destroyed the last hopes of its reviving passions.

*Thomas Wentworth Higginson, "Moral Significance of the Republican Triumph," *Atlantic Monthly* 23 (January-June, 1869), 124–28.

Those who are accustomed to recognize a providence in the direction of human affairs may find in the course and conduct equally of this military and political struggle the strongest confirmation of their faith. The great things that have been done appear to have been done through us, rather than by us. During the war, it seemed as if no mistakes could hinder us from gaining victories, no reverses obstruct our steady advance, no conservative prudence prevent us from being the audacious champion of radical ideas. The march of events swept forward government and people on its own path, converting the distrusted abstraction of yesterday into the "military necessity" of to-day and the constitutional provision of to-morrow. . . .

What was true of the military is true of the political contest. After the armed Rebellion was crushed by arms, and the meaner rebellion of intrigue, bluster, and miscellaneous assassination began, both parties had reason to be surprised at the issue. The Rebels found that their profoundest calculations, their most unscrupulous plottings, their most vigorous action, only led them to a more ruinous defeat. Their opponents had almost equal reason for wonder, for the plan on reconstruction, which they eventually passed and repeatedly sustained by more than two thirds of both Houses of Congress, would not have commanded a majority in either House at the time the problem of reconstruction was first presented. . . .

As it regards the right of the Government of the United States to dictate conditions of reconstruction, it must be remembered that the difference between the President's Plan and the Congressional Plan was not, in this respect, a difference in principle; and that the position held by the Democratic party—that the Rebellion was a rebellion of individuals, and not of States—equally condemns both. This position, however, can only be maintained by the denial of the most obvious facts. The enormous sacrifices of blood and treasure in putting down the Rebellion were made necessary by the circumstances that it was a rebellion of States. . . .

The intellect of the Democratic party is concentrated, to a great degree, in its Copperhead members; and these had become so embittered and vindictive by [Reconstruction policy], that their malignity prevented their ability from having fair play. [In the campaign of 1868, they] assailed the Republicans for not giving peace and prosperity to the nation, and then laid down a programme which proposed to reach peace and prosperity through political and financial anarchy. They selected unpopular candidates, and then placed them on a platform of which revolution and repudiation were the chief planks. Perhaps even with these drawbacks they might have cajoled a sufficient number of voters to succeed in the election, had it not been for the frank brutality of their Southern allies. To carry the North their reliance was on fraud, but the Southern politicians were determined to carry their section by terror and assassination, and no plausible speech could be made by a Northern Democrat the effect of which was not nullified by some Southern burst of eloquence, breathing nothing but proscription and war. The Democratic party was therefore not only defeated, but disgraced. To succeed as it succeeded in New York and New Jersey, in Louisiana and Georgia, did not prevent its fall, but did prevent it from falling with honor. To the infamy of bad ends it added the additional infamy of bad means; and it comes out of an overwhelming general reverse with the mortifying consciousness that its few special victories have been purchased at the expense of its public character. The only way it can recover its prestige is by discarding, not only its leaders, but the passions and ideas its leaders represent. . . .

143. THE END OF RECONSTRUCTION, 1877*

The inauguration of Rutherford B. Hayes marked the end of Reconstruction. A disputed election had raised once again the specter of insurrection, and most Americans celebrated the agreement that had averted yet

*From *A Compilation of the Messages and Papers of the Presidents, 1789–1897*, 10 vols. comp. James D. Richardson (Washington, D.C.; U.S. Government Printing Office, 1896–1899), IX:439–99.

another crisis. Moreover, the Compromise of 1877 showed that political leaders were anxious to leave sectional differences behind in order to heal the wounds that had festered for so long. In his inaugural address, the new president discussed some of the lingering results of the Civil War, but he also devoted attention to other matters. After 1877, concerns such as governmental reform and international affairs took on increasing importance. The war between the states was over.

FELLOW-CITIZENS: We have assembled to repeat the public ceremonial, begun by Washington, observed by all my predecessors, and now a time-honored custom, which marks the commencement of a new term in Presidential office. Called to the duties of this great trust, I proceed, in compliance with usage, to announce some of the leading principles, on the subjects that now chiefly engage the public attention, by which it is my desire to be guided in the discharge of those duties. I shall not undertake to lay down irrevocably principles or measures of administration, but rather to speak of the motives which should animate us, and to suggest certain important ends to be attained in accordance with our institutions and essential to the welfare of our country.

At the outset of the discussions which preceded the recent Presidential election it seemed to me fitting that I should fully make known my sentiments in regard to several of the important questions which then appeared to demand the consideration of the country. Following the example, and in part adopting the language, of one of my predecessors, I wish now, when every motive for misrepresentation has passed away, to repeat what was said before the election, trusting that my countrymen will candidly weigh and understand it, and that they will feel assured that the sentiments declared in accepting the nomination for the Presidency will be the standard of my conduct in the path before me, charged, as I now am, with the grave and difficult task of carrying them out in the practical administration of the Government so far as depends, under the Constitution and laws, on the Chief Executive of the nation.

The permanent pacification of the country upon such principles and by such measures as will secure the complete protection of all its citizens in the free enjoyment of all their constitutional rights is now the one subject in our public affairs which all thoughtful and patriotic citizens regard as of supreme importance.

Many of the calamitous effects of the tremendous revolution which has passed over the Southern States still remain. The immeasurable benefits which will surely follow, sooner or later, the hearty and generous acceptance of the legitimate results of the revolution have not yet been realized. Difficult and embarrassing questions meet us at a threshold of this subject. The people of those States are still impoverished, and the inestimable blessing of wise, honest, and peaceful local self-government is not fully enjoyed. Whatever difference of opinion may exist as to the cause of this condition of things, the fact is clear that in the progress of events the time has come when such government is the imperative necessity required by all the varied interests, public and private, of those States. But it must not be forgotten that only a local government which recognizes and maintains inviolate the rights of all is a true self-government.

With respect to the two distinct races whose peculiar relations to each other have brought upon us the deplorable complications and perplexities which exist in those States, it must be a government which guards the interests of both races carefully and equally. It must be a government which submits loyally and heartily to the Constitution and the laws—laws of the nation and the laws of the States themselves—accepting and obeying faithfully the whole Constitution as it is. . . .

The sweeping revolution of the entire labor system of a large portion of our country and the advance of 4,000,000 people from a condition of servitude to that of citizenship, upon an equal footing with their former masters, could not occur without presenting problems of the gravest moment, to be dealt with by the emancipated race, by their former masters, and by the General Government, the author of the act of emancipation. That it was a wise, just, and providential act, fraught with good for all concerned, is now generally conceded throughout the country. That a moral obligation rests upon the National Government to employ its constitutional power and influence to establish the rights of the people it has emancipated, and to protect them in the enjoyment of those rights when they are infringed or assailed, is also generally admitted.

The evils which afflict the Southern States can only be removed or remedied by the united and harmonious efforts of both races, actuated by motives of mutual sympathy and regard; and while in duty bound and fully determined to protect the rights of all by every constitutional means at the disposal of my Administration, I am sincerely anxious to use every legitimate influence in favor of honest and efficient local self-government as the true resource of those States for the promotion and contentment and prosperity of their citizens. In the effort I shall make to accomplish this purpose I ask the cordial cooperation of all who cherish an interest in the welfare of the country, trusting that party ties and the prejudice of race will be freely surrendered on behalf of the great purpose to be accomplished. In the important work of restoring the South it is not the political situation alone that merits attention. The material development of that section of the country has been arrested by the social and political revolution through which it has passed, and now needs and deserves the considerate care of the national Government within the just limits prescribed by the Constitution and wise public economy.

But at the basis of all prosperity, for that as well as for every other part of the country, lies the improvement of the intellectual and moral condition of the people. Universal suffrage should rest upon universal education. To this end, liberal and permanent provision should be made for the support of free schools by the State Goverments, and, if need be, supplemented by legitimate aid from national authority.

Let me assure my countrymen of the Southern States that it is my earnest desire to regard and promote their truest interests—the interests of the white and of the colored people both and equally—and to put forth my best efforts in behalf of a civil policy which will forever wipe out in our political affairs the color line and the distinction between North and South, to the end that we may have not merely a united North or a united South, but a unified country.

I ask the attention of the public to the paramount necessity of reform in our civil service—a reform not merely as to certain abuses and practices of so-called official patronage which have come to have the sanction of usage in the several Departments of our Government, but a change in the system of appointment itself; a reform that shall be thorough, radical, and complete; a return to the principles and practices of the founders of the Government. They neither expected nor desired from the public officers any partisan service. They meant that public officers should owe their whole service to the Government and to the people. They meant that the officer should be secure in his tenure as long as his personal character remained untarnished and the performance of his duties satisfactory. They held that appointments to office were not to be made nor expected merely as rewards for partisan services, nor merely on the nomination of members of Congress, as being entitled in any respect to the control of such appointments. . . .

In furtherance of the reform we seek, and in other important respects a change of great importance, I recommend an amendment to the Constitution prescribing a term of six years for the Presidential office and forbidding a reelection.

With respect to the financial condition of the country, I shall not attempt an extended history of the embarrassment and prostration which we have suffered during the past three years. The depression in all our varied commercial and manufacturing interests throughout the country, which began in September, 1873, still continues. It is very gratifying, however, to be able to say that there are indications all around us of a coming change to prosperous times.

Upon the currency question, intimately connected, as it is, with this topic, I may be permitted to repeat here the statement made in my letter of acceptance, that in my judgment the feeling of uncertainty inseparable from an irredeemable paper currency, with its fluctuation of values, is one of the greatest obstacles to a return to prosperous times. The only safe paper currency is one which rests upon a coin basis and is at all times and promptly converted into coin. . . .

Passing from these remarks upon the condition of our country to consider our relations with other lands, we are reminded by the international complications abroad, threatening the peace of Europe, that our traditional role of noninterference in the affairs of foreign nations has proved of great value in past times and ought to be strictly observed.

The policy inaugurated by my honored predecessor, President Grant, of submitting to arbitration grave questions in dispute between ourselves and foreign powers points to a new, and incomparably the best, instrumentality for the preservation of peace, and will, as I believe, become a beneficent example of the course to be pursued in similar emergencies by other nations.

If, unhappily, questions of difference should at any time during the period of my Administration arise between the United States and any foreign government, it will certainly be my disposition and my hope to aid in their settlement, in the same peaceful and honorable way, thus securing to our country the great blessings of peace and mutual good offices with all the nations of the world.

Fellow-citizens, we have reached the close of a political contest marked by the excitement which usually attends the contests between great political parties whose members espouse and advocate with earnest faith their respective creeds. The circumstances were, perhaps, in no respect extraordinary save in the closeness and the consequent uncertainty of the result.

For the first time in the history of the country it has been deemed best, in view of the peculiar circumstances of the case, that the objections and questions in dispute with reference to the counting of the electoral votes should be referred to the decision of a tribunal appointed for the purpose.

That tribunal—established by law for this sole purpose; its members, all of them, men of long-established reputation for integrity and intelligence, and, with the exception of those who are also members of the supreme judiciary, chosen equally from both political parties; its deliberations enlightened by the research and arguments of able counsel—was entitled to the fullest confidence of the American people. Its decisions have been patiently waited for, and accepted as legally conclusive by the general judgment of the public. For the present, opinion will widely vary as to the wisdom of the several conclusions announced by that tribunal. This is to be anticipated in every instance where matters of dispute are made the subject of arbitration under the forms of law. Human judgment is never unerring, and is rarely regarded as otherwise than wrong by the unsuccessful party in the contest.

The fact that two great political parties have in this way settled a dispute in regard to which good men differ as to the facts and the law no less than as to the proper course to be pursued in solving the question in controversy is an occasion for general rejoicing.

Upon one point there is entire unanimity in public sentiment—that conflicting claims to the Presidency must be amicably and peaceably adjusted, and that when so adjusted the general acquiescence of the nation ought surely to follow.

It has been reserved for a government of the people, where the right of suffrage is universal, to give to the world the first example in history of a great nation, in the midst of the struggle of opposing parties for power, hushing its party tumults to yield the issue of the contest to adjustment according to the forms of law.

Looking for the guidance of that Divine Hand by which the destinies of nations and individuals are shaped, I call upon you, Senators, Representatives, judges, fellow-citizens, here and everywhere, to unite with me in an earnest effort to secure to our country the blessings, not only of material prosperity, but of justice, peace, and union—a union depending not upon the constraint of force, but upon the loving devotion of a free people. . . .

Discussion

1. Compare the four Reconstruction plans presented in this chapter. What similarities or differences exist regarding power? To what degree do any of the documents express concerns for issues of liberty and equality?

2. How might southerners have viewed the law creating the Freedmen's Bureau as an unacceptable assertion of power? How might Radical Republicans have justified the act? To what degree, and how, does the act deal with issues of liberty and with issues of equality?

3. Why might the *Atlantic Monthly* have been so perturbed by the Democrats during the election of 1868? Does the document relate at all to matters of liberty and equality, or were Americans in 1868 primarily concerned with issues of power? How do you think southerners responded to the editorial? How might northern Democrats have reacted to it? What about Republicans?

4. Compare the inaugural address of Rutherford B. Hayes to the magazine editorial from 1868. Are there any differences or similarities in the two documents? How so? What do the two selections suggest about concepts of liberty, equality, and power in 1868 and in 1877?

5. Based on the black code document, how did the Mississippi state legislators respond to the emancipation of slaves in 1865? How do you react to their actions? How do you think northerners generally viewed the passage of these laws? How did the acts address the issues of liberty, equality, and power?

PHOTO CREDITS

Chapter 2 Title Page from Nova Britannia. Office of Special Collections, The New York Public Library. **Chapter 3** Announcement for the Sale of Newly Imported Slaves, Charles-Town, SC, May 6, 1763. Reproduced from the Collections of the Library of Congress. **Chapter 4** Collection of The New-York Historical Society. **Chapter 5** Paul Revere Engraving of the Boston Massacre. Courtesy American Antiquarian Society, Worcester, MA. **Chapter 6** The Federal Edifice from the Massachusetts *Centinel*, August 2, 1788. Collection of the New-York Historical Society. **Chapter 7** Venerate the Plow. Reproduced from the Collections of the Library of Congress. **Chapter 8** The Congressional Brawlers, 1798. Miriam and Ira D. Wallach Division of Art, Prints and Photographs. The New York Public Library. Astor, Lenox and Tilden Foundations. **Chapter 9** Title Page of *The Lowell Offering*, December 1845. Corbis /The Bettmann Archive. **Chapter 10** Reward Bill for Runaway Slaves. State Historical Society of Wisconsin. **Chapter 11** The Drunkard's Progress. Reproduced from the Collections of the Library of Congress. **Chapter 12** Despotism: Calhoun Reaching for the Crown. Miriam and Ira D. Wallach Division of Art, Prints and Photographs. The New York Public Library. Astor, Lenox and Tilden Foundations. **Chapter 13** "This Is the House that Polk Built." Corbis/The Bettmann Archive. **Chapter 14** "Southern Chivalry—Argument versus Club's," Print collection, Miriam and Ira Wallach Division of Art, Prints, and Photographs. New York Public Library, Astor, Lenox and Tilden Foundations. **Chapter 15** Feared Dissolution of Union **Chapter 16** Abe Lincoln's Last Card; or Rouge-et-noir. From *Punch*, London, October 18, 1862. **Chapter 17** A White Man's Government by Thomas Nast, 1868. The Library Company of Philadelphia.